*Cryptography,
Information Theory
and Error-Correction*

SERIES PAGE TITLE

A complete list of titles in this series appears at the end of this volume.

WILEY SERIES IN DISCRETE MATHEMATICS AND OPTIMIZATION

Cryptography, Information Theory and Error-Correction

A Handbook for the 21st Century

Second Edition

Aiden A. Bruen
Carleton University
Ottawa, Canada

Mario A. Forcinito
AP Dynamics, Inc., and
University of Calgary
Calgary, Canada

James M. McQuillan
Western Illinois University
Macomb, United States

WILEY

Dedications

Dedicated to the memory of my late parents, Edward A. Bruen and Brid Bean de Brún and to the memory of my late sister Antoinette.

Dedicated also to my siblings Phil and Bernard, to my beloved wife Katri, and to our children Trevor, Robin, and Merike. (Aiden A. Bruen)

Also dedicated to my parents, Alberto Forcinito and Olga Swystun de Forcinito, my beloved wife Claudia, and our children Dante, Lucas, and Diego. (Mario A. Forcinito)

Also dedicated to my parents, Archie and Muriel McQuillan, my siblings Dan, Mary, and Ian, my beloved wife Joy, and our children Anna and Christopher.
(James M. McQuillan)

Contents

Preface to the Second Edition

WELCOME, New Co-author

It is a privilege to welcome back our readers, past, present, and future to this second edition. We are delighted to introduce a third author, Dr. James McQuillan from Western Illinois University. We now have as co-authors a mathematician, a computer scientist, and an engineer which, we feel, provides a good balance.

Intended Readership, Connections Between the Areas

This new edition, like the first edition, is intended for a broad audience and our goals have not changed. Over the last 15 years, the three areas in the title have become more unified. For example, cryptographer **A** might exchange a key with **B** using public key cryptography. But in doing so, both would want to use error correction ensuring accuracy of transmission. Now that they have the common secret key they might use a symmetric-key protocol such as DES or AES to exchange messages or even a one-time pad. They need to know about security, and how it is measured, which brings in probability and entropy. This example is but the tip of the iceberg.

This book arose out of courses in cryptography and information theory at the University of Calgary. It is used as a text or a reference at universities in North America and Europe and of course can be used for self-study. Parts of the material have also been presented at various industrial gatherings. Material related to some of the topics in the book has been patented and used in the energy sector.

Problems with Solutions

The second edition has well over 350 worked examples and problems with solutions.

Style

As with the first edition, we have made a considerable effort to ensure that the chapters are as accessible as possible. We wanted this new edition to also have both depth and breadth, to read with ease, and to explain the content clearly. We feel that the updates, the incorporation of new applications of basic principles, and the new examples and worked problems added to this edition greatly enhance and complete the book. We hope that it will be an excellent source for academics (including undergraduate and graduate students!) and practitioners that want to understand the mathematical principles and their real-world consequences.

In a 2005 review of the first edition for the *Mathematical Association of America*, Dr. William Satzer states that the book is "lively and engaging, written with palpable enthusiasm." He mentions the "... clearly communicated sense of interconnections among the [three] parts [of the book]." In a review for *Mathematical Reviews* (MR2131191), Dr. Andrea Sgarro from the University of Trieste, Italy, noted that the first edition "... is meant for a wide audience ... and it can be used at various levels, both as a reference text and as a text for undergraduate and graduate courses; worked examples and problems are provided."

Possible Courses

Each chapter covers a lot of ground so a course might only cover part of it. For a basic course in cryptography, one could start with Chapter 2 having taken a quick look at Chapter 1. Chapter 2 introduces basic ideas on keys and security. Some of the material relates to weaknesses due to letter frequencies and requires some sophisticated mathematics described more fully in Beutelspacher, [Beu94]. Chapter 3 covers public key cryptography algorithms such as RSA and key-exchanges such as Diffie–Hellman, Elliptic curve cryptography and quantum cryptography are discussed in Chapter 6. Symmetric cryptography involving DES, AES, shift registers and perfect secrecy is discussed in

Chapters 2, 4, 5, 15, 16 and 21. Various attacks are covered in Chapter 7 Part II of the book is devoted to information theory and Part III mainly deals with error-correction. However, along the way all these topics, i.e., cryptography, information theory and error-correction merge. The unity is beautifully illustrated in Chapters 24, 25 and 26.

Recent algorithms related to some in industry are discussed in Chapter 24. For applications to Bitcoin, there is Chapter 26. There are lots of options in the book for an undergraduate or graduate course for a term or a year in all three topics.

On the more applied side, the book can be used for courses in Cybersecurity Foundations, IT Systems, Data Security, and Cryptanalysis which might include topics such as HTTP, SSL/TLS, brute-force, and birthday attacks.

What's New

We refer also to the preface of the first edition. Many new developments have taken place in this dynamic area since the first edition in 2005 and we have tried to cover them and to provide good references in this new edition. Chapters in the first edition have been updated. We have **six new chapters** dealing with Compression and Applications (Chapter 17), New Identities for the Shannon Function and an Application (Chapter 25), Blockchain and Bitcoin (Chapter 26), IoT, the Internet of Things (Chapter 27), In the Cloud (Chapter 28), and Review Problems and Solutions (Chapter 29). We touch only on a few of the changes and additions that have been made in various chapters, as follows:

- Chapter 4: homomorphic encryption is introduced, the discussion on quantum encryption is enlarged and post-quantum cryptography is discussed.

- Chapter 6 extends the usual algorithm for ECC and demonstrates corresponding new geometrical results.

- Chapter 7 contains details of many new attacks.

- Chapter 9 has a new extended discussion on entropy in weighing problems.

- Chapter 11 has an improved treatment of source coding.

- Chapter 12 now contains a full proof of the Fundamental Theorem of Information Theory.

- Chapter 13 features a more user-friendly approach to continuous signals and the Information Capacity Theorem for Band-Limited channels.

- The exposition for Chapter 15 has been polished and simplified.

- Chapter 16 includes background and full details of the Berlekamp–Massey algorithm.

- Chapter 17 has details of the WKdm algorithms.

- Chapter 18 outlines the proof by one of the authors on a long-standing conjecture regarding the next-to-minimum weights of Reed–Muller codes.

- Chapter 21 features a fresh approach to cyclic linear codes and culminates with a new user-friendly proof of a powerful result on the periodicity of shift registers in Peterson and Weldon, [PW72].

- The study of MDS codes leads to a very interesting and basic "inverse" problem in linear algebra over any field. It could be discussed in a first year linear algebra class. See Chapter 23 for the details.

- Chapter 24 introduces a new hash function and improvements to the main algorithm in the chapter.

- Chapter 25 brings readers of this book to the very forefront of research by exhibiting infinitely many new identities for the Shannon function.

- Chapter 26 features a simple new proof of the security of Bitcoin in the matter of double spending, avoiding the assumptions of the approximation by a continuous random variable in the original paper by Nakamoto ([Nak08]).

- Chapter 27 discusses privacy and security concerns relating to the Internet of Things (IoT). Important questions include: Who has access to the information that your smart device is collecting? Could someone remotely access your smart device?

- Chapter 28 focuses on the availability of data stored in the cloud and on homomorphic encryption, which allows computations to be done on data while it is in an encrypted form.

- Chapter 29 features another approach to MDS codes and, we hope, a very interesting discussion of the venerable topic of mutually orthogonal latin squares. There are also exercises in modular arithmetic, finite fields, linear algebra, and other topics to elucidate theoretical results in previous chapters, along with solutions.

Hardcover and eBook

The second edition will be available both as a hardcover book and as an eBook. The content will be the same in both. Besides traditional formatting for items in the bibliography, most of the items have accompanying URLs.

The eBook will have clickable links, including links to chapter and section numbers, to theorem numbers, from problems to their solutions, and to items in the bibliography. The URLs in the bibliography will also be clickable in the eBook.

Numbering of Definitions, Examples, Results.

When referring to a definition or result, we list the chapter number, a dot and then a number from an increasing counter for that chapter. For instance, Example 10.7 is the seventh numbered item in Chapter 10. Theorem 10.8 comes after Example 10.7 and is the eight such numbered item in Chapter 10.

Numbering of Problems, Solutions.

Most chapters have a section called Problems followed immediately by a corresponding section called Solutions at the end of the chapter. Problems and Solutions at the end of the chapter have their own counters. So, Problem 10.6 is the sixth problem in the Problems section (Section 10.15) of Chapter 10 and Solution 10.6 has the solution to that problem. It can be found in the subsequent section (Section 10.16).

Numbering of Equations.

Equation numbers follow their own counter for each chapter. For example, Equation (9.7) is the seventh equation in Chapter 9.

Acknowledgments for the Second Edition

The third author is extremely grateful to the first two authors for inviting him to be a co-author on the second edition! Thank you so much!

We are extremely grateful to a few individuals for their help with the second edition. We thank Professor Dan McQuillan from the Department of Mathematics at Norwich University in Vermont for a careful reading and many improvements to many chapters in the second edition. We thank Joy McQuillan for a careful reading and improvements to several chapters. We are indebted to Professor Sumesh Philip from the School of Information Technology at Illinois State University in Illinois for many significant improvements to the new content in the second edition. We thank Professor David Wehlau of the Department of Mathematics and Computer Science at the Royal Military College of Canada and the Department of Mathematics and Statistics at Queen's University in Kingston, Canada for valuable comments. We also thank Dr. Valery Ipatov from Petersburg State Electrotechnical University in Russia for numerous corrections to the first edition, and Burt Wilsker for corrections to the first edition. These were incorporated into the second edition.

We thank the *Wiley* staff including Kimberly Monroe-Hill, Kathleen Pagliaro, Blesy Regulas, Linda Christina E, Mindy Okura-Marszycki, and Kathleen Santoloci for their help with the second edition. We also thank Wiley staff Gayathree Sekar, Becky Cowan, and Aileen Storry.

Book Website

The website for the book is

    http://cryptohandbook.info

It will be a repository for additional information and updates.

We have done our best to correct the errors but, inevitably, some will remain. We invite our readers to submit errors to `mario@cryptohandbook.info`. We will post them, with attribution, on the website along with other clarifications as they arise.

About the Authors

Aiden A. Bruen was born in Galway, Ireland. He read mathematics for his Undergraduate and Master's degree in Dublin and received his Doctorate at the University of Toronto, supervised by F.A. Sherk. At Toronto, he also worked with H.S.M. Coxeter, E. Ellers, and A. Lehman. Dr. Bruen is an Adjunct Research Professor at Carleton University and a Professor Emeritus at the University of Western Ontario.

Mario A. Forcinito was born in Buenos Aires, Argentina where he took his Bachelor's degree in Engineering. He obtained his doctorate in Engineering at the University of Calgary under the supervision of M. Epstein. Dr. Forcinito is the CTO of *AP Dynamics*, an engineering company in Calgary. He currently holds an Adjunct Professor position at the Schulich School of Engineering, University of Calgary and is an industrial engineering consultant in the energy area in Calgary.

James M. McQuillan grew up in Ottawa, Canada. He obtained his Undergraduate and Master's degrees from Carleton University in Ottawa and the University of Vermont and his doctorate from the University of Western Ontario (now Western University) in London, Canada. Dr. McQuillan is a Professor in the School of Computer Sciences at Western Illinois University.

Part I

Mainly Cryptography

Chapter 1

Historical Introduction and the Life and Work of Claude E. Shannon

Goals, Discussion We present here an overview of historical aspects of classical cipher systems. Our objective is to give the reader a panoramic view of how the fundamental ideas and important developments fit together. This overview does not pretend to be exhaustive but gives a rough time line of development of the milestones leading to modern cryptographic techniques. The reader interested in a complete historical review is advised to consult the definitive treatise by Kahn [Kah67].

1.1 Historical Background

Cryptology is made up of two Greek words *kryptos*, meaning "hidden," and *lógos* meaning "word." It is defined [Bri19] as the science concerned with data communication and storage in secure and usually secret form. It encompasses both cryptography (from the Greek *graphia* meaning writing) and *cryptanalysis* or the art of extracting the meaning of a cryptogram.

Cryptography, Information Theory, and Error-Correction: A Handbook for the 21st Century, Second Edition.
Aiden A. Bruen, Mario A. Forcinito, and James M. McQuillan.
© 2021 John Wiley & Sons, Inc. Published 2021 by John Wiley & Sons, Inc.

Cryptography has a history that is almost as long as the history of the written word. Some four millennia ago (see [Kah67, p. 71]), an Egyptian scribe recorded in stone the first known hieroglyphic symbol substitution in the tomb of *Khnumhotep II*, a nobleman of the time. Although the intention in this case was to exalt the virtues of the person, rather than to send a secret message, the scribe used for the first time one of the fundamental elements used by cryptographers throughout the ages, namely **substitution**. He used unusual hieroglyphic symbols, known perhaps only to the elite, in place of the more common ones.

In substitution, the sender replaces each letter of a word in a message by a new letter (or sequence of letters or symbols) before sending the message. The recipient, knowing the formula used for the substitution – **the secret key** – is able to reconstruct the message from the scrambled text that was received. It is assumed that only the recipient and the sender know the secret key.

The other main cryptographic technique used is **transposition** (or permutation) in which the letters of the message are simply rearranged according to some prescribed formula which would be the secret key in that case.

The Greeks were the inventors of the first **transposition** cipher. The Spartans [Kah67] in the fifth century BCE, were the first recorded users of cryptography for correspondence. They used a secret device called a *scytale* consisting of a tapered baton around which was spirally wrapped either a strip of parchment or leather on which the message was written. When unwrapped, the letters were scrambled, and only when the strip was wrapped around an identically sized rod could the message be read.

Today, even with the advent of high-speed computers, **substitution** and **transposition** form the fundamental building blocks of ciphers used in **symmetric cryptography**.

To put it in a historical perspective, **asymmetric** or **public key** cryptography was not invented until the 1970s. Exactly when it was invented, or who should take most of the credit, is an issue still in dispute. Both the NSA[1] and the CESG[2] have claimed priority in the invention of public key cryptography.

Cryptography has had several reincarnations in almost all cultures. Because of the necessity of keeping certain messages secret (i.e. totally unknown to potential enemies) governments, armies, ecclesiastics, and economic powers of all kinds have been associated throughout history with the development of cryptography. This trend continues today.

The Roman General Julius Caesar was the first attested user of substitution ciphers for military purposes [Kah67, p. 83]. Caesar himself recounted this incident in his *Gallic Wars*. Caesar found out that Cicero's station was besieged and realized that without

---

[1] United States National Security Agency.
[2] Britain's Communications Electronics Security Group.

help, he would not be able to hold out for long. Caesar had a volunteer ride ahead, with an encrypted message fastened to a spear which he hurled into the entrenchment. Basically, Cicero was told to keep up his courage and that Caesar and his legions were on their way.

In the cipher form used by Caesar, the first letter of the alphabet "A" was replaced by the fourth letter "D," the second letter "B" by the fifth "E," and so on. In other words, each original letter was replaced by one three steps further along in the alphabet. To this day, any cipher alphabet that consists of a standard sequence like Caesar's is called a Caesar alphabet even if the shift is different from three.

Not much mention is made of the coding abilities of Augustus Caesar, the first Emperor of Rome and nephew of Julius Caesar. His cipher involved a shift of only one letter so that for the plain text (that is the original text) A was enciphered as B.

Mention of cryptography abounds in early literature: Homer's Iliad refers to secret writing. The *Kama-sutra*, the famous text book of erotics from the Indian subcontinent, lists secret writing as one of the 64 arts or yogas that women should know and practice [Kah67, p. 75]. One of the earliest descriptions of the substitution technique of encryption is given therein. One form involves the replacement of vowels by consonants and vice versa.

In Hebrew literature, there are also examples of letter substitution. The most prevalent is the **atbash** technique. Here the first and last, second and second last, and so on, letters of the Hebrew alphabet are interchanged. An example can be found in the Old Testament of the Bible. Kahn [Kah67, p. 77] cites Jeremiah 25: 26 and Jeremiah 51: 41, where the form "SHESHACH appears in place of *Babel* (Babylon)."

In Jeremiah 51: 41, the phrase with SHESHACH is immediately followed by one using "Babylon." To quote:

> How is SHESHACH taken!
>
> And the praise of the whole earth seized!
>
> How is Babylon become an astonishment
>
> Among the nations!

Through Aramaic paraphrases of the Bible, it is clear that SHESHACH is the same as Babel. With the atbash technique, the second letter of the Hebrew alphabet "b" or *beth* becomes the repeated SH or SHIN, the next to last letter in the alphabet. Similarly, the "l" of *lamed*, becomes the hard ch, or kaph of SHESHACH. Since Babylon appears below, the use of atbash here was not to actually hide the word but perhaps just a way for the scribe to leave a trace of himself in the work he was copying.

The first people to clearly understand the principles of cryptography and to elucidate the beginnings of cryptanalysis were the Arabs [Kah67]. While Europe was in the Dark Ages, Arab arts and science flourished and scholars studied methods of cryptanalysis, the art of unscrambling secret messages without knowledge of the secret key. A complete description of this work, however, was not published until the appearance of the multivolume *Subh al-a'sha* by about 1412.

European cryptology was being developed around this time in the Papal States and the Italian city-states [Kah67]. The first European manual on cryptography (c1379) was a compilation of ciphers by Gabriele de Lavinde of Parma, who served Pope Clement VII. The Office of *Cipher Secretary* to the Pope was created in 1555. The first incumbent was Triphon Bencio de Assisi. But considerably before this in 1474, Cicco Simonetta wrote a manuscript that was entirely devoted to cryptanalysis.

Cryptanalysis was to have tragic consequences for Mary, Queen of Scots. It was the decipherment of a secret message to Anthony Babington supposedly planning an insurrection against Elizabeth I [Lea96] that resulted in her tragic end. Having obtained this evidence, Sir Francis Walshingham, the head of Queen Elizabeth's secret service, sent his agent back to Fotheringay Castle, to intercept and copy more of Mary's secret messages with the result that Mary and all her coconspirators were finally arrested. As a result of the trial, all were executed but only Mary was beheaded. Walshingham later claimed that his agents had found the keys to as many as 50 different ciphers in Mary's apartments. (There has long been a conjecture that Mary was actually innocent and that the evidence was planted to remove this inconvenient rival to the English throne.)

The architect, Leon Battista Alberti born in Florence in 1404, is known as "the Father of Western Cryptology." In 1470, he published *Trattati in Cifra*, in which he described the first cipher disk. His technique led to a generalization of the Caesar cipher, using several shifted alphabets instead of just one alphabet. This gave rise to the so-called Vigenère cipher discussed in Chapter 2. (This is actually a misattribution as de Vigenère worked on auto-key systems).

In 1563, the Neapolitan, Giovanni Battista Porta published his *De Furtivis Literarum Notis* on cryptography, in which he formalized the division of ciphers into transposition and substitution.

Moving up several centuries, we find that cryptography was widely used in the American Civil War. The Federal Army [Bri97] made extensive use of transposition ciphers in which a key word indicated the order in which columns of the array were to be read and in which the elements were either plain text words or codeword replacements for plain text. Because they could not decipher them, the Confederacy, sometimes in desperation, published Union ciphers in newspapers appealing for readers to help with the cryptanalysis. To make matters worse for the Confederate Army, the Vigenère cipher which they themselves used was easily read by the Union Army.

Kahn reports [Kah67, p. 221] that a Vigenère tableau was found in the room of John Wilkes Booth after President Lincoln was shot. Because there was actually no testimony regarding any use of the cipher, could this have been a convenient method of linking Booth and the seven Southern sympathizers with the Confederate cause?

Lyon Playfair, Baron of St. Andrews, recommended a cipher invented in 1854 by his friend Charles Wheastone, to the British government and military. The cipher was based in a digraphic[3] substitution table and was known as the *Playfair Cipher*. The main difference when compared with a simple substitution cipher is that characters are substituted two at a time. Substitution characters depend on the positions of the two plain text characters on a secret 5×5 square table (the key) whose entries are the characters of the alphabet less the letter "J."

In 1894, Captain Alfred Dreyfus of the French military was accused of treason and sent to Devil's Island, because his hand writing resembled that of an encrypted document that offered military information to Germany. To prove his innocence, the note had to be cryptanalyzed. To be certain that the decipherers' work was correct, an army liaison officer with the Foreign Ministry managed to elicit another similarly encrypted note in which the contents were known to him. The plain text then showed that Dreyfus had not written the encrypted document, but it took several more years before he was to "receive justice, re-instatement and the Legion of Honour" [Kah67, p. 262].

Early in the twentieth century, Maugborne and Vernam put forth the basis for the cipher known as the one-time pad. Although – as was proven later by Shannon – this cipher is effectively unbreakable, its use is somewhat restricted because, in practice, a random key that is as long as the message must be generated and transmitted securely from **A** to **B**. Soviet spies used this cipher, and it is said that the phone line between Washington and Moscow was protected with a one-time pad during the Cold War era.

Edward Hugh Hebern [Bri97] of the United States invented the first electric contact rotor machine. In 1915, he experimented with mechanized encryption by linking two electric typewriters together using 26 wires to randomly pair the letters. In turn, this led to the idea of rotors which could not only mechanize substitution, but also alphabet shifts as well. The function of the rotor was to change the pairing of letters by physically changing the distribution of electric contacts between the two typewriters. By 1918, he had built an actual rotor-based encryption machine.

---

[3] *di* meaning two, *graph* meaning character or symbol.

At about the same time (1918–1919) three other inventors, the German Arthur Scherbius, the Dutchman Hugo Koch and the Swede Arvid Damm were filing patents of rotor-based encryption machines. The Scherbius idea, which included multiple rotors, materialized in the first commercial models having four rotors, ENIGMA A and ENIGMA B in 1923. Ironically, Hebern only filed for patent protection in 1921, received one in 1924 and lost a patent interference case against International Business Machines in 1941. Later modifications to the Scherbius machine including a reflector rotor, and three interchangeable rotors were implemented by the Axis Forces during World War II.

Rotor-based machines give the possibility to implement poly-alphabetic substitution ciphers[4] with very long keys or *cycles* in a practical way. With the advantage of mechanization, the ability of widespread deployment of cryptographic stations and widespread use became a reality. This translated into a larger volume of messages (potentially all messages) being encrypted. However, the increase in traffic gave more cipher text for cryptanalysts to analyze and the probability of operators making a deadly mistake in the management of keys was multiplied.

The timely breaking of the ENIGMA cipher by the Allies was due in part to inherent weaknesses in the encryption machine, mismanagement of keys by the operators and lots of mechanized, analytical work. The cipher was first broken, using only captured cipher text and a list of daily keys obtained through a spy, by the Polish mathematician Marian Rejewski. One of the important players in the mechanization of ensuing breaks was the English mathematician Alan Turing, who also contributed to the establishment of the basis for what is today called Computation Theory.

As a side note, after World War II, many of the ENIGMA machines captured by the Allies were sold to companies and governments in several countries.

Another very interesting cryptographic technique of a different kind was used by the US military in the Pacific campaign in World War II. Secret military messages were encrypted by translating them from English to the Navajo language. For decryption at the other end, of course, the Navajo was translated back into English. Some words describing military equipment did not exist in the original Navajo language, but substitutes were found. For example "tanks and planes" were described using the Navajo words for "turtles and birds." To avoid the possibility of the enemy getting a handle of the code, the whole system was committed – by means of an intensive training program – to the memory of the translators or "Code Talkers." This code was never broken.

Immediately after World War II, Shannon was publishing his seminal works on information theory. Almost simultaneously, thanks to the efforts of Ulam, von Neumann, Eckert, and Mauchly another key technological development was starting to make strident progress, the introduction of the newly invented digital computer as a mathematical tool [Coo87].

---

[4] A poly-alphabetic cipher uses several substitution alphabets instead of one.

(a) (b)

Figure 1.1: (a) Claude E. Shannon, Theseus, and the maze (see Section 1.4). (b) Claude E. Shannon. Source: Reused with permission of Nokia Corporation and AT&T Archives.

Because of the importance of his contributions to the issues in this book, we present here a brief biography of Shannon, before finishing the chapter with a review of modern developments (Figure 1.1).

1.2 Brief Biography of Claude E. Shannon

Claude Shannon has been described as the "father of the information age." His discoveries are everywhere. Waldrop [Wal01] gives an excellent example from the days, not so long ago, where most people listened to music on CDs, before streaming services became so popular.

> Pick up a favorite CD. Now drop it on the floor. Smear it with your fin-gerprints. Then slide it into the slot on the player-and listen as the music comes out just as crystal clear as the day you first opened the plastic case. Before moving on with the rest of your day, give a moment of thought to the man whose revolutionary ideas made this miracle possible: Claude Elwood Shannon.

Computers give us the power to process information. But Shannon gave us the capacity to understand and analyze information. Shannon demonstrated the unity of text, pictures, film, radio-waves, and other types of electronic communication, and showed how to use these media to revolutionize technology and our way of thinking.

1.3   Career

Shannon was born in Petoskey, Michigan in 1916. His father was a business man who later became a judge, and his mother was a high schoolteacher. As a youngster he was interested in, and became adept at, handling all kinds of contraptions such as model airplanes and boats as well as learning the workings of the telegraph system. At the age of 20, he graduated with degrees in Mathematics and Electrical Engineering from the University of Michigan.

In the summer of 1936, Claude joined the MIT Electric Engineering department as a research assistant to work on an analog computer (as opposed to our modern digital computers) under the supervision of Vannevar Bush. Bush's analog computer, called a differential analyzer, was the most advanced calculator of the era and was used mainly for solving differential equations. A relay circuit associated with the analyzer used hundreds of relays and was a source of serious study by Shannon, then, and later.

During the summer of 1937, Shannon obtained an internship at Bell Laboratories and returned to MIT to work on a Master's thesis. In September 1938, he moved to the Mathematics Department of MIT and wrote a thesis in genetics with the title *An Algebra for Theoretical Genetics* graduating in 1940 with his PhD degree in Mathematics and the S.M. degree in Electrical Engineering.

Dr. Shannon spent the academic year of 1940–1941 at the Princeton Institute where he worked with Herman Weyl, the famous group-theorist and geometer. Subsequently, he spent a productive 15 years at the Bell Laboratories in New Jersey returning to MIT in 1956, first as a visiting professor and then, in 1958, as Donner Professor of Science. This was a joint appointment between mathematics and electrical engineering. Here he did not teach ordinary courses but gave frequent seminars. According to Horgan and Claude [Hor90], he once gave an entire seminar course, with new results at each lecture!

He retired from MIT in 1978 but continued to work on many different problems including portfolio theory for the stock market, computer chess, juggling, and artificial intelligence. He died in 2001, at the age of 84 a few years after the onset of Alzheimer's Disease.

1.4   Personal – Professional

Dr. Shannon's Master's thesis [Sha40] and related publication in Transactions, American Institute of Electrical Engineers [Sha38] won him the Alfred Noble Prize along with fame and renown. The thesis has often been described as the greatest Master's thesis of all time; many feel that this may in fact understate the case.

At MIT, he was idolized by both the students and faculty. Golomb et al. [GBC+02], reports that Shannon was "somewhat inner-directed and shy, but very easy to talk to after the initial connection had been made."

In his spare time, Shannon built several items including Thrifty Roman numerical Backward-looking Computer (THROBAC) which was actually a calculator that performed all the arithmetic operations in the Roman numerical system. He also built Theseus, a mechanical mouse in 1950. Controlled by a relay circuit, the mouse moved around a maze until it found the exit. Then, having been through the maze, the mouse, placed anywhere it had been before, would go directly to the exit. Placed in an unvisited locale, the mouse would search for a known position then proceed to the exit, adding the new knowledge to its memory.

Shannon was the first to develop computerized chess machines and kept several in his house. He built a "mind-reading" machine that played the old game of penny-watching. As juggling was one of his obsessions, he built several juggling machines and worked hard on mathematical models of juggling. He was famous for riding his unicycle along the corridors at Bell Laboratories juggling all the while. On the more practical side, Shannon was also interested in portfolio management and the stock market which he connected to information theory, treating it as a noisy channel.

Over the course of his career, Dr. Shannon received umpteen awards, honors, prizes, honorary degrees, and invitations. In the end, it all became too much, and he "dropped out." To quote Waldrop [Wal01] "he turned down almost all the endless invitations to lecture or to give newspaper interviews. He didn't want to be a celebrity. He likewise quit responding to much of his mail. Correspondence from major figures in science and government ended up forgotten and unanswered in a file folder he labeled 'Letters I've procrastinated too long on.'." Dr. Shannon did attend one other Shannon lecture in Brighton, England, in 1985 (delivered by Golomb), where the shy genius created quite a stir. As Robert McEleice recalls (see [Hor90]): "It was as if Newton had showed up at a physics conference."

1.5 Scientific Legacy

Circuits

Shannon's Master's Thesis (see above and [Sha48]) was the first work to make him famous. He became intrigued by the switching circuits controlling the differential analyzer while working for Vannevar Bush. He was the first to notice that the work of a mathematics professor named George Boole in Cork, Ireland, done a century earlier, yielded the necessary mathematical framework for analyzing such circuits.

"On" and "Off" could be represented by "1" and "0." The Boolean logical operations of AND, OR correspond exactly to a circuit with two switches in series, or in parallel, respectively. He demonstrated that any logical statement, no matter how complex, could be implemented physically as a network of such switches. He also showed how the crucial Boolean decision operation could be implemented in a digital system marking the main qualitative difference between a calculator and the powerful digital computers to follow.

Cryptography

Shannon published just one paper in cryptography, namely "Communication theory of secrecy systems," [Sha49b]. Its contents had appeared in a war-time classified Bell Laboratories document which was then declassified. The beginning sentence is very revealing. It reads as follows:

> The problems of cryptography and secrecy systems furnish an interesting application of communication theory.

Indeed, this is precisely the point of view which inspired the authors of this book! We believe it is unrealistic to separate the study of cryptography from the study of communication theory embodying error-correction and information theory.

To illustrate this, Shannon points out that just as in error-correction, where the receiver tries to decode the message over a noisy channel so also, in cryptography, a receiver (this time, Eve, the eavesdropper) tries to decode the message over a noisy channel, the noise being the scrambling by the key which obfuscates the plain text to the cipher text.

In this paper, Shannon discusses at length his two famous principles of confusion and diffusion described in detail in Chapter 4. The Vernam cipher offers perfect security. We discuss perfect security in detail in Part II of the book where it is shown that, under appropriate conditions, perfect security corresponds precisely to a Latin square. Shannon's paper makes it quite clear that he was aware of this phenomenon though he did not explicitly state it.

In the paper, Shannon clearly differentiates between computational and unconditional security. Whether or not he "missed" public key cryptography is far from clear. However, in [Mas02] Massey points out that Hellman of Diffie–Hellman fame, has credited the following words from Shannon's paper as the inspiration for their discovery:

> The problem of good cipher design is essentially one of finding difficult problems .... We may construct our cipher in such a way that breaking it is equivalent to ... the solution of some problem known to be laborious.

Of course, the jury is still out, as Massey [Mas02] points out, on whether one-way functions, the foundations of public key cryptography, really exist. We refer to Chapters 3 and 4 on this point.

Shannon theory: information compression and communication.

Shannon's revolutionary paper [Sha49b] on information theory electrified the scientific world and has dominated the area of communication theory for over 50 years. No other work of the twentieth century has had greater impact on science and engineering.

First of all, Shannon unified what had been a diverse set of communications – voice, data, telegraphy, and television. He quantified and explained exactly what information means. The unit of information is the Shannon bit. As Golomb et al. [GBC$^+$02] so elegantly puts it, this is the "amount of information gained (or entropy removed) upon learning the answer to a question whose two possible answers were equally likely, a priori."

In the above, we can think of entropy as "uncertainty" analogous to entropy in physics (which is the key idea in the second law of thermodynamics). An example would be the tossing of a fair coin and learning which turned up – heads or tails. If the coin were biased, so that the probability of a head was p (and the probability of a tail was $1 - p$) with $p \neq 1/2$, the information gained, on learning the outcome of the toss, would be less than one. The exact amount of information gained would be

$$p \log(1/p) + q \log(1/q) \text{ where } q = 1 - p \text{ and where we take logs to the base 2} \quad (1.1)$$

Note that when $p = \frac{1}{2}$ and $q = \frac{1}{2}$, this works out to be 1. However if, for example $p = 2/3$, we gain only approximately 0.918 Shannon bits of information on learning the outcome of the coin toss.

It can be mathematically proven that the only information function that gives sensible results is the appropriate generalization to a probability distribution of Formula (1.1) above. Formula (1.1) ties in to the fundamental notion of entropy (or uncertainty). There are many examples of redundancy in the English language, i.e. the use of more letters or words or phrases than are necessary to convey the information content being transmitted. As Shannon points out, the existence of redundancy in the language is what makes crosswords possible.

This redundancy can be reduced in various ways. An example is by writing acronyms such as "U.S." for "United States." When information is to be electronically transmitted, we remove redundancy by data-compression. Shannon's formula for data compression is intimately related to entropy which is in turn related to the average number of yes–no questions needed to pin down a fact. Shannon showed that it is possible to obtain a bound for the maximum compression which is the best possible. The actual technique for compressing to that ultimate degree is embodied in the construction of the so-called Huffman codes, well known to all computer science undergraduates. Later, other compression techniques followed, leading to modern technologies used in, for example, mp3's (music compression). This part of Shannon's work is also connected to the later work of Kolmogorov on algorithmic complexity and the minimum length binary program needed for a Turing machine to print out a given sequence.

But this was only the beginning. Shannon then went on to prove his fundamental result on communication, based on entropy and the mathematical ideas delineated above. He showed that any given communications channel has a maximum capacity for reliably transmitting information which he calculated. One can approach this maximum by certain coding techniques – random coding and now turbo coding – but one can never quite reach it. To put it succinctly: *Capacity is the bound to error-free coding.* Thus, for the last 50 years, the study of error correction has boiled down to attempts to devise techniques of encoding in order to come close to the Shannon capacity. We will have much to say about this bound in Parts II and III of this book.

Shannon's work, theoretical and practical, still dominates the field and the landscape. To quote Cover in [Cov02]:

> This ability to create new fields and develop their form and depth surely places Shannon in the top handful of creative minds of the century.

Few can disagree with this assessment. Indeed, in Part III of this book, we describe protocols in cryptography and error-correction based squarely on C.E. Shannon's work in information theory.

1.6 The Data Encryption Standard Code, DES, 1977–2005

The *Data Encryption Standard*, or *DES*, was originally approved in 1977 as a block cipher algorithm that provides good cryptographic protection. Computational power has increased dramatically since 1977. DES is no longer considered to be secure. Since May 2005, it is recommended that DES no longer be used [Cen19].

The *Advanced Encryption Standard*, or *AES*, the replacement for DES, is detailed in Section 5.2.

1.7   Post-Shannon Developments

Cybersecurity

The first two decades of the twenty-first century have witnessed an explosive growth of global need for secure communications and the secure storage of data. Cybersecurity has become an area of major concern to governments and companies. Universities now offer entire degrees in cybersecurity. We discuss this more in Section 28.5.

Big data

In this big data era in which governments and private companies collect more and more information from, and make more information available to individuals in a variety of electronic formats. Along with the usual technological advances in the hardware and software of computers and networks that took place at the end of the twentieth century, there has been an increase in the variety and the uses of technology, including new devices such as smart phones, tablets, smart watches, apps on these devices, a multitude of devices from the Internet of Things (IoT), and cloud computing.

Memory (RAM)

Computers today often have 4, 8, 16, 32, or more GBs of main memory (RAM). Solid-state drives (SSDs) that are much faster (but more expensive) than hard drives (HDDs) are now prevalent in desktops and laptop computers. The memory hierarchy of a computer is discussed in Section 17.2.

Central processing unit (CPU) and graphics processing unit (GPU)

CPUs (processors, or central processing units) on desktops and laptops (and even portable devices such as smart phones) have progressed from mainly one-core processors to multicore processors with 2, 4, 8, or more cores. With multicore processors, multiple tasks can be done in parallel.

GPUs (graphics processing units), previously reserved for doing calculations to display graphics, can do some types of calculations, such as certain matrix manipulations, extremely quickly as they have many, many cores.

Moore's law

An empirical rule that has held true for a few decades is Moore's Law. In 1965, Intel cofounder Gordon Moore asserted that, **"The number of transistors incorporated in a chip will approximately double every 24 months"** (see [Int19]). For many years, the computing power of our desktop and laptop computers doubled every 18 months or so. As processor power increases, we must ensure that an adversary, Eve, who should not have the appropriate decryption keys, cannot decrypt our data and messages. This led in part to the replacement of DES with AES (see Section 1.6).

Recently, some have argued that Moore's law is dead. (See [Hea18, Sim16, Tib19], for example.) However, the performance of chips can still increase from changes in chip design. For example, multicore chips are now common-place. Multiple computations can be done in parallel (at the same time) on different cores in a chip. Other factors, such as artificial intelligence (AI), cloud computing, and quantum computing, mean that we must continue to keep our encryption algorithms up to date. The amount and types of data, some of which are very personal and/or sensitive (e.g. health records, financial records), have never been greater in quantity and sensitivity. The need for encryption using encryption algorithms that are not susceptible to attacks has never been greater.

Artificial intelligence (AI)

Artificial intelligence, AI, and machine learning are allowing cloud computing companies and even apps on phones to make predictions, such as what task should be performed next. We have progressed from having desktop and laptops to using smartphones, tablets, and smart watches, social media, cloud computing, and the IoT devices.

Smart phones

Cell phones have progressed from a basic cell phone (often a "flip phone") to Research in Motion's *BlackBerry 5810* in 2002 to Apple's first *iPhone* in 2007 to the first *Android* phone in 2008, to the smart phones of today. Phone apps allow users to video conference, watch movies, play video games, access important data, and make purchases.

Streaming – video and audio

Video and audio streaming have become so prevalent that a major portion of all Internet traffic is from streaming. We shall discuss streaming in Chapter 17.

Social media

Social media has seen exponential growth as well. For example, as of early 2019, Twitter had 126 million active daily users and Facebook had 1.2 billion daily users [Sha19]. In 2017, Facebook hit 2 billion monthly users. Yurieff notes in [Yur17] that, "It took the social network less than five years to go from 1 billion monthly users to 2 billion."

Cloud computing

Cloud computing is now extremely important, with companies offering impressive software, sometimes for free. Cloud computing providers have the ability to do some computations at much faster pace than we could with our personal devices. They have the advantage that they might have many computers at their disposal and so can use parallelism, artificial intelligence (AI) and other means to give results quickly. They can allow us to access our data from different devices from different locations in the world. Extremely important records, such as financial records and medical records, are accessible via browsers on computers and apps on phones. According to Gartner, "The worldwide public cloud services market is forecast to grow 17% in 2020 to total $266.4 billion, up from $227.8 billion in 2019...," [Gar19]. Chapter 28 deals with cloud computing.

Internet of Things (IoT)

The IoT is another major force today. It refers to any object or device that is connected to the Internet. A smart home can have many devices that can communicate with your phone, such as door bells to light bulbs to audio speakers. Amazon's Alexa is one example of IoT. In 2019, Amazon reported that over 100 million Alexa devices had been sold, [New19a]. Many IoT devices communicate by Bluetooth. The health-care field is also being transformed. As always, we need to be wary of security concerns. For example, in August 2019, *USA Today* had an article by Jefferson Graham entitled, "Sorry, readers. Your Bluetooth device is a security risk," [Gra19]. They quote Jovi Umawing, a research at Malwarebytes Labs:

> A year ago, I was on a ferry coming back from vacation and had a weird photo (a meme style image) pop up on my phone via Airdrop from a source I didn't recognize," he says. "I checked my settings, and it was open to anyone. I immediately shut it off and have left it off ever since. I turn it on to receive from people only when they are standing right in front of me."

Bluetooth has a limited range. So it is relatively safe around the home, unless there is an attacker nearby. But, in a public area, it might be best to turn it off. Graham also quotes Matt Lourens, a security engineering manager with Checkpoint software. He says,

> Another concern: shopping. Many retailers have Bluetooth beacons placed in-store to watch over you and track your location and shopping habits. Turning off Bluetooth before you enter will save your battery and keep prying eyes away from your device.

Bluetooth 5 devices have a range of up to 800 feet. (theoretically) The security of some IoT devices is of major concern. We shall discuss this further in Chapter 27 on the IoT.

Privacy concerns

Privacy and security go together. Biometrics are important as they have both applications and privacy concerns. You might use a fingerprint or facial recognition software on your phone, tablet, or computer to unlock it. Some airports now use facial recognition software to identify travelers so as to improve efficiency for processing the vast number of people that pass through an airport each day. See [Oli19] or [New19b], for example.

Security and privacy

Together, these add up to the need for security and privacy to be part of the decision-making in the development of software and hardware of devices at every stage and level. Security and privacy breaches are reported regularly on the news. Programmers must be ever vigilant to make sure that they write code in a "safe" way so as to ensure privacy and security. Will input provided to the code always be friendly, or could it be malicious? If input could arrive from an outside source (such as via the Internet), then you should assume that there will be malicious attacks. For example, for the C programming language, we recommend two wonderful books on this topic: *Secure Coding in C and C++*, second edition by Seacord, [Sea13], and *C Programming: A Modern Approach*, second edition, by King, [Kin08]. We discuss this more in Section 7.20.

Cryptography

Let us not forget cryptography. The twentieth century ended with DES, the United States Data Encryption Standard, being phased out and replaced. In 1999, Rijndael, a block cipher developed by Joan Daemen and Vincent Rijmen was selected as the AES.[5] AES is the current standard for symmetric cryptography [NIS19b]. Chapter 5 looks at these topics.

Postquantum cryptography

Less than 20 years after the adoption of AES, the United States is preparing for a postquantum world. See [NIS19f]. We will discuss this more in Section 4.12

Blockchains

Blockchains are being used increasingly because of their immutability. In April 2020, during the COVID-19 pandemic, IBM used blockchains to help the health-care industry. In [Wei20], Weiss writes that IBM is using blockchains to connect "pop-up medical mask and equipment makers with hospitals." They quote Mark Treshock, the IBM blockchain solutions leader for IBM healthcare and life sciences as saying, "It's the immutability component. If I am a supplier and I create a profile and include my information for onboarding as a new supplier, there's a qualification process I have to go through... It is done to determine if they are legitimate, ethical, that they comply with required laws and, in this case, with needed FDA certifications." [Wei20]. We will discuss this more in Chapter 26.

---

[5] Published as Federal Information Processing Standard (FIPS) standard 197.

Chapter 2

Classical Ciphers and Their Cryptanalysis

Goals, Discussion   In this chapter, we survey some historical ciphers which have been used since antiquity. (They are all symmetric ciphers. Public key ciphers were not invented until the 1970s and are discussed in Chapter 3.) Although the ciphers presented here are obsolete, they still provide good examples of cryptographic procedures. For example the Vigenère cipher, being a block cipher, is a forerunner of modern block ciphers such as Advanced Encryption Standard (AES). From these classical ciphers, we can also learn about various attacks in cryptography. This subject is pursued more fully in Chapter 7.

New, Noteworthy   We discuss the Vigenère cipher and show how it can be broken by finding the length of the keyword and then the keyword itself. We explain clearly the simple principles involved without getting bogged down in lengthy formulae. We also give a detailed but accessible description of the famous Enigma system used in World War II both from the mechanical and the mathematical point of view.

Cryptography, Information Theory, and Error-Correction: A Handbook for the 21st Century, Second Edition.
Aiden A. Bruen, Mario A. Forcinito, and James M. McQuillan.
© 2021 John Wiley & Sons, Inc. Published 2021 by John Wiley & Sons, Inc.

2.1   Introduction

Since the early stages of human civilization, there has been a need to protect sensitive information from falling into the wrong hands. To achieve such secrecy, mankind has relied on a branch of mathematics known as **cryptography**, which is the study of designing methods to securely transmit information over nonsecure channels. In order to achieve this goal, one must first **encipher**, or scramble, the intended message to prevent an eavesdropper from obtaining any useful information, should the message be intercepted. The message (referred to as **plain text**) is scrambled into **cipher text** using a predetermined key, known to both the sender and receiver. The encrypted message is constructed in such a way so as to be resilient against attack, while allowing the intended recipient to **decipher**, or unscramble the message with ease. The methods we will be investigating in this section to accomplish this task may be outdated and in some cases obsolete, but they can still provide us with valuable insight into some techniques that are still in use today.

2.2   The Caesar Cipher

While Julius Caesar was building his empire, he needed a method to transmit vital messages without risk of the enemy obtaining any crucial information. To achieve this goal, he employed one of the first known ciphering methods. The idea was to substitute each letter of the plain text with the letter appearing three spaces to the right in the alphabet, i.e. a is enciphered to D, b is enciphered to E, and z is enciphered to C (the alphabet wraps around). Thus, "six" is enciphered to "VLA."

In practice, this can be easily achieved using a simple device consisting of two disks, such as the one shown in Figure 2.1. Both disks have the alphabet engraved on their perimeter, and they can rotate with respect to each other. If we assign the inner disk to represent the plain text alphabet and the outer disk to represent the cipher text alphabet, enciphering is accomplished simply by rotating the outer disk by three letters counter clockwise and reading off the cipher text corresponding to the plain text. To decipher the message, one must only reverse the procedure. The "key" of the cipher is just the number of letters that the outer disk is shifted by, and is denoted by k. Both sender and recipient are in possession of this common secret key.

For a numerical explanation, suppose we label $a, b, \ldots, z$ by the numbers $0, 1, \ldots, 25$. Using Caesar's key of three, the plain text message "six" is enciphered as follows:

$$\text{six} \longrightarrow (18, 8, 23) \xrightarrow{k=3} (18 + 3, 8 + 3, 23 + 3) = (21, 11, 0) \rightarrow \text{VLA}$$

Figure 2.1: Caesar cipher wheel.

Note that in the above example, $23 + 3 = 26$. We replace 26 by $\text{Rem}[26, 26]$ which is the remainder when we divide by 26 (see Chapter 19 for details). In this case, the remainder is 0, corresponding to the letter A. Similarly, $24 + 11$ becomes $\text{Rem}[35, 26] = 9$. The number 9 corresponds to the letter J.

To decipher the message, reverse the operation (shift left by k spaces):

$$\text{VLA} \to (21, 11, 0) \xrightarrow{k=3} (21 - 3, 11 - 3, 0 - 3) = (18, 8, 23) \to \text{six}$$

In this case, we have $0 - 3 = 23$. If x is a negative number, then it is replaced by $26 + x$. So, for example -3 gets replaced by $26 + (-3) = 23$. The reasoning is that $\text{Rem}[-3, 26] = 23$ since $-3 = 26(-1) + 23$. Alternatively, (see Chapter 19) we have $-3 \equiv 23 \pmod{26}$.

The Caesar cipher is a simple example of a type of cipher known as a **monoalphabetic** cipher. Monoalphabetic ciphers belong to a class of ciphers known as **substitution**

ciphers, in which all of the plain text characters in the message are substituted for another letter. Mathematically speaking, the enciphering process of a monoalphabetic cipher can be represented by the mapping of a plain text character to a cipher text character:

$$x \to \mathrm{Rem}[x + k, 26]$$

Similarly, deciphering is represented by the mapping

$$x \to \mathrm{Rem}[x - k, 26]$$

where k is the **cipher key**, with $1 \le k \le 25$. In the case of the Caesar cipher, $k = 3$. If $x - k$ is negative, then, as explained above, $\mathrm{Rem}[x - k, 26] = 26 + (x - k)$.

To break such a cipher, one can decrypt the message by trying all 26 keys (this is referred to as an exhaustive search). For long messages, the likelihood of a cipher text decrypting to two intelligible messages is small.

We mention here briefly *affine ciphers*. They are similar to Caesar ciphers in that they are simple substitution ciphers, but they differ in that enciphering involves not only addition, but also multiplication as well.

2.3 The Scytale Cipher

The Scytale cipher was introduced around 500 BCE by the Spartans, who used this rather simple but effective method to send crucial planning data between generals and bureaucrats. Both the sender and receiver were in possession of a cylindrical tube of the same diameter. To encode the message, the sender would wrap a thin strip of paper around the tube, with the paper spiraling its way down the length of the tube. The message was then written on the strip, with letters being written one beneath the other until the end of the tube was reached. (The message was then continued by starting a new column of letters, and this process was repeated until the message was finished.) To encode, the sender would simply unwrap the paper, leaving a thin strip of unintelligible letters. To decode, the receiver only had to wrap the paper around their similar tube and read the message off in columns.

It is often much simpler to duplicate the Scytale process with pencil and paper. Using a preselected number of rows (this number is the cipher key), write the message in columns. Then, "unwrap" the message by writing a string of characters consisting of the concatenated rows. For example, the message "THE ENEMY WILL ATTACK AT DAWN" is encrypted as follows:

$$
\begin{array}{cccc}
T & M & A & A \\
H & Y & T & T \\
E & W & T & D \\
E & I & A & A \\
N & L & C & W \\
E & L & K & N \\
\end{array}
$$

$$\downarrow$$

TMAAHYTTEWTDEIAANLCWELKN

Knowledge of the cipher key reduces the decryption process to a trivial matter. Using the fact that the key for this example is six, count up the total number of characters and divide by six. Doing so yields the period of the sequence, which is four. Thus, by taking the first, fifth, ninth, . . . characters, one can reconstruct the columns. Upon completion, the message can be read off, column by column.

The Scytale concept can be modified to create very complex ciphers. By arranging the plain text in varying matrix patterns and "unwrapping" in different ways, messages can be scrambled very effectively. The Scytale cipher, along with its variants, belongs to a class of ciphers called **transposition ciphers**, in which all plain text characters are present in the cipher text, but they appear in a substantially different order.

2.4 The Vigenère Cipher

The next classical cipher of great interest is known as the Vigenère cipher. Although it is a relatively simple concept, it has influenced many ciphers used throughout history, including some that are still in use today. The idea is to modify the notion of Caesar ciphers, which were covered in Section 2.2. Instead of a single cipher key, we make use of an entire keyword, which is a key in the form of a string of letters chosen by the user. For example, suppose we decide to use the word "encode" as our keyword. The enciphering process is carried out as follows. The keyword is repeated as many times as necessary to span the length of the message. Each letter corresponds to a number between 0 and 25 (so $a = 0$, $b = 1$, . . ., $z = 25$). Then, to encipher, we add the corresponding numbers of the keyword and the message, subtracting 26 if the sum is bigger than 25. Then we switch back to letters to get the cipher text. For example, if the message letter is y ($= 24$), and the keyword letter is E ($= 4$), then the cipher text letter corresponds to $24 + 4 = 28$. However, 28 is larger than 26, so we subtract 26 to get 2, which is C. Thus, y enciphers to C.

Keyword:	E	N	C	O	D	E	E	N	C	O	D	E	E	N	C
Message:	t	h	e	s	k	y	i	s	f	a	l	l	i	n	g
Cipher text:	X	U	G	G	N	C	M	F	H	O	O	P	M	A	I

Notice that each letter of the cipher text is shifted by varying amounts, unlike the Caesar cipher. Interpreting this as many monoalphabetic ciphers acting on individual characters, it is easy to see why the Vigenère cipher is referred to as a **polyalphabetic cipher**.

To decipher, simply subtract the value of the respective key letters from each cipher text letter. For example, to decrypt the cipher text "XUGGNCMFHOOPMAI" from above, we use the keyword "ENCODE" as follows:

$$X - E = 23 - 4 = 19 \qquad = t$$
$$U - N = 20 - 13 = 7 \qquad = h$$
$$G - C = 6 - 2 = 4 \qquad = e$$
$$G - O = 6 - 14 = -8 = 18 = s$$

Repeat the process until all plain text characters have been determined. This enciphering process is easy if one has knowledge of the key. However, it can be difficult to break the cipher without such information. This will be investigated in Section 2.6.

The Vigenère cipher is known as a type of **block cipher**, where the block length is equivalent to the key length. In a block cipher procedure, the plain text or message is encrypted block by block, rather than character by character.

There are a few important remarks to be made regarding the use of the Vigenère cipher. First, because the same plain text character enciphers to different characters depending on the position, the cryptanalysis of such a cipher is much more complex than for a simple monoalphabetic substitution cipher. We also point out that the Vigenère cipher was invented to hide the frequencies of letters in the English language. The Caesar cipher, for example, does not do this. Also, if the key phrase "VIGENERECIPHERX" had been used instead of "ENCODE," in our previous example, the encrypted message would have had **perfect secrecy**. Perfect secrecy is achieved if the cipher text yields no information about the plain text, and this occurs, roughly speaking, when the keyword is as long as the message itself. Such a secure system can be obtained using **one-time pads**, which we investigate later in the book.

2.5   Frequency Analysis

The idea behind the use of frequency analysis in cryptanalysis is that all human languages have underlying statistical patterns and redundancies that can be exploited to help break a variety of ciphers. For the English language, it is well documented that the distribution of the most frequent characters is remarkably similar throughout texts of diverse style and length, as indicated in Table 2.1.

Letter	Frequency (%)	Letter	Frequency (%)
a	7.44	b	1.46
c	2.52	d	3.53
e	12.22	f	2.68
g	1.84	h	5.97
i	6.82	j	0.20
k	0.65	l	4.28
m	2.71	n	6.32
o	8.25	p	1.97
q	0.12	r	6.21
s	6.99	t	9.85
u	3.67	v	0.12
w	2.09	x	0.18
y	1.87	z	0.03

Table 2.1: Approximate frequencies of letters in the English language.
Source: These percentages are based on the book "The Tragical History of Doctor Faustus", by Christopher Marlowe, which is a book of approximately 100 000 characters that was chosen randomly from the *Project Gutenberg*.

Frequency analysis can be used for cryptanalysis. However, one needs a lot of craft in its use, along with any information that can be gathered about the contents of the message and the sender.

2.6 Breaking the Vigenère Cipher, Babbage–Kasiski

Now that the Vigenère cipher has been defined, we will show how to use the frequencies of letters in English, to break this cipher. We have two tasks.

- Find the keyword length.

- Find the keyword itself.

We have two methods to find the length of the keyword. The first method, the **Babbage–Kasiski method**, attempts to find repeated successive triples (or four-tuples, or five-tuples, etc.,) of letters in the cipher text. The second method treats the English language like a stationary or even ergodic source (see Chapter 11).

We will use two fundamental principles in carrying out our tasks.

- "E" is the most frequent letter of the English language.

- Informally, written English tends to "repeat itself." This means that the frequencies of a passage starting in position 1 are similar to the frequencies of the passage starting in position k when we slide the text along itself.

Once we obtain n, the key-length, we can find the keyword itself. We do this by using the first fundamental property above. Namely, we exploit the statistics of the letters in English, or pairs of letters (i.e. digrams), or trigrams, etc.

The second principle has two important interpretations. For the Babbage–Kasiski method, this means that if we find a repeated letter (or sequence of letters) in the cipher text there is a good chance that it comes from a given letter (or sequence of letters) in the plain text that has been enciphered by a given letter (or letters) in the key. Thus, there is a reasonable expectation that the distances between such repeated sequences of letters equals the key length or a multiple of the key length.

The second principle has an important implication in terms of our second method, called the method of "coincidences," as well. The basic idea is explained in an example below.

The Babbage–Kasiski method

To demonstrate this method for finding n, suppose we received the following cipher text:

EHMVL	VDWLP	WIWXW	PMMYD	PTKNF	RHWXS
LTWLP	OSKNF	WDGNF	DEWLP	SOXWP	HIWLL
EHMYD	LNGPT	EEUWE	QLLSX	TUP	

Our task is to search for repetitions in the above text. For a small cipher text, the brute-force method is not too difficult. We focus on trigrams, and highlight some as follows:

EHMVL	YDŴL̂P̂	WIWXW	PMM̃ỸD̃	PTKNF	RHWXS
LTŴL̂P̂	OSKNF	WDGNF	DEŴL̂P̂	SOXWP	HIWLL
EHM̃ỸD̃	LNGPT	EEUWE	QLLSX	TPU	

After having found these, we compute the distances between the trigrams.

EHM	-	60
WLP	-	25,15,40
XWP	-	39
MYD	-	45

We note that with the exception of 39, 5 divides all of the distances. In fact, if we proceed with frequency analysis, it turns out that we can decipher this message with a key length of 5. The codeword is "ladel," and the plain text is "Thor and the little mouse thought that they should douse the house with a thousand liters of lithium" (Who said that secret messages have to have a clear meaning!) Frequency analysis is used in our next example below.

It is purely by chance that we had the repeated trigram WXP – this repeated trigram was not the result of the same three letters being enciphered by the same part of the keyword. This highlights the fact that the above method is probabilistic.

The method of coincidences

We will now use the second principle of "coincidences," to find the length of the keyword. The sequence of plain text letters in positions 1 to n, $n + 1$ to $2n$, $2n + 1$, to $3n$, etc., should be approximately the same, especially if n is large. It follows that a similar result holds true for the corresponding sequences of cipher text letters. Thus, if we slide the cipher text along itself and count the number of coincidences (i.e. agreements) at each displacement, then on average the maximum number of coincidences will occur after an integer multiple of the keyword length n (i.e. the max occurs for some λn, $\lambda = 1, 2, 3, \ldots$). This technique can be illustrated using the following example: We will first determine the period n and use it to determine the nature of the keyword from a cipher text passage:

VVHZK	UHRGF	HGKDK	ITKDW	EFHEV	SGMPH
KIUWA	XGSQX	JQHRV	IUCCB	GACGF	SPGLH
GFHHD	MHZGF	BSPSW	SDSXR	DFHEM	OEPGI
QXKZW	LGHZI	PHLIV	VFIPH	XVA	

To find n, write the cipher text on a long strip of paper, and copy it onto a second strip of paper beneath the first strip. For a displacement of 1, move the bottom strip to the left by one letter and count the number of character coincidences. Repeat this process for several displacements until the maximum displacement is obtained. The shift shown below corresponds to a displacement of 3:

```
    V   V   H   Z   K   U   H   R   G   F   H   G   K   D           ...   ...
V   V   H   Z   K   U   H   R   G   F   H   G   K   D   K   I   T   ...   ...
```

By repeating this process for a number of displacements, we obtain Table 2.2:

Displacement	Number of coincidences
1	4
2	4
3	9
4	12
5	5
6	2
7	7
8	7

Table 2.2: Number of character coincidences corresponding to displacement

From our results, the maximum number of occurrences appears for a displacement of 4. Since we know the maximum displacement occurs for a scalar multiple of the period, the period is likely either 2 or 4.

Remark

In applying the second principle, we are using a probabilistic argument. That is, in the above example, we cannot be certain that the period is either 2 or 4; however, we can say with high probability that it is likely to be either 2 or 4. If we were unable to decipher the text with a keyword length of 2 or 4, we would then try with the next highest number of coincidences, which occurs for displacement 3.

Finding the keyword

Now that we know how to find n, we examine how to find the keyword itself. Suppose, for example, that the key-length is 7. Consider the plain text character in the $1^{st}, 8^{th}, 15^{th}, \ldots$ positions (i.e. characters at a distance of 7 spaces). If a particular letter occurs in positions 1 and 8, the cipher text letters in positions 1 and 8 will be the same (because we use the same key letter to encipher both characters). How can we deduce which cipher text characters correspond to which plain text characters? In the English language, the most frequently used letter is "e." Even if we restrict ourselves to the letters of the message in positions $1, 8, 15, \ldots$, this will still be the case. Therefore, the most frequent cipher text letter in positions $1, 8, 15, \ldots$ will have come from the enciphering of the letter "e". Thus, by computing the number of occurrences of each cipher text letter at intervals of 7 letters, we can determine the most frequently occurring cipher text letter and assign it to the plain text letter "e". Hence, we will have determined the first letter of the keyword. Similar remarks apply to positions $\{2, 9, 16, \ldots\}$, $\{3, 10, 17, \ldots\}$. In general, if we know the period n, we can capture the key using frequency analysis.

We will first try the case where the period is 4, and we will determine the character frequencies for the $\{1^{st}, 5^{th}, 9^{th}, \ldots\}$ letters, $\{2^{nd}, 6^{th}, 10^{th}, \ldots\}$ letters, and so on. Taking the $1^{st}, 5^{th}, 9^{th}, \ldots$ letters, we get

$$\text{VKGKT EVPUG JVCCP GDGPD DMGKG PVPA}$$

from which we obtain the following table of frequencies:

A	B	C	D	E	F	G	H	I	J	K	L	M
1	0	2	3	1	0	6	0	0	1	2	0	1

N	O	P	Q	R	S	T	U	V	W	X	Y	Z
0	0	5	0	0	0	1	1	4	0	0	0	0

Since G is the most frequently occurring letter, we make the assumption that "e" enciphers to G. Thus the first key letter might be "C." Similarly, for the second set of letters (i.e. the $2^{nd}, 6^{th}, 10^{th}, \ldots$ letters), we obtain the following table:

A	B	C	D	E	F	G	H	I	J	K	L	M
0	1	0	1	0	5	2	4	2	0	1	0	1

N	O	P	Q	R	S	T	U	V	W	X	Y	Z
0	1	0	1	0	4	0	1	2	1	0	0	1

Here there are three letters which could likely decipher to "e." To determine which letter is the right choice, consider each character separately. If "e" enciphers to "F," we have a key letter of "B." If "e" enciphers to "H," we have a key letter of "D." Finally, if "e" enciphers to "S," we have a key letter of "O." Now, we must examine each choice case by case. A key letter of "B" means that the most frequently occurring letters besides "e" are "g" and "r." Similarly, a key letter of "D" means that the most frequently occurring letters in the plain text (in positions $2, 6, 10, \ldots$) besides "e" are "c" and "p." Finally, a key letter of "O" means that the most frequently occurring letters besides "e" are "t" and "r.". From the results shown in Table 2.1, it seems that "O" is then the more likely key-letter. Therefore, we conclude that the second key letter is "O."

For the $3^{rd}, 7^{th}, 11^{th}, \ldots$ letters, we obtain the following frequency table:

A	B	C	D	E	F	G	H	I	J	K	L	M
1	1	0	1	1	2	2	8	0	0	2	2	0

N	O	P	Q	R	S	T	U	V	W	X	Y	Z
0	0	0	2	0	0	0	1	0	2	2	0	1

For this set of letters, the most frequently occurring letter is H. Therefore, we make the assumption that "e" enciphers to "H." This corresponds to a key letter of "D."

Finally, for the $4^{th}, 8^{th}, 12^{th}, \ldots$ letters, we compute the frequencies to be

A	B	C	D	E	F	G	H	I	J	K	L	M
1	0	1	0	2	0	1	2	5	0	0	1	1

N	O	P	Q	R	S	T	U	V	W	X	Y	Z
0	0	1	0	3	3	0	0	1	1	3	0	2

From this table, we deduce that since "e" likely enciphers to "I," our fourth and final key letter is "E."

Putting all of this together, we have determined that the period n is Four, and the corresponding keyword is the word "code." This gives the message, "The Vigenère cipher was created in the sixteenth century and was considered by everyone to be unbreakable until the twentieth century."

The method used above, though simple to use, is very effective in determining the keyword of a given cipher text passage. The reader should be aware that there may be times where it may take some more work to pin the keyword down, due to multiple period choices and ambiguities that may occur in the frequencies of cipher text letters.

Remark

In examining these methods for breaking the Vigenère cipher, we have stated many times that these methods are only probabilistic, that is, they are only likely to work, not guaranteed. It is possible that we could go through the above process, only to decipher a given cipher text incorrectly. The question of how many messages encipher to a given cipher text is discussed in Chapter 15, and it turns out that we can roughly expect there to be only one intelligible message fitting with a given cipher text when the cipher text has more than 28 letters.

2.7 The Enigma Machine and Its Mathematics

During World War II, German troops were able to march unopposed through much of Eastern Europe. At the heart of this war machine was an encryption scheme that allowed commanders to transfer crucial planning data with near total secrecy. Before the invasion of Poland, three Polish cryptologists by the names of Marian Rejewski, Henry Zygalski, and Jerzy Różycki were able to crack the majority of the Enigma code used by the German army. Fearing capture during the German invasion, they escaped to France, bringing with them vital secrets about the Enigma machine.

Mechanically speaking, the Enigma machine consists of three removable rotors, a keyboard, a reflector plate, and a plugboard (see Figure 2.2). Each rotor has 26 electrical

Figure 2.2: The German Enigma machine. (a) the Enigma machine type-K, (b) the German Enigma machine display at the Naval Museum of Alberta, Canada, (c) the caption on the display at the Naval Museum of Alberta, Canada, (d) the Enigma machine type-K, power supply, and additional lamp panel. Source: Used with permission of the Naval Museum of Alberta, Canada.

contacts on each face (with each one representing a value between 0 and 25), and wires connecting contacts on opposite faces in a variety of ways. The rotors rotate clockwise and are geared in such a way that the settings of the first rotor change with each plain text character that is enciphered and cycles through the values 0 to 25. Upon the transition between 25 back to 0, the second rotor rotates 1/26th of a turn. Following the transition between 25 back to 0 on the second rotor, the third rotor rotates 1/26th of a turn. This ensures that if the same character is sent twice in a row, it will likely be enciphered as two different cipher text letters. To increase the number of possible permutations, the rotors can be interchanged with one another. The reflector plate is a device with 26 contacts on the face adjacent to the last rotor, wired in such a way that the contacts are connected in pairs. Once a signal is sent to the reflector, it is sent through the corresponding wire and back into the third rotor. The plugboard consists of a series of sockets, and the board changes the identity of the input character based on the following conventions: if the given socket contains a plug, the character's identity is changed. If the socket is empty, the character remains unchanged. This device simply provides another set of permutations, meant to increase the complexity of the enciphering scheme. A basic block diagram of the system is depicted in Figure 2.3.

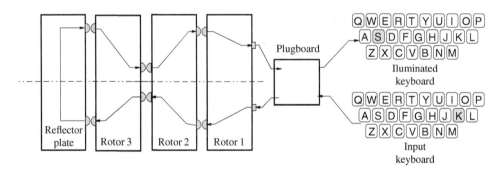

Figure 2.3: Block diagram of the Enigma machine.

To use the machine, an operator inputs the desired plain text into a keyboard, one character at a time. An electrical signal is passed from the keyboard through the rotors which are connected in series, until the charge reaches the reflector plate. Then, the signal is passed back from the plate through the rotors and back into the keyboard, where a separate panel consisting of light bulbs is illuminated. Each light bulb corresponds to a cipher text letter, which is recorded by the operator. As the signal passes through each rotor, the plain text character is continually substituted, depending on the daily settings of the rotor and the specific wiring between contacts, which govern the permutations of substitutions that are possible. When the enciphering process is complete, the operator sends the cipher text via radio to the intended receiver, who also possesses an Enigma machine. The receiver can then decode the message, given that the initial settings and the permutation sets of the machines are coordinated, by simply typing in the cipher text into the machine. The plain text message then appears on the illuminated keyboard.

It is worth noting some of the deficiencies in the machine design, as they made it possible for Allied cryptanalysts to eventually break the cipher. There is a very nice YouTube video, "Flaw in the Enigma Code - Numberphile," [Gri13], that talks about flaws in the Enigma machine. They note that a given letter of the alphabet might be mapped to any *other* letter, i.e. a letter is never encoded as itself. The number of permutations of n objects is $n!$, but if we insist that no object is mapped to itself, then the number of such permutations, i.e. the number of derangements of n objects, is reduced to approximately $\frac{n!}{e}$, (where $e \approx 2.72$ is the base of the natural logarithm). See Ryser [Rys63, p. 23]. Thus, some information about the encoding is revealed along with a coded message!

We will now investigate the machine from a mathematical standpoint. Each rotor is represented by a set of permutations containing all letter values between 0 and 25. The transition of each set runs left to right, with each bracket representing a wrap-around or cycle. The first, second, and third rotors have unique permutation sets denoted α_1, α_2, and α_3, respectively (each representing the possible transitions between letters). To aid in our analysis, we introduce the variables r_1, r_2, and r_3 to represent the initial rotor settings (taken to be the character currently located at the top of the rotor). For the purposes of this analysis, we will be ignoring the role of the plugboard. Finally, the reflector plate is modeled as a set of permutations between pairs of characters, denoted by β. The goal is to track a signal as it leaves the input keyboard, travels though the rotors and reflector, and back to the illuminated display. To determine the appropriate cipher text for each given plain text letter, we will calculate the shift of each rotor, the resulting reflector permutation and reflected signal shifts until we end up with a final cipher text character.

To show how the enciphering process works, consider the modified system shown in Figure 2.4.

The idea is to keep track of each intermediate substitution, in order to determine the final cipher text character. To illustrate the encoding process, consider the following example:

Example 2.1 *Suppose the permutation sets of each rotor and reflector are defined as follows:*

$$\alpha_1 = (0\ 15\ 6\ 10\ 14\ 8\ 19\ 17\ 22\ 18\ 11)\ (1\ 2\ 9\ 13\ 21\ 25)\ (3\ 4\ 23\ 5\ 24\ 7\ 12\ 16\ 20)$$
$$\alpha_2 = (0\ 7\ 9\ 4\ 6\ 18\ 23\ 25\ 8)\ (1\ 17\ 19)\ (2\ 20\ 10)\ (3\ 12)\ (5\ 11\ 13\ 21)\ (14\ 22\ 15\ 16\ 24)$$
$$\alpha_3 = (0\ 2\ 4\ 7\ 16\ 17\ 19\ 5)\ (1\ 6\ 3\ 8\ 21\ 24\ 11\ 13\ 9\ 10\ 25\ 12\ 14\ 15)\ (18\ 23\ 20\ 22)$$
$$\beta = (0\ 4)\ (1\ 7)\ (2\ 9)\ (3\ 16)\ (5\ 20)\ (6\ 8)\ (10\ 19)\ (11\ 17)\ (12\ 25)\ (13\ 18)\ (14\ 24)$$
$$(15\ 22)\ (21\ 23)$$

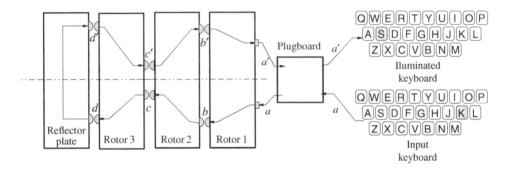

Figure 2.4: Simplified Enigma model.

So, with α_1, 0 gets moved to 15, 15 gets moved to 6, 11 moves to 0, etc.

Each permutation set possesses an inverse, which "undoes" the action of said permutation, as follows:

$$\alpha_1^{-1} = (11\ 18\ 22\ 17\ 19\ 8\ 14\ 10\ 6\ 15\ 0)\ (25\ 21\ 13\ 9\ 2\ 1)\ (20\ 16\ 12\ 7\ 24\ 5\ 23\ 4\ 3)$$
$$\alpha_2^{-1} = (8\ 25\ 23\ 18\ 6\ 4\ 9\ 7\ 0)\ (19\ 17\ 1)\ (10\ 20\ 2)\ (12\ 3)\ (21\ 13\ 11\ 5)\ (24\ 16\ 15\ 22\ 14)$$
$$\alpha_3^{-1} = (5\ 19\ 17\ 16\ 7\ 4\ 2\ 0)\ (15\ 14\ 12\ 25\ 10\ 9\ 13\ 11\ 24\ 21\ 8\ 3\ 6\ 1)\ (22\ 20\ 23\ 18)$$

The initial settings are defined with $r_1 = 22$ (i.e. the letter at the top of roter 1 is V), $r_2 = 7$, $r_3 = 12$.

For the signal traveling toward the reflector plate, the substitutions through the rotors are represented mathematically as follows:

$$b = \text{Rem}[a + r_1, 26]^{\alpha_1}$$
$$c = \text{Rem}[b + r_2, 26]^{\alpha_2}$$
$$d = \text{Rem}[c + r_3, 26]^{\alpha_3}$$

where raising a term to the exponent α_1 means locating the term in the permutation set and replacing it with the number to the right of the term. If there is a bracket adjacent to the term, wrap around to the beginning of the subset. For example, with our settings as above, $3^{\alpha_1} = 4$ and $8^{\alpha_2} = 0$.

Since the reflector has contacts which are only connected in pairs, we get

$$e = (d)^{\beta}$$

Once e has been output from the reflector, we follow the signal back to the keyboard:

$$c' = \text{Rem}[e^{\alpha_3^{-1}} - r_3, 26]$$
$$b' = \text{Rem}[c'^{\alpha_2^{-1}} - r_2, 26]$$
$$a' = \text{Rem}[b'^{\alpha_1^{-1}} - r_1, 26]$$

After the successful completion of the cipher text substitution, we need to update the rotor settings to take into account the rotation(s) that may have taken place:

r_1 *is redefined as* $\mathrm{Rem}[r_1 + 1, 26]$. *If* $r_1 = 25$ *and we add 1, the new* r_1 *becomes 0 and* r_2 *is advanced by one.*

Similarly, if $r_2 = 25$ *and we add 1, the new* r_2 *becomes 0 and* r_3 *is advanced by one.*

Let us see what happens when we encode the letter "k," which has numerical value 10.

$$
\begin{aligned}
a &= 10 \\
b &= \mathrm{Rem}[a + r_1, 26]^{\alpha_1} = \mathrm{Rem}[10 + 22, 26]^{\alpha_1} = 6^{\alpha_1} = 10 \\
c &= \mathrm{Rem}[b + r_2, 26]^{\alpha_2} = \mathrm{Rem}[10 + 7, 26]^{\alpha_2} = 17^{\alpha_2} = 19 \\
d &= \mathrm{Rem}[c + r_3, 26]^{\alpha_3} = \mathrm{Rem}[19 + 12, 26]^{\alpha_3} = 5^{\alpha_3} = 0
\end{aligned}
$$

Reaching the reflector, we get $e = (d)^\beta = 0^\beta = 4$. *Now following the signal back through the rotors, we obtain*

$$
\begin{aligned}
c' &= \mathrm{Rem}[e^{\alpha_3^{-1}} - r_3, 26] = \mathrm{Rem}[4^{\alpha_3^{-1}} - 12, 26] = \mathrm{Rem}[18 - 12, 26] = 16 \\
b' &= \mathrm{Rem}[c'^{\alpha_2^{-1}} - r_2, 26] = \mathrm{Rem}[16^{\alpha_2^{-1}} - 7, 26] = \mathrm{Rem}[15 - 7, 26] = 8 \\
a' &= \mathrm{Rem}[b'^{\alpha_1^{-1}} - r_1, 26] = \mathrm{Rem}[8^{\alpha_1^{-1}} - 22, 26] = \mathrm{Rem}[14 - 7, 26] = 7
\end{aligned}
$$

Therefore, the first cipher text character corresponds to 7, and is thus is "H."

Now, we must update the rotor settings: $r_1 = 23, r_2 = 7, r_3 = 12$.

If the settings were such that r_1 *was 25, the updating process would proceed as follows:* $r_1 = 0, r_2 = 8, r_3 = 12$.

As mentioned above, an interesting aspect about the Enigma enciphering scheme is the fact that deciphering a message follows the exact same process.

2.8   Modern Enciphering Systems

With the advent and ubiquity of computer-based encryption systems, cryptanalysis has shifted the emphasis from attacks based purely on the ciphering scheme to attacks on other aspects of cryptosystems, such as authentication, key exchanges, and digital signatures. We will detail some of these techniques later in the book, after the basis for modern ciphers, authentication, and digital signatures are developed.

2.9   Problems

2.1   Encipher the plain text message "encode" using the following Cipher: schemes:

1. Caesar cipher with $k = 3$.

2. Caesar cipher with $k = -5$.

(See Solution 2.1.)

2.2   Using the Scytale cipher with k = 2, encipher the plain text message "encode". Compare your results with those from Problem 2.1. (See Solution 2.2.)

2.3   Decode the following cipher text, given that it has been produced by a Caesar cipher: **JRYYQBAR** (See Solution 2.3.)

2.4   Is any additional security gained by enciphering a message using two monoalphabetic ciphers with different keys in succession? (See Solution 2.4.)

2.5   Encipher the first sentence of Homer's "Odyssey" using a Scytale cipher with key = 7.

> TELL ME O MUSE, of that ingenious hero who traveled far and wide after he had sacked the famous town of Troy.

(See Solution 2.5.)

2.6   Explain how frequency distribution can be used to determine if a given entry of cipher text was produced using a substitution cipher or a transposition cipher. (See Solution 2.6.)

2.7   Use the Vigenère cipher with keyword "ODYSSEY" to encipher the first sentence of Homer's "Odyssey." Compare the cipher text with the results obtained from Problem 2.5. (See Solution 2.7.)

2.8   Decipher the message below, using the fact that the keyword 'CIPHER' was used to encode it.

VPXZG   ZRTYM   JGIHF   XFDZT   HOZHW   CLOEQ   EHALV MMNDS IF

(See Solution 2.8.)

2.9   Suppose Caesar sends a message to one of his generals, and the message contains only one letter. What can you say about the message's security and why? (See Solution 2.9.)

2.10 Does the Enigma machine perform substitution enciphering or transposition enciphering? Explain. (See Solution 2.10.)

2.11 Ignoring the plugboard, how many possible initial settings are there for the three-rotor Enigma machine? (See Solution 2.11.)

2.12 Using the rotor and reflector permutation sets, along with the initial rotor settings, from the example in Section 2.7, encipher the following message: **"move out!"**. (See Solution 2.12.)

2.13 Find the period of the given cipher text, given that it was enciphered by the Vigenère cipher (see Section 2.6).

LVCKO GXKRR ITSKC XIPOG GZLCB GYXFC AYGDI RBMAU CFYAC FIPGM RRXFO JPSIB WELDI QDJPO USORA IHGCX PSFSD MMXEL NEJSX RVIJE GISXA KRZOH MXI (See Solution 2.13.)

2.14 Using the results of Problem 2.13, determine the keyword used to encipher the passage above (See Solution 2.14.)

2.15 Use the Enigma Machine with initial settings given in Section 2.7 to decipher the following message: **YDDMYU** (See Solution 2.15.)

2.16 Take a page of your favorite book and estimate the number of characters on the page. Count the number of times the letters e, t, a, and o appear on that page and calculate their relative frequencies. Compare your results with Table 2.1. (See Solution 2.16.)

2.10 Solutions

2.1 (a) Encode $\to (4, 13, 2, 14, 3, 4) \xrightarrow{k=3} (7, 16, 5, 17, 6, 7) \to$ HQFRGH

(b) Encode $\to (4, 13, 2, 14, 3, 4) \xrightarrow{k=-5} (25, 8, 23, 9, 24, 25) \to$ ZIXJYZ

2.2 Since $k = 2$, the number of rows is two. Thus, the message is encoded as follows:

$$\begin{matrix} E & C & D & \to & ECDNOE \\ N & O & E & & \end{matrix}$$

2.3 We use a brute-force attack, with results shown in the following table. The value k corresponds to a Caesar shift of magnitude k.

k	J	R	Y	Y	Q	B	A	R
1	I	Q	X	X	P	A	Z	Q
2	H	P	W	W	O	Z	Y	P
3	G	O	V	V	N	Y	X	O
4	F	N	U	U	M	X	W	N
5	E	M	T	T	L	W	V	M
6	D	L	S	S	K	V	U	L
7	C	K	R	R	J	U	T	K
8	B	J	Q	Q	I	T	S	J
9	A	I	P	P	H	S	R	I
10	Z	H	O	O	G	R	Q	H
11	Y	G	N	N	F	Q	P	G
12	X	F	M	M	E	P	O	F
13	W	E	L	L	D	O	N	E
14	V	D	K	K	C	N	M	D
15	U	C	J	J	B	M	L	C
16	T	B	I	I	A	L	K	B
17	S	A	H	H	Z	K	J	A
18	R	Z	G	G	Y	J	I	Z
19	Q	Y	F	F	X	I	H	Y
20	P	X	E	E	W	H	G	X
21	O	W	D	D	V	G	F	W
22	N	V	C	C	U	F	E	V
23	M	U	B	B	T	E	D	U
24	L	T	A	A	S	D	C	T
25	K	S	Z	Z	R	C	B	S
26	J	R	Y	Y	Q	B	A	R

After investigating the entries in the table, the only intelligible message exists for $k = 13$. The plain text message is "well done."

2.4   No. For example, if a message is enciphered with a key of 4, and the resulting cipher text is enciphered again using a key of 8, the final cipher text will be the same as if the message was enciphered with a key of 12.

2.5   Since the key is 7, we know that we need 7 rows. For the number of columns, count up the total number of characters and check if it is divisible by 7. Since it is not, we must add 4 Zs to the end. Therefore, we have 91 characters, and $\frac{91}{7} = 13$. Thus, we need 13 columns. Writing the message out in columns, we get the following matrix:

T	M	H	N	R	A	F	I	R	A	E	T	R
E	U	A	I	O	V	A	D	H	C	F	O	O
L	S	T	O	W	E	R	E	E	K	A	W	Y
L	E	I	U	H	L	A	A	H	E	M	N	Z
M	O	N	S	O	L	N	F	A	D	O	O	Z
E	F	G	H	T	E	D	T	D	T	U	F	Z
O	T	E	E	R	D	W	E	S	H	S	T	Z

After unwrapping, we obtain the encrypted message:

TMHNR AFIRA ETREU AIOVA DHCFO OLSTO WEREE KAWYL EIUHL
AAHEM NZMON SOINF ADOOZ EFGHT EDTDT UFZOT EERDW ESHST Z

2.6   Transposition ciphering will produce cipher text with roughly the same frequency distribution as the English language. Substitution ciphering, with a polyalphabetic cipher for example, will yield frequencies that can be much different, since the plain text letters are actually changed instead of reordered. Therefore, if the distribution "flattened," we can assume a substitution cipher was used. If it does not, we can assume that a transposition cipher was used.

2.7   The computations for the first few letters are shown.

Keyword:	O	D	Y	S	S	E	Y	O	D	Y
Plain text:	T	e	l	l	m	e	o	m	u	s
Cipher text:	H	H	J	D	E	I	M	A	X	Q

Continuing the process, the corresponding cipher text is

HHJDE IMAXQ WQJRV DRAFK CBHMM KLCFR UZGXP OYBDD IBTDP
SFHUW GCSXX CFKCZ SHQOF IWVXF SIYEG YQHRU FGJRF RW

2.8   We obtain the plain text by subtracting the cipher text from the keyword:

Keyword:	C	I	P	H	E	R	C	I	P	H
Cipher text:	V	P	X	Z	G	Z	R	T	Y	M
Plain text:	t	h	i	s	c	i	p	h	e	r

Working the rest of it out, we obtain the message.

"this cipher is easy to break if one knows the keyword"

2.9   The message has perfect security, because the message could be any of the 26 letters of the alphabet. That is, knowledge of the cipher text does not give any information regarding the message. Alternatively, one can think intuitively that "the key is as long as the message."

2.10   Substitution enciphering, because each letter of the plain text message is obtained by substituting different cipher text characters. Transposition enciphering is the reordering of the same letters, whereas substitution enciphering doesn't necessarily use the same characters.

2.11   Three rotors with 26 possible initial settings each $= 26^3$ initial settings $= 17\,576$. Since the three rotors can be interchanged, there are six ways to order them. Therefore, we have a total of $6 \times 26^3 = 105\,456$ different initial settings.

2.12   The corresponding cipher text is **JCJDUKJ**.

The initial settings are the following:

$\alpha_1 = (0\ 15\ 6\ 10\ 14\ 8\ 19\ 17\ 22\ 18\ 11)\ (1\ 2\ 9\ 13\ 21\ 25)\ (3\ 4\ 23\ 5\ 24\ 7\ 12\ 16\ 20)$

$\alpha_2 = (0\ 7\ 9\ 4\ 6\ 18\ 23\ 25\ 8)\ (1\ 17\ 19)\ (2\ 20\ 10)\ (3\ 12)\ (5\ 11\ 13\ 21)\ (14\ 22\ 15\ 16\ 24)$

$\alpha_3 = (0\ 2\ 4\ 7\ 16\ 17\ 19\ 5)\ (1\ 6\ 3\ 8\ 21\ 24\ 11\ 13\ 9\ 10\ 25\ 12\ 14\ 15)\ (18\ 23\ 20\ 22)$

$\beta = (0\ 4)(1\ 7)(2\ 9)(3\ 16)(5\ 20)(6\ 8)(10\ 19)(11\ 17)(12\ 25)(13\ 18)(14\ 24)(15\ 22)(21\ 23)$

$\alpha_1^{-1} = (11\ 18\ 22\ 17\ 19\ 8\ 14\ 10\ 6\ 15\ 0)\ (25\ 21\ 13\ 9\ 2\ 1)\ (20\ 16\ 12\ 7\ 24\ 5\ 23\ 4\ 3)$

$\alpha_2^{-1} = (8\ 25\ 23\ 18\ 6\ 4\ 9\ 7\ 0)\ (19\ 17\ 1)\ (10\ 20\ 2)\ (12\ 3)\ (21\ 13\ 11\ 5)\ (24\ 16\ 15\ 22\ 14)$

$\alpha_3^{-1} = (5\ 19\ 17\ 16\ 7\ 4\ 2\ 0)\ (15\ 14\ 12\ 25\ 10\ 9\ 13\ 11\ 24\ 21\ 8\ 3\ 6\ 1)\ (22\ 20\ 23\ 18)$

Also, the initial settings were defined as follows:

$r_1 = 22,\ r_2 = 7,\ r_3 = 12$

Using the given information, the cipher text was obtained as follows:

1st letter: $a = 12$ (m)

$b = \text{Rem}[a + r_1, 26]^{\alpha_1} = \text{Rem}[12 + 22, 26]^{\alpha_1} = 8^{\alpha_1} = 19$

$$c = \text{Rem}[b + r_2, 26]^{\alpha_2} = \text{Rem}[19 + 7, 26]^{\alpha_2} = 0^{\alpha_2} = 7$$

$$d = \text{Rem}[c + r_3, 26]^{\alpha_3} = \text{Rem}[7 + 12, 26]^{\alpha_3} = 19^{\alpha_3} = 5$$

Reaching the reflector, we get $e = (d)^\beta = 5^\beta = 20$

Now following the signal back through the rotors, we obtain

$$c' = \text{Rem}[e^{\alpha_3^{-1}} - r_3, 26]) = \text{Rem}[20^{\alpha_3^{-1}} - 12, 26] = \text{Rem}[23 - 12, 26] = 11$$

$$b' = \text{Rem}[c'^{\alpha_2^{-1}} - r_2, 26] = \text{Rem}[11^{\alpha_2^{-1}} - 7, 26] = \text{Rem}[5 - 7, 26] = 24$$

$$a' = \text{Rem}[b'^{\alpha_1^{-1}} - r_1, 26] = \text{Rem}[24^{\alpha_1^{-1}} - 22, 26] = \text{Rem}[5 - 22, 26] = 9$$

Therefore, the first cipher text character is J.

Now, we must update the rotor settings: $r_1 = 23, r_2 = 7, r_3 = 12$.

For the remaining characters, proceed through the same process. Remember, when r_1 changes from 25 back to 0, update r_2 to 8 (this occurs after the fourth cipher text character is computed).

2.13 After writing the cipher text on two strips of paper, we obtain the following table:

Displacement	# of coincidences
1	4
2	0
3	3
4	3
5	3
6	6
7	1
8	4

Here we note that the maximum number of coincidences occurs for a displacement of 6. Therefore, the period is either 3 or 6, because the displacement producing the largest number of coincidences is a scalar multiple of the period.

2.14 To complete the problem, we will try a period of 3 first. If it doesn't succeed, we will try the second choice of 6. With our results, we will find the most common letter and assume it deciphers to "e." If there are ties for the most frequent character, we will investigate each case individually to determine the most probable choice.

Starting with the first letter of the keyword, we create a table of cipher text frequencies:The first, fourth, seventh, ... letters of cipher text are

LKXRS   XOZBX   ZDBUY   FGROS   WDDOO   ICSDX   NSVES   KOX.

From this, we compute

A	B	C	D	E	F	G	H	I	J	K	L	M
0	2	1	4	1	1	1	0	1	0	2	1	0

N	O	P	Q	R	S	T	U	V	W	X	Y	Z
1	5	0	0	2	5	0	1	1	1	5	0	2

Here we note that the most frequent cipher text letters are O, S, and X. Now, we have to consider each letter to determine which is most likely the key letter. If O deciphers to "e"(yielding a key letter of "K"), then S → i, and X → n. Looking at Table 2.1, the number of occurrences of "i and n" in the cipher text are reasonable. Alternatively, if S deciphers to "e" (yielding a key letter of "O"), then O → "a" and X → "j". However, 5 occurrences out of 38 letters is far too high for j (the frequency of j is 0.002%). Finally, if X deciphers to "e," (yielding a key letter of "T"), then O → "v" and S → "y." Again, 5 occurrences for each "v" and "y" in 38 letters are far too high to be correct. Therefore, "K" is the most probable key letter.

We use the same reasoning for the next two key letters. For the second, fifth, eighth, ... letters, we compute:

A	B	C	D	E	F	G	H	I	J	K	L	M
1	0	1	0	3	2	3	2	8	2	2	1	3

N	O	P	Q	R	S	T	U	V	W	X	Y	Z
0	1	0	0	2	0	0	1	1	0	4	1	0

Here we have an overwhelming choice for "e," namely "I." Thus, if I deciphers to "e," we have a key letter of "E."

Similarly, for the third, sixth, nineth, ... letters, we compute

A	B	C	D	E	F	G	H	I	J	K	L	M
3	1	5	0	0	2	4	0	1	2	0	2	2

N	O	P	Q	R	S	T	U	V	W	X	Y	Z
0	0	5	1	4	2	1	0	0	0	0	1	1

This gives us two likely choices for "e," although two others are very close. If "C' deciphers to "e," we have a key letter of "Y." If this is the case, them G → "I," R → "t," and P→ "r," all of which have a reasonable number of occurrences. If, on the other hand, P deciphers to "e," then the key letter is "L." This would mean that C → "r," G → "v," and R → "g." However, the number of occurrences of both "v" and "g" are too high to be realistic. Therefore, we arrive at a key letter of "Y," producing a keyword of "key."

To make sure that 3 is the period, one can use the newly acquired keyword to decipher the message. For long messages, it is nearly impossible that two separate messages would appear out of the same piece of cipher text. Thus, if the first key works, we are done. If not, then the period is likely 6 instead. This problem illustrates the ambiguities one can run into when attempting to break the Vigenère cipher, and serves as a reminder to use the methods outlined here with diligence and care.

2.15 Repeat the exact same process as in Problem 2.14, inputting the letters YDDMYU with the same initial settings as before. The resulting output is the message "attack."

2.16 If the book contained typical English text, then the frequencies should be very similar to the table.

Chapter 3

RSA, Key Searches, TLS, and Encrypting Email

Goals, Discussion This chapter is important and does not require too much mathematical background. We avoid making essential use of number theory in the text, although it can be used to shorten the calculations. We discuss one of the main public key algorithms, namely RSA, as well as some of its applications to e-Commerce with Transport Layer Security (TLS) and to the encryption of email.

Public key and symmetric cryptography are discussed as well as the average number of guesses required when searching a key space for the key (Theorem 3.6). Some cryptographic attacks, both mathematical and real world are discussed here and in Chapter 7.

In Section 3.7, we discuss another important algorithm which straddles the border between symmetric and public-key exchanges, called the Diffie–Hellman key-exchange.

In Section 3.3, we denote by $Rem[u, v]$ the remainder w when the positive integer u is divided by the positive integer v. For example, $Rem[26, 4] = 2$. Another way of stating this is that $26 \equiv 2 \pmod 4$ or $u \equiv v \pmod v$. We are working here with the integers mod v. This is covered in detail in Chapters 5 and 19.

Let us briefly explain the idea. Alice wants to send a secret message to Bob. Bob has chosen a number N and another number e (for encryption). The pair $[N, e]$ represents *Bob's public key* and is listed in a "public key directory." Alice represents the secret message as a number M lying between 1 and $N - 1$. To encrypt or scramble the message

Cryptography, Information Theory, and Error-Correction: A Handbook for the 21st Century, Second Edition.
Aiden A. Bruen, Mario A. Forcinito, and James M. McQuillan.
© 2021 John Wiley & Sons, Inc. Published 2021 by John Wiley & Sons, Inc.

M, Alice multiplies M by itself e times, gets the remainder after dividing by N, and transmits the result to Bob. The result is called the cipher text C. An eavesdropper, noting C, realizes the message itself must be equal to the eth root of C, or $C + N$, or $C + 2N$, or $C + rN$ for some unknown r. Eve (the eavesdropper) cannot find M as there are too many values of r to try. *It is a remarkable fact that if there is just a single value of r, say $r = r_0$, such that the eth root of $C + rN$ is a whole number lying between 1 and $N - 1$.* To see this, let M_1 be any whole number, i.e. a positive integer not necessarily lying between 1 and $N - 1$ such that $M_1^e = C + N$. Then

$$M_1^e \equiv C \ (\text{mod } N). \tag{3.1}$$

Let d be a decryption index (there may be several). If M is the message, then, by definition,

$$M^e \equiv C \ (\text{mod } N). \tag{3.2}$$

Applying d, we have

$$M_1^{ed} \equiv M_1 \equiv C^d \ (\text{mod } N) \tag{3.3}$$

and

$$M^{ed} \equiv M \equiv C^d \ (\text{mod } N) \tag{3.4}$$

Therefore, $M \equiv M_1 \ (\text{mod } N)$. In particular, if M_1 lies between 1 and $N - 1$, as does M by assumption, then $M = M_1$. In effect, we are saying that the mapping $M \to M^e$ is 1 to 1 if M lies between 1 and $N - 1$.

Moreover, it can be shown that if for any positive integer r the eth root of $C + rN$ is a whole number v, then the remainder of v upon division by N must be M (see Chapter 19).

The recipient Bob, however, can calculate M immediately from a formula involving his private key consisting of a "decryption index" d along with two prime numbers p, q. The reason is that N is the product of p and q. Bob knows p and q. Anybody else, even knowing N, cannot in general determine what the factors p, q are in a reasonable amount of time.

Eve can try guessing the message without knowing d by guessing r_0. Alternatively, Eve can try guessing p and q from which she can calculate d. In other words, Eve can try to guess the private key and then determine the message.

We detail some potential weaknesses with public key algorithms such as RSA. However, this algorithm is still a central public key algorithm. Its security, when carefully implemented, seems to still be strong after many years of constant use.

A fact in cryptography is that in a **brute-force attack** on a key-space (one where we try all possible keys), the correct key is likely to be found after trying about half the total number of keys. In this chapter, we provide a short simple proof of this fact.

The encryption exponent e mentioned above must be chosen to have no factors in common with $p-1$ and no factors in common with $q-1$. The reason for assuming this is so that d exists. Another reason is that this condition must be satisfied in order that two different messages get two different encryptions. This comes up in Problem 3.1. We mention also that, for a given $[N, e]$, **the decryption index need not be unique!** We provide several examples. This is important because some attacks on RSA are possible if d is small; we refer to Chapter 7. So if d is not unique, this makes it more difficult to guard against this attack.

What we mean by "not unique" is that there may be more than one value of d such that the remainder of C^d, on division by N, is M. The reason for nonuniqueness is that, instead of working with $(p-1)(q-1)$, we can work with any number t that is divisible by $p-1$ and $q-1$, as explained in the algorithm description and in Chapter 19. It is often possible to find $t < (p-1)(q-1)$ so that the calculations are simplified, and we get a shortcut even if the resulting d is the same.

We present new insights on public key and symmetric encryption.

3.1 The Basic Idea of Cryptography

Cryptography is an old subject dating back at least as far as 1500 BCE. A technique developed by Porta associated also with Vigenère in the Middle Ages is close to the *cutting edge* of part of modern cryptography. Additionally, cryptography is closely connected to information theory and error-correction, with many fundamental ideas going back to Claude Shannon. Further details about Shannon and the history of cryptography are provided in Chapter 1.

Cryptography is the art of keeping messages secret. Imagine that **A, B** are two entities who wish to communicate in secret. Assume **A** wants to send a secret message to **B**.

The procedure is as follows (Figure 3.1). First, **A** scrambles the message using a ***cryptographic key***. The process of scrambling the message is called ***encryption***: alternatively, **A** *enciphers* the message.

The encryption or enciphering scrambles the message M, that is, the plain text, into unintelligible output called the cipher text. Next, the sender **A** transmits in the open (publicly) the cipher text C to the receiver **B**. When **B** receives the cipher text, **B** descrambles or deciphers the cipher text using a key that may or may not be the same

Figure 3.1: General encryption.

as the original key used by **A**. **B** can now recover the original message M that was transmitted by **A**.

In summary, the sender **A** encrypts or enciphers the message M into unintelligible cipher text C using an encrypting or enciphering key. The enciphering is done by a specific procedure involving a sequence of steps or rules called the ***enciphering algorithm*** (or ***encryption algorithm***).

Using the ***decryption*** or ***deciphering key***, and using the ***deciphering algorithm*** (***decryption algorithm***), the receiver **B** then ***decrypts*** or ***deciphers*** C and thus recovers the original message M that was transmitted by the transmitter **A**. Moreover, at least in theory, an intruder Eve cannot access the message M since Eve will not have the decryption key that is needed for decrypting (deciphering, inverting) C to recover M.

Evidently, everything depends on **B** being the sole possessor of the decryption key, apart possibly from **A**. (If the decryption and encryption keys are the same – as they are in symmetric encryption, then **A** also has the decryption key).

Generally speaking, a key is a mathematical object such as a number (or several numbers) or a string of zeros and ones, i.e. a ***binary string*** such as the binary string (1 1 0 1) of length 4.

The enciphering and deciphering operations are usually mathematical procedures. For example, let us suppose that the enciphering key is the number 7 and that the enciphering operation is "add 7." Suppose the secret message that **A** wants to transmit to **B** is the number 6. (For example **A** might be directing her stockbroker **B** to buy six thousand shares of a given security on the stock market).

Then, **A** calculates the cipher text 13 (= 6 plus 7) and transmits this to **B**. Now, **B** knows that the enciphering transformation is "add 7." To undo, or invert this, **B** subtracts 7 from 13 (as this is the deciphering operation) and ends up recovering the original message transmitted by **A**, namely 6.

It should be mentioned that the cryptographic keys above need not be mathematical objects: in fact, historically, they often were not. A famous example, mentioned in Chapter 1, occurred in World War II when, in effect, the key was an entire language! This was the Navajo language used by the Navajo tribe in Arizona and adapted for encryption purposes by the US armed forces around 1942. Enciphering consisted of translating messages from English into the Navajo language, while deciphering simply meant translating Navajo back to English at the other end. At that time, this symmetric encryption was extremely effective.

Using encryption for storing messages and files is another important function of encryption in today's society. As an example, we mention the encryption of a file – or even an entire hard drive (or solid state drive) – in a computer so that, if it is set aside (or stolen) an individual other than the owner cannot access the contents. (Apple and Windows both have encryption applications that use XTS-AES-128 encryption with a 256-bit key. Apple's MacOS uses it in FileVault 2, [App18], and Windows 10 version 1511 uses it in their Bitlocker feature, [Win19].) We can fit this into our previous general situation with the owner of the computer playing the role of both **A** and **B**.

We have been silent on how **A** and **B** get their enciphering and deciphering keys. This is discussed in a later chapter, but will depend on the kind of encryption being used. The two fundamentally different possibilities for cryptography are as follows:

1. *Symmetric Cryptography*

2. *Asymmetric Cryptography*, i.e. *Public Key Cryptography.*

Recall that as before **A**, **B** are the communicating entities and **A** wants to send a secret message M to **B** (Figure 3.2). In symmetric encryption, there are three features.

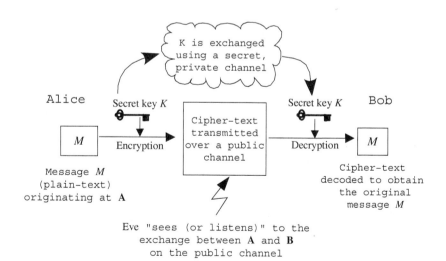

Figure 3.2: Symmetric encryption.

1. The enciphering key K used by the transmitter **A** is equal to the deciphering key used by the receiver **B** and this key is known only to **A** and **B**.

2. The enciphering algorithm, converting the plain text to cipher text, is such that the cipher text C can be calculated immediately given M and K.

3. The deciphering algorithm, converting C back to M, can be calculated immediately given C and K.

   The security depends on the fact that the secret key K is known only to **A** and **B**. Public key cryptography works differently (Figure 3.3). The procedure is as follows:

1. The enciphering key e_B used by **A** (or anybody else) to send a message M to **B** is publicly known, and is called the public key of **B**. However, the deciphering key d_B used by **B** to decrypt the cipher text is known only to **B** and is the **private key** of **B**. So the two keys are quite different.

2. The enciphering procedure, converting the plain text to cipher text C, can be immediately calculated given M and e_B.

3. The deciphering procedure, converting C back to M, can be calculated immediately by **B** using d_B. However, it is not possible for somebody else who is not in possession of d_B to convert C back to M in a reasonable amount of time.

   The security of public key cryptography rests on the assumption that it is not feasible to convert C back to M without knowledge of the private key d_B.

   Thus, in **public key cryptography** each user **B** in a network has a public key e_B and a private key d_B, which are supplied by a **public key authority** (**PKA**).

Symmetric cryptography (encryption) is also called *secret key cryptography* (encryption). The security depends, as stated above, on the assumption that only the communicating parties **A** and **B** know the (common) key. Note that **A**, **B** could also

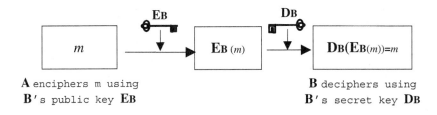

A enciphers m using   B deciphers using
B's public key **EB**   B's secret key **DB**

Figure 3.3: Asymmetric or public encryption.

denote groups of entities on a network and that **B** can also send a secret message to **A** using their common secret key.

Historically, cryptography meant symmetric cryptography. Nowadays, important symmetric algorithms in use are **AES** and the **One-Time Pad** which is sometimes derived from a shift register (see Chapter 16).

3.2 Public Key Cryptography and RSA on a Calculator

We now turn to some examples of asymmetric or public key cryptography. First, let us explain **RSA**, the main public key algorithm. As before, **A** wants to send a secret message M to **B**. For convenience, let us think of M as being the number 6, say, as in our previous example. We make the encryption more complicated. So instead of saying "add 7," we say "multiply 6 by itself 7 times" i.e. calculate $(6)(6)(6)(6)(6)(6)(6) = 6^7 = 279\,936$. As an extra complication, let us take some number N and declare the encryption algorithm to be "multiply 6 by itself 7 times and take the remainder of this number when divided by N to be the cipher text C." As a small working example, let $N = 55$. So our cipher text is the remainder of 6^7 upon division by 55. This remainder is easily calculated, using any calculator, as follows:

We want to find the (unique) remainder z that is left over when we divide 279 936 by 55. So we have

$$279\,936 = 55y + z \tag{3.5}$$

where z is one of $0, 1, 2, 3, 4, \ldots, 53, 54$. We are not really interested in the value of y: we just need z. Dividing across by 55 in Eq. (3.5), we get

$$\frac{279\,936}{55} = y + \frac{z}{55} \tag{3.6}$$

Pushing the divide button on the calculator, we get

$$\frac{279\,936}{55} = 5089.745\,455 \tag{3.7}$$

This indicates that y is 5089, $\frac{z}{55} = 0.745\,455$ so $z = 55(0.745\,455) = 41.000\,025$. *This is not what we were hoping for: z is supposed to be a whole number, namely the remainder when 279936 is divided by 55!* However, the calculator has made rounding errors, and we suspect that z is 41 (and y is 5089). This is easily checked. We can verify that Eq. (3.5) checks out with $y = 5089$, $z = 41$ since $279\,936 = (55)(5089) + 41$.

Principle 1 *To calculate the remainder of 279936 when divided by 55, perform the division on a calculator and multiply the decimal part by 55. Verify your answer by checking that Eq. (3.5) is satisfied. This also works to get the remainder whenever we divide a positive integer (= positive whole number) u by another positive integer v.*

Question *How do we know that z is unique? Maybe there are two possible values?*

Go back to Eq. (3.5), and suppose we have two solutions with y_1, y_2 being positive and z_1 and z_2 both lying between 0 and 54. So we have

$$279\,936 = 55y_1 + z_1 \tag{3.8}$$

$$279\,936 = 55y_2 + z_2 \tag{3.9}$$

Then $55y_1 + z_1 = 55y_2 + z_2$. Now, if $y_1 = y_2$ it follows that $z_1 = z_2$. So assume that $y_1 \neq y_2$. Call the larger one y_1, so $y_1 > y_2$.

We now have $55(y_1 - y_2) = z_2 - z_1$. Since y_1 is at least 1 bigger than y_2, we get that the left side is at least *55. Since z_1 and z_2 are between 0 and 54, we see that the right side is* at most *54. Since $55 > 54$, we conclude that the assumption $y_1 \neq y_2$ leads to a contradiction. Thus, $y_1 = y_2$ (and so also $z_1 = z_2$): end of story.* As a consequence, to check Eq. *(3.5)* in the future all we need to do in the case above is to ensure that $279\,936 - z$ is divisible by 55.

Getting back to our main narrative, **A** *transmits the cipher text* **C** $= 41$ *to* **B** *having calculated this from the message $M = 6$. How does* **B** *recover M from 41?* **B** *knows that $N = 55 = (5)(11)$. Since we are using a public cryptosystem, the enciphering algorithm is public knowledge (in this particular example), the enciphering algorithm is "multiply the message by itself seven times and take the remainder on division by N": this gives the cipher text 41.* **B** *calculates the deciphering index d as follows.*

There is a unique positive integer d between 1 and 39 such that 7d gives a remainder of 1 when divided by 40. In this case, it turns out that $d = 23$ (more on this later) since $(7)(23) = 161$ and 161 leaves a remainder of 1 on division by 40. Here, 40 comes from the fact that $(11 - 1)(5 - 1) = 40$ and 5, 11 are the factors of $N = 55$.

To recover the message, **B** *multiplies the cipher text, namely 41, by itself 23 times, gets the remainder on division by 55, and this should give the original message, namely 6. So we are claiming that $41^{23} - 6$ is divisible by 55.*

We will use the following principle to get the remainder of a product of two numbers.

Principle 2 *Calculate the product of the two individual remainders and then get its remainder, if necessary.*

*If we calculate 41^{23} – or in general any M^e – on a calculator or a computer, we run into overflow problems. To avoid them, we use this principle, combined with the **repeated***

squaring method. *Here is how this method works in the present case. We first express 23 as a sum of powers of 2. Thus, $23 = 7 + 16 = 1 + 2 + 4 + 16$. So if x is any number, we have $x^{23} = x^{1+2+4+16} = (x)(x^2)(x^4)(x^{16})$. Each number in this product is the square of the previous number except for x^{16} which is the square of the square of the previous number.*

Let us calculate 41^{23} and get the remainder upon division by 55.

*In detail, $x^1 = 41$, nothing more to do. Then, $x^2 = 41^2 = 1681$ gives a remainder of 31 when divided by 55. Proceeding, instead of calculating $x^4 = 1681^2$ by squaring x^2, we need only calculate 31^2 and get the remainder on division by 55 which is 26. Now, to get the next term in the product (namely x^{16}) instead of squaring x^4 – to get x^8 – and then squaring again to get x^{16} – we need only square 26, get the remainder and square the remainder again and finally get the remainder on division by 55 which is 36. So the four remainders for x, x^2, x^4, x^{16} are 41, 31, 26, 36. In principle, now we have to multiply 41 by 31 by 26 by 36 and get the remainder on division by 55. Again, we can take shortcuts using Principle 2. We can multiply 41 by 31 and get the remainder. We calculate $(26)(36)$ and get the remainder (on division by 55). Multiplying the 2 remainders together, and getting the remainder, on division by 55, gives us the answer. The two remainders are 6 and 1. Then $(6)(1) = 6$ and **B** ends up recovering the message which is 6. Note that in the example above, N is the product pq of two distinct primes p and q with $p = 11$ and $q = 5$. The **enciphering index** e is 7, M is 6, the cipher text C is 41, and the **deciphering index** d is 23.*

Several remarks are in order.

Remark 3.1

1. *The fact that **B** deciphers C to recover the message M by simply using the deciphering algorithm explained above is proved in Chapter 19.*

2. *Having found a decryption index by the official (hard) way, let us find an easier method. All we need is the unique integer, let us call it d', between 1 and 20, such that $7d'$ gives a remainder of 1 when divided by 20. Why 20? Well, instead of using $(p-1)(q-1)$, we can use any positive integer divisible by both $p-1$ and $q-1$. With $p = 11$ and $q = 5$, we choose the number 20, and get $d' = 3$. Then it is easy to check that the remainder of 41^3 upon division by 55 is 6. It is much easier to use the decryption index 3 instead of the decryption index 23.*

3. *The security of RSA rests on the mathematically unproven assumption that, even given C, e, N, an individual (other than **B**) cannot recover M in a reasonable amount of time if p and q are large.*

In technical language, the problem of recovering M is said to be **computationally infeasible** (= **infeasible**) or **intractable**. The enciphering function transforming M is conjectured to be a **one-way function**, i.e. it is easy to calculate C given M, but it is impossible to undo this calculation.

Given e and the two factors p, q of N it is easy to calculate d and thus to obtain M from C (see Chapter 19). Thus, if one can solve the problem of factoring N quickly one can calculate d quickly and thus M, given C. On the other hand, if we can find d, then we can get M (but also p and q).

It is now time to give a formal description of the RSA algorithm, as follows.

3.3   The General RSA Algorithm

A (=Alice) wants to send a secret message M to **B** (=Bob). Bob has already chosen two large unequal prime[1] numbers p and q. Bob multiplies p and q together to get $N = pq$. Bob also chooses some integer e bigger than 1. The integer e (e for enciphering) must have no factors in common with $p - 1$ and no factors in common with $q - 1$. In other words, the greatest common divisor of e and $p - 1$ is 1 (and similarly for e and $q - 1$). In symbols, we write $\gcd(e, p - 1) = 1$ and $\gcd(e, q - 1) = 1$. Thus, the only number dividing both e and $p - 1$ is 1, and the only number dividing both e and $q - 1$ is 1. We say also that e is **relatively prime** to $p - 1$ and to $q - 1$. It follows that $\gcd(e, (p - 1)(q - 1)) = 1$.

Because of the conditions imposed on e, namely that e is relatively prime to $(p - 1)(q - 1)$, there exists a unique integer d (d for deciphering) which is greater than 1 but less than $(p - 1)(q - 1)$ and is such that the remainder of de when divided by $(p - 1)(q - 1)$ is 1. It is easy for Bob to calculate d, using a method related to the Euclidean Algorithm (see Chapter 19), since Bob knows p, q which are the factors of N. There may be other deciphering indices that are easier to work with (see Remark 3.1 part 2 and a more general method in item 3 of the formal algorithm overleaf).

Bob puts the numbers e and $N(= pq)$ in a public directory under his name. He keeps secret the primes p and q: d is Bob's private key and the pair $[N, e]$ is Bob's public key.

Now, Alice has a secret message M to transmit to Bob. Alice converts M to a number between 1 and $N - 1$ represented in binary (which we also denote by M). If M is too large, Alice breaks M into blocks, each of which is less than N. Let us assume, for simplicity, that M is less than N. Then, Alice enciphers M by calculating the cipher text $C = \text{Rem}[M^e, N]$. Note that $\text{Rem}[u, v]$ **means the remainder when u is divided**

---

[1] Recall that a number is *prime* if it has no factors save itself and 1. So 11 is prime, but $6 = 2 \times 3$ is not since 2 and 3 divide 6, i.e. they are *factors* of 6.

by $\boldsymbol{v}$, so in other words Alice multiplies M by itself e times and gets the remainder upon division by N. This can be done quickly using the "repeated squaring" method and the principle described earlier. Note that e can be any positive integer relatively prime to $p-1$ and $q-1$. However, suppose $\text{Rem}[e, (p-1)(q-1)] = e_1$. Then it can be shown that $\text{Rem}[M^e, N] = \text{Rem}[M^{e_1}, N]$, *and so we may as well assume that* $e < (p-1)(q-1)$.

When Bob receives $C = M^e$, he in turn multiplies C by itself d times and gets the remainder upon division by N. As explained in our earlier example, the calculation can be simplified. This remainder is in fact equal to M, the original message.

Let us formalize the procedure.

The RSA Algorithm.

---

1. Bob chooses in secret two large primes p, q with $p \neq q$ and sets $N = pq$.

2. Bob chooses e bigger than 1 with e relatively prime to $p-1$ and to $q-1$, and with $e < (p-1)(q-1)$.

3. Bob calculates the decryption index d, where $d < (p-1)(q-1)$ is such that the remainder of de on division by $(p-1)(q-1)$ is 1. More generally, Bob calculates a decryption index d, where $d < t \leq (p-1)(q-1)$ is such that the remainder of de on division by t is 1. Here, t is any number divisible by both $p-1$ and $q-1$.

4. Bob announces his public key $[N, e]$ and keeps his private key d secret.

5. Alice wishes to send a secret message M and represents M as a number between 0 and $N-1$. Alice then encrypts the message M as the remainder C of M^e upon division by N and transmits C to Bob.

6. Bob decrypts C by calculating the remainder of C^d upon division by N: this gives the original secret message M.

Remark 3.2 *If p, q are odd, then $p-1, q-1$ are even, and so each is divisible by 2. So by choosing t to be the* least *common multiple of $p-1$ and $q-1$, we get that $t \leq (p-1)(q-1)/2$.*

Remark 3.3 *It is beneficial for Bob to also store p and q rather than just d. The reason is that some decryption algorithms work faster if he makes use of p and q rather than just d. Thus, the private key is sometimes defined as the triple $[p, q, d]$.*

Another example of the RSA algorithm

In the example below, we also briefly indicate how more sophisticated number theory can shorten the calculations.

Suppose Bob chooses the primes $p = 863$ and $q = 937$. So $N = pq = 808\ 631$, and $(p-1)(q-1) = 806\ 832$. A valid choice for e is 7, as $\gcd(806\ 832, 7) = 1$. Using the Euclidean Algorithm, Bob can also calculate d (see Chapter 19). Bob announces his public key $[N, e] = [808\ 631, 7]$ and finds $d = 461\ 047$. Bob keeps $[p, q, d]$ secret. When Alice wants to send $M = 205\ 632$ to Bob, she computes $C = \text{Rem}[205\ 632^7, 808\ 631]$ using the repeated squaring method to find that $C = 256\ 779$. Alice then transmits C in public, and when Bob receives it, he can either compute $M = \text{Rem}[C^d, N] = \text{Rem}[256\ 779^{461\ 047}, 808\ 631] = 205\ 632$ directly using the repeated squaring technique, or take a more efficient approach, as follows: Bob calculates $M_1 = \text{Rem}[256\ 779^{461\ 047}, p]$ and $M_2 = \text{Rem}[256\ 779^{461\ 047}, q]$, then uses the Chinese Remainder Theorem (of Chapter 19) to combine them to find M. Since $\text{Rem}[255\ 779, p] = \text{Rem}[255\ 779, 863] = 468$, Bob knows that $M_1 = \text{Rem}[256\ 779^{461\ 047}, 863] = \text{Rem}[468^{461\ 047}, 863]$, and by a theorem due to Fermat[2] this is equal to $\text{Rem}[468^{739}, 863] = 238$. Similarly, $M_2 = \text{Rem}[256\ 779^{461\ 047}, 937] = \text{Rem}[41^{535}, 937] = 429$. Bob then combines M_1 and M_2 to find $M = 205\ 632$.

Remark 3.4 *Note in the above that $461{,}047 - 739$ is divisible by $p - 1 = 862$.*

In general, suppose a, u, v are not divisible by p, $u > v$ and assume that $u - v$ is divisible by $p - 1$. Then $a^{u-v} = a^{(p-1)\lambda} = (a^\lambda)^{p-1} \equiv 1 \pmod{p}$. Therefore, $a^u = a^v \pmod{p}$ upon multiplying both sides by $a^v \pmod{p}$.

Remark 3.5 *Instead of using 461047 as the deciphering index, Bob can calculate that the least common multiple of $p - 1$ and $q - 1$ is $t = 403\ 416$. Then he can find that the remainder of $d'e$ when divided by t is 1, where $d' = 57\ 631$, and use this for a deciphering index instead.*

It is conceivable that the **RSA problem** of obtaining M from C is easier than the ***factoring problem**.* For some methods of obtaining M from C that work in special cases, we refer to the problems. *The factoring problem is to obtain p, q given $N = pq$.* Once p, q, e are known, it is easy to find the message M from C by calculating d: this is what Bob does. Mathematically, nobody has been able to prove that the factoring problem cannot

---
[2] Fermat's theorem says that $\text{Rem}[a^{p-1}, p] = 1$ when p is prime and a is not a multiple of p.

be solved in a reasonable amount of time. Similarly, it has not been shown that M cannot be obtained from C in a reasonable amount of time by some method or another. We point out also that given d we can find p, q, even when d is chosen so that $\text{Rem}[ed, t] = 1$, where $(p - 1)$ divides t and $(q - 1)$ divides t. (See Buchmann [Buc04]). ***Thus, the problem of finding d is equivalent to the factoring problem.***

Let us return again to our example of symmetric key encryption where the enciphering algorithm was "add 7." In order to avoid overflow and storage, we fix a large positive integer N. Let the message be some number M between 0 and $N - 1$, i.e. $0 \leq M \leq N - 1$. Our enciphering algorithm now reads: "increase M by 7 and get the cipher text C by calculating the remainder upon division by N." For example if N is 55 and $M = 50$, then $C = 2$. So **A** transmits the cipher text 2. Now, **B** must undo (or decrypt or decipher) 2 to get the original message. Before, our decryption algorithm read "subtract 7 from C," i.e. "add the inverse of 7 to C." We do this now. First, we must get *the additive inverse of 7 modulo N* i.e., *the inverse of 7 modulo 55* (see Chapter 19). In other words, we must find d such that $d + 7$ leaves a remainder 0 when divided by 55. In this case, d is 48. Then, to decipher C, we increase $C(= 2)$ by 48 and obtain the remainder upon division by 55. In this case, we obtain the number 50. This is the original message.

The kind of procedure just described seems remarkably similar to the RSA algorithm. A summary is as follows:

RSA Algorithm (Outline)	**Symmetric Algorithm (Outline)**
• **B** selects in private two large primes p, q with $p \neq q$ and sets $N = pq$.	• **A** and **B** publicly choose any positive integer N.
• **A** chooses a message M, $0 \leq M \leq N - 1$.	• **A** chooses a message M, $0 \leq M \leq N - 1$.
• **B** chooses any positive enciphering index e with $\gcd(e, (p - 1)(q - 1)) = 1$ and $1 \leq e < (p - 1)(q - 1)$.	• **A** and **B** secretly agree on an enciphering index e between 0 and $N - 1$.
• **A** forms the cipher text C, where C is the remainder when M^e is divided by N.	• **A** forms the cipher text C, where C is the remainder when $M + e$ is divided by N.
• Let d be the multiplicative inverse of e modulo $(p - 1)(q - 1)$, so that ed leaves a remainder of 1 upon division by $(p - 1)(q - 1)$. Then, to decipher, **B** raises C to the power d and gets the remainder of C^d upon division by N.	• Let d be the additive inverse of e modulo N. Then, to decipher, **B** adds d to C and gets the remainder of $d + C$ upon division by N: this yields M.

3.4   Public Key Versus Symmetric Key

The algorithms seem remarkably similar. However, by contrasting them we will glean the fundamental insights into the difference between public key and symmetric cryptography.

We note the following:

1. The integer e is kept secret in the symmetric case and is known only to **A** and **B**. In the RSA case, e is public knowledge.

2. The choice of the integer N in the symmetric case is unrestricted. In the RSA case, N must be the product of two large unequal primes p, q and furthermore, these primes are secret and are known only to **B**. The integer d constitutes the private key of **B** in the RSA case.

3. In this particular case, the symmetric algorithm provides perfect secrecy. *This means that knowledge of the cipher text provides no clue as to the message since any message will fit with the given cipher text. The cipher text does not narrow down the possibilities for the message in any way.* Thus, the only way for an intruder to get the message is by guessing; the eavesdropper Eve can try to guess the message but will have no way of verifying the guess is correct. For example, when $N = 55$ and we take any cipher text, C, say $C = 2$ (as above), then any message can be made to fit this cipher text. For example, the message 14 can be made to fit this cipher text by choosing $e = 43$.

Contrast this with the RSA situation. Only one message will fit with a given cipher text. If an intruder tries to guess the message, she can verify immediately whether or not the guess is correct. In particular, she can do this by enciphering the guess. Moreover, *given sufficient time and computing resources an adversary is certain to get the message.* (However, the adversary may need a very long time!)

Thus, the RSA algorithm affords only ***computational security*** as do all other public key algorithms. This means that the security comes from the unproven mathematical assumption that no deciphering algorithm can be computed in a reasonable amount of time (technically, in polynomial time) to obtain the message.

However, not all symmetric algorithms enjoy perfect secrecy. For this to happen, Shannon proved that roughly, "the key must be as long as the message." Symmetric algorithms like AES, where the key is much shorter than the message, are sometimes "insecure." The relative security offered by such a scheme depends on the length and the nature of the message, for example, a text message encoded in binary. Generally speaking, the knowledge of the cipher text will at least narrow down the possibilities for the message. We discuss this later in this chapter.

One of the main problems with RSA and public key systems is that somebody may come up with a fast method of deciphering or factoring. Also, as time progresses, the computational power that is available for an adversary to attempt an attack on an enciphering protocol increases, sometimes very quickly. (See Section 1.7 for further discussion.)

Thus, one needs longer and longer keys for public key systems to withstand computational attack. Nowadays, the industry uses mainly symmetric cryptography. The secret key needed for this can be supplied by a central server (as is the case with the **Kerberos system**) or by a public key methodology such as RSA, where the message M is the key to be used for the symmetric key session, i.e. the **session key**. The RSA algorithm is also widely used as the base for secure e-mail applications, such as PGP, and Internet security protocols such as TLS.

As mentioned, the computational power that an adversary Eve has at her disposal is increasing at a fast rate. Because of this one needs to work with bigger and bigger primes p, q to try to ensure that factoring N cannot be done quickly. Back in 1998, one needed to have p, q at least 154 digits (512 bits) each. However, that no longer provides adequate protection.

Table 2 of [Bar16, p. 53] gives estimated strengths for approved algorithms and key lengths. The **security strength** assigns a value to the amount of work that is required to break a cryptographic system. The higher the value, the more secure the system. NIST provides a recommendation for minimum security strengths and minimum numbers of bits for the various encryption algorithms that they recommend. *The minimum number of bits needed for adequate protection for RSA is a keysize of 2048 bits (see [Bar16, p. 53, Table 2] or [BD15, p. 12, Table 2]).* Therefore, p and q should have at least 308 digits (1024 bits) each. Of course, with longer keys, transmission errors become more and more prevalent.

Several additional remarks are in order.

1. P. Shor has proved that factoring numbers is computationally feasible with a quantum computer. Thus, if quantum computers ever become a reality, RSA will no longer be viable: it will be completely insecure.

2. The problem of transmission errors has to be addressed given that primes p, q should be at least 308 digits (1024 bits) each, ensuring a modulus N of 617 digits (2048 bits) for long-term security.

3. Despite the recent mathematical results of Agrawal et al., [AKS04] which shows that one can quickly test for primality[3] of a given number, one still has to generate large

---

[3] Testing for primality means to see whether the number in question is a prime number.

primes p, q of roughly the same size which are suitable for RSA use. In particular, they must be resistant to factorization algorithms, one of which is discussed later in the book.

4. For frequent RSA communications, one also needs a fast algorithm for ensuring that e has no factors in common with $p - 1$ and $q - 1$.

5. The RSA algorithm is slow relative to some comparable symmetric-key algorithms.

6. The security of RSA is in jeopardy without extensive "preprocessing" of plain text message units before encryption (see Mollin [Mol02]).

7. Other attacks on RSA include timing attacks and "man-in-the-middle" attacks. These are discussed in Chapter 7.

Apart from guaranteeing the secrecy of the message from **A** to **B** (or **B** to **A**), other fundamental issues in cryptography are as follows:

1. *Authentication*. Roughly, how can **B** be sure that the message came from **A**?

2. *Message integrity*. How can **B** be sure that the message has not been altered?

3. *Digital signatures*. How can a user "sign" a message?

4. *Nonrepudiation*. How can **B** prove (in court, for example) that **A** sent the message?

Technically, authentication has two aspects. One relates to the verification of the origin of received data. The other refers to verifying the identity of a user. Traditional methods include passwords, P.I.N. numbers, etc. Biometric data has been used in recent years as well, for example, for logging into a smart phone. We discuss this in Chapter 8.

Message integrity can be achieved using hash functions as described in Chapter 4. Digital Signatures can be carried out using either symmetric or public key encryption. This is also described in Chapter 4.

3.5   Attacks, Security, Catch-22 of Cryptography

There are many **attacks** on cryptosystems, i.e. attempts by an intruder to break the system by recovering the key and the message or the message directly. By far, the attack most difficult to defend against is an impersonation or **man-in-the-middle attack**. Another type of attack is a **brute-force attack** (see Section 7.3) in which the attacker systematically tries all possible keys on the key-space. A variety of attacks are discussed in Chapter 7.

A basic issue in cryptography is this: *If we are trying to guess one of n possible passwords in order to log on (or n possible keys say), then how many guesses will we have to make on average until we are successful? The answer is easy to find.*

Theorem 3.6 *On the average, when trying to guess one of n possible keys, we only need $(n+1)/2$ guesses.*

First, we explain the concept of average value which is discussed also in Chapter 9. Suppose that, in a class of 6 students, 3 get 70%, 2 get 80%, and 1 gets 92%. What is the average grade? One can write this average as $((3)(70) + (2)(80) + (1)(92))/6 = 77$. So the average grade is 77%. We could also calculate the average as $\frac{3}{6}(70) + \frac{2}{6}(80) + \frac{1}{6}(92)$, where $\frac{3}{6}, \frac{2}{6}, \frac{1}{6}$ are the probabilities of getting 70, 80, and 92, respectively. Now, we proceed to the proof.

Proof. The probability of guessing correctly the first time is $1/n$. To get it right in exactly 2 guesses, we must get it wrong on the first guess and then, having discarded the unsuccessful guess, we must guess correctly on the next attempt. So the probability of being successful in exactly 2 guesses is $(1 - \frac{1}{n})(\frac{1}{n-1}) = (\frac{n-1}{n})(\frac{1}{n-1}) = \frac{1}{n}$. Similarly, the probability of being successful in exactly $3, 4, \ldots, n-1, n$ guesses is also $1/n$. To get the average number of guesses, we multiply the number of guesses by the probability and add up. This gives the average number of trials until success to be $(1)(1/n) + (2)(1/n) + (3)(1/n) + \cdots + (n-1)(1/n) + n(\frac{1}{n}) = (1 + 2 + 3 + \cdots + (n-1) + n)(1/n) = (n+1)/2$. So on average, you get the correct password after $(n+1)/2$ attempts. ∎

Public key algorithms and symmetric algorithms were compared in Section 3.4. With any public key algorithm such as RSA (or elliptic curve cryptography), *given sufficient time and computing power, the eavesdropper is certain to recover the message.* In fact, with RSA it is generally quicker to try to solve the factoring problem than to try all possible values of d (brute-force). One of the main advantages of RSA is the convenience and low cost, especially for e-commerce. Advantages of symmetric systems include improved security and the speed.

A difficulty with key systems is the ***key distribution problem***, i.e. the problem of getting the common secret key to **A** and **B**. This is eloquently expressed by Professor Lomonaco when he writes about the Catch-22 of cryptography [Lom98].

Catch-22 of Cryptography:

To communicate in secret, we must first communicate in secret.

For symmetric encryption, the private key has to be given secretly to each entity, whereas the public keys for each entity are ... public!

We have spoken already of the assumption that the encryption algorithms for public key cryptography are assumed to be mathematical one-way functions. This means that enciphering has the property that its values are easily computed by a computer (i.e. are computed in polynomial time), yet the deciphering algorithm cannot be computed in a reasonable amount of time (even on a computer). In other words, the problem of deciphering the cipher text is intractable.

Of course, we emphasize again that the existence of such mathematical one-way functions is still in doubt since nobody has discovered a mathematical function that is provably one-way.

But one-way functions abound in the physical world, many of them related to time. For example, as Beutelspacher [Beu94] points out, most people are not getting any younger, i.e. the aging function is one-way!

Another analogy is the telephone directory of any big city. Here each name gets enciphered to the corresponding telephone number. The deciphering algorithm starts with a number and tries to find the corresponding name, a much more daunting task.

One can also make physical analogies concerning the two kinds of cryptography.

For public key cryptography, consider the following scenario: **A** wants to send a secret message to **B**. A number of mailboxes are available. **A** knows that the mailbox for **B** is number 3 (3 is the public key for **B**). All **A** has to do is to drop the message into mailbox number 3 for **B**. Then **B** (but nobody else) can recover the message since **B** has the key to mailbox number 3.

Another system for public key algorithms is as follows: **A** wants to send a secret message to **B**. He goes to the hardware store and buys a box and a combination lock marked **B** (this corresponds to the public key of **B**). Then **A** puts the message in the box, locks the box with the combination lock and mails it to **B**. When the box arrives, **B** opens it, and gets the message because he knows the combination for the lock. Nobody else can open the box to get the message.

The following is an analogy for symmetric encryption: If **A** wants to send a secret message to **B**, we can imagine **A** putting the message in a strong box, locking the box with a key and mailing it to **B**. When **B** receives the box, he opens it with his key and gets the message. Only **A** and **B** have a key for the box, so nobody else can get the secret message.

3.6 Summary of Encryption

We have seen what encryption is and the difference between public key and symmetric cryptography. Public-key algorithms such as RSA yield computational security which can be breached given sufficient time and computing resources. With RSA, security is weaker for a text message encoded in ASCII than if the message is a random binary string. This is also true for for some symmetric encryption systems. The reason for this reduction in security is attributed to the fact that consecutive characters in a text message are dependent upon each other.

The only mathematical way to assess the security of symmetric systems is through information theory, which is discussed later on in the book. The security depends on the uncertainty pertaining to the key and the uncertainty pertaining to the message. Roughly speaking, the longer the key the more secure the message. One reason for discussing historical ciphers, such as the Vigenère cipher, in this book is to furnish examples of how this works.

With public key algorithms, only one message can fit with a given cipher text. The keys have to be made longer and longer to withstand brute-force attacks. What the proper length should be is a matter of conjecture and it is one of the "hot-button" issues in modern cryptography. One the one hand, a financial institution using public key algorithms may not be in a hurry to report that its system has been broken. On the other hand, a successful intruder may not want to report success.

With symmetric systems, one can (at least in theory!) quantify the security which can be measured in ***Shannon bits***. In certain situations, it can be measured exactly; in other situations, it can be estimated experimentally (e.g. with text messages encoded in binary). In general, it may be the case that many messages will fit with a given cipher text so that, in the end, the determination of the message may still be a matter of guesswork. Nowadays, RSA keys should be several hundred decimal digits in length. In bits, they should be at least 2048 bits long.

We should also point out that in some situations, whether dealing with symmetric or public key algorithms, it may be easier or faster to try to guess the message than to guess the key and then to get the message. Furthermore, there is a strong probabilistic component running through all of cryptography, exacerbated by the possibility of transmission errors.

We have not touched on several practical issues here such as message compression, transmission errors, and checking for key equality. These will be dealt with in Parts II and III of the book when the appropriate machinery has been built up.

3.7   The Diffie–Hellman Key Exchange

This is one of the most mathematically elegant algorithms in cryptography. Communicating parties **A** and **B** end up generating a common secret key, so there is a connection with symmetric encryption. On the other hand, the method of generating the common key is quite similar to the RSA algorithm and indeed is said to have inspired the RSA algorithm. The security of DH, like the security of RSA, is computational.

The DH key exchange may proceed in the following way:

Participants **A**, **B** wish to generate a common secret key. First, a suitable prime p is publicly chosen and then a generator g for p. Here, a **generator** g (which always exists!) has the property that if we take all powers of g from 1 to $p-1$ and calculate their remainders when we divide by p, we obtain all possible numbers $1, 2, 3, \ldots, p-1$ in some order (see Chapter 19). Recall that $\mathrm{Rem}[u, v]$ means the remainder when u is divided by v. Here, in this section, and in the problems, $v = p$ and $\mathrm{Rem}[u, p]$ will be simply denoted by $\mathrm{Rem}(u)$.

Procedure. **A**, **B** choose secret numbers a, b and transmit $u = \mathrm{Rem}(g^a)$, $v = \mathrm{Rem}(g^b)$ to **B**, **A**, respectively.

B receives u and calculates $\mathrm{Rem}(u^b) = K_1$.

A receives v and calculates $\mathrm{Rem}(v^a) = K_2$.

Now, $K_1 = \mathrm{Rem}(g^{ab}) = \mathrm{Rem}(g^{ba}) = K_2$ and **A**, **B** are in possession of a common secret key $K_1 = K_2 = K$, since $g^{ab} = g^{ba}$.

An example with a small prime p

$p = 11$, $g = 2$, $a = 4$, $b = 3$. Then:

$$u = \mathrm{Rem}(g^a) = \mathrm{Rem}(2^4) = 5$$

$$v = \mathrm{Rem}(g^b) = \mathrm{Rem}(2^3) = 8$$

$$K_1 = \mathrm{Rem}(u^b) = \mathrm{Rem}(5^3) = 4$$

$$K_2 = \mathrm{Rem}(v^a) = \mathrm{Rem}(8^4) = 4$$

The common secret key possessed by **A**, **B** is 4. In calculating, we may use the shortcuts that were introduced earlier in Chapter 3.

The security of the Diffie–Hellman (DH) key-exchange rests on the assumption that the DH problem described now cannot be solved in a reasonable amount of time, i.e. is intractable.

Diffie–Hellman problem

Given a prime p, $u = \text{Rem}(g^a)$, and $v = \text{Rem}(g^b)$, find $w = \text{Rem}(u^b) = \text{Rem}(v^a)$.

A (potentially) more general problem is the discrete log problem.

(We remark that in the DH problem it suffices to consider the cases when $0 \leq a < p - 1$ and $0 \leq b < p - 1$.)

Discrete log problem

Given a prime p and $\text{Rem}(g^x)$, where x is one of the numbers $\{0, 1, 2, \ldots, p - 2\}$, find x.

It is called the discrete log problem because $\log(g^x) = x$ when g is chosen as the logarithmic base. A solution to the discrete log problem (i.e. finding an algorithm for calculating x in a reasonable amount of time) would imply a solution to the Diffie–Hellman problem. The converse statement is not known to be true, although there is experimental evidence pointing in that direction.

We should point out that, for security, one wants p to be well-behaved meaning that $p - 1$ has large factors. The ideal case is when $p - 1 = 2q$, where q itself is prime. For example, take $p = 11$ so $q = 5$. In the ideal case, p has the greatest possible number of different generators (for its size) so that it is easy to find a generator. However, such primes p, known as **Sophie-Germain** primes, are conjectured to be rare. In any event, only a finite number are known to exist.

Using the Diffie–Hellman idea, it is possible to construct a public-key cryptosystem called the **El Gamal Cryptosystem.**

El Gamal Cryptosystem

As before, we are given a prime p and a generator g. Each participant **B** has, as a private key, a secret integer b (which can be assumed to lie between 2 and $p - 2$) and a public key $\beta = \text{Rem}(g^b)$. Suppose **A** wants to send **B** a secret message m, which is in the form of a positive integer less than p. Let the integer a be the private key for **A**. **A** has, for a public key, $\alpha = \text{Rem}(g^a)$. **A** also computes the key $k = \text{Rem}((g^b)^a)$, obtained by getting the remainder upon raising β, the public key of **B**, to the power a, and dividing by p. (As in the DH key-exchange, **B** can also find k by raising α to the power of b and dividing by p to get the remainder.)

Finally, **A** transmits the cipher text $C = \text{Rem}(km)$ to **B** (as well as α). From α, **B** can calculate k. Since p is a prime **B** can calculate k^{-1}, where $\text{Rem}(kk^{-1}) = 1$. Then **B** calculates $m = \text{Rem}(k^{-1}(km))$. This is the El Gamal Cryptosystem.

Remark 3.7 *Instead of taking the cipher text* $C = \text{Rem}(km)$, *we could also choose the cipher text* $C_0 = f_k(m)$, *where* f_k *is any* keyed symmetric algorithm *such as AES.*

The RSA digital signature protocol is relatively easy because e and d are both defined on the same set, namely $\{0, 1, 2, \ldots, m - 1\}$. For a more complicated digital signature example, we present the El Gamal Digital Signature Scheme.

The El Gamal digital signature scheme

A wants to send a signed message M to **B**. **A** begins with a large prime p and a generator g (a primitive root) for that prime. Then **A** chooses an integer a such that $2 \le a \le p - 2$. The public key of **A** is (p, g, g^a) and the private key of **A** is a. Since p and g are publicly known, it is important that it be infeasible to calculate the solution x to $g^x \equiv g^a \bmod p$. This requires that p have a large number of bits. When signing a message M, **A** chooses an integer k relatively prime to $p - 1$ such that $1 \le k \le p - 2$. Then **A** transmits a signature in the form of the pair $(\text{Rem}(g^k), s)$, where

$$s \equiv k^{-1}(h - ag^k) \ (\text{mod } p - 1) \tag{3.10}$$

(In other words, $\text{Rem}[k^{-1}(h - ag^k), p - 1] = s$)

and h, the hash of the message M, is some integer such that $1 \le h \le p - 2$. (The hash function maps strings of 0's and 1's onto the integer h in the proper range).

The signature is verified by **B** who checks the conditions:

1. The left integer in the signature pair, namely $\text{Rem}(g^k)$, lies in the interval $[1, p - 1]$.

2. The congruence $g^{ag^k} g^{ks} \equiv g^h \bmod p$ is satisfied. In other words, we check that $\text{Rem}[g^{ag^k} g^{ks}] = \text{Rem}[g^h]$.

If both conditions hold, then **B** accepts the signature as coming from **A**. The reason for this is as follows: Substituting equation (3.10) into the second condition, we get

$$g^{ag^k} g^{k(k^{-1}(h - ag^k))} \equiv g^h \ (\text{mod } p) \tag{3.11}$$

This means that if **A** computed s, then condition 2 will be satisfied. Conversely, if condition 2 is satisfied, then (since g is a primitive root of p) the exponents must give the same remainder on division by $p - 1$. Hence,

$$ag^k + ks \equiv h \ (\text{mod } p - 1) \tag{3.12}$$

i.e.

$$\mathrm{Rem}[ag^k + ks, p-1] = \mathrm{Rem}[h, p-1]$$

which is a restatement of Eq. (3.10). So the computation carried out by **A** is the only way to satisfy the second condition.

For a simple example, let $p = 11$, $g = 2$, $a = 4$ and $k = 7$. Then **A** has the private key $a = 4$ and the public key $(p, g, g^a) = (11, 2, 5)$ since $g^a = 2^4 = 16$ and $\mathrm{Rem}(16) = 5$. Let the hash of the message M be $h = 1$. $\mathrm{Rem}[k^{-1}(h - ag^k), p - 1] = \mathrm{Rem}[3(1 - (4)(7)), 10] = \mathrm{Rem}[9, 10]$. Then $s = 9$. Thus, **A**'s signature is $(7, 9)$. Condition 2 is then satisfied for this signature.

3.8 Intruder-in-the-Middle Attack on the Diffie–Hellman (or Elliptic Curve) Key-Exchange

We concentrate on the Diffie–Hellman key-exchange. The Elliptic Curve key-exchange discussed in Chapter 6 is very similar, the main difference being that it uses a different group.

Basically, the intruder Eve impersonates **B** to **A** and **A** to **B**. We use the notation of Section 3.7. Eve chooses an exponent x, and intercepts both $g^a \pmod{p}$ from **A** to **B** and $g^b \pmod{p}$ from **B** to **A**. The procedures is as follows:

1. Eve intercepts g^a from **A** to **B** and sends g^x to **A**.

2. Eve computes $\mathrm{Rem}(g^x)^a$, i.e. $(g^x)^a \pmod{p}$.

3. **A** computes $(g^a)^x \pmod{p} = (g^x)^a \pmod{p} = E_{\mathbf{A}}$. Thus, Eve and **A** have a common secret key $E_{\mathbf{A}}$.

4. Eve intercepts $g^b \pmod{p}$ from **B** to **A** and sends $g^x \pmod{p}$ to **B**. Then Eve and **B** establish a common secret key $E_{\mathbf{B}}$. $E_{\mathbf{B}} = (g^x)^b \pmod{p} = (g^b)^x \pmod{p}$.

When **A** sends a message to **B** encrypted with $E_{\mathbf{A}}$ then Eve intercepts it, decrypts it with $E_{\mathbf{A}}$, encrypts it with $E_{\mathbf{B}}$ and sends it to **B**. **B** decrypts it with $E_{\mathbf{B}}$.

A and **B** have no idea that Eve is in possession of their secret. To avoid the attack, **A** and **B** need a procedure that authenticates **A** (**B**) to **B** (**A**). One way of achieving this is by using digital signatures.

3.9   TLS (Transport Layer Security)

TLS is used to protect data during communication via the Internet. Prior to TLS, the Secure Socket Layer (SSL) protocol was used for secure Internet transactions. The SSL protocol was developed by the Netscape corporation in the 1990s. It evolved into the TLS protocol [MC19,Res18,RNGC19], with the original TLS version 1.0 essentially being SSL version 3.1 [NIS20]. TLS is designed to provide *authentication, confidentiality, and data integrity protection* between two communicating entities. It is widely used to secure communications in online transactions, including financial transactions, such as online banking and online purchases, and healthcare transactions, such as viewing online medical records [MC19].

Most people will have encountered TLS on a regular basis while making purchases online, logging into accounts, such as social media accounts over the Internet. When doing these via a web browser (such as Google Chrome, Safari, Firefox, Microsoft Edge), these types of applications use HTTPS (Hyper-Text Transfer Protocol – Secure), which can use TLS. Note that HTTP should never be used to access websites when sensitive or valuable information is involved, such as login names and passwords, bank information. So before entering or accessing any sensitive or valuable information into a website via web browser, always be sure that the URL you are accessing has `https:` before it (e.g. `https://www.amazon.com`) as opposed to `http:`.

As mentioned, TLS is designed to provide authentication, confidentiality, and data integrity protection between two communicating entities. It uses an encrypted channel for communication between a client and a server (with the "client" often being one's web browser). This protects e-mail messages, for example, from man-in-the-middle attacks during message transmission. (See Section 7.4 for a discussion of Man-in-the-Middle attacks.)

TLS uses a combination of symmetric encryption (such as AES from Chapter 5) and asymmetric encryption (such as RSA from this chapter). Asymmetric cryptography is generally slower and is used for authentication and distributing a shared secret. Symmetric encryption is quicker but needs a shared secret which the asymmetric algorithm provides. The symmetric encryption is used for the actual encrypted transaction.

Before a secure TLS transaction occurs, the server (eBay, Amazon, PayPal, etc.) must generate a public key/private key pair, and then get this pair signed by an authority. This signed information is called the **certificate.** The person (or organization) that signs the certificate knows as the **certificate authority** (CA). Anyone may sign a certificate, but every machine maintains a list of trusted CAs, and if the server's certificate is not signed, a warning is usually produced.

The signing process is merely the CA using its private key to encrypt some known data. The client may then use the CA's public key to decrypt this data and compare it to the known value. If they match, then it must have been the CA who actually signed the certificate.

There are three subprotocols to the TLS protocol: the *handshake protocol*, the *change cipher spec protocol*, and the *alert protocol*. The handshake protocol is used to negotiate the session parameters. The change cipher spec protocol is used to change the cryptographic parameters of a session. The alert protocol notifies the client or server of any error conditions.

The handshake protocol consists of a series of messages between the client and server to negotiate the cryptographic algorithms that will be used so as to provide confidentiality, message integrity, authentication, and replay protection. Symmetric keys and other session parameters are established. There are three phases to the handshake protocol:

(i) *Key exchange.*

   The client sends a `ClientHello` message to the server. This message contains a random nonce, it notes which versions of TLS it supports, and it indicates which cryptographic protocols it can use.

   The server responds with a `ServerHello` message noting the version of TLS that will be used, and which cryptographic protocols will be used.

   The client and server exchange messages to determine shared keys and other cryptographic parameters.

(ii) *Server parameters.*

   In this (encrypted) phase, the client and server negotiate the other handshake parameters, including whether the client will be authenticated.

(iii) *Authentication.*

   In this (encrypted) phase, the server is authenticated. The client can be optionally authenticated as well.

As part of the establishment of keys during the TLS handshake protocol, a *premaster secret*, a *master secret* and the *session keys* are derived. The *premaster secret* depends on the key exchange method that is agreed upon by the client and server, and the version of TLS that is being used. The premaster secret together with values contained in the `ClientHello` and `ServerHello` messages are used in a pseudorandom function to compute the master secret. Session keys are derived from the master secret. These session keys are used to provide a secure channel for the client and server to communicate with each other. For further details, see [MC19] and [Res18].

When the client and server share the same secret key (in this case, the session keys), they may use a fast symmetric algorithm to communicate. When the two parties are finished communicating, then the session keys are forgotten, and would have to be regenerated for further transactions.

3.10   PGP and GPG

Pretty Good Privacy (or **PGP**) is a computer program which provides cryptographic privacy and authentication. It is a patented technology created by Phil Zimmerman and owned by the PGP Corporation. PGP may encrypt any type of data but it is most commonly used for e-mail.

OpenPGP is an open-source (free) alternative standard for digitally signing and encrypting e-mail. The most common implementation of OpenPGP is **GPG**, which stands for **GNU Privacy Guard**.

PGP and GPG are very similar in their uses and operation, but differ in the algorithms that they use. They both use algorithms such as RSA or Elliptic Curve cryptography (ECC) for asymmetric encryption but PGP uses patented symmetric encryption algorithms, while GPG uses public domain (free) algorithms.

Both programs may be used for encrypting/decrypting e-mail and signing/ authenticating messages.

Before using PGP or GPG, a user generates their own public key and private key pair. Then, the public key must be published so that others may access it. This may be done by putting it out on a website, sending out mass emails announcing the public key, or placing it on a **key server** and associating it to an e-mail address.

Encrypting/decrypting

To send an encrypted message, the user decides on a symmetric algorithm and then the computer will generate a random key for use with this message. The message is encrypted using this key, and the key is encrypted using the intended recipient's public key. Both the message and the encrypted key are sent by e-mail to the intended recipient. If the e-mail is intercepted in this form, the eavesdropper shouldn't be able to read the contents, because they don't possess the proper private key to decode the session key, nor do they possess the session key to decode the message.

Upon receipt of an encrypted e-mail, the user's computer will use his/her private key to decrypt the enclosed session key, and then will use the session key to decode the message. In many modern e-mail programs that support PGP or GPG, this is done without the user knowing. That way, the user isn't inconvenienced by the added security, but will still enjoy the benefits of encrypted e-mail.

Note that symmetric encryption is used for the actual message and asymmetric encryption is used for the key exchange. This is because symmetric cryptography is about 4000 times faster than asymmetric. That means that sending a large e-mail with large attachments would take quite some time to encrypt if you only used RSA.

Signing/authenticating

Just as the encryption algorithm for PGP and GPG are very similar to TLS, so is the authentication mechanism. A hash of the e-mail message is encrypted with the user's private key, and then appended to the end of the message. Then when the e-mail is received, the user's computer may decrypt this message with the sender's public key and check that the hash corresponds to the hash of the current message. This procedure may serve two purposes. It authenticates the original message sender (the person in possession of the private key used to encrypt the message hash), and it almost guarantees that the message wasn't altered since its signing since, with a strong enough hashing algorithm, it is highly unlikely that two messages hash to the same value.

For more information on the encryption of e-mail, see "Trustworthy Email" by Rose et al., [RNGC19].

3.11 Problems

Notation In some of the problems/solutions below, we used the $\text{Rem}[u, v]$ notation introduced in this chapter. Recall that $\text{Rem}[u, v]$ just means the remainder when u is divided by v. For example, $\text{Rem}[37, 16] = 5$. Later on, in Chapter 19 we will also use the equivalent $u \pmod{v}$ or $u \bmod v$ notation.

Some of these problems need background material and may be skipped on a first reading.

3.1 *An essential property.* In a cryptographic system suppose messages M_1, M_2 are encrypted, resulting in cipher texts C_1, C_2. If $C_1 = C_2$, must $M_1 = M_2$? (See Solution 3.1.)

3.2 In the RSA algorithm suppose that $1 < M_1 < N$, $1 < M_2 < N$ and $\text{Rem}[M_1^e, N] = \text{Rem}[M_2^e, N]$. Must $M_1 = M_2$? (See Solution 3.2.)
   Repeated squaring

3.3   Using the repeated squaring method, find the remainder when 5^{51} is divided by 97. (See Solution 3.3.)

3.4   Using the repeated squaring method, find the remainder when 11^{22} is divided by 167. (See Solution 3.4.)

RSA encryption

3.5   Using the RSA algorithm, given the cipher text $C = \text{Rem}[M^e, N]$ with $\gcd(e, (p-1)(q-1)) = 1$, can there be more than one decryption index d such that $\text{Rem}[C^d, N] = M$? (See Solution 3.5.)

3.6   In the RSA algorithm, we assume that p, q are large primes which must be unequal. Why is it that p, q must be unequal? (See Solution 3.6.)

3.7   Show that for security reasons in the RSA algorithm, p and q should not be chosen too close together. (See Solution 3.7.)

3.8   In the RSA algorithm, why must we choose e to be relatively prime to $(p-1)(q-1)$? (See Solution 3.8.)

3.9   In the RSA algorithm, show that e must be odd. (See Solution 3.9.)

3.10 In the RSA algorithm, the restriction is sometimes made – even in textbooks – that $\gcd(M, N) = 1$. Is this restriction necessary? (See Solution 3.10.)

3.11 Suppose an eavesdropper Eve knows $N = pq$ and also $\varphi(N) = (p-1)(q-1)$.[4] Show that Eve can then find p and q. (See Solution 3.11.)

Calculations using RSA (The Euclidean Algorithm of Chapter 19 can be used)

3.12 Find an RSA decryption exponent d given that $p = 41$, $q = 37$ and $e = 7$, using both methods as described in the text. (See Solution 3.12.)

3.13 Repeat the previous problem with $p = 17$, $q = 19$ and $e = 5$. (See Solution 3.13.)

3.14 Find an RSA decryption exponent d, given that $p = 47, q = 59$ and $e = 17$. (See Solution 3.14.)

3.15 Let $p = 29, q = 67$ so $N = 1943$ and $(p-1)(q-1) = 1848$. Let $e = 701$. Suppose $M = 23$. Find the cipher text C. (See Solution 3.15.)

3.16 Let p, q, e be as in the previous question. Suppose $C = 1926$. What is M? (See Solution 3.16.)

3.17 Find all possible values of e for $N = 55$. What is a compact formula for this quantity in general? (See Solution 3.17.)

Sending text messages with RSA

---

[4] $\varphi(N)$ is **Euler's Phi Function** see Chapter 19 for further details.

3.18 Suppose Alice wishes to send a text message M to Bob using the RSA algorithm. Bob's public key is the pair $[N, e] = [2867, 17]$. Note that $2867 = (47)(61)$. Alice encodes the 26 letters of the English alphabet by putting $A = 00, B = 01, \ldots, J = 09, K = 10, \ldots, T = 19, \ldots, Z = 25$. Alice transmits the message in blocks. Each block corresponds to two letters which are encoded into their numerical equivalents. For example the pair D, E becomes the block [0405] which then gets enciphered to $C = \text{Rem}[405^{17}, 2867]$, since the block corresponds to the decimal number 405. Now suppose Bob receives the cipher text 0300. What was the message transmitted by Alice? (See Solution 3.18.)

3.19 In the above problem, why can't we put more than 2 letters in a block? (See Solution 3.19.)

3.20 Are the text messages that are sent in this way secure? (See Solution 3.20.)

Elementary attacks, pitfalls and incorrect implementations of RSA

Small message, small exponent

3.21 Show that if the message M is a small integer and the enciphering index is a small integer, then RSA is not secure. (See Solution 3.21.)

3.22 For $[N, e] = [30\ 967, 3]$, decrypt $C = 29\ 791$ assuming that M is "small." (See Solution 3.22.)

3.23 Can you think of a real-world example of enciphering a small integer where the attack of Problem 3.22 might cause difficulties? (See Solution 3.23.)

3.24 Using the fact that $C = \text{Rem}[M^e, N]$, how can RSA be attacked if e is small? (This is similar to the above attack.) (See Solution 3.24.)

3.25 Decipher $C = 37$ given that $[N, e] = [51, 3]$, using the method of the previous problem. (See Solution 3.25.)

Semantic Security and RSA

3.26 RSA leaks information in various ways. For example, if C_1, C_2 are the cipher texts for messages M_1, M_2, respectively, then show that $C_1 C_2$ is the cipher text for $M_1 M_2$ (we are working here by taking remainders upon division by N, i.e. we are working mod N). (See Solution 3.26.)

Another way in which RSA leaks information is through the Jacobi symbol, since the Jacobi symbol of the cipher text C equals that of the message M. This reveals one bit of M. A cryptosystem has **semantic security** if no information is leaked.

Broadcast Attack

3.27 Given an enciphering index $e = 3$ show how a plain text message M can be recovered if it is enciphered and sent to three different entities having pairwise relatively prime moduli $N_1, N_2,$ and N_3. This is most easily solved using the Chinese Remainder Theorem of Chapter 19. (See Solution 3.27.)

3.28 Use the broadcast attack to find M when it is enciphered to 80 using $[N_1, e_1] = [319, 3]$; 235 using $[N_2, e_2] = [299, 3]$; and 121 using $[N_3, e_3] = [323, 3]$. (See Solution 3.28.)

Common Modulus Attack

3.29 Let Alice's public key be $[N_1, e_1]$ and let Bob's public key be $[N_2, e_2]$, with $N_1 = N_2$. Show that Bob can recover all messages sent to Alice. (See Solution 3.29.)

Cycling Attack

3.30 Given $C = M^e$, an eavesdropper can compute $C^e = (M^e)^e = M^{e^2}, (C^e)^e = C^{e^2} = M^{e^3}$, etc. How can the eavesdropper obtain the message M using this idea? (See Solution 3.30.)

3.31 For $[N, e] = [187, 3]$, decrypt $C = 173$ using the cycling attack. (See Solution 3.31.)

3.32 Find $\text{Rem}(5^{51})$, where $p = 97$. (See Solution 3.32.)

3.33 The following problem is an easy version of the discrete log problem: Find x if $p = 11$ and $\text{Rem}(2^x) = 9$. (See Solution 3.33.)

3.12   Solutions

3.1 Yes, we must have $M_1 = M_2$. First of all, we have $C_1 = e(M_1)$ and $C_2 = e(M_2)$, where e is the enciphering algorithm. Applying the decryption algorithm d, we have $d(C_1) = M_1$ and $d(C_2) = M_2$, since $d(C_1) = d(e(M_1)) = M_1$. Similarly, $d(C_2) = M_2$. Since $C_1 = C_2$, we have $d(C_1) = d(C_2)$; so $M_1 = M_2$.

3.2 This is a special case of Section 3.2. The reason is that if M is any message with $1 < M < N$, then the enciphering transformation e transforms M to $e(M)$ with $e(M) = \text{Rem}[M^e, N] = C$. As we will see in Chapter 19, the decryption algorithm d transforms C to $d(C) = \text{Rem}[C^d, N] = M$.

3.3 69.

3.4 7.

3.5   Yes, as we have seen in the first example discussed in the text, there can be more than one decryption index d. Here is another example. Suppose that **A** is transmitting a message to **B** whose public key is $[N, e] = [1541, 5]$. Now, we have $N = 1541 = (23)(67) = pq$ with $p = 23, q = 67$. Then, $(p-1)(q-1) = (22)(66) = 1452$. Now, $\text{Rem}[(5)581, 1452] = 1$. (In another notation, we have that 581 is the multiplicative inverse of 5 mod 1452.) So we can take $d = 581$. Then, for any cipher text $C = \text{Rem}[M^e, N] = \text{Rem}[M^5, 1541]$, it follows that $\text{Rem}[C^d, N] = \text{Rem}[C^{581}, 1541]$. However, instead of working with $(p-1)(q-1)$, we can work with any integer that is divisible by both $p-1$ and $q-1$. Such a number is 66. Note that $\gcd(e, 66) = \gcd(5, 66) = 1$. Thus, as will be shown in Chapter 19 in the general case, if d_1 is such that $\text{Rem}[(5)d_1, 66] = 1$, then d_1 also serves as a decryption index here. Now, $\text{Rem}[(5)(53), 66] = 1$. So $d_1 = 53$.

    Let us summarize. We have two decryption indices, namely, 581 and 53, for the same values of p and q. For any message M, in the form of an integer between 1 and $N = 1540$, we have $C = \text{Rem}[M^5, 1541]$, but also $\text{Rem}[C^{581}, 1541] = \text{Rem}[C^{53}, 1541] = M$.

3.6   Suppose a user announces his public key as $[N, e] = [pq, e] = [p^2, e]$. Then N is easily factored. Just take the square root of N to get p.

3.7   The idea goes back to Fermat, involving Fermat's "Difference of Squares Method," as follows. Suppose n factors as $n = pq$ with $p > q$. Recall that p, q are odd, so $p + q$ and $p - q$ are even. Then $p > \sqrt{n}$ and $q < \sqrt{n}$. Then $n = (\frac{p+q}{2})^2 - (\frac{p-q}{2})^2 = u^2 - v^2$ where u, v are integers with $u > v$. Thus, $n + v^2 = u^2$ or $u^2 - n = v^2$. If p is close to q, then u is bigger than, but close to, $\sqrt{n}$. So to factor n, which is our goal, we only need to try a few integers u until we find a u such that $u^2 - n$ is equal to a square integer denoted by v^2. For example, take $n = 2867$ as in Problem 3.18. Here, $\sqrt{n} = 53.54$ So start with $u = 54$ and immediately we get $54^2 - n = 49$ which is a square. Thus, $54^2 - n = 7^2, n = 54^2 - 7^2 = (54 - 7)(54 + 7)$ and we have factored $n = (47)(61)$.

3.8   One explanation is as follows. The official procedure for calculating the decryption index is to find d such that $\text{Rem}[ed, (p-1)(q-1)] = 1$. (In other language, d is the multiplicative inverse of e modulo $(p-1)(q-1)$). This can be carried out, as we shall see in Chapter 19, only if e is relatively prime to $(p-1)(q-1)$, i.e. only if $\gcd(e, (p-1)(q-1)) = 1$. For example, if $p = 5, q = 11, e = 2$, then it is impossible to find d so that the remainder of $2d$ on division by 40 is 1. To see that this is the case we would need to find d so that $2d - 40x = 1$ for some x. But the left side is even, the right side is odd. So, no such d exists. What happens if we break the rules and choose an enciphering index e such that $\gcd(e, (p-1)(q-1)) > 1$? Take $M = 2, p = 3, q = 5, e = 2$. Then $c = \text{Rem}[M^2, 15] = \text{Rem}[2^2, 15] = 4$. However, we also get $\text{Rem}[7^2, 15] = 4, \text{Rem}[13^2, 15] = 4$ and $\text{Rem}[8^2, 15] = 4$. In other words, four different messages namely 2, 7, 8, 13 all encipher to the same cipher text, namely 4. But we saw in Problem 3.1 that in a proper cryptographic system, two different messages cannot encipher to the same cipher text.

3.9   If e is even, then 2 divides e. For security, p and q must be large, certainly bigger than 2. Thus, p and q being primes bigger than 2 are odd numbers. So $p-1$ (and $q-1$) are even. Then 2 divides e as well as $(p-1)(q-1)$. This contradicts the assumption that $\gcd(e, (p-1)(q-1)) = 1$.

3.10   No, the algorithm works without that requirement. However, an attacker might test if $g = \gcd(M, N) > 1$, and if so, then $g = p$ or q. To see this, note that $g < N$, since $M < N$. Since g divides $N = pq$, and p is prime, this forces that g divides p or g divides q. Then, since $g > 1$ and both p and q are prime, this implies that $g = p$ or $g = q$. Thus, an attacker can easily factor N when $\gcd(N, M) > 1$.

3.11   We have $N - \varphi(N) + 1 = (pq) - (p-1)(q-1) + 1 = p + q$. Thus, Eve knows $p + q$ and pq. Now $(p+q)^2 - 4pq = (p-q)^2$ so Eve knows $(p-q)^2$. Eve can assume that p is bigger than q. So Eve calculates the positive square root of $(p-q)^2$ which is $p - q$. Since Eve knows both $p + q$ and $p - q$ then, by adding, she gets p and then q. For example, suppose Eve knows $N = 323$ and $\varphi(N) = 288$. Then $323 - 288 + 1 = 36 = p + q$. Now $36^2 - 4(323) = 1296 - 1292 = 4 = (p-q)^2$, so $p - q = 2$. Since $p + q = 36$ we get $p = 19$ and $q = 17$.

3.12   Solution (a). We find d such that $\text{Rem}[7d, (40)(36)] = 1$. This gives $d = 823$.
       Solution (b). Let $t = 360$. Then 40 divides t and 36 divides t. We find d such that $\text{Rem}[7d, t] = 1$. This gives $d = 103$.

3.13   Solution (a). We find d such that $\text{Rem}[5d, (16)(18)] = 1$. This gives $d = 173$.
       Solution (b). Let $t = 144$. Then 16 divides t and 18 divides t. We find d such that $\text{Rem}[5d, t] = 1$. This gives $d = 29$.

3.14   If $p = 47, q = 59, e = 17$ we get, using either method, that $d = 157$.

3.15 $C = 458$.

3.16   We can take $d = 29$ giving $M = 12$.

3.17 N factors as $p = 5$, $q = 11$, so we find all e for which there is a d so that $\text{Rem}[ed, (p-1)(q-1)] = 1$. That is, we find all integers relatively prime to, and less than, $(p-1)(q-1) = 40$. There are 16 (excluding the number 1), they are 3, 5, 7, 9,

11, 13, 17, 19, 21, 23, 27, 29, 31, 33, 37, 39. In general, this quantity is called **Euler's Phi function**, so $\varphi(40) = 17$ as $\phi(40)$ is the number of integers *including 1* that are less than 40 and relatively prime to 40. Note that, for any prime p, $\phi(p) = p - 1$. If u, v are relatively prime, i.e. have no nontrivial factors in common, then $\phi(uv) = \phi(u)\phi(v)$. This is further discussed in Chapter 19.

3.18 We can take $d = 2273$, so $M = 0408$ corresponding to the pair of letters EI.

3.19 If we put three letters in a block, we might have a block as large as 252 525 which is larger than $N = 2867$.

3.20 If we encode with, say two letters in a block, we know that there are only $26^2 = 676$ possible messages even though the largest message is encoded as 2525. So to increase the security (i.e. to make a brute-force attack more difficult), we need a large number of letters in a block and so a large modulus N. More economical methods of encoding are possible (see Mollin [Mol02] and [Mol00]).

3.21 If M^e is less than N, the message M is immediately obtained by getting the eth root of the cipher text C. For example, if $e = 3$, we need only calculate the cube root of C. The reason is that $\text{Rem}[M^e, N] = M^e = C$ so $M = C^{1/e}$.

3.22 $M = 29\,791^{\frac{1}{3}} = 31$.

3.23 Suppose **A** chooses a binary string of length 56 as a proposed session key K for the DES algorithm and transmits this key to **B** using RSA. When we represent K as an integer, it will be less than 2^{56}. Then the cipher text C is less than 2^{56e}. If e is small, say $e = 3$, then this may be much less than $N = pq$ when p and q are large. Then, by calculating the eth root of C an eavesdropper can recover the key K.

3.24 From the stated fact, it follows that $M = C^{\frac{1}{e}}$ or $(C + N)^{\frac{1}{e}}$ or $(C + 2N)^{\frac{1}{e}}$ or $(C + rN)^{\frac{1}{e}}$ for some r. If r is small, then RSA can be attacked.

3.25 For $r = 6$, we find $(C + rN) = 343$ so $M = 343^{\frac{1}{3}} = 7$ (One can verify from theory, or directly, that $\text{Rem}[M^e, N] = \text{Rem}[7^3, N] = 37 = C$).

3.26 We have $C_1 = \text{Rem}[M_1^e, N]$ and $C_2 = \text{Rem}[M_2^e, N]$. Therefore, $C_1 = M_1^e + \lambda_1 N$, $C_2 = M_2^e + \lambda_2 N$, $M_1 < N, M_2 < N$. Then $C_1 C_2 = (M_1 M_2)^e + \mu N$. Thus, $\text{Rem}[C_1 C_2, N] = \text{Rem}[(M_1 M_2)^e, N]$.

3.27 This follows from the Chinese Remainder Theorem discussed in Chapter 19. The main point is this. We have $\text{Rem}[M^3, N_1] = C_1, \text{Rem}[M^3, N_2] = C_2, \text{Rem}[M^3, N_3] = C_3$. By the Chinese Remainder Theorem, there is a unique x less than $N_1 N_2 N_3$

such that $Rem[x, N_1] = C_1, Rem[x, N_2] = C_2, Rem[x, N_3] = C_3$. Now M^3 also satisfies these three equations. Moreover, since $M < N_1, N_2, N_3$, we get $M^3 < N_1 N_2 N_3$. Thus, $x = M^3$. The cube root of x, then gives M. Note that this attack can be generalized to any small value of e.

3.28 First, we check that N_1, N_2 and N_3 are pairwise relatively prime. They factor as $N_1 = 11 \times 29$, $N_2 = 13 \times 23$ and $N_3 = 17 \times 19$, and are Thus, pairwise relatively prime. Now, x as described in the previous solution is 74 088, and so the answer is $M = 74\,088^{\frac{1}{3}} = 42$. [See Solution 3.28.]

3.29 By hypothesis, Bob knows the factors of N, i.e. he knows p, q, where $N = pq$.

In order to decrypt a cipher C sent to Alice, i.e. to find the message M sent to Alice, Bob merely has to find the inverse of e_1 modulo $(p-1)(q-1)$, i.e. to find d_1 such that $Rem[e_1 d_1, (p_1-1)(q_1-1)] = 1$. Then Bob raises C to the power d and gets the remainder of C^d upon division by N to find M.

3.30 Since e is relatively prime to $(p-1)(q-1)$, there are integers t, λ so that $e^t = 1 + \lambda(p-1)(q-1)$. This follows from a generalization to Fermat's Theorem. Using this fact, we have $C^{e^t} = C^{1+\lambda(p-1)(q-1)} = C(C^{\lambda(p-1)(q-1)})$. Now $Rem[C^{p-1}, p] = Rem[C^{q-1}, q] = 1$, by Fermat's Theorem. Then $Rem(C^{e^t}, N) = Rem[C(C^{\lambda(p-1)(q-1)}), pq] = C$. To see this, we are calculating

$$(C)(C^{\lambda(p-1)(q-1)}) \pmod{pq}. \tag{3.13}$$

This is equal to

$$(C(\text{mod } pq)\ C^{\lambda(p-1)(q-1)} \text{ mod } (pq)) \bmod(pq). \tag{3.14}$$

Now,

$$C^{\lambda(p-1)(q-1)} \pmod{p} = C^{\lambda(q-1)(p-1)} \pmod{p}$$

$$= (C^{\lambda(q-1)})^{p-1} \pmod{p}$$

$$= (C^{(q-1)} C^{(q-1)} \cdots C^{(q-1)})^{p-1} \pmod{p}$$

$$= (C^{q-1})^{p-1}(C^{q-1})^{p-1} \cdots (C^{q-1})^{p-1} \pmod{p}$$

$$\equiv 1 \pmod{p}.$$

Thus, $C^{\lambda(p-1)(q-1)} - 1$ is divisible by p. Similarly, it is divisible by q so that $C^{\lambda(p-1)(q-1)}$ is divisible by pq. From (3.14), we get $(C \text{ mod } (pq))(1 \text{ mod } (pq)) = C \pmod{pq} = C$. Then, given that $C = Rem[M^e, N]$, we conclude that

$\text{Rem}[C^{e^{t-1}}, N] = M$. Thus, if t is small, RSA can be attacked. Note that in using Fermat's Theorem, we have supposed that $\text{Rem}[C, p] \neq 0$ and $\text{Rem}[C, q] \neq 0$, but, we in fact can only be guaranteed that one of $\text{Rem}[C, p] \neq 0$ or $\text{Rem}[C, q] \neq 0$ is true, although it is possible that both are true. However, the result still holds in this case, and the proof is similar.

3.31   For $t = 4$, $\text{Rem}[C^{e^t}, N] = C$, so $M = \text{Rem}[C^{e^{t-1}}, N] = 24$.

3.32   69.

3.33 $x = 6$.

Chapter 4

The Fundamentals of Modern Cryptography

Goals, Discussion We present a summary of most of the important procedures and ideas in modern cryptography. The important question of authentication is pursued further in Chapter 8.

New, Noteworthy We discuss the material in such a way that mathematical prerequisites are minimized. For example, the RSA material discussed in Chapter 3 will give more than enough background for an understanding of digital signatures. On the question of the design of modern block ciphers, several authors will suggest that Shannon's diffusion principle comes down just to a permutation. However, quoting from the master, we point out that there is much more to diffusion than a mere permutation.

Issues from complexity theory, relating to computational security, are pursued in Chapter 19.

4.1   Encryption Revisited

Recall from Chapter 3 that cryptography is the art or science of keeping messages secret. Briefly, **A** (for Alice) wants to send a secret message M to **B** (for Bob). The message

Cryptography, Information Theory, and Error-Correction: A Handbook for the 21st Century, Second Edition.
Aiden A. Bruen, Mario A. Forcinito, and James M. McQuillan.
© 2021 John Wiley & Sons, Inc. Published 2021 by John Wiley & Sons, Inc.

M is also called the plain text. The message might be a text message or a binary string, such as $\{1\,1\,0\,1\,1\,0\}$, etc. As with all computer communications, the text message will first be converted to binary. One way of doing this is with the ASCII conversion code described in Appendix A.

A scrambles (encrypts, enciphers) M with an encryption key, often called the **session key** into unintelligible cipher text C. Then **A** transmits C **in the open** – that is, over a public channel – to **B**.

When the cipher text (=scrambled message) reaches **B**, it can be descrambled by **B** using the decryption key. Thus, **B** can recover the original message M. The security rests on two assumptions.

1. Only **B**, or an authorized representative has the descrambling (=decryption) key.

2. The message M cannot be recovered without the decryption key.

The procedure or algorithm for encryption is called a *cipher*. Several different kinds of ciphers – Caesar, Vigenère, affine – have been described in Chapter 2 on classical ciphers.

Cryptanalysis is the science of trying to "break the system," or trying to capture the message M from the cipher text C by first getting the key (or even by getting the message M directly). An attempted cryptanalysis is called an **attack**. An attack which involves trying all possible keys is called a **brute-force** attack. As we saw in Chapter 3, this involves trying only about half the key-space. A **cryptosystem** consists of an encryption and decryption algorithm, together with all possible messages (=plain texts), cipher texts and keys. Traditionally, a fundamental – if theoretical – principle in cryptography is known as **Kerchoff's principle**. It asserts that the security of a cryptosystem must depend only on the key. In other words, in assessing the security of a cryptosystem, one must assume that a possible intruder or eavesdropper has complete knowledge of the cryptosystem and its implementation. Of course, in practice, as little as possible is revealed.

Although we do not make extensive use of mathematical notation, we can summarize the encryption procedure in the following equation:

$$d(e(M)) = M \tag{4.1}$$

where e is the encryption (enciphering) transformation which scrambles the message M to give the cipher text C, so that $e(M) = C$. Further, d is the decryption or deciphering algorithm, so that $d(C) = d(e(M)) = M$.

An important mathematical consequence of Formula (4.1) is Formula (4.2):

$$e(d(M)) = M \tag{4.2}$$

Formula (4.1) says that we get the original message M back, if we first encrypt the message M and then decrypt the encrypted message (=the cipher text).

In Formula (4.2), the order is reversed. In other words, if we first perform the decryption algorithm on the message itself (not on the cipher text, as in (4.1)) and then perform the encryption algorithm on the result, we also end up with the message M. We are tacitly assuming here that the message set equals the set of cipher texts (see Chapter 15), so that e and d are defined on the same set.

Formula (4.2) is the basis for **digital signatures** as we will see later. The quantity $d(M)$ is called the signature. Note that, in (4.1) and (4.2), we should, strictly speaking, write $e_K(M)$ instead of $e(M)$ because the enciphering transformation e will depend on a key K. Similar remarks pertain to the deciphering transformation d.

As explained in Chapter 3, the enciphering and deciphering keys are equal in the case of symmetric cryptography; for public-key systems they differ. In the notation of Chapter 3, $e(M)$ is simply $\text{Rem}[M^e, N]$ for the RSA system, i.e. the remainder of M^e upon division by N.

The main public-key cryptosystem is RSA. Elliptic curve cryptography (ECC) is growing in use and popularity, as it requires smaller keys to achieve the same security strength (see [BD15, pp. 11–13]). For symmetric cryptography, the main algorithms are **AES** and (a modification of) the **Vernam Cipher** or **one-time pad**. Frequently, the lengthy random key that is needed for the one-time pad is approximated by the output of a suitable feedback shift register. In Section 3.7, we discussed the **Diffie–Hellman key-exchange**, which straddles the border between symmetric and public-key exchanges. Nowadays, in industry, a kind of **hybrid system** is used. This means that, using RSA for example, **A** transmits a message K to **B**. Then **A** and **B** use K as a session key for a symmetric encryption using Advanced Encryption Standard (AES).

One difficulty with transmitting messages with RSA is that it is quite slow, relatively speaking. AES is much faster. However, for **A** and **B** to use AES they must first be in possession of a common secret key.

In any cryptographic system, various other related issues besides encryption need to be addressed. These issues include the following:

1. *Authentication.* How does **B** (or **A**) know that the entity with whom **B** (or **A**) is communicating is really **A** (or **B**)?

2. *Message integrity.* How does **B** know that the message received from **A** has not been tampered with?

3. *Digital signatures/non-repudiation.* How do **A**, **B** arrange to obtain legally binding reassurances, similar to a signature, from each other?

In this chapter, we discuss some of these concerns. Authentication issues are also pursued in Chapter 8.

4.2   Block Ciphers, Shannon's Confusion and Diffusion

In some modern applications of symmetric cryptography, such as Global System for Mobile telecommunication (GSM) phones, a **stream cipher** encryption algorithm is used. The message, represented as a stream of binary digits (bits) is encrypted bit by bit. One advantage of stream ciphers is that an error will not affect future bits, i.e. the error is not propagated. One of the main examples of a stream cipher comes from a **linear feedback shift register** (LFSR), which is discussed in detail in Chapter 16.

In other applications of symmetric cryptography, **block cipher** encryption algorithms are used. The message is broken up into substrings (called blocks) of a fixed length $n > 1$ and encrypted block by block. The integer n is called the **block-length**. In the case of AES, $n = 128$, i.e. the block-length is 128 bits long and the key-length is either 128 or 192 or 256 bits.

At a basic level, AES is simply a combination of the two fundamental techniques for construction of ciphers advocated by Shannon in 1949, namely **confusion** and **diffusion**.

Confusion

This technique tends to block the cryptanalyst from obtaining statistical patterns and redundancies in the cipher text arising from the plain text. Thus, the statistical dependency of the cipher text on the plain text is obfuscated. The easiest way to cause confusion is through the use of substitutions. In the case of a binary string, we substitute various ones and zeros by zeros and ones, respectively, according to a predetermined formula.

Diffusion

This technique dissipates the redundancy of the plain text by spreading it over the cipher text. Redundancy will be precisely explained in Part II. For the moment, we can think of it informally as statistical patterns. Diffusion implies that, if we change just one letter or character in the plain text, we cause a big change in the cipher text. Thus, we will need a large amount of cipher text to capture redundancy in the plain text.

Several authors have suggested that, according to Shannon, diffusion simply means a permutation or rearrangement of the characters in the message string. However, this is not quite correct since a permutation will still preserve the frequency of characters. Shannon's recipe for diffusion also involves acting on a string with a diffusing function.

In the words of the master himself, Shannon [Sha49b]:

- In the method of diffusion, the statistical structure of M which leads to its redundancy is "dissipated" into long-range statistics, i.e. into statistical structure involving long combinations of letters in the cryptogram. The effect is that the enemy must intercept a tremendous amount of material to tie down this structure, since the structure is evident only in blocks of very small individual probability. Furthermore, even when he has sufficient material, the analytical work required is much greater, since the redundancy has been diffused over a large number of individual statistics.

An example of diffusion of statistics is operating on a message $M = m_1, m_2, m_3 \ldots$ with an "averaging" operation, for example

$$y_n = \sum_{i=1}^{s} m_{n+i} \ (\mathrm{mod}\ 26) \tag{4.3}$$

adding s successive letters of the message to get a letter y_n. One can show that the redundancy of the y sequence is the same as that of the m sequence, but the structure has been dissipated. Thus, the letter frequencies in the y sequence will be more nearly equal than in the m sequence, the diagram frequencies also more nearly equal, etc. Indeed any reversible operation, which produces one letter out for each letter in and does not have an infinite "memory," has an output with the same redundancy as the input. The statistics can never be eliminated without compression, but they can be "spread out."

We mention here that the historical ciphers discussed in Chapter 2, such as the Caesar and Vigenère ciphers, do not have the properties of confusion and diffusion. On the other hand, AES uses confusion and diffusion to good effect.

In general, the cipher texts in AES will reveal some information about the message, the amount depending on the nature of the message. The extreme case, mentioned in Chapter 3, is when knowledge of the cipher text reveals no information whatsoever about the message, as is the case with the Vernam cipher (=one-time pad). This extreme case is called **"perfect secrecy"** or **"perfect security"**. We will have much to say about this both in Section 4.3 and in Parts II and III of the book.

4.3   Perfect Secrecy, Stream Ciphers, One-Time Pad

We recall that in modern digital communications all numbers and symbols are converted to binary strings. All symbols consist of zeros and ones and are known as bits (=binary digits). The conversion to binary is made using some encoding table, such as the ASCII code (see Appendix A).

The *XOR operator (or exclusive OR)* is a well-known and important Boolean function. If $U = (u_1, u_2, \ldots, u_n)$, $V = (v_1, v_2, \ldots, v_n)$ are two binary sequences, then $U\ XOR\ V$ is the sequence $W = (w_1, \ldots, w_n)$, where $w_i = x_i + y_i$ (mod 2). For example, $(1, 1, 1)\ XOR\ (0, 1, 0) = (1, 0, 1)$.

To better explain how a one-time pad works, we use binary arithmetic in which we add according to the following four basic rules.

$$0 + 0 = 0, \quad 0 + 1 = 1, \quad 1 + 0 = 1 \quad , \text{and } 1 + 1 = 0 \tag{4.4}$$

An important property of binary arithmetic *is that subtraction is the same as addition*, i.e. $a - b = a + b$. For example, $0 - 1 = 0 + 1 = 1$, $1 - 1 = 1 + 1 = 0$, etc.

Note that these operations correspond to the XOR (= exclusive OR) Boolean function. Moreover, the usual rules of arithmetic are satisfied, namely

1. $a + a = 0$, no matter whether a is 0 or 1.

2. $a + b = b + a$, for all binary integers a, b.

3. $(a + b) + c = a + (b + c)$ for all binary integers a, b, c.

Multiplication in binary is also easy, since $1^2 = 1$, $0^2 = 0$ and $(1)(0) = (0)(1) = 0$. Thus, $x^2 = x$ for all binary variables x.

Let us suppose now that **A** wishes to send a secret message M to **B** in the form of a binary string of length n. We also assume that **A**, **B** are in possession of a secret key K, known only to them, which is also in the form of a random binary string of length n, *the same length as the message M*.

For example, assume that $n = 6$ and that K is the string $\{110010\}$. Suppose that the message M is $\{100011\}$. The enciphering algorithm is remarkably simple: add the two strings, bit by bit, using binary addition. Thus, we get

Plain-text M :	1	0	0	0	1	1
Key K :	1	1	0	0	1	0
Cipher-text C :	0	1	0	0	0	1

In symbols we can write $C = M + K$ (see Figure 4.1).

A transmits the cipher text C to **B**. When **B** receives C, he must undo the enciphering algorithm that **A** carried out on M. Since **A** added the key K to the message M to get the cipher text C, **B** must subtract the key K from the cipher text C. Since addition

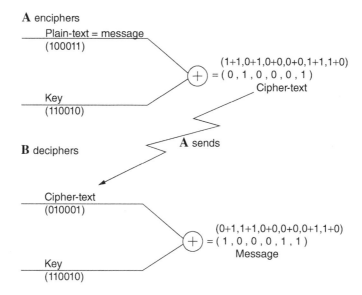

Figure 4.1: One-time pad.

and subtraction are the same in binary, **B** just adds the key K to C, without "carries" of course, to recover M.

Thus, **B** deciphers C by adding K to C to obtain:

$$C + K = (M + K) + K = M + (K + K) = M + 0 = M \qquad (4.5)$$

In other words, **B** recovers the original message M that was transmitted to **B** by **A**, as required.

This encryption procedure is known as the Vernam cipher or one-time pad since it is recommended that the key be used just once, for added security. This is discussed in more detail in Part II.

What does unconditional (=perfect) security mean? Why does the one-time pad yield unconditional security?

Answering these questions in a rigorous mathematical way requires the explanation of several concepts and formulae from the discipline of information theory, following the pioneering work of Claude E. Shannon.

It is not difficult to explain the main ideas.

An encryption algorithm gives unconditional or perfect security (= perfect secrecy), if knowledge of the cipher text gives no additional knowledge of the plain text. In the one-time pad, we can think of each 0 or 1 in K (i.e. each element of K) as having been obtained in a completely random way. For example, one can imagine a coin as having been tossed for each element of the key, with heads giving a zero and tails dictating that a one was chosen. Thus, the key K will have no known patterns in it.

In the example above, the plain text, key, and cipher text were, respectively, $M = \{100011\}$, $K = \{110010\}$, and $C = \{010001\}$. If an eavesdropper named *Eve*, recovers C, no inference on the contents of the message can be drawn by Eve. For all Eve knows, the real plain text might well be the message $M_1 = \{011110\}$ and the real key might be the key $K_1 = \{001111\}$, since when we encipher M_1 using the key K_1, we get the cipher text $C = \{010001\}$.

Indeed, for any binary string S of length 6, there is a unique key K of length 6 such that S, enciphered by binary addition using K, gives the plain text C. The total number of binary strings S of length 6 is easily calculated. There are two choices, zero or one, for the first digit, 2 for the second digit, ... and 2 for the sixth digit, giving $2 \times 2 \times \ldots \times 2 = 2^6 = 64$ total choices for S.

Thus, Eve can only guess which of these 64 strings is the real message, as the cipher text gives no information on the message (= plain text).

In the case where the message is a binary string of length n, the number of possible messages is 2^n and Eve can only guess which one of these 2^n possibilities is the correct one.

This indicates why the one-time pad is perfectly secure. Indeed, the probability that Eve makes the correct guess is $1/2^n$, which is vanishingly small as n gets large. *Moreover, even if Eve made the right guess, she would never know that she had done so.*

One-time pads form the most secure encryption algorithm. Nowadays, they are mainly used for ultra-secure low-bandwidth channels. To quote Schneier, [Sch96], "Many soviet-spy messages to agents were encrypted using one-time pads. These messages are still secure today and will remain that way forever."

We emphasize that for many applications the keys for one-time pads can only be used once and then discarded, as the name implies. If not, the security can be compromised.

It should also be pointed out that the general definition of perfect secrecy will not necessarily imply that the probability of getting the correct message is vanishingly small (as is the case for the one-time pad of length n, with n large). However, perfect secrecy means that the cipher text gives no extra information about the original message that was not available already.

Note that the Vernam cipher can be modified to work for any alphabet, not just the binary alphabet. Thus, **A** enciphers by adding a key element and **B** deciphers by subtracting the key element. For example we mention that the Vigenère cipher (see Chapter 2), where the key is as long as the message, is essentially equivalent to a one-time pad, but over an arbitrary alphabet, not just the binary alphabet.

A famous result of Shannon asserts that the key must be as long, roughly speaking, as the message for perfect secrecy. This is discussed in Part II.

Instead of using a random key in the Vernam cipher, we can modify it by using a **pseudo-random key**, which can be generated from a **LFSR**. This is discussed in more detail in Chapter 16.

4.4 Hash Functions

Hash functions are of fundamental importance in the design and implementation of cryptosystems. They arose in computer science where they are used for carrying out insertions, deletions, and searches of tables. There are many "off the shelf" hash functions that are readily available. However, in some situations, it can be advantageous to "custom design" hash functions using some theory, e.g. the theory of linear codes. We present a nice application in Chapter 24.

In many situations in data processing and communications alike, one has to condense a long binary string M representing a large message to a shorter binary string M_1 of a fixed length. We think of M_1 as providing a digest or "snapshot" of M. The formula which changes M to M_1 is called a **hash function**. The shorter string M_1 is called the **hash** of the longer string M. M is the *input* and M_1 is the *output*.

As a very simple example, if M is binary string $\{x_1 x_2 x_3\}$ of length 3, we could define M_1 to be the string of length 1 given by $M_1 = \{x_1 + x_2 + x_3\}$, addition being in binary.

Thus, if $M = \{011\}$, then $M_1 = \{0 + 1 + 1\} = \{0\}$.

An essential feature of hash functions is that the output ($= M_1$) can easily be calculated from the input M – but not the other way around! A desirable feature of hash functions is that each bit of the output depends – in a complicated way – on all the bits in the input. This is a recasting of Shannon's confusion and diffusion for hash functions rather than encryption transformations.

In general, the output of a hash function has a shorter length than the input.

From this, it follows that **collisions** necessarily occur (a collision being two different inputs that hash to the same output).

In order for a hash function to be useful for encryption it must be **secure**. This means that

(a) given an output M_1 it is not computationally feasible (=intractable) to find an input M such that $f(M) = M_1$.

(b) It is computationally not feasible to find collisions, i.e. to find messages $x_1 \neq x_2$ such that $f(x_1) = f(x_2)$.

Condition (a) implies that there will be no easy way of calculating any input which hashes to a given output.

Condition (b) is tied in with various kinds of attacks as described in Chapter 7.

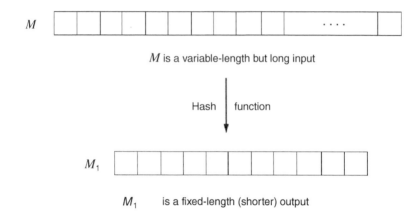

M is a variable-length but long input

Hash | function

M_1 is a fixed-length (shorter) output

As we will see later, secure hash functions are fundamental in digital signatures. Another application of hash functions concerns password-protection schemes such as that used in Unix. Characters of the password are converted to binary (using the ASCII encoding for example). To save storage space on the Computer, each password M is hashed to an output M_1 using a secure hash function f. When somebody logs in, their password is hashed, and a check is made with the valid list of stored hash values. If the hash checks out then access is granted; otherwise, it is denied.

There are several commercially available **"off the shelf" hash functions** such as MD4 and MD5 developed by R. Rivest using random permutations of bytes and various nonlinear compression functions. These give 128-bit hash values.

Together with the NSA, NIST has designed the so-called **SHA (Secure Hash Algorithms)**. The security strength of them depends in part on the number of bits. The choice of SHA-256 or SHA-384 depends on the security strength needed for the particular application. See [BD15, pp. 11–13] to determine which is best to use.

Later on in Part III of this book, we will show how to customize hash functions, suitable for the purpose at hand, using the theory of block designs and error-correcting codes. With such hash functions the security level can be calculated with more precision than the "off the shelf" hash functions mentioned above.

Another very important general application of hash functions is in the area of key-verification. For example, using public-key cryptography such as RSA, we assume that **A** has sent a secret message M to **B**. How do **A**, **B** verify that they both have the same message M? Because of the length of the keys in RSA, transmission errors are always a possibility. One suggested method is this: **A** and **B** publicly compare some number of corresponding bits, say 50 bits. If these 50 bits coincide, **A** and **B** can conclude with reasonably high probability, that they both have the same message M. The idea is that the 50 bits provide a hash function, then **A** and **B** conclude that if the hash functions are equal, then the corresponding messages are equal. We will have much more to say about this situation in Part III.

Hash functions are also widely used to check message integrity as described in Section 4.5.

4.5 Message Integrity Using Symmetric Cryptography

Here the evil *Eve* herself has designs on Romeo (see Figure 4.2) and, by altering the message, wishes to put Juliet out of the picture. In general, one is concerned with the question of whether the message itself has been transmitted without alteration. This is the quest for message integrity.

The procedure used to simultaneously ensure authentication and data integrity using symmetric encryption is simple (Figure 4.3). Suppose m is the message that **A** wants to send to **B**. **A** and **B** will work with a publicly known family of hash functions. Thus, this general family of hash function is also known to Eve. However, the specific hash function in the family to be used by **A** and **B** is, say the kth hash function, where k is a secret number or key is known only to **A** and **B**. So **A**, **B** work with a *keyed hash function*.

A calculates the hash $m^* = f_k(m)$ of the message m, appends this to m and transmits the package to **B**. It is entirely possible now that the pair (m, m^*) transmitted by **A** will be altered by Eve to the pair (m_1, m_2).

Now **B** must act. He simulates the procedure followed by **A**. Thus, he hashes the first half of the received message, namely, m_1 with the kth hash function (used by **A**) and checks if the result is equal to m_2.

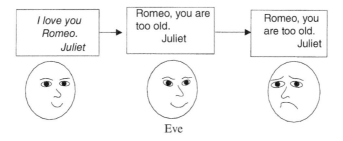

Figure 4.2: How does Romeo know that Juliet's message has not been altered?

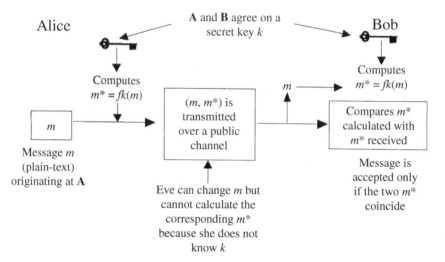

Figure 4.3: Authentication and message integrity check to ensure that nobody tampered with the message from **A** to **B**.

If they are not equal, **B** knows for sure that tampering has occurred, or that transmission errors may have occurred.

However, if they are equal, **B** can be quite certain that the message has not been tampered with *and* that the sender is **A**. After all, who else but **A** has the secret key k (apart from **B**)?

The more secure the hash function, the more certain B can be that

1. The message came from **A**. *and*

2. This message from **A** has not been altered.

Thus, in this way, we can use symmetric encryption both for authentication and for message integrity.

4.6   General Public Key Cryptosystems

In this situation, one assumes that each entity **B** in a network has a *pair of keys*, namely,

1. a public key E_B, known to all members of the network and,

2. a private key D_B, known only to **B**.

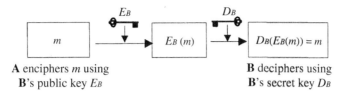

Figure 4.4: Public key encryption principle.

It is assumed that the enciphering algorithm E_B can be carried out easily and quickly. The keys E_B (E for enciphering) and D_B (D for deciphering) have the property that, for all messages m, $D_B(E_B(m)) = m$. The keys are created by a public key authority (PKA).

If **A** wants to send a message m to **B** (which will usually be a session key for a future communication), the procedure is as follows (Figure 4.4):

1. **A** looks up the public key E_B for **B**, or gets it from the PKA.

2. Using E_B, **A** enciphers the message m, yielding the cipher text $E_B(m)$. This cipher text is transmitted to **B**.

3. **B** applies the secret key D_B to the cipher text and recovers the original message since $D_B(E_B(m)) = m$.

This system using Public Key Cryptography for generating session keys between **A** and **B** will never have perfect (Shannon) security. We must settle instead for **computational security**. This means that the security rests on the assumption that, given the cipher text $E_B(m)$, it is infeasible to calculate m, in a reasonable time at least, and thereby break the system. It has been argued that, from the theoretical point of view, public key algorithms have **no real security at all**! This is because, given sufficiently large amounts of time and computational resources, an adversary is **certain** to break the system.

The main public-key algorithms in use, are RSA and ECC (=elliptic curve cryptography which is briefly described below and detailed in Chapter 6). The McEliece public-key cryptosystem, using error-correcting codes is briefly described below and is detailed in Part III.

It has been shown by P. Shor, that the factoring of integers can be carried out easily using a quantum computer. Thus, the physical construction of a *quantum computer* would kill off the RSA system but not necessarily the McEliece system or ECC.

First, we briefly discuss ECC. We focus on the key-exchange obtained from an **elliptic curve (=nonsingular cubic curve)**. Details are provided in Chapter 6.

In the Diffie–Hellman (DH) key-exchange described in Section 3.7, we worked with the p numbers, $\{0, 1, 2, \ldots, p-1\}$. In the elliptic curve case, we have n points on an elliptic curve $\mathbf{T}$ (which is a special kind of cubic curve). It turns out that any two points $\mathbf{P}$ and $\mathbf{Q}$ on $\mathbf{T}$ can be geometrically added to obtain a point $\mathbf{R}$ on $\mathbf{T}$. This geometric addition obeys all the usual rules of arithmetic and so we have a set of n numbers corresponding to the n points on $\mathbf{T}$. One can then construct a key-exchange, i.e. a common key for $\mathbf{A}$ and $\mathbf{B}$ using a method that is analogous to the Diffie–Hellman (DH) key-exchange. The analogous **discrete-log problem** is much more complex than DH. However, the overhead for implementing ECC is much larger than for DH.

There have been attacks on ECC that were successful in breaking messages encrypted with a 109-bit key. This is consistent with the assumption from Mollin [Mol00] that key-lengths starting at 300 bits for ECC are needed for even minimal security. NIST's recommendation for the minimum key lengths are 256 and 384 bits for the two ECC algorithms that they recommend. See [BD15, pp. 11–13].

We turn now to a brief description of the **McEliece cryptosystem**.

This ingenious public key system, discovered by McEliece in 1978, is of interest for a number of reasons. One of them is that, just like the other public-key systems, it provides only computational security, so that it can be broken by any adversary with sufficient time and computing resources. However, unlike the RSA system, the McEliece system cannot be directly broken by a quantum computer.

The McEliece system uses the theory of error-correcting codes. Rather than giving full mathematical details, we will explain the basic idea.

Each user $\mathbf{B}$ has a public key in the form of a binary code $\mathbf{G}_1$ (which is usually linear). This code is just a list of allowable binary strings called codewords, all of the same length.

Mathematically, if the code is linear, it can be described concisely by a binary matrix with k rows and n columns which we also denote by $\mathbf{G}_1$.

Suppose user $\mathbf{A}$ wishes to send a secret message m – such as a session key for a future communication with $\mathbf{B}$ – to $\mathbf{B}$.

First, $\mathbf{A}$ obfuscates the message m by introducing a random error vector $\mathbf{R}$. $\mathbf{R}$ is a binary vector having at most $t-1$ ones in it, where t is some predetermined positive integer. Then $\mathbf{A}$ encodes m using $\mathbf{G}_1$ and adds $\mathbf{R}$ to the result, yielding the cipher text $c = m\mathbf{G}_1 + \mathbf{R}$.

The public key for $\mathbf{B}$, as mentioned, is $\mathbf{G}_1$. $\mathbf{G}_1$ is obtained from the private key $\mathbf{G}$ of $\mathbf{B}$ by scrambling $\mathbf{G}$. Adversary Eve, knowing $\mathbf{G}_1$ and the cipher text, cannot recover the message m, but $\mathbf{B}$ can, by using $\mathbf{G}$.

G is a very special code: it is designed to correct up to t errors. Thus, **G** has the property that if a string is not equal to a codeword in **G** but is only off by a few digits, say at most $t-1$ digits, then **G** can match that string to the unique codeword in **G** which differs from that string in at most $t-1$ positions. Then **B** is able to get rid of the random error part of the cipher text and recover the message m.

One disadvantage of the system is that, offering only computational security, it is again vulnerable to the yearly increase in computational power (see Section 1.7) that is available to an adversary. To offer any kind of Security, the key-length must be very large.

4.7 Digital Signatures

Some attributes of the usual handwritten signature on a document signed by party **A** are as follows:

(a) Only **A** may produce this signature.

(b) Anyone can check or verify that the signature belongs to **A**.

We want to achieve these objectives electronically. One difference with respect to the handwritten signature is this: The handwritten signature is always the same, regardless of the message. On the other hand, the digital or electronic signature varies with the message. In the digital case, it will turn out that nobody can alter the message being signed without everyone involved seeing that the message has been tampered with: forgery is much more difficult!

Recall that any user **A** in the public-key network has a public key $e = e_A$ and a private key $d = d_A$. When **A** wants to sign a digital message m and send it to **B**, the following steps are carried out. We assume here that e and d act on the same set. (The El Gamal signature scheme discussed below and other signature schemes are not dependent on this assumption.)

1. **A** enciphers m with her private key d and sends the message m along with the enciphered message to **B**. Thus, **A** transmits the pair $(m, d(m))$ to **B**.

2. **B** applies the public key of **A**, namely e, to the second half of the received pair and verifies that the result is the first half of the received pair. In other words, **B** verifies that $e(d(m)) = m$. **B**, then concludes that the message m has been signed by **A** (see Figure 4.5).

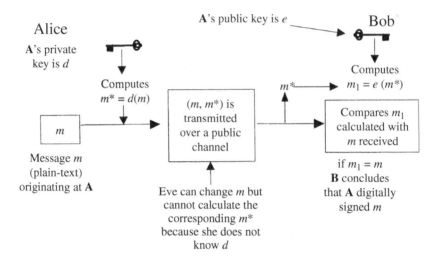

Figure 4.5: Digital signature scheme using Public Key Cryptography.

To reduce overhead, what frequently happens is that **A** calculates a hashed version, m_1 say, of the message m to **B**. The hash m_1 is obtained from m by applying a publicly known hash function f to m so that $f(m) = m_1$. Then **A** transmits the pair $(m, d(m_1))$ to **B**. When **B** receives the cipher text pair, **B** carries out the following steps.

(a) **B** applies the public key e that belongs to **A** (obtained from the PKA) to the second half of the received pair.

(b) **B** applies the publicly known hash function f to the first part of the message.

(c) **B** verifies that the answers from steps (a) and (b) are equal. In symbols, **B** verifies that $e(d(m_1))$ equals $f(m) = m_1$.

If this checks out, **B** concludes with very high probability that **A** has digitally signed the message m.

One can also construct digital signature schemes based on the Diffie–Hellman algorithm, which was discussed in Section 3.7.

Digital signatures using symmetric encryption

Theoretically, using public key algorithms for digital signatures is better for settling disputes between **A** and **B**. In the symmetric case, **A** and **B** both have the same key which might cause difficulties in the case of a dispute between **A** and **B**. It could conceivably be argued that the message that **A** reportedly signed was in fact a message created by **B** who then used the common key to produce the "signature"!

4.8 Modifying Encrypted Data and Homomorphic Encryption

If you have some data that is encrypted that you wish to modify, you can of course decrypt the data, modify it, and then encrypt the modified data. Suppose now that you have some encrypted data "in the cloud." With cloud computing (see Chapter 28), it is often desirable to use the cloud applications to modify data while it is in the cloud, rather than first transferring it to a local machine, modifying the copy on your machine, and then uploading the result to the cloud. However, for privacy reasons, you might not want the cloud to have access to your sensitive data in an unencrypted form. This is where homomorphic encryption can help.

Homomorphic encryption is a type of encryption in which computations can be done on encrypted data *while the data is in an encrypted form* (i.e. without first decrypting it). We discuss homomorphic encryption further in Section 28.4 as part of our cloud computing chapter, Chapter 28 "In the Cloud."

4.9 Quantum Encryption Using Polarized Photons

It was Stephen Wiesner at Columbia University who effectively invented quantum cryptography around 1970. He made the key breakthrough in his paper "Conjugate Coding." His fundamental paper entitled "Conjugate Coding" was rejected by IEEE Information Theory, but years later, it was eventually published in 1983 in SIGACT News [Wie83]. In the paper, he showed how to transmit two messages by encoding them in two "conjugate observables" such as linear and circular polarization of light, so that either, but not both, of which may be received and decoded. A decade later in 1983 Charles Bennett and Gilles Brassard, building on this unpublished work of Wiesner, proposed a method for a cryptographic key-exchange known as the *BB84 protocol* based on Wiesner's work (see [BB84]) which we discuss here. See David Darling, *Teleportation: the Impossible Leap*, [Dar05]. We also refer to the related paper by Bruen et al. [BWF06]. Before we do that, we want to discuss some classical and quantum physics.

Polarized light and photons

According to the classical "Maxwell equations," light is an electromagnetic wave. The electric and magnetic fields oscillate in a plane which is at right angles to the direction of motion. Think of the direction of motion as the x-axis with the electric field oscillating in the xy-plane and the magnetic field oscillating in the xz-plane. The electric field can oscillate in any direction in the xy-plane. Ordinary light, i.e. unpolarized light, can be visualized as a collection of oscillating electric fields oriented randomly.

However, polarized light results when the electric field is in one direction. A pair of polaroid spectacles reduces the glare because polarized glass has the property of only allowing one direction of electric oscillations to pass through. A polaroid plate oriented in the vertical direction polarizes light in the vertical direction. Think of the plate as having only vertical slits.

If light is polarized at an angle θ to the vertical, it can be broken down into vertical and horizontal components of polarized light. In terms of the electric field Ψ, we have the vector equation

$$\Psi = \cos\theta(\text{Vertical}) + \sin\theta(\text{Horizontal}) \tag{4.6}$$

If $\theta = 45°$, we have

$$\Psi = \frac{1}{\sqrt{2}}V + \frac{1}{\sqrt{2}}H \tag{4.7}$$

so the light has equal intensity in the vertical direction as in the horizontal direction.

In quantum mechanics, light such as a single photon must be *simultaneously* regarded as a wave and a particle, leading to the uncertainty principle. We will see how this fact and Eq. (4.7) come into the BB84 protocol.

The *BB84 protocol* uses photon polarization states to construct the key exchange. They assert that in fact any two *conjugate states* can be used. An example of conjugate states relates to position and momentum. If one has certainty regarding position, then one has no knowledge as to the momentum of the particle. This is the essence of the *uncertainty principle* in quantum mechanics. (As an aside, the uncertainty principle is well-known in mathematics. In physics, there is the identification of "conjugate variables" with the corresponding Fourier transforms. The uncertainty principle is then derived in detail in *Digital Files* by Hamming, [Ham89].)

BB84 uses two pairs of sates. Each pair is conjugate to the other pair. The two states within a pair are orthogonal to each other, forming a basis.

The usual state pairs are either the rectilinear basis of vertical (zero degrees) and horizontal of $90°$ or the diagonal basis of $45°$ and $135°$.

If a pulse is polarized in one direction, say horizontal–vertical, and we measure it in that direction, the correct count for the number of photons is obtained.

On the other hand, if we measure with a polarization detector whose axis is on the diagonal (at an angle of $45°$ to the vertical) we get a random result for the count.

Here is the protocol to generate a secret key.

1. **A** sends **B** a string of photon signals. Each photon is polarized in one of four directions, namely left-diagonal, right-diagonal, horizontal, and vertical. We denote the horizontal or vertical polarizations by the term "rectilinear." Denote the left or right diagonal polarizations by the term "diagonal."

2. **B** has a polarization detector with two settings, rectilinear or diagonal. In effect, both settings cannot be used at the same time by Heisenberg's uncertainty principle. Thus, **B** successively chooses one setting or the other at random, for measurement purposes.

3. At the end of the transmission **B** tells **A**, over a public authenticated channel, which of the two settings he has chosen in every reception.

4. **A** tells **B** which settings were correct, i.e. the polarization method that **A** used for each photon (rectilinear or diagonal) but not how the photon was polarized. For example, if the rectilinear polarization is used, **A** does not reveal whether a horizontal or vertical direction was favored. In effect, **A** does not announce, over the unsecured channel, which of 0 or 1 has been transmitted. However, **B** will have measured this accurately if **B** has chosen the rectilinear setting on his polarization detector, rather than the diagonal detector.

5. **A** and **B** only keep those polarizations that were correctly measured. For rectilinear polarization, assign 1 for vertical, 0 for horizontal. For diagonal, assign 1 for left-diagonal and 0 for right-diagonal. If A transmits using a rectilinear direction, and B receives with a diagonal detector, the probability that B receives 0 or 1 correctly is just 50%. This gets back to Eq. (4.7). The photon has only a 50% chance of correctly indicating 0 or 1, mirroring the fact that the wave function Ψ has equal intensity in the horizontal and vertical directions.

This generates a string of bits corresponding to the correct measurements by **B**. This bit string in principle is random and can be used as a one-time pad. Moreover, in theory, this one-time pad is absolutely unbreakable!

Note that, on the average, **B** will have correctly set the detector for about 50% of the measurements. So, in theory, if **A** transmits n photons, **A** and **B** will generate a secret key of length $\frac{n}{2}$ on the average.

However, this is not utopia. The most serious limitation of this scheme is the difficulty of transmitting photons accurately at a considerable distance without a loss of information due to the interaction between the photon and the medium.

Also, we have not brought the eavesdropper Eve positioned between **A** and **B** into account either. Eve can listen in and her eavesdropping can introduce errors in the pulse with 50% probability. Thus, **A** and **B** may end up with possibly different bit strings.

Brassard, Bennett and other colleagues worked on mathematically repairing the damage using the beginnings of techniques in **Privacy Amplification** and **Bit Reconciliation**.

However, it was discovered that the whole physical protocol was flawed. As Brassard himself later admitted, the devices that were used to polarize the photons made noticeably different noises depending on the type of polarization chosen. Thus, security was compromised. Nonetheless, the experiment became very well known and thus made its way into the literature. Furthermore, this ground-breaking attempt in the quantum domain, paved the way for much subsequent research and for repairing the protocol.

From the above, the protocol is such that if Eve is eavesdropping, this can be detected with high probability by **A** and **B**. However, in that case, the usual protocol calls for **A** and **B** to start all over again. We refer to Chapter 24 for further details.

4.10   Quantum Encryption Using Entanglement

The key exchange discussed in Section 4.9 seems to have been supplanted by one involving entangled particles and the Einstein–Podolsky-Rosen (EPR) paradox. The EPR paradox dates back to their paper in 1935 [EPR35]. The paper describes a thought experiment involving two entangled particles. It is pointed out that if, say, the momentum of particle A is measured, then the momentum of particle B is instantly determined no matter how far apart they are. Einstein referred to the phenomenon as "spooky action at a distance". It was deemed spooky and contradictory in that the correlation between A and B was instantaneous even though classical information cannot be transmitted faster than the speed of light. This was the EPR paradox.

The conclusion presented in the paper was that quantum theory was incomplete as the action at a distance could not be explained by the existing laws of quantum mechanics, and that a "hidden-variable" theory could explain things. In a famous paper [Bel64], John Bell, an Irish physicist, showed the correlations between particles A, B could not be explained away by any local hidden-variable theory, making use of the "Bell inequalities." Subsequent experiments by Alain Aspect and his group in France confirmed Bell's theorem indicating that "spooky action at a distance" does take place and is consistent with the laws of quantum mechanics.

Artur Ekert's scheme for a key exchange exploiting entanglement using entangled pairs of photons. Alice and Bob each have one photon from each pair.

The entangled states are correlated so that if Alice or Bob both measure whether their particles have vertical or horizontal polarizations, they always get the same answer. But it is impossible to predict, according to quantum mechanics, which measurement will be observed. Any attempt at eavesdropping by Eve destroys the correlations and can be detected.

4.11 Quantum Key Distribution is Not a Silver Bullet

Quantum key distribution (QKD) is a key exchange algorithm using quantum physics. As such, these are a few problems with QKD.

1. *Physics.* The physics part is constantly under siege and is still not settled.

2. *Main-in-the-middle attack.* To the same extent as any of the classical protocols, quantum distribution is vulnerable to a man-in-the-middle attack when used without authentication. See Chapter 7. No known principle of quantum mechanics solves the authentication problem. Alice and Bob cannot establish a secure connection without verifying each other's identities.

3. *Expense uncertain benefits.* Many resources are needed for QKD. As mentioned, it is only used to produce and distribute a key, not to transmit data. QKD requires an authentic classical channel for security. This involves a "shared secret." This implies that communicating parties Alice and Bob have already exchanged a symmetric key of sufficient length or used public keys of sufficient length for security. After this, the QKD can be used with any classical encryption algorithm to encrypt and decrypt a message which is distributed over a standard non-QKD channel. But if an authenticated public channel is available, one can readily achieve authenticated and secure communications *without using QKD* by using AES or other algorithms!

   In the 16 October 2008 edition of *Wired Magazine*, Bruce Schneier remarks that QKD "is as awesome as it is pointless" [Sch08]! It seems that he may have a point.

Addendum to Section 4.11

Public key algorithms rely on the presumed difficulty of various mathematical problems (the integer factorization problem, the discrete logarithm problem, the elliptic-curve discrete logarithm problem) for their security. But all of these problems can be easily solved on a sufficiently powerful quantum computer running Shor's algorithm [Sho97]. Of course, such a computer is still a long way off.

In contrast to the threat quantum computing poses to public-key algorithms, most current symmetric cryptographic algorithms and hash functions are considered to be relatively secure against attacks by quantum computers (see Daniel Bernstein et al. 2009, introductory chapter to [BBD09]).

4.12   Postquantum Cryptography

In the late 1990s, as computational power increased, Data Encryption Standard (DES) became susceptible to attacks. (See Section 1.6.) Therefore, the US government asked for submissions to be considered for AES, [NIS19b]. See Section 5.2.

Twenty years later, we are preparing for a postquantum cryptography world in a similar way. NIST has asked for proposals for "one or more quantum-resistant public-key cryptographic algorithms" to be submitted for evaluation, [NIS19f]. The first round of these evaluations of this NIST Post-Quantum Standardization Process has been completed. A status report was published in January 2019, [AASA+19]. There were 82 candidate algorithms that were submitted to NIST for consideration in 2017. Of those, 69 met the acceptance criteria. On 30 January 2019, 26 of them moved forward to the second round of the competition.

One of the finalists in NIST's Post-Quantum Cryptography Standardization Process is *CRYSTALS*, short for *Cryptographic Suite for Algebraic Lattices* by IBM. IBM has recently announced that they have used CRYSTALS in a practical application. They encrypted the data on a prototype drive, [Bus19].

4.13   Key Management and Kerberos

So far we have discussed several procedures using symmetric encryption. For this to work, the parties **A** and **B** who are communicating with each other use a particular encryption algorithm that is specified by a secret key, known only to **A** and **B**. Frequently, the key is used for just one particular communication session; it is time stamped and is called a session key.

However, we now come to the problem: *how does one get the key to* **A**, **B** *securely?* As mentioned earlier, this is a fundamental problem. In Chapter 3, we referred to it as the Catch-22 of cryptography.

Now, we briefly describe various methods that can be used to provide **A** and **B** with a secret key k.

(A) *Off line.* In this case, session keys are exchanged beforehand through a secure private channel such as a courier. This method is still used nowadays for certain financial transactions. Also, various encryption companies utilize this method by supplying sets of session keys to their clients at regular intervals.

(B) *Central server (Kerberos).* Each party **A** in a given network has established a secret authentication key T_A with the trusted central server T (for Trust). These passwords are often generated off-line. The basic procedure is very straight-forward (Figure 4.6).

1. **A** contacts **T** and request a session key to communicate with **B**.

2. **T** generates a random session key k (usually a binary string), encrypts k (which is now a message from **T** to **A**) with the key T_A – using a symmetric encryption algorithm that **A**, **T** have previously agreed upon – and transmits the encrypted message to **A** along with a time-stamp.

3. **A** decrypts the message from **T**, obtaining the session key k.

4. **T** encrypts k (treated as a message) with the key T_B and transmits this encrypted message to **B** along with a time-stamp.

   T informs **B** that **A** wishes to communicate with **B**.

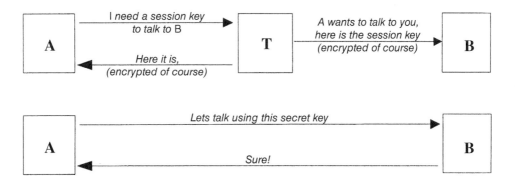

Figure 4.6: The basic Kerberos scheme for trusted server authentication.

5. **B** decrypts the message from **T**, obtaining the session key k.

6. **A** and **B** communicate using the session key k.

   Note that the role of the trusted central server in Kerberos is logically very similar to the role of the Certificate Authorities in the Public Key Infrastructure (PKI).

(C) *Pseudo-random keys.* This is usually accomplished by means of a LFSR, which is easily implemented in hardware. Using a shared secret, **A** and **B** generated a common pseudorandom sequence. A common (nonrepeating) portion of this pseudorandom sequence can be used by **A** and **B** as a session key for symmetric encryption or as a one-time pad.

   The security of the system can be improved by ensuring that the period of the sequence is very long. Also, instead of using a linear function f, one may use a nonlinear shift register.

   More general than LFSR's from the mathematical point of view are the so-called **Cellular Automata**. Introduced in the 1950s by Ulam and von Neumann, the theory of Cellular Automata provides a framework for the understanding of computing processes in digital machines.

   Several uses of Cellular Automata in cryptography have been proposed.

(D) *Quantum encryption.* Using properties of quantum physics, such as the Heisenberg uncertainty principle, one can construct a session key as described earlier.

(E) *Provable information-theory security by public discussion.* This is a very new technology. One can achieve unconditional security using classical physics and information theory. Such systems are only now coming on the market. The methods also apply to quantum encryption. Further details are in Part III.

(F) *Public key cryptosystems.* This has already been described in Section 4.7.

(G) *The Diffie–Hellman key-exchange.* This has already been described in Section 3.7.

4.14   Problems

4.1   Suppose **A**, **B** are in possession of the secret key $K = \{1010110\}$ and **A** has enciphered the message M (using K for a Vernam cipher). If **B** receives the cipher text C, where $C = \{0110111\}$, what is M? (See Solution 4.1.)

4.2 If in Problem 4.1, an eavesdropper **E** intercepts the communication and listens in to C, can **E** then narrow down possibilities for M? (See Solution 4.2.)

4.3 Let **A** be a binary matrix with k rows and n columns. Let M be a message in the form of a binary string of length n. Show how to use **A** to construct a hash function such that the hash of M has length k. (See Solution 4.3.)

4.4 Let M be the message 1101 and let **A** be the matrix $\begin{pmatrix} 1 & 0 & 1 & 1 \\ 0 & 1 & 0 & 0 \\ 1 & 1 & 0 & 1 \end{pmatrix}$. Use **A** to construct the hash of M as suggested in the previous problem. (See Solution 4.4.)

4.5 **B** receives the following message $m = (1101, 011)$, supposedly sent by his friend. In this case, the right part of the received message is an enciphered hash of the left part, using the matrix **A** given in the previous problem. The secret key $K = 001$ used to encipher the hash is a Vernam cipher key known only to **B** and his friend. Should **B** accept the message as a valid communication from his friend? (See Solution 4.5.)

4.6 Find all generators associated with the prime 11. (See Solution 4.6.)

4.7 Find all generators of the prime 7. (See Solution 4.7.)

4.15 Solutions

4.1 $M = \{1100001\}$. In general, $K + C = K + (M + K) = K + (K + M) = (K + K) + M = M$. So to get M, **B** simply adds K to C, where all operations are in binary.

4.2 No. Given C, then any message M can be made to fit with C: we just need to solve for K. We want $M + K = C$: this gives $K = C + M$ and with this choice of K it follows that M fits with C. In other words, enciphering M with K gives C. In this case, as far as an eavesdropper is concerned the number of possibilities for M is the number of binary strings of length 7, which is $2^7 = 128$, and the eavesdropper can only guess what M might be.

4.3 Make **M** into a column matrix and compute the matrix product **AM**. Suppose, for example that $m = 4$, $k = 3$ and

$$\mathbf{A} = \begin{pmatrix} 1 & 1 & 1 & 1 \\ 0 & 1 & 1 & 1 \\ 1 & 0 & 0 & 1 \end{pmatrix} \tag{4.8}$$

and $M = (1010)$. Then the column matrix form of $\mathbf{M}$ is

$$\mathbf{M} = \begin{pmatrix} 1 \\ 0 \\ 1 \\ 0 \end{pmatrix} \tag{4.9}$$

and the matrix product

$$\mathbf{AM} = \begin{pmatrix} 1 & 1 & 1 & 1 \\ 0 & 1 & 1 & 1 \\ 1 & 0 & 0 & 1 \end{pmatrix} \begin{pmatrix} 1 \\ 0 \\ 1 \\ 0 \end{pmatrix} = \begin{pmatrix} 1 + 0 + 1 + 0 \\ 0 + 0 + 1 + 0 \\ 1 + 0 + 0 + 0 \end{pmatrix} = \begin{pmatrix} 0 \\ 1 \\ 1 \end{pmatrix} \tag{4.10}$$

Therefore, the hash value of $M = (1010)$ is (011).

4.4   The matrix product $\mathbf{AM}$ (where $\mathbf{M}$ has been turned into a column matrix) gives the hash: (011).

4.5 $\mathbf{B}$ adds K to the right half of the received message to get (010). He also computes the hash of the left part of the message by multiplying by the matrix $\mathbf{A}$ on the left. The matrix product is the column matrix containing (011). Since (011) is not the same as (010), $\mathbf{B}$ should be doubtful about the source of the communication. (An error in transmission could account for the discrepancy. In cases where the message and key are much larger, this is much less likely to be a possible explanation.)

4.6   The possible remainders when a positive integer is divided by 11 are 0, 1, 2, 3, 4, 5, 6, 7, 8, 9, and 10. These integers are also known as the integers mod 11. Now 0 is not a generator since 0 raised to any power just gives 0. Similarly, 1 is not a generator. Let us try 2. So we take successive powers of 2 and get the remainder when we divide by 11. This gives us $2, 4, 8, 5, 10, 9, 7, 3, 6, 1$. Thus, 2 is a generator. Note that 9 is not a generator (even though 9 is the additive inverse of 2) since when we get successive powers of 9 and get the remainder upon division by 11 we just get $\{9, 4, 3, 5, 1\}$. The other generators, apart from 2, are 6, 7, and 8.

4.7   3, 5.

Chapter 5

Modes of Operation for AES and Symmetric Algorithms

Goals, Discussion   As discussed at the end of Chapter 4, modern encryption requires fast symmetric algorithms with relatively short keys. Several such ciphers are in use, notably the AES algorithm, which is studied here in detail. We briefly discuss some modes of operation for general block encryption algorithms, i.e. block ciphers.

5.1   Modes of Operation

There are several ways of applying a short block cipher for long texts. The simplest is called **Electronic Code Book (ECB) mode** and consists of breaking the long text into blocks of 64 bits that are then encrypted block-by-block, using the same key for each block. Therefore, if the plain text blocks are $B_1, B_2, \ldots, B_m$, then the encrypted text will be $C_1, C_2, \ldots, C_m$, where C_j is the cipher text for B_j. The problem with this mode is that some plain text blocks will be repeats of other plain text blocks such as in e-mail. If a large amount of the coded text is analyzed, it may be possible to determine the meaning of some encrypted blocks (from context) without having any knowledge of the key itself. A dictionary for the coded text could then be gradually built up and be used to break the cipher.

Cryptography, Information Theory, and Error-Correction: A Handbook for the 21st Century, Second Edition.
Aiden A. Bruen, Mario A. Forcinito, and James M. McQuillan.
© 2021 John Wiley & Sons, Inc. Published 2021 by John Wiley & Sons, Inc.

A method for ameliorating the problem with ECB is to use **Cipher Block Chaining** (**CBC**). Here, the encryption of a block depends on the encryption of previous blocks. (See [PM02, p. 84].) To encrypt the jth block to get the cipher block C_j, we XOR the jth plaintext M_j with the cipher block C_{j-1} and then encrypt. In symbols,

$$C_j = E(M_j \oplus C_{j-1})$$

To decrypt, and thus to find M_j, we decrypt C_j and XOR the answer with C_{j-1}. In symbols,

$$M_j = D(C_j) \oplus C_{j-1}$$

Suppose that we have a message consisting of n blocks $M_1, M_2, \ldots, M_n$ that are encrypted with a block cipher using a key K. For CBC mode, we have n cipher text blocks depending on all previous message blocks. To see this, note that C_1 depends on M_1. Since C_2 depends on M_2 and C_1, we have that C_2 depends on both M_1 and M_2. Similarly, C_3 depends on M_1, M_2, and M_3, and so on, each cipher text block thus depends on the corresponding plain text block and all previous plain text blocks. This virtually eliminates the possible underlying statistics of the message and the possibility that the cipher text can be manipulated. This has been achieved because each cryptogram block other than C_1 is obtained by encrypting the XOR of the corresponding message block with the previous cryptogram block. The first message block has to be treated separately. One option would be to let $C_1 = E_K(M_1)$. Another option is to use an initial value (IV) and to let C_1 be the result of encrypting $M_1 \oplus$ IV. The IV should be chosen randomly for each block in the interest of security.

A more secure mode of operation is called the **Cipher Feedback mode** (**CFB**). In this case, the plain text is broken up into blocks of 8 bits (or one byte), $A_1, A_2, \ldots, A_m$. A block of, say, 64 bits of plain text, B_1, is encrypted to produce the code block F_1. The next encryption block F_2 is obtained by applying the block cipher to the last (rightmost) 56 bits of B_1 followed by the 8 bits $A_1 \oplus G_1$, where G_1 is the first (leftmost) eight bits of F_1. Now, F_3 is obtained by applying the block cipher to the last 48 bits of B_1 followed by the 8 bits $A_1 \oplus G_1$, followed by the 8 bits $A_2 \oplus G_2$, where G_2 is the first eight bits of F_2. In general, G_j is the first eight bits of the jth coded block F_j. Continuing in this manner, we eventually compute F_{m+1} by applying the block cipher to the block which consists of $A_{m-7} \oplus G_{m-7}$ followed by $A_{m-6} \oplus G_{m-6}$ followed by $\ldots$ followed by $A_m \oplus G_m$. In this way, every block of 8 bits is eventually coded into one of the output text blocks. One of the advantages of this approach (over some other modes of operation that also involve feedback) is that errors in transmission only affect part of the decoded message. For example, if the first code block, F_1, contains an error, this will affect the interpretation of only the first nine bytes $A_1, \ldots, A_9$. The remaining bytes will be correctly decoded provided that there are no other errors in transmission. In other words, each error will only propagate through 9 bytes. Note that the block cipher is not limited to 64 bits: the method is quite general. Also, the block F_1 can be replaced by an initial vector (IV) X as in the CFB mode.

5.2 The Advanced Encryption Standard Code

The Advanced Encryption Standard (AES) code (also known as the Rijndael Code after its co-inventors Joan Daemen and Vincent Rijmen) is based on properties of the finite field of 256 elements (refer to Chapter 19 for mathematical details). Each byte can be associated with a unique element of this field. Since field elements can be multiplied and added, this association makes it possible to add and multiply bytes. Moreover, in a field, each byte has a multiplicative inverse. These algebraic properties make it possible to encode entire bytes at a time using matrix algebra operations which are nonlinear. The AES code was designed for use with keys of length 128, 192 or 256 bits. For simplicity, the discussion here is restricted to the case in which the key has length 128 bits. In this case, every round starts with the input of 16 bytes (or 128 bits) and has an output of 16 bytes (or 128 bits). There are ten rounds to promote diffusion of the bits, and each round has its own round key derived from the original round key.

Fields

Definition 5.1 A set S of algebraic elements together with a binary operation $\oplus$ defined on the elements of S is **associative** if $(a \oplus b) \oplus c = a \oplus (b \oplus c)$ for all elements a, b, and c in the set S.

Definition 5.2 A set S of algebraic elements together with a binary operation $\oplus$ defined on the elements of S is **commutative** if $a \oplus b = b \oplus a$ for all elements a and b in the set S.

Recall that matrix multiplication is not commutative. The fact that $(9 - 5) - 2 = 4 - 2 = 2$ while $9 - (5 - 2) = 9 - 3 = 6$ shows that the subtraction of integers is not associative.

Definition 5.3 A **field** $(F, +, *)$ is a set F together with two binary operations $+$ and $*$ defined on F (so that for a, b in F we have $a + b$ and $a * b$ in F), satisfying the following axioms:

1. The binary operation $+$ is associative and commutative on F. In other words, $(a + b) + c = a + (b + c)$ and $a + b = b + a$.

2. There is an identity element for $+$ in F, which is denoted by 0 and called the additive identity.

3. Every element a in the field F has an inverse for $+$ in F which is denoted by $-a$ and called the additive inverse of a.

4. The binary operation $*$ is associative and commutative on F.

5. The binary operation $*$ is distributive over $+$ in F. This means that $a * (b + c) = a * b + a * c$ for all elements a, b, and c in the field F.

6. There is a nonzero identity element for $*$ in F, which is denoted by 1 and is called the multiplicative identity.

7. Every element a in the field F EXCEPT 0 has an inverse for $*$ in F, which is denoted by $1/a$ and is called the multiplicative inverse of a.

For example, the set Z of integers satisfies 1, 2, 3, 4, 5, 6 but not 7. It is not a field since the number 3 has no multiplicative inverse *in the set Z*, even though it does have one outside of Z. The smallest field that contains all the integers is the field of rational numbers.

Let us give some important examples of fields. Example 1 is the real numbers. Example 2 is the field of rational numbers whose elements are all fractions of the form $\frac{u}{v}$, where u, v are integers (positive or negative), and v is not zero. When $v = 1$, we get an integer. So the integers are contained in the rational numbers which lie within the real numbers.

Z denotes the set of all integers. For finite systems, we study $Z \pmod n$. It is the set of integers $\{0, 1, 2, \ldots, n - 1\}$. If a and b are in this set, then so is $a + b$: we add them and the remainder c when divided by n is defined to be $a + b$. In symbols, $a + b = c \pmod n$. This says that the remainder when $a + b$ is divided by n is c. For example, $7 + 6 \equiv 4 \pmod 9$, since $7 + 6$ has remainder 4 when divided by 9. **In general, $u \equiv v \pmod n$ if $u - v$ is divisible by n.** The system $Z(n)$ is a field if and only if n is a prime number, i.e. has no factors except itself and 1. The reason is that if n is not a prime, not all nonzero of $\{0, 1, 2, \ldots, n - 1\}$ have an inverse. (Note: 0 never has an inverse.) For example, working $\pmod 9$, $0, 3, 6$ have no multiplicative inverses, whereas $\{1, 2, 4, 5, 7, 8\}$ have multiplicative inverses. They are $\{1, 5, 7, 2, 4, 8\}$, respectively.

If $n = p$, a prime, then $Z_n = Z_p$ is a field written as $\mathrm{GF}(p)$, the "Galois field" of order p. This is in honor of Évariste Galois, who developed the whole area by the age of 20 before being killed in a duel in France [KBG19].

Galois showed that, if p is a prime, such as 2, for example, and t is a positive integer, then there exists a finite field, i.e. a Galois field having p^t elements, i.e. of **order** p^t. Any two fields of order p^t are isomorphic, i.e. equivalent. Moreover, there are no other finite fields.

There is an analogy between (i) the "ring" of polynomials modulo $f(x)$ with coefficients in a field F and (ii) the ring Z_n. it turns out that this ring $F[x] \bmod f(x)$ is a field if and only if $f(x)$ is irreducible, i.e. has no factors in $F[x]$, the analog of being "prime" in $Z[n]$.

So how do we construct Galois fields of order p^t? We start with Z_p and construct a "field extension of degree n over Z_p." To do this, we construct a polynomial $f(x)$ of degree t with coefficients in Z_p which is irreducible, and go from there.

Example 5.4 *Let us construct a field of order $3^2 = 9$. We have $Z_3 = \{0, 1, 2\}$. Note that $2 \equiv -1 \pmod 3$ since $2 - (-1) = 2 + 1 = 3$ is divisible by 3.*

Claim The polynomial $x^2 + 1$ is irreducible in Z_3.

For otherwise, it would factor as a product of two factors, so $x^2 + 1 = (ax + b)(cx + d)$ in the polynomial ring $Z_3[x]$. Each of $ax + b = 0$, $cx + d = 0$ has a root α, β in Z_3, since $a \neq 0$, $b \neq 0$. Thus, $x^2 + 1 = (x - \gamma)(x - \delta)$ in $Z_3[x]$.

When $x = \gamma, \delta$, the right side is zero, so the left side is zero, i.e. $\gamma^2 + 1 = 0$ and $\delta^2 + 1 = 0$. But $0^2 + 1 \neq 0$, $1^2 + 1 \neq 0$, $2^2 + 1 \neq 0$. We have a contradiction. So the polynomial $x^2 + 1$ is irreducible. Now, we have our field of order $3^2 = 9$, i.e. $\mathrm{GF}(3^2)$. It is exactly the set of all nine elements of the form $a + b\alpha$, with a, b in Z_3 and with α satisfying $\alpha^2 + 1 = 0$, so $\alpha^2 = -1 \equiv 2 \pmod 3$. Addition and multiplication are done in the usual way. Example

$$(1 + 2\alpha) + (1 + \alpha) = 2 + 3\alpha = 2 + 0(\alpha) = 2$$
$$(1 + 2\alpha)(1 + \alpha) = 1 + \alpha + 2\alpha + 2\alpha^2 = 1 + \alpha + 2\alpha + 2(-1)$$
$$= -1 + 3\alpha = -1 \equiv 2 \pmod 3$$

So the product is also $2 + 0\alpha = 2$. We can do all the above with polynomials, but the above is a shortcut.

The field of 256 elements

To construct $\mathrm{GF}(2^8)$, the field with 256 elements: We are told that the polynomial $f(x) = x^8 + x^4 + x^3 + x + 1$ is irreducible in the ring $Z_2[x]$. Now, it is easy to construct $\mathrm{GF}(2^8)$

from this. The elements are all expressions of the form

$$c_0 + x_1 x + x_2 x^2 + c_3 x^3 + c_4 x^4 + c_5 x^5 + c_6 x^6 + x_7 x^7$$

where $c_0, c_1, \ldots, c_7$ are all either 0 or 1.

Addition is easy as is multiplication if we remember that

$$\alpha^8 + \alpha^4 + \alpha^3 + \alpha + 1 = 0 \tag{5.1}$$

so that $\alpha^8 = \alpha^4 + \alpha^3 + \alpha + 1$. Then $\alpha^9 = \alpha(\alpha^8) = \alpha(\alpha^4 + \alpha^3 + \alpha + 1) = \alpha^5 + \alpha^4 + \alpha^2 + \alpha$.

What is the additive inverse of α? It is $-\alpha = (-1)\alpha = \alpha$. Note that $\alpha + -\alpha = (1)\alpha + (-1)\alpha = (1 + -1)\alpha = 0(\alpha) = 0$.

What is the multiplicative inverse of α? From (5.1), $\alpha^8 + \alpha^4 + \alpha^3 + \alpha = 1$. Thus, $\alpha(\alpha^7 + \alpha^3 + \alpha^2 + 1) = 1$. So the multiplicative inverse of α is $\alpha^{-2} = (\alpha^{-1})(\alpha^{-1}) = (\alpha^7 + \alpha^3 + \alpha^2 + 1)(\alpha^7 + \alpha^3 + \alpha^2 + 1) = \alpha^{14} + \alpha^6 + \alpha^4 + 1 = \alpha^6(\alpha^4 + \alpha^3 + \alpha + 1) + \alpha^6 + \alpha^4 + 1 = \alpha^{10} + \alpha^9 + \alpha^7 + \alpha^6 + \alpha^4 + 1 = \alpha^2(\alpha^4 + \alpha^2 + \alpha + 1) + \alpha^5 + \alpha^4 + \alpha^2 + \alpha + \alpha^7 + \alpha^6 + \alpha^6 + \alpha^4 + 1 = \alpha^7 + \alpha^6 + \alpha^3 + \alpha + 1$. We are using a trick here, i.e.

$$(a + b + c + d)^2 = a^2 + b^2 + c^2 + d^2$$

since $2 = 0$ in binary.

A byte consists of eight bits $(c_7 c_6 \ldots c_0)$. The following one-to-one map from a byte to an element of F_{256} is central to the AES code construction: $(c_7 c_6 \ldots c_0) \to \sum_{j=0}^{7} c_j \alpha^j$. This shows that every byte can be associated with exactly one element of $\mathrm{GF}(2^8) = F_{256}$. This map allows the multiplication of bytes, since the elements of F_{256} can be multiplied together. The alternative one-to-one map $(c_7 c_6 \ldots c_0) \to \sum_{j=0}^{7} c_j 2^j$ maps every byte onto a unique integer in the range [0,255]. This map will be used to express the S-Box for the code. Thus, there are three interchangeable ways to express a byte, (i) as a series of 8 bits, (ii) as an element of the field F_{256}, and (iii) as an integer in the range [0,255].

5.3   Overview of AES

Using the S-box for the code

The S-box for the AES code is given by the following 16×16 matrix:

	0	1	2	3	4	5	6	7	8	9	10	11	12	13	14	15
0	99	124	119	123	242	107	111	197	48	1	103	43	254	215	171	118
1	202	130	201	125	250	89	71	240	173	212	162	175	156	164	114	192
2	183	253	147	38	54	63	247	204	52	165	229	241	113	216	49	21
3	4	199	35	195	24	150	5	154	7	18	128	226	235	39	178	117
4	9	131	44	26	27	110	90	160	82	59	214	179	41	227	47	132
5	83	209	0	237	32	252	177	91	106	203	190	57	74	76	88	207
6	208	239	170	251	67	77	51	133	69	249	2	127	80	60	159	168
7	81	163	64	143	146	157	56	245	188	182	218	33	16	255	243	210
8	205	12	19	236	95	151	68	23	196	167	126	61	100	93	25	115
9	96	129	79	220	34	42	144	136	70	238	184	20	222	94	11	219
10	224	50	58	10	73	6	36	92	194	211	172	98	145	149	228	121
11	231	200	55	109	141	213	78	169	108	86	244	234	101	122	174	8
12	186	120	37	46	28	166	180	198	232	221	116	31	75	189	139	138
13	112	62	181	102	72	3	246	14	97	53	87	185	134	193	29	158
14	225	248	152	17	105	217	142	148	155	30	135	233	206	85	40	223
15	140	161	137	13	191	230	66	104	65	153	45	15	176	84	187	22

The S-box is used to replace a byte with a coded byte in the following way: If the input byte is $(c_7 c_6 \ldots c_0)$, then the number in row $\sum_{j=4}^{7} c_j 2^{j-4}$ and in column $\sum_{j=0}^{3} c_j 2^j$ of the S-box is the integer representation of the new byte. For example, if the input byte is 10010101, then the row is $9 = 2^3 + 2^0$ and the column is $5 = 2^2 + 2^0$. Since both the rows and the columns start their numbering with 0, the corresponding output byte has integer representation $42 = 32 + 8 + 2$ and, therefore, the bits of the output byte are 00101010.

Algebraic interpretation of the S-box

We begin with a byte $\underline{x} = (x_7 x_6 x_5 x_4 x_3 x_2 x_1 x_0)$ of eight binary symbols, 0 or 1, and seek to find its S-box entry algebraically.

Step 1. Compute its inverse in the field $GF(2^8)$, yielding a byte $\underline{y} = (y_7, y_6, y_5, y_4, y_3, y_2, y_1, y_0)$. If the byte is the all-zero byte, then it has no inverse, and we use the all-zero byte instead in this step.

Step 2. Construct the column vector $\underline{y_1}$, where $\underline{y_1}$ is obtained from $\underline{y}$ transpose, but with the order reversed so that y_0 is on top and y_7 is at the bottom.

Step 3. Multiply $\underline{y}_1$ on the left by the 8×8 matrix T listed above. T is obtained by cycling repeatedly to the right the top row which is the row vector (10001111).

Step 4. Add the vector (11000110) as a column vector to the column vector from Step 3 obtaining the column vector $(z_0 z_1 z_2 z_3 z_4 z_5 z_6 z_7)$ so z_0 is on top and z_7 is on the bottom.

Step 5. Reversing again, from top to bottom, the byte $\underline{z} = (z_7 z_6 z_5 z_4 z_3 z_2 z_1 z_0)$ is the S-box entry for the byte $\underline{x}$.

Remark 5.5 *Steps 3 and 4 can be written as the affine mapping* $\underline{u} \to A\underline{u} + \underline{v}$

A is obtained from the row vector (10000111) by its 8 cyclic shifts to the right, including the identity shift. Thus,

$$A = \begin{pmatrix} 1 & 0 & 0 & 0 & 1 & 1 & 1 & 1 \\ 1 & 1 & 0 & 0 & 0 & 1 & 1 & 1 \\ 1 & 1 & 1 & 0 & 0 & 0 & 1 & 1 \\ 1 & 1 & 1 & 1 & 0 & 0 & 0 & 1 \\ 1 & 1 & 1 & 1 & 1 & 0 & 0 & 0 \\ 0 & 1 & 1 & 1 & 1 & 1 & 0 & 0 \\ 0 & 0 & 1 & 1 & 1 & 1 & 1 & 0 \\ 0 & 0 & 0 & 1 & 1 & 1 & 1 & 1 \end{pmatrix} \quad \text{and} \quad \underline{v} = \begin{pmatrix} 1 \\ 1 \\ 0 \\ 0 \\ 0 \\ 1 \\ 1 \\ 0 \end{pmatrix}$$

Example 5.6 *Our field* $\mathrm{GF}(2^{256})$ *is constructed modulo polynomials of the irreducible polynomial* $g(x) = x^8 + x^4 + x^3 + x + 1$. *Now,* $x^8 + x^4 + x^3 + x \equiv 1 \pmod{g(x)}$ *since the difference (which is the sum in binary) is divisible by* $g(x)$ *(with quotient 1). Thus,* $x(x^7 + x^3 + x^2 + 1) = 1 \pmod{g(x)}$. *Thus, the inverse of* $x^7 + x^3 + x^2 + 1$ *is* x, $\pmod{g(x)}$. *We start with the corresponding byte* $\underline{x} = (10001101)$. *Its inverse is* $(00000010) = \underline{y} = (y_7 y_6 y_5 y_4 y_3 y_2 y_1 y_0)$. *Thus,*

$$\underline{y}_1 = \begin{pmatrix} 0 \\ 1 \\ 0 \\ 0 \\ 0 \\ 0 \\ 0 \\ 0 \end{pmatrix}$$

Then,

$$A\underline{y_1} + \underline{v} = \begin{pmatrix} 0 \\ 1 \\ 1 \\ 1 \\ 1 \\ 1 \\ 0 \\ 0 \end{pmatrix} + \begin{pmatrix} 1 \\ 1 \\ 0 \\ 0 \\ 0 \\ 1 \\ 1 \\ 0 \end{pmatrix} = \begin{pmatrix} 1 \\ 0 \\ 1 \\ 1 \\ 1 \\ 0 \\ 1 \\ 0 \end{pmatrix}$$

Reversing, we get

$$\begin{pmatrix} 0 \\ 1 \\ 0 \\ 1 \\ 1 \\ 1 \\ 0 \\ 1 \end{pmatrix}$$

Thus, the byte $\underline{z} = (01011101)$. The entry for the byte (10001101) is the entry in Row number 8 and column number 13 which is 93. In binary, this equals $(01011101) = \underline{z}$.

Representing the input data

The input consists of 128 bits (or 16 bytes). If the input in byte form is

$$A_{0,0}, A_{1,0}, A_{2,0}, A_{3,0}, A_{0,1}, \ldots, A_{0,3}, A_{1,3}, A_{2,3}, A_{3,3}$$

then these bytes are arranged in a 4×4 matrix in the following way:

$$A = \begin{pmatrix} A_{0,0} & A_{0,1} & A_{0,2} & A_{0,3} \\ A_{1,0} & A_{1,1} & A_{1,2} & A_{1,3} \\ A_{2,0} & A_{2,1} & A_{2,2} & A_{2,3} \\ A_{3,0} & A_{3,1} & A_{3,2} & A_{3,3} \end{pmatrix} \tag{5.2}$$

The ByteSub transformation

The first step in a round of the code is called the ByteSub Transformation (BS), which is a nonlinear transformation and is therefore resistant to linear and differential attacks.

In this step, each of the 16 bytes in the matrix above is replaced with a new byte using the S-box and the procedure described above. The result is a new matrix

$$B = \begin{pmatrix} B_{0,0} & B_{0,1} & B_{0,2} & B_{0,3} \\ B_{1,0} & B_{1,1} & B_{1,2} & B_{1,3} \\ B_{2,0} & B_{2,1} & B_{2,2} & B_{2,3} \\ B_{3,0} & B_{3,1} & B_{3,2} & B_{3,3} \end{pmatrix} \tag{5.3}$$

where $B_{i,j}$ is the output byte which arises from using $A_{i,j}$ as the input byte. Thus, if $A_{3,2}$ is the byte 10010101 then $B_{3,2}$ is the byte 00101010.

The ShiftRow transformation

The second step is called the ShiftRow Transformation (SR). This linear step causes diffusion of the bits over multiple rounds. Row j of the matrix is shifted cyclically to the left by j offsets (recall that the rows are numbered starting with 0).

So the new matrix is

$$C = \begin{pmatrix} B_{0,0} & B_{0,1} & B_{0,2} & B_{0,3} \\ B_{1,1} & B_{1,2} & B_{1,3} & B_{1,0} \\ B_{2,2} & B_{2,3} & B_{2,0} & B_{2,1} \\ B_{3,3} & B_{3,0} & B_{3,1} & B_{3,2} \end{pmatrix} \tag{5.4}$$

The MixColumn transformation

The third step is called MixColumn Transformation (MC). This step creates high diffusion between the columns over multiple rounds of the code. In this step, the bytes in the matrix C are written as elements of the field F_{256} and multiplied on the left by a matrix M of elements from F_{256} as indicated below.

$$\text{MC} = \begin{pmatrix} \alpha & \alpha+1 & 1 & 1 \\ 1 & \alpha & \alpha+1 & 1 \\ 1 & 1 & \alpha & \alpha+1 \\ \alpha+1 & 1 & 1 & \alpha \end{pmatrix} \begin{pmatrix} B_{0,0} & B_{0,1} & B_{0,2} & B_{0,3} \\ B_{1,1} & B_{1,2} & B_{1,3} & B_{1,0} \\ B_{2,2} & B_{2,3} & B_{2,0} & B_{2,1} \\ B_{3,3} & B_{3,0} & B_{3,1} & B_{3,2} \end{pmatrix} \tag{5.5}$$

For example, if the elements in the first column of the matrix on the right have bit form

$$\begin{pmatrix} 10000001 \\ 00000000 \\ 00001001 \\ 00101010 \end{pmatrix} \tag{5.6}$$

then the entry in the left uppermost position of the product matrix is $\alpha(\alpha^7+1)+(\alpha+1)(0)+(1)(\alpha^3+1)+(1)(\alpha^5+\alpha^3+\alpha)=\alpha^8+\alpha^5+1=\alpha^5+\alpha^4+\alpha^3+\alpha$. The bit form of this byte would be 00111010.

Creating the W-matrix which contains the keys for the code

Initially, the key is a 128-bit number which is written as 16 bytes. These bytes are placed in the first four columns (columns w_0, w_1, w_2, and w_3) of the W-matrix, which is 4×44. The other columns of the W-matrix are generated recursively from the first four columns by the following procedure.

Let column $j+1$ of the W-matrix be denoted by w_j and assume that $j \geq 4$. Provided that j is not a multiple of 4, then $w_j = w_{j-4} + w_{j-1}$ (addition may be considered to take place in the field F_{256} or by using the XOR operation on the bit representation of the bytes). If j is a multiple of 4, then the computation is more complicated and should be regarded as a series of steps: (i) Every byte in column w_{j-1} is used to find a new byte in the S-box by using the ByteSub Transformation. (ii) The order of the new bytes is cyclically changed by moving the top byte to the bottom and moving every other byte up one place to create the column vector n_{j-1}. (iii) The new column vector in the W-matrix is $w_j = w_{j-4} + n_{j-1} + v_j$, where v_j is the column vector consisting of the bytes:

$$\begin{pmatrix} \alpha^{(j-4)/4} \\ 0 \\ 0 \\ 0 \end{pmatrix} \tag{5.7}$$

For example, if $j=16$, then $\alpha^{(j-4)/4}=\alpha^3$ which has bit form 00001000. Suppose that

$$w_{12} = \begin{pmatrix} 10110010 \\ 01100010 \\ 01101001 \\ 01001000 \end{pmatrix} \quad \text{and} \quad w_{15} = \begin{pmatrix} 10011110 \\ 11110000 \\ 01100110 \\ 10111111 \end{pmatrix} \tag{5.8}$$

Then using the S-box, we find that

$$n_{15} = \begin{pmatrix} 10001100 \\ 00110011 \\ 00001000 \\ 00001011 \end{pmatrix} \tag{5.9}$$

since $11 = 8 + 2 + 1$, $140 = 128 + 8 + 4$,   and $51 = 32 + 16 + 2 + 1$.   Therefore, $w_{16} = w_{12} + n_{15} + v_{16} =$

$$
\begin{pmatrix} 10110010 \\ 01100010 \\ 01101001 \\ 01001000 \end{pmatrix} + \begin{pmatrix} 10001100 \\ 00110011 \\ 00001000 \\ 00001011 \end{pmatrix} + \begin{pmatrix} 00001000 \\ 00000000 \\ 00000000 \\ 00000000 \end{pmatrix} = \begin{pmatrix} 00110110 \\ 01010011 \\ 01100001 \\ 01000011 \end{pmatrix} \tag{5.10}
$$

RoundKey addition

The final step is referred to as the RoundKey Addition (ARK) step. At the end of the jth round, the product matrix (MC) computed during the MixColumn Transformation is added (modulo 2) to the 4×4 matrix E_j obtained by taking columns w_{4j}, w_{4j+1}, w_{4j+2} and w_{4j+3} from the W-matrix.

Overview of the Rijndael encryption

Step 1. The W-matrix is computed from the key. The first four columns of this matrix (the original keyword) is added to the input data consisting of 16-bytes arranged in a 4×4 matrix.

Step 2. Nine rounds of BS, SR, MC, and ARK are processed, using the appropriate columns of the W-matrix for each application of ARK.

Step 3. The final round consists of BS, SR, and ARK, using the last round key (the final four columns of the W-matrix).

Notice that MC is not applied in the final round. This is to help with the decryption of the codeword.

Decryption of the AES Code

The decryption of the AES code is based on the fact that each of the steps BS, SR, MC, and ARK are invertible. The inverse of the BS step is based on the fact that the map from bytes onto integers in [0,255] is one-to-one and, hence, there is another lookup table called InverseByteSub (IBS) which inverts BS. The inverse of SR consists of shifting the rows to the right the same number of times that they were shifted to the left by SR. This operation is denoted by ISR. Moreover, the order of the operations BS and SR can be interchanged without changing the result. (In other words, these two operations commute with each other.) This means that the order of IBS and ISR can also be interchanged.

The inverse of MC is based on the fact that the 4×4 matrix M used in the MC operation is invertible over the field F_{256}. In fact, the inverse of M is the matrix

$$M^{-1} = \begin{pmatrix} \alpha^3 + \alpha^2 + \alpha & \alpha^3 + \alpha + 1 & \alpha^3 + \alpha^2 + 1 & \alpha^3 + 1 \\ \alpha^3 + 1 & \alpha^3 + \alpha^2 + \alpha & \alpha^3 + \alpha + 1 & \alpha^3 + \alpha^2 + 1 \\ \alpha^3 + \alpha^2 + 1 & \alpha^3 + 1 & \alpha^3 + \alpha^2 + \alpha & \alpha^3 + \alpha + 1 \\ \alpha^3 + \alpha + 1 & \alpha^3 + \alpha^2 + 1 & \alpha^3 + 1 & \alpha^3 + \alpha^2 + \alpha \end{pmatrix} \qquad (5.11)$$

Therefore, the inverse of MC, denoted by IMC, consists of multiplying the 4×4 matrix of 16 coded bytes by the matrix M^{-1} on the left. Since ARK is simply addition modulo 2, it is its own inverse. However, ARK does not commute with MC. MC followed by ARK has the form $MC + E_j = H$, where C is the matrix obtained at the end of the SR step and E_j as above is the key for the jth round. Solving this for the matrix C, we multiply by M^{-1} on the left to obtain $C + M^{-1}E_j = M^{-1}H$. So $C = M^{-1}H + M^{-1}E_j$ (since in modulo 2, $M^{-1}H - M^{-1}E_j = M^{-1}H + M^{-1}E_J$), which shows that the path from H back to C can be accomplished by first applying IMC to H and then adding the new key $M^{-1}E_j$. Because this key is directly computed from the key E_j (using the fixed matrix M^{-1}), we denote the operation of adding the key $M^{-1}E_j$ as IARK.

Overview of decryption of AES

Step 1. ARK using the last round key.

Step 2. Nine rounds of IBS, ISR, IMC, and IARK using the round keys in the opposite order, i.e. key 9 down to key 1.

Step 3. A final round consisting of IBS, ISR, and ARK using the original round key (the given key word).

Thus, decryption has essentially the same format as encryption.

Concluding comments

As mentioned earlier, a major modern cryptography involves a two-step process.

Step 1. Communicating parties A, B establish a common secret key. This is frequently done using public key cryptography such as RSA or the El Gamal cryptosystem or using Diffie–Hellman or Elliptic curve cryptography or methods from coding theory such as the McEliece cryptosystem. More recently, A and B have keys which are close to being equal and use privacy amplification by public discussion to equalize the keys. This method is used in quantum cryptography and is discussed in Chapter 24. (Of course, there are several other issues coming into play such as digital signatures, authentication, hash algorithms, to mention a few.)

Step 2. Once the secret key is in place, A and B can use block-encryption symmetric algorithms such as AES making use of design principles of Shannon such as confusion. For Step 2, public key cryptography such as RSS is normally not used as it is slow compared to AES.

Previously, DES was a choice in Step 2 in addition to AES, but security issues related to the key-length have been raised about DES. Since May 2005, it is recommended that DES no longer be used [Cen19].

In 1998, the US National Institute of Standards and Technology put out a call for candidates to replace DES. For a brief history and other issues, we refer to Mollin [Mol00] and NIST's report [Cen19]. Five finalists were chosen: MARS (IBM), RC6 (from RSA), Serpent (Anderson, Bilham, Knutsen), Twofish (Schneier, Kelsey, Whiting, Wagner, Hall, Ferguson) and Rijndael (Daemen and Rijmen). Rijndael was ultimately chosen as the "Advanced Encryption Standard." The other four candidates were highly regarded and are also used.

Rijundael has several advantages. The construction of the S-boxes is nonlinear, improving security and resistance to differential and the equivalent of linear cryptanalysis. The ByteSub is nonlinear mixing layer promoting "confusion" in the cipher. The ShiftRow step introduces high diffusion over multiple rounds and interacts with the next step. The MixColumn step creates intercolumn confusion.

Concerning key-size, in Luenberger [Lue06, p. 196], we read that,

for DES ... the effective key size is 56 bits. A primary weakness of DES is that there are only $2^{56} \approx 7.2 \times 10^{16}$ possible keys. There are therefore fewer keys than that of ... the Enigma machine.

The 128-bit AES system has $2^{128} \approx 3.4 \times 10^{38}$ possible keys. Hence, there are about 10^{21} times more AES keys than DES keys. To illustrate this magnitude, suppose that it were possible to test all DES keys in 1 second. At that speed it would take 149 trillion years to check all AES keys. The age of the universe is estimated to be (only!) 13.7 billion years.

Of course, we can argue that this is a worst-case scenario. In Section 3.5, we showed that on average, the correct one of n keys is found in about $(n+1)/2$ attempts (Theorem 3.6). But this will not make much difference in this argument.

Remark

An important source in this chapter is Mollin [Mol00]. Two others are [DR99,NIS19b]. The authors believe that, apart from Mollin's description of fields, they also may have made use of another source for some of the finer points relating to the algorithm, but their notes and memory are unhelpful on this point. We apologize to the unknown source if this is so, and will make amends in the web-page by acknowledgment if the source comes to light or gets in touch.

Chapter 6

Elliptic Curve Cryptography (ECC)

Goals, Discussion   We present an overview of elliptic curves as well as some cryptographic and geometric applications.

Elliptic curves were introduced into cryptography in the 1980s. They can be used as a key exchange, analogous to the Diffie–Hellman key exchange. They can also be used for public key encryption and digital signatures analogous to the El Gamal algorithms, based on Diffie–Hellman, which are discussed in Chapter 4. A modification of the standard procedure is presented in Section 6.14. The geometrical result in Section 6.10 is extended in the paper that is cited there.

New, Noteworthy   We present some historical background and also some of the geometry of elliptic curves. In particular, we present a detailed derivation of the algebraic formula for addition on the curve based on the geometrical definition. We also give a detailed overview of the idea of a nonsingular cubic curve, i.e. an elliptic curve. Related work in finite geometries due to the author and others is presented. (In fact, one of the results here will be mentioned again in Part III in connection with MDS codes). We also briefly describe the brilliant insight due to Frey, which was a major catalyst for the solution to Fermat's last theorem. Frey showed that the Fermat problem – which

Cryptography, Information Theory, and Error-Correction: A Handbook for the 21st Century, Second Edition.
Aiden A. Bruen, Mario A. Forcinito, and James M. McQuillan.
© 2021 John Wiley & Sons, Inc. Published 2021 by John Wiley & Sons, Inc.

can be phrased as a question on curves of *unknown degree* – could be solved if the solution to a question on *cubic* curves could be found. This led to the famous result by A. Wiles that the Fermat equation $x^n + y^n = z^n$ has no nontrivial solution in integers when $n > 2$.

The *National Institute of Standards and Technology (NIST)* continually updates their recommendations as to which cryptographic protocols should be used. Information about the NIST Elliptic Curve Cryptography (ECC) project can be found from the NIST website, https://www.nist.gov, [NIS19c]. In 2013, they recommended 15 elliptic curves of various security levels. NIST is considering which elliptic curves to recommend for the future, including some new elliptic curves which the "designers claim to offer better performance and are easier to implement in a secure manner" [NIS19c].

6.1 Abelian Integrals, Fields, Groups

The subject of elliptic curves is indeed a venerable one. In fact, it has been asserted that more mathematical papers have been written on topics related to elliptic curves (= nonsingular cubic curves) than on the rest of mathematics put together.

Historically, elliptic curves arose in connection with doubly periodic functions. For the motivation, recall from calculus that $\int_0^x \frac{1}{\sqrt{1-t^2}} dt$ is a function of x, say $f(x)$, that arises in the computation of the arc-length of a circle. (Note that the integral measures arc length on the unit circle starting from $(0,1)$ (i.e. from $x = 0$) rather than from $(1,0)$ (i.e. from $x = 1$).) In the familiar notation, we have $y = f(x) = \arcsin x$. Then $x = \sin y$, so the inverse function is the sine function. So, when "inverting the integral," we end up with the sine function – which has some fundamental properties. In particular, although not an algebraic function, it is periodic of period 2π, i.e. $\sin(x + 2\pi) = \sin x$.

It was Gauss, in 1797, who studied the integral $\int_0^x \frac{1}{\sqrt{1-t^4}} dt$ in connection with the arc length of the leminiscate which looks like the infinity symbol and whose equation in polar coordinates is $r^2 = a^2 \cos 2\theta$. According to Whittaker and Watson [WW46] this gave rise to one of the earliest new functions defined by the inversion of an integral. Long before Gauss, Count Fagnano had investigated similar integrals, but not their inversion.

The study of elliptic integrals and elliptic functions was developed in the eighteenth and nineteenth centuries giving rise to doubly periodic functions in general and the Weierstrass function $W(z)$ in particular. It was observed that W and W' satisfy a cubic relationship and parameterize a cubic curve that, topologically, can be made to correspond to the period lattice and thus, to a torus. Moreover, the "group law" defined on the cubic played a major role in Abel's theory of Abelian Integrals: See Shafarevich [Sha77] for an account of this along with Clemens [Cle80].

Algebraically, nonsingular cubic curves are an order of magnitude more complicated than second-degree curves such as circles. For example, the unit circle $x^2 + y^2 = 1$ in the Euclidean plane has a "rational parameterization." This is because if we put $x = \frac{1-t^2}{1+t^2}$, $y = \frac{2t}{1+t^2}$ and let t vary over all real numbers, we get all points on the circle. Contrast that with cubic nonsingular curves (= elliptic curves) which have no such rational parameterization. Of course, there also exist rational cubic curves (such as the familiar calculus curve given by $y = x^3$).

In the twentieth century, cubic curves have been intensively studied mainly on the algebraic side, related to theta functions, number theory, and algebraic geometry. Few people have not heard of the solution of the three-hundred and fifty year-old problem known as "Fermat's last theorem" by Andrew Wiles. The proof of Wiles built on the work of Frey and Ribet, who were able to reduce the question on curves of *arbitrary degree* to to a problem on *cubic curves*. However, many deep questions in number theory related to cubic curves still remain unsolved. We mention in particular the so-called "Birch Swinnerton-Dyer" conjectures. Some brief remarks connecting the Fermat problem and cubic curves are presented at the end of this chapter.

Fields

As mentioned in Chapter 19, a field is an algebraic system with two operations, addition and multiplication, obeying all the usual rules so we can add, subtract, multiply, and divide. Addition and multiplication are abelian, i.e. $a + b = b + a$ and $ab = ba$. They are connected by the distributive law, namely $a(b + c) = ab + ac$. The rational numbers (comprised of all fractions $\frac{u}{v}$ with $v \neq 0$, where u, v are integers) form a familiar example as do the real numbers (calculus again!). The reals can be extended to the complex numbers.

The above fields are infinite, but there also exist finite fields. The number of elements in the field is called the **order** of the field. The work of Galois shows that the order of a finite field F must be equal to a power of a prime p. In symbols, $|F| = q = p^n$. (In honor of Galois, a finite field of order q is known as a Galois field and is written GF(q).) Conversely, if we take any prime power such as 25 ($=5^2$), there is a field F with exactly 25 elements. In fact, as shown by Galois there is essentially only one such field. Sitting inside F is the field Z_5 consisting of the remainders $\{0, 1, 2, 3, 4\}$ when we divide by 5. Thus, $4 + 4 = 3$, $(4)(3) = 2$, etc.

Note especially that in the field F of order 25, we have $1 + 1 + 1 + 1 + 1 = 0$. In general, the **characteristic** of a field is the smallest number of ones that add up to zero. For example, if $|F| = p^n$, then the characteristic of F is p. If no sum of ones equals zero the field (such as the reals or the complexes or the rationals) is said to have **characteristic zero**.

To construct a field of order 5^n, we use Z_5 together with an equation of degree n that does not factor over Z_5: see Chapter 19.

Groups

A group is a nonempty set with just one operation, unlike a field, which has two operations. The operation in a group is usually called addition or multiplication. We work mainly with abelian groups. For example, in the Diffie–Hellman key-exchange, the set is $\{1, 2, 3, \ldots, p-1\}$ for some prime p and the operation is multiplication. Another example of a group is also given by $\{0, 1, 2, \ldots, p-1\}$ where we add two elements and get the remainder upon division by p. In a field, the nonzero elements form a group under multiplication and all of the elements form a group under addition. In this chapter, we will construct a group from the points on an elliptic curve.

6.2 Curves, Cryptography

Here we develop a key exchange using elliptic curves. As Hendrik Lenstra showed, elliptic curves can also be used to factor integers (see [Len87]).

Start off in the plane $\mathrm{AG}(2, F)$ over F, where F is any field. Let us define this plane, denoted by π. It has points and lines. The points of π are all possible ordered pairs (a, b) with a, b in F. The lines are all sets of points satisfying linear equations of the type $y = mx + b$ or $x = c$, where m, b, c are fixed in F. There are no surprises here: when F is the reals, π is just the Euclidean plane, following Descartes.

In what follows now, we assume in order to get a nonsingular curve that *the characteristic of F is neither two nor three*. (We explain in detail the reason for this in the problems at the end of this chapter.) By an **elliptic curve** E, we mean all ordered pairs (x, y) satisfying the following equation:

$$y^2 = x^3 + ax + b \tag{6.1}$$

In addition, we impose the following condition:

$$4a^3 + 27b^2 \neq 0 \tag{6.2}$$

to make the curve *nonsingular* (see Section 6.2). Finally, apart from the solutions in (6.1), which in $\mathrm{AG}(2, F)$ are known as the **affine points**, we decree that E also contains the infinite point P_∞ with coordinates $(0, 1, 0)$. We think of this point as the "point of intersection" of all vertical lines in the plane: they meet at infinity (at P_∞). For example,

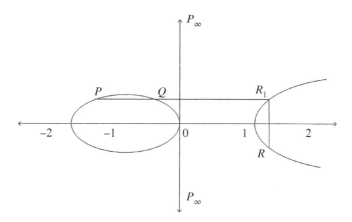

Figure 6.1: The group law.

think of P_∞ of lying at both ends, extended infinitely, of the y-axis. This can all be explained rigorously using projective or homogeneous coordinates. Later on, we give a brief discussion of homogeneous coordinates. In homogeneous coordinates, P_∞ does lie on the curve, and we have

$$P_\infty = (0, 1, 0) \tag{6.3}$$

For example if we take the curve $y^2 = x^3 - 4x$ over the real numbers, (see Figure 6.1), from the equation we see that if (x, y) is on the curve, then so also is $(x, -y)$. In other words, the curve is symmetric about the x-axis. *If we reflect the top half in the x-axis, we get the bottom half of the curve.* Note that Eq. (6.1) is a cubic equation because of the x^3 term. *This implies that any line meets the curve in at most three points.*

The condition in Eq. (6.2) can be explained in two different ways. Geometrically, it implies that each point of the curve is a "simple point," in that it has a unique tangent at each point. Algebraically, we have that at no point P on the curve are the three partial derivatives equal to zero. The reason why we must assume that the characteristic of $F \neq 2, 3$ is to ensure nonsingularity. All this is discussed in the problems at the end of the chapter. There are algebraic complications: When checking if the partial derivatives are all equal to zero, we have to make sure that they cannot all be zero even when we work in an extension of the ground field.

6.3 The Hasse Theorem, and an Example

Given a curve E such as in Eq. (6.1), where we are working with a finite field $F = \mathrm{GF}(q)$, we may ask how many points including P_∞ are there on E? The number of elements in

F is denoted by q, where q is necessarily a prime power, say $q = p^n$. Denote the number of points on the curve by N. We have the following famous result due to Hasse.

Theorem 6.1 N *lies between* $q + 1 - 2\sqrt{q}$ *and* $q + 1 + 2\sqrt{q}$. *In symbols, we have* $q + 1 - 2\sqrt{q} \leq N \leq q + 1 + 2\sqrt{q}$.

There is also the following result in Waterhouse [Wat69].

Theorem 6.2 *If* $q = p$,, *a prime with* $p > 3$ *and if* N *is any integer such that* $p + 1 - 2\sqrt{p} < N < p + 1 + 2\sqrt{p}$ *there exists an elliptic curve satisfying Eqs. (6.1) and (6.2) and having exactly N points.*

To get a very rough idea of why Theorem 6.1 works, suppose we have a curve as in Eq. (6.1). There are q possible values for x. Now, in any field of characteristic other than 2 (where every element has a square root), about half the elements are squares, i.e. half the elements have square roots. (This is similar to what we expect from the real numbers where "about half" the elements, namely the positive elements, have square roots.) If $x^3 + ax + b$ is not zero and has a square root y, it will also have a square root $-y$: For fields of characteristic not 2, $y \neq -y$. So, roughly, the total number of points should be about $2\left(\frac{1}{2}q\right) = q$.

As mentioned earlier, (for the real numbers) a nonsingular cubic curve, i.e. an elliptic curve over a field has no rational parameterization, unlike a rational cubic curve. However, subject to minimal conditions, any cubic over any field can be obtained as the projection of a quartic, i.e. a curve of degree 4, in three dimensions. Such a quartic can be regarded as the intersection of two quadrics in three dimensions. Then by space dualizing (point to plane, line to line), we get two different quadrics and a different quartic. This then easily leads to the following result, in Bruen and Hirschfeld [BH88, Theorem 8.4].

Theorem 6.3 *For every rational cubic or elliptic curve C with exactly N points over* $\mathrm{GF}(q)$ *there is a curve C_1 with N_1 points over* $\mathrm{GF}(q)$ *such that* $N + N_1 = 2(q + 1)$.

The proof of Theorem 6.3, by algebraic methods and involving two projectively distinct curves with the same absolute invariant, is in Cicchese [Cic65,Cic71].

In fact, Theorem 6.2 has been extended by Rück in 1987 (see [Ř87]), as follows.

Theorem 6.4 *For every N with* $q + 1 - 2\sqrt{q} \leq N \leq q + 1 + 2\sqrt{q}$, *there exists an elliptic curve E with exactly N points. Moreover, the group of E is cyclic.*

We will explain the meaning of cyclic again below, but we have met the idea already. It simply means that the group has a generator as in the Diffie–Hellman protocol when the group is the multiplicative group of integers (mod$p$).

6.4 More Examples

We work with the field GF(7), also known as Z_7. The elements of Z_7 are $0, 1, 2, 3, 4, 5, 6$. These are just the remainder when we divide any integer by 7. To add or multiply, we add or multiply in the usual way and take the remainder upon division by 7. Thus $4 + 5 = 2$, $(3)(5) = 1$. The additive inverse of 5, for example, is 2 since $5 + 2 = 0$. Thus, $5 = -2$ and $-5 = 2$. The multiplicative inverse of 5 is 3 since $(5)(3) = 1$, so $\frac{1}{5} = 3$.

Which elements of GF(7) are squares, i.e. which elements have square roots?

We have $0^2 = 0$, $1^2 = 1$, $2^2 = 4$, $3^2 = 2$, $4^2 = 2$, $5^2 = 4$, $6^2 = 1$. So the squares are $0, 1, 2, 4$. Note that the calculations above can be shortened since $5 = -2$, $5^2 = (-2)^2 = 2^2$. For a general prime p, $p > 2$, we only need to calculate $0^2, 1^2, 2^2, \ldots, \left(\frac{p-1}{2}\right)^2$ from which we get the rest.

Now, consider the curve E given by

$$y^2 = x^3 + 2 \tag{6.4}$$

so that $a = 0$, $b = 2$, in Eq. (6.1). Since $(27)(2^2)$ is not divisible by 7 it is not zero in the field GF(7) so Eq. (6.2) is satisfied and we have a nonsingular cubic curve C. We can now make up the following table.

Values of x	0	1	2	3	4	5	6
Values of x^3	0	1	1	6	1	6	6
Values of $x^3 + 2$	2	3	3	1	3	1	1
Values of y from (6.4)	± 3			± 1		± 1	± 1
Affine points on E	$(0,3), (0,4)$			$(3,1), (3,6)$		$(5,1), (5,6)$	$(6,1), (6,6)$

Thus, including the infinite point P_∞, the number of points on E is exactly $9 = q + 2$.

From the point of view of cryptography, the crucial fact is that the points on any elliptic curve actually form an abelian group. For example, if we add P_∞ to $(3, 1)$ in this group, we get $(3, 1)$. If we add $(5, 1)$ to $(3, 1)$, we get $(6, 6) = (-1, -1)$. This is explained below.

6.5 The Group Law on Elliptic Curves

Theorem 6.5 *The set of points on any elliptic curve over any field F forms an additive abelian group G. If $F = \mathrm{GF}(q)$ then $q + 1 - 2\sqrt{q} \le |G| \le q + 1 + 2\sqrt{q}$.*

The first part of this theorem is one of the show pieces of classical algebraic geometry. A formal proof can be constructed from the theorem of the "nine associated points" to wit: Given 9 points which form the intersection of 2 cubic curves, any other cubic curve passing through 8 of the 9 points automatically passes through the ninth.

The definition of addition on the curve is very simple. First of all, P_∞ is the identity element so $P_\infty + P = P$ for all points P on the curve including $P = P_\infty$.

Next, let $P = (x_1, y_1)$ and $Q = (x_2, y_2)$ be any two affine points. To find $P + Q$, perform the following two steps (see Figure 6.1).

(i) Let the line PQ meet the curve again in R_1.

(ii) Reflect R_1 in the x-axis to get $R = -R_1$.

   Then define $P + Q$ to be the point R.
   A few remarks are in order.

1. The reflection of P_∞ in the x-axis is defined to be P_∞: As P_∞ is on either end of the y-axis, this makes sense. So $-P_\infty = P_\infty$, and we can define $P + Q$ even if $R_1 = P_\infty = R$.

2. The definition of addition can be extended to any two points on the curve, not just to two affine points.

3. If $P = Q$, then the line PQ is defined to be the (unique!) tangent to the curve at $P = Q$.

4. R is on the curve. To see this, the line l joining P, Q has two roots. When we substitute the linear equation for l into the curve, we end up with a cubic with two roots and therefore three roots. Thus, given P and Q, we have that $P + Q$ is one of the points on the curve. Thus, we have *"closure under addition."* It is clear that $P + Q = Q + P$, so the group is *abelian*. The point P_∞ acts as the identity element. Each element (=point) P in the group has an inverse, namely $-P$, its reflection in the x-axis.

   In general, the axioms for a general group involve closure, an identity element, inverses, and associativity. For an abelian group, we need that $P + Q = Q + P$. (This will imply that, when adding any number of points, the order does not matter). From the above definition, all axioms for a group (in fact, an abelian group) are satisfied save for the associative law. This law says that $(P + Q) + R = P + (Q + R)$ and is the big stumbling block. As mentioned earlier, it can be proved using the theorem of the nine associated points.

5. The addition on the cubic is not the same as the usual vector addition whereby, if $P = (x_1, y_1)$ and $Q = (x_2, y_2)$, then $P + Q = (x_1 + x_2, y_1 + y_2)$. Also, to get a formula for the sum of a point with itself on a cubic, one needs to calculate the tangent at a point on the curve $y^2 = x^3 + ax + b$. This can be done (calculus again) by noting that, from implicit differentiation, $2y\frac{dy}{dx} = 3x^2 + a$.

The geometrical definition of addition above gives rise to the following algebraic result.

Theorem 6.6 *Let $P = (x_1, y_1)$, $Q = (x_2, y_2)$. Let $(x_1, y_1) + (x_2, y_2) = P + Q = R = (x_3, y_3)$, where $+$ denotes addition on the cubic. We have two cases.*

1. *$x_1 = x_2$. Then if $y_1 \neq y_2$, we have $P + Q = R = P_\infty$. However, if $y_1 = y_2$ (i.e. $P = Q$), then*

$$x_3 = \gamma^2 - x_1 - x_2$$
$$y_3 = \gamma(x_1 - x_3) - y_1$$

and $\gamma = 3x_1^2 + \frac{a}{2y_1}$.

2. *$x_1 \neq x_2$. Then x_3, y_3 are as described above, except that in this case $\gamma = \frac{y_2 - y_1}{x_2 - x_1}$, so that γ is the slope of the line through the points.*

Proof. Suppose $x_1 = x_2$ and $y_1 = y_2$ so $P = Q$. The equation of the tangent at P is obtained by using implicit differentiation on the curve $y^2 = x^3 + ax + b$. We get $2y\frac{dy}{dx} = 3x^2 + a$. Thus, $\frac{dy}{dx} = \frac{3x^2 + a}{2y}$. Thus, the slope of the tangent at (x_1, y_1) is $\frac{3x_1^2 + a}{2y_1}$. If $y_1 = 0$, then the tangent line is vertical and $P + Q = P_\infty$. Suppose $y_1 \neq 0$. The equation of the tangent line at P is as follows.

$$y - y_1 = \frac{3x_1^2 + a}{2y_1}(x - x_1) \tag{6.5}$$

i.e. $y = y_1 + \gamma x - \gamma x_1$, where $\gamma = \frac{3x_1^2 + a}{2y_1}$. Substituting into the cubic we get

$$(y_1 + \gamma x - \gamma x_1)^2 = x^3 + ax + b \tag{6.6}$$

Write this out as a cubic in x of the form $x^3 + Ux^2 + Vx + W = 0$. If the roots are x_1, x_1, and x_3 (we have a double root at x_1) we get

$$x^3 + Ux^2 + Vx + W = (x - x_1)^2(x - x_3) \tag{6.7}$$

So $-\gamma^2 = U = -(x_1 + x_2 + x_3)$ on comparing the coefficients of x^2. Thus, $x_3 = \gamma^2 - x_1 - x_2$. Now, $y_3 = y_1 + \gamma x_3 - \gamma x_1$ by substituting in the equation of the tangent line. Thus, $y_3 = \gamma(x_3 - x_1) + y_1$. So when we join P to Q, i.e. when we take the tangent at P

we get the point $(\gamma^2 - x_1 - x_2, \gamma(x_3 - x_1) + y_1)$. To get the sum we get the negative of the x-coordinate and use the same y-coordinate. Thus,

$$P + P = (\gamma^2 - x_1 - x_2, \gamma(x_1 - x_3) - y_1) \qquad (6.8)$$

The case $x_1 \neq x_2$ is handled in the same way. ∎

Going back to our curve over GF(7) we see that, for example, $(3,1) + (5,1) = (6,1) = (-1,1)$.

6.6 Key Exchange with Elliptic Curves

Given an elliptic curve E satisfying Eqs. (6.1) and (6.2) over GF(q), we have a group G. It is convenient to assume that G is cyclic or has a generator. This means that there is a point $P = (u, v)$ on the elliptic curve such that all points on the curve are of the form $P, 2P = P + P, 3P = P + P + P, \ldots, nP = P + P \ldots + P$ (n times).

Let A, B be communicating parties. Then A, B (Alice, Bob) proceed exactly analogous to the situation in Diffie–Hellman as follows:

A, B choose secret integers a, b, respectively. Suppose P is a given generator for the elliptic curve. Then A, B transmit aP, bP openly to each other. When A, B receive bP, aP they calculate $a(bP)$, $b(aP)$, respectively. They end up with a common secret key $(ab)P = (ba)P$. The discrete log problem in DH comes out to the following in ECC.

Given P, xP, find x.

In the above if P is a generator and the group G has order n, then $nP = P_\infty$, which is the zero element of the group, giving that $(n+1)P = P$, $(n+2)P = 2P$ and, in general, $mP = Rem[m, n]P$.

We can also develop a cryptographic system in ECC analogous to that for DH as well as a digital signature scheme.

6.7 Elliptic Curves mod n

Instead of working with elliptic curves over a field, it is possible to work over the integers mod n which is the set $Z_n = \{0, 1, 2, 3, \ldots, n-1\}$. Recall from Chapter 3 that the only numbers in Z_n that have a multiplicative inverse are those that are relatively prime to n. Thus, Z_n is not a field unless n is a prime. However, one can get important results such as algorithms for factoring n, called elliptic curve factorization, developed by H. Lenstra in 1987 [Len87]. When $n = pq$ is the product of two distinct primes, this can be used on the RSA cryptosystem developed in Chapter 3.

6.8   Encoding Plain Text

Let m be a message, represented as a binary string. To use an ECC cryptosystem, how do we make m correspond to a point on an elliptic curve E? We can initially make m be a part of the x-coordinate of a point on E by ensuring that the length of m is suitably small and by appending zeros to m. If the corresponding y-value for $x = m$ is not a square (we need this to ensure that (x, y) is on the curve and there is only about half a chance that it will be) we can use a method developed by Koblitz and append bits suitably in such a way that the y-value is now a square (with very high probability).

6.9   Security of ECC

This is analogous to the security of DH. For example in the above notation we have the following questions:

Problem 1 Elliptic Curve Problem.   *Given aP, bP, P, how does one find (ab)P?*

Problem 2 Discrete Log Problem for Elliptic Curves.   *Given xP, P, how does one find x?*

Given a solution to Problem 2, we obtain a solution to Problem 1. Whether the converse holds is not clear.

It seems that the security of ECC may be a bit stronger than the security of DH (the Diffie–Hellman key exchange) and RSA. One reason is that the size of the prime (or field) used in ECC need not be as large as that in DH or RSA to guarantee comparable security. In any event, ECC is still in its infancy even though the subject of elliptic curves is a venerable one.

6.10   More Geometry of Cubic Curves

Working over an algebraically closed field (such as the complex numbers), let $F(x, y, z) = 0$ be a cubic curve in homogeneous coordinates – see Section 6.12. We consider the equation

$$y_1 Fx + y_2 Fy + y_3 Fz = 0 \tag{6.9}$$

where F_x denotes the partial derivative of F with respect to x. We can interpret this in two ways (see [SR85]).

1. Suppose P is on the curve. Then, varying y_1, y_2, y_3 we get an equation of the form

$$y_1 a + y_2 b = y_3 c = 0 \qquad (6.10)$$

with $a = F_x(P)$, $b = F_y(P)$, $c = F_z(P)$. Then it follows that (if the curve F is nonsingular), $(a, b, c) \neq (0, 0, 0)$. As a result, the above, in homogeneous coordinates, is the equation of a line. The line is in fact the tangent line to the curve at P.

On the other hand, think of a point $P = (y_1, y_2, y_3)$ as being a point that is not necessarily on the curve. Now, if F has degree n, then F_x, F_y, F_z all have degree $n - 1$. Then Eq. (6.9) yields a curve of degree $n - 1$ called the *polar curve* of P with respect to F. This polar curve represents the points lying on the "feet of the tangents" from P to the curve $F = 0$.

A basic fact from algebraic geometry, called Bezout's theorem, asserts that two curves of degree u, v intersect in exactly uv points. (This is valid only for algebraically closed fields so in the smaller field we may have less.) The conclusion is that, in general, a point P off F lies on exactly $n(n - 1)$ tangents to F.

6.11   Cubic Curves and Arcs

Let Γ be an elliptic curve in the plane over $F = \mathrm{GF}(q)$. We then have $q + 1 - 2\sqrt{q} \leq |\Gamma| \leq q + 1 + 2\sqrt{q}$, where $|\Gamma|$ denotes the number of points on Γ, which is the number of elements in the group G.

Suppose now that $|\Gamma|$ is even, so 2 divides $|\Gamma|$. Recall that P_∞ serves as the identity element for the group G associated with Γ: denote it by 0. From our earlier definition, we know that $P + Q + R = 0$ if and only if P, Q, R are collinear. By hypothesis, two divides $|G|$. Since G is abelian, there exists a subgroup H of G with $2|H| = |G|$. So we can write G as the disjoint union of H and the coset L where $|H| = |L|$. Then, from group theory, we have that

(a) the sum of any two elements in L lies in H.

(b) the sum of any three elements in L lies outside H.

From (b) it follows that the sum of any three elements in L is never 0, since 0 is in H. Thus, the set L gives rise to an **arc** with size $|L|$, i.e. a set of $|L|$ points in the plane with no three collinear, where $|L| = \frac{1}{2}|G|$. Such large arcs have been intensively studied in connection with Segre's theorem and a generalization of the Hasse theorem known as the Hasse–Weil theorem. We refer the reader to [Bru84] for more detail. As pointed out there, the arc L was independently discovered by A. Zirilli and by P.M. Neumann (see [Bru84]). In fact, building on the work of J. Voloch, Alderson et al. [ABS07] show that in many cases, the *code* associated with L is maximal.

6.12 Homogeneous Coordinates

Given any "Euclidean" or "affine" equation such as Eq. (6.1), namely $y^2 = x^3 + ax + b$, we can convert it (by adjoining appropriate powers of z for each term) to a homogeneous equation in which each term now has degree 3. Thus, the above equation becomes

$$y^2 z = x^3 + ax^2 z + bz^2 \tag{6.11}$$

On the other hand, given Eq. (6.11), we can get the Euclidean equation by putting $z = 1$. The point (x, y) corresponds to the point $(x, y, 1)$ in homogeneous coordinates. In fact, two triples $(u_1, v_1, w_1) \neq (0, 0, 0)$ and $(u_2, v_2, w_2) \neq (0, 0, 0)$ represent the same point if and only if $u_2 = \lambda u_1$, $v_2 = \lambda v_1$, $w_2 = \lambda w_1$ with $\lambda \neq 0$, i.e. if and only if one triple is a nonzero scalar multiple of the other.

The advantage of homogeneous coordinates is that algebraically they are easier to work with, compared to the usual Euclidean coordinates. Also, the behavior at infinity is captured by putting $z = 0$. If we do this in Eq. (6.11), we get $x^3 = 0$ giving $x = 0$. So the point(s) at infinity of Eq. (6.1) are all points corresponding to the triples $(0, y, 0)$ with y in F. By "scalar multiples," we just get one point at infinity, namely, the point corresponding to the triple $(0, 1, 0)$, which is the point P_∞.

6.13 Fermat's Last Theorem, Elliptic Curves, Gerhard Frey

Fermat's last theorem is the assertion that the equation $x^n + y^n = z^n$ has no solutions when x, y, z are nonzero integers and $n > 2$ is an integer. Fermat, from Toulouse in France, stated this around 1630, but it was not proved, despite many attempts, until 1997, by A. Wiles.

In fact, it suffices to prove the equation has no solutions when $n > 2$ is an odd prime. For, let $n = pq$, where p is an odd prime. Since $x^n + y^n = z^n$, we have $(x^q)^p + (y^q)^p = (z^q)^p$, where now also x^q, y^q and z^q are nonzero positive integers.

Suppose then that we are looking at the equation $x^p + y^p = z^p$ for p an odd prime and let $x = a$, $y = b$, $z = c$ be a solution. Thus, we have $a^p + b^p = c^p$, where a, b, c are nonzero integers. Then, $a^p + b^p - c^p = 0$. Frey's insight then was to study the Frey elliptic curve with equation given by $y^2 = x(x - a^p)(x - b^p)$. He predicted that this curve would be incompatible with the Taniyama–Shimura conjecture. This is a central conjecture about curves which states that rational elliptic curves are **modular** so that they arise from modular forms. Wiles then proved the Taniyama–Shimura conjecture for a large class of rational elliptic curves including the so-called **semistable** curves. Since Frey's elliptic curves were semistable, Fermat's result followed as a corollary.

6.14 A Modification of the Standard Version of Elliptic Curve Cryptography

We refer to "Cubic Curves, Finite Geometry and Cryptography" by Bruen et al. [BHW11].

In Cryptography, the following views of an elliptic curve over a particular field K are common.

(a) A curve of genus 1.

(b) A plane nonsingular cubic curve.

(c) A plane nonsingular cubic curve with an inflection.

(d) $\{(x, y) \mid y^2 = x^3 + ax + b\}$.

For many fields, (c) is equivalent to (d). However, to perform ECC on a nonsingular cubic curve, it is not necessary to assume that the curve has an inflection point. This then widens the choice of the curve for the ECC. If only nonsingular cubics with more than one point are considered, then since an inflection point other than the zero has order 3 and the order of a subgroup divides the order of the group, this restricts to curves whose group size is divisible by 3.

Let us suggest a modification of the usual version of ECC. Parties A, B are working with a given elliptic curve which may or may not have an inflection. In the usual version of ECC, the line at infinity is a tangent at the inflection $O = (0, 1, 0)$. The identity element for the group structure is always chosen to be at the inflection point O. In the proposed variation, A and B share a secret. This secret, which will be digitized, is the choice of the identity element which is known only to A and B and which can be any point on the curve C. The choice of the identity point determines the group operation.

The unknown identity of the identity point makes the task of an eavesdropper that much more difficult. Also, the computerized attacks are programmed in accordance with the usual version of ECC.

6.15 Problems

6.1 For the elliptic curve E with equation $y^2 = x^3 + 2$ given in the text over the field $GF(7)$, describe some calculations for the group G associated with E. In particular, determine whether or not G is cyclic. (See Solution 6.1.)

Nonsingular Curves

6.2 We examine the curve E given in the text, where E has the equation $y^2 = x^3 + ax + b$ over a field K. In homogeneous coordinates, E has equation $y^2 z = x^3 + axz^2 + bz^3$. Under what conditions does there exist a point P in the plane such that $F_x(P) = F_y(P) = F_z(P) = 0$? (See Solution 6.2.)

6.3 If $F_x(P) = F_y(P) = F_z(P) = 0$ for some homogeneous polynomial F, must P lie on E (defined above)? (See Solution 6.3.)

6.4 Use the equation $y_1 F_x + y_2 F_y + y_3 F_z = 0$ to find the equation of the tangent line to E (defined above) at a point. Reconcile this with the calculus approach suggested in the text. (See Solution 6.4.)

6.5 In general, how many tangents can be drawn to E from a point P? (See Solution 6.5.)

6.6 Give an easy example of a curve which does not factor over a field F but does factor over a larger field K containing F. (See Solution 6.6.)

An Application of Nonsingularity

6.7 Show that the Fermat curve $F = 0$, given by $x^n + y^n - z^n = 0$ over any field K, where the characteristic of K is zero or does not divide n, is irreducible (i.e. does not factor). (See Solution 6.7.)

6.8 For the elliptic curve with equation $y^2 = x^3 + 4x + 4$ over Z_{13}, what is the size of the group G? (See Solution 6.8.)

6.9 If G is the group in Problem 6.8, what is the structure of G? (See Solution 6.9.)

6.16   Solutions

6.1   As shown in the text, $|G| = 9$. We know that G has P_∞ as the neutral or zero element 0. Take any nonzero point P such as, say, $(3,1)$. To find $P + P$, we have $\gamma = \frac{3x_1^2 + a}{2y_1} = \frac{3\,3^2 + 0}{2} = \frac{27}{2} = (27)(4) = (6)(4) = (-1)(4) = 3$. Then $P + P = (x_3, y_3)$, where $x_3 = \gamma^2 - x_1 - x_2 = 9 - 3 - 3 = 3$ and $y_3 = \gamma(x_1 - x_3) - y_1 = 3(3 - 3) - 1 = -1$. So $(3,1) + (3,1) = (3,-1)$ and $(3,1) + (3,1) + (3,1) = (3,1) + (3,-1) = P_\infty$. Thus, $(3,1)$ and in fact all points $Q \neq P_\infty$ have the property that $3Q = P_\infty = 0$. Thus, there is no point P such that all points on the curve E are of the form xP, $1 \leq x \leq 9$, i.e. there is no generator. So G is not cyclic.

6.2   We have $y^2 z = x^3 + axz^2 + bz^3$ giving

$$x^3 + axz^2 + bz^3 - y^2 z = 0 \tag{6.12}$$

$F_x = 0$ implies $3x^2 + az^2 = 0$.
$F_y = 0$ implies $-2yz = 0$.
$F_z = 0$ implies $2axz + 3bz^2 - y^2 = 0$.

   Suppose $z = 0$. Then $F_x = 0$ implies $3x^2 = 0$. Assume that the characteristic of the field is not 3. Then x must equal 0. So a point satisfying $F_x = 0$ and $F_y = 0$ must look like $(0, y, 0)$. For this triple to be a point, we must have $y \neq 0$. But then $F_z = 0$ is not satisfied by $(0, y, 0)$.

   Conclusion. If the characteristic of K is not 3, then no point with $z = 0$ satisfies $F_x = 0$, $F_y = 0$, $F_z = 0$. However, if char $K = 3$ the point $(1, 0, 0)$ satisfies $F_x = 0$, $F_y = 0$, $F_z = 0$. Note that this point $(1, 0, 0)$ is **not** on the curve. (See also Problem 6.3.)

   Now, suppose $z \neq 0$. Because of scalar multiples we can take $z = 1$. Our equations become

$$3x^2 + a = 0$$

$$-2y = 0$$

$$2ax + 3b - y^2 = 0$$

We have three cases.

   char $K = 2$. Then, since $1 + 1 = 2 = 0$, we have $x^2 + a = 0$, $y^2 + b = 0$. Since $-1 = +1$ and since each element has a unique square root, we end up with the point $(\sqrt{a}, \sqrt{b}, 1)$. This point lies on the curve, because $1 + 1 = 0$.

   So we have solutions if $x^2 = \frac{-a}{3}$, $y^2 = 3b$.

char $K = 3$. Then our conditions become $a = 0$, $y = 0$, $2ax - y^2 = 0$.

That is, $a = 0$, $y = 0$. Substituting in the equation of the curve gives a singular point $(v, 0, 1)$ on the curve where $v^3 = -b$.

char $K \neq 2, 3$ (and $z \neq 0$).

We have $3x^2 + a = 0$, $y = 0$, $2ax + 3b = 0$. Suppose $a = 0$. Then $3b = 0$. So $4a^3 + 27b^3 = 0$. Thus, $a \neq 0$. Then $x = \frac{-3b}{2a}$. But $3x^2 + a = 0$, giving $3\left(\frac{-3b}{2a}\right)^2 + a = 0$. This implies $(3)\frac{9b^2}{4a^2} + a = 0$, $27b^2 + 4a^3 = 0$, i.e. $4a^3 + 27b^2 = 0$.

Conclusion. If char $K = 2$ or char $K = 3$ there can be points P on the curve with $F_x(P) = F_y(P) = F_z(P) = 0$ even if $4a^3 + 27b^2 \neq 0$. However, if char $K \neq 2$ and char $K \neq 3$ and $4a^3 + 27b^2 \neq 0$, there are no points P in the plane and thus no points on the curve with $F_x(P) = F_y(P) = F_z(P) = 0$.

6.3   The Euler identity says that

$$xF_x + yF_y + zF_z = nF \tag{6.13}$$

Now, if $F_x(P) = F_y(P) = F_z(P) = 0$ this implies that $nF(P) = 0$. Thus, if the characteristic of the field does not divide n, we conclude that $F(P) = 0$ so P is on F. In particular, if F is a cubic, so $n = 3$ there are situations where the partial derivatives at P are zero, yet P is not on the cubic curve.

6.4   We work with the equation $y^2z = x^3 + axz^2 + b^3$ i.e. $x^3 + axz^2 + bz^3 - y^2z = 0$. Suppose $P = (u, v, w)$ is on the curve. Then the equation of the tangent line at P can be calculated. We have $F_x = 3x^2 + az^2$, $F_y = -2yz$, $F_z = 2axz + 3bz^2 - y^2$. So the equation of the tangent line at P is

$$x(3u^2 + aw^2) + y(-2vw) + z(2auw + 3bw^2 - v^2) = 0 \tag{6.14}$$

Assume $w \neq 0$. So P is not equal to P_∞. So we can assume $w = 1$. Then the point $(u, v, 1)$ satisfies the equation

$$x(3u^2 + a) + y(-2v) + (2au + 3b - v^2) = 0 \tag{6.15}$$

The affine equation of the curve is

$$y^2 = x^3 + ax + b \tag{6.16}$$

From calculus, we have $2y\frac{dy}{dx} = 3x^2 + a$ so $\frac{dy}{dx} = \frac{3x^2+a}{2y}$. The equation of the tangent at (u, v) is as follows:

$$y - v = m(x - u) = \frac{3u^2 + a}{2v}(x - u) \tag{6.17}$$

and so

$$2vy - 2v^2 = (3u^2 + a)(x - u) \tag{6.18}$$

This gives

$$x(3u^2 + a) - 2vy - 3u^3 - au + 2v^2 = 0 \tag{6.19}$$

Since (u, v) is on the curve, $v^2 = u^3 + au + b$, $u^3 = v^2 - au - b$. The constant term in Eq. (6.19) becomes $-3(v^2 - au - b) - au + 2v^2 = -v^2 + 2au + 3b$. So Eqs. (6.15) and (6.19) give the same answer.

6.5   If P is off the curve, we get in general 6 tangents. If P is on the curve, we get 4 tangents. (Note that $6 = n(n - 1) = (3)(2)$.)

6.6   Let us work with the curve $x^2 + y^2 = 0$. This does not factor over the real numbers. However, over the complex numbers, which contain the reals (i.e. are an extension of the reals), we have $x^2 + y^2 = (x + iy)(x - iy)$ with $i^2 = -1$. So over the complex numbers, the curve $x^2 + y^2 = 0$ factors into the product of 2 lines with slope $i, -i$.

6.7   Suppose F factors as GH. Then G, H are homogeneous with $\deg(G) = n_1$, $\deg(H) = n_2$ and $n_1 + n_2 = n = \deg(F)$. Now, by Bezout's theorem, there must exist a point P defined over $\overline{K}$, the algebraic closure of K, such that $G(P) = 0$ and $H(P) = 0$. It follows that $F_x(P) = G_x(P)H(P) + H(P)G_x(P)$. Thus, $F_x(P) = 0$. Similarly, $F_y(P) = 0$, $F_z(P) = 0$. But F_x is nx^{n-1}, $F_y = ny^{n-1}$, $F_z = nz^{n-1}$. Let $P = (u, v, w)$. Then $F_x(P) = nu^{n-1}$. So $F_x(P) = 0$ with characteristic of K not dividing n implies $u = 0$. Similarly, $F_y(P) = 0$ implies $v = 0$ and $F_z(P) = 0$ implies $w = 0$. So $P = (0, 0, 0)$ which is the one triple that does not represent a point in homogeneous coordinates. We conclude that F does not factor over a field K if the characteristic of K does not divide n.

   In summary, the moral is this: *F is nonsingular implies* that *F is irreducible.*

6.8 G has exactly 15 elements.

6.9 G is an abelian group with the order of G being pq, where $p \neq q$ are primes with $p = 3$, $q = 5$. From group theory G must be cyclic. For example the point $(1, 3)$ or the point $(-1, -5)$ is a generator.

   Further remarks. There exists $g_1 \neq 1$ with $g_1^3 = 1$. Also there exists $g_2 \neq 1$ with $g_2^5 = 1$. Then $g = g_1 g_2$ is a generator, i.e. $g^{15} = 1$ and no smaller power of g equals one. Then g^m is also a generator, $1 \leq m < 15$ proved m is relatively prime to 15. The number of integers relatively prime to 15 is $\phi(15) = \phi[(3)(5)] = \phi(3)\phi(5) = (2)(4) = 8$ (see Chapter 19). So all told there are exactly eight generators.

Chapter 7

General and Mathematical Attacks in Cryptography

Goals, Discussion Some of the classical cryptanalytic techniques were already introduced in Chapter 2 for what are often known as "pencil and paper" ciphers. In Chapter 3 we also discussed several attacks on various implementations of RSA and on Diffie–Hellman. Here we introduce several techniques, mathematical and otherwise, developed for the breaking of modern ciphers and other components of crypto-systems used in real-life applications and protocols. These are in addition to the attacks on insecure implementations of RSA discussed in various problems in Chapter 3.

New, Noteworthy We give a comprehensive overview of the most common attacks on privacy. A classic attack – relay attacks – (not to be confused with replay attacks) has gained new attention in recent years with adversaries using this type of attack to gain entry to cars with keyless entry systems.

7.1 Cryptanalysis

Technically speaking, we can define **cryptanalysis** (or cryptanalytics or cryptoanalysis) as the art and science of solving unknown codes and ciphers. Cryptanalysts try to

Cryptography, Information Theory, and Error-Correction: A Handbook for the 21st Century, Second Edition.
Aiden A. Bruen, Mario A. Forcinito, and James M. McQuillan.
© 2021 John Wiley & Sons, Inc. Published 2021 by John Wiley & Sons, Inc.

break the codes and ciphers created and used by cryptographers. This can sometimes be achieved either by obtaining the key or by directly obtaining the message. By extension, the art of exploiting weaknesses in protocols used to communicate secure information (authentication, key-management, software/hardware defects, etc.) also fall within the bounds of cryptanalysis. Practitioners often refer to the cryptanalytic process as "breaking the crypto-system."

In general, cryptanalysts are faced with the task of first determining the language being used for the communication, the general type of cipher or code being used, the specific key(s), and finally, the reconstruction of the message or plain text. These determinations have to be made based on variable amounts of cipher text and related information such as the identity of sender and receiver, statistical analysis of traffic, knowledge of some specific information about the contents of the message.

A famous literary example of these ideas can be found in Edgar Allan Poe's tale "The Golden Bug" [Poe93]. In this tale, the principal character describes, in vivid detail, the entire process of cryptanalysis of a simple substitution cipher based only on the cipher text and a scant knowledge of the sender's identity and intent. In real life, examples abound of broken secrecy systems based on knowledge of side information or weaknesses of the system rather than on the breaking of the cipher itself. Frequently, in cryptanalysis, we try to piece together various existing probable pieces of information in order to determine the secret key or the message.

7.2 Soft Attacks

No matter how sophisticated the attack techniques become, one must not forget that when the ultimate goal is to obtain the secret message, **coercion** or **social engineering** is often the most effective attack techniques. These attacks are based on using physical or psychological threats, robbery, bribery, embezzlement, etc. The attacks are mostly directed to human links of the data security chain. Extensive consultation with experienced professionals and security experts is a good defense against these attacks. In a sense, design of the whole data security system includes the selection of hardware, software, and human resources, as well as the implementation of mechanisms to check the proper functioning of all these elements. However, as so many high-profile cases have shown, no matter how much effort is spent on keeping information secret, human nature will always conspire against, and defeat, even the best-designed secrecy systems.

The particular techniques used in physically securing information is beyond the scope of this book. We will concentrate instead on mathematical aspects of attacks and assume that physical and operating data security has been implemented. The interested reader can consult the extensive literature on the subject from authors such as Schneier [Sch03] and Mitnick et al. [MSW02].

In the problems in Chapter 3, we have already described various mathematical attacks on Rivest–Shamir–Adleman (RSA). We proceed with other kinds of general attacks, which are so numerous that we can only give a very short summary here. Many attacks are based on Internet vulnerabilities and are described in detail in books on Internet security. Schneier [Sch96] also presents several examples.

7.3   Brute-Force Attacks

Assuming, as **Kerckhoffs's principle** recommends, that the algorithm used for encryption and the general context of the message are known to the cryptanalyst, the brute-force attack involves the determination of the specific key being used to encrypt a particular text. When successful, the attacker will also be able to decipher all future messages until the keys are changed. One way to determine the key is by exhaustive search of the **key-space**,[1] or **brute-force**. In Chapter 3, we have described some mathematical results applicable to brute-force attacks.

A brute-force attack could be a passive or **off-line attack**. The attacker (*Eve* in this case) passively eavesdrops on the communication channel and records cipher text exchanges for further analysis, without interacting with either **A** or **B**.

Brute-force attacks can be carried out knowing only a small portion of cipher text and the corresponding plain text (such a collection of data commonly referred to as a **crib**). The attack consists of systematically trying all possible keys on the key-space until the key that enciphers the plain text into the cipher text (or vice-versa) for the particular encryption algorithm being used. To estimate the time that a successful brute-force attack will take we need to know the size of the key-space and the speed at which each key can be tested. If N_k is the number of valid keys, and we can test N_s key per second, it will take, on average $\frac{1}{2}\left(\frac{N_k}{N_s}\right)$ seconds to find the proper key by brute-force: see Chapter 3.

If no amount of plain text is known with certainty or the amount of cipher text is small, the brute-force attack may not even be practical; more than one guessed key may yield meaningful messages from which the attacker may not be able to decide, with certainty, the correct one. For a brute-force attack to succeed, the attacker must have sufficient information about the contents of the message to be able to recognize the right key, when it is found. In the case of public key algorithms it is possible to check, with certainty that the correct key has been guessed.

---

[1] Defined as the set of all possible valid keys for the particular crypto-system.

The threat that a brute-force attack poses cannot be underestimated in the real world. The US *Cybersecurity & Infrastructure Security Agency (CISA)* from the Department of Homeland Security noted in 2020, [Age20].

According to information derived from FBI investigations, malicious cyber actors are increasingly using a style of brute force attack known as password spraying against organizations in the United States and abroad.

They note that possible impacts of brute-force attacks can include

1. Temporary or permanent loss of sensitive or proprietary information;

2. Disruption to regular operations;

3. Financial losses incurred to restore systems and files; and

4. Potential harm to an organization's reputation.

Brute-force analysis can be used in combination with other attacks as was the case for the deciphering of the Enigma. The famous **bombes** [Bau02] designed by M. Rejewski were an example of the brute-force approach working in combination with a mathematical method that provided an important reduction of the key-space.

7.4   Man-in-the-Middle Attacks

This is a generalization to previous impersonation attacks such as **IP address spoofing** and it is by far the most powerful attack in cryptography. **A** and **B** are communicating with each other, supposedly, along with *Malone* (or *Mallory* or *Middle*, the Malicious active attacker). Consider a scenario in which **A** wishes to send a message to **B**, and then **B** sends a response to **A**. It might play out differently. Instead, **Malone** intercepts the message from **A** to **B**. **Malone** then, pretending to be **A**, sends an altered or different message to **B**. **B**, thinking that the message came from **A**, then sends a reply to **Malone**. **Malone**, impersonating **B** this time, sends a reply (possibly an altered version of **B**'s message) to **A**. An example relating to the Diffie–Hellman key-exchange was given in Section 3.8.

Note that *Malone* is much more powerful than the traditional passive attacker *Eve*. Not only can *Malone* listen in to the cipher text of messages between **A** and **B**: he can alter messages, delete messages, or even create fictitious messages on his own by impersonating **A** to **B** and **B** to **A**.

Figure 7.1: Man-in-the-middle attack on symmetric key encryption.

This kind of attack has been known since antiquity, and all ciphers are susceptible to it. It will fail if **A** and **B** have a proper system of authentication (such as the use of **digital signatures**) which are discussed in Chapter 4. Moreover, one can say that this type of attack is one of the main reasons why an authentication system is needed, so that **A** and **B** can be certain that they are communicating with each other. Widely used e-commerce applications, such as the SSL protocol, are susceptible to the man-in-the-middle attack.

In the case in which both parties are using a shared secret key scheme, M has to intercept the initial key in transit from **A** to **B** to be successful (Figure 7.1). It is always good practice to use an independent channel to transmit keys. In the case in which a public key scheme is being used (Figure 7.2), a successful **man in the middle** M replaces **A**'s public key being transmitted to **B** and **B**'s public key being transmitted to **A** with public keys generated adhoc, for which M has the corresponding private keys. **Public key infrastructure** (PKI) addresses this problem by creating a **Certificate Authority** (CA) that issues special files called **certificates**. These certificates can be used by **B** (or **A**) to verify the authenticity of **A**'s key (or **B**'s key). By querying the CA, **B** can independently assert whether or not the given public key is uniquely associated with the identity of **A**. This system is logically equivalent to a **Trusted Server** which provides authentication and session keys for symmetric encryption system, as in the **Kerberos** system.

In any case, the idea is to replace trust between **A** and **B**, who at this point might not know each other, by a third party which **A** and **B** independently trust. It has been often pointed out that shifting the trust in this way removes the problem of the man in

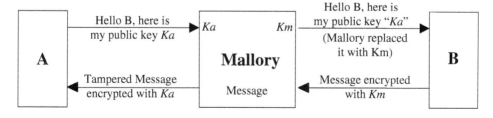

Figure 7.2: Man-in-the-middle attack on public key encryption.

the middle but generates new potential weaknesses such as the certification of the CA or the level of trust that can be accorded to the Trusted Server.

7.5   Relay Attacks, Car Key Fobs

Relay attacks are not to be confused with replay attacks (which are covered in Section 7.10)! In a *relay attack*, messages are forwarded, or relayed, by an adversary. For example, consider a message m that **Alice** wishes to send to **Bob** to determine if **Bob** is nearby. Message m could be intercepted by adversary **Eve** and forwarded on to **Bob**. **Bob** might then send an acknowledgment back. Again, **Eve** could intercept the message and forward it to **Alice**. **Alice** might incorrectly conclude that **Bob** is nearby. (**Eve** could even have an accomplice to help with this. That is, **Eve** could forward a message to the accomplice who then forwards the message to the desired recipient.) See Figure 7.3.

Eve could perform a *passive relay attack* in which she forwards the data, unaltered. Alternatively, an *active relay attack* would exist if, in addition, **Eve** altered the data.

Relay attacks have become a major concern in the last several years as the use of Near Field Communication (NFC) for short-range communications has increased. See [VR15], for example.

Here, we offer an example that is of importance to many of us, namely **cars with keyless entry systems**. Over the last one to two decades, more and more new cars have come with a keyless entry system. Traditionally, of course, a physical key was inserted into a keyhole of a car door to unlock the door, and into a second keyhole inside the car to start the car. In cars with a Passive Keyless Entry and Start (PKES) system, the driver carries a key fob with them – perhaps in their pocket. If the key fob is close enough to the car door, the door can be unlocked without the need to insert a physical key into a key hole. Similarly, if the key fob is inside the car, that might allow the car to be started with the push of a button. This gives us the convenience of not having to get our key out of our pockets, or not having to find our keys in a bag that we are carrying.

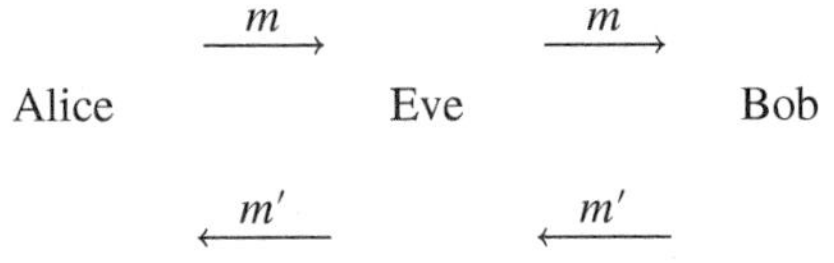

$$\text{Alice} \quad \xrightarrow{\;m\;} \quad \text{Eve} \quad \xrightarrow{\;m\;} \quad \text{Bob}$$

$$\xleftarrow{\;m'\;} \qquad \xleftarrow{\;m'\;}$$

Figure 7.3: A passive relay attack in which encrypted message m is sent by **Alice**. **Eve** intercepts it and forwards it, unaltered, to **Bob**. Acknowledgement message m' is then sent by **Bob**. **Eve** intercepts it and forwards it, unaltered, to **Alice**.

There is no need to insert a traditional physical key into a keyhole. There is no need to remove the key fob from our pocket.

In 2011, Francillon et al., [FDC11], showed how to compromise PKES keyless entry systems on cars by using a relay attack using equipment costing between \$100 and \$1000 USD. With one antenna device close to the door handle of a car, and the other antenna device relatively close to the key (if you know roughly where the owner with the key is), they were able to relay messages between the key and the car.

This is an ongoing concern, as described by Mills in a CBC News article, [Mil19]. Mills notes that a spokesperson for a major car company warned owners to "... never leave their key fobs near the front door of their home." The company "... suggests buying a radio frequency shielding 'faraday pouch' to prevent unwanted radio waves from reaching the device."

Consider the following car key fob scenario. Message m_1 is sent by Alice's **car**. If Alice's **key fob** was close enough to her **car**, the **key fob** would receive the message and send an acknowledgment back to the **car**. At the moment, the **fob** is not close enough to the **car**. *However*, **Eve** "assists" this process by quickly forwarding message m_1 to the **fob**, so the **fob** does indeed receive the message in the required short amount of time. **Eve** also assists in getting the **fob**'s reply m_1' back to the **car** in the required short amount of time. Therefore, the **car** initiates a challenge-response protocol, to determine if it should allow the doors to be unlocked. The **car** sends Challenge message m_2, again with the unwelcome and unknown relay assistance of **Eve**'s transmitters. **Eve** assists once again in getting the **fob**'s response to the challenge back to the **car** in a timely fashion. (For more details, see [FDC11], including Figures 1 and 3.) See Figure 7.4.

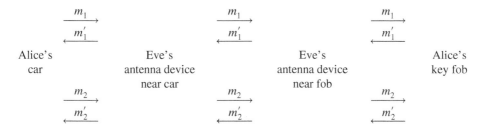

Figure 7.4: A relay attack. Message m_1 is sent by Alice's **car**. **Eve** relays (forwards) message m_1 to the **fob** so that it is received quickly enough. **Eve** also assists in relaying the **fob's** reply m_1' back to the **car** in a timely fashion. Subsequently, using a challenge-response protocol, challenge message m_2 is sent by the **car**, and relayed by Eve's transmitters to the bf fob. The **key fob**'s response to the challenge is sent, and relayed by **Eve**'s transmitters back to the **car**. See [FDC11, Figures 1 and 3].

Thus, an attacker could unlock a car door, and even start the car, without having a key themselves. Francillon et al. (see [FDC11]) were able to excite a smart key from up to 8 m away from the key. That is, while an attacker needs to put one of the transmitting devices near the driver's key fob in order to carryout such an attack, the transmitting device doesn't need to be right next to the key fob.

These relay attacks, "... are completely independent of the modulation, protocol, or presence of strong authentication and encryption." The relay attacks were successful because the PKES systems were designed to verify that the key fob was able to communicate with the car, rather than verifying that the key fobs were close to the car. Verification of physical proximity is needed. See [FDC11].

In a 2018 Washington Post article, [Tsu18], author Hayley Tsukayama notes that not every type of car with a key fob is equally affected. She also quotes Michael Calkins, manager of technical services at American Automobile Association (AAA): "But we do know that there are some people who are at a higher risk than others. People with high-end cars are bigger targets, Calkins said. Cars that have valuables in plain sight on the seat are also a target." People who are concerned can always remove the batteries from their fob or keep it in a pouch or bag that blocks electromagnetic signals, or wrapping the fob in tinfoil. The inconvenience of this comes when using the key fob to unlock or drive your car. Car manufacturers are working on solutions to this problem. For example, another major car manufacturer introduced a new fob in 2019. This company "has launched an aftermarket key fob upgrade that makes its keyless entry models far less vulnerable to theft via relay attack." "The new fob is equipped with a motion sensor that detects when the key has been stationary for more than 40 seconds." See [SH19]. As noted above, a good piece of advice from [Mil19] is to "never leave their key fobs near the front door of their home."

7.6   Known Plain Text Attacks

In this situation the adversary *Eve*, who is listening in, is assumed to possess a considerable length of message text and corresponding cipher text (i.e. a "crib"), and from this seeks to find the key. This situation is a realistic one, especially for public key algorithms when the same key is used for a lengthy period.

E-mail and **e-commerce** applications are susceptible to attack in this way because the plain text for addresses, routing and headers are known or fairly easy to guess. There is plenty of software available on the Internet to stage this type of attack. Attacks using cribs were effective for the Allied forces in World War II. Since the German military even encrypted trivial data such as weather forecasts, the Allies were able to obtain very useful cribs which helped crack the Enigma machine.

7.7 Known Cipher Text Attacks

In this scenario, the adversary *Eve* only knows a piece of the cipher text and tries to obtain the plain text and the key from it. This type of attack always involves a large amount of work but is the one that requires the least input as the cipher text is almost always available to the attacker. We already discussed some particular cases such as the methods presented in Chapter 2 to attack the Vigenère cipher. Gillogly [Gil95] presented a classical example of a known cipher text attack only on the Enigma cipher.

7.8 Chosen Plain Text Attacks

In this type of attack the cryptanalyst must be able to define a particular plain text, feed it into the encryption device, and retrieve and analyze the resulting cipher text. This could be used to attack RSA, for example, where the public key is known.

It is not necessary for the cryptanalyst to have access to the enciphering device. In some cases, it is possible to get the victim to help carry out the attack by "planting" the chosen plain text in a normal exchange, in such a way that does not raise the victim's suspicions.

There are several well-known historical examples in which one side, directly or indirectly, revealed a purportedly "secret text" and then eavesdropped on the communication lines of the enemy to see what the corresponding cipher text was, therefore, gaining information about the enemy's cipher-system.

As mentioned, public key ciphers (in particular RSA) are vulnerable to this type of attack. In general, any system that uses the same keys to encrypt large volumes of data will be vulnerable to a chosen plain text attack. As an example, one can mount an attack of this kind to obtain the encryption keys from a wireless network using Wired Equivalent Privacy (WEP) by sending a large number of chosen plain text messages (spamming) to one user and eavesdropping on the traffic between the user and the wireless server.

7.9 Chosen Cipher Text Attacks, Digital Signatures

In this type of attack, the analyst chooses a cipher text and tries to get the victim to decrypt it in order to find the key. An alternative approach is to decrypt the cipher text with different random keys in order to get some information about the real key.

If RSA is also being used for digital signatures, *Eve* can generate a random number r and ask *Bob* to sign the message $C' = r^e C$, which looks like a random message to *Bob*. If he signs the message, *Eve* will have $C'^d = r^{ed} C^d = rM$. She needs only to divide by r

to obtain the message. To avoid this situation, a **hash function** must be used when an unknown message is digitally signed.

This type of attack can be employed against popular e-mail encryption systems such as Pretty Good Privacy (PGP), although it seems to fail if compression is used in addition to encryption.

7.10 Replay Attacks

Replay attacks are not to be confused with relay attacks (which are covered in Section 7.5)! Under certain conditions, an attacker may use parts of a previous encrypted exchange between *Alice* and *Bob* to gain access to their resources.

Suppose that *Alice* sends an encrypted request to transfer funds to her bank. The key used to sign the message is only know to *Alice*. By copying and later replaying the encrypted transfer request, *Eve* can repeat the same transaction without Alice's knowledge. To be successful, *Eve* need to guess or otherwise determine which part of the cipher text corresponds to the transfer request, copy the encrypted request and replay it at another time, without ever having to decrypt.

In general, a *replay attack* occurs any time an intruder manages to capture a message (or part of a message) with the intention of using it at a later time. There are two variants of this attack. In the first variant, the original message is allowed to reach the destination unimpeded, but it is copied to be replayed later. In the second variant, the original message is prevented from arriving at the intended destination and is copied to be used later. See [Syv94] for further details.

To guard against such attacks, many protocols, such as Kerberos, include a time-stamp of some type or other. The protocol is designed in such a way that when **A** sends a request, **B** has a limited amount of time to acknowledge and complete the transaction. In that way when the intruder copies the encrypted exchange and later tries to replay it, **B** can decrypt and checks the time stamp, refusing the transaction if the delay is bigger than a predetermined amount.

7.11 Birthday Attacks

Suppose we have n people in a room. An individual's name is encoded as a binary string. Denote the corresponding variable by x. So altogether x has n distinct values, one for each person in the room. Each of the n people has a birthday which can be described by a short binary string y representing a number between 1 and 365 (or 366 in the case of a leap year).

We can now construct a hash function f which associates the string y with the string x. One can then ask the following question: what is the probability that f does not have a collision? In other words, what is the probability that no two people have the same birthday?

Of course, if n is greater than 365 (or 366) that probability is zero: some two people must have the same birthday. But what if $n < 365$ (or 366)?

For the following discussion, assume that the current year is not a leap year. If we arrange the n people in some order, the total number of possible strings of length n that we obtain if we have n distinct birthdays is

$$(365)(364)(363)\cdots(365 - (n-1)) \tag{7.1}$$

The total number of birthday strings of length n, distinct or not, is

$$(365)(365)\ldots(365) = (365)^n \tag{7.2}$$

Thus, the probability that we end up with n birthdays such that not two are equal is (7.1) divided by (7.2) which gives

$$\left(1 - \frac{1}{365}\right)\left(1 - \frac{2}{365}\right)\cdots\left(1 - \frac{n-1}{365}\right) \tag{7.3}$$

If n is 23, the probability that we end up with no two people having the same birthday is $0.49 < 0.5$, so if we have 24 or more people, it is likely that some two have the same birthday. We can generalize the argument above as follows.

Recall (calculus again) that $\ln(1 - \lambda)$ is approximately equal to λ for λ small. This follows because $e^\lambda \approx 1 + \lambda$ so $e^{-\lambda} \approx 1 - \lambda$. If we generate n numbers independently, at random (i.e. with replacement) from a set $1, 2, 3, \ldots, t$ the probability that they are all distinct, denoted by $P(t, n)$, is, as above,

$$\prod_{j=0}^{n-1}\left(1 - \frac{j}{t}\right) \tag{7.4}$$

Now

$$\ln(P(t,n)) \approx \sum_{i=0}^{n-1}\ln\left(1 - \frac{j}{t}\right) \approx -\sum_{j=0}^{n-1}\frac{j}{t} = -\frac{n(n-1)}{2t} \tag{7.5}$$

If n is much smaller than $\sqrt{t}$, $P(t, k) \approx 1 - \frac{n^2}{2t}$. Thus, for birthdays, $P(365, 23) \approx 0.5$.

As t gets large, one can show that the expected number of draws until a collision, i.e. until two of the drawn numbers coincide, is $\sqrt{\frac{\pi t}{2}}$.

In the case of a hash function whose output is m bits, so $t = 2^m$, the average number of trials until a collision is about $2^{\frac{m}{2}} = \sqrt{t}$, which is the square root of the total number of possible outputs. Because the average number of trials until a collision is $2^{\frac{m}{2}}$, rather than, 2^m, we can say informally that the output's value should be "twice as long as it usually is" in order to withstand a brute-force collision attack.

7.12 Birthday Attack on Digital Signatures

The following attack is due to Yuval [Yuv79].

Alice wants to cheat *Bob*. She prepares two contracts X, Y with Y being favorable to *Bob* and X being favorable to *Alice*. *Alice* makes small harmless changes to X, such as inserting spaces, etc., and also to Y.

If each document has m lines, *Alice* can easily construct 2^m versions of X and 2^m versions of Y. If *Alice* is using a hash function with n bits and m is about $\frac{n}{2}$, the chances are good that some version of X, say X_1, hashes to the same value as some version Y_1 of Y.

Now *Alice* asks *Bob* to digitally sign Y_1 using a signing protocol whereby *Bob* only signs the hash value. Then down the road, *Alice* can replace Y_1 by X_1 – the contract favorable to *Alice* – and claim that this is what *Bob* has signed.

Birthday attacks can also be used on Diffie–Hellman and on Double DES (which is why Double DES is not used). The technique used is similar to the previous signature scheme.

7.13 Birthday Attack on the Discrete Log Problem

Given a prime p and a generator g, we want to solve the **discrete log problem** given by the equation $Rem[g^x, p] = v$, i.e. $g^x \pmod{p} = v$, where we are also given v. We construct two lists (analogous to the variation on the two contracts in the previous discussion) called X and Y.

X consists of numbers $g^t \pmod{p}$ for about $\sqrt{p}$ values of t.

Y consists of numbers $vg^{-s} \pmod{p}$ for about $\sqrt{p}$ values of s. Note that g^{-s} is just the multiplicative inverse of $g^s \pmod{p}$.

Now, since the number of elements in X multiplied by the number of elements in Y is around p, there is a collision probability greater than $(\frac{1}{2})$, i.e. that there are t, s with $g^t \pmod{p} = vg^{-s} \pmod{p}$, or, $Rem[g^t, p] = Rem[vg^{-s}, p]$. Thus, $Rem[g^t - vg^{-s}, p] = 0$. Therefore, $Rem[g^{t-s} - v, p] = 0$, i.e. $g^{t-s} = v \pmod{p}$ and we have solved the discrete log problem.

7.14 Attacks on RSA

We continue our discussion with some specific attacks on the RSA algorithm. However, as pointed out by Boneh [Bon99], "although 20 years of research have led to a number of fascinating attacks, none of them is devastating. They mostly illustrate the dangers of improper use of RSA." One such attack is the "factoring attack." If we can factor $N = pq$, we can break RSA. One such factoring technique which works in certain cases is called the *Pollard* $p - 1$ *method* and is discussed in Chapter 19. Advances in computing power and in mathematical Methods, over the last 45 years can be gauged by the increase in the length of numbers that are practical to factor. From a 39-digit number in 1970, to a 129-digit number in 1994,[2] to a 155-digit number in 1999, which is equivalent to a binary 512-bit number, the progress has been faster than predicted. As of 2020, NIST recommends that key lengths have *at least* 2048 bits for RSA, if not 3072 bits or higher. See Table 2 of [Bar16], for example.

Another possibility an attacker has is to re-encrypt the cipher text (anybody can do this because the public encryption exponent and the modulus are public) and iterate the encryption step on each new cipher text thus obtained, until the message is recovered. This attack is a consequence of one of the properties of the RSA algorithm, that for each M, there exists a unique number k called the iteration exponent or period of M such that $C_{k+1} = C_0$, where $C_{k+1} = C_k^e \pmod{N}$ and $C_0 = M$. This attack can be efficiently staged only for relatively small p, q and e.

As mentioned, as of 2020, NIST recommends that key lengths have *at least* 2048 bits for RSA, if not 3072 bits or higher. See Table 2 of [Bar16], for example. This is a hot topic of discussion for practical applications because in the case of RSA, Diffie–Hellman and ECC systems, increasing the key length increases the computational effort required to solve the underlaying problem even though, the entropy of the longer key is still 0. Meeting the needs of secure communication for portable wireless systems becomes an increasingly difficult task as key-lengths grow to reach acceptable security levels. Many of the proposed attacks on RSA are effective only if RSA is not properly implemented. To increase the security offered by RSA, one option is to "pad" the message M by appending random bits to the message. While padding does add some randomness to the message, there exist attacks (suc as the Coppersmith Short Pad Attack) that exploit random padding to determine M.

for further details on correct RSA implementation and RSA attacks we refer the reader to Mollin [Mol00] and Boneh [Bon99].

---

[2] The challenge to factor a 129-digit number known as RSA129 was set forth in 1978 when the original RSA paper was Published.

7.15   Attacks on RSA using Low-Exponents

To save computational effort, users may be tempted to select small encryption and decryption exponents. Because they make the modular exponentiation operation faster, Fermat primes $e = 2^1 + 1 = 3$, $e = 2^4 + 1 = 17$, or $e = 65\,537 = 2^{16} + 1$ are commonly chosen for the exponent e in practical implementations of RSA. Once e is fixed, it is easier to conduct the tests $\gcd(e, p - 1) = 1$ and $\gcd(e, q - 1) = 1$, while generating and testing the primes p and q, rejecting the primes that fail this test. The mathematics of RSA is such that this practice could make it vulnerable to attacks.

When the encryption exponent e is less than the number of recipients k of a given message M, an eavesdropper may recover the message as follows: *Eve* sees k cipher texts M^e (mod N_i). She knows that for all recipients to be able to uniquely decipher the message the condition $M < N_i$ must hold for $i = 1, 2, \ldots, k$. Therefore, $M^e < N_1 N_2 \ldots N_k$. If the N_i are relatively prime, *Eve* can compute M^e (mod $N_1 N_2 \ldots N_k$), where $e < k$ using the Chinese Remainder Theorem. She then has a perfect integer power over the integers, namely, M^e, from which she can calculate the eth root and recover M. Otherwise, *Eve* can factor the N_i's and compute M.

To avoid these types of attacks a large encryption exponent e must be selected.

The possibility of a successful attack arises when a small decryption exponent is used to reduce decryption time. Wiener [Wie90] published a detailed description of a method for recovering the decryption key when a small decryption exponent d is used. We present here the main theorem without proof.

Theorem 7.1 *Let $N = pq$ with $q < p < 2q$. Let $d < \frac{1}{3}\sqrt[4]{N}$. Given (N, e) such that $ed \equiv 1$ (mod $\phi(N)$) then an attacker can efficiently recover d.*

This means that for a 1024-bit modulus, d needs to be at least 256-bits long to be secure. There is a potentially damaging avenue here for an attack that utilizes the results presented in Chapter 3 regarding the nonuniqueness of the decryption exponent.

Partial knowledge of the decryption exponent can also be exploited. This, if $N = pq$ is an n-bit RSA modulus and $n/4$ least significant bits of the decryption exponent d are known, there is an algorithm that can be used to efficiently reconstruct the whole decryption exponent and the factorization of N. We refer the reader to Boneh et al. [BDF98].

7.16   Timing Attack

In 1996, Kocher proposed a simple algorithm to obtain bits of an RSA key by measuring the slight time differences in the computations times for a series of decryptions [Koc96].

For each particular implementation of the algorithm, there is a correlation between the time the decryption takes and whether the bits of d, the decryption exponent, are 0 or 1. If the least significant bits of the decryption key are known, by carefully measuring the average time that decrypting several (known) cipher texts takes, one can guess whether the next bit of the decryption exponent is 1 or 0. The process can be repeated to obtain one additional bit of the decryption exponent per repetition. Diffie–Hellman and Digital Signature Standard (DSS) are also susceptible to this type of attack. The attack is passive but needs to be staged on-line because the attacker needs to know the time taken by the system to decrypt each cipher text C.

7.17   Differential Cryptanalysis

This method works in a similar way to the chosen plain text attack. Originally, the method was developed to attack ciphers based on **Feistel algorithms**, such as DES. (See Section 1.6 for historical information about DES.) The attack consists of looking at differences produced in the cipher text by known differences in the plain text. The chosen plain text is carefully designed by the attacker to contain known differences that will result in a particular statistical distribution of the cipher text bits as they are shuffled through the successive rounds. A search is then made for the cipher texts corresponding to those patterns. (With this information, it is possible to make inferences about S-boxes in DES and the bits of the key with increasing certainty, as more plain texts are used.) Of course, the internal details of the algorithm need to be known to give the attacker the ability to generate meaningful statistics for different patterns.

The method of differential attack was rediscovered in the late 1980s by den Boer (see [dB88]) who applied it to a four-round FEAL cipher. Later, it was extended to a reduced eight-round DES by Biham and Shamir [BS90].

In general, the shorter the key compared to the length of the message, the more vulnerable the message is – especially a text message. Differential cryptanalysis is one of the standard attacks.

7.18   Attacks Utilizing Preprocessing

Preprocessing in general can be extremely powerful. It can dramatically speed up the run-time of many algorithms. The idea is simple. For any algorithm that you wish to run, you might have some of the data in advance. That data can be *preprocessed*. That might mean that it is put into a nice tree data structure, for example, for efficient access later on. The main goal of preprocessing is that when the final data arrives later on, any computations using the preprocessed data can be done extremely quickly because of the work already done in the preprocessing stage.

A nice example of preprocessing is a Search engine (e.g. Google or DuckDuckGo). If you search for a term such as "encryption," the search engine can almost immediately give you many matches. Fast results are possible because of the tremendous amount of work that was done ahead of time. They did a lot of preprocessing.

The same idea can be used by an adversary in cryptography. If they have a bit of data now, then can preprocess it. Then, later, when you send a message, they might be able to break your encryption code faster.

In January 2019 issue of *Communications of the ACM*, there were two articles [ABD+19] and [Bon19] about preprocessing and Diffie–Hellman. (Diffie–Hellman was discussed previously in Sections 3.7 and 3.8.)

In [ABD+19], Adrian et al. note that

The current best technique for attacking Diffie–Hellman relies on compromising one of the private exponents (a, b) by computing the discrete logarithm of the corresponding public value ($g^a \bmod p$, $g^b \bmod p$). With state-of-the-art number field sieve algorithms, computing a single discrete logarithm is more difficult than factoring a RSA modulus of the same size. However, an adversary who performs a large precomputation for a prime p can then quickly calculate arbitrary discrete logarithms in that group, amortizing the cost over all targets that share this parameter. Although this fact is well known among mathematical cryptographers, it seems to have been lost among practitioners deploying cryptosystems.

In [Bon19], Boneh notes,

The authors of the following paper show that, in practice, implementations that use Diffie–Hellman tend to choose a universally fixed prime p (and fixed g). For example, many SSH servers and IPsec VPNs use a fixed universal 1024-bit prime p. The same is true for HTTPS Web servers, although to a lesser extent.

The authors speculate that a precomputation attack on discrete-log modulo a fixed 1024-bit prime is within reach for a nation state. Because a small number of fixed primes is employed by a large number of websites, a precomputation attack on a few primes can be used to compromise encrypted Internet traffic at many sites.

An attacker's ability to preprocess information has to be taken into account when analyzing the security of any cryptographic protocol.

7.19 Cold Boot Attacks on Encryption Keys

For this type of attack, we consider the main memory, or RAM, of a computer. (See Section 17.2 for background information on RAM.) The RAM for most desktop and laptop computers is DRAM, which is *volatile*, meaning that, if it does not have power, it loses its contents. There is newer, more expensive nonvolatile (NVM) memory as well. (Nonvolatile RAM will become more common after it has been in use for a while and the price decreases.) In this section, we only consider DRAM memory, which is volatile.

We consider the scenario in which an attacker obtains physical access to a computer. Therefore, they have physical access to main memory. What type of attack could they perform? Could they possibly retrieve any cryptographic information?

Halderman et al. noted in 2008 at the *17th USENIX Security Symposium*, [HSH+08], that

> Most security experts assume that a computer's memory is erased almost immediately when it loses power, or that whatever data remains is difficult to retrieve without specialized equipment. We show that these assumptions are incorrect. Ordinary DRAMs typically lose their contents gradually over a period of seconds ...

This means that it is harder for an operating system to protect cryptographic keys from an attacker that has physical access to the computer or device. The authors used cold reboots to mount attacks with out the need for specialized devices. They note that,

> ... data will persist for minutes or even hours if the chips are kept at low temperatures. Residual data can be recovered using simple, nondestructive techniques that require only momentary physical access to the machine.

Halderman et al. present multiple attacks that can exploit physical access to DRAM with the goal of recovering cryptographic keys. For more details, see [HSH+08].

7.20 Implementation Errors and Unforeseen States

It is very difficult to write software free of errors or unexpected responses to unforeseen inputs. The variety and complexity of modern hardware/software combinations makes the notion of error-free systems utopian, to say the least. Readers following the science and technology section of any major news source these days would have the feeling that security holes or bugs, susceptible to be used by hackers, are discovered almost weekly in popular software applications. Computer system administrators and end users find it hard to keep up with the installation of a stream of security patches released by major software vendors.

One recent example of this is "Flaw in billions of Wi-Fi devices left communications open to eavesdropping" [Goo20]. The flaw affected "billions of devices." The good news is that, at the time of that article, many of the devices had already been patched. This speaks to the importance of keeping the operating systems of our computers, tablets, smart phones, etc., uptodate. But, how many of people regularly update the firmware on their Wi-Fi routers? A *zero day vulnerability* is a flaw in the software that it is unknown to the software vendors before it is being exploited to gain unauthorized access. If found by responsible, security researchers, these flaws are disclosed to the coders to be fixed within a grace period before the finding is made public. When found by black hat hackers, zero day flaws are typically used to compromise the security of computer systems for nefarious purposes or sold to a third party. Depending on the severity of the flaw and the popularity of the software, zero-day vulnerabilities can fetch high prices in the black market where the buyer could be organized crime actors or even intelligence agencies.

In *Small Business Information Security: The Fundamentals*, a National Institute of Standards and Technology (NIST) publication by Paulsen and Toth, [PT16], they note that,

> Vulnerabilities found in software applications are the most common avenue of attack for hackers.

Similarly, Richard Pethia, former Director of CERT, a division of Carnegie Mellon University's Software Engineering Institute, states in the Forward to Robert Seacord's important book [Sea13],

> Today, software vulnerabilities are being discovered at a rate of 4000 per year. These vulnerabilities are caused by software designs and implementations that do not adequately protect systems and by development practices that do not focus sufficiently on eliminating implementation defects that result in security flaws.

In the Preface to [Sea13], Seacord states, "Analysis of existing vulnerabilities indicates that a relatively small number of root causes accounts for the majority of vulnerabilities."

It is a fact of life that an army of hackers is working around the clock to find the next buffer overrun on popular software applications or how to fool operative systems into allowing malicious code to run undetected. Although it seems unfair, this situation is only to be expected. Many authors have already described the conflict between code-makers and code-breakers as an ongoing battle. Both sides know that any little advantage could tip the balance one way or the other.

Increasingly, artificial intelligence (AI) is being used to carry out attacks. Choudhury notes in [Cho19] that "Artificial intelligence used to carry out automated, targeted hacking is set to be one of the major threats to look out for in 2020, according to Etay Maor from IntSights." Choudhury also notes that, "With AI, an attacker can carry out multiple and repeated attacks on a network by programming a few lines of code to do most of the work."

From the cryptographical point of view, it is very important to know the implementation details for each particular algorithm, or at least to be confident that the necessary precautions had been taken at the moment of writing software. For implementations of standard algorithms such as RSA, Advanced Encryption Standard (AES), there is in place a validation program set up by the National Institute of Standards of Standards and Technology that ensures the compliance of the software to the corresponding FIPS[3] standard. From the commercial point of view, it is very important to achieve certification if one hopes to sell to governments or large organizations. New (or old) cryptographic methods, not covered by existing standards, cannot be certified under FIPS.

The FIPS certification gives some reassurance of quality to users of cryptographic modules. However, it does not guarantee that the underlying operative system or the network structure is secure. There are cases of features found in widespread applications that can be used to steal information from the victim's computer. For example, *Malone* can send *Alice* an innocent looking text file for review. Unknown to *Alice*, *Malone* added a special, legitimate instruction to embed a given file (or several files) to the document. When *Alice* opens the document for editing, the special, hidden field will embed the indicated files from *Alice's* computer without *Alice* ever knowing what is happening. When *Alice* returns the corrected file to *Malone*, the stolen files will be embedded in it, and *Malone* will have no problem retrieving the information. This technique works even if encryption is used to transmit the files back and forth.

As the industry pushes programmers and software engineers for more features in hardware/software, unforeseen states and responses leave open doors for **viruses**, **worms** and **trojan horses** that can take control or extract data from the victim's computer. Mobile phones are vulnerable to attacks as well, such as phishing voice calls ("vishing") and phishing text message ("smishing"), [RF11]. Defense against these types of threats has become a flourishing business with many companies dedicated to produce software and hardware able to stop the attacks. Above all, the best defense is to keep software

---

[3] Federal Information Processing Standards.

patches updated and be on the alert for new developments. All major antivirus software include links to a network of websites that keep user updated on current security threats. This is extremely important for cell phones as well, as cell phones increasingly contain a lot of personal information, including apps that might have access to financial records or health records.

System administrators need to be especially careful, as they have additional privileges that regular users do not have. If you own a laptop or desktop computer, then you are probably the system administrator for that computer. The code that system administrators run can alter the operating system and the files of other users. We need to be extremely careful if code takes input from outside sources, such as the Internet, but this is especially true for system administrators for the reasons just mentioned. Many pieces of malware are designed to search for administrative accounts or to elevate user accounts privileges by exploiting otherwise harmless flaws in software.

An example of a system administration program that takes input from users is a request for a login name and password. We note here that a malicious user might respond with undesirable input. For example, what happens if a particularly long string is entered as input? Is it possible that the software might run out-of-bounds of a data structure? What effect could that have? Different programming languages have different vulnerabilities because of the way in which they handle data input. Programmers need to be aware of the shortcoming each language has, in particular how strictly validation of input data and memory management is controlled at runtime. System administrators need to be particularly aware of such vulnerabilities peculiar to operating systems and database management software.

Section 1.5 of Robbins and Robbins' book, [RR03], gives a lot of important advice. It is worth reading that section (and the book!). In particular, they say,

> ... Unfortunately, most people learn to program for an environment in which programs are presented with correct or almost correct input ...
>
> Real-world programs, especially systems programs are often long-running and are expected to continue running after an error ...
>
> Long-running programs must release resources, such as memory, when these resources are longer needed. Often, programmers release resources such as buffers in the obvious places but forget to release them if an error occurs.
>
> ... the C run-time system does not complain if you modify a nonexistent array element – it writes values into that memory (which probably corresponds to some other variable). ... Because overwritten variables are so difficult to detect and so dangerous, newer programming languages, such as Java, have runtime checks on array bounds.

For any application with a user interface, investing effort in making the data input validation robust against errors and malicious attempts is a must, in particular in network-facing applications. On a desktop or laptop, creating an extra account or two can be helpful. You might create at least two system administration accounts and at least one regular user account. One system administration account is necessary for updating or modifying the operating system and for installing most software. A second system administration account can sometimes be very helpful if there are issues with the first one. For day-to-day use of your computer, use a regular user account whenever possible. If additional privileges are needed in order to install software, for example, then you'll need to use a system administrator account.

Why take this approach? Depending on the operating system, a regular user account might have far fewer privileges than a system administrator account. If so, then if you do something accidentally, or come across some unfriendly software, the nasty effects of the software will hopefully be limited to the resources accessible via that account.

Keep your operating system uptodate (this applies to your desktop and laptop computers, tablets, smart phones and watches, and your other devices). If the operating system is no longer being supported, then upgrade to a newer operating system (after first making copies of your files!).

7.21 Tracking. Bluetooth, WiFi, and Your Smart Phone

Your smart phone will let you make phone calls, send and receive text messages, audio and video conference, surf the web, and access an incredible variety of apps. Having WiFi turned on means that you can use WiFi to access some of these rather than using your cell phone data. Bluetooth is often used to allow communication between devices, such as that between a phone and wireless headphones.

If you walk around with Bluetooth and WiFi turned on, then others may track you. See [CBC14,Fun13], for example. Stores are interested in data – the more specific, the better. It might help them decide what items to stock, where to place certain items, what displays are effective, etc.

As you enter a store, they are interested in: How often do you visit the store? How long do you typically stay when you visit? How many items do you tend to buy? If you stood in front of a particular display, what did you buy afterwards? Cell phones and security cameras can help them to gather specific information about their shoppers. Turning off Bluetooth and WiFi before entering a store can limit the amount of data that they collect.

At the time of writing the Second Edition of this book, the world experienced the COVID-19 pandemic. In an effort to slow down the spread of the virus, government health authorities of several countries developed and implemented contact tracing applications that use Bluetooth signals to track whether the user was in close proximity to a person that tested positive for the virus that causes the illness. Although the technology is readily available for mass deployment in everybody's pocket, in many countries adoption of such systems were hampered by the obvious privacy concerns people have. Mandating the populace to download the application worked only in some countries and was vigorously opposed in others. Bluetooth is the best technology for the purposes of tracking contacts because it is predicated on the physical proximity of the devices for it to work.

Similar privacy concerns apply to any other commercial applications that can trace the location of an individual's phone, in particular when the information is stored in servers beyond the control of the individual and can be associated with the user. Disabling WiFi, Bluetooth, and NFC capabilities will hinder attempts to identify and track your steps (unless the cell phone company gets involved). It is also a good practice to disable wireless capabilities when you are traveling with a laptop. Rogue Wi-Fi routers can be setup to imitate the public credentials of legitimate open access routers to which your laptop has connected before, thus fooling your computer into connecting and sharing information. This attack is commonly called the *Evil Twin* or *Wifiphisher attack*.

7.22   Keep Up with the Latest Attacks (If You Can)

Keeping up with the latest attacks and security breaches on computers and IoT devices is a full-time job for a small team of researchers. It is not recommended for the average person to even try. However, because of its importance and the devastating consequences that a successful attack can have, the reader is encouraged to search for and follow one or more of the good online resources that provide timely and reliable information to stay out of trouble. Here we mention a handful of reliable and current sources: Schneier's "Crypto-Gram Newsletter" https://www.schneier.com/crypto-gram/ and SANS Institute's "OUCH! Newsletter" https://www.sans.org/security-awareness-training/ouch-newsletter, both are free and easy to subscribe to and easy to follow. Steve Gibson's "Security Now!" https://www.grc.com/securitynow.htm, one of the longest running podcasts on the subject, is a good source of up-to-date information and features extensive searchable archives. Kaspersky's "Threatpost podcasts" https://threatpost .com/category/podcasts/ carry up-to-the-minute information on cyberattacks. Due to the importance of the subject, the list of competent and, at times, entertaining shows on the subject grows by the day.

Chapter 8

Practical Issues in Modern Cryptography and Communications

Goals, Discussion   In real life, mathematical concepts are not the only factors to be considered in the design of communication systems. Systems intended for commercial, military, and governmental use interact with a variety of hardware and software applications, management systems, and data security policies. The systems must also be able to handle diverse networking protocols. We briefly describe here some of the principal issues.

New, Noteworthy   In this chapter, we discuss various practical issues which are of fundamental importance to the development and deployment of digital communication systems. The ideas expressed are based on our experience and industrial research.

8.1   Introduction

It is no secret that the volume of information transmitted over the Internet and the demand for connectivity have been explosively increasing over the last two decades and will continue at a sustained rate. To stay competitive and maintain revenues,

Cryptography, Information Theory, and Error-Correction: A Handbook for the 21st Century, Second Edition.
Aiden A. Bruen, Mario A. Forcinito, and James M. McQuillan.
© 2021 John Wiley & Sons, Inc. Published 2021 by John Wiley & Sons, Inc.

communication service providers are constantly looking at more effective ways to deliver a growing variety of data services. The above-mentioned growth in volume and complexity makes this task difficult. In particular, from the engineering point of view, as designs for hardware and software become more varied and complex, communication protocols have to be designed more carefully to meet the two competing goals of interoperability and security. In our experience in industry, we have found that in this complex and competitive environment some of the fundamental constraints are as follows:

- *Technical.* The system (hardware/software/protocol) must perform the task for which it was designed under a wide variety of conditions, many of which are beyond designers' control. The variety and complexity of modern systems often makes the task of designing them well beyond the abilities of code-developers.

- *Commercial.* The business model used to commercialize new applications must make sense. One of the golden rules of business (know thy customers) is sometimes forgotten in the excitement of developing new products or services. Equally damaging is the tendency to ignore the need for official validation or certification. This can make a product unacceptable for certain market segments, no matter how good it is technically.

- *Property rights.* Patents are essential to protect and commercialize any technological advantage. There are many lawyers who offer advice on patenting issues. However, the real value of a patent resides on having a good grasp of issues related to the **prior art**, the correct mathematics, and proper engineering practices, issues which are outside the field of expertise of most lawyers. It is your responsibility to make sure you have access to good technical advice on these aspects. Do not rely on lawyers or patent agents.

- *Legal.* The provision for encryption and protection of online services users' private data has now become the defacto standard without which it will be laughable to offer any kind of service over the Internet. This has serious, and sometime onerous, implications for the design and implementation of information systems, communications systems, and data repositories. Also, for auditing purposes for example, information may need to be stored for several years, bringing issues of robust file encryption to the forefront.

The above constraints should be taken into account in the design/development cycle. We will briefly outline some specific concerns and how to address them in this chapter. In the specific area of applications of encryption, the reader can consult Graff [Gra00] and Ferguson and Schneier [FS03].

8.2 Hot Issues

Perhaps the most important issue to be addressed by any system designer is that related to **user authentication**. Openness and accessibility are desirable characteristics for the legitimate user of a network, and a nightmare for administrators charged with the task of keeping out illegitimate users and attackers.

An adequate authentication system, if available, would solve the problem by admitting only those users that can produce the proper **credentials**. However, the implementation of an "adequate authentication system" is easier said than done. We have briefly described several systems for the authentication of network users by utilizing one form or another of encryption keys, usually known as **credentials**, in the technical jargon. Here we will give more details on the practical aspects.

To give the reader a brief overview, we will discuss below some of the topics that are generating intense debate and are relevant to the application of cryptography. Authentication is at the core of many of these unresolved problems. We start here with a brief summary of the subject and refer those interested in more details to the book by Smith [Smi02]. For related issues on e-commerce, see the book by Graff [Gra00].

8.3 Authentication

What is Authentication? In general, authentication has to do with protecting identity and privacy. For example, when withdrawing money from the bank or from an ATM machine, it is necessary to provide evidence (account number, PIN, bank card, etc.) that one is the legal owner of the bank account. Authentication is a key component for securing data and communication systems. Any failure of this component will invalidate even the best-designed encryption systems by allowing adversarial parties to access sensitive information or computer resources. Shortcomings of the authentication protocols and imperfections in its implementation are constantly being sought by hackers as the entry points for attacks. The vast majority of successful attacks can be traced to failures of the authentication system to stop unauthorized users to gain access privileges to malicious agents. Authentication is a vast subject, the large number of different authentication system and the wide variety of technologies used to achieve authentication deserve a few volumes of their own for a complete and deep treatment. This chapter should not be considered an exhaustive treatment of the subject, we are giving here an overview of the principles and a few practical notions that will orient the reader when looking for additional information. Due to the speed of technological change in this area, the interested reader is encouraged to visit on-line resources specialized in the subject to keep abreast of developments in this fascinating area. User authentication is based on one or more of the following:

1. Something you know, for example a password or PIN number.

2. Something you have, for example a smart card or an ATM card.

3. Something that is physically connected to the user such as biometrics, voice, hand-writing.

What are some of the advantages and disadvantages of the various authentication systems based on 1, 2, or 3 above?

For computer and network access, **passwords** have been the main tool for verifying identity and granting access. Indeed, around 99% of all computer identification operates by means of password authentication. There are many different kinds of password schemes and mechanisms. The potential weaknesses are well known. Also, passwords, if sent unencrypted, i.e. in plain-text over a network, are vulnerable to "sniffing attacks" (i.e. electronic interception).

Password guessing has become big business. Many web sites sell, for quite a modest price, password-cracking software. Frequently, but not always, password-cracking software is based on dictionary brute-force attack. The passwords dictionaries were compiled by hackers using simple statistical analysis of millions of passwords obtained from data breaches over the years, and they are publicly available on the Internet. Dictionary attacks work very well in practice because users tend to pick weak passwords that are easy to remember. As it was discovered, after hackers release 32 million passwords that were stored in plain text in Rockyou servers, "123456" was the most popular password protecting almost 300 000 user's accounts.

More mathematically sophisticated attacks are also used by password cracking software programs. Law-enforcement agencies make use of these commercially available programs for forensic work, whenever they need to decrypt confiscated files and cyber-criminals have been brought to justice because they reused credentials in more than one account. The security of a password is based on the **Shannon entropy** of the password. Shannon entropy is a measure of the difficulty in guessing the password. This entropy is measured in **Shannon bits**. For example, a random 10-letter English text would have an estimated entropy of around 15 Shannon bits, meaning that on average we might have to try $\frac{1}{2}(2^{15}) = 2^{14} = 16\,384$ possibilities to guess it. In practice, the number of attempts needed would be considerably less because of side information available and redundancy (= patterns and lack of randomness). A major weakness of passwords is that the entropy is usually too small for security since users cannot remember long passwords and also they are prone to use very well-known methods for constructing their passwords. It is wellknown to hackers that users commonly select passwords that include variations of the user name, make of the car they drive, name of some family member, etc. Additionally, 54% of consumers use five or fewer passwords for all of their accounts (see [NIS19a]) which gives hackers access to multiple accounts if they guess one password correctly. As we mentioned in Chapter 7, social engineering is one of the most powerful tools being used by hackers. To avoid these pitfalls, these simple rules are recommended: create strong passwords, use different passwords at different sites, use a password manager and use two-factor (or multifactor) authentication. What is a good way to choose a password that is both strong and easy to remember? One approach is as follows:

Remark 8.1 (Choosing a strong password) *Think of a sentence with at least eight words in it. Construct a password using the first letter from each of the words of the sentence, being sure to use at least one capital letter. Additionally, include at least one special character such as # or %, and at least one digit in the password. Make sure that your password has at least eight characters, or for a stronger password, at least 12 characters. Also, make sure that it is not similar to any word in the English dictionary, and that it does not include part of your name or some other thing that an adversary might be able to guess.*[1] *In addition, make sure to never reuse a password and never, ever, send a password in an e-mail message.*

When logging on to a remote server, passwords are also subjected to **sniffing** attacks whereby the attacker eavesdrops on the traffic between the user and the server and looks for occurrences of the password. Even if an encrypted version or the hash of the password is sent to the server, the attacker can use this information to log in by replaying this portion of data. To avoid these type of attacks, modern systems use a protocol based on **challenge and response** or encrypt the traffic using a protocol called **TLS** (Transport Layer Security). TLS works in the following way. The server sends the user its RSA public key, and the user then generates a secret random number and encrypt this number with the server's public key. The server decrypts and use the secret random number as a symmetric secret key for encryption. From this point on, all the traffic is encrypted and the authentication of the user can now proceed over an encrypted channel. To avoid the potential problem of an attacker setting up a fake server to obtain user information, "**Public Key Certificates**" issued by official **Certificate Authorities** are used to authenticate or validate the user to the server. See Chapter 3 for more information on TLS.

Concerning authentication based on "something you have," the most common method involves plastic cards with a magnetic stripe such as **ATM cards**, credit cards, drivers licenses. Some of the weaknesses are as follows: These cards can be transferred

---

[1] This strategy for choosing a strong password that is easy to remember was communicated to the third author by Michael Rodriguez, a former Chief Technology Security Officer at Western Illinois University.

to other individuals (by lending the card, losing it or having the card stolen), sometimes without the user's knowledge. Just as it is easy to copy keys, it is also very easy to copy such magnetic stripes. Unscrupulous personnel have been known to copy magnetic stripes using adhoc modified electronic readers or by installing malware on point of sales computers. Cards can also be cloned easily. PIN numbers, usually in the format of four-digit numbers, are easily guessed or surreptitiously recorded by hidden cameras located on top of point of sale terminals and should be protected by the user from the view of others when you enter it. The information on the magnetic tape or the chip can be retrieved by adversaries by using special (and inexpensive) hardware called "card skimmer" that need to be surreptitiously attached to the card reader. ATM machines and fuel pumps at gas stations are often targeted by hackers because they are easily accessible.

Some newer cards come with an additional embedded chip, which may or may not be used by the card reader. The chip contains information that is used by the reader to authenticate the card and the PIN entered by the use. It also has the ability to produce a unique, one-time-use cryptogram for each transaction, making it more secure than a magnetic stripe card.

Access cards can be classified within the general category of "security tokens," which includes any physical device that contains specific authentication information. Tokens can contain static data or they can perform complex functions such as the generation of a one-time cryptographic key for validation. They can also store biometric information such as hashed information for fingerprints or iris scans and some are designed to be tamper resistant. Many include a keypad to allow entry of a PIN, although the most common type includes a single button to activate the cryptographic data generating routine.

There are tokens that connect into the USB port of a computer and send the one-time key directly to the authentication server when the user press a button. Near-field communication (NFC), radio-frequency identification (RFID), or Bluetooth link are also used to connect the token to the computer. All active tokens use cryptographic techniques for authentication that are immune to sniffing attacks. Since they generate **one-time passwords** they are also immune to replay attacks.[2] Thus, it does an attacker no good to try to replay a previous message or set of messages. However, inevitably, they have weaknesses. Some of the devices are vulnerable to off-line attacks. There is also the fundamental "lost or stolen" problem. Also there is a security risk for a network based on the fact that the owner of the token can lend (or even sell) the token to unauthorized individuals. In some sense, these devices have the same weakness that PKI has. Here, PKI means "public key infrastructure," i.e. they keys, authentication protocols, etc. associated with systems using public key cryptography as explained in Chapters 3

---

[2] An attack in which the eavesdropper records the traffic and later forward the relevant information to gain access to the server.

and 4. Namely, one can only be confident, but not certain, that on the other side of the line, somebody has the authentication device, be it an electronic certificate (a file) or a token. However, one can never have the same level of confidence that the authentic user is there. When transactions involve legal or financial liability, trusting a device that can be stolen or lost it is a very risky proposition.

The so-called "soft tokens" are software-based security token applications that run on a smartphone and generate the one-time key to authenticate with the server. They leverage mobile phones computational power and their communication networks. A one-time key can be send to the phone by SMS, voice call or to an app that displays a QR code. Among the advantages of using mobile phones, the ubiquity of such devices make unnecessary to spend on adhoc pieces of hardware, users are almost guaranteed to carry the "token" at all times and reported its lost immediately. Software tokens are easier to distribute and update through an app.

Biometric authentication

Any characteristic uniquely associated with an individual and that can be discriminated by mechanical means, can be used for an authentication system. Such characteristics are commonly referred to as **biometrics**. The idea of using biometrics as an identification means is not new. In 1880, Dr. Henry Faulds published an article where he discussed fingerprints as a means of personal identification. He is also credited with the first fingerprint identification greasy fingerprint left on an alcohol bottle. The first documented use of a fingerprint to prevent document forgery was that by Gilbert Thompson of the US Geological Survey in 1882. By 1892, Sir Francis Galton, a cousin of Charles Darwin, published his book, *Fingerprints*, in which he established the individuality[3] and permanence of fingerprints as well as the first classification system for fingerprints. In the same year, the first criminal fingerprint identification was made by Juan Vucetich, an Argentine Police Official, who also began to systematically file the fingerprints of the general population as a mean of identification. Even today, some countries include a copy of a thumbprint on **ID cards**.

Newer technologies are able to recognize a person based on physical characteristics such as differences in the iris pattern, retina, facial features shape and size, voice, earlobes, and hand geometry. Continuously tracking behavior and user computer interaction including left/right handedness, hand tremors, and pressure, as well as cognitive factors, such as eye–hand coordination, usage preferences, and device interaction is being used to supplement other factors for authentication. Biometric authentication is taking off.

---

[3] According to his calculations, the odds of two individual fingerprints being the same were 1 in 64 billion.

Many smart phones offer facial recognition or fingerprint recognition as an alternative to a password for logging in. Biometrics devices are nowadays used for household entry in conjunction with other security measures. Airports are increasingly making use of biometric technology (see [Dav19,Eco18], for example). In the United States, several states such as California use biometric indicators such as fingerprints to authenticate individuals and trusted travellers programs use iris scans to identify and authorize passengers at member countries ports of entry. Some details of the process, involving the digitizing of fingerprints are described below. The process should satisfy several major requirements. Two of these requirements are as follows:

1. A detailed statistical analysis to ensure that the number of "false positives" and "false negatives" are minimized. This means that

   (a) another person's fingerprint will not be accepted and;

   (b) the valid owners fingerprint will be accepted by the validator checking the authentication.

2. The entropy of the digital signature is sufficiently high (as measured in Shannon bits) that it is not vulnerable to attack.

Biometrical devices are not vulnerable to "transference" (the "lost or stolen" syndrome). Theoretically, biometric devices are vulnerable to forgery. For example, a thumbprint could be copied to a plastic mold. However, this is much more difficult than stealing a smart card or guessing a password. We should point out that in the case when biometric readers are physically attached to the computer a viable attack can be launched whereby the attacker makes a mold of the user's fingerprint and uses it to gain access in the absence of the user. The main impediment to the adoption of a biometric solution might be an individual's concern that the biometric data could fall into the wrong hands. However, with proper cryptographic techniques and security policies in place, this concern can be allayed.

For example, FIPS 201-2 and related Standards,[4] define procedures for the lifecycle management of biometric and personal verification information. Activities covered include identity proofing, registration, credential issuance and re-issuance, chain-of-trust operations, and credential usage, as well as the guidelines for cryptographic protection of the biometric data.

---

[4] FIPS 201 Personal Identity Verification (PIV) for Federal Employees and Contractors, http://dx.doi.org/ 10.6028/NIST.FIPS.201-2.

Two-factor authentication (2FA) and multifactor authentication (MFA)

These are obtained by combining two or more well-established authentication techniques, i.e. biometric signatures and event-synchronization. If an unauthorized user, denoted by **X**, by a stroke of fortune, guesses the biometric signature, he still has to guess the number in the events counter. Moreover, in the statistical sense, these guesses are independent and so provide mathematically independent authentication guarantees. To illustrate this point, suppose that the probability of **X** guessing the biometric signature is unrealistically high, say 0.001, i.e. **X** succeeds once in every 1000 trials. Similarly, assume that the probability of **X** guessing the number in the event counter is 0.003. Then, because the two methodologies are working independently, the probability of guessing both simultaneously is only 0.000003, i.e. 3 out of 1 000 000, which is a dramatic reduction in the probability of a malfunction. This applies also to the security. If there is a 1 in 1000 chance to break one method of authentication and 3 in 1000 of break a second, independent method of authentication, there will be only 3 in 1 000 000 chances of breaking a system that combines the two methods. Indeed, there is no doubt that employing biometrics dramatically increases authentication levels over devices where the ownership can be transferred. For organizations with authentication concerns for their communications and network devices, we recommend that at least two-factor authentication should be the standard.

Multifactor authentication decreases the chances of misidentification even further by factoring in additional independent probabilities. The system thus become tolerant to faults on any single authentication method. Systems using MFA are said to have **strong authentication**.

The use of strong authentication based on MFA is being touted as the solution to the problem with password authentication. The perception among industry analysts is that about 80% of the data breaches can be traced to problems with passwords and elimination of password for authentication have been a long time held aspiration by many. In February 2013, after a few years of preparation, the FIDO Alliance (Fast IDentity Online) was launched by a group of companies[5] with vested interest in easy to use and strong user authentication. The FIDO Alliance[6] mandate is the development of standard-based open authentication protocols and in the short years since its creation, it has attracted the attention of government agencies, mayor computer manufacturers, software companies and Internet, and communication service providers.

---

[5] Agnitio, Infineon Technologies, Lenovo, Nok Nok Labs, PayPal, and Validity.
[6] https://fidoalliance.org/what-is-fido/.

Their authentication paradigms are based on a standardized architecture that authenticate the user with respect to the local device (e.g. laptop, phone) and communicate with the server by means of a secure cryptographic protocol. The authentication server provides the credentials necessary for the local device to access the requested service without the need for the user credentials or personal information to leave the local device. If in the local authentication is biometric, the FIDO paradigm has the advantage that there is no need for biometric template to be stored on the server, reducing potential threads to privacy.

At the time of writing the FIDO2 specifications, they were adopted by the World Wide Web Consortium's as the Web Authentication specification and FIDO Alliance's corresponding Client-to-Authenticator Protocol (CTAP).

One of the latest trends on authentication is the so-called **Contextual Authentication**. It uses the information that is present in the signals exchanged between the authentication server and the user device as part of the authentication protocol to establish contextual information such as IP address, geo-location tags, and time-stamps. This information is stored and aggregated by the server to be used as a baseline to detect irregularities and anomalies in later exchanges. Thus, if a transaction request has some anomaly, i.e. a credit card transaction request coming from a town far away from the user's registered places, the system will flag this as potentially fraudulent and can take actions to further validate the user or denied access.[7] All this is transparent to the user (normally hidden from view) and helps to prevent unauthorized access in certain situations. It has the drawback that this contextual information, if leaked, will be extremely valuable to attackers. We will not recommend this method to be used as a single factor authentication, however, a strong authentication can be built by using contextual authentication of a secondary device that the user is supposed to carry, such as a mobile phone, as another factor of a MFA system.

The latest news related to Internet security (or lack thereof) leads us to believe that one-step authentication with a username and password is well past its due date and is totally inadequate to support an increasing demand for on-line services.

8.4   User Anonymity

The use of encryption methods does not guarantees anonymity. Even if Alice and Bob can exchange secret messages between them, it will not be too hard for Eve to find out that Alice and Bob are communicating, or how much or how often. This knowledge gives Eve a positive advantage to guess the nature and content of Alice and Bob exchanges. Personal

---

[7] Readers using Google services are certainly familiar with the notification that a "new" device logged in to the account.

safety and privacy concerns sometimes require that the parties communicating be at the same time authenticated between them while the fact that they are communicating remain hidden to third parties. Cryptographic protocols provide a way to achieve these seemingly opposite requirements. One way to achieve both has been implemented in practice by **The Onion Routing** protocol (TOR). It has been implemented as a free service over a voluntary network of connected servers that advertise their cryptographic credentials to all the users on the network; it enables users to communicate without being seen by third parties. In simple terms, the Onion Routing works as follows: Alice wants to communicate with Bob without Eve's knowledge; To do so, Alice selects a random route (or circuit) of n servers belonging to the network, $(\mathbf{OS_1}, \mathbf{OS_2}, \dots, \mathbf{OS_n})$; Alice encrypts her message (including headers) M with Bob's key M' and creates a duple $\langle M' - \text{Bob IP address} \rangle$ and encrypts it with the key for $\mathbf{OS_n}$; then it encrypts the result together with the IP address of $\mathbf{OS_n}$ with the key for server $\mathbf{OS_{n-1}}$; the process is repeated until the message is encrypted using the key for $\mathbf{OS_1}$; Alice sends the message to $\mathbf{OS_1}$ that decrypts the message and reads the address of the next server in the circuit $\mathbf{OS_2}$; $\mathbf{OS_1}$ forwards this message to server $\mathbf{OS_2}$ that repeats the process of decryption and forwarding to the next server in the circuit. The process ends when the last server decrypts the message and finds Bob address, the message is forwarded to him that can decrypt it and find out it is from Alice. Bob can follow the same protocol using a different circuit than Alice. None of the routers in the network can decrypt the message nor can they get the addresses of the two endpoints of the communication. TOR is susceptible to end-to-end timing attacks. In this attack, Eve can watch the traffic coming out of Alice's computer and also the traffic arriving at Bob's computer. Using statistical analysis of the timing between arrival of messages at both ends, Eve can find out whether they are part of the same circuit. In practice, TOR type protocols direct traffic through a free, worldwide, volunteer network. These networks can consist of thousands of relay servers, and the more they get used, the more difficult is to find out a user's location or usage through network traffic analysis.

8.5 E-commerce

Worldwide retails sales through e-commerce were a staggering 3.53 trillion US dollars in 2019, and e-retail revenues are projected to grow to 6.54 trillion US dollars in 2022.[8] At this pace, it is expected that e-commerce will represent about 22% of all retail sales by the year 2023, with the consequential reshaping of the retail business landscape at the

---

[8] https://www.statista.com/statistics/379046/worldwide-retail-e-commerce-sales/.

global scale. PayPal (one of the main payment processing companies) had well over 300 Million active accounts at the end of 2019.

On the technical side, data encryption, authentication, message integrity, and nonre-pudiation are essential for on-line commerce. The spread of E-commerce and the amounts of money that are in play are making identity theft, either by eavesdropping on legit-imate transactions, exploitation of security holes in the Internet browsers and servers, viruses, trojan horses, spy-ware or the so-called **phishing**,[9] a big problem. Research firm Gartner estimates that 57 million Americans in the past year received phishing e-mail messages. Gartner estimates that phishing related fraud cost banks and credit-card com-panies about $1.2 billion in direct losses in the last year alone. The cost to businesses, of all these attacks combined, amounts to many billions of dollars a year.

Individuals need to be wary of phishing attacks as well. An adversary might send you a message via e-mail, text message, or a traditional phone call that makes it look like or sound like they work for a company that you know or trust. They might tell you that there is a "problem with your account," or that you won something. They just need some personal information to proceed. With personal information, they might try to sell it, or illegally open credit card accounts and loans in your name, for example. For more examples of phishing, see [RNGC19]. The Federal Trade Commission's Consumer Information website notes that, "The FBI's Internet Crime Complaint Center reported that people lost $30 million to phishing schemes in one year" [FTC19].

More secure technologies for on-line transactions need to be implemented at all levels, from secure protocols to secure applications and better authentication methods, designed with security in mind. Indeed, problems such as e-mail spam cannot be solved unless the Internet protocol is modified in such a way as to force every packet of data to have a valid return address.

8.6 E-government

Another emerging area of communications that is quickly expanding and for which data security and strong authentication are fundamental, is the so-called **e-government**, that is, all the on-line exchanges between any level of government and its citizenry. Trans-actions can be of different kinds. The simplest and most frequent case is the searching for information about services or the downloading official forms from a government web-site. Transactions such as renewing a driver's license, responding to jury summons and answering preliminary questions, changing an address with a government agency, such as the post office, and having it disseminated automatically to all specified government

---

[9] The technique known as phishing is often based on fraudulent e-mail sent to lure people to phony Web sites asking for financial information.

agencies, are often more convenient for both the government and the public if carried out on-line. More complex transactions such as those involving the exchange of sensitive information (i.e. filing taxes on-line or exchanging health records) are becoming common as well. Some other transactions, such as on-line voting, have proven very difficult to implement giving the current state of the technology. For example, in a 90-day period near the end of 2019, there were 3.58 billion visits to US government websites [USA19]. In the United States, the 2020 Census will be the first time that people have the opportunity to respond online, which has been the case in Canada since 2006. Mobile phones can be used as well [USC19].

A national **ID card** system would be necessary for more complex transactions, but such an idea has proven controversial. The majority of users in the United States and Canada oppose this idea, although there is more support for such a system in many European countries.

If a system such as **PKI** is used for this purpose, the normal ID card can be replaced by a smart card with built-in public keys and corresponding electronic certificates issued by the government (which will play the role of the Certificate Authority). However, as noted in a 2003 GAO report,[10] there are serious logistical problems for the deployment of PKI within large organizations such as the federal government. The deployment of such systems in the general population will be even more difficult. In particular, the general population must be given sufficient training on key use, management, and protection issues. As electronic transactions are much easier to track by automatic means, concerns about the invasion of citizen privacy may prove to be the most difficult obstacle for widespread adoption of e-government. The only viable route for the introduction of e-government might be a system that rewards the voluntary and incremental adoption of electronic IDs by interested users.

One example of ID cards is driver's licenses in the United States. In some states, both "REAL ID" drivers licenses and those that are not REAL ID compliant are available. There are advantages, however, to having a REAL ID one. The Department of Homeland Security notes on their website [DHS19] that, "The Transportation Security Administration is reminding travelers that beginning October 1, 2020, every traveler must present a REAL ID-compliant driver's license, or another acceptable form of identification, to fly within the United States."

Another hot issue closely related to the government is the possibility of casting electronic votes. Such a system would encourage more people to participate in the democratic process, be it in electing representatives or in referendums on important issues. It would also make vote-counting faster, cheaper, and more accurate.

---

[10] General Accounting Office, Status of Federal PKI Activities 2003, http://www.gao.gov/new.items/d04157 .pdf.

Currently, there is no single scheme or technology proposed that can meet the required anonymity, authorization, and transparency at the scale of a Country. However, based in advances on BlockChain and PKI systems, some researchers are predicting the advent of workable solutions over the next decade [Orm19].[11]

Many states in the United States already allow some form of on-line voting. In a 2016 article, [Hor16] they quote Neil Jenkins, from the Office of Cybersecurity and Communications at the Department of Homeland Security, as saying, "We believe that online voting, especially online voting in large scale, introduces great risk into the election system by threatening voters' expectations of confidentiality, accountability and security of their votes and provides an avenue for malicious actors to manipulate the voting results." It is easy to see why this is a difficult problem. There are many requirements. Some of them are the following: It is crucial, of course, to ensure that the software used is correct. If someone votes, that vote/message should arrive at its destination and be counted exactly once and correctly. There are additional requirements. If someone votes, it is necessary to determine that they are a registered voter and that they are not somehow voting for someone else. It is also necessary to ensure that no one votes multiple times. Also, it is necessary to ensure that afterwards, it is impossible for anyone to determine who or what a particular individual voted for. It is also important that the software being used is self-explanatory enough that the voter doesn't accidentally spoil their ballot, and then, because noone can vote multiple times, not be able to go back and correct whatever mistake they made. Blockchains might be very helpful with some of these issues. See [Orm19]. They note that West Virginia and Denver, CO, are both experimenting with a mobile voting app that uses blockchains. Blockchains are discussed in detail in Chapter 26.

8.7   Key Lengths

There is a lot of contradictory information coming from vendors on the length of keys needed to ensure adequate security. This is of particular concern to public key systems, Rivest–Shamir–Adleman (RSA), or Elliptic Curve Cryptography (see Chapters 3 and 4). Proponents of the different algorithms regularly arrange public challenges, offering monetary rewards to the first that can break a cipher obtained with a given key-length. The value of such challenges is dubious at best. There is no easy answer to the question of how long the key must be; it all depends on the particulars of each implementation. Unfortunately, in this particular aspect, the best advice is *caveat emptor*! It should be borne in mind that an institution whose security has been breached may not wish to publicize this. On the other hand, the attacker also may want to keep a good thing going and restrain to reveal its advantage.

---

[11] The US Defense Department's Defense Advanced Research Projects Agency (DARPA) has destined 10 Million USD to build an open source, secure voting system https://www.vice.com/en_us/article/yw84q7/darpa-is-building-a-dollar10-million-open-source-secure-voting-system.

8.8 Digital Rights

The most popular web-based businesses are centered around the selling of any kind of content in digital format on-line, as there is no need for physical exchange of goods. Content, be it text, software, music, films, TV, etc., can be downloaded by the buyer from the server and paid through an electronic money transfer, giving the buyer the advantages of convenience and instant gratification and eliminating the cost to the seller of maintaining and transporting physical inventories.

Indeed, the publishing, music recording, and motion pictures industries have invested heavily in on-line content, with streaming of video and audio commonplace. The ability to watch, listen, or read your favorite movie, show, song whenever and wherever you are is an enormous advantage. Video rental stores have disappeared. One of the main requirements is that of restricting the unauthorized access and reproduction of the content once it is off-line. The problem is akin to that of authentication. Many streaming services allow you to download content for off-line viewing, while some others still do not allow this feature.

Digital rights management (DRM) is a very divisive issue because the rights that the content owner chooses to grant are not necessarily the same as the actual legal rights of the content consumer. Opponents claim that digital restrictions management is a more accurate description of the real functionality.

Attempts to prevent unauthorized access to content that has been delivered using some other electronic channels such as radio and satellite signals have the same type of technical and management problems. In some jurisdictions, it is illegal to receive satellite broadcasts from certain providers, even if the equipment and the content were purchased from the provider.

In lieu of technically feasible solutions that work with the variety of recording/reproducing systems available in the market, publishing industries have resorted to the enforcement of stricter copyright laws such as the **Digital Millennium Copyright Act** (DMCA) which make the attempt of circumventing digital protection systems illegal. Thus, the publishers are mainly relying on the justice system to fight unauthorized access and reproduction of copyrighted material.

8.9 Wireless Networks

Wireless LANs have experienced an explosive growth and are pervasive everywhere. The reader will be hard-pressed to think of a spot without wireless network coverage of one way or another. WiFi hot-spots can be found at stores, cafés, airports, and libraries. Even high-end cars and planes have their own wireless network to provide connectivity to passenger's devices. And we have a plethora of such devices; phones, watches, tablets, and laptops that can access the Internet using WiFi.

There are certain differences between **Wireless Wide Area Network** (WAN) and **Wireless Local Area Network** (LAN) or **Wireless Personal Area Network** (PAN) technologies. However, from the security point of view, the problem of keeping data secure while it is being transmitted is a common one for any kind of wireless network.

Some quick facts about Internet use (see [Pew19a] and [Pew19b]) include the following:

1. Nine in ten American adults use the Internet.

2. Approximately three-quarters of them have broadband Internet at home.

3. Three-quarters of US adults have a desktop or laptop, and half own a tablet.

4. 81% of Americans have a smartphone.

5. Smart phones are now so fast and powerful that one in five American adults use their smart phone for accessing the Internet and do not have home broadband service in addition to their phone.

Be extra careful if you are using public WiFi. If this is something that you do often, you might consider subscribing to a **virtual private network** (**VPN**) that you trust to give you extra security. Many companies offer VPNs to their employees for work-related tasks. You should strongly consider using them for work-related tasks when you are away from your company's networks. When using wireless communication, encryption is essential in keeping your data safe. Make sure that websites that you visit start with "https" rather than "http," especially if you are accessing anything that you don't want. For additional tips, see [FCC19,PT16]. You should set your wireless router to use **WiFi Protected Access 2** (**WPA2**) with the Advanced Encryption Standard (AES) for encryption. See [PT16]. Do **NOT** use Wired Equivalent Privacy, WEP as it is no longer considered to be secure.

8.10   Communication Protocols

Internet traffic moves over a heterogeneous media. Physically, signals that represent bits move over copper wires, optic fiber, and air. Logically, bits move across a variety of platforms, ranging from cell-phones to supercomputers, which invariably have different ways to encode information. The fundamental parts that make all these systems work together and transport the information without errors is what we call **communication**

protocols such as the **TCP/IP** protocol. These protocols need to be sanctioned as standards, so manufacturers of communication hardware and software developers can produce equipment that works within a common framework. In particular, the Internet Standards are normative specifications of methodologies applicable to the Internet. Internet Standards are created and published by the Internet Engineering Task Force (IETF),[12] an open standards organization, which develops and promotes voluntary Internet standards, in particular the standards that comprise the Internet protocol suite (TCP/IP).

One of the protocols that works for the basic layer of data transport is the **ATM** (Asynchronous Transfer Mode) that parses the information into a fixed-size cell for transport across the network. This protocol developed in the late 1980 supports voice, video, and data simultaneously, and it is used for applications that need fast transmission. ATM technology was eventually superseded by Internet Protocol (IP)-only technology. The **IP** is the most widely adopted data transport protocol that routes packet by including network, source, and destination information together with the data. It traces its origins to a 1974 paper by Cerf and Kahn [CK74] and its underlaying features proved very adaptable over the last several decades.

The Bluetooth protocol, which is used for wireless communication between devices over short distances has been widely adopted by "smart"[13] devices and peripherals. The protocol, initially developed as a wireless alternative to RS-232, a serial communication protocol introduced in 1960, is used by a growing list of small devices to communicate sound, video, and data over a "wireless personal area network" (WPAN) built around a computer or a mobile phone. The protocol has been designed to work with low-power devices. The Bluetooth Special Interest Group (SIG) oversees the development of standards and licensing of the technology (already in its core specification version 5.2 at the time of writing). There have been many security concerns affecting the protocol over the years. In 2017, NIST released a Special Publication[14] that provides information on the security capabilities of Bluetooth devices and gives recommendations on securing them effectively.

The protocols used for exchanging communication are in themselves codes. In a sense, an encrypted message sent over a **TCP/IP** connection can be considered as a code riding on top of another code. Nothing prevents us from designing a protocol (code) that can provide transport, error correction encryption, and compression of the message. It is also desirable to have standard protocols that can be adhered to by all the players in the communication industry. Hybrid protocols have been developed, for example, **IPSEC**,

---

[12] https://ietf.org/standards/.

[13] More details about smart devices are provided in Chapter 27.

[14] NIST Special Publication 800-121 Revision 2, Guide to Bluetooth Security (https://doi.org/10.6028/NIST.SP.800-121r2).

to address the inherent security weaknesses of the IP protocol, which was not designed with security concerns in mind.

At the time of writing of this chapter, new communication protocols that work on and take advantage of specific features of Quantum Networks are being proposed and actively developed by researchers [DdOFH+19].

Parts II and III of this book address information theory and error-correction, both of which are integral to modern secure communications.

Part II

Mainly Information Theory

Chapter 9

Information Theory and its Applications

Goals, Discussion We present a fairly complete but accessible survey of the subject involving ideas from mathematics, physics, and engineering. Not much mathematical background is required.

New, Noteworthy We briefly discuss two of the main results from information theory relating to source coding and channel capacity for transmission. Shannon's bandwidth-limited theorem for the capacity in bits/second of continuous channels is covered in Chapter 11. (One can usually think of a bit either as an abstract unit of information or as an electronic storage bit.) We also explain a connection between weighing problems and information theory in Section 9.8. We show in Section 9.4 how information theory can be used in a fundamental way in cryptography. Connections between physics and information theory are touched upon. We refer here also to Pierce [Pie79, pp. 184–207] for a discussion of entropy in statistical physics and information theory.

Cryptography, Information Theory, and Error-Correction: A Handbook for the 21st Century, Second Edition.
Aiden A. Bruen, Mario A. Forcinito, and James M. McQuillan.
© 2021 John Wiley & Sons, Inc. Published 2021 by John Wiley & Sons, Inc.

9.1   Axioms, Physics, Computation

Information theory can be approached from many different points of view. It has many strands. In some treatments, it is an arcane mathematical subject concerned with axioms, measure theory, and abstract probability theories. In other treatments, it is described in terms of formulae that are the underpinnings of practical questions in modern communication theory in science and engineering. To others, it is a subject that is inextricably linked with physics, notably statistical physics, heat, energy, and the theory of computation as in Feynman [Fey00]. Another approach is to tie the subject to complexity and randomness as developed by Solomonoff, Kolmogorov, Chaitin, and others. In this chapter, we will try to touch on some of these ideas.

As pointed out in Chapter 3, the subject has been dominated by Claude Shannon for over 50 years, but there have been new applications and developments. For example, in nanotechnology, the parallel theory of quantum information is coming to the fore Nielsen and Chung [NC10]. In this book, we present, in Part III, new applications of information theory to cryptography. In particular, in Chapter 25, we use a result on entropy to obtain new identities for the Shannon function.

Basically, information theory has to do with converting knowledge about probabilities to **Shannon bits**. Ideas of randomness and redundancy follow closely. Rather than launching into definitions we first skirmish, informally, with some ideas.

9.2   Entropy

We start off with numbers. Any positive integer such as 43 can be expressed uniquely as $3 \times 10^0 + 4 \times 10^1 = 43$ using the powers of ten, but we can use any other base, or number system, such as binary. For example, in binary, 43 can be written as the binary string of length 6 given by 101011. To explain this, we have $43 = 3 \times 10^0 + 4 \times 10^1$ if we read from the right. Also, reading from the right, $43 = 1 \times 2^0 + 1 \times 2^1 + 0 \times 2^2 + 1 \times 2^3 + 0 \times 2^4 + 1 \times 2^5$.

Now, suppose we are told that a given number is written as a binary string of length 6, and we are asked to guess that number. What are our chances of success? The total number of possibilities is 64, ranging from the number 0 to the number 63. To see this, the rightmost slot can be filled in two ways, and similarly for all the other slots. Thus, we have $2 \times 2 \times 2 \times 2 \times 2 \times 2 = 64$ possibilities, ranging from 0 to 63, since $2^6 = 64$. So our probability of success in guessing is $\frac{1}{64}$. In general, if the binary string is of length n, i.e. has n bits, each of which is chosen independently, randomly deciding between 0 and 1 at each stage, there would be 2^n possible numbers from which to choose. But, n

binary digits can indicate any one of 2^n possible numbers. In this case, the **uncertainty** or **entropy** of the string is defined to be n since $n = \log(2^n)$. In this book, log invariably means log to the base 2. In general, we can say that, for a binary string, with all strings equally likely to occur, we have

$$entropy = \log\ (number\ of\ possible\ strings) \tag{9.1}$$

Getting back to the case $n = 6$, the number of possible numbers or outcomes would be reduced if we had some extra algebraic information. For example, if we knew that the six bits $a_5, a_4, a_3, a_2, a_1, a_0$ added up to zero with addition in binary, i.e. $a_5 + a_4 + a_3 + a_2 + a_1 + a_0 = 0$ (mod 2), then any one of the six bits, for example the sixth bit, is **redundant**. It can be calculated from the other five bits and thus causes no extra uncertainty. In this case, the string of length 6 is **less random** than before. The entropy now is just 5. So we have roughly three principles:

$$
\begin{array}{lll}
Entropy & = & Randomness \\
Entropy & = & Uncertainty \\
Redundancy & = & Lack\ of\ Randomness
\end{array}
$$

But now, suppose we just have some **probabilistic** knowledge of the binary sequence. For example, suppose we know that the probability of getting 1 in any bit is equal, say, to 0.85, independent of the other bits. In other words, for each bit a "free choice" is made as to the content, be it 1 or 0, apart from the condition that, overall, a one is chosen with probability 0.85. What are the possibilities now? What is the entropy? This is a very special case of one of the problems solved by Shannon.

Of course, all 2^n binary strings are still possible. For a string of length n, the average number of ones appearing will be $n(0.85)$. However, in all probability, only a **typical sequence** will materialize and the probability of a **nontypical sequence** will tend to zero as n gets large. For example, suppose $n = 100$. In this case, the number of typical sequences is about 2^{61} (see below — this section — for details). Since $\log_2(2^{61}) = 61$, the entropy of a typical binary sequence of length 100 (which would be 100 if the sequence were random) is now just 61.

Let us explain. The **Shannon function** $H(p)$ is defined as follows:

$$H(p) = p \log\left(\frac{1}{p}\right) + q \log\left(\frac{1}{q}\right) = -[p \log p + q \log q] \tag{9.2}$$

where $q = 1 - p$ and logs are to the base 2. If $p = 0.85$, then $H(0.85)$ is about 0.61 and $100H(0.85)$ is about 61. (See the Entropy Table in Appendix B.)

A rough sketch of $H(p)$ is as follows:

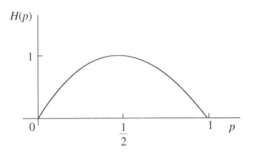

From the diagram, we see that $H(p) \leq H(\frac{1}{2}) = 1$. Since $p = 0.85$, the average number of ones in a binary sequence of length 100 is $100 \times 0.85 = 85$. *We define a typical sequence here to be one in which the total number of 1s is close to 85.* The details are in Chapter 12. *Shannon's work on entropy, as indicated below, implies that the number of typical sequences will be, in this case, about* $2^{nH(p)} = 2^{100 \times 0.61} = 2^{61}$.

In this particular case, we can get an idea as to why this is so without explicitly using Shannon's work, as follows. As indicated above, the number of 1s on average is np, where p is the probability of a one appearing. To make life easy, we assume np is an integer like 85 in the above. Then the number of sequences of length n that have exactly np 1s is the binomial coefficient $\binom{n}{np}$.

We just choose the np out of n positions where we want the 1s to appear. If we take the log of this number to the base 2, then, when n is large the log to the base 2 of $\binom{n}{np}$ is approximately $nH(p)$ which is the number of "typical sequences." So we are choosing from $\binom{n}{np}$ equally likely possibilities. Thus, the entropy is $\log_2 \binom{n}{np} \approx nH(p)$. The proof uses an approximation for binomial coefficients known as Stirling's expansion. The details are in Feynman [Fey00].

In summary then, the entropy has been reduced from n to $nH(p)$.

9.3 Information Gained, Cryptography

Let us look at this from another point of view. Suppose that cryptographic station **A** is sending a secret message M to cryptographic station **B** in the form of a binary string of length n. Let us assume that an eavesdropper E (for Eve) by listening has acquired sufficient information that E knows each bit that **A** has transmitted, independently, with a probability of 0.85. How much information about M does E really have?

Compare the string that E has with that of **A**. The probability that E has the right bit is $p = 0.85$. Thus, E knows that with high probability, as above, the total number of strings from which the message M has been chosen is about $2^{nH(p)}$. The calculation is as above. The probability of "getting 1" is analogous, for Eve, to getting "Yes" for a bit, where "Yes" means that E and $\mathbf{A}$ agree in that bit. Thus, from the point of view of E, the number of possible strings from which the message M has been chosen has been reduced from 2^n to about $2^{nH(p)}$. Therefore, the entropy has been reduced from n to $nH(p)$ $(= \log_2(2^{nH(p)}))$. Thus, the loss of uncertainty is $n - nH(p) = n(1 - H(p))$. Therefore, the **gain in information** that E has is $n(1 - H(p))$. When $n = 100, p = 0.85$, Eve gets about $100(1 - 0.61) = 39$ units of information.

Here we are coming very close to the idea of channel capacity. This was mentioned in the Preface and comes in again in the last chapter.

We can look at it this way. On average, Eve will agree with $\mathbf{A}$ in 85 positions. However, because she does not know where the corresponding positions of agreement are, Eve only knows "with certainty" about 39 units of information. We record the following principle: *Entropy Reduced = Uncertainty Removed = Information Gained.*

Definitions

It is high time to give some definitions. Suppose that we have a probability space with probabilities $p_1, p_2, \ldots, p_m$. For example, we might be rolling a fair die, so $m = 6$, $p_1 = p_2 = \cdots = p_6 = \frac{1}{6}$. The individual probabilities always lie between 0 and 1 and add up to 1. We define the **entropy**, following Shannon, as follows:

$$H(p_1, p_2, \ldots, p_m) = p_1 \log\left(\frac{1}{p_1}\right) + p_2 \log\left(\frac{1}{p_2}\right) + \cdots + p_m \log\left(\frac{1}{p_m}\right) \quad (9.3)$$

Examples

If we roll a fair die so that $p_1 = p_2 = \cdots = p_6 = \frac{1}{6}$, then $H = \log 6 = 2.59$. To give another example, suppose we are tossing a coin in which the probability of getting heads is p. Then, $H(p, 1 - p)$ is frequently abbreviated to $H(p)$, where $H(p)$ is the Shannon function (Section 9.2, see the graph). If $p = 0.85$, we get $H(0.85)$ which is equal to 0.61 approximately. Then $H(0.85)$ is the amount of entropy or uncertainty we have about the result of the coin toss *before* the toss. We can also think of $H(0.85)$ as the amount of information received *after* the toss, i.e. the amount of information received when the outcome of the toss is revealed.

Suppose that $p = \frac{1}{2}$. Then

$$H\left(\frac{1}{2}, \frac{1}{2}\right) = H\left(\frac{1}{2}\right) = \frac{1}{2}\log 2 + \frac{1}{2}\log 2 = 1 \quad (9.4)$$

This is taken as the unit of information: it is one Shannon bit. As Golomb et al. [GBC⁺02] eloquently puts it: A **Shannon bit** "is the amount of information gained (or entropy removed) upon learning the answer to a question whose two possible answers were equally likely, a priori." With this measure, when the die is rolled as above, a knowledge of the outcome reveals 2.59 Shannon bits of information.

This connection between entropy and "yes or no" questions also suggests the following principle:

Entropy = number of yes or no questions needed, on average, to determine the outcome of an experiment.

Another approach to information and entropy is as follows. Think of information as "surprise." If the probability p of an event is small, then $\frac{1}{p}$ is big so we receive a big surprise if the event occurs. Actually, it is more convenient to work with $\log(\frac{1}{p})$ rather than $\frac{1}{p}$. Another idea is to think of $\log(\frac{1}{p})$ as **the information content** of the event. The formula above for entropy suggests another principle:

Entropy = Average Surprise = Average Information Content.

If p is small, $\log(\frac{1}{p})$ is big, but the product $p\log(\frac{1}{p})$ balances things out in the product when calculating H. In the coin-tossing experiment above, when $p = 0.85$ the entropy $H(0.85)$ is around 0.61. How does one talk about 0.61 questions? The solution is to use "block coding" whereby we toss the coin n times and determine the outcome of the n tosses with about $nH(0.85)$ questions. We can also identify tossing a coin n times with our previous discussion of the entropy of a binary string of length n.

(Note that a "bit" can mean a binary digit with values 0 or 1 or a "Shannon bit," i.e. a unit of information.)

As above, $H(p) = H(p, 1 - p)$ is the information revealed by knowledge of the outcome of one experiment, where p is the probability of getting "heads" or by being informed that a one is in a given position in a binary string. Then, if we perform either experiment n times independently, the information revealed by the outcome is $nH(p)$.

In general, for a binary string of length n, with the probability of getting 1 in any given position being some number p, $0 \le p \le 1$, the entropy or uncertainty removed or information gained upon learning what the string is will be bounded as follows: $0 \le nH(p) \le n$. In this case, we see an example of the following principle:

The entropy or information content of a binary string of n bits is at most n Shannon bits and is at least 0 bits (since entropy is always nonnegative).

9.4   Practical Applications of Information Theory

Data compression

Suppose that we want to transmit a file consisting of 1000 characters. Each character is one of five possibilities, say $A, B, C, D,$ or E. Altogether, the symbols A, B, C, D, E appear

400 times, 200 times, 150 times, 150 times, and 100 times, respectively. We want to encode each symbol as a binary string in such a way that the resulting binary "superstring" corresponding to the file is as short as possible. We also impose the condition that the superstring can be unambiguously decoded to give the original file at the receiving end. It turns out that the answer, due to Shannon, is closely related to the entropy $H(0.4, 0.2, 0.15, 0.15, 0.1)$ and that the most economical encoding of the file is around 2200 bits as 2200 is bigger than, but close to $1000H(0.4, 0.2, 0.15, 0.15, 0.1)$. This is a big improvement on the uncompressed approach whereby each character is encoded as an 8-bit binary string in ASCII for a total of 8000 bits. One encoding method is **Huffman coding** discussed in Chapter 11.

Channel capacity

Suppose that we are sending one of a set of M possible messages across a noisy channel. Our goal is to minimize the probability of error. To take an example, suppose $M = 2$ so that we have just two messages, namely, the bits 0 or 1. One way to minimize the probability of error is to encode 0, 1 as the messages $(0, \ldots, 0)$ and $(1, \ldots, 1)$, respectively, both of length n with n large. Then, even if one or two bits get corrupted, the probability of correct decoding (using "majority wins" here) is very high. The downside is that the transmission rate is very small. The rate here is the number of "information bits" M per codeword divided by the length n of the codeword. So the rate is $\frac{1}{n}$, which goes to 0 as n gets large. Shannon, in his famous noisy channel theorem, showed that the rate does not have to go to 0 for accurate decoding. In fact, so long as the rate is less than a number known as the **channel capacity**, accurate decoding is possible. As an example, suppose that A is transmitting n bits to B and assume that the probability of any given bit being corrupted is p, independent of the other bits. Then the channel capacity is our old friend $n(1 - H(p))$.

In engineering, the channel capacity C of a **continuous channel of bandwidth B hertz**, perturbed by additive white Gaussian noise of power spectral density $\frac{N_0}{2}$ is given by the formula $C = B\log_2(1 + \frac{P}{N_0 B})$ bits per second, where P is the average power. For many people, this formula ranks above $E = mc^2$!

Cryptography

Information Theory has several applications here. We mention Shannon's "perfect secrecy" criterion in Chapter 15 which quantifies perfect secrecy. Entropy also gives a measure of the "search space" of various cryptographic procedures such as AES discussed in Chapters 3, 4, and 5. The higher the entropy, the better the security. You do not want to choose a password that is easy to guess. The entropy of the average eight character password is around 14 bits – bearing in mind that one only has to try about half the keyspace in a brute-force search (Chapter 3). It is also important to have a good estimate of the entropy of a message, for example a text message in English. This is discussed in Chapter 14. Another very fundamental application occurs in the new protocols for an encryption key exchange described in Part III, where one first has to estimate the information an eavesdropper may have, as we did above in a special case.

In "Probability," Lecture Notes by John N. Guidi on MIT Course 18.313 by Professor Gian-Carlo Rota [Rot98, p. SC4.13], it is pointed out that entropy plays a fundamental role in such practical topics as Image Reconstruction and Pattern Recognition. There are many other applications of information theory. In Section 9.8, we show how information theory comes to the rescue in several weighing problems.

9.5   Information Theory and Physics

The word "entropy" was first coined by Clausius in physics around 1865. Entropy is used mainly in statistical mechanics and thermodynamics. Roughly, it measures the amount of energy lost to heat in an irreversible physical process.

It was Boltzmann in 1896 who was the first to show that the physical entropy of a system could be expressed as the average value of the logarithm of the probabilities of the states of a physical system. If the probability of a particular gas configuration is W, we have $S = k \log W$, where k is Boltzmann's constant. As Feynman [Fey00] puts it *"Generally speaking, the less information we have about a state the higher the entropy."*

If F is the free energy, U the total energy (which remains unchanged), T the temperature and S the entropy, we have

$$F = U - TS \quad \text{(see Feynman [Fey00])} \tag{9.5}$$

Denoting an infinitesimal change at constant temperature by δ, we have

$$\delta S = -\frac{\delta F}{T} \quad \text{since} \quad \delta T = 0 \tag{9.6}$$

As in [Fey00] this is "a variant of the standard formula $\delta S = -\frac{\delta Q}{T}$ for the infinitesimal change in entropy resulting from a thermodynamically reversible change in state where at each stage, an amount of heat δQ enters or leaves the system at absolute temperature T. For an irreversible process, the equality is replaced by an inequality, ensuring that the entropy of an isolated system can only stay constant or increase – this is the Second Law of Thermodynamics.

In fact, there is an analogy to the idea that "high randomness corresponds to high entropy." In thermodynamics also, as Feynman puts it "the less information we have about a state the higher the entropy." To conclude this brief discussion, we quote from

Shannon and Weaver [SW49] who quote from Eddington's work "The Nature of the Physical World" as follows:

> Suppose that we were asked to arrange the following in two categories – *distance, mass, electric force, entropy, beauty, and melody.*
>
> I think there are the strongest grounds for placing entropy alongside beauty and melody, and not with the first three. Entropy is only found when the parts are viewed in association, and it is by viewing or hearing the parts in association that beauty and melody are discerned. All three are features of arrangement. It is a pregnant thought that one of these three associates should be able to figure as a commonplace quantity of science. The reason why this stranger can pass itself off among the aborigines of the physical world is that it is able to speak their language, viz., the language of arithmetic.

9.6 Axiomatics of Information Theory

In our discussions above, we encountered the situation where an eavesdropper E was trying to determine a message M that was being transmitted by cryptographic station **A**. Assume that M is 1000 bits long and that E knows, with probability 0.85, what each bit is in M. Then, on the average, E "knows" 850 bits, i.e. Eve is aware that 850 of her bits are identical to those in M. The problem for Eve is not knowing where the places of agreement and disagreement with M lie in Eve's binary string. In fact, in terms of "hard information," Eve's knowledge only comes out to

$$1000(1 - H(0.85)) = 1000(1 - 0.6098) = 1000(0.3902) \tag{9.7}$$

which is approximately 390 Shannon bits. This seems a bit small compared to the 850 bits above. Perhaps we have the wrong measure for information?

To justify our definition of entropy axiomatically, let us suppose that H is some information measure which assigns a number $H(E)$ to each event E in a sample space. We assume that $H(E)$ only depends on the probability of E and not on the nature of E. Thus, we can think of H as being defined on a probability space, so $H = H(p_1, \dots, p_n)$, with $0 \le p_i \le 1$, $1 \le i \le n$ and $p_1 + \dots + p_n = 1$.

We make the following eight assumptions or axioms.

1. $H(p_1, \dots, p_n)$ achieves a maximum when $p_1 = p_2 = \dots = p_n = \frac{1}{n}$,

2. $H(p_1, \dots, p_n)$ is unaffected by the ordering of $p_1, \dots, p_n$ (so $H(p_1, p_2) = H(p_2, p_1)$ if $n = 2$, etc.),

3. $H(p_1, \dots, p_n) \ge 0$. $H = 0$ if and only if one of $p_1, \dots, p_n$ is 1 and the rest zero,

4. $H(p_1, \ldots, p_n, 0) = H(p_1, \ldots, p_n)$,

5. $H(\frac{1}{n}, \ldots, \frac{1}{n}) \leq H(\frac{1}{n+1}, \ldots, \frac{1}{n+1})$,

6. $H(p_1, \ldots, p_n)$ is a continuous function in each of $p_1, \ldots, p_n$,

7. $H(\frac{1}{mn}, \ldots, \frac{1}{mn}) = H(\frac{1}{m}, \ldots, \frac{1}{m}) + H(\frac{1}{n}, \ldots, \frac{1}{n})$,

8. Let $p = p_1 + \cdots + p_m$ and $q = q_1 + \cdots + q_n$, where each p_i and q_j are nonnegative. Then if p, q are positive with $p + q = 1$,

$$H(p_1, \ldots, p_m, q_1, \ldots, q_n) = H(p, q) + pH\left(\frac{p_1}{p}, \ldots, \frac{p_m}{p}\right) + qH\left(\frac{q_1}{q}, \ldots, \frac{q_n}{q}\right).$$

These axioms all have convincing intuitive explanations as pointed out in Welsh [Wel88]. For example, Axiom 1 says that the uncertainty is maximized when all outcomes are equally likely. Axiom 3 says that entropy is always nonnegative. Axiom 5 says there is more uncertainty, in the equiprobable case, when we increase the number of possible outcomes. Axiom 6 says that if we only change the probabilities slightly then H changes only slightly. Axiom 7 has to do with independence. Axiom 8 says that we can break down the total uncertainty involving the uncertainty as to whether one of the p_i or the q_i is chosen (or occurs). Then we have uncertainty involving weighted averages.

We then have the following result (see [Wel88]).

Theorem 9.1 *If H satisfies axioms* (1) *to* (8), *then*

$$H(p_1, \ldots, p_n) = -\lambda \sum_{i=1}^{n} p_i \log p_i \tag{9.8}$$

where λ is some positive constant and the sum is over all the nonzero numbers p_j, $1 \leq j \leq n$.

These axioms, originally proposed by Shannon, are not minimal. Many other systems have been published. The axioms are chosen in [Wel88].

9.7   Number Bases, Erdös and the Hand of God

In this book, we generally work in base 2. However, many of the results hold for *any* number base. We mention in particular the results of Kraft and McMillan in the next chapter. Also, we mention the important set of examples for source coding given by DNA coding where the alphabet has size 4.

Here we want to talk briefly about number bases and their properties. Let us fix on an arbitrary positive integer $d > 1$. Then every positive integer n can be written as nonnegative combinations of the nonnegative powers of d. Thus, $n = c_0 + c_1 d + c_2 d^2 + \cdots + c_t d^t$, where $0 \leq c_i < d$. Also, this expression is **unique**. In particular then, the set S of positive integers given by

$$S = \{d^0 = 1, d, d^2, d^3, \ldots\} \tag{9.9}$$

satisfies the following interesting property which we will call property E (for Erdös).

Property E

A set S of positive integers is said to satisfy **Property** E if two different subsets of S must have different sums.

It is clear that the nonnegative powers of d satisfy this property. Otherwise, we would have

$$n = \alpha_0 + \alpha_1 d + \alpha_2 d^2 + \cdots = \beta_0 + \beta_1 d + \beta_2 d^2 + \cdots \tag{9.10}$$

where $\alpha_i, \beta_i \in \{0, 1\}$. Thus, n would have two different expansions in powers of d, which is impossible.

If we were trying to construct a set S satisfying Property E one way to do it would be to pick each new number x of the set to be a suitably large number. This will work, but then, when x is big, $\frac{1}{x}$ is small. Note that the powers of d "barely work" since each new power of d is the sum of all the previous powers of d plus 1. There are no gaps. This leads naturally to the Erdös problem (or we should say an Erdös problem. The legendary Erdös posed many fascinating problems).

Erdös problem

Given a set S of positive integers satisfying Property E, find a least upper bound for $\sum_{x \in S} \frac{1}{x}$.

Let us try the number bases.

$$
\begin{array}{lll}
\text{base} = 2 & 1 + \frac{1}{2} + \frac{1}{4} + \frac{1}{8} + \cdots & \text{which tends to } 2 \\
\text{base} = 3 & 1 + \frac{1}{3} + \frac{1}{3^2} + \frac{1}{3^3} + \cdots & \text{which tends to } \frac{3}{2} \\
\vdots & \vdots & \vdots \\
\text{base} = d & 1 + \frac{1}{d} + \frac{1}{d^2} + \frac{1}{d^3} + \cdots & \text{which tends to } \frac{d}{d-1}
\end{array}
$$

So just looking at the case when S is the set of nonnegative powers of d leads us to conjecture that the least upper bound might be 2. But what about the general case where we only know that S satisfies Property E?

One of the authors, in joint work with David Borwein [BB75], was fortunate enough to solve the problem. The least upper bound is indeed 2. In his book "Mathematical Gems III," Professor Honsberger devotes an entire chapter, Chapter 17, entitled "A Problem of Paul Erdös", to this problem. In the chapter, he discusses the Borwein–Bruen solution and offers the following comment concerning the solution. "Professor Erdös has the theory that God has a book containing all the theorems of mathematics with their absolutely most beautiful proofs, and when he wants to express the highest application of a proof he explains: This is one from the book! Erdös does not do this very often, but across the top of the note he sent me is the inscription 'I think this proof comes straight out of the book!' "

The proof that the least upper bound is 2 uses nothing but high school algebra. We also point out that the problem was first solved by Erdös and Benkoski. For details, we refer the reader to Honsberger [Hon85].

In fact, the Borwein–Bruen proof goes through for all number bases, not just powers of 2. This result was also rediscovered by Eric Lenstra. Here is the result.

Theorem 9.2 (Number bases theorem) *Let $0 < a_1 < \cdots < a_k$ be a set of positive integers such that all sums $\sum_i \varepsilon_i a_i$ are distinct, where $\varepsilon_i = 0, 1, \ldots, n-1$. Then*

$$\frac{1}{a_1} + \cdots + \frac{1}{a_k} \leq \left(\frac{n}{n-1}\right)\left(1 - (\frac{1}{n})^k\right) \tag{9.11}$$

with equality exactly when $a_i = n^{i-1}$.

We also mention here a related paper in the binary case by Richard Guy [Guy82].

9.8 Weighing Problems and Your MBA

Several years ago a colleague of one of the authors, Desmond ffolliott, was associated with the Ivey Business School at the University of Western Ontario. Another colleague, Dave Johnson, an oil and gas expert also lived in London, Ontario, and had Ivey connections. In conversation Desmond and Dave mentioned that "the 12 weights problem" was often used to instill the right attitude into prospective MBA students. If they were good, they might be able to solve it. If not, the attempt would build character!

Here is the problem. You are provided with a certain number of weights, say 12, and a balance. You are told that exactly one of the weights is defective, being too light or too heavy. You are not told whether the culprit is too light or too heavy.

Problem

Determine which of the 12 weights is defective and determine whether it is too light or too heavy in 3 weighings or less.

Why 12? In fact, the case of 9 weights and 3 weighings is stated as a problem in Welsh [Wel88]. But we solve the problem here for 12 weights. Why 3 weighings? Can we generalize this problem? What does it have to do with information theory? We will try to outline the answers to some of these questions.

First of all, we mention some abstract theory. We have 12 weights numbered 1 to 12. One of these is defective, say the i-th weight. Moreover, it is either too heavy, so we have (i, H), or too light, so we have (i, L). So altogether we have a list of 24 possible outcomes, namely, $(1, H), (1, L), \ldots, (12, H), (12, L)$, which are all equally likely. Moreover, exactly one outcome materializes. Think of a horse race with 24 horses in the race and exactly one winner, and all of them equally likely to win. One uncertainty about the winner is then $H(\frac{1}{24}, \ldots, \frac{1}{24})$ which is $\log 24$. Each weighing gives three possible results: heavy to the left or right or balanced. The maximum amount of information we can get from a weighing (see Axiom 1) is $H(\frac{1}{3}, \frac{1}{3}, \frac{1}{3}) = \log 3$.

This is why it is not a good idea to weight 6 against 6 at the beginning. If we do this, there are only 2 possible outcomes instead of 3, and so we won't acquire enough information.

This occurs when the 3 outcomes are equally likely. So with x weighings, we get at most $x \log 3$ Shannon bits of information. But from the above, we need $\log 24$ Shannon bits of information. Thus, $x \log 3 \geq \log 24$. This gives

$$x \geq \frac{\log 24}{\log 3}. \tag{9.12}$$

Logs are taken to the base 2, but we get the same answer no matter which base we choose, because of the ratio. Thus, $x \geq 2.89$. So we are going to need at least three weighings! In general, with n weights and x weighings, we get the following inequality.

General inequality

$x \log 3 \geq \log(2n)$.

So for n weights, we need at least x weighings, where x satisfies the above inequality.

How can we discover the culprit in at most three weighings? First, we choose four at random on one side of the balance and another four on the other side.

Case 1. They balance. Then the culprit is among the four left. Next, we balance three of these potential culprits with three good weights.

> Subcase a. They balance. Then we balance the remaining weight, which we know to be the culprit, with one of the good weights, to see if the culprit is too heavy or too light. We have found the answer in three weighings.

> Subcase b. They don't balance. So we have three potential culprits one of which is the real culprit. We can also tell if the culprit is heavy or light. Next, balance one of these three against another one of the three, and all will be revealed whether or not they balance.

Case 2. They do not balance and the balance tilts to the left say. Label the four weights on the left as H_1, H_2, H_3, H_4 and the four weights on the right as L_1, L_2, L_3, L_4. Thus, either one of the H weights is too heavy or one of the L weights is too light.

Next, we perform the following move. We put H_1, H_2, L_1 on the left against H_3, H_4, L_2 on the right. We have $H_1\ H_2\ L_1 \mid H_3\ H_4\ L_2$.

> Subcase a. They balance. The culprit must be either L_3 or L_4. Then put these two opposing each other on the balance to identify the culprit as the lighter of the two.

> Subcase b. They do not balance. If the right side rises, the culprit is H_1, H_2, or L_2. If the left side rises, the culprit is H_3, H_4, or L_1.

In any case, we have as possible culprits two potentially heavy weights denoted by H_5, H_6 and one potentially light weight, say L.

Now, weight H_5 against H_6. If they balance, the culprit is L. If they do not, then the culprit is the heavier of the two.

Additional weighing problems

In [Rot98] the author considers the following problem: We are given a set of 3^N coins, all but one of which is a gold coin. The remaining coin, a fake coin, is too light. The question is this: how many weighings are required to discover the fake coin and how can this be done?

We approach this question as follows: We have 3^N coins labelled $L_1, L_2, \ldots, L_{3^N}$, where L stands for "Light" representing 3^N equally likely possibilities for the fake coin. Our uncertainty about the outcome is $H\left(\frac{1}{3^N}, \frac{1}{3^N}, \ldots, \frac{1}{3^N}\right) = \log_2(3^N)$. This is equal to $N \log_2 3$.

If we weight 3^{N-1} against 3^{N-1}, there are 3 possible outcomes, i.e. the scales tilt left or right or balance. Thus, each weighing yields at most $H(\frac{1}{3}, \frac{1}{3}, \frac{1}{3}) = \log_2 3$ bits of information. So the number of weighings required to detect the fake coin is at least $\frac{N \log_2 3}{\log_2 3} = N$. We show that we can detect the fake coin in N weighings. We proceed by induction on N.

If $N = 1$, we have 3 coins. Weigh one coin against another. If the balance tilts down to the left, the coin on the right is light and is the fake. If they balance, the remaining coin is fake.

Assume the proposition is true for 3^m coins. Suppose we have 3^{m+1} coins. Put 3^m coins against 3^m coins on the scale. If they balance, the remaining 3^m coins contain the fake. By induction, the fake is detected in m weighings. So we have detected the fake in $m + 1$ weighings.

If they do not balance, but tilt down to the left, say, then the set of 3^m coins on the right has the fake as it is known to be light. Again we detect the fake in $m + 1$ weighings, and the result is proven.

Now, we examine a more difficult problem. Let us suppose that we have 3^N coins of which one is fake, but it is not known whether it is too heavy or too light. We want to find out which is the fake and also whether the fake is too heavy or too light in a minimal number of weighings.

We now have $(2)(3^N)$ equiprobable possibilities as a coin may be too light or too heavy. The entropy in bits is now

$$H\left(\frac{1}{3^N}, \ldots, \frac{1}{3^N}, \frac{1}{3^N}, \ldots, \frac{1}{3^N}\right) = \log_2(2(3^N)) = \log_2 2 + \log_2(3^N) = 1 + N \log_2 3$$

As in the previous case, each weighing yields at most $H\left(\frac{1}{3}, \frac{1}{3}, \frac{1}{3}\right) = \log_2 3$ bits of information. [The three outcomes might not be equiprobable, so the entropy might be less than $\log_2 3$ bits.] Therefore, the number of weighings required is at least

$$\frac{1 + N \log_2 3}{\log_2 3} = \frac{1}{\log_2 3} + \frac{N \log_2 3}{\log_2 3} = \log_3 2 + N \approx N + (0.63)$$

It follows that the required number of weighings is at least $N + 1$. To find the fake coin – which may be heavy or light – we weigh a set S_1 of 3^{N-1} coins versus a set S_2 of 3^{N-1} coins.

Case 1. They balance. Then the remaining 3^{N-1} coins can be weighed against one of Set 1 or Set 2. This will tell us if the fake coin is light or heavy.

Now, we have a set of 3^{N-1} coins containing a fake coin which is too light, say. From the above, we can identify it in $N-1$ weighings. We have done two weighings before this. All told, we identify the fake in $N+1$ weighings.

Case 2. S_1 and S_2 do not balance, and tilt down to the left, say. So S_1 on the left has a fake which is too heavy or S_2 on the right has a fake which is too light. Weigh S_1 against the remaining coins, i.e. S_3. We end up with 3^{N-1} coins which contain a fake coin which is known to be too light if S_1 and S_3 balance or too heavy if they do not balance. Again, we find the culprit in $N+1$ weighings.

9.9   Shannon Bits, the Big Picture

It should be emphasized that the abstract unit of information is the Shannon bit. A priori, this is not connected to a regular physical bit such as a "voltage bit" or binary digit. However, a wonderful feature of information theory, reaffirming Shannon's genius and the verification of the correctness of his theories, is the correspondence between Shannon bits and physical storage bits, i.e. $(0,1)$ voltages [Ale02].

For example, Shannon's first theorem shows that the entropy of a given source, measured in Shannon bits, is arbitrarily close to the number of physical $(0,1)$ bits on average needed for efficient encoding of the source.

Shannon's second theorem shows that the maximum value of a conditional entropy, i.e. the **channel capacity** measured in Shannon bits is the maximum transmission rate, measured in physical bits, for accurate communication across the channel.

So, in these two theorems, the motto, roughly speaking, is that:

$$Theory = Practice$$

$$Shannon\ \ Bit = Physical\ \ Bit$$

Finally, we should mention the famous Whittaker–Shannon Sampling Theorem for sampling continuous information which is covered in detail in Chapter 13.

Chapter 10

Random Variables and Entropy

Goals, Discussion In subsequent chapters, we focus on communicating over various channels. In preparation for this, we need to develop background on random variables, conditional probability, entropy, conditional entropy and mutual information.

We discuss these topics here in an elementary way. We present several worked examples. Related topics come in again, notably in Chapter 12.

New, Noteworthy We discuss sample spaces, basic probability theory and random variables. Conditional probability leads to tree diagrams and the Bayes formula. Bernoulli trials pave the way for typical sequences. Axiomatics of entropy have been discussed in Chapter 9. Here we develop the important basic concepts of entropy and conditional entropy.

10.1   Random Variables

A **Random Variable** X associates with each possible outcome of an experiment or observation a value of X. For example a source may be emitting symbols chosen from an alphabet with certain probabilities. The value of the random variable X is defined to be the symbol emitted. Or the experiment might consist of choosing an individual from a set of n people and measuring his or her weight in pounds. In this case, the value X is a real number corresponding to an individual's weight in pounds.

Cryptography, Information Theory, and Error-Correction: A Handbook for the 21st Century, Second Edition.
Aiden A. Bruen, Mario A. Forcinito, and James M. McQuillan.

Throughout this chapter, we assume that X has only finitely many possible values. Generally, X is discrete, although the continuous case is discussed in Chapter 13.

Consider the following examples:

Example 10.1 *Suppose we roll a six-sided die. The number on a side or face of the die is one of 1, 2, 3, 4, 5, 6. If each face is equally likely to show up (with probability $\frac{1}{6}$) the die is said to be* **fair**.

This is really a bit like the source example above. The source, which is the die, selects a number from the set $\{1, 2, 3, 4, 5, 6\}$.

Example 10.2 *We have a set of five individuals. An experiment consists of choosing one of the five at random and measuring that individual's height in inches. Here the source is the set $\Omega = \{A, B, C, D, E\}$ consisting of the five individuals. The random variable X is the height of the individual in inches.*

Note that in Examples 10.1 and 10.2, the values of X are real numbers. But this is not always the case as is shown by the following kind of example which is examined in detail in Chapter 11.

Example 10.3 *A source emits a finite number of symbols of an "alphabet" with pre-assigned probabilities. For instance, the symbols might be the binary symbols 0 or 1. Here the source can be identified with the symbols emitted. If the possible symbols are $\{x_1, x_2, \ldots, x_n\}$, we say that the set $\{x_1, x_2, \ldots, x_n\}$ is the target space of the random variable X.*

For example, in the string (x_3, x_2, x_4), the source assigns the first, second, and third positions of the string to the symbols x_3, x_2, x_4, respectively.

Abstractly, let Ω be a source or "sample space" (see below) and X a random variable defined on Ω. Denote the values of X by $x_1, x_2, \ldots, x_n$. Given any value x_i, $1 \leq i \leq n$, we can define "the probability that $X = x_i$" which is denoted $\Pr(X = x_i)$. This is simply the sum of the probabilities of all outcomes e in the sample space which map to x_i. In symbols:

$$\sum_{X(e)=x_i} \Pr(e) = \Pr(X = x_i)$$

Another approach to sources and random variables is via the idea of a **sample space** with **probability measure** or function (i.e. a "**probability space.**")

A (finite) sample space is a finite set E of "elementary events." An **event** is simply any subset of E. A probability measure assigns to each element in E a positive number (probability) such that the sum of the probabilities of the elementary events add up to 1. If A is an event (i.e. any subset of the sample space), we denote the probability of A by $\Pr(A)$. Two basic rules are as follows:

(a) If A, B are events, then

$$\Pr(A \cup B) = \Pr(A) + \Pr(B) - \Pr(A \cap B)$$

(b) Events A, B are said to be **independent** if

$$\Pr(A \cap B) = \Pr(A) \Pr(B)$$

(We can think of sets with $A \cup B$, the union of A, B, counting the elements contained in set A or set B. The overlap, i.e. the intersection $A \cap B$, is contained twice in the first two terms. It should only be counted once, so we must subtract it.)

Example 10.4 *Suppose each of the five individuals in Example 10.2 has an equal probability of being chosen. Since the probabilities add up to 1, this means that each of A, B, C, D, and E has a probability equal to $\frac{1}{5}$ of being chosen. Now, assume that the heights in inches of A, B, C, D, and E are, respectively, 67, 67, 69, 72, and 70. Then*

$$\Pr(X = 67) = \frac{2}{5}, \ \ \Pr(X = 69) = \frac{1}{5}, \ \ \Pr(X = 72) = \frac{1}{5}, \ \ \Pr(X = 70) = \frac{1}{5}$$

In the future, we will occasionally be informal and write "$\Pr(x_i)$" instead of "$\Pr(X = x_i)$."

The **average** or **expected value** or **mean** of X is denoted by $E(X)$. It is defined as follows:

$$E(X) = \sum_{i=1}^{n} x_i \Pr(X = x_i)$$

In other words, to calculate the average value of X, we multiply each possible value of X by the corresponding probability. In Example 10.4, the average value of X is $\frac{1}{5}(67) + \frac{1}{5}(67) + \frac{1}{5}(69) + \frac{1}{5}(70) + \frac{1}{5}(72) = 69$ (in). Thus, the expected value of the height is 69 in.
Sometimes the symbol μ is used for expected value.

The **Variance** of X is defined as follows:

$$V(X) = \sum_{i=1}^{n} (x_i - E(X))^2 \Pr(X = x_i) = \sum_{i=1}^{n} (x_i - \mu)^2 \Pr(x_i)$$

In other words, the variance of X is the average value of the variable $(x_i - E(X))^2$.

The **Standard Deviation** $\sigma(X)$ is defined to be the positive square root of the variance. Thus,

$$\sigma(X) = \sqrt{V(X)}$$

Example 10.5   *Now, suppose we assume that A, B, C, D, E, are chosen in accordance with a different probability distribution from that in Example 10.4, where we used the equiprobable distribution. Let* $\Pr(A) = 0.1$, $\Pr(B) = \Pr(C) = 0.2$, $\Pr(D) = 0.4$, $\Pr(E) = 0.1$.

To find $E(X)$, *the average value, we construct the following table. Recall that the heights of A, B, C, D, and E in inches are, respectively, 67, 67, 69, 72, 70.*

Possible Values of X	67	69	70	72
Corresponding Probabilities	*0.3*	*0.2*	*0.1*	*0.4*

Then $E(X) = (67)(0.3) + (69)(0.2) + (70)(0.1) + (72)(0.4) = 69.7$ *(in).   We can now calculate the variance of X. This involves the average value of* $(x_i - E(X))^2 = (E(X) - x_i)^2$.

Possible Values of $(E(X) - x_i)^2$	$(2.7)^2$	$(0.7)^2$	$(0.3)^2$	$(2.3)^2$
Corresponding Probabilities	*0.3*	*0.2*	*0.1*	*0.4*

$$V(X) = (0.3)(2.7)^2 + (0.2)(0.7)^2 + (0.4)(2.3)^2 + (0.1)(0.3)^2$$

$$= 2.187 + 0.098 + 0.009 + 2.116$$

$$= 4.41$$

Then, $\sigma(X) = \sqrt{4.41} = 2.1$.

A formula for calculating the variance which is sometimes easier to use than the one above is as follows:

$$V(X) = E(X^2) - (E(X))^2$$

To calculate $E(X^2)$, the expected value of X^2, we simply multiply the possible values of X^2 by their corresponding probabilities and then sum up. In Example 10.5, we know that $E(X) = 69.7$, and we calculate that

$$E(X^2) = (0.3)(67^2) + (0.2)(69^2) + (0.1)(70^2) + (0.4)(72^2)$$

$$= 4862.5$$

We finish by finding the variance.

$$V(X) = E(X^2) - (E(X))^2 = 4862.5 - 69.7^2 = 4.41$$

10.2 Mathematics of Entropy

Given a random variable X let the possible values of X be $x_1, x_2, \ldots, x_n$ and set $p_i = \Pr(X = x_i)$, $1 \leq i \leq n$. We will only be concerned with the probability space $\{p_1, p_2, \ldots, p_n\}$ and not with the nature of X.

As such we define the **Entropy of X** as follows:

$$H(X) = \sum_{i=1}^{n} p_i \log\left(\frac{1}{p_i}\right) = -\sum_{i=1}^{n} p_i \log(p_i)$$

Here the second equality is obtained by using the fact that $\log\left(\frac{1}{t}\right) = -\log(t)$ for any number $t > 0$. **The logarithms are taken to the base 2**, and this is usually the case throughout this book.

The preceding sum is taken over all *non-zero p_i*. Additionally, we take $0 \log\left(\frac{1}{0}\right)$ to be zero with respect to our definition of $H(X)$ as above. One justification for this is that the entropy should be continuous, and we know from calculus that $\lim_{x \to 0} x \log(x) = 0$.

An especially interesting case occurs when $n = 2$. In this case, we have two possible outcomes for the random variable, with probabilities p and q where $q = 1 - p$. So we have a probability distribution $[p, 1 - p]$. Then

$$H(p) = H(p, 1 - p) = p \log\left(\frac{1}{p}\right) + q \log\left(\frac{1}{q}\right) = -(p \log(p) + q \log(q))$$

This is the famous **Shannon Function** whose diagram is given below and whose values are tabulated in the Appendix. We refer also to Chapters 9 and 25.

We can think of $H(p)$ as the amount of information received upon learning the outcome of an experiment or trial that has just two possible outcomes occurring with probabilities p, q, where $q = 1 - p$ and $0 \leq p \leq 1$. $H(p)$ is 0 at $p = 0$ and $p = 1$. In either of these cases, we know the outcome already so no information is revealed and $H(p) = 0$. When $p = \frac{1}{2}$, $H(p)$ achieves its maximum value, which is one. **So we receive maximum information, upon learning the outcome, when the outcome is completely random to begin with.** The amount of information received in this case is 1 (**The Shannon Bit**), which is the unit of information and entropy. Thus, information and entropy is measured in Shannon bits. As mentioned in Chapter 9, a *Shannon bit is the amount of information received (or uncertainty removed) upon learning the outcome* *of an experiment with two possible outcomes, both of which were, a priori, equally likely* Golomb et al. [GBC$^+$02].

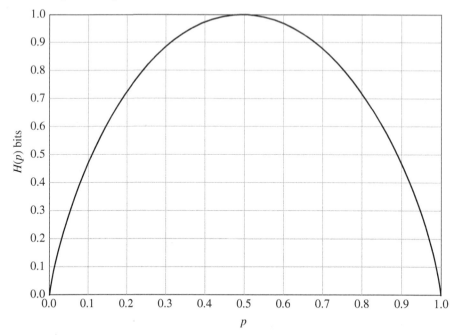

We note that the Shannon function is **concave down** (as can be seen by calculating the second derivative). This means that the graph lies above the line segment joining any two points on the graph, and below the tangent line to the graph.

Caution about notation

The symbol p is a dangerous one! When we discussed cryptography, p is a prime. Now, p is a probability relating to a source. When we discuss channels, such as the binary symmetric channel (BSC) p will denote the probability of a transmission error. In Chapter 25, p is again the probability relating to a source.

10.3   Calculating Entropy

The procedure for calculating the entropy of a random variable X is similar to that for calculating the average value or variance of X. We simply make up a table as follows:

Possible Values of X	x_1	x_2	$\cdots$	x_n
Corresponding Probabilities	p_1	p_2	$\cdots$	p_n
Entropy $H(X)$	$p_1 \log\left(\frac{1}{p_1}\right)$ +	$p_2 \log\left(\frac{1}{p_2}\right)$ +	$\cdots$ +	$p_n \log\left(\frac{1}{p_n}\right)$

Note that when X is a source (Chapter 11), the units for $H(X)$ are *Shannon bits per symbol*. Additionally, notice that in the definition of entropy, we only need the probabilities $\Pr(X = x_i)$, rather than the actual values of X. Thus, for entropy, we only need a probability distribution for its calculation. Then, for a probability distribution $(p_1, p_2, \cdots, p_n)$ we have

$$H(p_1, p_2, \cdots, p_n) = \sum_{i=1}^{n} p_i \log\left(\frac{1}{p_i}\right) = -\sum_{i=1}^{n} p_i \log(p_i)$$

Here, as usual, logs are taken to the base 2. Another way of looking at the matter is to say that *entropy is the average value of the* log *of one over the probability to the base 2*.

If $p_i \neq 0$, we know that p_i is positive. Now since $p_i \leq 1$, $\frac{1}{p_i} \geq 1$, and we have that $\log\left(\frac{1}{p_i}\right) \geq 0$. Thus, each term in the sum defining entropy is nonnegative. As will be seen in Chapter 11, the maximum value of entropy (for a fixed n) occurs when $p_1 = p_2 = \cdots = p_n = \frac{1}{n}$ in which case we find that $H(X) = \log(n)$.

In summary, given n, we have $0 \leq H(X) \leq \log(n)$.

Example 10.6 *For the six-sided die in Example 10.1, the entropy is*

$$H(X) = \frac{1}{6}\log(6) + \frac{1}{6}\log(6) + \frac{1}{6}\log(6) + \frac{1}{6}\log(6) + \frac{1}{6}\log(6) + \frac{1}{6}\log(6)$$
$$= \log(6)$$

Since we are using logs to the base 2, we have $H(X) = \log_2(6) = 2.59$ and, recalling that the unit of entropy is the Shannon bit, we have $H(X) = 2.59$ Shannon bits.

Calculating tip

If your calculator only has logs to the base 10 and you want the log to the base 2, just use the **conversion formula**, i.e.

$$\log_2 x = \frac{\log_{10} x}{\log_{10} 2}$$

10.4 Conditional Probability

As above, in a sample space Ω (= a list of possible outcomes) an **Event** is any set of possible outcomes. Let U, V be the events in a sample space Ω. We want to define $\Pr(U|V)$, the **probability of U given V** or the **Conditional Probability** (of U given V). We define this as follows:

$$\Pr(U|V) = \frac{\Pr(U \text{ and } V)}{\Pr(V)} = \frac{\Pr(U \cap V)}{\Pr(V)} \qquad (10.1)$$

where we assume that $\Pr(V) \neq 0$.

We think of $\Pr(U|V)$ roughly as the proportion of outcomes of U lying in V.

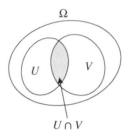

Example 10.7 *Urn 1 contains 2 black balls and 1 white ball. Urn 2 contains 3 white balls and 1 black ball. A ball is first drawn from Urn 1 and then placed in Urn 2. A ball is then drawn from Urn 2. Let U be the event that a white ball is drawn from Urn 1. Let V be the event that a black ball is drawn from Urn 2. Calculate*

(a) $\Pr(U)$

(b) $\Pr(V)$

(c) $\Pr(U \cap V)$

(d) $\Pr(V|U)$

(e) $\Pr(U|V)$

   Here are the solutions.

(a) Since we have 3 balls in Urn 1 and one of them is white, $\Pr(U) = \frac{1}{3}$.

(b) Suppose we draw a white ball from Urn 1 and put it in Urn 2. Urn 2 now has 5 balls, 4 of which are white. When we now draw, the probability of drawing black is $\frac{1}{5}$. Thus, $\Pr$(white ball is from 1 and black ball from 2) is $\frac{1}{3} \cdot \frac{1}{5} = \frac{1}{15}$. Similarly, $\Pr$(black from 1 and black from 2) is $\frac{2}{3} \cdot \frac{2}{5} = \frac{4}{15}$.

   Thus, the total probability of drawing a black ball from Urn 2 is $\frac{1}{15} + \frac{4}{15} = \frac{1}{3} = \Pr(V)$.

(c) $\Pr(U \cap V) = \Pr$(white from Urn 1 and black from Urn 2)$= \frac{1}{15}$.

(d) We have

$$\Pr(V|U) = \frac{\Pr(V \text{ and } U)}{\Pr(U)} = \frac{\Pr(V \cap U)}{\Pr U} = \frac{\Pr(U \cap V)}{\Pr U} = \frac{\frac{1}{15}}{\frac{1}{3}} = \frac{1}{5}$$

Alternatively, from the probability tree below $\Pr(V|U) = \frac{1}{5}$. *We just get the probability of moving from "white ball from Urn 1" to the left to black.*

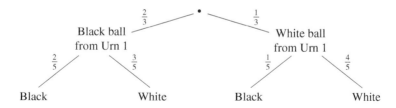

(e) $\Pr(U|V) = \frac{\Pr(U \cap V)}{\Pr(V)} = \frac{\frac{1}{15}}{\frac{4}{15}} = \frac{1}{4}$

Note that $\Pr(U|V)$ involves the **Bayes formula** whereby we have the "forward probabilities" and we want to find the "backward probabilities." In this example, the Bayes formula gives the following result:

$$\Pr(U|V) = \frac{\Pr(U)\Pr(V|U)}{\Pr(U)\Pr(V|U) + \Pr(U^c)\Pr(V|U^c)} \qquad (10.2)$$

where U^c denotes the complement of U, so $\Pr(U^c) = 1 - \Pr(U)$.

Note also that $\Pr(V|U)$ can easily be read from the tree diagram. However, $\Pr(U|V)$ (i.e. the probability of the earlier given the latter) has to be calculated from the formula for conditional probability (10.1). In general, the Bayes formula computes "backward probabilities" $\Pr(x|y)$ given the "forward probabilities" $\Pr(y|x)$ as follows:

$$\Pr(x|y) = \frac{\Pr(x)\Pr(y|x)}{\Pr(y)}$$

To explain the Bayes formula for $Pr(U|V)$, think of the probability of all paths on the tree leading from U to V and divide by the probability of all paths leading to V. In the tree diagram for $\Pr(U|V)$, we get

$$\frac{\left(\frac{1}{3}\right)\left(\frac{1}{5}\right)}{\left(\frac{1}{3}\right)\left(\frac{1}{5}\right) + \left(\frac{2}{3}\right)\left(\frac{2}{5}\right)} = \frac{1}{5}$$

We say that events U and V are **Independent** if $\Pr(U|V) = \Pr(U)$. This means, from (10.1), that $\Pr(U|V) = \frac{\Pr(U \cap V)}{\Pr(V)} = \Pr(U)$. Thus, for independence, we have

$$\Pr(U \cap V) = \Pr(U)\Pr(V)$$

In Example 10.7, $\Pr(U|V) = \frac{1}{5} \neq \frac{1}{3} = \Pr(U)$. Thus, U and V are **Not Independent**.

Events U, V are independent if the value of V does not affect the value of U, so that V gives no information about U (and vice versa).

It may be the case that we need to combine two (or several) random variables. For example, with a channel, we can measure both the input X and the output Y. In this way, we may **combine two random variables X and Y to obtain a single joint variable** (X, Y) whose values are ordered pairs (x, y), where x is the value of X and y is the value of Y. The probability of (x, y) is the probability that $X = x$ and, simultaneously, $Y = y$. That is, $\Pr(x, y) = \Pr[(X = x) \text{ and } (Y = y)]$.

Theorem 10.8 *From the definition of conditional probability in Eq. (10.1), we have* $\Pr(x, y) = \Pr(x) \Pr(y|x)$.

This will be important when we discuss channels where we will be given in advance the "forward probabilities" $\Pr(y|x)$.

Example 10.9 *Suppose we roll two fair dice and note the numbers appearing on each, corresponding to X, Y, respectively. So our sample space consists of all possible ordered pairs (x, y) with $1 \leq x \leq 6$ and $1 \leq y \leq 6$. There are 36 such pairs. Let Z denote the sum of X and Y. Let U denote the event that X is even, and let V denote the event that Y is odd. Then*

$$\Pr(U|V) = \frac{\Pr(U \cap V)}{\Pr(V)}$$

Now to calculate $\Pr(V)$, we know that the total number of ordered pairs of values is 36. These pairs are $(1, 1), \dots, (1, 6), (2, 1), \dots, (2, 6), \dots, (6, 1), (6, 2), \dots, (6, 6)$.

Since the event V corresponds to the pairs, where the second component is 1, 3, or 5, we have that $\Pr(V) = \frac{18}{36} = \frac{1}{2}$. Similarly, $\Pr(U) = \frac{1}{2}$. For $\Pr(U \cap V)$, the total number of ordered pairs corresponding to this event is 9, so $\Pr(U \cap V) = \frac{9}{36} = \frac{1}{4}$. The event $U \cap V$ corresponds to the nine pairs: $(2, 1), (2, 3), (2, 5), (4, 1), (4, 3), (4, 5), (6, 1), (6, 3), (6, 5)$.

Thus,

$$\Pr(U|V) = \frac{\Pr(U \cap V)}{\Pr(V)} = \frac{\frac{9}{36}}{\frac{18}{36}} = \frac{9}{18} = \frac{1}{2}$$

In Example 10.9 U, V *are independent*, since both of $\Pr(U \cap V)$ and $\Pr(U) \times \Pr(V)$ are equal to $\frac{1}{4}$.

Example 10.10 *Let U be the event that X is even and let V be the event that $Z = 4$. As above, we have $\Pr(U) = \frac{1}{2}$. The number of ordered pairs (x, y) for which $x + y$ is 4 is 3. Thus, $\Pr(U) = \frac{1}{2}$, $\Pr(V) = \frac{3}{36} = \frac{1}{12}$. The event $U \cap V$ is represented by all pairs (x, y) with x being even and $x + y = 4$: this gives the pair $(2, 2)$. Therefore, $\Pr(U \cap V) = \frac{1}{36}$. But $\Pr(U) \Pr(V) = \frac{1}{24} \neq \frac{1}{36}$. We conclude that the events U, V are not independent.*

Now, we move from sample spaces to random variables. If X, Y are random variables, they are said to be **independent** or **Statistically Independent** if

$$\Pr(X = x \text{ and } Y = y) = \Pr(X = x)\Pr(Y = y)$$

for all possible values x of X and y of Y. In the previous example of the two dice, X and Y are independent, but X and Z are not independent random variables and Y and Z are not independent. For example, $P(X = 3) = \frac{1}{6}$. But $\Pr((X = 3) \mid Z = 2) = 0 \neq \frac{1}{6}$.

In recent years, questions regarding independence of events have become a major legal issue. In our discussions of sources and channels in Chapters 11 and 12, we will be assuming independence in various situations. Whether or not X and Y are independent, we have that

$$E(X + Y) = E(X) + E(Y)$$

and in general:

$$E(X_1 + X_2 + \cdots + X_n) = E(X_1) + E(X_2) + \cdots + E(X_n)$$

If X, Y are independent, then also:

$$E(XY) = E(X)E(Y)$$
$$\text{and } V(X + Y) = V(X) + V(Y)$$

Similarly, if $X_1, X_2, \ldots, X_n$ are independent, then

$$V(X_1 + X_2 + \cdots + X_n) = V(X_1) + V(X_2) + \cdots + V(X_n)$$

10.5　Bernoulli Trials

Suppose Ω is a sample space with two possible outcomes. We can think of tossing a coin with the two outcomes being "Heads" and "Tails." Let the probability of "Heads" be p and let "Tails" have probability q with $p + q = 1$. If we toss just once and let X_1 denote the number of heads obtained, then $E(X_1) = p$ and $V(X_1) = pq$, where $V(X_1)$ denotes the variance of X_1. Recall that the variance of a random variable X means the expected value of the quantity $(X - E(X))^2$.

This can be seen by constructing the following table (to get the average value of any random variable X multiply the possible values of X by the corresponding probabilities)

Possible Values of X_1	1	0
Corresponding Probabilities	p	q

Then $E(X_1) = (1)(p) + (0)(q) = p$. Also, since $V(x_1) = E(X - \mu)^2$, where μ is the average, as in (10.1), we get

$$V(X_1) = (1 - p)^2 p + (0 - p)^2 q = q^2 p + p^2 q = pq(p + q) = pq$$

If we toss the coin n times corresponding to the n **independent and identically distributed (i.i.d.)** random variables $X_1, X_2, \ldots, X_n$ we are looking at the outcome of n independent trials with two possible outcomes, i.e. n **Bernoulli trials**. Thus, if $Z = X_1 + X_2 + \cdots + X_n$, we have

$$E(Z) = E(X_1 + X_2 + \cdots + X_n) = E(X_1) + E(X_2) + \cdots + E(X_n) = np$$

$$\text{Also } V(Z) = V(X_1 + X_2 + \cdots + X_n) = nV(X_1) = npq$$

Then the **standard deviation** of Z, denoted by $\sigma(Z)$ is defined by

$$\sigma(Z) = \sqrt{V(Z)} = \sqrt{npq}$$

In summary, if we have n Bernoulli trials and p is the probability of "success," then the **average number of successes is np and the standard deviation is $\sqrt{npq}$.**

It can be seen that the probability of having exactly t successes in n trials is

$$\binom{n}{t} p^t q^{n-t}, \quad 0 \le t \le n$$

The **normal** or **Gaussian curve** is characterized by its two parameters μ and σ. The high point occurs at $x = \mu$. A small σ means that the curve is highly peaked. A large σ means a large dispersion.

From the Law of Large Numbers (Section 10.7) it follows that when n is large, the outcome of n Bernoulli trials can be estimated by a **Normal** or **Gaussian Curve** ("bell curve") with mean equal to np and standard deviation equal to $\sigma = \sqrt{npq}$.

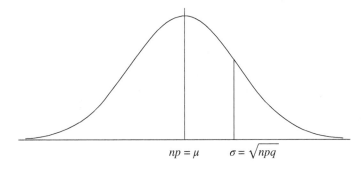

$$np = \mu \qquad \sigma = \sqrt{npq}$$

10.6 Typical Sequences

We can also relate Bernoulli trials to "typical sequences." Suppose we obtain a binary sequence of length n from a series of n Bernoulli trials, in which the probability of a one appearing in any given position is p and the probability of a zero appearing in that position is q, with $p + q = 1$. So the average number of ones appearing is np. (To make things convenient assume that np is an integer.) The average number of zeros is then $n - np = n(1 - p) = nq$.

Pick any $\epsilon > 0$. Let k be any integer such that $k^2 > \frac{2}{\epsilon}$. Let N denote the number of ones in a sequence. We say that a sequence is **typical** if either $\frac{N-np}{\sigma}$ is less than k or greater than $-k$: in other words the *absolute value* of $\frac{N-np}{\sigma}$ is less than k. From this we have the following result, as shown in [Ash90].

Theorem 10.11

(a) The set of nontypical sequences has total probability less than ϵ.

(b) The total number of typical sequences is approximately $2^{nH(p)}$, where $H(p) = p \log \left(\frac{1}{p} \right) + q \log \left(\frac{1}{q} \right)$ is the entropy of the Bernoulli variable X_i with probability of success p, $1 \leq i \leq n$.

(c) Each typical sequence has a probability of occurring that is close to $2^{-nH(p)}$ so that all typical sequences are essentially equiprobable.

The proof uses the well-known Chebyshev Inequality ("the probability of being very far from the average – for any distribution – is fairly small") together with the Normal approximation for n Bernoulli trials mentioned above.

For reference, we include the statement of **the Chebyshev Inequality**, valid for any probability distribution X with mean μ and standard deviation σ as follows:

$$\Pr(|X - \mu| \geq k\sigma) \leq \frac{1}{k^2}$$

Here, k is any positive real number.

As a side-note, the Chebyshev Inequality will be very useful in Section 26.8 regarding the security of Bitcoins. Also, the Chebyshev Inequality is a crucial component in the proof of the Fundamental Theorem in Chapter 12.

Explanation of typical sequences

The concept of a "typical sequence" can be explained, informally, as follows. In a typical sequence, the number of ones and zeros is close to the expected numbers, namely np

and $n(1-p)$, respectively. The difference between the actual and expected numbers is of the order of $\sqrt{n}$ and therefore, *when divided by* n, tends to zero. (Remember that in information theory, we are usually talking about *bits per symbol*.)

We should point out that the theory of typical sequences works not just for two possible outcomes (heads and tails) but for an arbitrary number of outcomes.

Let us discuss typical sequences in a slightly different way. Suppose we have a binary memoryless source emitting 1 with probability p and 0 with probability $q = 1 - p$.

Each sequence then has a probability associated with it. For example the sequence of length 3 given by 101 has probability given by $pqp = p^2q$. This follows from the independence of the source.

For a sequence $\mathbf{x}$ of length n, we expect that $\mathbf{x}$ should have roughly np ones and nq zeroes. (Let us assume that np is an integer for convenience.) If $\mathbf{x}$ has exactly np ones and nq zeroes, then the probability of $\mathbf{x}$, $\Pr(\mathbf{x})$, is given by the equation $\Pr(\mathbf{x}) = p^{np}q^{nq}$. Then $\log \Pr(\mathbf{x}) = np \log p + nq \log q$. Dividing by n, we get $\frac{1}{n} \log \Pr(\mathbf{x}) = p \log p + q \log q$. Thus, $-\frac{1}{n} \log \Pr(\mathbf{x}) = -p \log p - q \log q$, i.e. $\frac{1}{n} \log \left(\frac{1}{\Pr(\mathbf{x})} \right) = p \log \frac{1}{p} + q \log \frac{1}{q} = H(p)$. From this, we can also get that $\log(\Pr(\mathbf{x})) = -nH(p)$. Therefore, we have $\Pr(\mathbf{x}) = 2^{-nH(p)}$. In other words, for the "ultra-typical" sequence $\mathbf{x}$ above, we have $\Pr(\mathbf{x})$ exactly equal to $2^{-nH(p)}$.

This motivates an **alternative definition** of a typical sequence. A typical sequence $\mathbf{x}$ of length n and error γ is defined to be one for which

$$\left| \frac{1}{n} \log \left(\frac{1}{\Pr(\mathbf{x})} \right) - H(p) \right| < \gamma$$

where γ is an arbitrarily small given positive number. Thus, a typical sequence will have probability of occurrence which is close to $2^{-nH(p)}$, so that typical sequences are close to being equiprobable, the total number of typical sequences being, roughly, $2^{nH(p)}$.

10.7   Law of Large Numbers

First, we want to talk informally about (a special case of) the law of large numbers. Let us suppose we toss a fair coin n times. Then $p = \frac{1}{2}$ is the probability of getting heads on a single toss. Now the probability of getting **exactly** x **heads** in n tosses is $\binom{n}{x} p^x q^{n-x}$, $q = 1 - p$, which is $\binom{n}{x} (\frac{1}{2})^x (\frac{1}{2})^{n-x} = \binom{n}{x} \frac{1}{2^n}$. To see this, just pick out the x slots where you want heads to appear and multiply by the probabilities. For example, the probability of getting exactly 2 heads in 10 tosses of a fair coin is $\binom{10}{2} \frac{1}{2^{10}} = 0.0439$. The most likely number of heads occurring is approximately $(10)(\frac{1}{2}) = 5$. The probability of getting exactly 5 heads is $\binom{10}{5} \frac{1}{2^{10}} = 0.246$.

As n gets larger, the normal curve estimating these probabilities gets much more peaked. The number of heads may not be exactly equal to $\mu = np$. However, the probability that the total number of heads obtained (*when divided by* n) is close to μ is very high.

In fact, the **law of large numbers** says just this. It has to do with a probability limit. It states that

$$\lim_{n \to 0} \Pr \left(\left| \frac{(\text{total number of heads})}{n} - \mu \right| > \epsilon \right) = 0$$

where ϵ is any positive number (no matter how small) and $|\ |$ denotes the absolute value. In other words, when n is large, we can say with high probability of being correct that $\frac{\text{total heads}}{n} = \mu$.

Concerning the "Law of Large Numbers," we should mention that Richard Guy makes some amusing and interesting observations on numbers that are not large, but small [Guy88]!

In his paper entitled "The Strong Law of Small Numbers," Guy discusses the difficulty of gauging a mathematical pattern. He points out that "Capricious coincidences cause careless conjectures" and also warns that "initial irregularities inhibit incisive intuition." But we digress.

10.8   Joint and Conditional Entropy

The following lemma (The Entropy Lemma) is proved in Chapter 11.

Lemma 10.12 *Let* $(p_i, 1 \le i \le n)$ *be a given probability distribution with* $0 < p_i \le 1$ *and* $p_1 + p_2 + \cdots + p_n = 1$. *Let* $(q_i, 1 \le i \le n)$ *be another probability distribution with* $0 < q_i \le 1$. *Then*

$$\sum_{i=1}^{n} p_i \log q_i \le \sum_{i=1}^{n} p_i \log p_i$$

with equality if and only if $p_i = q_i$, $1 \le i \le n$.

(In Chapter 11, among other things, this result will be used to show that if X is a random variable with probabilities $p_1, p_2, \ldots, p_n$ then $H(X) \le \log(n)$ with equality if and only if $p_i = \frac{1}{n}$, $1 \le i \le n$.)

Next, let X, Y be random variables associated with the same experiment and each having only finitely many values. Then we can construct a random variable (X, Y) from the joint probability distribution (see Theorem 10.8), as follows:

If X has values $x_1, x_2, \ldots, x_s$ (with probabilities $p_1, p_2, \ldots, p_s$), and Y has values $y_1, y_2, \ldots, y_t$ (with probabilities $q_1, q_2, \ldots, q_t$), then (X, Y) has values $x_i y_j, 1 \le i \le s$ and

$1 \leq j \leq t$. We denote $\Pr(X = x_i \text{ and } Y = y_j)$ by p_{ij}. We sometimes put $p_i = \Pr(X = x_i)$ and $q_j = \Pr(Y = y_j)$. From this joint distribution, we have

$$\sum_j p_{ij} = p_i, \text{and} \sum_i p_{ij} = q_j$$

Using the definition of the joint probability distribution (X, Y), we have

$$H(X, Y) = -\sum_i \sum_j p_{ij} \log(p_{ij})$$

From this definition, it follows that $H(X, Y) = H(Y, X)$.

Theorem 10.13 $H(X, Y) \leq H(X) + H(Y)$ *with equality if and only if X, Y are independent.*

Proof.

$$H(X) + H(Y) = - \left(\sum_{i=1}^{s} p_i \log(p_i) + \sum_{j=1}^{t} q_j \log(q_j) \right)$$

$$= - \left(\sum_i \sum_j p_{ij} \log(p_i) + \sum_j \sum_i p_{ij} \log(q_j) \right)$$

$$= - \sum_i \sum_j p_{ij} \log(p_i q_j) \quad \text{since } \log(uv) = \log(u) + \log(v)$$

We now denote the expression $p_i q_j$ by q_{ij}.

At this point, we can invoke Lemma 10.12. The fact that we have a double summation here is not important, since we can reduce this to a single summation by re-indexing. So we have

$$H(X) + H(Y) = - \left(\sum_i \sum_j p_{ij} \log(q_{ij}) \right)$$

$$\geq - \sum_i \sum_j p_{ij} \log(p_{ij}) = H(X, Y)$$

From Lemma 10.12, equality occurs if and only if $p_{ij} = q_{ij}$, i.e. if and only if $p_i q_j = p_{ij}$. In other words, we have equality if and only if

$$\Pr(X = x_i \text{ and } Y = y_j) = \Pr(X = x_i) \Pr(Y = y_j)$$

which is equivalent to saying that the random variables X, Y are independent.   □

Example 10.14 *Going back to our previous example of the two dice (Example 10.9), it is easy to calculate $H(X,Y)$ since X, Y are independent. We have $H(X,Y) = H(X) + H(Y) = \log(6) + \log(6) = 5.18$. We can see that $H(X) = \log(6)$ because there are 6 equiprobable outcomes. $H(Y)$ is calculated in the same way, and is equal to $\log 6$ also.*

Informally, Theorem 10.13 says that the uncertainty of (X,Y) is at most the uncertainty of X plus the uncertainty of Y. But if the value of X is known, then it may actually give information about the outcome of Y so that the remaining uncertainty of (X,Y), once X is known, may be less than $H(Y)$. It will only equal $H(Y)$ if X, Y are independent.

Since $H(X,Y) = H(Y,X)$ an analysis like the above can be carried out with the roles of X, Y being interchanged.

Theorem 10.13 may be easily generalized as follows:

Theorem 10.15 *Given n random variables $(X_1, X_2, \ldots, X_n)$, then*

$$H(X_1, X_2, \ldots, X_n) \leq H(X_1) + H(X_2) + \cdots + H(X_n)$$

with equality if and only if the variables $X_1, X_2, \ldots, X_n$ are independent.

We now are in a position to discuss **Conditional Entropy**.

If X, Y are random variables, then for a given y, the variable $(X|y)$ denotes a random variable with probabilities

$$\Pr(X = x_i|y), \quad i = 1, 2, \ldots, n$$

where X has the n values $x_1, x_2, \ldots, x_n$. This is a probability distribution since

$$\sum_x \Pr(x|y) = 1$$

Example 10.16 *In Example 10.9, suppose y has the value 4. Now $\Pr(Y = 4)$ is $\frac{1}{6}$. There are 6 ordered pairs (x, y) with $y = 4$. We have, for example,*

$$\Pr(X = 1 \mid Y = 4) = \frac{\Pr(X = 1 \text{ and } Y = 4)}{\Pr(Y = 4)} = \frac{\frac{1}{36}}{\frac{1}{6}} = \frac{1}{6}$$

In fact, $\Pr(X = x_i \mid Y = 4) = \frac{1}{6}$ for $x_i = 1, 2, 3, 4, 5, 6$.

We have

$$H(X \mid Y) = \sum_y H(X \mid y) \Pr(y)$$

$$= -\sum_y \left\{ \sum_i \Pr(X = x_i \mid y) \log \Pr(X = x_i \mid y) \right\} \Pr(y)$$

$$= -\sum_y \left\{ \sum_i \Pr(X = x_i) \log \Pr(X = x_i) \right\} \Pr(y), \text{since } X, Y \text{are independent}$$

$$= -\sum_y H(X) \Pr(y) = H(X) = H\left(\frac{1}{6}, \frac{1}{6}, \frac{1}{6}, \frac{1}{6}, \frac{1}{6}, \frac{1}{6}\right)$$

$$= \log 6 \approx 2.59$$

Or we can use Theorem 10.18 to show that, in general, if X, Y are independent then $H(X \mid Y) = H(X)$.

We can now relate $H(X|Y)$ to $H(X,Y)$. The basic idea for joint probabilities is as follows:

If x_i, y_i are values for X and Y, then we have that $\Pr(X = x_i$ and $Y = y_j) = \Pr(X = x_i) \Pr(Y = y_j | X = x_i)$.

To abbreviate, we say that $\Pr(x_i y_j) = \Pr(x_i) \Pr(y_j | x_i)$.

Theorem 10.17

$$H(X,Y) = H(X) + H(Y|X) = H(Y) + H(X|Y)$$

Proof.

$$H(X,Y) = -\sum_{i=1}^{m} \sum_{j=1}^{n} \Pr(x_i y_j) \log(\Pr(x_i y_j))$$

$$= -\sum_{i=1}^{m} \sum_{j=1}^{n} \Pr(x_i y_j) \log[\Pr(x_i) \Pr(y_j | x_i)]$$

Using the fact that $\log(uv) = \log(u) + \log(v)$ we get:

$$H(X,Y) = -\sum_{i=1}^{m}\sum_{j=1}^{n}\Pr(x_iy_j)\log(\Pr(x_i)) - \sum_{i=1}^{m}\sum_{j=1}^{n}\Pr(x_iy_j)\log(\Pr(y_j|x_i))$$

$$= -\sum_{i=1}^{m}\sum_{j=1}^{n}\Pr(x_iy_j)\log(\Pr(x_i)) - \sum_{i=1}^{m}\sum_{j=1}^{n}\Pr(y_j|x_i)\log(\Pr(y_j|x_i))\Pr(x_i)$$

$$= -\sum_{i=1}^{m}\sum_{j=1}^{n}\Pr(x_iy_j)\log(\Pr(x_i)) + H(Y|X)$$

$$= -\sum_{i=1}^{m}\Pr(x_i)\log\Pr(x_i) + H(Y|X)$$

$$= H(X) + H(Y|X)$$

But $H(X,Y) = H(Y,X)$, so reversing the roles of X, Y, we get

$$H(Y,X) = H(Y) + H(X|Y)$$

and this completes the proof. $\square$

Theorem 10.17 says that the weighted average of $H(X,Y)$ equals the weighted average value of Y plus the weighted average value of X.

Theorem 10.17 is called the **chain rule** for entropies. It generalizes to any number of variables. For example, we have

$$H(X,Y,Z) = H(X) + H(Y|X) + H(Z|X,Y)$$

$$= H(Y) + H(Z|Y) + H(X|Y,Z)$$

From Theorem 10.17, we have $H(X|Y) = H(X,Y) - H(Y)$.

Thus, $H(X) - H(X|Y) = H(X) + H(Y) - H(X,Y)$.

We define the **Information conveyed about** X **by** Y to be

$$I(X:Y) = H(X) - H(X|Y) \; [= H(X) + H(Y) - H(X,Y)]$$

From Theorem 10.17 we have

$$H(X,Y) = H(X) + H(Y|X) = H(Y) + H(X|Y)$$

Therefore,

$$H(X) - H(X|Y) = H(Y) - H(Y|X)$$

Thus,

$$I(X : Y) = I(Y : X)$$

and we can call $I(X : Y)$ the **Mutual Information** of X, Y. Thus, the information conveyed about X by Y equals the information conveyed about Y by X. For a homely example, we could say that the information conveyed about the political truths by a politician's speech equals the information conveyed about the politician's speech by the political truths. The mutual information can thus be an elusive quantity.

Combining Theorems 10.13 and 10.17 we have:

Theorem 10.18 $H(X|Y) \leq H(X)$ *with equality if and only if X and Y are independent.*

Proof. From Theorem 10.17, we have

$$H(X|Y) = H(X, Y) - H(Y)$$

From Theorem 10.13, we have

$$H(X, Y) \leq H(X) + H(Y)$$

(with equality if and only if X and Y are independent). Thus,

$$H(X|Y) \leq H(X)$$

with equality if and only if X and Y are independent.   □

Corollary 10.19 $I(X:Y)=0$ *if and only if X, Y are independent.*

Comments

The formula for mutual information can be explained as follows: The uncertainty about X has been reduced from its original value of $H(X)$. By observing Y the new uncertainty is now just $H(X|Y)$. Thus, the *reduction in uncertainty* is $H(X) - H(X|Y)$.

Another way of looking at this from the Shannon point of view (See Shannon and Weaver [SW49]) is that $H(X) - H(X|Y)$ is the amount of information that we have to add on to the information obtained about X by observing Y to get the full information about X.

Or we can say, thinking of a channel with X transmitting and Y receiving, that $H(X) - H(X|Y)$ is the amount of information transmitted that has been lost by noise in the channel. Since $H(X) = H(X|Y) + (H(X) - H(X|Y))$. The quantity $H(X) - H(X|Y)$ is the amount of information that the "correcting channel" must restore so that full information is received. Once again, we can interchange the roles of X, Y in the above.

We should point out that Theorem 10.18 implies that *uncertainty can never be increased by side conditions, i.e. knowing Y cannot make X less certain.*

When could $H(Y|X)$ be zero? This would seem to say that once we know X we know Y so that Y is a function of X. This is indeed the case: we discuss this in the problems.

We can draw a kind of Venn diagram for entropies, where products of variables correspond to unions. (For more than three variables the corresponding diagram can be a bit misleading because some of the Venn regions may correspond to negative numbers.)

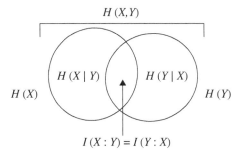

10.9   Applications of Entropy

Entropy is a measure of randomness or uncertainty. Entropy also describes information as the reduction in uncertainty. In cryptography and information security, for example we want to choose a password with high entropy to make it harder to guess.

In information theory, as we will see in the next chapter, entropy tells us how efficiently a source coding can be achieved. Also, in a subsequent chapter (Chapter 12), we will see how conditional entropy is the crucial concept for determining the channel capacity, i.e. the largest possible rate for the secure transmission of information.

10.10   Calculation of Mutual Information

The following example may be found in Ash [Ash90, p. 23] – using a different solution than the one here – and provides a nice illustration of $I(X : Y)$.

Example 10.20 *Two coins are available, one being a fair coin and one being a two-headed coin. A coin is selected at random and tossed twice. The total number of heads is recorded. How much information is conveyed, about which coin has been chosen, by the total number of heads that are obtained?*

Recall that

$$I(X : Y) = H(X) + H(Y) - H(X, Y)$$

Let X be a random variable that has value 0 or 1 according as to whether or not the fair coin or the two-headed coin is chosen. Let Y be the total number of heads obtained when the coin is tossed twice.

Now $H(X) = \log_2(2) = 1$ since the choice of coin is random.

To calculate $H(X, Y)$, we calculate the probabilities corresponding to $X = 0$, $Y = 0$, i.e. the probability of the pair $(0, 0)$, and similarly, the probabilities of $(0, 1)$, $(0, 2)$ and $(1, 2)$. Note that if $X = 1$, Y must be 2. Thus,

$$H(X, Y) = H\left(\frac{1}{2} \cdot \frac{1}{4}, \frac{1}{2} \cdot \frac{1}{2}, \frac{2}{4}, \frac{1}{2} \cdot \frac{1}{4}, \frac{1}{2} \cdot 1\right)$$

$$= H\left(\frac{1}{8}, \frac{1}{4}, \frac{1}{8}, \frac{1}{2}\right) = \frac{1}{8}\log(8) + \frac{1}{4}\log(4) + \frac{1}{8}\log(8) + \frac{1}{2}\log(2)$$

$$= \frac{3}{8} + \frac{2}{4} + \frac{3}{8} + \frac{1}{2} = \frac{14}{8}$$

Now the possible values for Y are 0, 1, 2 with probabilities $\frac{1}{8}, \frac{1}{4}, \frac{5}{8}$, so that

$$H(Y) = \frac{1}{8}\log(8) + \frac{1}{4}\log(4) + \frac{5}{8}\log\left(\frac{8}{5}\right) = \frac{3}{8} + \frac{2}{4} + \frac{5}{8}(\log(8) - \log(5))$$

$$= \frac{3}{8} + \frac{2}{4} + \frac{15}{8} - \frac{5}{8}(\log(5)) = \frac{22}{8} - \frac{5}{8}(\log(5))$$

$$I(X : Y) = H(X) + H(Y) - H(X, Y) = 1 + \frac{22}{8} - \frac{5}{8}\log 5 - \frac{14}{8} = 2 - \frac{5}{8}\log 5 = 0.55$$

For questions on conditional entropy and conditional probability such as the question above, it is convenient to use a **probability tree**. For the question above, our tree would look like the following:

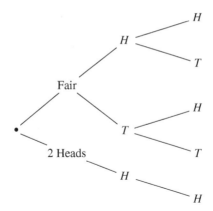

10.11   Mutual Information and Channels

Suppose A is transmitting to B in binary. Assume that the source A is **memoryless** so A chooses a zero with probability α and a one with probability $\beta = 1 - \alpha$, independently of what has already been transmitted.

We also assume that the channel is a **BSC**. Thus, the probability of an error in transmission is always a fixed number p, regardless of whether 1 or 0 is transmitted. These channels will be discussed in great detail in subsequent chapters.

Let X denote a binary variable which has the value 1 or 0, depending on whether A chooses 1 or 0. Let Y be a binary variable which has the value 1 or 0, depending on whether or not B receives 1 or 0.

We want to find $H(X) - H(X|Y)$, i.e. the information revealed about X by Y.

One probability tree is as follows:

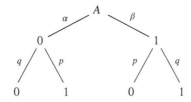

Then

$$H(X) = H(\alpha, \beta) = \alpha \log\left(\frac{1}{\alpha}\right) + \beta \log\left(\frac{1}{\beta}\right)$$
$$H(Y) = H(\alpha p + \beta q, \alpha q + \beta p)$$

since Y receives a one with probability $\alpha p + \beta q$ and a zero with probability $\alpha q + \beta p$.

We want to calculate the information about X that is revealed by knowledge of Y. This information is given by

$$I(X:Y) = H(X) + H(Y) - H(X,Y)$$

The outcome $X = 0, Y = 0$, i.e. the pair $(0,0)$, has probability αq. Similarly, the pairs $(0,1), (1,0), (1,1)$ have probabilities $\alpha p, \beta p, \beta q$. Thus, (X,Y) gives rise to the probability space $(\alpha q, \alpha p, \beta p, \beta q)$. Then

$$H(X,Y) = H(\alpha q, \alpha p, \beta p, \beta q)$$
$$= \alpha q \log\left(\frac{1}{\alpha q}\right) + \alpha p \log\left(\frac{1}{\alpha p}\right) + \beta p \log\left(\frac{1}{\beta p}\right) + \beta q \log\left(\frac{1}{\beta q}\right)$$

Using the facts that $\log(uv) = \log(u) + \log(v)$, $\alpha + \beta = 1$ and $p + q = 1$, we finally obtain the mutual information $I(X:Y)$ given by the following formula:

$$I(X:Y) = p\log(p) + q\log(q) - (\alpha p + \beta q)\log(\alpha p + \beta q) - (\alpha q + \beta p)\log(\alpha q + \beta p)$$

10.12   The Entropy of $X + Y$

Earlier on in the chapter we discussed rolling two fair dice, independently. We have that $H(X) = \log(6), H(Y) = \log(6)$.

Thus, $H(X) + H(Y) = \log(6) + \log(6) = 2.59 + 2.59 = 5.18$. If $Z = X + Y$, it can be calculated that $H(Z) = 3.2 < H(X) + H(Y)$. This is true in general.

We now show that whether or not the real variables X and Y are independent, we have the following result:

Theorem 10.21
$$H(X + Y) \leq H(X,Y)$$

Equality occurs if and only if given any value z in $Z = X + Y$, there is exactly one ordered pair (x,y) of values x in X and y in Y with $x + y = z$.

Sketch of Proof: Suppose that for a given value of z, we had say two ordered pairs (x_1, y_1) and (x_2, y_2) with $(x_1 + y_1) = z = (x_2 + y_2)$. Denote the probabilities

$\Pr(X = x_i \text{ and } Y = y_j)$ by p_{ij} with $i = 1, 2$. Then $H(X, Y)$ will contain the term $-p_{11} \log p_{11} - p_{22} \log p_{22}$. The corresponding term when calculating $H(X + Y)$ will be the term $-(p_{11} + p_{22}) \log(p_{11} + p_{22})$ which is smaller, as can be seen by using properties of the function $x \log(x)$ (see Section 10.13). If the pair (x_1, y_1) is the only ordered pair with $x_1 + y_1 = z$ then $H(X, Y)$ and $H(X + Y)$ will both contain just the term $-p_{11} \log(p_{11})$. $\qquad\square$

Since $H(X, Y) \leq H(X) + H(Y)$, we get a corollary.

Corollary 10.22

$$H(X + Y) \leq H(X) + H(Y)$$

Theorem 10.21 and the corollary can be extended to any number of variables. The reason why Theorem 10.21 holds is that when we "merge two terms" the entropy goes down. An interesting example of this occurred in Example 10.20 and in Theorem 10.21: see also the problems.

10.13   Subadditivity of the Function $-x \log x$

If x, y are positive numbers, then

$$x \log x + y \log y \leq x \log(x + y) + y \log(x + y) = (x + y) \log(x + y)$$

since $\log x$ is an increasing function.

The fact that $x \log x + y \log y \leq (x + y) \log(x + y)$ is shown in [Tur76] under the assumption that x, y and $x + y$ are probabilities. However, as is clear from the above, this assumption is not needed. We thank Paul Tarjan for this useful observation.

The usual definition of a **subadditive function** f is that $f(x + y) \leq f(x) + f(y)$. Thus, the above implies that $-x \log x$ is subadditive.

10.14   Entropy and Cryptography

In Problem 10.13, we show that $H(f(X)|X) = 0$. **This formula proves that the entropy of, for example, RSA is 0.** To see this put $X = C$, the cipher text, and let f be the decryption function. We are given the cipher text C and $f(C) = C^d = M$, the message. In other words, all the uncertainty of the message is stored in the cipher text, which is known.

What this means is that public key systems, such as RSA, provide only **computational security**. That is, given sufficient time and resources, anyone can break RSA and various other public key systems. However, in practice, the amount of time required seems to be infeasibly large, so that RSA and public key cryptography in general still serve to protect important information.

10.15   Problems

10.1   A pair of fair die are rolled. If X, Y denote the numbers showing up on the faces find the average value of Z, the sum of the face-numbers. (See Solution 10.1.)

10.2   Find the variance and the standard deviation of Z. (See Solution 10.2.)

10.3   Find (a) $H(X)$ (b) $H(Y)$ (c) $H(X, Y)$. (See Solution 10.3.)

10.4   Find (a) $H(Z)$ (b) $H(Z|X, Y)$. (See Solution 10.4.)

10.5   Find $H(X|Z)$, $I(X : Z)$. (See Solution 10.5.)

10.6   A fair die is tossed 720 times and the random variable X measures the number of sixes obtained in the 720 tosses. Find the mean and the standard deviation of X. (See Solution 10.6.)

10.7   Use the normal approximation to find the approximate probability of getting exactly 121 sixes. (See Solution 10.7.)

10.8   An urn contains 4 red balls and 3 white balls. A ball is selected at random from the urn and replaced by 5 balls of the other color. Then a second ball is selected at random from the urn.

   Draw a probability tree diagram for this experiment, labeling all the branch probabilities. (See Solution 10.8.)

10.9   Find the probability that both selected balls are of the same color. (See Solution 10.9.)

10.10   Given that both selected balls are of the same color, what is the probability that they are both white? (See Solution 10.10.)

10.11   A source emits a binary string of length 3 subject only to the condition that the binary sum of the three digits is zero. What is the entropy of this string? (See Solution 10.11.)

10.12   Prove that for any random variable X, $H(X|X) = 0$. (See Solution 10.12.)

10.13   Show that $H(Y|X) = 0$ if and only if Y is a function of X. (See Solution 10.13.)

10.14 If $\Pr(U|V) = 0$ must $\Pr(V|U) = 0$? (See Solution 10.14.)

10.15 A is transmitting binary digits to B. A chooses a one with probability 0.8 and a zero with probability 0.2. Because of transmission error, there is a 10% chance of error no matter what is transmitted to B. How much information about what A has transmitted is revealed by what B has received? (See Solution 10.15.)

10.16 A coin is tossed n times in a row. The probability of getting heads is p at each toss of the coin. Show that

$$\sum_{t=0}^{n} t \binom{n}{t} p^t q^{n-t} = np$$

(See Solution 10.16.)

10.17 With the same notation as in Problem 10.16, let $n = 2$. Show that $H(p^2, pq, qp, q^2) = 2H(p)$, where H denotes the Shannon function. (See Solution 10.17.)

10.18 Can the result in Problem 10.17 be generalized for arbitrary n? (See Solution 10.18.)

10.19 Using the notation in Problem 10.17, show that $H(p^2, 2pq, q^2) \leq 2H(p)$. (See Solution 10.19.)

10.20 Can the result in Problem 10.19 be generalized for larger values of n? (See Solution 10.20.)

10.16 Solutions

10.1 $E(Z) = E(X + Y) = E(X) + E(Y) = 3.5 + 3.5 = 7$.

10.2 It is convenient to use the formula for the variance given by $V(X) = E(X^2) - (E(X))^2 = \frac{91}{6} - \left(\frac{7}{2}\right)^2 = \frac{35}{12}$. Now $V(X + Y) = V(X) + V(Y)$, since X, Y are independent $V(Z) = V(X + Y) = \frac{35}{6}$ and $\sigma = \sqrt{\frac{35}{6}}$.

10.3 $H(X) = H(Y) = \log_2 6 = 2.59$. Since X, Y are independent $H(XY) = H(X) + H(Y) = 5.18$.

10.4 By straight forward calculation, we get $H(Z) = H(X + Y) = 3.27$. Once we know X and Y, we know Z so $H(Z|XY) = 0$ (because $H(1, 0) = 0$).

10.5 We need $H(X|Z)$

$$H(X|Z) = \sum_{z=2}^{12} H(X|Z=z)\Pr(Z=z)$$

$$= \frac{1}{36}\log_2 1 + \frac{2}{36}\log_2 2 + \frac{3}{36}\log_2 3 + \frac{4}{36}\log_2 4 + \frac{5}{36}\log_2 5 + \frac{6}{36}\log_2 6$$

$$+ \frac{5}{36}\log_2 5 + \frac{4}{36}\log_2 4 + \frac{3}{36}\log_2 3 + \frac{2}{36}\log_2 2 + \frac{1}{36}\log_2 1$$

$$\approx 1.9$$

Thus, $H(X|Z) = 1.9$. It follows that $I(X:Z) = H(X) - H(X|Z) = 2.59 - 1.9 = 0.69$.

10.6 $E(X) = \frac{1}{6}(720) = 120$, $\sigma(X) = \sqrt{720 \cdot \frac{1}{6} \cdot \frac{5}{6}} = 10$.

10.7 We estimate $\Pr(X = 121)$ by $\Pr(120.5 < X < 121.5)$, i.e. we are estimating a histogram by a piece of an area under the normal curve.

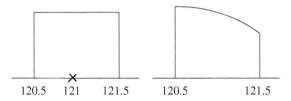

The approximating normal variable Y has mean 120 and standard deviation 10. To convert Y to a standard normal variable Z, which we can look up in tables, we proceed as follows:

$$\Pr(X = 120) \approx \Pr(120.5 < Y < 121.5)$$

$$= \Pr\left(\frac{120.5 - 120}{10} < Z < \frac{121.5 - 120}{10}\right)$$

$$= \Pr(0.05 < Z < 0.15)$$

$$= 0.5596 - 0.5199 = 0.0397$$

So there is about a 4% chance of getting exactly 121 heads.

10.8 Here is the probability tree.

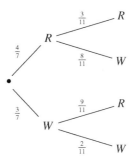

10.9 $\frac{4}{7} \cdot \frac{3}{11} + \frac{3}{7} \cdot \frac{2}{11} = \frac{18}{77}$.

10.10 Let's calculate $\Pr(\text{both } W | \text{both same color})$:

$$\Pr(\text{both } W | \text{both same color}) = \frac{\Pr(\text{both } W \text{ and both same color})}{\Pr(\text{both same color})}$$

$$= \frac{\Pr(\text{both } W)}{\Pr(\text{both same color})} = \frac{\frac{3}{7} \cdot \frac{2}{11}}{\frac{4}{7} \cdot \frac{3}{11} + \frac{3}{7} \cdot \frac{2}{11}} = \frac{1}{3}$$

10.11 The entropy is 2 Shannon bits.

10.12 We have

$$H(X|X) = \sum_{x_0 \in X} H(X|x_0) \Pr(X = x_0)$$

In the calculation of $H(X|x_0)$, the only nonzero probability is 1, corresponding to $x = x_0$, so $H(X|x_0) = 0$ since $\log 1 = 0$. That is,

$$H(X|x_0) = -\sum_{x \in X} \Pr(X = x | X = x_0) \log \Pr(X = x | X = x_0)$$

and since $\Pr(X = x | X = x_0) = 0$ or 1, we have that $H(X|x_0) = 0$. Thus, $H(X|X) = 0$.

10.13 Remember that

$$H(Y|X) = \sum_{x \in X} H(Y|x) \Pr(X = x)$$

The right-hand side is a sum of nonnegative terms. If $H(Y|X) = 0$, then each term in the sum is zero. Since $H(Y|x) = -\sum_y \Pr(y|x) \log \Pr(y|x)$, we know that $\Pr(y|x)$ is defined. From Eq. 10.1, we have that $\Pr(x)$ must then be nonzero, and so we may restrict to the case, where $\Pr(X = x)$ is nonzero. Then, in calculating $H(Y|x)$ all the probabilities must be 0 or 1 since $H(Y|x) = 0$.

To see this, note that a term such as $p \log p$, with p a probability, can only be zero if $p = 0$ or $p = 1$. Now, let x be any value of X such that $\Pr(X = x) \neq 0$. It will follow that there is exactly one value y_0 of Y such that $\Pr[(Y = y_0)|(X = x)] = 1$. For all other $y \neq y_0, \Pr(y|x) = 0$. Thus, there is determined a function mapping x to y_0 and Y is a function of X. The converse follows easily.

10.14 For these two conditional probabilities, to be defined we must have that $\Pr(V) \neq 0$ and $\Pr(U) \neq 0$. Now,

$$\Pr(U|V) = \frac{\Pr(U \text{ and } V)}{\Pr(V)}$$
$$\Pr(V|U) = \frac{\Pr(V \text{ and } U)}{\Pr(U)}$$

Thus, if $\Pr(U|V) = 0$, then $\Pr(U \text{ and } V) = 0$, so it follows that $\Pr(V \text{ and } U) = 0$, i.e. $\Pr(V|U) = 0$.

10.15 Let X be the random variable corresponding to the transmission by A and let Y denote the random variable corresponding to what is received by B.

We have $I(X : Y) = H(X) + H(Y) - H(X, Y)$. Now $H(X) = H(0.2) = 0.7219$.

The possible values for Y are $0, 1$ with probabilities given by $\alpha = (0.2)(0.9) + (0.8)(0.1) = 0.26$ and $\beta = 1 - \alpha = 1 - 0.26 = 0.74$. Thus, $H(Y) = H(0.26) = 0.8267$.

The possible values for (X, Y) are $(0, 0)$, $(0, 1)$, $(1, 0)$, $(1, 1)$ with probabilities $(0.2)(0.9)$, $(0.2)(0.1)$, $(0.8)(0.1)$, $(0.8)(0.9)$. Thus,

$$H(X, Y) = H(0.18, 0.02, 0.08, 0.72)$$

$$= -(0.18 \log(0.18) + 0.02 \log(0.02) + 0.08 \log(0.08) + 0.72 \log(0.72))$$

$$= 0.18 \cdot 2.473 + 0.02 \cdot 5.644 + 0.08 \cdot 3.644 + 0.72 \cdot 0.4739$$

$$= 1.1907$$

Thus, $I(X : Y) = 0.7219 + 0.8267 - 1.1907 = 0.3579$ Shannon bits.

10.16 Let X be the event corresponding to tossing a coin n times in a row, and let X_i correspond to individual ith coin toss, $1 \leq i \leq n$. To calculate $E(X)$, we can make a table, where X is the number of heads, as follows:

Possible Values of X	1	$\ldots$	t	$\ldots$	n
Corresponding Probability	$\binom{n}{1} p^1 q^{n-1}$		$\binom{n}{t} p^t q^{n-t}$		$\binom{n}{n} p^n q^{n-n}$

Then $E(X) = \sum_{t=0}^{n} t \binom{n}{t} p^t q^{n-t}$. But $E(X) = E(X_1 + X_2 + \cdots + X_n) = E(X_1) + E(X_2) + \cdots + E(X_n) = p + p + \cdots + p = np$. The result follows:

10.17 If X_1, X_2 correspond to Bernoulli trials with probability of success p, then $H(X_1, X_2) = H(p^2, pq, qp, q^2)$. Since X_1, X_2 are independent, $H(X_1, X_2) = H(X_1) + H(X_2) = 2H(p)$. The result can also be verified by direct calculation.

10.18 Yes. Since $X_1, X_2, \ldots, X_n$ are independent, we have

$$H(X_1, X_2, \ldots, X_n) = H(X_1) + H(X_2) + \cdots + H(X_n) = nH(p)$$

The expression on the left will be the sum of 2^n terms.

10.19 We use the subadditivity of the function $-x \log x$ as discussed in the text at Section 10.13.

$$\begin{aligned} H(p^2, 2pq, q^2) &= -(p^2 \log p^2 + 2pq \log(2pq) + q^2 \log q^2) \\ &= -(p^2 \log p^2 + (pq + qp) \log(pq + qp) + q^2 \log q^2) \\ &\leq -(p^2 \log p^2 + pq \log(pq) + qp \log(qp) + q^2 \log q^2) \\ &= H(p^2, qp, pq, p^2) = 2H(p) \end{aligned}$$

10.20 Yes, using subadditivity from Section 10.13, we can say for $n = 3$ that

$$H(p^3, 3p^2 q, 3pq^2, q^3) \leq 3H(p)$$

For arbitrary n, we get an analogous result by using the random variable X which denotes the number of successes in n trials. We then have $H(X) \leq nH(p)$. In other words, we have

$$H(x_1, \ldots, x_n) \leq H(x_1) + \cdots + H(x_n) \; (= nH(p))$$

In the case $n = 2$, this is just Corollary 10.22.

Chapter 11

Source Coding, Redundancy

Goals, Discussion In this chapter, we discuss source coding. At this point, we are not yet transmitting data over a possibly noisy channel. Instead, we are mainly involved with formatting source words from a source into binary strings that can then be transmitted. The source can have many different forms such as an analog, biological, digital, or some other kind of source.

We cover source coding in detail including the basic results of Kraft and McMillan leading to Shannon's First Theorem. This result gives the amazing connection between source coding and entropy, the subject of Chapter 10. Arithmetic coding and the fundamental Huffman coding algorithm are also discussed. A crucial component of source coding, from a practical point of view, is to encode data so that it takes up less space so as to require less storage space and to speed up the transmission of messages. Since this aspect is so important, there is some discussion of data compression in this chapter, and even more algorithms and applications in Chapter 17. Compression is crucial for such applications as data transfer or downloading from a source such as the Internet.

The mathematical requirements in this chapter are not unreasonable even though we cover everything in full mathematical detail. One reason for doing this is that the remarkable connection between entropy and encoding must be seen to be believed.

New, Noteworthy The well-known Entropy Lemma in Section 11.2 is at the heart of all source coding.

Cryptography, Information Theory, and Error-Correction: A Handbook for the 21st Century, Second Edition.
Aiden A. Bruen, Mario A. Forcinito, and James M. McQuillan.
© 2021 John Wiley & Sons, Inc. Published 2021 by John Wiley & Sons, Inc.

The proof that the Huffman algorithm is optimal is tricky. Various authors make an unnecessary assumption as follows: Given an optimal encoding and a source word of smallest probability, the corresponding codeword will have maximal length. This codeword will then have a "sibling" on the tree. The assumption, often made, is that the corresponding source word will have the smallest probability or the next smallest probability. In our proof here, we show how to avoid this assumption.

11.1   Introduction, Source Extensions

Let us start off with a **source** which is a mechanism for emitting a continuous stream of **source words** chosen from the set $X = \{x_1, x_2, \ldots, x_m\}$ with corresponding probabilities $p_1, p_2, \ldots, p_m$, where $p_1 + p_2 + \cdots + p_m = 1$ and $0 \leq p_i \leq 1$, $i = 1, \ldots, m$. The set X is known as the **alphabet** of the source. These source words might be actual text words taken from a book, for example, or letters from the English alphabet, where $m = 26$ or 27 (depending on whether or not we allow spaces as well as letters). In this case we have $p_1 = 0.064 =$ probability of A, $p_5 =$ probability of $E = \Pr(E)$, etc. The source words might also be signals from a radio antenna. Pierce [Pie79] discusses at length the case, where the source emits musical notes. Another example would be a DNA sequence in molecular biology.

Frequently, we assume that the source is **memoryless**. This means that the probability p_i that the source emits the symbol x_i is independent of what has been emitted previously. This assumption is not really valid when we write in a language such as English, where the probability that a given letter appears depends very much on the letter or sequence of letters or spaces that precede it. Later on in the book, we discuss **ergodic sources**, generalizing from memoryless sources. Ergodic sources yield a better approximation to a written language when regarded as a source.

Given a source Γ with source words chosen from X, we can construct a new source, called the **sth order extension of** Γ, denoted by Γ^s. The alphabet of Γ^s consists of all possible strings of length s chosen from the alphabet X. If Z is a word in Γ^s, then $Z = y_1 y_2 \cdots y_s$ with y_i in X, $i = 1, \ldots, s$. The probability of Z is defined to be the product of the probabilities of $y_1, y_2, \ldots, y_s$. In symbols, $\Pr(Z) = \Pr(y_1) \cdots \Pr(y_s)$. The sum of the probabilities of elements such as Z add up to 1.

Example 11.1 *Let $X = \{x_1, x_2\}$ with $p_1 = \Pr(x_1) = 0.4$ and $p_2 = \Pr(x_2) = 0.6$. Then the **second extension** X^2 of X has source words (or alphabet) $X^2 = \{x_1 x_1, x_1 x_2, x_2 x_1, x_2 x_2\}$ with corresponding probabilities 0.16, 0.24, 0.24, 0.36. When encoding (see Section 11.2 below), it can be more efficient to encode blocks of consecutive* *source words rather than individual source words, which is why we sometimes use extensions of sources. This process is known as* **block coding.**

By independence, we have the following important result.

Theorem 11.2 *If Γ is a source with alphabet X, and Γ^s denotes the sth order extension of Γ, then*

$$H(\Gamma^s) = sH(\Gamma)$$

Intuitively, we can think that since we are making s choices from a source with uncertainty $H(\Gamma)$, the uncertainty of the resulting string will be s times the uncertainty of $H(\Gamma)$.

11.2 Encodings, Kraft, McMillan

An **encoding** f maps each source word chosen from X to a string with symbols in the alphabet Y. For example, Y might be the binary alphabet, so $Y = \{0, 1\}$, X might be the upper-case English alphabet and f the ASCII encoding which encodes each letter as a binary string of length 8 (see also Chapter 3).

Another possibility is that f might be the encoding given by the **Morse code** so that Y consists of dots, dashes, and spaces.

We always assume that for source words x_i, x_j with $i \neq j$, $f(x_i) \neq f(x_j)$. A **message** is defined to be any string of source words from $X = \{x_1, x_2, \ldots, x_m\}$. For example, the message M might be given by $M = x_3 x_1 x_3$. Then M gets encoded by stringing together or concatenating the strings $f(x_3)f(x_1)f(x_3)$. So we have $f(M) = f(x_3)f(x_1)f(x_3)$. The particular strings over Y of the form $f(x_i)$, $1 \leq i \leq m$ are called **code words**. The set of codewords $f(x_i)$ is a **code** C.

Example 11.3 *Let X consist of the three source words u, v, w with probabilities $0.3, 0.5, 0.2$, respectively. Then, from Chapter 9,*

$$H(X) = (0.3) \log\left(\frac{1}{0.3}\right) + (0.5) \log\left(\frac{1}{0.5}\right) + (0.2) \log\left(\frac{1}{0.2}\right)$$

$$= 0.5211 + 0.5 + 0.4644 = 1.4855$$

An encoding f from X to Y with $Y = \{0, 1\}$ is given as follows:

$$f(u) = 01, \quad f(v) = 1, \quad f(w) = 101.$$

Then if $m = vu$, $f(m) = f(v)f(u) = 101$ The **average length** of an encoded source word is $(0.3)(2) + (0.5)(1) + (0.2)(3) = 1.7$.

An encoding f is said to be **uniquely decipherable** (u.d.) if there do not exist two different messages M_1, M_2 with $f(M_1) = f(M_2)$. Note that, in Example 11.3, f is not u.d, because there are two messages that get encoded to the same codeword. For example, $f(vu) = f(w) = 101$. The encoding f is an **instantaneous code** (or **prefix code**) if there do not exist two distinct source words x_i, x_j such that $f(x_i)$ is a prefix of $f(x_j)$. This means that we cannot have $f(x_j) = f(x_i)y$, where y is some string over Y. Thus, a prefix code can be uniquely decoded from left to right without "look ahead."

Remark 11.4 *It could be argued that the term "prefix" should be replaced by "prefix free."*

Lemma 11.5 *If f is instantaneous, then f is u.d.*

Proof. Suppose M_1, M_2 are two messages with $f(M_1) = f(M_2)$, so the two encodings are equal. Let $M_1 = x_a z_1$ and $M_2 = x_b z_2$, where z_1, z_2 are strings over X, and x_a, x_b are source words. Then, by definition of the encoding function f, we have $f(x_a)f(z_1) = f(x_b)f(z_2)$, because $f(M_1) = f(M_2)$. Suppose $x_a \neq x_b$. Then $f(x_a) \neq f(x_b)$. Then, depending on the length, either $f(x_a)$ is a prefix of $f(x_b)$ or $f(x_b)$ is a prefix of $f(x_a)$. We conclude from this that $x_a = x_b$. Continuing, if $z_1 = x_c u$ and $z_2 = x_d v$ we get $x_c = x_d$. Proceeding we get that $M_1 = x_a x_c u$ and $M_2 = x_b x_d u$. Continuing in this way, we conclude that if $f(M_1) = f(M_2)$ then $M_1 = M_2$. ∎

Lemma 11.6 *There exist u.d. codes which are not instantaneous.*

Proof. Let $X = \{a, b\}$ with $f(a) = 1$, $f(b) = 10$. Then $f(a)$ is a prefix of $f(b)$ so f is not instantaneous. However, f is u.d. as we can see by working to the left each time a zero appears in the output. For example the string 1101 is the encoding of the string aba. ∎

Example 11.7 *Let $X = \{a, b\}$, $f(a) = 1$, $f(b) = 1110$. Here again f is u.d. but not instantaneous because $f(a)$ is a prefix of $f(b)$.*

This example brings up essential differences between u.d. and prefix codes. In a prefix code we can decode "*on line*" moving from left to right as indicated in the proof of Lemma 11.5. Thus, given a message M, and an encoding $f(M)$, proceed from left to right until a codeword $y = f(x)$ is formed. Then x must be the first source word in M, then we just iterate this procedure.

A fundamental result which we only prove now for the *binary alphabet* but which can be immediately generalized to any alphabet is as follows:

Theorem 11.8 (Kraft's inequality) *A necessary and sufficient condition for the existence of an instantaneous encoding $f : X \to Y^*$ with word-lengths $l_1, l_2, \ldots, l_m$ is that $\sum_{i=1}^{m} 2^{-l_i} \leq 1$. Here Y^* denotes the set of all possible strings over the alphabet Y.*

Proof. For convenience of notation, we assume that $l_1 \leq l_2 \leq \cdots \leq l_m$, and construct an associated **binary tree** of depth l_m. We can also think of this tree as a **decision tree** with, say, 0 corresponding to "No" and 1 corresponding to "Yes." For example, let $m = 2$, $X = \{x_1, x_2\}$ and let $f(x_1) = 1$, $f(x_2) = 01$. Then $l_1 = 1$, $l_2 = 2$ and the corresponding tree is in Figure 11.1. This tree has depth 2. There are $2^2 = 4$ **terminal points** labeled $11, 10, 01$ and 00. The **initial vertex** or **root** is V. Any prefix code gives rise to a binary tree such that, if $u \neq v$, the vertex $f(u)$ (or $f(v)$) is not a predecessor of $f(v)$ (or $f(u)$) on the tree, i.e. there is no path on the tree between $f(u)$ and $f(v)$.

To prove Theorem 11.8, we first assume the existence of a binary instantaneous code with word-lengths $l_1 \leq l_2 \leq \cdots \leq l_m$. We associate with this code a binary tree of depth l_m.

A codeword of length l_1 excludes $\frac{2^{l_m}}{2^{l_1}} = 2^{l_m - l_1}$ terminal points, because this is the number of terminal points to the right of the codeword, i.e. the number of terminal points for which the codeword is a predecessor. Note that if u, v are distinct codewords of length l_i, l_j, then by the prefix condition, any terminal point excluded by u is different from a terminal point excluded by v.

Thus, given a prefix code with word-lengths $l_1, l_2, \ldots, l_m$, the total number of excluded terminal points is $\sum_{i=1}^{m} 2^{l_m - l_i}$. Since the total number of terminal points is 2^{l_m} and since $l_1 \leq l_2 \leq \cdots \leq l_m$, we have that

$$\sum_{i=1}^{m} 2^{l_m - l_i} \leq 2^{l_m}$$

Dividing by 2^{l_m} gives $\sum_{i=1}^{m} 2^{-l_i} \leq 1$.

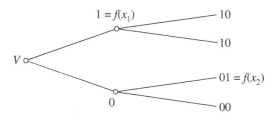

Figure 11.1: Decision tree.

For the converse, suppose we are given positive integers $l_1, l_2, \ldots, l_m$ with $1 \leq l_1 \leq l_2 \leq \cdots \leq l_m$ and satisfying the condition that $\sum_{i=1}^{m} 2^{-l_i} \leq 1$.

To construct a prefix code with word lengths $l_1, l_2, \ldots, l_m$, choose any point P on a binary tree of depth l_1, where P is l_1 steps from the root or initial vertex V.

As above, P excludes $2^{l_m - l_1}$ terminal points. In fact, no vertex of the tree on a path from P to one of these terminal points can correspond to another codeword.

Since $\sum_{i=1}^{m} 2^{-l_i} \leq 1$, we get multiplying by 2^{l_m}, that $\sum_{i=1}^{m} 2^{l_m - l_i} \leq 2^{l_m}$. It follows that $2^{l_m - l_1} < 2^{l_m}$. Thus, at least one terminal point is not excluded by P. It follows that any point on a path from V to one of the nonexcluded terminal points can be chosen as another point on the tree. We choose such a point Q which has distance l_2 from the root (or left end-point) V of the tree. Then, proceeding, we get the required prefix tree with code-lengths $l_1, l_2, \ldots, l_m$ with $l_1 \leq l_2 \leq \cdots \leq l_m$. ∎

Note For a code alphabet of size D the Kraft inequality becomes $\sum_{i=1}^{m} D^{-l_i} \leq 1$.

Remark 11.9 *If the number of codewords of length i is denoted by λ_i the condition in Theorem 11.8 can be written as $\sum_{j=1}^{t} \lambda_j 2^{-j} \leq 1$, where $t = l_m$ is the maximum length of a codeword.*

In the sequel, the following lemma will be fundamental.

Lemma 11.10 (The Entropy Lemma) *Let $p_i, 1 \leq i \leq n$ be a given probability distribution so that $0 < p_i \leq 1$ with $p_1 + p_2 \cdots + p_n = 1$ and let $q_i, 1 \leq i \leq n$ be another probability distribution with $q_i > 0$. Then, taking logs to the base 2, we have $\sum_{i=1}^{n} p_i \log q_i \leq \sum_{i=1}^{n} p_i \log p_i$ with equality if and only if $p_i = q_i, 1 \leq i \leq n$.*

Proof. Recall from calculus the function $y = \ln x = \log_e x$. When $x = 1$, $y = \ln x = 0$. The equation of the tangent line is $y - 0 = 1(x - 1)$, i.e. $y = x - 1$. Since $y'' < 0$, the function y is concave down. From calculus, we know that the graph of a function that is concave down lies below the tangent line at P (no matter, where P is chosen on the curve). Thus, by taking the tangent at $x = 0$ we see that, for all x, $\ln x \leq x - 1$, with equality if and only if $x = 1$. So $\ln\left(\frac{q_i}{p_i}\right) \leq \frac{q_i}{p_i} - 1$, with equality if and only if $q_i = p_i$, $1 \leq i \leq n$. Therefore,

$$\sum_{i=1}^{n} p_i \ln\left(\frac{q_i}{p_i}\right) \leq \sum_{i=1}^{n} p_i \left(\frac{q_i}{p_i} - 1\right) \leq \sum_{i=1}^{n}(q_i - p_i) = \sum_{i=1}^{n} q_i - \sum_{i=1}^{n} p_i = 0$$

Thus, $\sum_{i=1}^{n} p_i \ln(q_i) - \sum_{i=1}^{n} p_i \ln(p_i) \leq 0$ giving

$$\sum_{i=1}^{n} p_i \ln(q_i) \leq \sum_{i=1}^{n} p_i \ln(p_i)$$

with equality if and only if $p_i = q_i$, $1 \le i \le n$. Now, since for any number v, $\log_e v \log_2 e = \log_2 v$ (and $\log_2 e$ is positive) the result follows. ∎

We can also use the above argument to prove our next result. Here $X = \{x_1, x_2, \dots, x_n\}$ is a source with probabilities $p_1, p_2, \dots, p_n$, and $H(X)$ is the entropy of X (see Chapter 9).

Theorem 11.11 $H(X) \le \log_2 n$ *with equality if and only if* $p_1 = p_2 = \dots = p_n = \frac{1}{n}$ *so that* X *is equiprobable. In other words, to maximize the entropy make the probabilities equal.*

Proof. In Lemma 11.10 put $q_1 = q_2 = \dots = q_n = \frac{1}{n}$. Then, from the above $\sum_{i=1}^n p_i \log \left(\frac{1}{n}\right) \le \sum_{i=1}^n p_i \log(p_i)$. Since, for any number v, $\log \left(\frac{1}{v}\right) = -\log v$, we get that $\sum_{i=1}^n p_i \log \left(\frac{1}{p_i}\right) \le \sum_{i=1}^n p_i \log n = \log n$, because $\sum_{i=1}^n p_i = 1$. Thus, $H(X) \le \log n$ with equality if and only if $p_1 = p_2 = \dots = p_n = \frac{1}{n}$. (Intuitively, to increase randomness, equalize the probabilities.) ∎

The next result gives a fortuitous reduction from u.d. to prefix codes.

Theorem 11.12 (McMillan's inequality) *A uniquely decipherable code with word-lengths* $l_1, l_2, \dots, l_n$ *exists if and only if an instantaneous (or prefix) code exists with these word-lengths. (This is in turn equivalent to the statement*

$$2^{-l_1} + 2^{-l_2} + \dots + 2^{-l_n} \le 1.$$

Proof. The condition can be written as $\sum_{j=1}^t \lambda_j 2^{-j} \le 1$, as described in the remark above, where the longest codeword has length t.

The "if" part of the theorem is clear, since every prefix code is u.d. We proceed to the converse. Thus, we assume that we have a u.d. code with word-lengths $l_1, \dots, l_n$. We will show that there exists a prefix code with these word-lengths by proving that the Kraft inequality above holds.

Write

$$\left(\sum_{j=1}^t \lambda_j 2^{-j}\right)^s = \sum_{k=s}^{ts} N_k 2^{-k} \tag{11.1}$$

where s is an arbitrary positive integer that in the sequel goes to infinity. Equation (11.1) is obtained by multiplying out the s terms on the left. To explain (11.1), note that when written out, the left side will have t^s terms, each of the form $2^{-w_1 - w_2 - \dots - w_t} = 2^{-k}$ with $k = w_1 + w_2 + \dots + w_t$. Thus, k lies between t and st.

We claim that N_k is the total number of (source) messages M, where $M = u_1 u_2 \cdots u_s$ is obtained by concatenating exactly s (not necessarily distinct) source words whose coded representation $f(M)$ has a length of exactly k code symbols. To see this, note that by unique decipherability, any sequence of code characters corresponds to at most one message. The number of distinct binary sequences of length k is 2^k.

To summarize, we have $N_k \leq 2^k$.

Substituting in Eq. (11.1), we have

$$\left(\sum_{j=1}^{t} \lambda_j 2^{-j} \right)^s \leq \sum_{k=s}^{ts} 2^k 2^{-k} = ts - s + 1 \leq ts$$

Raising both sides to the power $\frac{1}{s}$, we get

$$\sum_{j=1}^{t} \lambda_j 2^{-j} \leq t^{1/s} s^{1/s}$$

Letting s go to infinity (and using some calculus) gives us the result that $\sum_{j=1}^{t} \lambda_j 2^{-j} \leq 1$, as required. ■

We now proceed to one of the main results for source coding.

Noiseless coding theorem

The setup is this. A memoryless source emits source words chosen from $X = \{x_1, x_2, \ldots, x_m\}$ with corresponding probabilities $p_1, p_2, \ldots, p_m$. We have a binary u.d. encoding f which minimizes the average length t of $\{|f(x_i)|\} = \{n_i\}$, where $|f(x_i)| = n_i$ is the length of $f(x_i)$, $1 \leq i \leq m$. Our goal is to obtain an estimate for t. (Note that t here has a different meaning than what it had in the previous theorem, i.e. Theorem 11.12!) The entropy of a binary string of length t is at most t (see Chapter 9). So we suspect that $t \geq H(X)$ since $H(X)$ is the average uncertainty of a source word. This turns out to be the case.

Theorem 11.13 (Noiseless coding theorem) *If a memoryless source has entropy H, then the average length of a binary, uniquely decipherable, encoding of that source is at least H. Moreover, there exists such a code having average word-length less than $1 + H$, on the assumption that the emission probability p_i of each source word is positive, $1 \leq i \leq m$.*

Proof. We have $H = -\sum_{i=1}^{m} p_i \log p_i$. The average length of a codeword is $t = \sum_{i=1}^{m} p_i n_i$. From Theorem 11.8, we have $A = \sum_{i=1}^{m} 2^{-n_i} \leq 1$. Now, define $q_i = \frac{2^{-n_i}}{A}$. Then

$q_i \geq 0$ and $\{q_i\}$ gives a probability distribution. From Lemma 11.10, we have $H \leq -\sum_{i=1}^{m} p_i \log q_i = -\sum_{i=1}^{m} p_i(-n_i - \log A)$. Thus,

$$H \leq \sum_{i=1}^{m} p_i n_i + \left(\sum_{i=1}^{m} p_i\right) \log A$$

Since $A \leq 1$ and $\sum_{i=1}^{m} p_i = 1$, we have $H \leq \sum_{i=1}^{m} p_i n_i$, as required since $\log A \leq 0$. To prove the last sentence of the theorem, we choose $n_1, n_2, \ldots, n_m$ such that, for each i, n_i is the smallest positive integer satisfying $\frac{1}{p_i} \leq 2^{n_i}$. Since $p_1 + p_2 + \cdots + p_m = 1$ this gives $\sum_{i=1}^{m} 2^{-n_i} \leq 1$. Thus, there exists a u.d. code (in fact, a prefix code) with these word lengths. From the definition of n_i, we have $n_i \geq -\log p_i$, and by minimality of n_i we get $n_i < -\log p_i + 1$. Then

$$t = \sum_{i=1}^{m} p_i n_i < \sum_{i=1}^{m} p_i(-\log p_i) + \sum_{i=1}^{m} p_i = H + 1$$

so $t < H + 1$. ∎

Note Suppose we use, instead of the binary alphabet, a general alphabet of size D. Then the lower bound for the average length becomes $\frac{H}{\log D}$. The upper bound becomes $1 + \frac{H}{\log D}$.

11.3 Block Coding, the Oracle, Yes–No Questions

Now, suppose that instead of assigning a codeword $f(x_i)$ to each source word x_i, we use "**block coding**" to construct the s-fold extension or sth extension of X denoted by X^s (see Section 11.1) and assign a codeword to each source word Z in X^s. In other words, we take a sequence of s independent measurements of X and assign a codeword, using f, to a source word Z in X^s as follows. For $Z = (x_1, x_2, \ldots, x_s)$, put $f(Z) = f(x_1)f(x_2)\cdots f(x_s)$. We have that $\Pr(Z) = \Pr(x_1)\Pr(x_2)\cdots\Pr(x_s)$, where $\Pr$ denotes "probability." If $|X| = m$, then $|X^s| = m^s$. Let t_s denote the average length of an encoded word of Z. From Theorem 11.13, we have $H(Z) \leq t_s < H(Z) + 1$. Since Z is obtained from s **independent** measurements of X, $H(Z) = sH(X)$. Then $sH(X) \leq t_s < sH(X) + 1$.

Dividing by s (which is $>$ positive 0), we get

$$H(X) \leq \frac{t_s}{s} < H(X) + \frac{1}{s}$$

Now $\frac{t_s}{s}$ represents the *average codeword length per value of* X and can be made as close as we wish to $H(X)$ by increasing s. Thus, $H(X)$ can be regarded as the minimum number of binary digits needed on average to encode a source word from X.

Harking back to Chapter 10, if we use a binary tree for encoding a source X, $H(X)$ can be thought of as the minimum number of "yes–no" questions needed, on average, to find out the value of X. Given the tree, we determine the outcome by asking "Yes or No" questions, for example "Is the first entry of the codeword 0?," "Is the second 0?," etc., from an "oracle." This is also closely related to the **binary search algorithm** in computer science.

Example 11.14 *We have a biased coin in which* $\Pr(Head) = 0.7$ *and* $\Pr(Tail) = 0.3$. *We toss it twice. To find out the final outcome, we could just ask for the outcome of each toss separately. This would take two questions.·*

However, if we asked, "Is it heads then heads?," we would get a yes answer with probability $0.7 \times 0.7 = 0.49$. *If we got a no answer, we can ask "Is it heads then tails?," which would be correct with probability* $0.7 \times 0.3 = 0.21$. *Finally, if the answer to that is no, we could ask "Is it tails then heads?," which is correct with probability 0.21 and incorrect with probability equal to 0.09. On average, this yields* $1 \times 0.49 + 2 \times 0.21 + 3 \times 0.21 + 3 \times 0.09 = 1.6$ *questions to determine the outcome of the two tosses which is fewer questions than the naïve approach.*

N*ote: This setup is the encoding function* f, *where* $f(HH) = 1$, $f(HT) = 01$, $f(TH) = 001$, $f(TT) = 000$.

11.4   Optimal Codes

We now look to the problem of actually constructing encodings f and codes C that minimize the average length t of the codewords. If C is the code that minimizes $t = L(C)$ in the class of prefix codes we claim that C minimizes $L(C)$ in the class of *all* u.d. codes. For, if C_1 minimizes t in this larger class, then there exists a *prefix code* C_2 with the same codeword lengths as C_1. The claim now follows from the optimality of C.

(Technically, one needs to prove that an optimal code C actually exists, i.e. that we don't have to get involved in some kind of limiting process involving the greatest lower bound. In fact, the existence can be shown using the Kraft inequalities above).

So we restrict attention to prefix codes C *(= instantaneous codes).* We assume that C is an encoding of a source, with source words drawn from $X = \{x_1, x_2, \ldots, x_m\}$ with the corresponding probabilities

$$p_1 \geq p_2 \geq \cdots \geq p_{m-1} \geq p_m$$

The source word x_i is encoded by an encoding function f, and we denote the length of the binary string $f(x_i)$ by N_i, $1 \le i \le m$. Our notation is also chosen so that source words with the same probability are listed in increasing order of codeword length. We claim that if C is optimal (i.e. minimizes the average codeword length), then C satisfies the following two properties:

Property 1 *Let* **c** *denote any longest codeword in an optimal encoding by a code C. Then there must also exist another codeword* **d** *agreeing with* **c** *in all digits except the last, so* **c** *and* **d** *are siblings. (Think of a family tree.)*

    Proof. Suppose this were not true. Then we could cancel the last digit of **c** and still have a prefix code which would then have a shorter average length than C, contradicting the optimality of C. ∎

Property 2 *Higher probability symbols have shorter codewords. Thus, if $p_i > p_j$, then $N_i \le N_j$.*

    Proof. If this were not the case, we could construct an instantaneous code C_1 by interchanging the codewords $f(x_i)$ and $f(x_j)$. The average length of C_1 minus the average length of C is $p_j N_i + p_i N_j - (p_j N_j + p_i N_i) = (p_j - p_i)(N_i - N_j)$, which is negative (given that $p_i > p_j$) or if we assume that $N_i > N_j$. That is, C_1 has shorter average word length than C, but now we have a contradiction to the optimality of C, i.e. to the minimality of $L(C)$. ∎

    Concerning the construction of codes C, with $L(C)$ small, where $L(C)$ denotes the average length we see one way to do this, which is embedded in the proof of Theorem 11.13. Namely, assuming that all p_i are positive, we define N_i to be the smallest positive integer satisfying $\frac{1}{p_i} \le 2^{N_i}$. Then, from the Kraft inequality, we can construct a prefix code C so that $L(C) < 1 + H$ because $\sum_{i=1}^{m} 2^{-N_i} \le \sum_{i=1}^{m} p_i = 1$. The actual construction of C can be carried out as in the proof of Theorem 11.8.

    This method of constructing codes with small average codeword length is called **Shannon–Fano** encoding. For the Shannon–Fano encoding, $L(C)$ is within 1 of the optimal length.

    In fact, it is possible to construct an optimal encoding by a remarkably simple procedure called **Huffman coding**.

11.5   Huffman Coding

This procedure will lead to an instantaneous (or prefix) code C such that $L(C)$ is less than or equal to $L(C_1)$ for any u.d. code C_1 associated with the given source.

We start off with a given source $S = S_0$ that emits source words which are drawn from $X_0 = X = \{x_1, x_2, \ldots, x_m\}$. Our notation is as in Section 11.4, so $p_1 \geq p_2 \geq p_3 \geq \cdots \geq p_{m-1} \geq p_m$, where $p_i = \Pr(x_i)$, $1 \leq i \leq m$.

First, we "merge" the two source words with smallest probability into a single new source word. Thus, in the first iteration we merge x_{m-1} and x_m to give a new "heavier" vertex W_1 with probability $y = x_m + x_{m-1}$.

Simultaneously, we are constructing, inductively, a graph. When we start off we have m distinct points in the graph and no edges. Then, when we merge, we have an edge from each of the vertices representing x_m and x_{m-1} to W_1.

Thus, initially our graph G_0 looked like Figure 11.2

After the first merge, we have a new "source" S_1 with $m - 1$ source words $x_1, x_2, \ldots, x_{m-2}, W_1$. Our graph G_1 now has vertices $x_1, x_2, \ldots, x_{m-2}, x_{m-1}, x_m, W$ and looks like Figure 11.3.

The net effect is that we have *increased* the number of vertices in the graph by one, and the number of edges by two. Simultaneously, the number of source words in our source has *decreased* by one.

At the next stage, we iterate the process. Thus, we adjoin a new vertex W_2 to the existing graph G_1 together with two new edges emanating from the two source words in S_1 with smallest probability, where S_1 draws its source words from $X_1 = \{x_1, x_2, \ldots, x_{m-2}, W_1\}$. In what follows, given any graph G, we denote the vertices and edges of G by $V(G)$ and $E(G)$.

Associated with our Huffman procedure we have the following table arising from the iterative procedure above, which terminates when the number of source words is 1.

Figure 11.2: Initial graph.

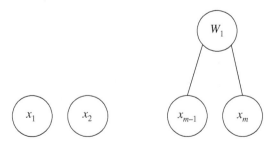

Figure 11.3: After one merge.

Source	Number of source words	Graph G	$|V(G)|$	$|E(G)|$
S_0	m	G_0	m	0
S_1	$m-1$	G_1	$m+1$	2
S_2	$m-2$	G_2	$m+2$	4
$\vdots$				
S_i	$m-i$	G_i	$m+i$	$2i$
$\vdots$				
S_{m-1}	1	G_{m-1}	$2m-1$	$2(m-1)$

Note that at the end of our procedure, we have a connected graph G_{m-1}, which is a **tree** because the number of edges is 1 less than the number of vertices. The set of new vertices is $\{W_1, W_2, \ldots, W_{m-1}\}$. Using the tree, we can encode the original source S and obtain a prefix encoding f of S – which turns out to be optimal. Each source word of S will correspond to a **leaf** on the tree, i.e. a vertex with just one edge on it. All other vertices (or nodes) on the tree are called **internal vertices** (or nodes).

Note that the tree and the encoding will not be unique. For one thing, we may have ties among the probabilities. There is also a left–right ambiguity. A small example can now be presented.

Let $X_0 = X = \{a, b, c, d, e\}$, where the corresponding probabilities are $0.45, 0.2$, $0.15, 0.1$, and 0.1. Our initial graph, and the corresponding probabilities, look as follows:

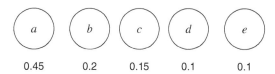

After the first merge, we have the following picture:

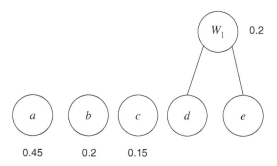

Our probability set now is $\{0.45, 0.2, 0.2, 0.15\}$. So we have a choice. We can merge b and c or we can merge W_1 and c. Either procedure works to give an optimum code, although the coding will be different.

Our diagram after the second merge will be more manageable if we merge b and c. We then have the following.

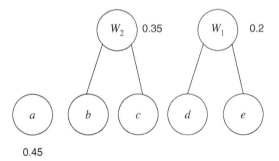

After this merger, our probability set is $\{0.45, 0.35, 0.2\}$. So we merge W_1 and W_2. When we do this, we have the following diagram.

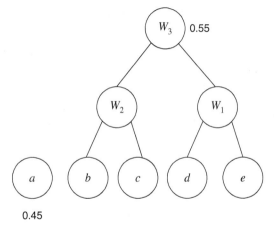

Our probability set is now $\{0.55, 0.45\}$. So we merge a and W_3 to get our encoding tree.

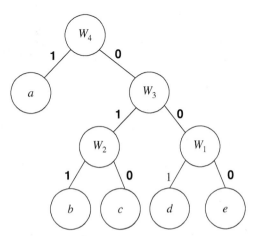

Now starting from the top vertex W_4, we construct our encoding f. Imagine the encoder starting out from W_4 and coming down. If the encoder goes right, she puts in a 0; if she goes left, she puts in a 1. So with this convention, we have $f(a) = 1$, $f(b) = 011$, $f(c) = 010$, $f(d) = 001$, $f(e) = 000$. Note that $H(X) = (0.45)\log\left(\frac{1}{0.45}\right) + (0.2)\log\left(\frac{1}{0.2}\right) + 0.15\log\left(\frac{1}{0.15}\right) + 2(0.1)\log\left(\frac{1}{0.1}\right) = 1.7$. The average length is $(0.45)(1) + 3[0.2 + 0.15 + 0.1 + 0.1] = 2.1$.

Calculating the average length

There is a shortcut here. One way of getting the average length is by multiplying the length of $f(x_i)$ by p_i, and adding, as we have just done. But there is a shorter approach, as follows: Each time we merge, we get a new vertex W_i, $i = 1, 2, \ldots, m - 1$ with associated probability, say q_i. We have the following result:

Theorem 11.15 *The average length is $q_1 + q_2 + \cdots + q_{m-1}$.*

Proof. Our final graph which, being connected and having no circuits is a tree G_{m-1}, also gives a prefix encoding f and a sequence of codes $C_1, C_2, \ldots, C_{m-1}$ for the sources $S_1, S_2, \ldots, S_{m-1}$.

The source C_{m-1}, containing just one source word with probability 1, is encoded by the null string. (In our example, W_4 is encoded by the null string, a is encoded as 1, W_3 is encoded by 0, W_2 by 01, and so forth). Denoting the average length of C_i by $L(C_i)$ we have the following:

$$L(C) = L(C) - L(C_1) + [L(C_1) - L(C_2)] + \cdots + [L(C_{m-2}) - L(C_{m-1})] + L(C_{m-1})$$

Since $L(C_{m-1}) = 0$, we need only calculate $[L(C_{i-1}) - L(C_i)]$. To get from the graph G_{i-1} to the graph G_i, we merge two words with probability u, v say into a single vertex W_i with probability $u + v$. Thus, the average length is changed, as follows: For some integer ℓ, which is the length of the codeword corresponding to the node W_i, we have

$$L(C_{i-1}) - L(C_i) = (\ell + 1)u + (\ell + 1)v - \ell(u + v) = u + v.$$

So we get that $L(C_{i-1}) - L(C_i) = u + v$, which is the probability associated with the vertex W_i, $1 \leq i \leq m - 1$. ∎

Remark 11.16 *In the previous example, associated with W_1, W_2, W_3, W_4, we have the probabilities $0.2, 0.35, 0.55, 1$ for a total of 2.1, which agrees with our previous calculation for the average of length of $L(C)$.*

Remark 11.17 *Note, too, that when merging we can put either one of the merged nodes on the left and the other on the right, giving different encodings.*

Example 11.18 *Let X be a memoryless source which emits heads with probability 0.7 and tails with probability 0.3. Let X^2 denote the second extension of X. We want to find an optimal encoding of X^2.*

The possibilities after two coin tosses are HH, HT, TH, and TT with respective probabilities 0.49, 0.21, 0.21, and 0.09. When we run the Huffman algorithm, we come up with a tree as follows:

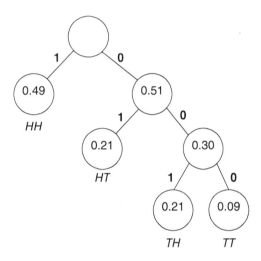

Which offers the encoding f, where $f(HH) = 1$, $f(HT) = 01$, $f(TH) = 001$ and $f(TT) = 000$, which is exactly the encoding we had in Example 11.14 of Section 11.3.

11.6   Optimality of Huffman Coding

Proof of the optimality of Huffman coding

As mentioned in the proof of Theorem 11.15, the tree constructed from the Huffman encoding C_0 of a source $S = S_0$ yields a sequence of Huffman encodings $C_1, \ldots, C_{m-1}$ for the sources $S_1, \ldots, S_{m-1}$.

To prove the result we induct on m, where the source $S_0 = S$ chooses source words from $X = \{x_1, \ldots, x_m\}$.

If $X = \{x_1, x_2\}$ consists of just two source words, then the Huffman encoding gives an encoding function f with $f(x_1) = 1$, $f(x_2) = 0$ which is optimal.

Let us construct the Huffman encoding for S_0. Moving down from the top of the corresponding tree, assume that the source S_i is optimally encoded by C_i (so that the average length $L(C_i)$ is minimal) and that the code C_{i-1} is not an optimal encoding of S_{i-1}. Then there exists an optimal prefix encoding f of S_{i-1} and a code D obtained from f such that $L(C_{i-1}) > L(D)$.

Let l be the maximum length of $f(\mathbf{x})$, where $\mathbf{x}$ is any source word. Then there must exist a codeword $\mathbf{u}$ in S_{i-1} of minimal probability such that $|f(\mathbf{u})| = l$, where $|\ |$ denotes length. For if not, we could construct a new prefix code by interchanging $f(\mathbf{x})$ with $f(\mathbf{u})$, where $|f(\mathbf{x})| = l$ and $\mathbf{u}$ has minimal probability. Then using the same argument as in Property 2 of Section 11.4 we could show that D is not optimal.

From Property 1 in Section 11.4 there exists a sibling codeword $f(\mathbf{v})$ to $f(\mathbf{u})$ in D, where $\mathbf{v}$ is another source word in S_{i-1}.

We want to show that we may assume that either $\Pr(\mathbf{v}) = \Pr(\mathbf{u})$ or else that $\Pr(\mathbf{v})$ has the next smallest probability of any source word in S_{i-1}. Suppose there exists $\mathbf{w}$ in S_{i-1} with $\Pr(\mathbf{v}) > \Pr(\mathbf{w})$. Then by Property 2 in Section 11.4, $|f(\mathbf{v})| = |f(\mathbf{w})|$. By interchanging $f(\mathbf{v})$, $f(\mathbf{w})$, we then have a prefix code E with $L(D) = L(E)$ with E being optimal and having the desired property.

So we can assume that there exists an optimal prefix encoding f of S_{i-1} with code D such that the following holds. There are two source words $\mathbf{u}, \mathbf{v}$ having the two smallest probabilities q_1, q_2 in S_{i-1} such that the codewords $f(\mathbf{u})$ and $f(\mathbf{v})$ are siblings.

By merging the two source words $\mathbf{u}$ and $\mathbf{v}$, we get a new source T and an encoding D_1 of T. Now $\mathbf{u}, \mathbf{v}$ may not be the same two source words of smallest probability in S_{i-1} that were merged to form the source S_i. However, as sources, T and S_i are the same, and D_1 gives an encoding of S_i.

So we have, with L denoting the average codeword length, that

$$L(D) = L(D_1) + q_1 + q_2$$

$$L(C_{i-1}) = L(C_i) + q_1 + q_2$$

Thus, $L(D) - L(C_{i-1}) = L(D_1) - L(C_i)$.

If $L(D) < L(C_{i-1})$, then $L(D_1) < L(C_i)$. But this contradicts the optimality of the code C_i. We conclude that $L(D) = L(C_{i-1})$ so that C_{i-1} is an optimal encoding of S_{i-1}.

This completes the induction and the proof of the optimality of Huffman encoding.

11.7 Data Compression, Redundancy

We have seen the fundamental theoretical connection between the average length of a codeword when the source is encoded into a code C and the entropy of the source. If the source has alphabet X and none of the probabilities are 0, and $L(C)$ is the average codeword length, we have

$$H(X) \le L(C) < H(X) + 1.$$

If we allow zero probabilities, the above statement must be modified, and we get

$$H(X) \le L(C) \le H(X) + 1.$$

(To go to the zero probability case, we can use a limiting process, but then we have to allow equality in the upper bound.)

Arithmetic coding

We have already met two important compression algorithms, namely Shannon–Fano encoding and Huffman encoding. In Section 11.2, we talked about "block coding," where we use the s-fold extension of a source to show that the average word length is close to $H(X)$. Another way of encoding, suitable for the s-fold extension, is called "**Arithmetic Coding**." Let us give the main idea.

Suppose our source is $X = \{x_1, x_2\}$ with probabilities given by $\frac{3}{5}, \frac{2}{5}$, and we want to encode length 2 messages. We can write down the $2^2 = 4$ possible source words lexicographically giving the words $x_1 x_1, x_1 x_2, x_2 x_1, x_2 x_2$ with probabilities $\frac{9}{25}, \frac{6}{25}, \frac{6}{25}, \frac{4}{25}$. We can make the following diagram:

$x_1 x_1$	$x_1 x_2$	$x_2 x_1$	$x_2 x_2$

$0 \qquad\qquad \frac{9}{25} \qquad\qquad \frac{15}{25} \qquad\qquad \frac{21}{25} \qquad\qquad 1$

The probabilities above in decimal form are $0.36, 0.24, 0.24, 0.16$ and the cumulative probabilities are $0.36, 0.60, 0.84, 1$. To encode a message, we just need to indicate the corresponding segment unambiguously. For example, the point $\frac{1}{4}$ is in the first segment, the point $\frac{1}{2}$ is in the second, the point $\frac{3}{4}$ is in the third segment, and the point $\frac{7}{8}$ is in the fourth segment. This is represented in Figure 11.4.

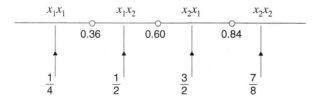

Figure 11.4: Arithmetic coding.

Now, all we have to do is to calculate $\frac{1}{4}, \frac{1}{2}, \frac{3}{4}, \frac{7}{8}$ as *binary decimals*. We have $\frac{1}{4} = 0.01$, $\frac{1}{2} = 0.1$, $\frac{3}{4} = 0.11$, $\frac{7}{8} = 0.111$. This gives the following encoding:

$$x_1x_1 \to 01$$
$$x_1x_2 \to 1$$
$$x_2x_1 \to 11$$
$$x_2x_2 \to 111$$

The average length (per alphabet symbol) is

$$\frac{1}{2}\{(0.36)2 + (0.24)1 + (0.24)2 + (0.16)3\} = 0.96$$

On the other hand, $H(X) = \frac{3}{5}\log\left(\frac{5}{3}\right) + \frac{2}{5}\log\left(\frac{5}{2}\right) = 0.9710$.

For arithmetic coding, the number of bits is determined by the size of the interval. In general, a shorter interval will have smaller probability and will require more bits, giving a nice tie-in with Shannon's measure of $\log(\frac{1}{p})$ for entropy. It can be shown that arithmetical coding is optimal in the limit as the size of the source (= the length of the message) goes to infinity.

11.8 Problems

11.1 Carry out the other Huffman encoding for the source with probabilities $0.45, 0.2, 0.15, 0.1, 0.1$. (See Solution 11.1.)

11.2 Is the following code C optimal, where C is a set of codewords given by $C = \{1, 100, 101, 1101, 1110\}$? (See Solution 11.2.)

11.3 What is the maximum number of source words in a prefix binary code with maximum word length 5? (See Solution 11.3.)

11.4 Find a Huffman code for a source with probabilities $0.1, 0.15, 0.15, 0.2, 0.4$. (See Solution 11.4.)

11.5 Let X be the source which emits heads with probability 0.8 and tails with probability 0.2. Find an optimal encoding for X^2, the second extension of X. What is the average word length? (See Solution 11.5.)

11.6 Let X be as in problem 11.5. Find an optimal encoding for X^3, the third extension of X. What is the average word length? (See Solution 11.6.)
weight 1?

11.7 If a source with N source words is encoded as an instantaneous code and the codeword lengths are $\ell_1, \ell_2, \ldots, \ell_N$, show that $\ell_1 + \ell_2 + \cdots + \ell_N \geq N \log_2 N$. (See Solution 11.7.)

11.8 What does the Huffman code look like for a source with 2^m source words, where each source word is equally likely? (See Solution 11.8.)

11.9 Solutions

11.1 First, begin by merging 0.1 and 0.1 to give a new source $\{0.45, 0.2, 0.15, 0.2\}$. Combine the 0.15 to the 0.2 to get $\{0.45, 0.2, 0.35\}$. Merge 0.2 and 0.35 to get $\{0.45, 0.55\}$. Finally, merge those to get the full tree. Now we get the following encoding:

$$0.45 \rightarrow 0$$
$$0.2 \rightarrow 10$$
$$0.15 \rightarrow 110$$
$$0.1 \rightarrow 1110$$
$$0.1 \rightarrow 1111$$

Notice that this is an optimal code as defined in Section 11.4. The average word length is 2.1.

11.2 No. The longest strings, 1101 and 1110, should be siblings.

11.3 You can't fill any of the spots above the 5th level without blocking off other codeword spots at the fifth level. So the maximum number of source words occurs when the whole 5th level is full, which is $2^5 = 32$ source words.

11.4 Combine 0.1 and 0.15 to get a new source $\{0.4, 0.2, 0.15, 0.25\}$. Now, merge 0.15 and 0.2 to get $\{0.4, 0.35, 0.25\}$. Join 0.25 and 0.35 to get $\{0.4, 0.6\}$, and then join the last two. This yields an encoding of

$$0.4 \rightarrow 0$$
$$0.2 \rightarrow 100$$
$$0.15 \rightarrow 101$$
$$0.15 \rightarrow 110$$
$$0.1 \rightarrow 111$$

The average word length is 2.2.

11.5 The source X^2 has possibilities HH, HT, TH, TT with associated probabilities 0.64, 0.16, 0.16, and 0.04. An optimal encoding is

$$HH \to 1$$

$$HT \to 01$$

$$TH \to 001$$

$$TT \to 000$$

with average word length 1.56.

11.6 The source X^3 is tabulated as follows:

Source symbol	HHH	HHT	HTH	THH	HTT	THT	TTH	TTT
Probability	0.512	0.128	0.128	0.128	0.032	0.032	0.032	0.008
Codeword	1	011	010	001	0001	00 001	000 001	000 000

The average word length is 2.192.

11.7 The given encoding will still give an instantaneous encoding for any probability distribution, including the equiprobable case. In that case, we have $H(X) \leq t$, where t is the average word length. Thus,

$$\log N = \sum_{i=1}^{N} \frac{1}{N} \log N = H(X) \leq t = \frac{\ell_1}{N} + \frac{\ell_2}{N} + \cdots + \frac{\ell_N}{N}$$

and from this the conclusion follows.

11.8 All source words will end up in the bottom level, because after merging any two source words, you will get a node whose probability is bigger than any other pure source word. So you will get a code C, where each codeword has length m, and, furthermore, C will contain *all* codewords of length m.

Chapter 12

Channels, Capacity, the Fundamental Theorem

Goals, Discussion The material here is fundamental. We want to give detailed explanations of these topics, not just statements of theorems. In Chapter 11, we have seen how data can be efficiently encoded in binary form. We discussed how to get rid of "bad" redundancy that adds nothing to the information content of the source.

Here is an example. Let a source S emit symbols a, b, c, d, e with probabilities 0.45, 0.2, 0.15, 0.1, 0.1. As we saw in Chapter 11, the Huffman encoding, which is the most efficient coding, is such that, on average, 2.1 bits per emitted symbol are required. If we are constructing a file of 1000 successive source symbols from S, we require about 2100 bits. We point out that the individual source letters have been encoded into binary strings of *variable length.*

Using, for example, a Huffman encoding, we can get rid of "bad Redundancy." But now we introduce *"good redundancy"*! Let us explain.

We want to transmit our file of approximately 2100 bits over some kind of **noisy channel**, denoted by Γ.

What we do is this. We divide our data stream of 2100 bits into blocks of a *fixed* size k. We then "encode" our block of length k – so we have k **information digits**, or **message digits** (or **bits**) – into a longer block of length n, called a **codeword**, by adjoining $n-k$ bits which add "good redundancy." These $n-k$ bits, in the case of

Cryptography, Information Theory, and Error-Correction: A Handbook for the 21st Century, Second Edition.
Aiden A. Bruen, Mario A. Forcinito, and James M. McQuillan.
© 2021 John Wiley & Sons, Inc. Published 2021 by John Wiley & Sons, Inc.

linear codes, are "**check bits**" or "**parity bits**" or "**parity checks**". For example with our 2100 bits, we could let $k = 7$ and adjoin just one parity bit. This single parity bit adjoins 0 or 1 as the case may be to ensure that *the total number of ones in the enlarged message of length 8 is an even number*. For example the block (0 1 1 1 1 0 1) which has 5 ones, gets encoded as (0 1 1 1 1 0 1 1) which has 6 ones. On the other hand, a block (0 1 1 1 0 0 1) that has 4 ones, gets encoded as (0 1 1 1 0 0 1 0) which still has 4 ones. Then, if a binary string with an odd number of ones is Received, we know that there has been a transmission error and can ask for a resend. This is an example of **error detection**.

In the general case, each check bit will be a binary sum (or linear combination, for bigger fields) of message bits. The idea is that if only a few bits of a codeword are corrupted by the channel, the receiver can decode correctly (perform **error correction**) or **detect** errors and ask for a resend.

Our task then is to determine exactly the maximum rate of transmission whereby the codewords can be decoded in such a way that the probability of error is vanishingly small over a given channel. This famous problem was solved by Claude Shannon in the 1940s. His result is the fundamental result in communication theory. A more engineering-type aspect of the same problem is discussed in Chapter 13.

New, Noteworthy   We explain the fundamental concepts of information rate and channel capacity by means of several examples. We show how to calculate channel capacity in a very easy manner using elementary probability tree diagrams. We are able to quickly obtain the limiting value of the **cascade** of a channel with itself n times by using some of the mathematical results behind Markov chains. The basic idea is that, mathematically, certain kinds of channel matrices can be regarded as the matrix of a Markov chain.

12.1   Abstract Channels

We start off with a **channel** Γ which is a mechanism for transmitting data messages. We will give several examples shortly.

Abstractly, the input and output of the channel correspond to discrete random variables X, Y. Our channels will be discrete and X, Y **will have only finitely many values**. Y will not be a function of X in the sense that, knowing X, we cannot predict exactly what Y will be. We think of Y as a "noisy version" of X. This noise could correspond to thermal noise in a circuit, for example. X might correspond to a source, or to a source obtained by encoding X. For each input x in X, there is an output determined by the **forward probabilities** or **transition probabilities** $\Pr(y \mid x)$ for y in Y. If these probabilities do not change with time and are independent, i.e. they correspond to independent random variables, the channel is **memoryless** (and discrete). Then, the probability of a given symbol being output depends only on the input symbol.

Thus, given a channel Γ, there corresponds a pair X, Y of statistical variables and a set of forward probabilities, $\Pr(Y = y \mid X = x)$.

On the other hand, given a join pair (X, Y) of random variables, we can construct a discrete channel with forward probabilities

$$\Pr(y \mid x) = \Pr((Y = y) \mid (X = x))$$

That is, knowing $\Pr(x, y)$ and $\Pr(x)$, we can find $\Pr(y \mid x)$ using the formula for conditional probability of Chapter 10, which says that

$$\Pr(y \mid x) = \frac{\Pr[(X = x) \text{ and } (Y = y)]}{\Pr(X = x)}, \qquad \Pr(X = x) \neq 0$$

We can summarize as follows:

Theorem 12.1 *Channels are equivalent to discrete joint probability distributions. That is, given a channel, we can construct a discrete joint probability distribution, and vice versa.*

12.2   More Specific Channels

Let us examine the situation in more concrete terms. We suppose that the channel accepts input symbols from an alphabet $A = \{a_1, \ldots, a_m\}$ and outputs symbols from the alphabet $B = \{b_1, \ldots, b_n\}$. Given any input symbol a_i, there is a certain probability that b_j is the output, namely $p_{ij} = \Pr(b_j \mid a_i)$. These probabilities are independent and never change with time. Given these probabilities, we can form the **channel matrix** $P = (p_{ij})$, which is a matrix with m rows and n columns in which each entry lies between 0 and 1 and the sum of the entries in each row is 1. Very often, $A = B = \{0, 1\}$.

Example 12.2   *Let $A = B = \{0, 1\}$. Suppose that the channel Γ has the following two properties:*

(a) Whenever 0 is the input, then 0 is the output with probability 0.8.

(b) Whenever 1 is the input, then 1 is the output with probability 0.9.

The channel matrix P is then as follows:

$$P = \begin{matrix} \\ 0 \\ 1 \end{matrix} \begin{matrix} 0 & 1 \\ \left(\begin{matrix} 0.8 & 0.2 \\ 0.1 & 0.9 \end{matrix} \right) \end{matrix}$$

The general binary channel matrix P for a memoryless channel will look like this:

$$P = \left(\begin{matrix} q_1 & p_1 \\ p_2 & q_2 \end{matrix} \right)$$

Here p_1, p_2, q_1, q_2 are probabilities, i.e. they are real numbers lying between 0 and 1. Moreover, $p_i + q_i = 1$, $i = 1, 2$. We see that p_1 (p_2) is the probability that 0 (respectively, 1) is incorrectly received.

As a very important special case, suppose $p_1 = p_2 = p$. Then $q_1 = q_2 = q$. Our matrix P is now as follows:

$$P = \left(\begin{matrix} q & p \\ p & q \end{matrix} \right) = \left(\begin{matrix} 1-p & p \\ p & 1-p \end{matrix} \right)$$

The number p is then called the **parameter** of the channel. **Thus, p is the probability of a transmission error** regardless of whether 0 or 1 is sent over the channel Γ. This channel is then called the **binary symmetric channel** (BSC), because P is now a **symmetric matrix**.

We can diagram this channel as follows:

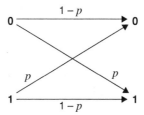

If $p > \frac{1}{2}$, then by reversing the output, i.e. by interchanging 0,1 in the output, we have a new channel with parameter less than or equal to $\frac{1}{2}$. **Thus, we can always assume that $p \leq \frac{1}{2}$.** If $p = \frac{1}{2}$, the channel is **completely random**.

12.3   New Channels from Old, Cascades

Given two channels Γ_1, Γ_2 with the number of outputs of Γ_1 equalling the number of inputs of Γ_2, we can compose them and form the **cascade** of the two channels by putting the channels in series with the input of Γ_2 being the output of Γ_1 in order to obtain a new channel called the cascade of the two original channels. We have

$$\text{input} \; \to \Gamma_1 \to \Gamma_2$$

Example 12.3 *Suppose* Γ_1, Γ_2 *are channels with respective channel matrices*

$$P_1 = \begin{pmatrix} 0.6 & 0.4 \\ 0.4 & 0.6 \end{pmatrix}$$

and

$$P_2 = \begin{pmatrix} 0.8 & 0.2 \\ 0.1 & 0.9 \end{pmatrix}$$

We have the following probability tree diagram for the cascade of the two channels.

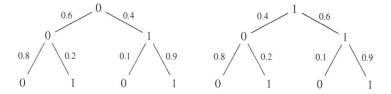

We note the following:

If 0 is the input, the probability of outputting 0 is $(0.6)(0.8) + (0.4)(0.1)$.

If 0 is the input, the probability of outputting 1 is $(0.6)(0.2) + (0.4)(0.9)$.

If 1 is the input, the probability of outputting 0 is $(0.4)(0.8) + (0.6)(0.1)$.

If 1 is the input, the probability of outputting 1 is $(0.4)(0.2) + (0.6)(0.9)$.

Thus, the channel matrix for the cascade $\Gamma_1 \Gamma_2$ *is*

$$P = \begin{pmatrix} (0.6)(0.8) + (0.4)(0.1) & (0.6)(0.2) + (0.4)(0.9) \\ (0.4)(0.8) + (0.6)(0.1) & (0.4)(0.2) + (0.6)(0.9) \end{pmatrix} = \begin{pmatrix} 0.52 & 0.48 \\ 0.38 & 0.62 \end{pmatrix}$$

Note that for any channel matrix, the rows must add up to 1, but the columns need not add up to 1. But another key fact here is that the matrix P for the cascade of the two channels is just the **matrix product** of the two channels. In general, we have the **cascade theorem**.

Theorem 12.4 (Cascade theorem) *The matrix Q for the cascade of s memoryless channels $\Gamma_1, \ldots, \Gamma_s$ with channel matrices $P_1, \ldots, P_s$ of size $n \times n$ is the matrix product $P_1 \cdots P_s$. In particular, if $\Gamma_1 = \cdots = \Gamma_s = \Gamma$ has matrix P of size $n \times n$, then $Q = P^s = \underbrace{P \cdots P}_{s \ times}$ is the cascade matrix.*

This last fact is very useful, for the following reason. The matrix P is what is called a **Markov transition matrix**, it is then easy to use Markov theory and obtain an approximation of P^s. P^s will in fact tend to a matrix such that every row is equal to **the fixed probability vector of P.**

Example 12.5 *Let*

$$P = \begin{pmatrix} 0.6 & 0.4 \\ 0.7 & 0.3 \end{pmatrix}$$

Find an approximation for P^6.

To do this we calculate the fixed probability vector $\mathbf{w}$ of P. This is a vector $\mathbf{w} = (x, y)$ determined by the following two conditions:

(1) $\mathbf{w}P = \mathbf{w}$

(2) $x + y = 1$.

*It is a remarkable fact of Markov theory that – assuming P is irreducible (Chapter 14)–these equations can always be solved uniquely so that x, y are **positive**. The vector $\mathbf{w}$ will be a probability vector. We have*

$$(x, y) \begin{pmatrix} 0.6 & 0.4 \\ 0.3 & 0.7 \end{pmatrix} = (x, y)$$

This gives

$$0.6x + 0.3y = x$$

$$0.4x + 0.7y = y$$

and

$$x + y = 1$$

The second equation can be seen to follow from the third and first equations by subtracting them, so we can ignore it. From the first and third equations, we get $x = \frac{3}{7}$

and $y = \frac{4}{7}$. Thus, P^s tends to the matrix $\begin{pmatrix} \frac{3}{7} & \frac{4}{7} \\ \frac{3}{7} & \frac{4}{7} \end{pmatrix}$ *as s gets large. In particular, P^6 is approximately equal to* $\begin{pmatrix} \frac{3}{7} & \frac{4}{7} \\ \frac{3}{7} & \frac{4}{7} \end{pmatrix}$.

Example 12.6 *Let Γ be the BSC with parameter $p \le \frac{1}{2}$ and channel matrix*

$$P = \begin{pmatrix} 1-p & p \\ p & 1-p \end{pmatrix}$$

Describe the channel that is obtained by composing Γ with itself, i.e. the channel that corresponds to the cascade of Γ with Γ.

We calculate the matrix

$$PP = \begin{pmatrix} q & p \\ p & q \end{pmatrix} \begin{pmatrix} q & p \\ p & q \end{pmatrix} = \begin{pmatrix} q^2 + p^2 & 2pq \\ 2pq & p^2 + q^2 \end{pmatrix}$$

where $q = 1 - p$. This gives that

$$PP = P^2 = \begin{pmatrix} 1 - 2p(1-p) & 2p(1-p) \\ 2p(1-p) & 1 - 2p(1-p) \end{pmatrix}$$

This matrix is symmetric so the cascade is again a BSC. It has parameter $2p(1-p)$. This parameter is the probability of a transmission error in the cascade channel $\Gamma\Gamma$. Examining the quadratic $2p(1-p)$, we see that $2p(1-p) \le \frac{1}{2}$. Since $p \le \frac{1}{2}$, we have $1 - p > \frac{1}{2}$. Multiplying by $2p > 0$, we thus have $p < 2p(1-p) \le \frac{1}{2}$. This means that the cascade has parameter $\le \frac{1}{2}$ but is less reliable *because the probability of a transmission error is larger.*

In fact, the reliability decreases as we construct the cascades $\Gamma\Gamma, \Gamma\Gamma\Gamma, \ldots$. In the limit, we get the result (discussed in the problems) that the parameter tends to $\frac{1}{2}$ so that the channel becomes completely unreliable, i.e. random, in the limit, with parameter $\frac{1}{2}$.

12.4 Input Probability, Channel Capacity

So far we have only discussed the channel. We also need to pin down some facts about the source and the input probability. Having done so we can define the **channel capacity**.

In general, let X and Y be random variables corresponding to the input and output as in Section 12.1. Recall that from Chapter 10 we can calculate the entropy $H(X)$, which is defined as $-\sum_{x \in X} \Pr(x) \log \Pr(x)$. We will restrict attention in this chapter to **memoryless** sources X as defined in Chapter 11. This just means that, if a is an input symbol, $\Pr(X_i = a)$ does not vary with i and is independent of the probability of emission of other symbols. We can think of starting off with a source S, as in the introduction, and then encoding S in binary or in some other alphabet. We now have a new binary source X from the encoding that provides the channel input. Recall that there is associated with the channel the "forward probabilities" that can also be regarded as a "source" emitting symbols with certain probabilities, as follows:

Given any y in Y, we have $\Pr(y) = \sum_x Pr(y \text{ and } x)$. From Chapter 10, we have

$$\Pr(U|V) = \frac{\Pr(U \cap V)}{\Pr(V)}$$

where $\Pr(V) \neq 0$. Applying this, we get

$$\Pr(y) = \sum_x \Pr(y \mid x) \Pr(x)$$

Then we can calculate $H(Y)$, $H(X|Y)$, $H(X,Y)$ and

$$I(X:Y) = H(X) + H(Y) - H(X,Y)$$

We define the **capacity** of the channel as follows:

$$\mathbf{capacity} = \max_{\Pr(X)} I(X:Y)$$

where $\Pr(X)$ denotes the probability distribution of the input X. In other words, we take the maximum, over all possible input probability distributions, $\Pr(X)$, of the mutual information $I(X:Y)$. (Strictly speaking, in rigorous mathematical terms, we should define capacity to be $\sup_{\Pr(X)} I(X:Y)$, i.e. the supremum of $I = I(X:Y)$ taken over all input probabilities. However, in our case, because I is a continuous function of X, there will exist an input distribution X which actually attains the supremum. So we are justified in using the maximum in the definition. We encountered this kind of issue before in Chapter 11 when discussing optimal encodings.)

The capacity will be a number that *will depend only on the channel matrix*. Its **units** are Shannon bits per symbol or Shannon bits per time unit depending on the context.

To understand the concept more fully, let us do some calculations. Our first concern is the BSC.

Channel capacity for binary symmetric channels

As usual, let p denote the parameter of a BSC, i.e. the probability of a transmission error.

The beginning of the calculation here is the same – apart from notation – as that in Section 10.11.

Let x denote the probability that 0 is input so that $1 - x$ is the probability that 1 is input. As usual, all our logs will be to the base 2.

Therefore, we have

$$H(X) = -(x \log x + (1-x) \log(1-x))$$

Setting $q = 1 - p$, we get that the probability that a zero is output is $x(1-p) + (1-x)p = \alpha$ and the probability that a one is output is $(1-x)(1-p) + xp = \beta$. Therefore,

$$H(Y) = H(\alpha, \beta) = -(\alpha \log \alpha + \beta \log \beta)$$

The possible outcomes (x, y), corresponding to the random variable (X, Y), are easily obtained.

The possible values for the input X are $0, 1$ with probabilities $x, 1 - x$. The possible values for the output Y are $0, 1$ with probabilities α, β. Thus, the possible values for (X, Y) are $\{(x, y)\} = \{(0, 0), (0, 1), (1, 0), (1, 1)\}$. Then, $\Pr((x, y) = (0, 0)) = \Pr(0$ is input and 0 is output$) = x(1 - p)$. Probabilities for the other values of (x, y) can be calculated in a similar fashion. It follows that

$$H(X, Y) = H(x(1-p), xp, (1-x)p, (1-x)(1-p))$$

We then have

$$I(X : Y) = H(X) + H(Y) - H(X, Y)$$

$I(X : Y)$ is now just a function of a single variable x, denoted by $f(x)$, where x denotes the probability that the source emits a zero. What we have to do is to find the maximum value of $f(x)$, where $0 \le x \le 1$. By a well-loved calculus principle, this maximum can be obtained where the derivative of f is zero (having first checked the value of f at the end points 0 and 1). We need first to simplify using the fact that $\log(uv) = \log u + \log v$. Set $q = 1 - p$. We have

$$H(X) - H(X, Y) = -x \log x - (1-x) \log(1-x) + xq \log(xq) + xp \log(xp)$$

$$+ (1-x)p \log((1-x)p) + (1-x)q \log((1-x)q)$$

$$= \log x(-x + xq + xp) + \log(1-x)(x - 1 + (1-x)p + (1-x)q)$$

$$+ \log q(xq + (1-x)q) + \log p(xp + (1-x)p)$$

$$= q \log q + p \log p \quad \text{(since the first two terms are 0).}$$

Thus, $I(X : Y) = H(X) + H(Y) - H(X, Y) = p \log p + q \log q - (\alpha \log \alpha + \beta \log \beta)$.

As before, we have $f(x) = I(X : Y)$. We want to find the maximum value of $f(x), 0 \le x \le 1$.

Suppose $x = 0$. Then $\alpha = p$, $\beta = q$, and

$$I(X : Y) = p \log p + q \log q - (p \log p + q \log q) = 0$$

Suppose $x = 1$. Then $\alpha = q$, $\beta = p$. We have

$$I(X : Y) = p \log p + q \log q - (q \log q + p \log p) = 0$$

Next, differentiating $f(x)$ and setting the derivative to 0 gives $x = \frac{1}{2}$. Then $\alpha = \frac{1}{2}$ and $\beta = \frac{1}{2}$. So

$$I(X : Y) = p \log p + q \log q - \left(\frac{1}{2} \log \left(\frac{1}{2} \right) + \frac{1}{2} \log \left(\frac{1}{2} \right) \right)$$

Since $\log \left(\frac{1}{2} \right) = -\log 2 = -1$, we get

$$I(X : Y) = 1 + p \log p + q \log q = 1 - H(p)$$

We have now our channel capacity.

Theorem 12.7 (Capacity theorem for the binary symmetric channel)   *The channel capacity Λ of the BSC with parameter p is equal to $1 - H(p) = 1 + p \log p + q \log q$, where $q = 1 - p$.*

A diagram for this capacity function $\Lambda = \Lambda(p)$ is as follows:

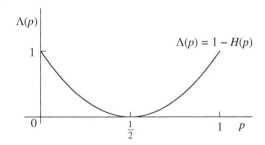

Remarks

When $p = \frac{1}{2}$, the channel is purely random and $\Lambda = 0$.

When $p = 1$, the channel is completely reliable and $\Lambda = 1$.

When $p = 0$, the channel is not only completely unreliable but also $\Lambda = 1$.

We refer to the Appendix B for tables of values of $H(p)$.

12.5 Capacity for General Binary Channels, Entropy

In general, capacities are difficult to calculate. Let us examine the general binary memoryless channel with channel matrix P as follows:

$$P = \begin{pmatrix} q_1 & p_1 \\ p_2 & q_2 \end{pmatrix}$$

with

$$\begin{cases} p_1 + q_1 &= 1, \\ p_2 + q_2 &= 1. \end{cases}$$

Let the input probability for 0 be denoted by x so that the input probability for 1 is $1 - x$. Using a probability tree as in Section 12.3, we deduce the following:

The probability that 0 is output is $xq_1 + (1 - x)p_2 = \alpha$.

The probability that 1 is output is $xp_1 + (1 - x)q_2 = \beta$.

Then the capacity Λ is given by the maximum value of $f(x)$, where

$$f(x) = H(x, 1 - x) + H(\alpha, \beta) - H(xq_1, xp_1, (1 - x)p_2, (1 - x)q_2)$$

To actually calculate this maximum is slightly complicated and is best done using Lagrange multipliers. However, in any given case, we can calculate the capacities as indicated below.

A discussion of the general case is given by Ash ([Ash90], p. 304) who uses the inverse of the channel matrix. The conclusion is as follows. Let the capacity be Λ. Then

$$\Lambda = \log(2^u + 2^v)$$

where $u = \frac{q_2 H(q_1) - p_1 H(p_2)}{p_2 - q_1}$, $v = \frac{-p_2 H(q_1) + q_1 H(p_2)}{p_2 - q_1}$.

Let us return to the symmetric case with $p_1 = p_2 = p$, $q_1 = q_2 = q$ so that we have a BSC with parameter p. Note that Λ above then simplifies to $1 - H(p)$ as expected.

Using the notation of Section 12.4, the input entropy is

$$H(X) = -(x \log x + (1 - x) \log(1 - x)) = H(x)$$

The entropy of the output Y is

$$H(Y) = H(x(1 - p) + (1 - x)p, xp + (1 - x)(1 - p)) = H(x(1 - p) + (1 - x)p)$$

(See also below, this section.) We now have the following result for the BSC.

The entropy of the input of a binary symmetric channel is less than or equal to the entropy of the output.

To see this, let us study the graph of the Shannon function $y = H(x)$. As can be seen from the graph (or by taking the second derivative and verifying that it is negative between 0 and 1), this function is (strictly) concave down (=convex). This implies that if we join 2 points A, B on the graph, the y value at a point on the curve, whose x-value lies between the x-values of A, B is greater than the corresponding y-value on the line AB.

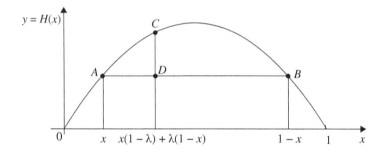

Here, the y-value of C is greater than the y-value of $D = H(x)$. A point on the axis between x and $1 - x$ has x-coordinate equal to $x + \lambda(1 - x - x) = x(1 - \lambda) + \lambda(1 - x)$ for some number λ with $0 \le \lambda \le 1$. Replacing λ by p, the result above follows.

Algebraic relation between input and output

Over a binary channel let $(x, 1 - x)$ be the input probability distribution so that the probability of 0 being transmitted is x. Then, if P is the channel matrix, the output is obtained by calculating $(x, 1 - x)P$. For a BSC with parameter p, we get

$$(x, 1 - x) \begin{pmatrix} 1 - p & p \\ p & 1 - p \end{pmatrix} = (x(1 - p) + (1 - x)p, \, xp + (1 - x)(1 - p))$$

for the output, where the first element of the pair is the probability that 0 is output.

12.6   Hamming Distance

Suppose $\mathbf{x}$ and $\mathbf{y}$ are two **vectors** of length n, i.e. two strings of length n over some alphabet. Then the **Hamming distance** between $\mathbf{x}$ and $\mathbf{y}$, denoted by $d(\mathbf{x}, \mathbf{y})$, is defined to be the number of positions in which $\mathbf{x}$ and $\mathbf{y}$ *disagree*.

Example 12.8 *Suppose the alphabet is the binary alphabet, $n = 4$, $\mathbf{x} = (1\,0\,1\,1)$, $\mathbf{y} = (0\,1\,0\,1)$. Then $\mathbf{x}$ and $\mathbf{y}$ differ in the first three positions, agreeing on the fourth, so the Hamming distance is 3, i.e. $d(\mathbf{x}, \mathbf{y}) = 3$.*

The important point about this definition is that the Hamming distance is a distance in the mathematical sense, similar to the Euclidean distance. That is, it satisfies the following three properties.

(a) $d(\mathbf{x}, \mathbf{y}) \geq 0$. Also $d(\mathbf{x}, \mathbf{y}) = 0$ if and only if $\mathbf{x} = \mathbf{y}$.

(b) $d(\mathbf{x}, \mathbf{y}) = d(\mathbf{y}, \mathbf{x})$ (symmetry).

(c) $d(\mathbf{x}, \mathbf{z}) \leq d(\mathbf{x}, \mathbf{y}) + d(\mathbf{y}, \mathbf{z})$ for any three vectors $\mathbf{x}$, $\mathbf{y}$, $\mathbf{z}$ of the same length over the same alphabet.

Property (c) is called the **triangle inequality**. It says that the distance between two points of a triangle is less than or equal to the sum of the other two distances in the triangle. See the following picture.

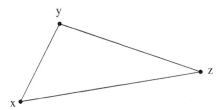

We can easily visualize what is going on in the binary case by drawing an n-cube. For $n = 3$, we get the following picture.

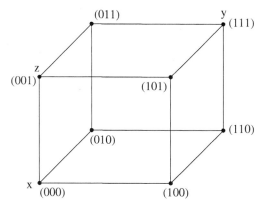

We have $2^3 = 8$ possible binary strings of length 3 represented by the 8 vertices of a cube.

The Hamming distance between any 2 vertices is not the Euclidean distance but rather the number of cube edges that one has to traverse in going from one of the vertices to the other. For example if $\mathbf{x} = (000)$ and $\mathbf{y} = (111)$, then $d(\mathbf{x}, \mathbf{y}) = 3$ because the shortest path of edges between $\mathbf{x}$ and $\mathbf{y}$ contains three edges. Similarly, if $\mathbf{z} = (001)$, we get $d(\mathbf{x}, \mathbf{z}) = 1$, $d(\mathbf{y}, \mathbf{z}) = d(\mathbf{z}, \mathbf{y}) = 2$.

12.7   Improving Reliability of a Binary Symmetric Channel

Suppose A is transmitting binary vectors or strings of length n to B over a BSC Γ with parameter p. We want to calculate some error probabilities and to devise means for improving the reliability of the channel.

Example 12.9   *Let $n = 1$, so A has just two possible messages, namely, "yes" and "no" encoded as 1 and 0, respectively. Then the probability of a message getting corrupted is p.*

Example 12.10   *Let $n = 3$ and suppose A has eight possible messages corresponding to the eight possible binary strings of length 3. We calculate the probability that a given message of length 3 will undergo a transmission error, as follows: The probability that the first bit gets transmitted properly is $q = 1 - p$. Independently, the probability that the second and third bits are transmitted correctly is also q. So the probability that* all *three bits are correctly received is q^3. Thus, the probability of at least one transmission error is $1 - q^3$. For example, if $p = 0.01$, then the probability of at least one error is $1 - (0.99)^3 = 0.0297$. This is almost 3p.*

In general, these error probabilities can become unacceptably large. We want to devise a strategy to reduce the error.

A related problem concerns the *average* number of transmission errors.

Example 12.11   *A transmits a binary string of length n to B over the channel Γ. On the average, how many transmission errors will there be?*

On average, as follows from Chapter 10, there will be np transmission errors.

12.8   Error Correction, Error Reduction, Good Redundancy

A wants to transmit messages chosen from a set M of possible messages to **B** and to minimize the possibility of error. Each message is presumed to be a binary string of fixed length k. Thus, the total number M of possible messages is at most $(2) \cdots (2) = 2^k$.

The strategy is this. A encodes each message $\mathbf{x}$ of length k in a longer message $f(\mathbf{x})$ of length n, using some encoding rule f. So we have

$$\mathbf{x} = (x_1, \ldots, x_k) \xrightarrow{f} (y_1, \ldots, y_k, y_{k+1}, \ldots, y_n)$$

Thus, the encoding function now adds "good redundancy" for correct decoding as opposed to the "bad, wasteful" redundancy of Chapter 11. The string or vector $f(\mathbf{x})$ is called a **codeword**.

We can often assume that $x_1 = y_1, \ldots, x_k = y_k$ and that the extra bits $y_{k+1}, \ldots, y_n$ are just parity bits, i.e. they are linear combinations of the **message bits** or **information bits** $x_1, \ldots, x_k$.

Example 12.12 *Suppose W is the message set consisting of all possible binary strings of length 2. So $W = \{(0,0), (0,1), (1,0), (1,1)\}$ and the number of messages M is 4. Our encoding function f maps (x_1, x_2) to $(x_1, x_2, x_1, x_2, x_1 + x_2)$. Then*

$$(00) \xrightarrow{f} (00000)$$
$$(01) \xrightarrow{f} (01011)$$
$$(10) \xrightarrow{f} (10101)$$
$$(11) \xrightarrow{f} (11110)$$

In general, we need to make several assumptions about the encoding function f. Of course, we assume that no errors occur in this encoding. Also, f only makes sense if it is one to one. This means that if $\mathbf{x}_1 \neq \mathbf{x}_2$ then $f(\mathbf{x}_1) \neq f(\mathbf{x}_2)$. Then, *given any codeword there is exactly one message corresponding to it so if* $\mathbf{B}$ *decodes the correct codeword,* $\mathbf{B}$ *can then calculate the message.*

The total number of codewords is equal to M, which is the total number of messages. *Transmitter $\mathbf{A}$ and receiver $\mathbf{B}$ are both equipped with a list of the set of all possible code words $f(\mathbf{x})$.* This list C is called the **code list** or simply, the **code**. Since f is one to one, *the number of words in C equals the number of messages M. In symbols, $M = |C|$.*

We want the Hamming distance between any two codewords in C to be large. We have seen that, on the average, only a certain number of transmission errors, namely, np errors, can be made. Now, when $\mathbf{B}$ receives a string $\mathbf{z}$ of length n it is likely that this string came from (corresponds to, is a corruption of) the codeword closest to $\mathbf{z}$, i.e. the codeword $\mathbf{u}$ such that $d(\mathbf{z}, \mathbf{u}) \leq d(\mathbf{z}, \mathbf{v})$ for any $\mathbf{v}$ in C.

In other words, we use **nearest neighbour decoding** (sometimes called **minimum distance decoding**). In the event of a tie, we make an arbitrary choice between the competing codewords. Having found $\mathbf{u}$, we can then reconstruct the original message because f is one to one.

Example 12.13 *Let us assume, using the code C in the previous example, that we transmit the codeword $\mathbf{u} = (01011)$ (over the BSC channel Γ with parameter p) and that the string $\mathbf{z} = (11011)$ is received. Then $d(\mathbf{z}, \mathbf{u}) = 1$. Moreover, $d(\mathbf{z}, \mathbf{v}) \geq 2$ if $\mathbf{v}$ is in C with $\mathbf{v} \neq \mathbf{u}$. Thus $\mathbf{z}$ is decoded as $\mathbf{u}$.*

Probability of error

Suppose we did not first encode the four messages of length 2 in Example 12.12 into longer codewords of length 5 but, instead, tried a direct transmission. The probability that no error occurs is $q^2 = (1-p)^2$. Thus the probability of at least one error when a message of 2 bits is transmitted is $1 - (1-p)^2$. For example, if $p = 0.05$ this is equal to 0.0975. This represents the probability that an incorrect message is received.

Now suppose we encode into codewords of length 5 in the code C of Example 12.13. As can be checked, the Hamming distance between any 2 words in C is at least 3. So the receiver decodes correctly with nearest neighbour decoding if there is at most 1 error. This follows from the triangle inequality. In general, if the Hamming distance between any 2 words in C is at least $2e + 1$, then decoding is correct provided that there are at most e transmission errors. (This and similar issues will be discussed in Part III.)

We want to find the probability that the wrong message is received. The probability of zero errors is q^5, where $q = 1 - p$. The probability of exactly one error is $\binom{5}{1} pq^4$. So the probability of at most one error is $q^5 + 5q^4 p = q^4(q + 5p)$. For $p = 0.05$, we have $q = 0.95$ and $q^4(q + 5p) = (0.95)^4(0.95 + 0.25) = 0.9774$. Thus the probability that the wrong message will be received has been reduced from 0.0975 to $1 - 0.9774 = 0.0226$.

We obtain an even more dramatic improvement in our next example.

Example 12.14 *Suppose our message set W contains just two messages, namely, 0 and 1. Then the probability that the wrong message is received over Γ is p. If $p = 0.05$ this means that there is a 5% chance that the wrong message is received.*

Now, use the encoding function f, which maps $\mathbf{x} = (x_1)$ to $f(\mathbf{x}) = (x_1, x_1, x_1)$. The resulting code, which has just 2 codewords, namely $(0, 0, 0)$ and $(1, 1, 1)$, is called the **binary repetition code** *(of length 3). Thus we have*

$$(0) \xrightarrow{f} (000)$$

$$(1) \xrightarrow{f} (111)$$

The Hamming distance between the 2 codewords is 3. Using nearest neighbour decoding we ask the following question: What is the probability that an incorrect message is received?

The correct message will be decoded provided that there are no errors or exactly one error. The probability of this happening is

$$q^3 + 3pq^2 = q^2(q + 3p) = (0.95)^2(0.95 + 0.15) = 0.9928$$

where we assume again that $p = 0.05$. Thus the probability of an error has been reduced from 0.05 to $1 - 0.9928 = 0.0072$.

In Examples 12.13 and 12.14, we have shown how to drastically reduce the probability of receiving the wrong message. But there is a price to be paid. In Example 12.13 we are using 5 bits for encoding a message with 2 bits. In Example 12.14 we use 3 bits to encode a 1-bit message.

In general, let W denote the set of all possible messages to be transmitted, with each message being of length k. Each message in W is first encoded to a codeword in a code C. So $|C| = |W| = M$, say. Each codeword has length n. Since the maximum number of binary strings of length k is 2^k, we get $M \le 2^k$. For example, suppose $M = 2^k$. Then we can define the information rate or rate of the code C as $\frac{k}{n} = \frac{\log M}{n}$. We want to handle the more general case when M may be less than 2^k. We have $M = 2^{\log M}$ and we can think of W as containing all possible binary strings of "length" $\log M$ — even though $\log M$ may not be an integer.

This motivates the general definition of the **transmission rate** or **information rate** or simply the **rate** of C. It is defined as $\frac{\log M}{n}$, where M is the total number of possible messages being transmitted, which is also the total number of codewords in the code list (or code) C, and n is the length of each codeword in C.

Now we are encountering one of the most fundamental issues in coding theory, which is the tension between two competing goals for a code C. These goals are as follows.

(1) A large Hamming distance between any 2 codewords in C, but

(2) a large transmission rate for C.

Note that in Example 12.13 the rate is $\frac{2}{5}$. In Example 12.14, the rate is $\frac{1}{3}$. Again, the code in Example 12.14 is a binary repetition code of length 3. We can use the encoding formula given by

$$f(\mathbf{x}) = f(x_1) = (x_1, \dots, x_1)$$

with 3 replaced by n, where the parity bits are $x_1, x_1, \dots$. Then the probability of receiving the wrong message is arbitrarily small, since the Hamming distance between the two codewords in C is n. This is because the two code words are $(0, \ldots, 0)$ and $(1, \ldots, 1)$. However, the rate is $\frac{1}{n}$, which tends to zero as n gets large.

The question then becomes the following.

To get the probability of incorrect decoding to be arbitrarily small must the transmission rate tend to zero? If not, how large can the rate be?

This question is at the heart of communication theory. We pursue it in Section 12.9.

12.9   The Fundamental Theorem of Information Theory

We are now in a position to reconcile the two competing considerations for a noisy channel, namely,

1. a high transmission rate and

2. a low error probability.

In this section, we assume that we have a memoryless source denoted by an input random variable X. The source emits binary strings of length n over a channel Γ. Any set of these binary strings is called a code, and the strings in the code are codewords. Although the result that we discuss will work over any channel, we assume that Γ is a BSC. Later on in Chapter 14, we show how the requirements on the source can be relaxed. As discussed earlier in this chapter, one way in which these binary strings arise is as follows. We have a data stream arising from a previous source. This stream is blocked off into binary strings of length k and then we adjoin a total of $n - k$ parity bits (as discussed in detail also in Part III) to end up with codewords of length n.

The result we want to discuss is a special case of a more general result which holds for memoryless discrete channels and even for ergodic channels.

The fundamental theorem of information theory for binary symmetric channels

Let Γ be a BSC with parameter $p < \frac{1}{2}$ and resulting capacity $\Lambda = \Lambda(p) = 1 + p \log p + q \log q$. Let R be any information rate with $R < \Lambda$. Let $\varepsilon > 0$ be an arbitrarily small positive quantity. Then, if $N = N(\varepsilon)$ is sufficiently large, there is a code C of length N with the following properties. C has rate R. Moreover, the average probability of error, using nearest neighbour decoding, is less than ε.

This theorem involves two basic questions.

1. Why does the capacity Λ give the upper bound for accurate communication?

2. Having surmised this, how can we prove it?

Rather than launching into a proof immediately, we prefer to take several preliminary informal approaches using a memoryless source. However our discussion and informal proofs cover all the mathematical tools used in a formal proof of the theorem.

Approach 1

An input n-sequence $\mathbf{x} = (x_1, x_2, \ldots, x_n)$ is chosen at random with the components x_i being chosen independently and is transmitted through the channel. Let $\mathbf{y}$ be the corresponding received sequence.

Define $H(X)$ as the common uncertainty $H(x_i)$, $i = 1, \ldots, n$ and similarly define $H(Y)$, $H(X|Y)$, $H(Y|X)$, $H(X,Y)$. For example, for a BSC $H(X) = H(p, 1-p)$.

There are approximately $2^{nH(X)}$ typical n-sequences, each with probability approximately $\frac{1}{2^{n(H(X))}} = 2^{-nH(X)}$. We have $2^{nH(Y)}$ typical output sequences and $2^{nH(X,Y)}$ typical pairs of input and output sequences.

A typical pair is generated by choosing a typical input n-sequence $\mathbf{x}$ and then selecting output sequence $\mathbf{y}$ such that $(\mathbf{x}, \mathbf{y})$ is a typical pair.

The number of typical input n-sequences is $2^{nH(X)}$ and the number of typical pairs is $2^{n(H(X,Y))}$. Then for each input sequence $\mathbf{x}$ there are

$$\frac{2^{nH(X,Y)}}{2^{nH(X)}} = 2^{n[H(Y,X)-H(X)]} = 2^{nH(Y|X)}$$

output sequences $\mathbf{y}$ such that $(\mathbf{x}, \mathbf{y})$ is a typical pair.

Basically we want to find the **maximum number of distinguishable inputs**. Two inputs are **distinguishable** if their "output fans" do not overlap.

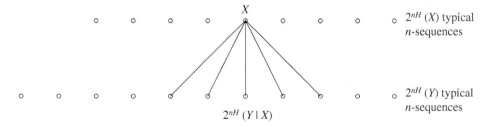

$$2^{nH} (Y|X)$$

If we have M inputs and we want their output fans not to overlap we want

$$M \leq 2^{n[H(Y)-H(Y|X)]} = 2^n I(Y:X)$$

since $I(Y:X)$ denotes the maximum value of

$$\{H(Y) - H(Y|X) = H(X) - H(X|Y) = \text{channel capacity } \Lambda\}$$

Then $M \leq 2^{nI(Y:X)}$ because $I(Y:X)$ represents the maximum value of $H(Y) - H(X|Y)$. Moreover it will turn out that this upper bound can be achieved. In the case of the BSC with parameter p we have $I(Y:X) = \Lambda(p)$ the channel capacity. Thus our argument suggests that $M \leq 2^{n\Lambda(p)}$ so that $\log M \leq n\Lambda(p)$. Since the rate R is $\frac{\log M}{n}$ we get $R \leq \Lambda(p)$. Our argument above suggests the following Fundamental Principle.

Fundamental principle. The capacity of a channel is the log of the maximum number of distinguishable inputs.

Let us reconcile this principle with our result above. Above we got that $\log M \leq n\Lambda$. The BSC accepts one bit and transmits one bit. When a binary string of length n is successively transmitted (and received) over a BSC the correct channel for this is the **n-th extension of the binary symmetric channel**, which has capacity $n\Lambda$ (rather than Λ). This channel transmits binary n-strings to binary n-strings. We can think of it as n copies of a single BSC operating independently and in parallel.

Approach 2

This is a bit like Approach 1. We will also sketch a proof as to why any rate less than the channel capacity will work for accurate transmission. It is similar to Shannon's original informal argument, and is described by Ash [Ash90].

As above we have approximately $2^{nH(X)}$ typical input n-sequences; similarly, we have $2^{nH(Y)}$ typical output n-sequences. We are always assuming that n is suitably large. Then there will also be about $2^{nH(X,Y)}$ typical pairs of input–output n-sequences. Here a typical pair is obtained by first choosing a typical output n-sequence $\mathbf{y}$ and then selecting a typical input n-sequence $\mathbf{x}$ such that $(\mathbf{x}, \mathbf{y})$ is a typical pair.

There are approximately $2^{nH(Y)}$ typical output n-sequences $\mathbf{y}$. Because the total number of typical pairs $(\mathbf{x}, \mathbf{y})$ is $2^{nH(X,Y)}$, it follows that for each typical output sequence $\mathbf{y}$ there are, on average,

$$2^{n[H(X,Y)-H(Y)]} = 2^{nH(X|Y)}$$

input sequences $\mathbf{x}$ for which $(\mathbf{x}, \mathbf{y})$ is a typical pair. So the input fan of $\mathbf{y}$ has about $2^{nH(X|Y)}$ sequences when n is large.

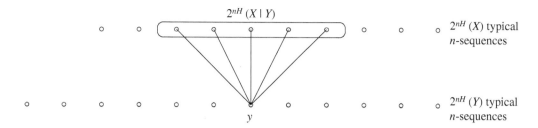

For accurate decoding of a code C we want disjoint fans. So, if W is the set of codewords in C, with $|W| = M$ we have

$$M 2^{nH(X|Y)} \leq 2^{H(X)}$$

Then

$$M \leq 2^{n(H(X)-H(X|Y))} \leq 2^{nI(X:Y)}$$

Thus $\frac{\log M}{n} \leq I(X : Y)$. Again, this shows that the rate is bounded above by the capacity.

Remark

In Approach 1, we had that the allowable rate is at most $I(Y : X)$. Here we get the rate to be at most $I(X : Y)$. So we have another way of looking at the fact that $I(X : Y) = I(Y : X)$.

Next we want to give a plausible argument as to why an accurate code *can* be constructed with a rate R, $R < \Lambda$, Λ being the capacity. Construct a code C randomly as follows. Let C be a set of $2^{nR} < 2^{n\Lambda}$ typical n-sequences with the sequences chosen successively, at random, such that the $2^{nH(X)}$ possible typical n-sequences are equally likely to be chosen at each stage. Here X is chosen in accordance with the input distribution that achieves channel capacity. Suppose a typical sequence $\mathbf{u}_i$ is transmitted and the typical sequence $\mathbf{y}$ is received. We have a decoding error if at least one other typical sequence or codeword $\mathbf{u}_j \neq \mathbf{u}_i$ belongs to the set T of possible typical input n-sequences that output to $\mathbf{y}$.

The probability that at least one other sequence $\mathbf{u}_j$ belongs to T is less than or equal to the sum

$$\sum_{j=1, j \neq i}^{2^{nR}} \Pr(\mathbf{u}_j \text{ in } T) = \theta, \text{ say}$$

(Here, we are invoking the **union bound**, i.e., the fact that the probability of a union of events is at most the sum of the probabilities. For example, $\Pr(A \text{ or } B) \leq \Pr(A) + \Pr(B)$). Now

$$\theta \leq (2^{nR} - 1)\frac{2^{nH(X|Y)}}{2^{nH(X)}} < \frac{2^{nR}}{2^{n\Lambda}}$$

since $\frac{H(X|Y)}{H(Y)}$ gives the fraction of the typical input n-sequences that are in T. Thus the probability, on average, that $\mathbf{x}_i$ is decoded incorrectly tends to zero as n gets large because $R < \Lambda$.

Remark

In upper-bounding θ we appeal to our choice of X.

Approach 3

This is a bit like the first part of Approach 2 but is more specialized. $\mathbf{A}$ is transmitting codewords chosen from a code C consisting of binary n-sequences to $\mathbf{B}$ over a BSC Γ with parameter p. Suppose that a sequence $\mathbf{y}$ of length n is received by $\mathbf{B}$. $\mathbf{B}$ knows that $\mathbf{y}$ is the corruption of $\mathbf{x}$, where $\mathbf{x}$ is a codeword of length n. On average, the number of transmission errors is $np = \lambda$. For convenience, let's assume that np is an integer. Thus the Hamming distance between $\mathbf{x}$ and $\mathbf{y}$ is np, so $\mathbf{x}$ differs from $\mathbf{y}$ in about np positions. For example, if $\mathbf{y}$ is the all-zero vector then $\mathbf{x}$ in all likelihood is an n-string with about np ones in it and $n - np$ zeros. There are $\binom{n}{np}$ ways of choosing the np positions where the ones occur, giving about $\binom{n}{np}$ choices for $\mathbf{x}$, where $\binom{n}{np}$ is the binomial coefficient.

Thus the input fan associated with $\mathbf{y}$ is about $\binom{n}{\lambda}$. If the input fans are disjoint, we get that $|C| \binom{n}{\lambda} \leq 2^n$. Now, using Stirling's expansion as in Chapter 9, we get that $\log\binom{n}{\lambda} = \log\binom{n}{np}$, which is approximately $nH(p)$. Thus, $\log|C| \leq n(1 - H(p)) = n(1 + p\log p + q\log q)$. This gives that the largest transmission rate that C can have is the capacity of Γ, namely, $\Lambda(p) = 1 + p\log p + q\log q = 1 - H(p)$.

Stirling's expansion

For reference, we include here Stirling's expansion. It says that

$$\ln n! \approx \frac{1}{2}\ln n + n\ln n - n$$

where ln denotes the natural logarithm, and $n!$ means n factorial, or $n(n-1)(n-2)\cdots(2)(1)$.

Approach 4

Again, this is similar to Approach 2. We choose a code C at random. Suppose codeword $\mathbf{x}$ of length n is transmitted over the BSC with parameter p. Let $\mathbf{y}$ be the received string. We have the following facts:

Fact 1 The Hamming distance between $\mathbf{x}$ and $\mathbf{y}$, on average, is np.

Fact 2 The probability that another codeword $\mathbf{x}_i$ is within a Hamming distance t of $\mathbf{y}$ is, roughly,

$$\sum_{i=0}^{t} \binom{n}{i} 2^{-n}$$

To see Fact 2, we count the total number of words at distance $0, 1, \ldots, t$ from $\mathbf{y}$.

Fact 3 Using the union bound, the upper bound for the probability that there is a decoding error is around $\frac{(|C|-1)}{2^n} \sum_{i=0}^{t} \binom{n}{i}$. This is bounded by $\frac{|C|}{2^n} \sum_{i=0}^{t} \binom{n}{i}$, because $|C| - 1 < |C|$. To get the upper bound, note that the total number of n-sequences is 2^n. We are choosing the words in C at random.

Fact 4 Let $0 < p < \frac{1}{2}$. Then $\sum_{i=0}^{np} \binom{n}{i} \leq 2^{nH(p)}$. This is an interesting result on the "tail" of the binomial coefficients and known as the **tail inequality** – see Welsh [Wel88].

From the above, then, since $|C| = 2^{nR}$, by setting $t = np$, an approximate upper bound on the probability of a decoding error (on average) is

$$\frac{2^{nR}}{2^n} 2^{nH(p)} = \frac{2^{nR}}{2^{n\Lambda}}$$

This tends to zero when n gets large because $R < \Lambda$.

Remark

If you look at this proof in Approach 4, there is a lot of averaging and estimating going on. To really make the proof rigorous, we have to average over all possible random codes, as Shannon did, and show that the decoding error tends to zero. The theorem will then follow. We refer the reader to Ash [Ash90] and van Lint [vL98] for details.

Approach 5

This is discussed by Feynman [Fey00]. The idea is as follows. We have a message consisting of k bits. We adjoin $n - k$ parity check bits so that our codeword now has n bits. The $n - k$ parity check bits need to be able to describe the location of all the possible error patterns as we need to **correct** all errors when decoding. Let $\lambda = np$. Let us assume that it is an integer. So λ is the average number of errors. The total number of error patterns is then around $\binom{n}{\lambda}$. So we get that

$$2^{n-k} \geq \binom{n}{\lambda}$$

Using Stirling's expansion, we get that

$$n - k \geq n[H(p)]$$

Thus, $1 - \frac{k}{n} \geq H(p)$, so $\frac{k}{n} \leq 1 - H(p)$. Since the transmission rate R is $\frac{k}{n}$, we get

$$R \leq 1 + p \log p + q \log q$$

Thus, $R \leq \Lambda(p)$, the capacity of the binary symmetric channel Γ.

Feynman [Fey00] goes on to develop two other arguments in support of the fundamental theorem. One of these is a "sphere-packing" argument relating to error-correction. The other argument relates to physics and free energy.

We want to make some further comments on the fundamental theorem.

1. As mentioned earlier, we need not restrict ourselves to a BSC. Also, the source need not be memoryless. In practice, ergodic sources are extensively used.

2. The length n of the codewords may have to be quite large to get the error-rate close to zero.

3. No specific recipe is given for constructing the codes in the theorem.

4. We can think of the theorem as saying that for the BSC the maximum transmission rate is just under the capacity $\Lambda(p)$, where $0 \leq \Lambda(p) \leq 1$. So we can safely send $\Lambda(p)$ bits per second across the channel if, physically, the channel can transmit 1 bit per second.

5. In the Fundamental Theorem of Information Theory in Section 12.9, we assume that $R < \Lambda$. This is, in fact, the best rate possible, i.e. we have a kind of Converse Theorem.

Converse

For a memoryless channel of capacity Λ and rate $R > \Lambda$, there cannot exist a sequence of codes C_n, $n = 1, 2, \ldots$ with the property that C_n has 2^{nR} codewords of length n and error probability tending to zero as n gets large.

We refer the reader to Welsh [Wel88]. A much stronger result due to Wolfowitz [Wol61] shows that the maximum probability of error tends to 1 as n gets large. It can be shown by using the **Hamming codes** that the error probability p can tend to 1 in the limit.

6. It can be shown that the fundamental theorem holds if we restrict ourselves just to **linear codes**. The following result has been shown by Elias (see Welsh [Wel88, p. 71]).

For $\epsilon > 0$ and $R < 1 + p \log p + (1 - p) \log(1 - p)$ then, assuming that N is sufficiently large, there exists a binary linear code C having 2^{RN} words of length N such that, on the BSC with bit error p the error probability is less than ϵ.

12.10   Proving the Fundamental Theorem

So far we have given several informal arguments to show that for accurate decoding of a code C of length n with M codewords, we need to have $M \leq 2^{nI(X:Y)}$. Here, $I(X:Y)$ is the mutual information of X, Y defined in Chapter 10 as the maximum value over all inputs of the quantity $H(X) - H(X|Y) = H(Y) - H(Y, X)$. Now, we want to prove the fundamental theorem for BSCs as stated in Section 12.9. For such channels, $I(X : Y)$ is the channel capacity $\Lambda(p)$. But first we need the following result, relating to probabilities in a simple space (see Chapter 10).

Lemma 12.15 (The union bound)   *If A, B are events in a sample space, then* $Pr(A \cup B) \leq Pr(A) + Pr(B)$.

Proof. To see this, think of the events A, B as corresponding to two circular disks in the plane. If the disks are disjoint, then $Pr(A \cup B) = Pr(A) + Pr(B)$. If they have an overlap, we don't count this intersection twice. Thus, we get $Pr(A \cup B) = Pr(A) + Pr(B) - Pr(A \cap B) < Pr(A) + Pr(B)$. In words, we have that "the probability that at least one of two possible events will occur is at most the sum of the individual probabilities that each will occur." ■

From Chapter 10, we have the formulae for the *mean* μ of n Bernoulli trials and the *standard deviation* σ of the n trials. If each trial has two outcomes with probabilities p

and q, where $q = 1 - p$, we have

$$\mu = np, \qquad \sigma = \sqrt{npq}$$

From Chapter 10, we also have the *Chebyshev Inequality*, i.e. $Pr(|X - \mu| \geq k\sigma) \leq \frac{1}{k^2}$ or, alternatively $Pr(|X - \mu| \geq a) \leq \frac{\sigma^2}{a^2}$, where σ^2 denotes the *variance* of the random variable X.

Proof of the fundamental theorem (for the binary symmetric channel)

We denote by V_n the set of 2^n binary strings of length n. (As an example, we think of a vector space of dimension n which has 2^n vectors where each vector has length n.)

We work with a channel which is in the nth extension of a BSC with p denoting the probability of error. This channel has 2^n possible inputs and 2^n possible outputs of binary strings of length n, i.e. elements of V_n.

We seek a set of M codewords $\mathbf{c_i}, 1 \leq i \leq M$ which can be transmitted in an error-free manner over the channel. Our method is "random coding". That is, we choose (encode) a vector $\mathbf{c_i}$ at random from V_n, independently for each i, $1 \leq i \leq M$. So we send M messages through the channel by selecting M of the 2^n possible inputs as *codewords*.

We decode as follows. Fix an integer $t > 0$. For any vector $\mathbf{y}$, the t-sphere $S_t(\mathbf{y})$ about $\mathbf{y}$ is given by

$$S_t(\mathbf{y}) = \{\mathbf{z} \text{ in } V_n, \ d(\mathbf{y}, \mathbf{z}) \leq t\}$$

(Here $d(\mathbf{y}, \mathbf{z})$ means the Hamming distance between $\mathbf{y}$ and $\mathbf{z}$.) If $\mathbf{y}$ is the received vector, we decode $\mathbf{y}$ as $\mathbf{c_j}$ if $\mathbf{c_j}$ is the unique codeword in $S_t(\mathbf{y})$. Otherwise, we decode $\mathbf{y}$ as some arbitrary codeword $\mathbf{c_a}$.

Proceeding with the proof, let $\mathbf{Y}$ denote the received vector when codeword $\mathbf{c}$ is transmitted. An error can only occur if either

(1) $d(\mathbf{c}, \mathbf{Y}) > t$ or

(2) $d(\mathbf{c}, \mathbf{Y}) \leq t$ and $d(\mathbf{c'}, \mathbf{Y}) \leq t$ for another codeword $\mathbf{c'}$.

From Lemma 12.15 the probability of an error is at most $Pr(1)$, the probability of (1) plus $Pr(2)$, the probability of (2). We consider (2). Since the codewords in C are chosen at random, the probability that a codeword $\mathbf{c_j}$ is within a distance t of $\mathbf{Y}$ is given by $\frac{N_t}{2^n}$, where $N_t = \sum_{k=0}^{t} \binom{n}{k}$ counts the number of vectors in V_n that lie in $S_t(\mathbf{y})$ for any vector $\mathbf{y}$. The probability that at least one of the other vectors in C not equal to $\mathbf{c}$ lies within a distance t of the received vector $\mathbf{Y}$, i.e. $Pr(2)$, is at most $\frac{M-1}{2^n}\sum_{k=0}^{t}\binom{N}{k}$. (Note that two of the other code vectors might be the same.)

The average number of errors transmitting a codeword is np, so we could choose $t = np$. However, we enlarge the radius of the sphere by putting $t = \lfloor n(p+\epsilon)\rfloor$, the integer part of $np + n\epsilon$, where ϵ is an arbitrarily small positive number.

Using the *tail inequality* in Section 12.9, we have

$$Pr(2) \leq \frac{M}{2^n}(2^{nh(p+\epsilon)})$$

We next calculate $Pr(1)$, the probability of an error from part (1), i.e., $Pr(d(\mathbf{c},\mathbf{Y})) > t$. Let U denote the number of symbols in error when transmitting codeword $\mathbf{c}$. Then

$$Pr(1) = Pr(U > t) = Pr(U > n(p+\epsilon)) \quad \leq Pr(|U - np| > n\epsilon)$$
$$\leq \tfrac{npq}{n^2\epsilon^2}\text{ by Chebyshev\'s inequality}$$

Then

$$Pr(1) + Pr(2) \leq \frac{pq}{n\epsilon^2} + M(2^{-n(1-h(p+\epsilon))})$$

Thus, for $Pr(E)$, the average probability of an error E, we have

$$Pr(1) + Pr(2) = Pr(E) \leq \frac{pq}{n\epsilon^2} + M2^{-n\Lambda(p+\epsilon)}$$

where Λ is the capacity function of the BSC. The term $\frac{pq}{n\epsilon^2}$ can be made arbitrarily small for sufficiently large n. The term $M2^{-n\Lambda(p+\epsilon)} = \frac{M}{2^{n\Lambda(p+\epsilon)}}$ can also be made arbitrarily small if $\log M < n\Lambda(p+\epsilon)$, i.e. if $\frac{\log M}{n} < \Lambda(p+\epsilon)$.

Since by hypothesis $0 < p < \frac{1}{2}$ (p being the probability of error in the BSC), we have $\Lambda(p+\epsilon) < \Lambda(p)$. By taking ϵ small, we can make $\Lambda(p+\epsilon)$ arbitrarily close to $\Lambda(p)$. Also, we can have any number M of messages as close to $2^{n\Lambda(p)}$ as we want and still force the average probability of an error to be arbitrarily small for n sufficiently large. There must be at least one code which does as well as the average. Thus, we are assured that there exists a code C with $M = 2^{nR}$ codewords with error probability arbitrarily small, where $R < \Lambda(p)$ with C having rate R. This completes the proof of the Fundamental Theorem for the Binary Symmetric Channel.

12.11 Summary, the Big Picture

We want to summarize again one of the main guiding principles in this chapter. The transmitter (but also the receiver!) has a list C of allowable codewords. The receiver decodes by nearest neighbour decoding. In the event of a tie, the receiver makes a random decision among the competing codewords. If the codewords in the list are very well spread out, their output fans will be disjoint, and we will have correct decoding. But, if they are too far apart, the transmission rate, which is related to the number of codewords in the list, becomes too small. The biggest transmission rate that you can get away with for accurate decoding is the channel capacity. *Capacity is the upper bound to accurate communication.* The main theorem guarantees the existence of a code C with information rate less than the channel capacity such that no matter what codeword from C is transmitted the receiver will decode it accurately.

Again, we remind the reader that the Fundamental Theorem holds also even if we restrict to just linear codes.

We should point out that the capacity of other structures such as graphs has also been of considerable interest. A particularly famous problem suggested by Shannon was to find the capacity of a 5-cycle, C_5. This problem was finally solved by Laci Lovasz [Lov79].

12.12   Postscript: The Capacity of the Binary Symmetric Channel

Here we offer a "calculus-free" proof that the capacity is $1 - H(p) = 1 + p \log p + q \log q$ where p is the probability of a transmission error and $q = 1 - p$ (see Sections 10.11 and 12.4). Recall that the channel matrix

$$A = \begin{array}{c} \\ 0 \\ 1 \end{array} \begin{array}{c} 0 \quad\; 1 \\ \begin{pmatrix} 1 - p & p \\ p & 1 - p \end{pmatrix} \end{array}$$

The capacity can be defined as the maximum, maximized over all possible input distributions, of $H(Y) - H(Y|X)$. Now,

$$H(Y|X) = H(Y \mid X = 0)Pr(X = 0) + H(Y \mid X = 1)Pr(X = 1)$$

$$= H(p, 1 - p)Pr(X = 0) + H(p, 1 - p)Pr(X = 1).$$

Since $Pr(X = 0) + Pr(X = 1) = 1$, we get that $H(Y|X) = H(p, 1 - p)$. We sometimes write $H(p, 1 - p)$ simply as $H(p)$.

So $H(Y|X)$ is independent of the input distribution. To find the capacity, we thus have to maximize $H(Y)$. We know that $H(Y)$ is maximized when and only when all values of Y (i.e. 0 or 1) are equally likely so that the (probability that $Y = 0$) = (probability that $Y = 1$) = $\frac{1}{2}$. We claim that this can be achieved with the uniform distribution for the inputs.

To see this put $Pr(X = 0) = \frac{1}{2}$ and $Pr(X = 1) = \frac{1}{2}$. Then

$$Pr(Y = 0) = Pr(X = 0 \text{ and } Y = 0) + Pr(X = 1 \text{ and } Y = 0) = \frac{1}{2}[(1 - p)] + \frac{1}{2}[p] = \frac{1}{2}$$

Similarly, $Pr(Y = 1) = \frac{1}{2}$. Thus,

$$H(Y) = \frac{1}{2} \log \frac{1}{\frac{1}{2}} + \frac{1}{2} \log \frac{1}{\frac{1}{2}} = \log_2 2 = 1$$

Then the capacity of the BSC being the maximum of

$$H(Y) - H(Y|X) = 1 - H(p) = 1 - [-(p \log p + q \log q)] = 1 + p \log p + q \log q$$

Remark

As pointed out in Ash [Ash90], the same argument works when the channel is "symmetric." The channel matrix A of size $M \times L$ need not itself be symmetric. What is required is that

(a) Each row of A consisting of the entries $Pr(y_j \mid x_i)$ contain the same set of numbers $p_1, p_2, \ldots, P_L$ as any other row.

(b) Each column of A contain the same numbers as any other column.

In other words, the rows of A are identical except for permutations and, similarly, for the columns of A.

The most celebrated example is the BSC as illustrated again here

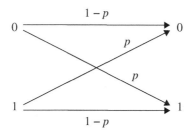

12.13   Problems

12.1   A BSC with parameter 0.2 is used for transmitting the codeword 011. What is the probability that there is a transmission error? (See Solution 12.1.)

12.2   The code $C = \{(1,0),(0,1)\}$ is being transmitted over a binary symmetric channel with parameter p. Find the probability that the codeword $(1,0)$ is decoded as $(0,1)$ by using nearest neighbour decoding. (See Solution 12.2.)

12.3   A binary source emitting binary strings (x_1, x_2, x_3, x_4) is encoded as the codeword $(x_1, x_2, x_3, x_4, x_1 + x_3, x_2 + x_4)$ of length 6 in the code C and transmitted sequentially over a BSC with parameter p. Decoding is carried out using nearest neighbor decoding.

(a) Does the (information) rate depend on p?

(b) Does the (information) rate depend on the decoding rule?

(c) Does the channel capacity depend on p?

(See Solution 12.3.)

12.4   What is the rate in Problem 12.3? (See Solution 12.4.)

12.5   A message of N bits is transmitted over a BSC with parameter p. An "error burst" is defined to be a sequence of three consecutive bits each of which is incorrectly transmitted. Find the average number of error bursts in the transmission. (See Solution 12.5.)

12.6   What is the probability that two random binary strings of length N have Hamming distance at most 4? (See Solution 12.6.)

12.7   A binary memoryless channel Γ transmits 0 correctly with a probability of 0.8 and transmits 1 correctly with probability of 0.7. What is the capacity of Γ? (See Solution 12.7.)

12.8   If we take the cascade of the BSC with itself n times and let n go to infinity, what is the capacity of the resulting channel? (See Solution 12.8.)

12.9   See [Wel88]. Prove that if $\frac{1}{2} < \lambda < 1$ and λn is an integer, then

$$\sum_{k=\lambda n}^{n} \binom{n}{k} \le 2^{nH(\lambda)}$$

(See Solution 12.9.)

12.14   Solutions

12.1   The probability that there is no error is $(0.8)^3 = 0.512$. Thus, the probability that there is at least one error is $1 - 0.512 = 0.488$.

12.2   We transmit $(1,0)$. The probability that $(0,1)$ is received is p^2. If $(0,1)$ is received, we decode it as $(0,1)$. Suppose $(0,0)$ is received: the probability for this is pq. The Hamming distance of $(0,0)$ from $(1,0)$ and $(0,1)$ is 1. So with probability $\frac{1}{2}$, we decode $(0,0)$ as $(0,1)$. Similarly, with probability $\frac{1}{2}$, we decode $(1,1)$ as $(0,1)$. Therefore, the probability of incorrect decoding is $p^2 + \frac{1}{2}pq + \frac{1}{2}pq = p^2 + pq = p(p+q) = p$.

12.3   (a) No.   (b) No.   (c) Yes, since for a BSC the capacity is $\Lambda(p) = 1 + p\log p + q\log q$.

12.4   The size M of the code (or code list) is 2^4. The rate is $\frac{\log M}{n} = \frac{4}{6} = \frac{2}{3}$.

12.5   There are $N-2$ sequences of 3 consecutive bits. The probability of a burst error is p^3. So the average number of burst errors is $(N-2)p^3$.

12.6   Having Hamming distance at most four means that there is either 0 disagreements or 1 disagreement or 2 or 3 or 4. In general, the probability of exactly x disagreements is $\binom{N}{x}\left(\frac{1}{2}\right)^x\left(\frac{1}{2}\right)^{N-x} = \binom{N}{x}\left(\frac{1}{2}\right)^N$. So we get

$$\frac{1}{2^N}\left[\binom{N}{0} + \binom{N}{1} + \binom{N}{2} + \binom{N}{3} + \binom{N}{4}\right]$$

Another approach is as follows. Let S_1 be the first string and S_2 the second. Given S_1, if S_2 has Hamming distance 0 from S_1, there is just one possibility for S_2, namely, S_1. If the Hamming distance is one, then, for S_2, the number of choices is the position of the disagreement which is $\binom{N}{1}$. For distance 2, 3, 4, we have $\binom{N}{2}$, $\binom{N}{3}$, $\binom{N}{4}$ choices. Thus, we get the probability being $\binom{N}{0} + \binom{N}{1} + \binom{N}{2} + \binom{N}{3} + \binom{N}{4}$ out of a total of 2^N possibilities which gives the answer above.

12.7   We can calculate directly, using a probability tree or using the formula in the text from Ash, [Ash90, p. 304], with $\alpha = p_1 = 0.2$, $q_1 = 0.8$, $\beta = p_2 = 0.3$, $q_2 = 0.7$. Our formula is $\log(2^u + 2^v)$, where

$$u = \frac{q_2 H(q_1) - p_1 H(p_2)}{p_2 - q_1}, \qquad v = \frac{-p_2 H(q_1) + q_1 H(p_2)}{p_2 - q_1}$$

which gives a capacity of 0.1912.

12.8   We have the transmission matrix P given by the following formula

$$P = \begin{pmatrix} 1-p & p \\ p & 1-p \end{pmatrix}$$

Let $\mathbf{w} = (x, y)$ be the fixed probability vector. Then, since $\mathbf{w}P = \mathbf{w}$, we get

$$(x, y) \begin{pmatrix} 1-p & p \\ p & 1-p \end{pmatrix} = (x, y)$$

Then

$$\begin{aligned} x(1 - p) + yp &= x \\ xp + y(1 - p) &= y \end{aligned}$$

and also $x + y = 1$. The second equation is obtained by subtracting the first equation from the third equation. Using the first and third equations, we get

$$x(1 - p) + (1 - x)p = x$$

This gives $x = \frac{1}{2}$ so $y = \frac{1}{2}$. Then the fixed vector is $(\frac{1}{2}, \frac{1}{2})$. It follows that P^n tends to $\begin{pmatrix} \frac{1}{2} & \frac{1}{2} \\ \frac{1}{2} & \frac{1}{2} \end{pmatrix}$ — see Chapter 13. Then the capacity tends to $1 + \frac{1}{2} \log(\frac{1}{2}) + \frac{1}{2} \log(\frac{1}{2}) = 0$, since the parameter of P^n tends to $\frac{1}{2}$, leading to a purely random channel.

12.9   By the symmetry of the binomial coefficients, we have $\binom{n}{k} = \binom{n}{n-k}$.

The left side is

$$\sum_{k=0}^{\lambda n} \binom{n}{k} \qquad \text{where } 0 \le \lambda \le \frac{1}{2}$$

Set $n - k = t$. As k varies between 0 and λn, $t = n - k$ varies between

$$n - \lambda n, \; n - \lambda n + 1, \; \ldots, n - 1, n$$

So t varies between $n(1 - \lambda)$, $n(1 - \lambda) + 1$, $\ldots$, $n - 1$, n. Put $\mu = 1 - \lambda$. Then $\frac{1}{2} < \mu < 1$, and t varies between $n\mu, n\mu + 1, \ldots, n$. The left side becomes $\sum_{t=\mu n}^{n} \binom{n}{t}$, $\frac{1}{2} < \mu < 1$. From the tail inequality (see Fact 4 in text), we get that this sum is at most $2^{nH(\mu)} = 2^{nH(1-\lambda)} = 2^{nH(\lambda)}$.

Chapter 13

Signals, Sampling, Coding Gain, Shannon's Information Capacity Theorem

Goals, Discussion In this chapter, we mainly study continuous random variables, rather than finite discrete variables. The entropy is in the form of an integral, rather than a finite sum. Still, the work connects up with the fundamental principles relating to entropy and channel capacity in Chapters 1, 8, 9, 10, 11 and 12.

We prove the Whittaker–Shannon sampling theorem and outline a proof of Shannon's celebrated information capacity theorem for band-limited, power-limited Gaussian channels.

New, Noteworthy Claude Shannon discovered three fundamental theorems. They are the following:

1. The source coding theorem provides the mathematical tool, i.e. entropy for data compression (Chapters 11 and 17).

Cryptography, Information Theory, and Error-Correction: A Handbook for the 21st Century, Second Edition.
Aiden A. Bruen, Mario A. Forcinito, and James M. McQuillan.
© 2021 John Wiley & Sons, Inc. Published 2021 by John Wiley & Sons, Inc.

2. The channel coding theorem, Shannon's second theorem, is both the most surprising and the single most important result in all of information theory (Chapter 12).

3. His third remarkable theorem is the Information Capacity theorem, telling us, inter alia, how there is a maximum to the rate at which any communication system can operate free of errors when the system is constrained in power.

13.1   Continuous Signals, Shannon's Sampling Theorem

We will be dealing with a continuous signal of finite energy that is band-limited, having no frequency component higher than W hertz.

The **sampling theorem**, which Feynman [Fey00] refers to as "another of Claude Shannon's babies" has two equivalent parts that apply to the transmitter and the receiver of a pulse modulation system, respectively.

Theorem 13.1 (The sampling theorem)

(a) A band-limited signal of finite energy, which has no frequency components higher than W hertz, is completely described by specifying the values of the signal at instants of time separated by $\frac{1}{2W}$ seconds.

(b) A band-limited signal of finite energy, which has no frequency components higher than W hertz, may be completely recovered from a knowledge of its samples taken at the rate of 2W samples per second.

The sampling rate of $2W$ samples per second for a signal bandwidth of W hertz is called the **Nyquist rate** and the reciprocal $\frac{1}{2W}$ (in seconds) is called the **Nyquist interval**.

In practice, an information signal will not be band-limited, leading to **undersampling**. Two correcting mechanisms can be used.

1. The high-frequency components of the signal can be attenuated by a filter.

2. The filtered signal is sampled at a rate somewhat higher than the Nyquist rate.

In what follows, we outline a proof of the sampling theorem. Although Shannon developed applications for the sampling theorem, it seems that the result in mathematical form goes back to Whittaker [Whi15]. The method of proof is based on a combination of the Fourier series and the Fourier integral in their complex form.

Mathematically, a signal is a function $f(t)$ defined for all of t. We have the **Fourier integral** representation of $f(t)$ as follows:

$$f(t) = \int_{-\infty}^{\infty} g(\lambda)e^{i\lambda t}d\lambda \tag{13.1}$$

We are just saying that $f(t)$ is a "sum" of orthogonal exponential functions e^{iwt}. For example, we can write any vector $\mathbf{f}$ in three dimensions as a linear combination of three basic vectors. Then

$$\mathbf{f} = g_1\mathbf{u} + g_2\mathbf{v} + g_3\mathbf{w} \tag{13.2}$$

where $\mathbf{u}, \mathbf{v}, \mathbf{w}$ are pairwise orthogonal vectors (of length 1, say) in three Euclidean dimensions.

To find the number g_1, we take the dot product of both sides with $\mathbf{u}$. We get

$$\mathbf{f} \cdot \mathbf{u} = g_1\mathbf{u} \cdot \mathbf{u} + g_2\mathbf{v} \cdot \mathbf{u} + g_3\mathbf{w} \cdot \mathbf{u} \tag{13.3}$$

This gives, by using the orthogonality, that $\mathbf{f} \cdot \mathbf{u} = g_1$. Similarly, $\mathbf{f} \cdot \mathbf{v} = g_2$, $\mathbf{f} \cdot \mathbf{w} = g_3$, and we have then found the coefficients g_1, g_2, g_3. Analogously, we get

$$g(\lambda) = \frac{1}{2\pi}\int_{-\infty}^{\infty} f(t)e^{-i\lambda t}dt \tag{13.4}$$

We assume that the signal is **band-limited**, meaning that $g(\lambda) = 0$ for $|\lambda| > w$ where w is the **cut off frequency**. Then Eq. (13.1) becomes

$$f(t) = \int_{-w}^{w} g(\lambda)e^{i\lambda t}d\lambda \tag{13.5}$$

Now, since $g(\lambda)$ vanishes outside $[-w, w]$, we can extend g periodically, with period $2w$ and then use a discrete Fourier series, as follows.

$$g(\lambda) = \sum_{n=-\infty}^{\infty} c_n e^{\frac{in\pi\lambda}{w}}, -w < \lambda < w \tag{13.6}$$

The coefficients c_n, which are complex numbers, are given by

$$c_n = \frac{1}{2w}\int_{-w}^{w} g(\lambda)e^{\frac{-in\pi\lambda}{w}}d\lambda \tag{13.7}$$

The integral for c_n is actually the value of $f(t)$ for some t. In fact, from Eq. (13.5) and the restriction on λ, we get

$$c_n = \frac{1}{2w}f\left(\frac{-n\pi}{w}\right) \tag{13.8}$$

Then, from (13.6),

$$g(\lambda) = \frac{1}{2w} \sum_{n=-\infty}^{\infty} f(\frac{-n\pi}{w}) e^{\frac{in\pi\lambda}{w}} \tag{13.9}$$

$$= \frac{1}{2w} \sum_{n=-\infty}^{\infty} f(\frac{n\pi}{w}) e^{\frac{-in\pi\lambda}{w}}, \quad -w < \lambda < w. \tag{13.10}$$

From Eq. (13.5), we have

$$f(t) = \int_{-w}^{w} g(\lambda) e^{i\lambda t} d\lambda = \frac{1}{2w} \sum_{n=-\infty}^{\infty} f(\frac{n\pi}{w}) \int_{-w}^{w} e^{\frac{-in\pi\lambda}{w}} e^{i\lambda t} d\lambda \tag{13.11}$$

We now evaluate the integral on the right using the fact that

$$\sin z = \frac{e^{iz} - e^{-iz}}{2i} \tag{13.12}$$

This gives

$$f(t) = \sum_{-\infty}^{\infty} f(\frac{n\pi}{w}) \frac{\sin(wt - n\pi)}{wt - n\pi} \tag{13.13}$$

Note that, when $t = \frac{n\pi}{w}$, we also get $f(\frac{n\pi}{w})$ on the right-hand side (using the fact from calculus that $\lim_{x\to 0} \frac{\sin x}{x} = 1$) since all other values in the sum over n are zero.

The above formula (13.13) says that f can be reconstructed exactly by sampling f at $t = 0, \pm\frac{\pi}{w}, \pm\frac{2\pi}{w}, \ldots$. Now, as in Feynman [Fey00] the bandwidth W is given as $W = \frac{w}{2\pi}$, so $\frac{1}{2W} = \frac{\pi}{w}$. Thus, by sampling the signal at time instants separated by $\frac{1}{2W}$ seconds, we capture the entire signal. This completes the proof of the sampling theorem.

This result will be the basic building block in the proof of Shannon's information capacity theorem for band-limited, power-limited Gaussian channels.

13.2   The Band-Limited Capacity Theorem

We follow Haykin, *Communication Systems*, 4th Edition, Wiley, 2001, [Hay01]. We are now working with random variables $X, Y, \ldots$. The *(differential) entropy* of the random variable X is defined as

$$h(X) = -\int_{-\infty}^{\infty} f_X(X) \log_2 (f_X(X)) \, dX,$$

where the probability density function associated with X is $f_X(X)$, with X a dummy variable. An important example is the Gaussian probability density function (= distribution).

Figure 13.1: The German 10 Deutsche Mark featured Gauss in the 1990s.

Here

$$f_X(X) = \frac{1}{\sqrt{2\pi}} \frac{1}{\sigma} \, exp\left(-\frac{(x-\mu)^2}{2\sigma^2}\right),$$

where σ is the variance of X. This is just the well-known Bell Curve. It is associated with the names of the Belgian mathematician Abraham de Moivre, who discovered it and the German mathematician Carl Gauss who developed its properties. We refer to the picture of the old German 10-mark note in Figure 13.1

There is no formula to calculate the integral $\int_a^b f_X(X) \, dX$ which yields the probability that X lies between the values a and b. However, a very useful fact is that $h(X)$ can be integrated in the Gaussian case. In this case,

$$h(X) = -\int_\infty^\infty f_X(X) \log_2 (f_X(X)) \, dX$$

$$= \frac{1}{2} \log_2 (2\pi e \sigma^2).$$

This comes about because

(a)

$$\int_{-\infty}^\infty f_X(X) \, dX = 1 \qquad \text{and}$$

(b)

$$\int_{-\infty}^\infty (x-\mu)^2 f_X(X) \, dX = \sigma^2.$$

Using a fundamental result on entropy (see Lemma 11.10) one can show the following.

1. For a finite variance σ^2, the Gaussian random variable has the largest (differential) entropy attained by any random variable.

2. The entropy of a Gaussian random variable X is uniquely determined by the variance of X (i.e. it is independent of the mean of X).

We consider a continuous stationary random variable $X = X(t)$, where the mean of X is zero and where X is band-limited to W hertz. We let $X_1, \ldots, X_m$, with $m = 2W$ be the random variables corresponding to uniform sampling of $2W$ samples per second (the Nyquist rate). The samples are transmitted over a noisy channel that is also band-limited to W hertz. If the duration of transmission is T seconds, then, altogether, $2WT$ samples are transmitted.

We have seen that a continuous signal of bandwidth W can be completely characterized by its amplitude at $2W$ sample points per second with the amplitude measured in units such as volts. Using suitable units, we can define the **energy** as the square of the sample amplitude.

Conversely, given the samples, we can construct a unique band-limited signal of band width W passing through $2W$ sample points per second.

The variables $X_1, \ldots, X_m$ corresponding to the $m = 2W$ amplitude samples are independent. *The signal source is assumed to be ergodic.* Define the **average transmitted power** P as the average of the variable X_i^2, $i = 1, \ldots, 2W$. In symbols,

$$E(X_i^2) = P, \qquad i = 1, \ldots, 2W \tag{13.14}$$

The channel output is perturbed by **additive white Gaussian noise** (AWGN) with mean zero and variance $\sigma^2 = \frac{N_0}{2}$, where $\frac{N_0}{2}$ is the power spectral density. Let $(X_1, \ldots, X_m)$ denote an input signal and $(Y_1, \ldots, Y_m)$ its received signal. We have

$$Y_i = X_i + N_i, \qquad i = 1, \ldots, m = 2W \tag{13.15}$$

with N_i being a normal (Gaussian) variable with mean zero and variance equal to $\frac{N_0}{2}$, with the noise also being band-limited to W hertz. We assume that the samples $Y_1, \ldots, Y_m$ are statistically independent. We assume also that the variables X_i, N_i are independent.

The noise sample N_k is Gaussian with zero mean and variance given by

$$\sigma^2 = N_0 W \tag{13.16}$$

A channel for which the noise and the received signal are as in Eqs. (13.15) and (13.16) is called a **discrete-time memoryless Gaussian channel**.

Equation (13.14) states that the channel is *power-limited* with P as the average transmitted power.

The capacity C of the channel is defined to be the mutual information $I(X_k : Y_k)$ maximized with respect to the incoming probability density function f subject to Eq. (13.14). In symbols,

$$C = \max_{f_{X_k}(X)} [I(X_k : Y_k) \; : \; E(X_k^2) = P] \tag{13.17}$$

Now, as in earlier chapters,

$$I(X_k : Y_k) = h(Y_k) - h(Y_k|X_k) \tag{13.18}$$

Since X_k and N_k are independent, and their sum equals Y_k, we get

$$h(Y_k|X_k) - h(N_k).$$

Thus,

$$I(X_k : Y_k) = h(Y_k) - h(N_k) \tag{13.19}$$

Since $h(N_k)$ is independent of the distribution of X_k, maximizing $I(X_k : Y_k)$ requires maximizing Y_k. But, as above (see Section 13.2), that requires Y_k to be Gaussian. Since N_k is Gaussian and $X_k = Y_k + N_k$, X_k must also be Gaussian. We can then formulate Eq. (13.17) as

$$C = I(X_k : Y_k), \qquad X_k \text{ Gaussian}, \qquad E(X_k^2) = P.$$

Now, $Y_k = X_k + N_k$. Since X_k and N_k are independent, the variance of Y_k is the variance of X_k plus the variance of N_k. Thus, the variance of Y is $P + \sigma^2$.

Thus,

$$h(Y_k) = \frac{1}{2} \log_2 [2\pi e(P + \sigma^2)]$$

$$h(N_k) = \frac{1}{2} \log_2 [2\pi e\sigma^2], \text{ since } N_k \text{ has variance } \sigma^2.$$

From this, using formula (13.17) we have

$$C = \frac{1}{2} \log_2 \left(1 + \frac{P}{\sigma^2}\right) \text{ bits per transmission} \tag{13.20}$$

The channel is used $2WT$ times giving

$$C = W_n \log_2 \left(1 + \frac{P}{N_0 W}\right) \text{ bits per second} \tag{13.21}$$

Using here (13.16), that $\sigma^2 = N_0 W$ (where $\frac{N_0}{2}$ is the power spectral density), we get the following:

Information capacity theorem

The information capacity C is given by the formula $C = W \log(1 + \frac{P}{\sigma^2})$ bits per second, where P is the average power.

Since $\sigma^2 = N_0 W$, we get the following equivalent formulation for C.

Capacity Formula 2

$C = W_n \log(1 + \frac{P}{N_0 W}) = W_n \log(1 + \frac{P}{N})$ *bits per second, where $N = N_0 W$ and P is the average power.*

Capacity Formula 3

$C = B \log(1 + \text{SNR})$. *This is the traditional formulation where B stands for "Bandwidth" and $\text{SNR} = S/N$ denotes the "Signal to Noise Ratio."*

This formula is of great practical importance and gives the precise connection between the information capacity, the bandwidth and the average power. Again, the **information capacity** is defined as the maximum rate at which information can be transmitted across the channel without error, which is the log of the number of distinguishable inputs. We can regard the term $\frac{P}{N_0 W}$ as the average "signal to noise ratio" (SNR).

From the capacity formula, C varies in a linear fashion with W versus only a logarithmic growth with P. It follows that to increase capacity, it is easier to increase C by widening the band width, rather than by increasing the power for a prescribed noise variance. For further details, we refer the reader to Pierce [Pie79] and Haykin [Hay01].

Haykin also gives an intuitive argument for these results.

From Eq. (13.14), we also have

$$E(X_1^2 + \cdots + X_m^2) = mP, \qquad m = 2W \qquad (13.22)$$

If $(x_1, \ldots, x_m)$ denotes observed amplitude values we have that, on average,

$$x_1^2 + \cdots + x_m^2 = mP \qquad (13.23)$$

Thus, the points $(x_1, \ldots, x_m)$ lie close to the surface of a hypersphere in a Euclidean m-dimensional space, $m = 2W$, with center the origin and radius $\sqrt{mP}$.

Our input signal $(X_1, \ldots, X_m)$ has band-limit W, and the sampling rate is $2W$ samples per second. If the signal duration is T seconds, and the average power per sample is denoted by P, it follows that the points representing the samples at different times lie close to the surface of a sphere having radius $\sqrt{2WPT}$.

The received message corresponding to Y lies in a small sphere *centered at the input signal* with radius equal to $\sqrt{2WT\sigma^2}$. To see this, we have $Y_i = X_i + N_i$, so $Y_i - X_i = N_i$. Thus, $E(Y_i - X_i) = E(N_i)$, where E denotes the expected value. Since N_i has mean 0 and variance σ^2, we have from Chapter 10 $\sigma^2 = E(N_i - 0)^2 = E(N_i^2)$. Then $E[(Y_1 - X_1)^2 + (Y_2 - X_2)^2 + \cdots + (Y_m - X_m)^2] = m\sigma^2$. Thus, on average the received message corresponding to Y lies on a sphere centered at X with radius equal to $\sqrt{2WT\sigma^2}$.

In a time T, the total received energy is $2WT(P + \sigma^2)$ and the point representing whatever signal was sent plus whatever noise was added to it lies within a hypersphere of radius $\sqrt{2WT(P + \sigma^2)}$ and is close to the surface of that hypersphere.

To see this, take $T = 1$. We have $Y_i = X_i + N_i$ so $Y_i^2 = (X_i + N_i)^2$. Thus, $E(Y_i^2) = E(X_i + N_i)^2 = E(X_i^2 + N_i^2 + 2X_iN_i)$. Since X_i, N_i are independent, $E(X_iN_i) = E(X_i)E(N_i) = E(X_i)0 = 0$ (see Chapter 10). Therefore, we have $E(Y_i^2) = E(X_i^2) + E(N_i^2) = P + \sigma^2$. Thus, $E(Y_1^2 + Y_2^2 + \cdots + Y_m^2) = m(P + \sigma^2)$.

So we have a collection of M small hyperspheres of radius $\sqrt{2WT\sigma^2}$ all lying within a larger hypersphere of radius $\sqrt{2WT(P + \sigma^2)}$ in m dimensions, where $m = 2WT$. For accurate decoding these spheres should be disjoint.

How large can M be in order that the hyperspheres be disjoint? The argument is reminiscent of our work in Chapter 11, where we were filling up a finite set (e.g. of size $2^{nH(X)}$) with a family of disjoint subsets, all of the same size (e.g. of size $2^{nH(X|Y)}$).

In the case $n = 2$, we have a collection of small circles, each having the same radius, being packed into a larger circle with no two of the small circles overlapping.

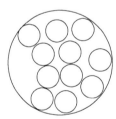

We think of each sample as an input source word. As discussed in Chapter 12, we have the following relation:

Channel capacity $=$ log(number of distinguishable inputs).

The inputs are distinguishable here if their output fans, in this case the small spheres, are disjoint.

Now in m dimensions (with $m = 2WT$ here), the volume of a hypersphere is proportional to R^m, where R is the radius.

In symbols, the volume is $V_m(m(P + \sigma^2))^{\frac{m}{2}}$, where V_m is a constant. The volume of each smaller sphere is $V_m(m\sigma^2)^{\frac{m}{2}}$.

The ratio is

$$\left(1 + \frac{P}{\sigma^2}\right)^{\frac{m}{2}} = 2^{\frac{m}{2}\log(1+\frac{P}{\sigma^2})} \tag{13.24}$$

where logs are taken to the base 2, as usual. It follows that if M is the maximum number of disjoint small spheres, we get

$$M \leq 2^{\frac{m}{2}\log(1+\frac{P}{\sigma^2})} \tag{13.25}$$

Since $m = 2WT$, we get

$$M \leq 2^{WT\log(1+\frac{P}{\sigma^2})} \tag{13.26}$$

Taking logs we get

$$\log M \leq WT \log\left(+\frac{P}{\sigma^2}\right) \tag{13.27}$$

As the message is T seconds in duration, then dividing by T, we get an upper bound on the channel capacity as $W \log(1 + \frac{P}{\sigma^2})$.

13.3   The Coding Gain

In many practical situations, there is a choice between the number U of user bits that need to be accurately transmitted through a noisy channel and the available power P (Figure 13.2). There is a trade-off. For example, in deep space transmission, U determines the number of pictures that can be sent and P is the power available from solar panels. The transmitter will have an average energy of

$$E_b = \frac{U}{P} \tag{13.28}$$

When we encode, we use up more bits. Given that the available power is fixed, there is then a loss of energy per bit and the "dividing line" between 0 and 1 becomes blurred. The probability of a bit error will, therefore, increase. In van Lint [vL98], the author gives the example of the 32×32 Hadamard code used in the spacecraft Mariner '69. In the case of no coding, the bit error probability is about $\frac{10^{-4}}{6}$. With coding, the bit error probability increases by a factor of about 2000 to about 0.036. However, the *message error probability* improves from about 10^{-4} (with no coding) to 1.4×10^{-5} with coding!

Another way of looking at the situation is as follows: *We can use coding not to reduce message error probability but to improve the SNR, keeping the error probability the same.* In the Mariner example this allows for the reduction of the solar panels by almost 15%. For further details, we refer the reader to van Lint [vL98].

Figure 13.2: The late Professor J. H. van Lint, one of the world's leading coding theorists.
Source: Photo courtesy of Professor H. van Tilborg.

Chapter 14

Ergodic and Markov Sources, Language Entropy

Goals, Discussion So far, our sources have been discrete. In the real world, this need not be the case. Sometimes we need to utilize continuous sources such as continuous electromagnetic signals used in engineering. Also, even in the discrete case, memoryless sources can be too restrictive. Ergodic sources form a bridge. For discrete sources, we have a hierarchy: Memoryless sources are the most specialized. Stationary sources are more general than ergodic sources which are more general than the special kinds of Markov sources featured in Theorem 14.16. Languages can be modeled as ergodic sources. From this, we can estimate the redundancy of a language such as English. This has obvious ramifications in cryptography.

New, Noteworthy Conceptually, these topics are complex. We give several examples in the text and in the problems to illustrate some of the subtleties. On the Markov side, we give clear statements about the main results. We discuss the fixed probability vector for an irreducible Markov chain and emphasize that this probability vector must have all components **positive**. We use the fixed probability vector to compute the entropy of a Markov source. Markov sources form a basic part of discrete mathematics both from the theoretical and practical point of view. In fact on p. 34 [McE78] McEliece points

Cryptography, Information Theory, and Error-Correction: A Handbook for the 21st Century, Second Edition.
Aiden A. Bruen, Mario A. Forcinito, and James M. McQuillan.
© 2021 John Wiley & Sons, Inc. Published 2021 by John Wiley & Sons, Inc.

out that *for any communication system the random vectors* $(\mathbf{u}, \mathbf{x}, \mathbf{y}, \mathbf{v})$ *corresponding to input→encodes→channel→decodes form a Markov chain.*

14.1   General and Stationary Sources

Useful sources for this chapter include Welsh [Wel88], Ash [Ash90], and Goldie and Pinch [GP91]. Let S be any source emitting symbols from some alphabet A. We denote the random variables corresponding to the values of the alphabet emitted by the source by $X_1, X_2, \ldots$, where X_n corresponds to the nth letter that the source outputs.

Then, for any n, we will show how $H(X_1, X_2, \ldots, X_n)$ can be calculated in various ways.

Example 14.1   *Suppose S produces symbols from $A = \{0, 1\}$ such that S independently emits 0 with probability 0.3 and 1 with probability 0.7 in each position. Calculate $H(X_1, X_2)$.*

The possible values of (X_1, X_2) are $(0,0), (0,1), (1,0), (1,1)$ with corresponding probabilities $0.09, 0.21, 0.21, 0.49$, respectively. Then

$$H(X_1, X_2) = -[(0.09)\log(0.09) + (0.21)\log(0.21) + (0.21)\log(0.21) + 0.49\log(0.49)]$$

Alternatively, $H(X_1, X_2) = 2H(X_1) = 2(H(0.7)) = 2(0.8813) = 1.7626.$

In general, we want to define $H(S)$, the entropy of an arbitrary source S. This is done as follows: **The entropy of S**, denoted by $H(S)$, is defined to be a limit, namely $\lim_{n\to\infty} \frac{H(X_1, X_2, \ldots, X_n)}{n}$, if such a limit exists.

Note that if S is memoryless, as in Example 14.1, then

$$\frac{H(X_1, X_2, \ldots, X_n)}{n} = \frac{H(X_1) + H(X_2) + \cdots + H(X_n)}{n} = \frac{H + H + \cdots + H}{n} = H$$

where $H = H(X_i)$, $1 \leq i \leq n$.

To see that $H(X_1, X_2, \ldots, X_n) = H(X_1) + H(X_2) + \cdots + H(X_n)$, we use the fact that the X_i are *independent*.

Here is another formula that we might propose for the definition of entropy.

$$H(S) = \lim_{n\to\infty} H(X_n \mid X_1, X_2, \ldots, X_{n-1}) \quad \text{(if this limit exists)}$$

In fact, we have the following result.

Theorem 14.2 *If* $\lim_{n\to\infty} H(X_n \mid X_1, \dots, X_{n-1})$ *exists, then* $\lim_{n\to\infty} \frac{H(X_1, X_2, \dots, X_n)}{n}$ *exists and the two limits are equal.*

Proof. We refer to the problems for a proof. ∎

However, as pointed out by Welsh [Wel88] it may be the case that $\lim_{n\to\infty} \frac{H(X_1, X_2, \dots, X_n)}{n}$ exists even though $\lim_{n\to\infty} H(X_n \mid X_1, X_2, \dots, X_{n-1})$ does not exist. Here is an example.

Example 14.3 *Let a source S emit a sequence $(X_1, X_2, X_3 \dots)$ in such a way that $X_2, X_4, X_6, \dots, X_{2m}, \dots$ are zero and such that $(X_1, X_3, X_5, \dots)$ are chosen independently at random from the alphabet $\{0, 1\}$.*

Then (see Problems) $H(X_1, X_2, X_3, \dots, X_n)$ is $\frac{n+1}{2}$ if n is odd and $\frac{n}{2}$ if n is even. It follows that $\lim_{n\to\infty} \frac{H(X_1, X_2, \dots, X_n)}{n}$ exists and is equal to $\frac{1}{2}$. However, if n is even, $H(X_n \mid X_1, X_2, \dots, X_{n-1}) = 0$. If n is odd, then $H(X_n \mid X_1, X_2, \dots, X_{n-1}) = 1$. Thus, $\lim_{n\to\infty} H(X_n \mid X_1, X_2, \dots, X_{n-1})$ does not exist.

We now come to **stationary sources**. The source S is **stationary** if it is "**time-invariant.**" This means that $\Pr(X_{i_1} = a_1, X_{i_2} = a_2, \dots, X_{i_n} = a_n) = \Pr(X_{i_1+w} = a_1, X_{i_2+w} = a_2, \dots, X_{i_n+w} = a_n)$, where $w \geq 0$ is any nonnegative integer, and $i_1, i_2, \dots, i_n$ is any set of nonnegative indices.

Let us examine this condition. Take the alphabet to be binary. As a very special case, we have that $\Pr(X_i = 1) = \Pr(X_{i+w} = 1)$ for any integer $w \geq 0$. Thus, $\Pr(X_1 = 1) = \Pr(X_2 = 1) = \cdots = \Pr(X_n = 1) = p$. Doesn't this say that the sequence is in fact memoryless? Not quite. We refer to the problems.

Another example of the definition is this. The probability that both the 8th and the 11th symbol are 1 equals the probability that both the 15th and the 18th symbol are 1. We get this by taking $w = 7$.

Any memoryless source is stationary. This follows because in the memoryless case the variables X_i are, by definition, independent and identically distributed random variables.

Example 14.4 *Let S be a binary memoryless source, where the probability of emitting 1 is 0.7, and the probability of emitting 0 is 0.3. Then*

$$\Pr(X_8 = X_{11} = 1) = \Pr(X_8 = 1)\Pr(X_{11} = 1) = (0.7)^2 = 0.49$$

$$\Pr(X_{15} = X_{18} = 1) = \Pr(X_{15} = 1)\Pr(X_{18} = 1) = (0.7)^2 = 0.49.$$

However, not all stationary sources are memoryless

Example 14.5 *A source S emits $\{X_1, X_2, \dots\}$ as follows. An unbiased coin is tossed. If the result is heads, then $X_n = 1$ for all n. If the result is tails, then $X_n = 0$ for all n. We pose the following questions:*

(a) Is S memoryless?

(b) Is S stationary?

The answer to (a) is "No," but it is worth discussing, and we do so in the problems. The answer to (b) is "Yes."

To see this, observe that $\Pr(X_{i_1} = X_{i_2} = X_{i_3} = \dots = 0) = \frac{1}{2} = \Pr(X_{i_1+w} = X_{i_2+w} = X_{i_3+w} = \dots = 0)$. If we replace 0 by 1 above the conclusion is the same. For example, $\Pr(X_1 = X_2 = 1) = \Pr(X_9 = X_{10} = 1) = \frac{1}{2}$. We remark that the only subsequence that has a nonzero probability of occurring is either the all-zero or the all-one subsequence.

Theorem 14.6 *Any stationary source has an entropy. This entropy is the limit given by $\lim_{n \to \infty} H(X_n \mid X_1, X_2, \dots, X_{n-1})$.*

Proof. $H(X_n \mid X_1, X_2, \dots, X_{n-1}) \leq H(X_n \mid X_2, \dots, X_{n-1})$ as can be seen from the fact that side-information, in this case X_1, "never increases entropy" – see Chapter 10. By stationarity the right side equals $H(X_{n-1} \mid X_1, X_2, \dots, X_{n-2})$. Therefore, $v_n = H(X_n \mid X_1, X_2, \dots, X_{n-1}) \leq H(X_{n-1} \mid X_1, X_2, \dots, X_{n-2}) = v_{n-1}$. So $\{v_n\}$ is a *decreasing* sequence, and $v_n \geq 0$. By a basic property of the real numbers the limit of $\{v_n\}$ exists as n tends to infinity, since $\{v_n\}$ is bounded below by zero. The result now follows from Theorem 14.2. ■

14.2 Ergodic Sources

The fact that a source S is stationary pins down S to some extent. But we need more structure in the source. The type of source that we need is called an **ergodic source**.

We assume that S is a stationary source emitting symbols $(X_1, X_2, \dots, X_n)$ according to some known probability distribution over some alphabet A. Let $\mathbf{a} = (a_1, \dots, a_t)$ denote some sequence over A. We define $f_n(\mathbf{a})$, the **frequency** of $\mathbf{a}$ for an output $(X_1, X_2, \dots, X_n, \dots)$ of the source, to be the number of times that $\mathbf{a}$ occurs in the first n terms of the output.

Example 14.7 *Let $\mathbf{a} = (0,1)$ with S binary and $(X_1, X_2, \dots, X_n) = (100110100110)$. Here $n = 12$, $f_{12}(\mathbf{a}) = 3$.*

The stationary source is **ergodic** if $\Pr\left(\lim_{n\to\infty} \frac{f_n(\mathbf{a})}{n} = \Pr(X_1 = a_1, \ldots, X_t = a_t)\right) = 1$, where $\mathbf{a} = (a_1, a_2, \ldots, a_t)$. As Ash [Ash90, p. 197] puts it, *"In other words, the long-run relative frequency of a sequence converges stochastically to the probability assigned to the sequence."* More briefly, the time average equals the ensemble average. In page 512 of "The Princeton Companion to Mathematics," [GBGL09, p. 512], they discuss some very informative examples on how ergodicity works due to Von Neumann and "similar questions about the relationship between time and space averages."

Example 14.8   *Let S be the source in Example 14.5 of Section 14.1. Is S ergodic?*

Let $t = 1$ and $\mathbf{a} = (0)$. Then either $f_n(\mathbf{a}) = n$ or $f_n(\mathbf{a}) = 0$. Thus, either $\lim_{n\to\infty} \frac{f_n(\mathbf{a})}{n} = 1$ or $\lim_{n\to\infty} \frac{f_n(\mathbf{a})}{n} = 0$. Now, $\Pr(X_1 = 0) = \frac{1}{2}$. Thus, $\Pr\left(\lim_{n\to\infty} \frac{f_n(\mathbf{a})}{n} = \Pr(X_1 = 0)\right) \neq 1$. Thus, S is stationary, but not ergodic.

Example 14.9   *This example is found in Pierce [Pie79]. The source S emits*

(i) *the sequence $A, B, A, B, A, B \ldots$ with probability $\dfrac{1}{3}$*

(ii) *the sequence $B, A, B, A, B, A \ldots$ with probability $\dfrac{1}{3}$*

(iii) *and the sequence $E, E, E, E, E, E \ldots$ with probability $\dfrac{1}{3}$*

Then if $\mathbf{a} = (A)$, we have $\frac{f_n(\mathbf{a})}{n} = \frac{1}{2}$ for the first kind of sequence, $\frac{f_n(\mathbf{a})}{n} = \frac{1}{2}$ for the second kind of sequence and $\frac{f_n(\mathbf{a})}{n} = 0$ for the third kind of sequence. But $\Pr(X_1 = A) = \frac{1}{3}$. Again, S is stationary but not ergodic.

Discussion

If a source is stationary it is time invariant, so we can calculate meaningful **time averages** for a *given* output. For a source to be ergodic, we need these time averages to be equal to the **ensemble averages**.

These are averages taken over all possible outputs obtained from the given probability distribution of the source. The idea is important, if a bit complicated. Pierce [Pie79] offers the following discussion.

Let us think of a very large number of writers in a given language, say English. For a given message (i.e. for a given writer), the frequency of occurrence of a letter such as S does not vary much along the length of the message. As we analyze a longer and longer piece of a message, our estimate of the statistics of a message (e.g. the frequency of occurrence of a letter such as S or of a diagram such as AE) and the associated probabilities converges.

The point about a source being ergodic is that these statistics or probabilities apply equally well to all possible messages or outputs, i.e. to all possible writers of English in this case.

The ergodic idea applies also in the physical world, where we are dealing with electromagnetic sources of various sorts.

From our point of view, the main property about ergodic sources is that they satisfy the **asymptotic equipartition property** (AEP). This is called the **Shannon–McMillan Theorem**. It means that most sequences of length N, with N large, from an ergodic source are "typical" and equiprobable with probability of occurrence equal to 2^{-NH}, where H is the entropy of the source. Using this, one can show that the channel capacity theorem for a binary symmetric channel discussed in Chapter 12 holds, not just for memoryless sources but also for ergodic sources.

Example 14.10 *Every memoryless source is ergodic.*

The proof of this is not immediate and involves proving a special case of "the law of large numbers" in the theory of probability.

In Section 14.3 we discuss the examples "par excellence" of ergodic sources which are not memoryless. They are obtained from certain Markov sources.

14.3 Markov Chains and Markov Sources

A source S is said to be a **Markov source** if $\Pr(X_{n+1} = a_{n+1} \mid X_n = a_n, \ldots, X_1 = a_1) = \Pr(X_{n+1} = a_{n+1} \mid X_n = a_n)$, where $a_1, a_2, \ldots, a_n, a_{n+1}$ are elements of the alphabet A of S. In other words, the probability of the event that $X_{n+1} = a_{n+1}$ only depends on the source output immediately preceding X_{n+1}. The **transition probability** p_{ij} is defined as follows.

$$p_{ij} = \Pr(X_{n+1} = a_j \mid X_n = a_i)$$

Here, if the alphabet A has m letters in it, we have $1 \leq i, j \leq m$. Then the transition probabilities form the **transition matrix** $P = (p_{ij})$.

Each entry in P, being a probability, lies between 0 and 1. The entries in each row of the matrix add up to 1. We regard the elements $a_1, a_2, \ldots, a_m$ of the alphabet A as "states" and p_{ij} as the probability of moving from state i to state j. If we are in a given state i, we either have to remain in state i or move to a new state. Thus, the entries in any row of P add up to 1. If we know the initial value X_1, we can find the probability of subsequent values $X_2, X_3, \ldots$ from the transition matrix P.

Example 14.11 *Suppose the source is an English writer. So we have 27 states, say, corresponding to the 26 letters and a space. Then, if A is letter 1, B is letter 2, C is letter 3, etc., we get $p_{2,5} = p_{25}$ the probability of moving from state 2 to state 5 = the probability that the next letter to be written is E given that the present letter is B.*

The matrix P of size 27×27 can be constructed from the statistics of the language.

Example 14.12 *A binary source operates as follows. The next entry equals the present entry with probability p and equals the opposite of the present binary entry with probability $1 - p$.*

Here, the transition matrix P is as follows:

$$P = \begin{matrix} & \begin{matrix} 0 & \quad 1 \end{matrix} \\ \begin{matrix} 0 \\ 1 \end{matrix} & \begin{pmatrix} p & 1-p \\ 1-p & p \end{pmatrix} \end{matrix}$$

If $p = 0.7$, then P becomes $\begin{pmatrix} .7 & .3 \\ .3 & .7 \end{pmatrix}$.

Question

If the first entry in the output of the source above is 1, what is the probability that the 3rd element is in fact 0?

We want to calculate $\Pr(X_3 = 0 \mid X_1 = 1)$.

It is easier to visualize this with a "**state diagram**," where we have two states named 0 and 1 along with a "**transition diagram**" as indicated below.

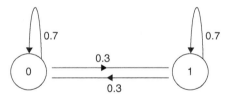

Our question is this. What is the probability of moving from state 1 to state 0 in exactly 2 transitions (denoted by $p_{1,0}^{(2)}$)?

We can move from state 1 to state 1 and then from state 1 to state 0. The probability of this happening is $(0.7)(0.3)$. Or, we can move from state 1 to state 0 and then from state 0 to state 0. The probability of this happening is $(0.3)(0.7)$. Thus, the total probability is $(0.7)(0.3) + (0.7)(0.3) = 0.42$

This can all be handled easily from the algebraic point of view. We have

$$P = \begin{pmatrix} p & 1-p \\ 1-p & p \end{pmatrix} = \begin{pmatrix} .7 & .3 \\ .3 & .7 \end{pmatrix}$$

Now, $P^2 = PP$ is a transition matrix. In fact P^n, for any positive integer n is also a transition matrix. This means that each entry of P^n is a probability and that, moreover, each row of P^n adds up to 1.

Significance of P^n

The (ij)th entry of P^n, i.e. $(P^n)_{i,j}$ tells us what the *probability is of moving from state i to state j in exactly n steps or transitions.* Here, $P^2 = \begin{pmatrix} 0.58 & 0.42 \\ 0.42 & 0.58 \end{pmatrix}$.

So 0.58 represents the probability of moving from state 0 to state 0 in exactly two steps or transitions. Similarly, 0.42 represents the probability of moving from state 0 to state 1 (and also, the probability of moving from state 1 to state 0) in exactly two steps.

Caution

Here p has a different meaning than it had when we discussed the BSC in earlier chapters. There, p was the probability of a mistake being made, so we had $p < \frac{1}{2}$. Here, p is the probability of moving from state 0 to state 0 or state 1 to state 1 so $p = 0.7$.

In general, if we have some initial probability distribution (α, β) for the two states, then the vector $(\alpha, \beta)P^n$ tells us the probability distribution after exactly n steps (transitions). To calculate $(\alpha, \beta)P^n$ it is much shorter, instead of calculating P^n, and then getting $(\alpha, \beta)P^n$ to calculate $((((\alpha, \beta)P)P)P \ldots)$ In this approach, we are only multiplying a vector by a matrix at each stage. This is much easier than multiplying an entire matrix by itself at each stage.

We now come to the key results about Markov chains that show their power and utility.

First, we say that a Markov source (or Markov chain) with transition matrix P is **irreducible** if there exists some power of P, say P^m, such that all entries of P^m are *positive*.

Example 14.13 *Let*

$$P = \begin{pmatrix} \frac{1}{3} & \frac{1}{3} & \frac{1}{3} \\ 0 & \frac{1}{2} & \frac{1}{2} \\ \frac{1}{3} & \frac{1}{3} & \frac{1}{3} \end{pmatrix}$$

Then $P = P^1$ has some zeros. But P^2 has no zeros as is easily checked, and so, P is irreducible.

Here is our first main result.

Theorem 14.14 *Let P be an irreducible Markov source with transition matrix P. Then there exists a unique fixed probability vector $\mathbf{w}$ such that the following holds.*

(a) $\mathbf{w}P = \mathbf{w}$.

(b) each entry in $\mathbf{w}$ is positive.

(c) As n gets large, P^n tends to W, where each row of W is $\mathbf{w}$.

(d) No matter what the initial probability vector $\mathbf{p}_0$ is, $\mathbf{p}_0 P^n$ tends to $\mathbf{w}$ as n gets large. In other words, the probability of being in state number i tends to the ith component of the fixed probability vector $\mathbf{w}$ regardless of the initial probability distribution.

This theorem is one of the major results in discrete mathematics. The proof is quite involved. For a discussion, we refer the interested reader to Ash [Ash90], Feller [Fel50], and Goldie-Pinch [GP91]. Part (d) is especially important as it shows that **long range predictions** such as weather forecasts can easily be derived from the Markov model.

Example 14.15 *Let P be as above. We want to calculate the fixed probability vector $\mathbf{w}$.*

Let $\mathbf{w} = (x, y, z)$. We have $\mathbf{w}P = \mathbf{w}$, so

$$(x, y, z) \begin{pmatrix} \frac{1}{3} & \frac{1}{3} & \frac{1}{3} \\ 0 & \frac{1}{2} & \frac{1}{2} \\ \frac{1}{3} & \frac{1}{3} & \frac{1}{3} \end{pmatrix} = (x, y, z)$$

Then

$$\frac{1}{3}x + \frac{1}{3}z = x$$

$$\frac{1}{3}x + \frac{1}{2}y + \frac{1}{3}z = y$$

$$\frac{1}{3}x + \frac{1}{2}y + \frac{1}{3}z = z.$$

Since $\mathbf{w}$ is a probability vector we also demand that

$$x + y + z = 1$$

In solving these equations we see from the second and third equations that $y = z$. Substituting and using the forth equation gives that $\mathbf{w} = \left(\frac{1}{5}, \frac{2}{5}, \frac{2}{5}\right)$.

Now, we come to the *coup de grâce*, a fundamental result which goes back to A.A. Markov.

Theorem 14.16 *Suppose P is the transition matrix for an irreducible Markov source S. If the fixed probability vector $\mathbf{w}$ is used as the initial distribution, then S is an ergodic source.*

The distribution $\mathbf{w}$ is sometimes called the **stationary distribution** as well as the **fixed probability vector**.

14.4 Irreducible Markov Sources, Adjoint Source

If S is irreducible, then the source S is stationary. Let P denote the transition matrix. Thus, from Section 14.1, S has an entropy which can be defined as

$$\lim_{n \to \infty} H(X_{n+1} \mid X_1, X_2, \dots, X_n) = \lim_{n \to \infty} H(X_{n+1} \mid X_n)$$

since the source is Markov.

Recall that $H(X \mid Y)$ can be written as the average value of $H(X \mid y)$. Thus,

$$H(X, Y) = \sum_y H(X \mid y) \Pr(y)$$

Let a_i be the ith element of the alphabet $A = \{a_1, a_2, \dots, a_m\}$. We regard the possible elements of the alphabet as the possible states. (Thus, for example, we could model the English language using 26 states for the 26 letters.) Then, $H(X_{n+1} \mid X_n) = \sum_{i=1}^m H(X_{n+1} \mid X_n = a_i) \Pr(X_n = a_i)$. Now, $\Pr(X_n = a_i)$ is, (in the limit, as n gets large) w_i, where $\mathbf{w} = (w_1, w_2, \dots, w_m)$ is the fixed probability vector of P: This follows from Theorem 14.14 in Section 14.3.

Also, $H(X_{n+1} \mid X_n = a_i)$ is easily calculated simply by thinking of the ith state as a source with emission probabilities p_{ij}. Recall that p_{ij} is the probability of moving from state i to state j. The source corresponding to the ith state, then has an entropy H_i. So we get the following result: The entropy H of an irreducible Markov source is given by the following formula

$$H = -\sum_{i=1}^m w_i \sum_j p_{ij} \log p_{ij}$$

Alternatively, we have, from the above, that

$$H = \sum_{i=1}^{m} w_i H_i$$

where H_i is the entropy corresponding to the ith state. Now, if S is an ergodic Markov source with alphabet $A = \{a_1, a_2, \ldots, a_m\}$ and fixed probability vector $\mathbf{w}$, we can ignore the transition matrix P and form the **adjoint source** S^*, which is memoryless, with alphabet A and with w_i defined to be the probability that S^* emits a_i, $1 \leq i \leq m$. This source will then have its own entropy $H^* = H(S^*)$.

Theorem 14.17 (Comparison theorem for entropies) *The entropy of an ergodic Markov source is less than or equal to the entropy of the adjoint source. In symbols, we have $H \leq H^*$.*

Example 14.18 *Let the Markov source have transition matrix*

$$P = \begin{pmatrix} \frac{1}{3} & \frac{1}{3} & \frac{1}{3} \\ 0 & \frac{1}{2} & \frac{1}{2} \\ \frac{1}{3} & \frac{1}{3} & \frac{1}{3} \end{pmatrix}$$

As we have seen, $\mathbf{w} = \left(\frac{1}{5}, \frac{2}{5}, \frac{2}{5}\right)$. Then

$$H^* = \frac{1}{5}\log 5 + \frac{2}{5}\log\left(\frac{5}{2}\right) + \frac{2}{5}\log\left(\frac{5}{2}\right)$$

$$= \frac{1}{5}\log 5 + \frac{2}{5}(\log 5 - \log 2) + \frac{2}{5}\log(5 - \log 2)$$

$$= \log 5 - \frac{2}{5}\log 2 - \frac{2}{5}\log 2 = \log 5 - \frac{4}{5} = 1.5222.$$

The source corresponding to the ith state has entropy $H_i = -\sum_j p_{ij}\log(p_{ij})$. Alternatively, $H_i = \sum_j p_{ij}\log\left(\frac{1}{p_{ij}}\right)$. Then

$$H_1 = \left(\frac{1}{3}\log 3 + \frac{1}{3}\log 3 + \frac{1}{3}\log 3\right) = \log 3 = 1.585$$

$$H_2 = \frac{1}{2}\log 2 + \frac{1}{2}\log 2 = \log 2 = 1$$

$$H_3 = \frac{1}{3}\log 3 + \frac{1}{3}\log 3 + \frac{1}{3}\log 3 = \log 3 = 1.585.$$

Now, the entropy of H is

$$w_1 H_1 + w_2 H_2 + w_3 H_3 = \frac{1}{5}(1.585) + \frac{2}{5}(1) + \frac{2}{5}(1.585) = \frac{3}{5}(1.585)^- + \frac{2}{5}$$

$$= 1.351.$$

Since $1.351 < 1.522$ we have $H < H^*$.

14.5   Cascades and the Data Processing Theorem

Given three random variables X, Y, Z, we can define the mutual information $I(X, Y : Z)$, which we can think of as the amount of information that (X, Y) provide about Z (or as the amount of information that Z provides about (X, Y)).

Using the work in Chapter 10, we can see that for two variables X, Y, we have $I(X : Y) = \sum_{x,y} \Pr(x, y) \log \left(\frac{\Pr(y|x)}{\Pr(y)} \right)$. Similarly,

$$I(X, Y : Z) = \sum_{x,y,z} \Pr(x, y, z) \log \left(\frac{\Pr(z \mid x, y)}{\Pr(z)} \right)$$

In [McE78], McEliece discusses convex functions (up or down) and Jensen's inequality. If $F(X)$ is a probability distribution then, for a random variable X, the expected value of $F(X)$ satisfies the inequality $E(f(X) \geq F(E(X))$ or its reverse, depending on the convexity of F.

Applying Jensen's inequality, as in McEliece [McE78] it can be shown that $I(X, Y : Z) \geq I(Y : Z)$ with equality if and only if $\Pr(z \mid x, y) = \Pr(z \mid y)$ for all (x, y, z) with $\Pr(x, y, z) > 0$.

We want to study the case of equality. Suppose X, Y, Z form a "Markov triple" as in the diagram.

We have a channel connecting X and Y described by the forward probabilities $\Pr(y \mid x)$ and a channel connecting Y and Z with forward probabilities $\Pr(z \mid y)$. By saying that X, Y, Z form a Markov triple, we mean that $\Pr(z \mid x, y) = \Pr(z \mid y)$. So from the above we have $I(X, Y : Z) \geq I(Y : Z)$ with equality if and only if X, Y, Z is a Markov triple (i.e. Z depends on X only through Y).

We have the following result:

Theorem 14.19

(a) $I(X, Y : Z) \geq I(Y : Z)$ *with equality if and only if the sequence* (X, Y, Z) *can be viewed as a Markov chain.*

(b) *If* (X, Y, Z) *is a Markov triple, then*

$$I(X : Z) \leq \begin{cases} I(X : Y) \\ I(Y : Z) \end{cases}$$

This important result says that the "extra processing" involving Z cannot increase mutual information.

14.6 The Redundancy of Languages

This is an important topic for various reasons and is much-studied. For example, in cryptography, one needs to know how much **redundancy** is carried by a language such as English to ensure that encryption is secure. Also, the question is of interest in linguistics and in mathematical modeling for testing the assumption that a suitable ergodic source can give a reasonable mathematical model of a language.

First, let us talk about some definitions. Suppose we are working with some language over an alphabet Γ. For English, we can use 26 letters and a space, so $|\Gamma| = 27$.

We regard the language as an ergodic source. (Then, assuming the Shannon–McMillan theorem, the number of typical sequences Y_n of length n is about 2^{nH}, where H denotes the entropy per symbol in Shannon bits.)

From our work with source coding and block coding – which is easily generalized to the non-binary case – we know that a source with entropy H can be efficiently encoded in such a way that the average length L_n of a typical sequence of length n is given by the formula

$$L_n \log|\Gamma| = nH$$

since

$$L_n = \frac{nH}{\log|\Gamma|} \tag{14.1}$$

This follows since the average encoding length per symbol is $\frac{H}{\log|\Gamma|}$ from Shannon's noiseless coding theorem. This average length is a certain fraction of n. If there were no redundancy, it would be n. So we define R as follows:

$$L_n = n(1 - R) \tag{14.2}$$

(In terms of percentages for the redundancy, a redundancy of 40% translates to $R = 0.4$.) Combining Eqs. (14.1) and (14.2), we get our **formula for redundancy**

$$R = 1 - \frac{H}{\log|\Gamma|}$$

where H is the entropy per symbol.

We observe that for the binary alphabet, this gives $R = 1 - H$.

Formula (14.1) says that a typical sequence of length n can be recoded using just L_n characters without loss of information about the sequence. Of course, we need to estimate H or R.

The redundancy R is usually measured in percentages. Calculating R is not an exact science. Estimates suggest that, for English, redundancy is about 70%. As a very rough, if not incorrect approximation, this might suggest that only about 30% of a message – suitably chosen – is needed to recover the entire message. Or we can think of having only a "free choice" with 30% of the message with the rest of the message, being determined by statistical patterns and grammatical structure.

(A colleague, Ernest Enns, has passed on an interesting message on the Internet concerning the redundancy of English. As we mentioned earlier redundancy can be "good" or "bad." The piece is entitled "clever student" and "reads" as follows:

> Aoccdrnig to a rscheearch at Cmabrigde Uinervtisy, it deosn't mttaer in waht oredr the ltteers in a wrod are, the only iprmottent thing is that the first and lsat ltteer be at the rghit pclae. The rset can be a total mses and you can still raed it wouthit problem. Tihs is bcuseae the human mnid deos not raed every ltetter by itself, but the wrod as a wlohe.
>
> (amzanig huh?)

The *correct mathematical interpretation of R* is that in an optimal encoding, we can reduce the length of the message from n characters to L_n characters.

As an example, let us suppose $H = 1.4$. Then we get $L_n = \frac{n(1.4)}{\log 27} = n\left(\frac{1.4}{4.76}\right) = n(0.2941)$. This means that say a 100-letter message can be recoded as a message using only around 29.4 characters without losing any information.

How would we go about calculating the redundancy or entropy of English?

The first crude approximation is to think of a 27-symbol alphabet (including the space) and to regard English as a memoryless source and one in which each symbol is equally likely to occur. This gives the entropy as $\log 27 = 4.76$ Shannon bits per symbol.

Our next approximation involves taking account of the probabilities of occurrence of the symbols. The most probable symbol is a space with probability 0.18, followed by the letter E with probability approximately equal to 0.13.

This approximation will be an **upper bound** for the following reason. In Chapter 10, we saw that $H(X, Y) \leq H(X) + H(Y)$ with equality if and only if X, Y are independent. Thus, we get

$$H \leq -\sum_{i=1}^{27} p_i \log p_i$$

giving $H \leq 4.03$.

Similarly, we get upper bounds using diagrams, trigrams, etc., and the probabilistic interdependence of the symbols.

Thus, from digrams, $H \leq \frac{1}{2}\sum_i\sum_j \Pr(i,j) \log p_{i,j}$, where $p_{i,j}$ is the estimated probability of the ordered pair (i, j) of symbols and zero-probability pairs are thrown out. This method gives $H \leq 3.32$. One can experiment with trigrams, getting $H \leq 3.10$.

Other approaches included estimating the quantity $H(X_{n+1} \mid X_1, \ldots, X_n)$ that was discussed earlier in this chapter. This estimate can be carried out by estimating the average number of guesses needed to obtain the $(n + 1)$th letter given the previous n letters.

Also, Shannon proposed a different approach to finding the entropy of English by working with words and finding the "word-entropy."

The conclusion of all this is that the entropy (per symbol) of English comes out to a little over 1 Shannon bit (giving a redundancy of around 70% for average English).

14.7 Problems

14.1   Assume that source S is emitting $X_1, X_2, \ldots$ and that $\lim_{n\to\infty} H(X_n \mid X_1, X_2, \ldots, X_{n-1})$ exists. Show that $\lim_{n\to\infty} H(X_1, X_2, \ldots, X_n)$ exists and that the two limits are equal. (See Solution 14.1.)

14.2   Let S be a binary stationary source.

    (a) Show that $\Pr(X_1 = 1) = \Pr(X_2 = 1) = \cdots = \Pr(X_n = 1)$ for all n.

    (b) Why does it not follow that S is memoryless?

    (See Solution 14.2.)

14.3   A memoryless source emits symbols in blocks of size 2 according to the following probability distribution:

$$\Pr(0,0) = \frac{1}{4}, \quad \Pr(0,1) = \frac{3}{4}$$

(a) Is S stationary?

(b) Find the entropy of S.

(See Solution 14.3.)

14.4   Suppose we now regard the source S in Question 14.2 as a source T which emits single binary symbols, not symbols in blocks of size 2.

(a) Is T stationary?

(b) Calculate the entropy (*per symbol*) of T.

(See Solution 14.4.)

14.5   Let S be a memoryless binary source emitting the sequence $X_1, X_2, \ldots$ with the following probability distribution:

$$\Pr(0) = 0.8, \quad \Pr(1) = 0.2$$

(a) Calculate $H(X_1, X_2)$ from first principles.

(b) Calculate $H(X_1, X_2)$ using the fact that S is memoryless.

(See Solution 14.5.)

14.6   For the source S in Problem 14.5 estimate the number of typical output sequences of length 1000. (See Solution 14.6.)

14.7   A binary source S emits symbols 0 and 1 as follows: The first 100 entries are all zero. After that the source is memoryless with probability 0.7 (or 0.3) of emitting 0 (or 1).

Estimate the number of typical output sequences of length 1000 from this source. (See Solution 14.7.)

14.8   Let a Markov source S with 3 states have a transition matrix

$$P = \begin{pmatrix} \frac{1}{4} & 0 & \frac{3}{4} \\ \frac{2}{3} & \frac{1}{6} & \frac{1}{6} \\ \frac{1}{2} & \frac{1}{2} & 0 \end{pmatrix}$$

Find the entropy of S. (See Solution 14.8.)

14.9   Given that the initial probability distribution of the three states is $\left(\frac{6}{14}, \frac{3}{14}, \frac{5}{14}\right)$, calculate the approximate number of output sequences of length n emitted by the source. (See Solution 14.8.)

14.10   With reference to the source S in Problem 14.8 find the entropy of S^*, the adjoint source. (See Solution 14.10.)

14.8   Solutions

14.1   Put $v_n = H(X_n \mid X_1, X_2, \ldots, X_{n-1})$. $w_n = H(X_1, X_2, \ldots, X_n)$, $n \geq 1$, with $w_0 = 0$. Using the fact that $H(A, B) = H(A) + H(B \mid A)$ with $A = (X_1, X_2, \ldots, X_{n-1})$ and $B = X_n$, we get

$$w_n = w_{n-1} + v_n$$

This gives that $w_n = v_1 + v_2 + \cdots + v_n$.
Thus, $\lim_{n \to \infty} \frac{w_n}{n} = \lim_{n \to \infty} \left(\frac{v_1 + v_2 + \cdots + v_n}{n}\right)$. This last limit is the limit of the average of a sequence that tends to a definite limit A, (where $A = \lim_{n \to \infty}(H(X_n \mid X_1, X_2, \ldots, X_{n-1}))$ and so, in the limit, is itself equal to A.

14.2   Part (a) is explained in the text in Section 14.1.
      Part (b) is trickier. S may not be memoryless because the random variables X_n, X_{n+1} may not be independent. For X_n, X_{n+1} to be independent it must be the case that, for example, $\Pr(X_{n+1} = 0 \mid X_n = 1) = \Pr(X_{n+1} = 0)$. But, in Example 14.5 of Section 14.1, $\Pr(X_{n+1} = 0) = \frac{1}{2}$ and $\Pr(X_{n+1} = 0 \mid X_n = 1) = 0$.

14.3   (a) Yes: think of S as a memoryless source emitting possible letters corresponding to two symbols with probabilities equal to $\frac{1}{4}$ or $\frac{3}{4}$.

(b) $H(S) = H(0.25) = H(0.75) = 0.8113$.

14.4   (a) No, T is not stationary. To see this we have that $\Pr(X_n = 0) = 1$ if n is odd but $\Pr(X_n = 0) = \frac{1}{4}$ if n is even. But, from Problem 14.2, we have that if S is stationary then $\Pr(X_1 = 0) = \Pr(X_2 = 0) = \cdots = \Pr(X_n = 0)$ for all n.

(b) The entropy of T is $\frac{1}{2}$(entropy of S) = $\frac{1}{2}(.8113) = 0.4057$.

14.5   (a) The possible values corresponding to the ordered pair (X_1, X_2) are $(0,0)$, $(0,1)$, $(1,0)$, $(1,1)$. Then, the corresponding probabilities are $0.64, 0.16, 0.16,$ 0.04. Thus,

$$H(X_1, X_2) = -[0.64 \log(0.64) + 0.32 \log(0.16) + (0.04) \log(0.04)]$$

(b)

$$H(X_1, X_2) = H(X_1) + H(X_2) \quad \text{(by independence)}$$
$$= 2H(0.8) = 2(0.7219) = 1.4438.$$

14.6 $2^{nH(0.8)} = 2^{(1000)(0.7219)} = 2^{722}$

14.7 $2^{900 H(0.8)} = 2^{(900)(0.7219)} = 2^{650}$

14.8   The fixed probability vector is $\left(\frac{6}{14}, \frac{3}{14}, \frac{5}{14}\right)$. Thinking of the first state as a source with entropy H_1, we have

$$H_1 = -\left[\frac{1}{4} \log\left(\frac{1}{4}\right) + \frac{3}{4} \log\left(\frac{3}{4}\right)\right] = 0.8113$$

Similarly,

$$H_2 = -\left[\frac{2}{3} \log\left(\frac{2}{3}\right) + \frac{1}{6} \log\left(\frac{1}{6}\right) + \frac{1}{6} \log\left(\frac{1}{6}\right)\right] = 1.2516,$$

$$H_3 = -\left[\frac{1}{2} \log\left(\frac{1}{2}\right) + \frac{1}{2} \log\left(\frac{1}{2}\right)\right] = 1.$$

Then the entropy of S is $H = \frac{6}{14}H_1 + \frac{3}{14}H_2 + \frac{5}{14}H_3 = 0.9730$, say.

14.9 Because the initial distribution is **w**, S is ergodic (see Theorem 14.16 in Section 14.3). Then, by the Shannon McMillan Theorem, we have that most sequences emitted are "typical sequences," where the number of typical sequences is $2^{nH} = 2^{0.9730n}$. Here H is the number indicated in Problem 14.8.

14.10 The fixed probability distribution is $\left(\frac{6}{14}, \frac{3}{14}, \frac{5}{14}\right)$. Thus, $H(S^*)$ is as follows:

$$H(S^*) = -\left[\frac{6}{14}\log\left(\frac{6}{14}\right) + \frac{3}{14}\log\left(\frac{3}{14}\right) + \frac{5}{14}\log\left(\frac{5}{14}\right)\right] = 1.5305$$

Chapter 15

Perfect Secrecy: The New Paradigm

Goals, Discussion This chapter links encryption and information theory. We want to study the idea of "perfect secrecy" in cryptography from both concrete and abstract points of view involving entropy. We have seen (Section 4.3) that the one-time pad affords perfect secrecy. This ties in with our discussion in Chapter 2 of the Vigenère cipher where the key is shorter than the message and which can be broken because of this. For discussion, we refer to Shannon's paper [Sha49b].

New, Noteworthy We clarify the idea that for perfect security the key must be as long as the message. We show that a fundamental concept for symmetric key cryptosystems including the one-time pad is a latin square of size $n \times n$, for **any** positive integer n. We show (see the example at the end of Section 15.1 and Problems 15.13 and 15.14) how the one-time pad can be lifted in to the latin square framework. We also present problems illustrating Shannon's idea that cryptography is a bit like error-correction where an eavesdropper tries to decode the message over a noisy channel.

Cryptography, Information Theory, and Error-Correction: A Handbook for the 21st Century, Second Edition.
Aiden A. Bruen, Mario A. Forcinito, and James M. McQuillan.
© 2021 John Wiley & Sons, Inc. Published 2021 by John Wiley & Sons, Inc.

15.1   Symmetric Key Cryptosystems

We begin with the idea of a *symmetric key cryptosystem*. Here we have a cipher system involving a finite set $\mathbf{M} = \{m_1, m_2, \ldots\}$ of **possible messages**, together with a finite set of **cipher texts** $\mathbf{C} = \{c_1, c_2, \ldots\}$ and a finite number of **keyed enciphering transformations** e_k. The key k in the enciphering transformation is chosen, with various nonzero probabilities, from a finite set $\mathbf{K}$ of keys. It is assumed that each message m has a nonzero probability of transmission. Otherwise we could delete it.

Each enciphering transformation e_i associated with key number i, has a unique deciphering transformation d_i associated with it such that d_i undoes e_i. Thus, for any message m we have a cipher text $e_i(m)$. Applying d_i, we recover m since $d_i(e_i(m)) = m$.

Let m_1, m_2 be messages. Suppose $e_k(m_1) = e_k(m_2)$. Applying d_k, we get $d_k(e_k(m_1)) = d_k(e_k(m_2))$. Therefore, $m_1 = m_2$. We conclude that a given e_k maps different messages (= **plain texts**) to different cipher texts. In other words, e_k is one to one.

Thus, let $\mathbf{M} = \{m_1, \ldots, m_n\}$ be the set of n messages in $\mathbf{M}$. Fix the key k. Then $\{e_k(m_1), \ldots, e_k(m_n)\}$ is a set of n distinct cipher texts in $\mathbf{C}$. Then $|\mathbf{C}|$, which is the number of cipher texts in $\mathbf{C}$, is at least equal to the number of messages in $\mathbf{M}$. In symbols

$$|\mathbf{C}| \geq |\mathbf{M}| \tag{15.1}$$

Let us now suppose that our cryptosystem enjoys **perfect secrecy**. By definition then, for any message-cipher text pair m, c we have that $\Pr(m|c) = \Pr(m)$. This means that the conditional probability that the particular message m was transmitted, given that cipher text c is observed, is equal to the probability that m was transmitted. In other words, we have *independence* of the plain text and cipher text; the cipher text reveals nothing about the plain text.

Let us explore some consequences of this. Let (m, c) be any plain text-cipher text pair. So $\Pr(m|c) = \Pr(m)$. Since $\Pr(m) \neq 0$, we have $\Pr(m|c) \neq 0$. Thus, there is a nonzero probability that c was "caused" by the message m. Thus, given any c in $\mathbf{C}$ and any message m in $\mathbf{M}$ there is at least one key k and an enciphering transformation e_k with $e_k(m) = c$, since otherwise we would have $\Pr(m|c) = 0$.

Now fix m and vary the key k in $\mathbf{K}$. It follows that the set $\{e_k(m) \mid k \in \mathbf{K}\}$ contains all cipher texts and so is equal to $\mathbf{C}$ since $e_k(m)$ is in $\mathbf{C}$. (We must allow for the possibility that some members of the set $\{e_k(m)\}$ might be equal.) We then conclude that

$$|\mathbf{K}| \geq |\mathbf{C}| \tag{15.2}$$

Combining with (15.1), we get

$$|\mathbf{K}| \geq |\mathbf{M}| \tag{15.3}$$

This says that for perfect secrecy, the total number of (enciphering) keys is at least as big as the possible number of messages.

Example illustrating the one-time pad

Let $\mathbf{M}$ denote the set of all binary strings m of length u, say. Let $\mathbf{K}$ be the set of all binary strings k of length u. The enciphering transformation $e_k(m)$ maps m to the ciphertext string which is defined as $m\ XOR\ k$. (The XOR operator was defined in Section 4.3.) We have $\mathbf{M} = \mathbf{K} = \mathbf{C}$ (where $\mathbf{C}$ is the set of ciphertexts) and each has size 2^u.

In Chapter 2, we studied other examples of cryptosystems such as the Vigenère and Caesar ciphers.

15.2 Perfect Secrecy and Equiprobable Keys

The case of equality in formula (15.3), when $|\mathbf{K}| = |\mathbf{M}|$ gives rise to an elegant mathematical theory, some of which we now want to explore.

Since $|\mathbf{C}| \geq |\mathbf{M}|$ from formula (15.1) and $|\mathbf{K}| \geq |\mathbf{C}|$ from formula (15.2), it follows that the assumption that $|\mathbf{K}| = |\mathbf{M}|$ leads to the fact that $|\mathbf{K}| = |\mathbf{M}| = |\mathbf{C}| = n$, say. From the above, for each ordered pair (m, c) there is then a unique enciphering transformation e_{k_i} such that $e_{k_i}(m) = c$. Choose the pair $(m, c) = (m_1, c)$ with $e_{k_1}(m_1) = c$ in such a way that $\Pr(k_1) \geq \Pr(k_i)$, $1 \leq i \leq n$. (Recall from the opening paragraph in Section 15.1 that the keys have various probabilities associated with them.) We have the following kind of diagram.

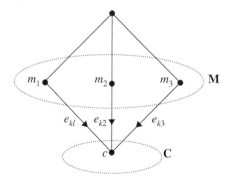

From the Bayes formula (see Chapter 10) and the fact that $\Pr(C|m_i) = \Pr(k_i)$, we get

$$\Pr(m_1|c) = \frac{\Pr(m_1)\Pr(k_1)}{\Pr(m_1)\Pr(k_1) + \cdots + \Pr(m_n)\Pr(k_n)} \tag{15.4}$$

Now, from perfect secrecy,

$$\Pr(m_1|c) = \Pr(m_1) \tag{15.5}$$

Combining formulae (15.4) and (15.5) and dividing by $\Pr(m_1) \neq 0$, we get that

$$\Pr(k_1) = \Pr(k_1)\Pr(m_1) + \cdots + \Pr(k_n)\Pr(m_n)$$

Since $\Pr(m_1) + \cdots + \Pr(m_n) = 1$, we get

$$\Pr(k_1)[\Pr(m_1) + \cdots + \Pr(m_n)] = \Pr(k_1)\Pr(m_1) + \cdots \Pr(k_n)\Pr(m_n)$$

This gives that

$$\Pr(m_2)(\Pr(k_1) - \Pr(k_2)) + \cdots + \Pr(m_n)(\Pr(k_1) - \Pr(k_n)) = 0$$

Since $\Pr(k_1) \geq \Pr(k_i)$, $1 \leq i \leq n$, we know that the above is a sum of nonnegative terms summing to zero. It follows that each term in the above sum is zero, and since $\Pr(m_i) \neq 0$, $2 \leq i \leq n$, we get that

$$\Pr(k_1) = \cdots = \Pr(k_n) = \frac{1}{n}$$

We have shown the following result.

Theorem 15.1 (The equiprobable keys result) *For perfect secrecy, each key has an equal probability of being chosen, namely $\frac{1}{n}$, assuming $n = |\boldsymbol{M}| = |\boldsymbol{C}| = |\boldsymbol{K}|$.*

Conversely, if $\Pr(k_i) = \frac{1}{n}$, $1 \leq i \leq n$, we see by applying the formula analogous to formula (15.4) to any plain text-cipher text pair (m, c) that $\Pr(m|c) = \Pr(m)$, using the fact that $\sum_{i=1}^{n} \Pr(m_i) = 1$.

To summarize, we have perfect secrecy with $|\boldsymbol{M}| = |\boldsymbol{C}| = |\boldsymbol{K}|$ if and only if $\Pr(k_i) = \frac{1}{n}$, $1 \leq i \leq n$.

15.3   Perfect Secrecy and Latin Squares

Assume we have a cryptosystem with perfect secrecy with $|\mathbf{K}| = |\mathbf{M}| = |\mathbf{C}| = n$, say. Let us denote our message set $\mathbf{M}$ by the set $\{1, \ldots, n\}$ with the messages written in that order. We take $\mathbf{C} = \{1, \ldots, n\}$: our set of enciphering transformation is $\{e_1, \ldots, e_n\}$. We have seen earlier that, for fixed i, the set $\{e_i(1), \ldots, e_i(n)\}$ consists of distinct cipher texts. Thus, for a fixed i with $1 \leq i \leq n$, the set $\{e_i(1), \ldots, e_i(n)\}$ is a rearrangement of the sequence $\{1, \ldots, n\}$. We examine the matrix $L = (e_i(j))$, $1 \leq i, j \leq n$. We have seen that each row of L, such as the ith row above, is a re-arrangement of $\{1, \ldots, n\}$. As seen earlier, for fixed m, the set $\{e_k(m) \mid k \in \mathbf{K}\}$ equals the set $\mathbf{C}$ of all cipher texts. It follows also that each column of L is some permutation of $\{1, \ldots, n\}$. The conclusion is that L is a **latin square** of size $n \times n$. That is, each entry of L is some number t, $1 \leq t \leq n$. No element t is repeated in any row or any column.

Using the notation above, we have the following result.

Theorem 15.2 (Characterization of perfect secrecy) *Let* Γ *be a symmetric key system with perfect secrecy with* $|\mathbf{C}| = |\mathbf{M}| = |\mathbf{K}| = n$, *so we may take* $\mathbf{M}$ *and* $\mathbf{C}$ *as the set* $\{1, \ldots, n\}$. *Each enciphering transformation* e_k *yields a unique row of an* $n \times n$ *latin square* $L = (e_{ij})$, $1 \leq i, j \leq n$, *i.e. a permutation of* $\{1, \ldots, n\}$ *and the key is the index of that row. Each key is chosen with probability* $\frac{1}{n}$. *If the message is* j *and the enciphering key is* e_i, *we have* $e_i(j) = e_{ij}$, $1 \leq i, j \leq n$.

Conversely, given any $n \times n$ *latin square* L *we may construct a cryptosystem with perfect secrecy as above.*

Now we see the true nature of a symmetric cryptosystem with perfect secrecy having $|\mathbf{K}| = |\mathbf{M}|$, not as a one-time pad but as an $n \times n$ latin square. The number of latin squares of order n, denoted by $f(n)$, grows exponentially with n. So there is no shortage of such symmetric cryptosystems!

Example

Let $n = 4$, so our message set is $\{1, 2, 3, 4\}$. Choose the latin square given by

$$
L = \begin{pmatrix} 2 & 3 & 4 & 1 \\ 3 & 4 & 1 & 2 \\ 1 & 2 & 3 & 4 \\ 4 & 1 & 2 & 3 \end{pmatrix}
$$

Let us suppose that $\mathbf{A}$ and $\mathbf{B}$ are in possession of the secret key 2 and that $\mathbf{A}$ transmits the cipher text 4 to $\mathbf{B}$. $\mathbf{B}$ seeks the message X such that $e_2(X) = 4$. Now the second row of L, which is the row $(3, 4, 1, 2)$, equals $(e_2(1), e_2(2), e_2(3), e_2(4))$. Therefore, we have that $e_2(2) = 4$ so $X = 2$, i.e. the message is 2.

So we see from Theorem 15.2 that perfect secrecy corresponds to message sets of size n, for arbitrary n, not just for $n = 2^t$ (which is the case for a binary one-time pad). The number of latin squares of order n, as mentioned earlier, grows exponentially with n.

One easy specific example that works for all n is the cyclic latin square of order n. For $n = 3$, we get

$$\begin{pmatrix} 1 & 2 & 3 \\ 2 & 3 & 1 \\ 3 & 1 & 2 \end{pmatrix}$$

where each row gets shifted one place to the right and around.

The one-time pad can be filled into this theory. Indeed, if the key is a binary string of length 2^w then, we must have $n = 2^w$ and a suitable latin square of order n can then be constructed to correspond to the one-time pad. For an example we refer to Problem 15.13. The following example, discussed in Chapter 3 can also be fitted in. Our message set and cipher text set is $\{0, 1, \dots, n-1\}$. Each key k is also a number between 0 and $n-1$. The cipher text for the message x, given by the key k, is $e_k(x) = Rem[x + k, n]$. We refer to Problem 15.14. Note the change of notation from $\{1, 2, \dots, n\}$ to $\{0, 1, \dots, n\}$.

Remark

In Theorem 15.2, we made no initial assumption concerning the probability of the messages.

15.4   The Abstract Approach to Perfect Secrecy

Let $X = (x_1, \dots, x_n)$ denote the random variable corresponding to a plain text message of n bits: we are taking the alphabet to be binary here but this is not really necessary. Let $Y = (y_1, \dots, y_n)$ denote the corresponding cipher text of n bits. Then, the mutual information $I(X : Y)$ between X and Y as defined in Chapter 11 is given by the formula

$$I(X : Y) = \max_{\Pr(X)} (H(X) - H(X|Y))$$

This is the measure of secrecy here. **Perfect secrecy** is defined by the criterion that $I(X : Y) = 0$. Thus, for perfect secrecy

$$H(X) = H(X|Y) \tag{15.6}$$

Switching to a more familiar notation where we replace X by M and Y by C, we get the following *criterion for perfect secrecy*:

$$H(M) = H(M|C) \tag{15.7}$$

This says that the uncertainty of M given C equals the uncertainty of M so that M, C are independent.

Now let K denote the random variable corresponding to the key space. We have

$$H(M) = H(M \mid C) = H(M, K \mid C) - H(K \mid M, C) \qquad \text{(see Problem 15.15)}$$

Since entropy is always nonnegative, we have

$$H(M) \leq H(M, K \mid C) = H(K \mid C) + H(M, C \mid K) \qquad \text{(see Problem 15.15.)}$$

Now K and C determine M uniquely: if we know the key and the ciphertext, we can recover the message with certainty. Thus, $H(M \mid C, K) = 0$. It follows that

$$H(M) \leq H(K \mid C) \leq H(K)$$

In summary, $H(M) \leq H(K)$. Thus, the entropy of the key space is at least as big as the entropy of the message space. This is also consistent with formula (15.3), and reminds us of the principle that perfect secrecy can only occur when "the key is at least as long as the message." This holds for the one-time pad but does not hold for algorithms such as DES and AES.

15.5 Cryptography, Information Theory, Shannon

One of the early important ideas of Claude Shannon was that these two subjects are very closely related, due to the following very basic idea. We simply think of an eavesdropper Eve as attempting to recover the message from the cipher text. In other words, Eve can be thought of as trying to recover the message from a "noisy channel" version of the message, namely the cipher text! We can think of a communication channel in which the messages form a zero memory source with the encrypting function and keys serving as the channel. We refer to the problems for a further discussion of this.

15.6 Unique Message from Ciphertext, Unicity

Given a cipher text C in a symmetric key cryptosystem, it seems reasonable to suppose that the longer that C is the fewer the number of message-key pairs from which C could have arisen. Shannon indicated that there exists a critical length U called the **unicity point**, such that for cipher texts longer than this length, there is likely to be just one corresponding pain text. If the length of a cipher text C is much shorter than U then there will be many messages which can in principle encrypt to C thereby increasing security.

Shannon showed that U can be calculated as roughly the point where the message entropy plus the key entropy is less than or equal to the cipher text entropy. This is discussed in Welsh [Wel88].

Let $H(\Gamma)$ denote the entropy per symbol of the language Γ being used. We estimate the cipher text entropy on the basis that all U-sequences of letters are equally likely to occur as a cipher text. Then our cipher text entropy is approximated by $U \log |\Gamma|$ where $|\Gamma|$ is the number of letters in Γ. The unicity point can be approximated on the basis of the following equality, where $H(K)$ denotes the entropy of the key-space.

$$U \cdot H(\Gamma) + H(K) = U \cdot \log |\Gamma|$$

If all keys are equally likely to occur then $H(K) = \log |K|$ and we get

$$U = \frac{\log |K|}{\log |\Gamma| - H(\Gamma)} \tag{15.8}$$

Example 15.3 *Let us work with substitution ciphers over the English alphabet. Then* $|K| = 26!$. *By Stirling's expansion,* $\log(26!)$ *is approximately 88 and* $\log 26$ *is about 4.7. Take the entropy of English to be about 1.5 Shannon bits per letter. Then*

$$U \approx \frac{88}{4.7 - 1.5} \approx 28$$

Thus, if a cipher text has length 28 or more, we expect there to be just one meaningful plain text.

This is in accordance with Shannon's estimate of a unicity point between 20 and 30, as pointed out in Welsh [Wel88].

We can also write Eq. (15.8) as follows:

$$U = \frac{\log |K|}{\log |\Gamma| \left(1 - \frac{H(\Gamma)}{\log |\Gamma|}\right)}$$

This gives

$$U = \frac{\log |K|}{R \, \log |\Gamma|}$$

where R is the redundancy.

For security we want U to be big so that it is desirable that R is small. Note that in the hypothetical case when $R = 0$ we get U to be infinite.

15.7 Problems

15.1 Let L be a latin square of order 6 as follows.

$$L = \begin{pmatrix} 2 & 3 & 4 & 5 & 6 & 1 \\ 3 & 4 & 5 & 6 & 1 & 2 \\ 4 & 5 & 6 & 1 & 2 & 3 \\ 5 & 6 & 1 & 2 & 3 & 4 \\ 6 & 1 & 2 & 3 & 4 & 5 \\ 1 & 2 & 3 & 4 & 5 & 6 \end{pmatrix}$$

Suppose **A**, **B** are in possession of the secret key 4 and **A** sends the cipher text 3 to **B**. What message does **B** recover? (See Solution 15.1.)

15.2 Let

$$L = \begin{pmatrix} 1 & 2 & 3 & 4 & 5 \\ 2 & 3 & 4 & 5 & 1 \\ 3 & 4 & 5 & 1 & 2 \\ 4 & 5 & 1 & 2 & 3 \\ 5 & 1 & 2 & 3 & 4 \end{pmatrix}$$

Similar to Problem 15.1, let the secret key be 4 and the cipher text be 1. What is the message (= plain text)? (See Solution 15.2.)

15.3 Let the message space in a symmetric cryptosystem Γ be $\{0,1\}$ with $Pr(0) = x$, $Pr(1) = 1 - x$ and let the cipher texts be the set $\mathbf{C} = \{0,1\}$. The key-set has two keys k_1 and k_2. The key k_1, i.e. the enciphering transformation e_{k_1} maps 0 to 0 and 1 to 1. The enciphering transformation e_{k_2} switches 0 and 1. We have $Pr(k_1) = 1 - p$, $Pr(k_2) = p$. For what values of p does Γ have perfect security? (See Solution 15.3.)

Problems 15.4 to 15.9 use the setup in Problem 15.3.

15.4 If Γ has perfect secrecy, what is the corresponding latin square? (See Solution 15.4.)

15.5 Calculate $H(M)$, $H(C)$. (See Solution 15.5.)

15.6   Calculate $H(K)$. (See Solution 15.6.)

15.7   Can you think of a channel corresponding to the setup in Problem 15.3? (See Solution 15.7.)

15.8   (a) Find $H(M|C)$.

(b) For what value of p is $H(M|C) = H(M)$?

(c) Explain your answer in (b).

(See Solution 15.8.)

15.9   (a) What is the maximum value of $H(M) - H(M|C)$ as we vary x.

(b) What does this number represent?

(See Solution 15.9.)

15.10 A symmetric cryptosystem Γ having perfect secrecy has $|M| = |K| = |C| = n$, say. What is $H(K)$? (See Solution 15.10.)

15.11 Let $m = (m_1, m_2)$ be a message in the form of a binary string of length $2n$ obtained by concatenating two different random binary strings, each of length n. Let $k = (k_1, k_1)$ be a key in the form of a random binary string k_1 of n bits concatenated with itself.

(a) Find $H(m)$.

(b) Find $H(k)$.

(See Solution 15.11.)

15.12 In Problem 15.11, does the corresponding cryptosystem have perfect security? (See Solution 15.12.)

15.13 Show how to construct a latin square corresponding to a one-time pad based on binary messages of length 2. (See Solution 15.13.)

15.14 In a symmetric key cryptosystem let $M = C = \{0, 1, \dots, n-1\}$ and let the possible keys be $0, 1, \dots, n-1$, chosen at random. Let key k encipher message x to the cipher text $c_k(x) = Rem[x + k, n]$. Show how to obtain a latin square from this system when $n = 5$. (See Solution 15.14.)

15.15 Show that $H(Y, Z \mid X) = H(Y \mid X) + H(Z, X \mid Y)$. (See Solution 15.15.)

15.8 Solutions

15.1 5.

15.2 3.

15.3 $p = \frac{1}{2}$. (For perfect security the keys must be equiprobable so $p = 1 - p$, $p = \frac{1}{2}$.)

15.4 $\begin{pmatrix} 0 & 1 \\ 1 & 0 \end{pmatrix}$. Here we use the alphabet $\{0, 1\}$ instead of $\{1, 2\}$.

15.5 $H(x)$, $H(x(1-p) + (1-x)p)$. In these solutions if u, v are nonnegative with $u + v = 1$ we sometimes use the abbreviation $H(u)$ for $H(u, v)$.

15.6 $H(p)$.

15.7 The binary symmetric channel with parameter p.

15.8 (a) We start by noting that $H(M|C) = H(M, C) - H(C)$. Now, (M, C) is a random variable with four possible events, for example, "the message is zero, and the cipher text is zero" is one such event. The probabilities are xp, $x(1-p)$, $(1-x)p$, $(1-x)q$, where $q = 1 - p$. Thus,

$$H(M, C) = H(xp, x(1-p), (1-x)p, (1-x)q)$$
$$= H(x) + H(p)$$

where the last equality follows from algebraic manipulation. $H(C)$ can be calculated by noting that C is zero with probability $xq + (1-x)p$ and 1 with probability $xp + (1-x)q$. It follows that

$$H(M|C) = H(M, C) - H(C)$$
$$= H(x) + H(p) - H(xp + (1-x)q)$$

(b) $H(xp + (1-x)q) \geq H(p)$ by convexity, as in Section 12.5. Thus $H(M|C) = H(M) = H(x)$ if and only $p = q$, i.e. $p = \frac{1}{2}$.

(c) $H(M|C) = H(M)$ corresponds to perfect secrecy which in turn corresponds to $p = \frac{1}{2}$: also see Problem 15.3.

15.9 (a) $1 + p \log p + (1 - p) \log(1 - p)$.

(b) the maximum amount of information concerning M that could be gained by an eavesdropper on learning C. It is also the channel capacity of the BSC with parameter p.

15.10 $\log n$ as the n keys are equiprobable.

15.11 (a) $2n$ as we have 2^{2n} equiprobable strings and $\log(2^{2n}) = 2n$.

(b) n.

15.12 No, since $H(k) < H(m)$.

15.13 Our message M is as follows: $M = \{(0,0), (0,1), (1,0), (1,1)\}$. We abbreviate M
to $M = \{a, b, c, d\}$, where $a = (0,0)$, $b = (0,1)$, $c = (1,0)$, $d = (1,1)$. The set C
of cipher texts is also equal to $\{a, b, c, d\}$. Each key is one of a, b, c, d, chosen at
random. Suppose for example that k is $b = (0,1)$. How do we find $e_b(d)$, say? We
have, by addition mod 2 (i.e. XORing), using the one-time pad construction that

$$e_b(d) = (0,1) + (1,1) = (1,0) = c$$

The rows of our latin square L will have the rows $e_a(M), e_b(M), e_c(M), e_d(M)$.
The rows are indexed by the keys in this way. Then,

$$\begin{aligned}
e_a(M) &= (0,0) + \{(0,0), (0,1), (1,0), (1,1)\} &= \{a, b, c, d\} \\
e_b(M) &= (0,1) + \{(0,0), (0,1), (1,0), (1,1)\} &= \{b, a, d, c\} \\
e_c(M) &= (1,0) + \{(0,0), (0,1), (1,0), (1,1)\} &= \{c, d, a, b\} \\
e_d(M) &= (1,1) + \{(0,0), (0,1), (1,0), (1,1)\} &= \{d, c, b, a\}
\end{aligned}$$

where $e_i(M)$ means the ordered set $\{e_i(a), e_i(b), e_i(c), e_i(d)\}$. So the latin square
(with rows indexed by a, b, c and d) is as follows:

$$L = \begin{pmatrix} a & b & c & d \\ b & a & d & c \\ c & d & a & b \\ d & c & b & a \end{pmatrix}$$

In fact, $L = \begin{pmatrix} A & B \\ B & A \end{pmatrix}$ where A, B are latin squares with $A = \begin{pmatrix} a & b \\ b & a \end{pmatrix}$ and
$B = \begin{pmatrix} c & d \\ d & c \end{pmatrix}$. This is because of the one-time pad construction.

15.14   We have that the message set is $M = \{0, 1, 2, 3, 4\}$. We tabulate our results.

Key k	Enciphering transform	Row of L
0	$e_k(x) = x$	$e_0(M) = \{0, 1, 2, 3, 4\}$
1	$e_k(x) = Rem[x + 1, 5]$	$e_1(M) = \{1, 2, 3, 4, 0\}$
2	$e_k(x) = Rem[x + 2, 5]$	$e_2(M) = \{2, 3, 4, 0, 1\}$
3	$e_k(x) = Rem[x + 3, 5]$	$e_3(M) = \{3, 4, 0, 1, 2\}$
4	$e_k(x) = Rem[x + 4, 5]$	$e_4(M) = \{4, 0, 1, 2, 3\}$

and in this case, $e_i(M)$ means the ordered set $\{e_i(0), e_i(1), e_i(2), e_i(3)\}$. We end up with the latin square

$$L = \begin{pmatrix} 0 & 1 & 2 & 3 & 4 \\ 1 & 2 & 3 & 4 & 0 \\ 2 & 3 & 4 & 0 & 1 \\ 3 & 4 & 0 & 1 & 2 \\ 4 & 0 & 1 & 2 & 3 \end{pmatrix}$$

15.15
$$H(Y, Z \mid X) = -\sum_{i,j,k} \Pr(x_i, y_j, z_k) \log \Pr(y_j, z_k \mid x_i)$$

$$= -\sum_{i,j,k} \Pr(x, y_j, z_k) \log[\Pr(y_j \mid x_i) \Pr(z_k \mid x_i, y_j)]$$

$$= H(Y \mid X) + H(Z \mid X, Y).$$

(Note: we use the fact that $\log(AB) = \log A + \log B$.)

Chapter 16

Shift Registers (LFSR) and Stream Ciphers

Goals, Discussion Shift registers are at the heart of cryptography, error-correction, and information theory. In cryptography, they are the main tools for generating long pseudo-random sequences which can be used as keys in symmetric cryptography.

In information theory, the output of shift registers forms a very good testing ground for fundamental questions involving the entropy of a sequence.

In error correction, as we will see, the linear feedback shift registers (LFSRs) are the basic building blocks for the theory of cyclic linear codes. According to Schneier [Sch96], "most practical stream-cipher designs center around LFSRs," and "stream ciphers based on shift registers have been the workhorse of military cryptography since the beginning of electronics."

This chapter will provide a thorough analysis of LFSRs.

New, Noteworthy The theory is quite intricate. Given a recurrence relation generated from the equation $x_m = c_0 x_0 + c_1 x_1 + \cdots + c_{m-1} x_{m-1}$. Usually, we need to assume that $c_o \neq 0$. If this is not the case, all the usual results break down such as the impossibility of moving from a nonzero state to a zero state. We provide results and counter-examples. A very well-known folklore result states that $2m$ consecutive bits determine the output

Cryptography, Information Theory, and Error-Correction: A Handbook for the 21st Century, Second Edition.
Aiden A. Bruen, Mario A. Forcinito, and James M. McQuillan.
© 2021 John Wiley & Sons, Inc. Published 2021 by John Wiley & Sons, Inc.

of a linear feedback shift register with m states. We give a formal proof of this. Part of the proof requires that $c_0 \neq 0$. The condition that $c_0 \neq 0$ can be rephrased as a linear algebra condition and this is discussed in Section 16.2. We also point out that the LFSR provides a very nice example of a **cyclic code** discussed in Chapter 21. We also discuss issues related to the celebrated Berlekamp–Massey algorithm at the end of the chapter.

16.1   Vernam Cipher, Psuedo-Random Key

In the Vernam cipher (= one-time pad), communicating parties **A** and **B** must both be in possession of a common secret key in the form of a random binary string. This key must have the same length as the message and hence, may be very long. The Vernam cipher is a *stream cipher* in which the secret message is encrypted bit by bit. For a block cipher, such as Advanced Encryption Standard (AES, discussed in Chapter 5, the message is first divided up into blocks of a fixed length before encryption.

It can be difficult to arrange for the two parties to have such a long common random key. However, instead of using a long random secret key, **A** and **B** can use a common pseudo-random binary key. A powerful way for achieving this is to use a *linear feedback shift register* (an LFSR). There are also **nonlinear shift registers**. In this chapter, we deal only with the linear case, and we will use "shift register" and "LFSR" interchangeably. Shift registers are used extensively, both commercially and in industry. They are easily implemented in hardware and are very fast, generating several million bits per second.

The main idea is this. Assume that **A** and **B** are already in possession of a common binary secret key of length $n = 2m$. The first m of these $2m$ bits correspond to the initial state vector of a shift register of length m. The other m bits give the recurrence (i.e. they are the coefficients of the binary recurrence relation associated with the LFSR). These $2m$ bits can generate a much longer sequence of N bits, where N can be as large as $2^m - 1$. These N bits serve as a longer pseudo-random secret key K. Then, each bit of a secret message M of length N is XOR'ed with K (i.e. N and K are added, using binary addition) by **A** to yield a cipher text C, which is transmitted in the open to **B**. **B** then XORs C with K to recover M (As usual, XOR refers to the exclusive OR operator).

For example, if $2m = 20$, then the pseudo-random key K could be as long as $2^{10} - 1 = 1023$ bits. How does a secret random key of just 20 bits get transformed into a secret random key K of over 1000 bits? The answer is that K is not really random. To quantify this precisely, we need to use the ideas of entropy and information theory discussed earlier in Part II. However, if K has length $2^m - 1$, then K has many of the statistical properties that make K appear to be random.

16.2 Construction of Feedback Shift Registers

Let us describe how an LFSR having m binary registers, i.e. having **length** m works. We start with m binary registers in a row from left to right named $R_{m-1}, R_{m-2}, \ldots, R_1, R_0$. The contents of each register is either a zero or a one. These registers can be considered storage devices such as flip flops.

Denote the entry or value in the first or right-most register by x_0, the value in the second register by $x_1, \ldots$ and the value in the left-most register by x_{m-1}.

An electronic clock controls proceedings.

$$\boxed{x_{m-1}} \to \boxed{x_{m-2}} \to \quad \ldots \quad \to \boxed{x_1} \to \boxed{x_0} \to \text{Output}$$
$$R_{m-1} \qquad R_{m-2} \qquad\qquad\qquad R_1 \qquad R_0$$

Initial binary values for $x_0, x_1, \ldots, x_{m-1}$ are in place. At the first clock-pulse, the following happens: The entry x_{m-1} is pushed over to the right by one unit to occupy the register R_{m-2}. Simultaneously, x_{m-2} becomes the new entry in R_{m-3}, etc. So each entry gets shifted over by one place to the right, apart from the right-most element which is fed into the **Output Sequence**. For example, suppose $m = 5$ and the initial configuration is as follows:

$$\boxed{1} \to \boxed{0} \to \boxed{0} \to \boxed{1} \to \boxed{1}$$
$$R_4 \qquad R_3 \qquad R_2 \qquad R_1 \qquad R_0$$

So $x_4 = 1$, $x_3 = 0$, $x_2 = 0$, $x_1 = 1$, $x_0 = 1$. After the first clock pulse, we now have the following configuration:

$$\boxed{} \to \boxed{1} \to \boxed{0} \to \boxed{0} \to \boxed{1}$$
$$R_4 \qquad R_3 \qquad R_2 \qquad R_1 \qquad R_0$$

The output sequence at the moment just consists of 1. We can symbolically describe what has happened as follows.

$$(x_4, x_3, x_2, x_1, x_0) \to (-, x_4, x_3, x_2, x_1).$$

How should we fill in the blank? In other words, what should we put in register R_4? Let us denote this element by x_5. The element x_5 will depend on the initial values x_0, x_1, x_2, x_3, x_4 so x_5 is a function of $x_0, x_1, \ldots, x_4$. We can write $x_5 = f = f(x_0, x_1, x_2, x_3, x_4)$. Figure 16.1 gives a graphic representation of this process.

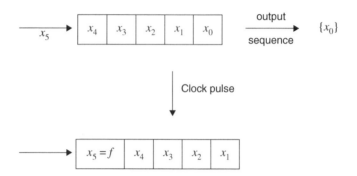

Figure 16.1: One clock pulse.

For a linear feedback shift register (= LFSR), x_5 must be a *linear* function of x_0, x_1, x_2, x_3, x_4. Hence,

$$x_5 = c_4 x_4 + c_3 x_3 + c_2 x_2 + c_1 x_1 + c_0 x_0 \qquad (16.1)$$

where $c_0, c_1, \ldots, c_4$ are binary variables and the addition and the multiplication are binary (see the previous section). Note that if c_0 were zero, we could do away completely with the register R_0 holding x_0. *Thus, we usually assume that $c_0 = 1$. That condition has a very important implication as detailed in Result 16.18.* It is shown there that each transition from a state vector to the next is the result of a transition matrix A and that A is nonsingular, i.e. invertible if and only if $c_0 = 1$.

The sequence of elements occupying the registers at any given time ($\{x_4, x_3, x_2, x_1, x_0\}$ for example) is called the **state vector**. Thus, at each clock pulse, a state vector gets changed to another state vector as in Figure 16.1 and some x_j is adjoined to the output sequence.

For example, assume that $x_5 = x_0 + x_2 + x_4$ and that the initial state vector is $\{10011\}$ (see Figure 16.2). Then $x_5 = 1 + 0 + 1 = 0$ in binary. After one pulse, the state vector is $\{01001\}$ with output sequence $\{1\}$. Then, after two clock pulses, the state vector is $\{10100\}$ with output sequence $\{11\}$.

After three clock pulses, the state vector is $\{01010\}$ with output sequence $\{110\}$.

After four pulses, the state vector is $\{00101\}$ with output sequence $\{1100\}$.

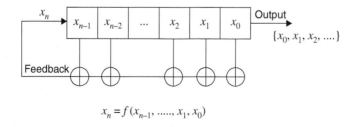

$$x_n = f(x_{n-1}, \ldots\ldots, x_1, x_0)$$

Figure 16.2: A general LFSR.

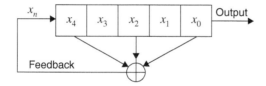

Figure 16.3: The 5-bit LFSR generated by $x_5 = x_0 + x_2 + x_4$.

The above results were computed from the equations

$$x_5 = x_0 + x_2 + x_4$$
$$x_6 = x_1 + x_3 + x_5$$
$$x_7 = x_2 + x_4 + x_6$$

and so on.

The general situation is as follows. **A (binary) recurrence relation of length** m (corresponding to m registers) is a relationship of the form

$$x_{i+m} = \sum_{j=0}^{m-1} c_j x_{i+j} \tag{16.2}$$

Here $m \geq 0$ is a fixed positive integer equal to the number of registers and i can be any nonnegative integer. All variables x_i are binary and $c_0 = 1$.

For $i = 0$, we get

$$x_m = c_0 x_0 + c_1 x_1 + c_2 x_2 + \cdots + c_{m-1} x_{m-1}$$

Our old formula (16.1) is this result in the case where $m = 5$.

The m given binary numbers $c_0, c_1, \ldots, c_{m-1}$ are called the **recurrence coefficients**.

The recurrence relation in formula (16.2) can be generated by an LFSR (i.e. a shift register) of length m which is easily and economically implemented in hardware. (To avoid trivial cases, we must assume that the initial state vector, namely $(x_{m-1}, x_{m-2}, \ldots, x_1, x_0)$ is not the all-zero state vector. Also, as mentioned earlier, we assume that $c_0 = 1$.) So we have a correspondence between linear recurrence relations and linear shift registers.

16.3   Periodicity

From the above, the **output sequence** will be $\{x_{m+n}, \ldots, x_{m+1}, x_m, \ldots, x_1, x_0\}$, where we start off with the state vector $\{x_{m-1}, x_{m-2}, \ldots, x_0\}$. We think of the outputs as going down a vertical tunnel, but to save space, we use a row vector rather than a column vector. The full mathematical details of an LFSR are complex and intricate. We refer to the books by Golomb [Gol82], and to Rueppel [Rue86]. Beutelspacher [Beu94] and Mollin [Mol00] also give details.

However, we are able to describe many of the main results here. For the most part, we will not distinguish between an LFSR and the corresponding recurrence relation.

Suppose we have a recurrence relation of length m (*where the initial state vector is not the all-zero string and the coefficient $c_0 = 1$*). At the outset, and after each clock-pulse, the registers hold a binary digit or **bit**, a 0 or a 1. Thus, the m bits in the current state vector give a binary string of length m. The total number of binary strings of length m is 2^m since there are 2 choices for the first bit, 2 for the second, 2 for the third, ..., and 2 for the mth bit, giving a total of $(2)(2)(2) \ldots (2) = 2^m$ possible strings. This includes the all-zero string. So, apart from the all-zero string these are at most $2^m - 1$ distinct state vectors. Thus, after at most $2^m - 1$ clock pulses, some state vector is repeated. Assume that state vector is repeated after exactly t clock pulses. Then all state vectors are repeated after exactly t clock pulses.

To see this, let the state vectors be successively the column vectors $s_0, s_1, \ldots$ and assume that s_j is repeated after t clock pulses so that $s_{j+t} = s_j$. Using the notation of Result 16.18, we have

$$A^t s_j = s_j. \tag{16.3}$$

(Caution: A^t denotes A to the power t, not A transpose!)

Thus, $A^t A(s_{j-1}) = As_{j-1}$, i.e. $A^{t+1}(s_{j-1}) = A(s_{j-1})$. Multiplying on the left by A^{-1} gives $A^t(s_{j-1}) = s_{j-1}$. Iterating this, we get that all state vectors before s_j are repeated after t clock pulses.

From equation (16.3) multiplying by A on the left we get that $A^{t+1}s_j = As_j$ so $A^t A(s_j) = A(s_j)$. Therefore, $A^t s_{j+1} = s_{j+1}$. This all state vector after s_j is repeated after t clock pulses. Thus, *all* state vectors are repeated after t clock pulses.

Result 16.1 Let Γ_m be a linear shift register of length m with initial state vector

$$\{x_{m-1}, x_{m-2}, \ldots, x_1, x_0\}$$

and recurrence relation $x_m = \sum_{i=0}^{m-1} c_i x_i$. Provided that $c_0 = 1$, there exists some positive integer t where $1 \leq t < 2^m$ and some state vector s_j such that s_j is repeated after t clock pulses (i.e. such that $s_{j+t} = s_j$). It follows that all state vectors are repeated after t clock pulses; hence, $s_{i+t} = s_i$ for all $i > 0$ and the output sequence $\{x_0, x_1, \ldots, x_{m-1}, x_m, \ldots, x_{m+n}\}$ satisfies

$$x_{i+t} = x_i, \quad i = 1, 2, \ldots$$

Conversely, if there exists and integer t so that $x_{i+t} = x_i$ for every i, then $s_{j+t} = s_j$ for every state vector s_j.

We say that t is a **period** of the recurrence relation. The next result is a logical consequence of the result above:

Result 16.2   Let t_0 be chosen as small as possible in Result 16.1. Then, if $s_{j+t} = s_j$ for every state vector s_j for some positive integer $t > 1$, then t_0 must divide t.

Proof. Divide t by t_0 to get a remainder u with $0 \le u < t_0$. If u were nonzero, then $s_{j+u} = s_j$, contradicting the minimality of t_0.   ∎

The integer t_0 in Result 16.2 is called the **fundamental period**. From the above results, periodicity can be phrased either in terms of state vectors or in terms of the output sequence.

In the proof of Result 16.1, we used the fact that $c_0 \ne 0$. This assumption is needed.

Remark 16.3 *Result 16.1 need not be true if $c_0 = 0$.*

(a) *To construct an example of this, let $m = 3$, let the initial state vector be $s_0 = \{x_2, x_1, x_0\} = \{001\}$ and let the recurrence be generated by $x_3 = x_2 + x_1$.*
Then after one pulse, the state vector is $\{000\} = s_1$.
Then, $s_2 = \{000\}$.
It follows that $s_1 = s_{1+1}$, but $s_0 \ne s_{0+1}$ since $s_0 \ne s_1$. So Result 16.1 fails with $t = 1$.

Remark 16.4 *The condition $c_0 \ne 0$ guarantees periodicity, as we have seen in Results 16.1, 16.2. However, the converse does not hold. In other words, we can have periodicity even when $c_0 = 0$. As an example, take $m = 4$ with initial state vector $s_0 = (1011) = (x_3 x_2 x_1 x_0)$ and with the recurrence generated by $x_4 = x_3 + x_1$. Then $s_0, s_1, \ldots, s_6$ all differ and $s_7 = s_0$, from which it follows that $s_{j+7} = s_j$ for all state vectors s_j. Thus, we have periodicity even though $c_0 = 0$.*

Using ideas in Result 16.18, we can show the following.

Result 16.5   Given a recurrence relation of length m, any m consecutive terms of the output sequence determines uniquely all past and future elements of the sequence.

Proof. Any m consecutive elements can be regarded as a state vector $\mathbf{u}$. Since the recurrence coefficients are given, the matrix A can be constructed as in Result 16.18. Thus, $A\mathbf{u} = \mathbf{v}$ is known, as is $A\mathbf{v}, \ldots$. So all output elements after $\mathbf{u}$ are known. Also, by applying A^{-1}, all previous elements are known. For this part we need A^{-1}, and A^{-1} exists if $c_0 = 1$.   ∎

As a counterpoint, we have the following:

Remark 16.6 *The conclusion of Result 16.5 is sometimes false if $c_0 = 0$.*

Example 16.7 *Let $m = 3$ and let the shift register Γ_1 have initial state vector $s_0 = \{x_2 x_1 x_0\} = \{001\}$ and recurrence $x_3 = x_2$. Then $s_1 = s_2 = s_3 = \cdots = \{000\}$.*

Let Γ_2 have the initial state vector $\{011\}$ and recurrence generated also by $x_3 = x_2$, so $s_1 = \{001\}$ and $s_2 = s_3 = s_4 = \cdots = \{000\}$.

The output sequence for Γ_1 is $\{100000 \ldots\}$.

The output sequence for Γ_2 is $\{110000 \ldots\}$.

So we have 2 different linear shift registers agreeing on $m = 4$ consecutive output elements, namely, a sequence of four consecutive zeros. The assertion concerning forward elements in Result 16.5 is always correct, whether or not $c_0 = 0$.

16.4   Maximal Periods, Pseudo-Random Sequences

By algebraic means (see Peterson and Weldon [PW72]), the following can be shown.

Result 16.8   For every positive integer m there exists a linear shift register of length m with period equal to $2^m - 1$.

For some theory behind this, see Result 16.14.

When using the LFSR for secure communication between **A** and **B**, each bit of the secret message M (in the form of a binary string that **A** is sending to **B**) is XOR'ed with the key K which is the output of the linear shift register Γ. If $\Gamma = \Gamma_m$ of length m has maximal period equal to $2^m - 1$, then the output sequence of Γ_m is a binary sequence of $2^m - 1$ bits.

Thus, Result 16.8 gives us a way to construct arbitrarily long keys. Although the key K obtained from Γ_m is not random, it does satisfy various statistical tests for randomness if the period of the LFSR Γ_m equals $2^m - 1$.

Before discussing this, it is appropriate to take another look at a linear shift register.

Suppose our initial state vector is $\{x_{m-1}, x_{m-2}, \ldots, x_1, x_0\}$.

After one clock pulse, the new state vector is $\{x_m, x_{m-1}, \ldots, x_2, x_1\}$ where $x_m = c_0 x_0 + c_1 x_1 + c_2 x_2 \ldots + c_{m-1} x_{m-1}$. We can form the $m \times m$ matrix P where

$$P = \begin{pmatrix} x_0 & x_1 & \cdots & x_{m-1} \\ x_1 & x_2 & \cdots & x_m \\ \vdots & \vdots & \ddots & \vdots \\ x_{m-1} & x_m & \cdots & x_{2m-1} \end{pmatrix}.$$

Note the rows of P give the successive register state vectors *in reverse order* after $0, 1, 2, 3, \ldots, m-1$ clock pulses. Moreover, the first column of P gives the output sequence after m clock pulses, namely $\{x_0, x_1, \ldots, x_{m-2}, x_{m-1}\}$. The j-th column of P gives the last m outputs after $m + j - 1$ clock pulses.

Result 16.9 Given any finite binary sequence $(u_0, u_1, \ldots, u_{m-1})$ there exists a linear shift register whose output sequence contains this sequence.

Proof. Just take any LFSR Γ, of length m, whose initial state vector is $\{u_{m-1}, \ldots, u_1, u_0\}$. Then the output sequence starts with the given sequence. ■

Frequently, we can find an LFSR of shorter length. For example, if the binary sequence is the output sequence of length $2^n - 1$ obtained from an LFSR of length n and period $2^n - 1$, then n is very small compared to $2^n - 1$. In this case, the length n of the shift register is approximately the *log* of the length of the sequence.

In general, the **linear complexity** of a binary sequence is the minimum length of a LFSR generating the sequence as a consecutive subsequence of its output sequence. One algorithm for finding this is the *Berlekamp–Massey algorithm*; we refer to Section 16.7.

A **block of length** k is a sequence of the form $\{011 \ldots 110\}$, i.e. it is an all-ones sequence of length k with zeros at both ends. Similarly, a **gap of length** k is a sequence of the form $\{100 \ldots 001\}$, i.e. it is an all-zero sequence of length k with ones at both ends. As an indication of the random nature of the output of a LFSR with maximum period, we have the following result.

Result 16.10 Suppose the linear shift register ($=$ LFSR) of length m has maximum period equal to $2^m - 1$. Then the output sequence of length $2^m - 1$ has the following properties.

(a) It has exactly $2^{m-1} - 1$ zeros and 2^{m-1} ones.

(b) For any k with $1 \leq k \leq n - 2$, it contains 2^{n-k-2} blocks of length k and an equal number of gaps of length k.

We refer to Welsh [Wel88, page 130].

16.5 Determining the Output from $2m$ Bits

Recall that cryptographic stations **A** and **B** use the output of a linear shift register of length m as a common secret key K. Once the $2m$ bits consisting of the m bits and the m binary coefficients $c_0, c_1, \ldots, c_{m-1}$ are known, the entire output is known. It is a remarkable fact that the entire key can be obtained (and the cipher broken) given any $2m$ consecutive bits of K. Hence, if any $2m$ consecutive bits of the cipher text can be correctly decoded to the plain text, the entire cipher text can be decoded.

This is a well-known (in the mathematical folklore) result which is fundamental from a theoretical point of view. Following the proof, we will present an alternative proof using the approach in Result 16.18. The part of the proof involving the subsequent bits of the output sequence is reasonably easy to follow. The part involving the prior bits is more difficult.

Theorem 16.11 *Let Γ_m be a linear shift register of length m with initial state vector*

$$\{x_{m-1}, x_{m-2}, \ldots, x_1, x_0\}$$

and recurrence relation $x_m = \sum_{i=0}^{m-1} c_i x_i$. Then, the entire output sequence of Γ_m can be determined from any $2m$ consecutive output bits of this sequence, provided that $c_0 = 1$.

Proof. Assume that $2m$ consecutive output bits are known and denoted by $\alpha_0, \alpha_1, \ldots, \alpha_{2m-1}$. Then, the recurrence relation for Γ_m can be expressed using the recurrence coefficients by the following matrix equation:

$$\begin{pmatrix} \alpha_0 & \alpha_1 & \cdots & \alpha_{m-1} \\ \alpha_1 & \alpha_2 & \cdots & \alpha_m \\ \vdots & \vdots & \ddots & \vdots \\ \alpha_{m-1} & \alpha_m & \cdots & \alpha_{2m-2} \end{pmatrix} \begin{pmatrix} c_0 \\ c_1 \\ \vdots \\ c_{m-1} \end{pmatrix} = \begin{pmatrix} \alpha_m \\ \alpha_{m+1} \\ \vdots \\ \alpha_{2m-1} \end{pmatrix} \qquad (16.4)$$

We will represent this equation by $PC = Z$. If the $m \times m$ matrix P on the left is invertible, then we can solve for the recurrence coefficients by multiplying equation (16.4) on the left by P^{-1}. Once the recurrence coefficients are known, the entire output sequence can be computed.

If P is not invertible, then $PY = \mathbf{0}$ for some column vector $Y \neq \mathbf{0}$, with $\mathbf{Y}$ of length n. Thus, $P(Y + C) = Z$ so the equation $PX = Z$ will have more than the one solution $X = C$. Let D be any solution different than C. Then $PD = Z$ and hence, $P(C + D) = PC + PD = Z + Z = \mathbf{0}$ since the addition is binary. Taking the transpose of this matrix equation, we get $(C + D)^t P^t = \mathbf{0}^t = \mathbf{0}$, or

$$UP = \mathbf{0} \qquad (16.5)$$

where $U = (C + D)^t$ is a nonzero row matrix and $P = P^t$ since P is a symmetric matrix.

The vector $\mathbf{0}$ denotes the all zero row vector of length m.

We wish to show **that the entire output sequence for C equals that of D** given that they agree on some consecutive $2m$ output bits. Now the two output sequences will also agree on the next bit – i.e. bit number $2m + 1$ – if and only if equation (16.4), shifted by one bit, as explained below, is true. Let

$$
P_1 = \begin{pmatrix} \alpha_1 & \alpha_2 & \cdots & \alpha_m \\ \alpha_2 & \alpha_3 & \cdots & \alpha_{m-1} \\ \vdots & \vdots & \ddots & \vdots \\ \alpha_m & \alpha_{m+1} & \cdots & \alpha_{2m-1} \end{pmatrix}.
$$

We want to show that $P_1 C = P_1 D$ where, by assumption, $P_1 C = \begin{pmatrix} \alpha_{m+1} \\ \alpha_{m+2} \\ \vdots \\ \alpha_{2m} \end{pmatrix}$. We have

$PC = Z$. From equation (16.5), $UP = \mathbf{0}$. Thus, $U(PC) = (UP)C = \mathbf{0}$. Thus, the matrix product of U with each column of P and also with the right column Z is zero. Each column of P_1, apart from the last, is a column of P. Also Z is the same as the last column of P_1. Hence, $UP_1 = \mathbf{0}$, i.e. $(C + D)^t P_1 = \mathbf{0}$. Transposing, we get $P_1^t(C + D) = \mathbf{0}$, i.e. $P_1(C + D) = \mathbf{0}$, since P_1 is symmetric. This gives $P_1 C = P_1 D$, as required.

So we have shown that if the two sequences agree on any $2m$ consecutive bits, then they agree on all subsequent bits.

What about preceding bits? Here we assume that $P_1 C = P_1 D = \begin{pmatrix} \alpha_{m+1} \\ \alpha_{m+2} \\ \vdots \\ \alpha_{2m} \end{pmatrix}$ and try

to show that $PC = PD$ where $PC = \begin{pmatrix} \alpha_m \\ \alpha_{m+1} \\ \vdots \\ \alpha_{2m-1} \end{pmatrix}$. As before we have $UP_1 = \mathbf{0}$. Thus,

$UP = \begin{pmatrix} \lambda & 0 & 0 & \cdots & 0 \end{pmatrix}$, since the matrix product of U with all columns of P, save possibly the first, is zero. Also, since the matrix product of U with the last column of P_1 is zero, and this column is PC, we have $U(PC) = \mathbf{0}$. Now by associativity, $\mathbf{0} = U(PC) =$

$$
(UP)C = \begin{pmatrix} \lambda & 0 & 0 & \cdots & 0 \end{pmatrix} \begin{pmatrix} c_0 \\ c_1 \\ \vdots \\ c_{m-1} \end{pmatrix}.
$$

Thus, $\lambda c_0 = 0$. By our fundamental assumption, $c_0 \neq 0$, i.e. $c_0 = 1$. Hence, $\lambda = 0$ and $UP = 0$, giving $(C + D)^t P = 0$. Transposing gives $P^t(C + D) = 0$, i.e. $P(C + D) = 0$ so $PC = PD$. So C and D agree on all preceding bits and the proof is now complete. ∎

Alternative proof of Theorem 16.11   As in (16.5) $UP = \mathbf{0}$ where $U \neq \mathbf{0}$. Let $U = (u_0, \dots, u_n, \dots)$, where n is the largest integer for which the vector U has a nonzero component. Then $(u_0, u_1, \dots, u_n)P = \mathbf{0}$, with $n \leq m - 1$. This induces a relation between the rows of P, i.e.

$$u_0 R_0 + u_1 R_1 + \cdots + u_n R_n = \mathbf{0}$$

so that, since we are working in binary,

$$R_n = u_0 R_1 + u_1 R_1 + \cdots + u_{n-1} R_{n-1} \tag{16.6}$$

Applying the matrix A of Result 16.18 to (16.6) we get

$$
\begin{aligned}
AR_n &= A(u_0 R_0 + u_1 R_1 + \cdots + u_{n-1} R_{n-1}) \\
&= u_1 A(R_0) + u_1 A(R_1) + \cdots + u_{n-1} A(R_{n-1}).
\end{aligned}
$$

Thus,

$$R_{n+1} = u_0 R_1 + u_1 R_2 + \cdots + u_{n-1} R_n.$$

Thus, (16.6) holds for the subsequent $n + 1$ consecutive rows $R_1, R_2, \dots, R_n, R_{n+1}$ corresponding to $n + 1$ state vectors in the original LFSR Γ. By applying A^{-1} we get that A holds for the previous consecutive $n + 1$ rows of Γ. (Note that if Γ has period t, then $A^t =$ identity, so $A^{-1} = A^{t-1}$.) Applying (16.6) to each column of the rows we get that (16.6) yields a recurrence relation for Γ of length n. Since $n \leq m - 1$, Γ can be replaced by a shorter-length LFSR Δ, i.e. Γ and Δ have the same output. ∎

We should also mention that the possibility envisaged in the proof of Theorem 16.11 can occur.

Result 16.12   There exist two different shift registers of length m, both having the same initial state vector and the same output sequence, and both having a one in the recurrence relation for the coefficient of x_0.

For a proof, see Example 16.20.

Result 16.13   Theorem 16.11 need not hold if we only assume that the two sequences have $2m$ (not necessarily consecutive) outputs in common.

Result 16.14 Let Γ be an LFSR of length $m > 1$. Let P be the matrix corresponding to any $2m$ consecutive output bits of Γ as in Theorem 16.11.

(a) Assume that $det\ P = 0$. Then the output of Γ is replicated by that of a shorter LFSR Δ, i.e. Δ has length less than m.

(b) If the output of Γ is replicated by that of a shorter LFSR Δ, then $det\ P = 0$.

(c) The shortest LFSR whose output replicates that of Γ is unique.

Proof.

(a) If $det\ P = 0$ then there exists a row vector $U \neq \mathbf{0}$ such that $UP = \mathbf{0}$. U then yields a nonzero linear combination of rows of P summing to zero from which we derive a shorter LFSR Δ whose output replicates Γ.

(b) A shorter LFSR Δ whose output replicates Γ gives a nonzero linear combination of the rows of P summing to $\mathbf{0}$, where P corresponds to any $2m$ consecutive output bits as in Theorem 16.11. Then $det\ P = 0$.

(c) Let Δ_1 be a shortest LFSR. If there exists any other LFSR whatsoever whose output equals that of Δ_1, then there exists an LFSR which is shorter than Δ_1 and replicates its output. This contradicts the fact that Δ_1 is a shortest LFSR. In particular, there cannot exist Δ_2 having the same length as Δ_1 and replicating its output. ∎

16.6 The Tap Polynomial and the Period

Next, let the linear shift register Γ_m of length m replace each state vector $(x_{m-1}, x_{m-2}, \ldots, x_1, x_0)$ by the next state vector $(x_m, x_{m-1}, \ldots, x_1)$, with $x_m = c_0 x_0 + c_1 x_1 \cdots + c_{m-1} x_{m-1}$. For the (binary) **tap polynomial** $t(x) = x^m + c_{m-1} x^{m-1} + c_{m-2} x^{m-2} + \cdots + c_1 x + c_0$, associate with Γ_m the **reverse** of the tap polynomial, i.e. the polynomial $h(x) = c_0 x^m + c_1 x^{m-1} + \cdots + c_{m-1} x + 1$, where we assume $c_0 \neq 0$. We say that $t(x)$ is **primitive** if

1. $t(x)$ has no proper nontrivial factors and

2. $t(x)$ does not divide $x^d + 1$ for any d less than $2^m - 1$.

Result 16.15   (See Welsh [Wel88])

(a) Γ_m has period $2^m - 1$ if its tap polynomial $t(x)$ is primitive.

(b) For every m, there exists a primitive polynomial.

Example 16.16 *Suppose that the tap polynomial for LFSR Γ is $t(x) = x^8 + x^6 + x^5 + x^3 + 1$. Then $t(x)$ has no factors i.e. is irreducible and does not divide $x^n - 1$ for any $n < 255$. (It does divide $x^{255} - 1$.) Therefore, the length of the periodic output sequence is $2^{255} - 1$ and Γ is of maximum period.*

The following result is from Peterson and Weldon [PW72] and is discussed in Chapter 21.

Result 16.17 Let Γ be an LFSR with tap polynomial $t(x)$. Suppose that n is the smallest integer such that the polynomial $t(x)$ divides $x^n - 1$. Then for any initial state, the fundamental period of Γ divides n. Moreover, for some initial state, the fundamental period is exactly n.

Result 16.18 Let the linear shift register Γ_m of length m be constructed from the recurrence relation $x_m = c_0 x_0 + c_1 x_1 + \cdots + c_{m-1} x_{m-1}$ with $c_0 = 1$. Assume the initial state vector is not the zero vector. Then, no subsequent state vector is the zero vector.

Proof. Let the initial state vector be $\mathbf{u} = (x_{m-1}, x_{m-2}, \ldots, x_2, x_1, x_0)$. Then the next state vector is $\mathbf{v} = (c_0 x_0 + \cdots + c_{m-1} x_{m-1}, \ldots x_2, x_1)$. Writing of $\mathbf{u}$, $\mathbf{v}$ as columns, we see that $A\mathbf{u} = \mathbf{v}$ where the $m \times m$ matrix A is given by

$$A = \begin{pmatrix} c_{m-1} & c_{m-2} & \cdots & c_1 & c_0 \\ 1 & 0 & \cdots & 0 & 0 \\ 0 & 1 & \cdots & 0 & 0 \\ \vdots & \vdots & \ddots & \vdots & \vdots \\ 0 & 0 & \cdots & 1 & 0 \end{pmatrix}.$$

Now, by expanding along the rightmost column, we find that the determinant of A is c_0 where, by assumption, $c_0 = 1 \neq 0$. Thus, A is nonsingular. Each state vector can be represented as a column matrix of the form $A^j \mathbf{u}$, $j = 1, 2, 3, \ldots, t - 1$, with t being the fundamental period. Since $\det(A^j) = (\det A)^j = 1$, A^j is nonsingular. Also, $\mathbf{u} \neq \mathbf{0}$. Thus, each state vector is nonzero. ∎

Remark 16.19 (Remark on periodicity) *Suppose that an LFSR Γ of length m has period t, say. Thus, each **state vector** returns to itself after t clock pulses. Since a state vector is an **ordered** array of m field elements (usually binary digits), it follows that each **element** of the output returns to itself after t clock pulses.*

Instead of using a *linear* shift register generated by the recurrence

$$x_m = c_0 x_0 + c_1 x_1 + \cdots + c_{m-1} x_{m-1}$$

we can also devise a shift register generated by the output sequence $x_m = f(x_{m-1}, x_{m-2}, \ldots, x_1, x_0)$ where f is a suitable **nonlinear** function. An example would be: $x_k = x_{k-1} \cdot x_{k-2} + x_{k-2} \cdot x_{k-3}$. This can improve security. Another technique is to combine the output sequences of different synchronized shift registers to get a single output. For more discussion, we refer the reader to Mollin [Mol00].

16.7 Short Linear Feedback Shift Registers and the Berlekamp-Massey Algorithm

As mentioned earlier, shift registers are used in constructing cryptographic stream ciphers Γ. The cryptographics problem then relates to constructing Γ given a small sequence of consecutive outputs. In effect, we are interested in finding an LFSR of shortest length containing the given sequence.

In Chapter 22, we see how this exact same problem arises when decoding Reed–Solomon codes in finding the shortest LFSR that generates the syndromes.

For this general problem, we can make use of Theorem 16.11 which underscores its importance. As mentioned before, two linear shift registers with the same initial state vector but different recurrence polynomials can yield the same output (see Example 16.20 below). However, the determinant of a P-matrix will be zero. If Γ is a shortest LFSR for a given output it is unique, $det\, P = 1$ and we only need $2n$ bits to determine the entire sequence.

Example 16.20 *It can be shown that Γ_4 and Γ^* with initial state vector given by $\{x_3 x_2 x_1 x_0\} = \{1011\}$ both generate the same sequence. Here, Γ_4 has the recurrence*

$$x_4 = x_3 + x_1 + x_0 \quad and \quad \Gamma^* \quad has \quad the \quad recurrence \quad x_4 = x_2 + x_0. \quad So, \quad C = \begin{pmatrix} 1 \\ 1 \\ 0 \\ 1 \end{pmatrix} \quad and$$

$$D = \begin{pmatrix} 1 \\ 0 \\ 1 \\ 0 \end{pmatrix}. \quad Then \quad U = (C + D)^t = (0111). \quad Now, \quad UP = \mathbf{0} \quad implies \quad that \quad 0(Row\ 0) +$$

$1(Row\ 1) + 1(Row\ 2) + 1(Row\ 3) = \mathbf{0}$. *In other words, $Row\ 3 = Row\ 1 + Row\ 2$.*

This relationship extends to $P_1, P_2, \ldots$, etc. The conclusion is that the output sequence generated by Γ_4 and Γ^* is also generated by a shorter shift register of length 3 with recurrence $x_3 = x_2 + x_1$ (i.e. a "Fibonacci" recurrence) and initial state vector $\{x_2x_1x_0\} = \{011\}$. The common output of all 3 shift registers is then $\{x_0x_1x_2x_3 \ldots\} = \{110110110 \ldots\}$.

Note. In Algorithm 16.21, = denotes the assignment operator. The operator == evaluates to "true" if the objects on the left and right of it evaluate to the same value, and "false" if they evaluate to different values.

A well-known general algorithm for finding a shortest LFSR is the Berlekamp–Massey algorithm – "the LFSR Synthesis Algorithm," [Mas69, p. 124].

Algorithm 16.21   (Massey – the LFSR Synthesis Algorithm, [Mas69])   *Here, we take as input, a binary string $s = s_0s_1 \ldots s_{n-1}$. We will output the minimum length λ, and the recurrence polynomial*

$$P(X) = p_0 + p_1X + p_2X^2 + \cdots + p_\lambda X^\lambda, \quad p_0 = 1.$$

Initialize: $P(X) = 1$, $Q(X) = 1$, $k = 1$, $\lambda = 0$, $m = 1$, $j = 0$
```
while j < n
   d = s_j + \sum_{i=1}^{\lambda} p_i s_{j-i}
   if d == 0 //current LFSR works
      k = k + 1
   else //must modify the LFSR
      if 2\lambda > j //update LFSR but length okay
         P(X) = P(X) - dm^{-1}X^kQ(X) //update P(X)
         k = k + 1
      else //update LFSR and length
         T(X) = P(X) //save the old P(X) before modifying P(X)
         P(X) = P(X) - dm^{-1}X^kQ(X) //update P(X)
         \lambda = j + 1 - \lambda //update the length of the LFSR
         Q(X) = T(X) //save the old P(X)
         m = d
         k = 1
   j = j + 1
```

Algorithm 16.21 will output (one of) the shortest LFSR(s) to produce that given output string. Here is an example output that shows the recurrence relation after each iteration of j.

Example 16.22 *We find the shortest LFSR that generates the string $s_n s_{n-1} \cdots s_1 s_0 =$ 01101110011110 over $GF(2)$.*

j	output $s_j s_{j-1} \cdots s_1 s_0$	$P(X)$	λ	recurrence
0	0	1	0	$x_0 = 0$
1	10	$1 + X^2$	2	$x_2 = x_0$
2	110	$1 + X + X^2$	2	$x_2 = x_1 + x_0$
3	1110	$1 + X$	2	$x_2 = x_1$
4	11110	$1 + X$	2	$x_2 = x_1$
5	011110	$1 + X + X^4$	4	$x_4 = x_3 + x_0$
6	0011110	$1 + X^2 + X^4$	4	$x_4 = x_2 + x_0$
7	10011110	$1 + X^2 + X^4$	4	$x_4 = x_2 + x_0$
8	110011110	$1 + X^2 + X^4$	4	$x_4 = x_2 + x_0$
9	1110011110	$1 + X^2 + X^4$	4	$x_4 = x_2 + x_0$
10	01110011110	$1 + X^2 + X^4 + X^5 + X^6$	7	$x_7 = x_5 + x_3 + x_2 + x_1$
11	101110011110	$1 + X + X^2 + X^3 + X^4 + X^6$	7	$x_7 = x_6 + x_5 + x_4 + x_3 + x_1$
12	1101110011110	$1 + X + X^2 + X^3 + X^4 + X^6$	7	$x_7 = x_6 + x_5 + x_4 + x_3 + x_1$
13	01101110011110	$1 + X + X^2 + X^3 + X^4 + X^6$	7	$x_7 = x_6 + x_5 + x_4 + x_3 + x_1$

So our final recurrence is $x_7 = x_6 + x_5 + x_4 + x_3 + x_1$, with initial configuration equal to the right-most 7 bits $= 0011110$. In this case, the recurrence is unique because of Theorem 16.23.

It may well be that two different shift registers will produce the same output. In some important situations this cannot happen. The following theorem is also proven by Massey [Mas69].

Theorem 16.23 *Let a linear shift register Γ_m of length m with recurrence polynomial $x_m = c_0 x_0 + c_1 x_1 + \cdots + c_{m-1} x_{m-1}$ be the shortest LFSR generating the sequence $S = \{s_0, s_1, s_2, \ldots, s_n\}$, where we assume that $n \geq 2m - 1$. Then, Γ_m is unique.*

Sketch of proof Let Γ^* be another LFSR of length m with recurrence polynomial $x_m = d_0 x_0 + d_1 x_1 + \cdots + d_{m-1} x_{m-1}$ generating S. In particular, Γ_m and Γ^* generate the sequence $\{s_0, s_1, s_2, \ldots, s_{2m-1}\}$. Using the notation and proof of Theorem 16.11 we have that $UP = \mathbf{0}$ where $U = (C + D)^t$ is a nonzero row vector. Thus, U annihilates all columns of P, P_1, P_2, etc., as in the proof of Theorem 16.11. Then, U causes a dependency relation among the rows of $P, P_1, P_2, \ldots$. This in turn will yield an LFSR of length $v < m$ that outputs S. But this contradicts the minimality of Γ_m.

Note that Theorem 16.23 does not hold without restrictions on n relative to m. For example, consider the string 011110. Note that this is a substring of the one in Example 16.22; looking at the row for $j = 5$ in the table of Example 16.22, we have $x_4 = x_3 + x_0$ for a minimum LFSR. But $x_4 = x_2 + x_0$ is a recurrence for a different LFSR.

Remarks

1. Theorem 16.23 first shown by Massey [Mas69] is central in connection to the Reed–Solomon decoding procedure in Chapter 22 as it shows uniqueness for the shortest LFSR.

2. In Theorem 16.11, the fact that $UP = \mathbf{0}$ leads to a shorter LFSR is also shown in Trappe and Washington [TW01].

16.8   Problems

16.1   Let the linear shift register Γ of length 5 have the initial state vector

$$s_0 = \{x_4, x_3, x_2, x_1, x_0\} = \{10011\}$$

and a recurrence generated from the relation $x_5 = x_0 + x_2 + x_4$ (see Figure 16.3) so that

$$x_{n+5} = x_n + x_{n+2} + x_{n+4}, \quad n \geq 0.$$

(a) What is the period of Γ?

(b) What is the output sequence of Γ?

(See Solution 16.1.)

16.2   Let the linear shift register Γ of length 4 have the output sequence $x_0 x_1 x_2 1100 \ldots$ and the recurrence relation $x_4 = x_0 + x_2 + x_3$. What are the values of x_0, x_1 and x_2? (See Solution 16.2.)

16.3   Let the linear shift register Γ of length 6 have the recurrence relation $x_6 = x_0 + x_3 + x_4$.

(a) What is the tap polynomial $h(x)$ for Γ?

(b) Is $h(x)$ a primitive tap polynomial?

(See Solution 16.3.)

16.4   Let the linear shift register Γ_m have maximal period equal to $2^m - 1$. Show that the output sequence has $2^{m-1} - 1$ zeros and 2^{m-1} ones. (See Solution 16.4.)

16.5   Give an example of a linear shift register Γ with nonzero initial state vector such that a subsequent state vector is the all-zero state vector as are all subsequent state vectors. (We will need $c_0 = 0$.) (See Solution 16.5.)

16.6   Show that if a linear shift register Γ_m with a given initial state vector $\mathbf{x} \neq \mathbf{0}$ has maximal period equal to $2^m - 1$, then the linear shift register obtained from Γ_m by changing only the initial input $\mathbf{x}$ to any other input $\mathbf{y} \neq \mathbf{0}$ also has period equal to $2^m - 1$. (See Solution 16.6.)

16.7   Give an example of two different linear shift registers with the same initial state vector, the same output sequences but with different tap polynomials. (See Solution 16.7.)

16.8   Let Γ_4 be a linear shift register with initial state vector $\{1101\}$ which maps $\{x_3 x_2 x_1 x_0\}$ to $\{c_0 x_0 + c_1 x_1 + c_2 x_2 + c_3 x_3, x_3, x_2, x_1\}$ at each pulse, where $c_0 = c_3 = 1$ and $c_2 = c_1 = 0$.

(a) Find the period of Γ_4.

(b) Find the output sequence of Γ_4.

(c) Find the associated tap polynomial of Γ_4.

(See Solution 16.8.)

16.9   Suppose that the linear shift register Γ of length 4 has period 1. Assuming that the initial state vector is not all zeros, what are the possibilities for Γ? (See Solution 16.9.)

16.10   (a) What is the shortest LFSR that will yield an output of 10110110?

       (b) What is the shortest LFSR that will yield an output of 101101100?

       (c) What is the shortest LFSR that will yield an output of 010110110?

       (See Solution 16.10.)

16.9   Solutions

16.1   (a) The period is 15 so there are 15 register state vectors starting with $(x_4x_3x_2x_1x_0) = (10011)$ and ending with (00110).

       (b) The output sequence is the following sequence of length 15

$$\{110010100001110\}.$$

16.2 $(x_0x_1x_2) = (101)$

16.3   (a) The tap polynomial is $h(x) = x^6 + x^4 + x^3 + 1$.

       (b) Since $x = 1$ is a root of $h(x)$, $h(x)$ has the proper factor $x + 1$ and hence, is not primitive.

16.4   Any register state vector is a nonzero binary sequence of length m and so is the binary representation of a positive integer N between 1 and $2^m - 1$. To see this just take the ordered sequence of the state vector contents as the binary representation of the integer: the rightmost digit, which is the current output, tells us whether N is odd or even.

       Each nonzero binary m-tuple shows up just once as the machine travels through the $2^m - 1$ state vector registers. So we need only calculate how many odd and even integers N there are. (Note that each bit of the output sequence shows up just once as the current output, namely just after it is the rightmost entry of a register state vector).

16.5   Let Γ_2 have initial state vector $\{01\}$ with recurrence generated by $x_2 = x_1$. Then the next state vector, and all subsequent state vectors, are the all-zero state vector.

16.6   The $2^m - 1$ state vectors $A^0\mathbf{x}, A\mathbf{x}, A^2\mathbf{x}, \ldots, A^{2^m-2}\mathbf{x}$ are distinct and give all possible nonzero vectors of length m. Thus, $\mathbf{y} = A^i\mathbf{x}$ for some i, with $0 \leq i \leq 2^m - 2$. Now consider the vectors $\mathbf{y}, A\mathbf{y}, A^2\mathbf{y}, A^{2^m-2}\mathbf{y}$. If some two of these, say $A^u\mathbf{y}$ and $A^v\mathbf{y}$ with $1 \leq u, v \leq 2^{m-2}$, and $u \neq v$, were equal, we would have $A^u\mathbf{y} = A^v\mathbf{y}$, so $A^u A^i\mathbf{x} = A^v A^i\mathbf{x}$. Multiplying on the left by $(A^{-1})^i = A^{-i}$ (recall that det $A = c_0 = 1 \neq 0$) gives $A^u\mathbf{x} = A^v\mathbf{x}$, a contradiction. Thus, $A^u\mathbf{y} \neq A^v\mathbf{y}$ for $1 \leq u, v \leq 2^{m-2}$ with $u \neq v$, and so it follows that we have max period since the $A^u\mathbf{y}$ range over all possible states.

16.7   Let the initial state vector be $\{x_3 x_2 x_1 x_0\} = \{1011\}$. Let Γ_1 be the LFSR generated by the recurrence $x_4 = x_0 + x_2$ and let Γ_2 be the LFSR generated by the recurrence $x_4 = x_3 + x_1 + x_0$. Then the output sequence for both LFSRs has fundamental period 3 and is $110110110 \ldots$. The tap polynomial for Γ_1 is $h_1(x) = x^4 + x^2 + 1$ and the tap polynomial for Γ_2 is $h_2(x) = x^4 + x^3 + x + 1$. Note. The output sequence is generated by a shorter LFSR with initial state vector $\{10\}$ and recurrence given by $x_3 = x_1 + x_2$, consistent with the general theory.

16.8   (a) The period is 15.

   (b) The output sequence is $\{101100100011110\}$.

   (c) The tap polynomial is $h(x) = x^4 + x^3 + 1$. Note that $x^{15} + 1 = (x^4 + x^3 + 1)$ $(x^{11} + x^{10} + x^9 + x^8 + x^6 + x^4 + x^3 + 1)$ and that $h(x)$ does not divide $x^d - 1$ for any divisor d of 15.

16.9   The only outputs of period 1 are $\{0000 \ldots\}$ and $\{1111 \ldots\}$. Since the initial state vector is not the all zero vector, it follows that the output must be $\{1111 \ldots\}$. This implies that the initial state vector is $\{1111\}$.

16.10   (a) $x_2 = x_1 + x_0$, Initial configuration = 10.

   (b) $x_3 = x_2 + x_1$, Initial configuration = 100.

   (c) $x_7 = x_6 + x_5 + x_0$, Initial configuration = 0110110.
     Further, the above shortest LFSR is unique.

Chapter 17

Compression and Applications

Goals, Discussion Data compression is a major area because of the many applications when transmitting or downloading text, audio, video, etc. Like shorthand, it is a method for encoding data in an economical way, that is, a noiseless economical encoding of a source that can easily be decoded to give the original message.

Compression is extremely important to streaming. Streaming – both video streaming and audio streaming – have become so prevalent that a major portion of all Internet traffic is from streaming. Netflix alone consumes a substantial percentage of all Internet traffic [Luc15, Mor18], as does Amazon Prime Video, and YouTube. New streaming services are currently being added at a steady rate.

In this chapter, we continue the discussion of Chapter 11, but here we focus on data compression and related applications. The Lempel–Ziv (LZ) and WKdm algorithms are presented in Sections 17.4 and 17.5, respectively. Applications include general compression and compressed memory.

New, Noteworthy We noted in Chapter 11 that compression is crucial for applications such as data transfer or downloading from a source such as the Internet when there is a large amount of data or when we need the data to be transmitted quickly. There, we included topics such as arithmetic coding (Section 11.7) and Huffman coding (Section 11.5). We continue here with the extremely important Lempel–Ziv and

Cryptography, Information Theory, and Error-Correction: A Handbook for the 21st Century, Second Edition.
Aiden A. Bruen, Mario A. Forcinito, and James M. McQuillan.
© 2021 John Wiley & Sons, Inc. Published 2021 by John Wiley & Sons, Inc.

WKdm algorithms, in Sections 17.4 and 17.5, respectively, as well as a focus on related applications in Sections 17.1 and 17.3.

One application is compressed memory (also known as RAM compression, or compressed caching in main memory), which will be discussed throughout this chapter. This took on mainstream use by Apple's MacOS (OS X), by Linux, and by Microsoft's Windows 10 around the years 2013–2015. For example, Microsoft began using memory compression in its Windows operating system with its Windows 10. The result for Windows 10 is that **compressed pages take approximately 30% of the space of the original pages.** See [Shu18] for further details. Other applications include the mainstream compression algorithms `gzip` and `zip`, which are based on Lempel–Ziv.

17.1   Introduction, Applications

Streaming video and audio on watches, phones, tablets, laptops, and desktops have become commonplace, especially for those who have access to the Internet via fiber-optic cables or 4G or better cell-phone network speeds. Even those with slower download speeds may have access to these services because the data is normally compressed before it is transmitted. Additionally, buffering may be used to store some of the data before one begins to listen to music or watch a TV show or movie, for example, so as to not incur as many annoying delays while listening or watching your favorite shows or movies.

Compressing data before transmitting it means that audio and video can be often be transmitted in real-time. Services that stream live events such as championship sporting events rely on this, as do video and audio conferencing for business or personal use. Streaming video or music on our phones, tablets, etc. at a real-time rate mean that we do not have to store the video or music on our devices before we begin watching or listening.

In general, compressing data before storing it means that less space is required for storage. Compressing data before it is transmitted means that it can be transmitted at a faster rate.

The uses of compression are certainly not limited to streaming. The heavily used `gzip` compression algorithm [gzia] can be used to compress your favorite file before storing it or emailing it to a friend, for example. `Gzip` is free software [gzib]. It uses Lempel–Ziv coding (LZ77) [gzib, ZL77], which we will discuss in Section 17.4.

Microsoft uses the NT file system (NTFS) file system for its Windows operating system. The NTFS file system also uses Lempel–Ziv for its compression algorithm [Cen18]. Graphics formats that you might be using to store your digital photos include GIF and TIFF formats, both of which use Lempel–Ziv–Welch [gif, Lic].

Central processing units (CPUs) have transitioned toward multi-core architectures. With a multi-core CPU, multiple tasks can be done at the same time, or some tasks can proceed at a faster pace if there are sub-tasks that can be done at the same time. Additionally, the use of hand-held devices such as tablets and smart phones has exploded; this must be factored-in. Handheld devices might have fewer resources than a desktop, including less memory, and there will be battery life restrictions as well.

In the early 1990s, Wilson [Wil99,Wil91] proposed a partial solution to the disk-latency problem: *memory compression*, which is also known as *RAM compression* or *compressed caching in main memory*. The idea is simple: store some pages in main memory in compressed form. With this, main memory can effectively hold more pages. Therefore, one could be less likely to have to wait for data to be transferred from permanent storage to main memory, and our fast CPUs could be kept busy. The trade-off is that, sometimes the CPU might have to wait for data to be uncompressed before the CPU can use it.

As mentioned at the beginning of this chapter, memory compression became standard in Apple's OS X, the Linux kernel, and Windows 10 around 2013–2015. Apple's MacOS (OS X) started using a variant of WKdm for compressed memory in 2013 in OS X 10.9 Mavericks. Compressed memory also became stable in Linux 3.14, which was released on 30 March 2014. They use a variant of Ziv-Lempel. Microsoft started using memory compression in Windows 10 [Shu18].

The main idea for applications of this is (for operating systems) to store some information in main memory (RAM) in compressed form. This effectively gives us more space in main memory. Consider a computer or hand-held device with a finite amount of memory. If we could fit more applications and their data into main memory, then we might be able to speed up the applications. As an added benefit, we might be able to improve the battery life of hand-held devices at the same time!

An interesting question: Why did Apple, Linux, and Microsoft Windows all rush to incorporate compressed caching around 2013–2015?

One answer is **battery life**! There is a strong desire (in essence, a requirement!) to have batteries for tablets, phones, laptops, etc. to last for a full day. It takes less energy to compress and uncompress data than it takes to transfer the data between permanent storage and main memory. Usually, there is a trade-off when deciding to use new technologies. But, here, you win twice! Compressed memory improves not only the performance of applications (apps) but **at the same time** it improves the battery life of portable devices. These advantages, together with the mainstream use of multi-core processors (CPUs) explain why the major operating systems all incorporated compressed memory around the years 2013–2015.

17.2   The Memory Hierarchy of a Computer

We are almost ready for a major application of compression – memory compression, which we introduced in Section 17.1. Before we discuss memory compression further (Section 17.3), we give some background on the memory hierarchy of a computer. If you have taken a course in computer organization or computer architecture, or you are already familiar with the memory hierarchy, then please proceed to the next section.

The *CPU* performs most of the main computations for your computer (desktop, laptop, tablet, etc.) The applications or "apps" that you want to run, along with the data that they need, have to be loaded into main memory (RAM) in order for the CPU to access them. The code and data for the apps are often stored in a solid state drive or a hard drive, or perhaps some external storage device like a thumbdrive. When you click or double-click on an icon to open an app, it is loaded into main memory (if it is not already there) to create a process. A *process* consists of a program, including both its code and its data, that is loaded into main memory and is executing. (See [SGG18].)

A general computer science principle is that information that is used now might very well be used again in the near future. So, "caching" is a frequently used computer science concept. A *cache* is a store of recently used information that is closer (quicker to access) than the information itself. There may be multiple caches to store recently used information. A CPU can access data in one of its caches quicker than it can access information from main memory. Unfortunately, caches also cost more (per byte of information they can contain) than main memory. Therefore, they are smaller. Figure 17.1 shows the memory hierarchy of a computer. For more details on this and other topics in computer architecture, please see [HP17].

Before leaving this section, we briefly mention a recent breakthrough in memory technology. Traditionally, the RAM of a computer has been "volatile," meaning that when there is no power to the RAM, it loses its contents. There is now newer, more expensive *nonvolatile memory*, or *NVM*. For example, Intel and Micron have developed some NVM [Int15, Int18]. They are using this to make a new line of high-endurance, high-performance solid-state drives (SSDs). As it is more expensive, NVM will tend to be used for specialized tasks or perhaps in smaller devices initially, and then NVM-expand in use as it becomes cheaper.

17.3   Memory Compression

If some of the code or data in main memory was there in a compressed form, then effectively we would have more memory, or more RAM. Figure 17.1 shows the memory hierarchy of a computer. Figure 17.2 shows it when compressed caching is used.

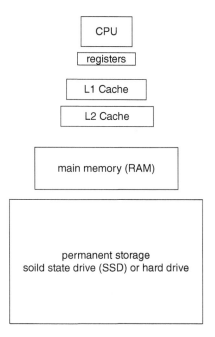

Figure 17.1: Memory hierarchy.

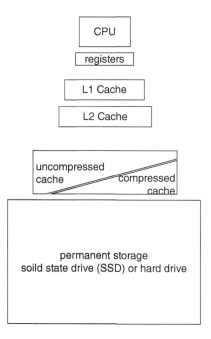

Figure 17.2: Memory hierarchy with compressed caching included.

Figure 17.3: Compressed caching in main memory.

Figure 17.3 is often used when main memory is split into two parts – the *compressed cache* (the part in which data is stored in compressed form) and the uncompressed part, called the *uncompressed cache*.

Note:

Figure 17.3 is deceiving. This is how it is often drawn. One goal of this figure is to show that there are two parts (a compressed and an uncompressed part) to main memory. Sometimes there is an additional goal of showing the relative sizes of the compressed and uncompressed caches. However, the figure gives the impression that the information that is stored in compressed form in main memory needs to be contiguous, i.e. next to each other. This need not be the case.

Question:

Since having a compressed memory means you can store more information in main memory, shouldn't we compress as much of the information in main memory as possible so as to fit in as much information as possible?

The answer is no, it is not that simple. If it were, then it would make sense to compress everything that goes into main memory so as to fit as much code and data as possible in memory. Unfortunately, anything that the CPU needs to use for calculations etc. needs to first be decompressed if it is in compressed form. There might also be some additional overhead associated with keeping track of the compressed information.

Rodrigo de Castro started working on an undergraduate research project that led to his master's thesis on compressed caching. A paper by de Castro, do Lago, and Da Silva on this can be found at [dCdLS03]. The Compcache project was selected in the *Google Summer of Code* program [Goo]. Compcache was then implemented in the Linux operating system as zRAM. Compressed caching was considered stable in Linux 3.14, which was released on 30 March 2014 [Kera] Memory compression was improved in Linux 3.15, which was released on June 8, 2014 [Kerb]. We discuss this more in Section 17.6.

17.4 Lempel–Ziv Coding

The LZ algorithm, [ZL77,ZL78], as well as the Lempel-Ziv-Welch (LZW) algorithm, [Wel85], are very important for general compression algorithms as well as memory compression algorithms. The LZ algorithm has, in large part, displaced the Huffman algorithm for data compression. Haykin [Hay01] reports that LZ achieves a **compression of around 55%** when applied to ordinary English text as opposed to a figure of 43% for Huffman. One reason is that the Huffman encoding does not seem to exploit statistical dependencies in English as well as LZ. In general, a disadvantage of Huffman (as opposed to LZ) is the fact that one needs to know in advance (or estimate) the probabilities of the source words. The LZ algorithm is simple and easy to implement. **Unix compression** uses general LZ methods, as do the various **zip** and **unzip** algorithms.

The LZ technique is remarkably simple. The method is this. We parse the source stream into segments that are the **shortest** subsequences not yet encountered. Each new subsequence is longer than some previously encountered sequence by one symbol. By keeping track of this, the desired compression is obtained; i.e. if we keep track of the previously encountered sequences, then each new sequence consists of a pointer to an old sequence plus one additional character. We can also construct trees (or "tries") for encoding/decoding. Each new subsequence not yet encountered will be equal to an old subsequence with a single letter (innovation symbol) added on at the end.

An example will clarify the method. Suppose our alphabet has just two letters x and y and that our sample input stream is

$$x \, y \, y \, y \, x \, x \, y \, x \, x \, x \, x \, y \, x \, y \, x \, x \, y \, x \, x \, x$$

Our algorithm or procedure is as follows.

Procedure

Proceeding from the left, break up the remaining stream into segments that represent the shortest subsequences not yet encountered. Also, index these segments. This gives us the following.

x	y	$y\,y$	$x\,x$	$y\,x$	$x\,x\,x$	$y\,x\,y$	$x\,x\,y$	$x\,x\,x\,x$
1	2	3	4	5	6	7	8	9

These index numbers from 1 to 9 are used to label the segments and construct the tree.

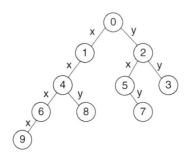

Figure 17.4: Lempel–Ziv tree for the string $x\ y\ y\ y\ x\ x\ y\ x\ x\ x\ x\ y\ x\ y\ x\ x\ y\ x\ x\ x\ x$.

The empty string corresponding to the start of the text has index 0. The segment numbered 1 is x. Thus this segment gets the label $0x$.

Similarly, the segment y in slot 2 gets labeled $0y$. The string in slot 3 is yy. This can be regarded as the concatenation of the old string in slot 2, namely y, with the new or innovation symbol y. So slot 3 is labeled $2y$. Slot 4 becomes $1x$. Slot 5 is $2x$. Slot 6 is $4x$. Slot 7 is $5y$. Slot 8 is $4y$. Slot 9 is $6x$. So we now have the following

Labels	$0x$	$0y$	$2y$	$1x$	$2x$	$4x$	$5y$	$4y$	$6x$
Slots	1	2	3	4	5	6	7	8	9

Now we see the compression at work. For example, in slot 8 we have (uncompressed) 3 letters xxy which cost $3(8) = 24$ bits when encoded in ASCII. With the compression we only need to encode $4y$, which takes just 13 bits. In effect, we are replacing long strings of text with just a number and a text letter for each slot.

We can also construct a tree associated with the encoding. This tree will have as its root the label 0 corresponding to the empty string. It will have, in addition, 9 vertices corresponding to the 9 indexes 1 to 9. See Figure 17.4.

17.5   The WKdm Algorithms

As mentioned in Section 17.1, in computer science, there is often a trade-off between various goals. We might want to improve battery life as well as the speed of an application. A new feature might improve one at the expense of the other. But, with compressed memory, we can improve both. Apple has used compressed memory (https://www.apple.com/osx/all-features/pdf/osx_elcapitan_core_technologies_overview.pdf) [Appb] since 2013, and they continue to use it today. They started using WKdm compression in OS X 10.9 Mavericks [Dil13]. Apple notes (https://support.apple.com/guide/mac-help/save-energy-mh35848/mac) that compressed memory has **several advantages**, including reducing the sizes of items in memory and improving power efficiency. They also note the compression algorithms (based on WKdm) are extremely efficient, "compressing or decompressing a page of memory in just a few millionths of a second." They also note that they take advantage of your multi-core machines, "Unlike traditional virtual memory, Compressed Memory can run in parallel on multiple CPU cores ...." See (https://www.apple.com/osx/all-features/pdf/osx_elcapitan_core_technologies_overview.pdf) for more details.

As noted in Section 17.2, a general computer science principle is that something that is used now might very well be used again in the near future. (As a result, caching is used extensively in computer science.) A compression algorithm might be based on that principle. The idea is to watch out for duplicates. We have already talked about Huffman coding, which relies on some characters in a file occurring more often than other characters in the file. As with Huffman coding, we wish to exploit the possibility of there being duplicate words.

The WKdm algorithms, [WKS99], take this idea a step further. The key insight in their algorithms is, not only is it beneficial to keep track of exact matches, but one should watch out for partial matches as well.

Suppose that one is reading a string of 32-bit words that are to be stored in main memory in compressed form. Consider an algorithm that reads one 32-bit input word at a time. The output of a compression algorithm, called the **compressed output**, will also be a string of bits. (The hope is that the output string will be much shorter than the input string.) A *dictionary* is used to keep track of *new* words. If the word is a duplicate, we would like to avoid writing the word a second time (to the compressed output). To achieve this, the WK algorithm checks to see if the word is an exact match to a word in the dictionary. Therefore, the WKdm algorithms use a table (a data structure) called a *dictionary* to keep track of some of the recent words that have been seen.

Wilson et al. realized [WKS99] that this strategy could be substantially improved by not only looking for exact matches of words but by also looking for "partial matches," i.e. words that are fairly similar. Their idea is that if the upper 22 bits of a 32-bit word are the same, then they should be considered as a *partial match*. Then, only the low-order 10 bits could have differences.

The idea of partial matches is a key to the success of the WKdm algorithms for compression in main memory. There tend to be a lot of partial matches in main memory. This is because, if you convert two integers that are close to each other into binary representations, then most of the bits for the two numbers will be the same, i.e. we have a partial match. The same goes for the memory addresses. If two addresses are close to each other, most of the bits in their addresses will be the same. Sometimes we want to keep track of some addresses (e.g. pointers). This happens a lot in main memory.

We are almost ready to give the WKdm algorithm [WKS99] from 1999.

Notation 17.1 *If $x = w_1 \cdots w_t$ is a string consisting of 32-bit words $w_1, \ldots, w_t$, we use l_i to represent 10 low-order bits of w_i, and the upper 22 bits of w_i are represented by u_i. We write $w_i = u_i l_i$.*

Definition 17.2 A **dictionary** D for the WKdm algorithms is a table (data structure) of recently seen 32-bit words. Words are removed from the dictionary in least recently used (LRU) order; i.e. if a word is to be added to the dictionary and the dictionary is full, then an item that was used the least recently is removed from the dictionary before adding in the newest word.

The WKdm algorithms will use a two-bit tag for each word to identify what type of word it is. There are four possibilities for a string consisting of two bits, namely, $00, 01, 10, 11$.

Definition 17.3 A **two-bit tag** for the WKdm algorithms is a string consisting of two bits that represents the type of word that was read. For each 32-bit word w, there are four possibilities:

(a) *new word case*: If the word w is a new word, i.e. it is not an exact match or partial match to any current dictionary word, and if it is not the all zero word, then the tag 01 is used.

(b) *exact match* case: If the word w is an exact match to a word currently in the dictionary, then the tag 11 is used.

(c) *partial match case*: If the word w is a partial match to a word currently in the dictionary, then the tag 10 is used.

(d) *zero word* case: If the word w is the all zero word, then the tag 00 is used.

It is arbitrary, of course, as to which tag corresponds to which case in Definition 17.3. One just needs to be consistent.

Algorithm 17.4 (WKdm compression) *Let $x = w_1 w_2 \cdots w_t$ be a string consisting of the 32-bit words $w_1, \ldots, w_t$. We write $w_i = u_i l_i$, where u_i represents the upper 22 bits* *of w_i and l_i represents the 10 low-order bits of w_i, $i = 1, \ldots, t$. Let D be a table or (a data structure) that will be used for the dictionary (as in Definition 17.2).*

We will read one word at a time in the order $w_1, \ldots, w_t$. For each word read, we will compare it to the entries in the dictionary D, and write a corresponding word to the compressed output.

For the word w_i, there are four possibilities:

(a) new word case*: If w_i is a "new word," i.e. it is not an exact nor a partial match to a word that is currently in the dictionary, and it is not the zero word, then do each of the following:*

    (i) Insert w_i into the dictionary. If the dictionary is full, first remove the least recently used word from the dictionary.

    (ii) Write the 2 bit tag for this case, 01, to the compressed output.

    (iii) Write the entire word w_i to the compressed output.

    (Notice that in this case, the "compressed" version of w_i is 34 bits, which is more than the original 32 bits.)

(b) exact match case*: If w_i is an exact match to a word that is in the dictionary, then do all of the following:*

    (i) Leave the dictionary as it is.

    (ii) Write the 2 bit tag for this case, 11, to the compressed output.

    (iii) Write the dictionary index of the match to w_i in the dictionary to the compressed output.

    (iv) Do not write any of w_i to the compressed output.

(c) partial match case*: If w_i is a partial match to a word in the dictionary, meaning the upper 22 bits of w_i matches the upper 22 bits of some word in the dictionary but the full words are not identical, then do all of the following:*

    (i) Leave the dictionary alone.

    (ii) Write the 2 bit tag for this case, 10, to the compressed output.

    (iii) Write the dictionary index of the partial match to w_i in the dictionary to the compressed output.

   (iv) Write the low order 10 bits l_i of w_i to the compressed output.

   (v) Do not write the upper order 22 bits u_i of w_i to the compressed output.

(d) zero word case: If w_i is the all zero word, then do the following:

   (i) Leave the dictionary alone.

   (ii) Write the 2-bit tag 00 corresponding to this case to the compressed output.

   (iii) Do not write w_i to the compressed output.

For Algorithm 17.4, notice that, if we never have any exact or partial matches, then the compressed output will actually be bigger than the uncompressed input! Fortunately, in computer science, there tend to be a lot of exact matches because we often using data multiple times. Moreover, in main memory, there tend to be a lot of partial matches because integers that are close together will agree in mast of the upper bits, and memory addresses that are close to each other will also agree in most upper bits. So, there tends to be a lot of partial matches in information stored in main memory.

We now give an example in which a string is compressed using the WKdm algorithm in Algorithm 17.4.

Example 17.5 *We wish to compress the string $x = w_1 w_2 w_3 w_4 w_5$, where $w_1, \ldots, w_5$ are 32-bit words. Using Notation 17.1, we write $w_i = u_i l_i$, u_i are the upper 22 bits of w_i, and l_i are the lower 10-bits of w_i, $i = 1, 2, \ldots, 5$. Assume that $w_1, \ldots, w_5$ have the following properties:*

  (i) w_1 is any nonzero 32-bit word,

  (ii) w_2 is identical to w_1,

  (iii) w_3 is the zero word,

  (iv) w_4 is an arbitrary nonzero 32-bit word that is different enough from w_1 so that $u_4 \neq u_1$,

  (v) w_5 is an arbitrary nonzero 32-bit word with the property that $u_5 = u_1$ but $l_5 \neq l_1$.

We wish to compress x.

  Assume that the 2-bit tags corresponding to cases (a), (b), (c), and (d) in Definition 17.3 are $01, 11, 10$, and 00, respectively. Assume that the dictionary table (data *structure) used by the algorithm holds 16 32-bit words and that the addresses are 0000 through 1111, with the first new word being added at address 0000. With a dictionary of size 16, a dictionary address requires 4 bits.*

In the compressed output, the appropriate 2-bit code will be written first. For cases (b) and (c), the dictionary index will be written next. For case (c), the low-order 10 bits l_i will be written after that.

The algorithm proceeds as follows:

(i) *Starting with w_1, we are in Case (a) of Algorithm 17.4. We add w_1 to the dictionary at index 0000. To the compressed output, we add the corresponding 2-bit tag 01 followed by the entire word w_1.*

(ii) *For w_2, we are in Case (b). The dictionary remains the same. We add the 2-bit tag 11 corresponding to the exact match case followed by dictionary index 0000 to the compressed output.*

(iii) *For w_3, we are in Case (d). The dictionary remains the same. The only addition to the compressed output is the 2-bit tag 00.*

(iv) *For w_4, we are in case (a). We add w_4 to the dictionary at index 0001. To the compressed output, we add the 2-bit tag 01 and the entire word w_4.*

(v) *For w_5, we are in case (c). We leave the dictionary alone. To the compressed output, we add the 2-bit tag 10, the dictionary index 0000, and the low-order 10 bits l_5 of w_5.*

Thus, the string $x = w_1 w_2 w_3 w_4 w_5$, which consists of $5 \times 32 = 160$ bits is compressed to form the string $01w_1 1100000001w_4 1000000l_5$, which has only $(2 + 32) + (2 + 4) + (2) + (2 + 32) + (2 + 4 + 10) = 92$ bits. At that point, the dictionary looks like Figure 17.5.

0000 0001 0010 0011 0100 0101 0110 0111 1000 1001 1010 1011 1100 1101 1110 1111

Figure 17.5: Dictionary immediately after compressing w_5 in Example 17.5. After the string x is compressed, this dictionary is no longer needed, and can be deleted.

Remark 17.6 *Note: Algorithm 17.4 does not save the dictionary after it finishes. Instead, the associated decompression algorithm, Algorithm 17.7 rebuilds the dictionary as it decompresses the string.*

The decompression algorithm corresponding to Algorithm 17.7 undoes Algorithm 17.4; i.e. given a compressed string as input, Algorithm 17.7 returns a string identical to the original uncompressed string. Note that the dictionary was thrown out after the compression algorithm. The decompression will rebuild it.

Algorithm 17.7 (WKdm decompression) *Let z be the output from Algorithm 17.4. We wish to decompress it. Let D be a table (data structure) that will be used for the dictionary (as in Definition 17.2). We assume that it has 16 entries in it so that four bits are needed for a dictionary index.*

Initialize i *to* 1.

Until we have read all the compressed input, do the following:Read 2 bits (which is the 2-bit tag for the ith word of the original uncompressed string) There are four possibilities for that tag:

(a) new word case*: If the tag corresponds to Case (a) from Definition 17.2 (the "new word" case), then do the following:*

   (i) *Read the next 32-bits from the input. This is the string w_i.*

   (ii) *Add w_1 to the dictionary.*

   (iii) *Write w_i to the uncompressed output.*

   (iv) *Increment* i.

(b) exact match case*: If the tag corresponds to the exact match case, then do the following:*

   (i) *Leave the dictionary as it is.*

   (ii) *Read the next four bits of the input, which corresponds to the dictionary index containing the match for w_i.*

   (iii) *Read the 32 bits from that dictionary entry. Write that string to the uncompressed output.*

   (iv) *Increment* i.

(c) partial match case*: If the tag corresponds to the partial match case, then do the following:*

  (i) *Leave the dictionary alone.*

  (ii) *Read the next four bits of the input, which corresponds to the dictionary index containing the match for w_i.*

  (iii) *Read the 22 bits from that dictionary entry. They represent u_i. Write that string to the uncompressed output.*

  (iv) *Read the next 10 bits from the compressed input. They represent l_i. Write then to the uncompressed output.*

  (v) *Increment* i.

(d) zero word case*: If the tag corresponds to the zero word case, then do the following:*

  (i) *Leave the dictionary alone.*

  (ii) *Write the zero word to the uncompressed output.*

  (iii) *Increment* i.

In the next example, we decompress the output from Example 17.5.

Example 17.8 *Let $z = 01w_1 1100000001 w_4 100000l_5$ be the string obtained from Example 17.5. We wish to decompress it.*

  (i) *Read the first two bits 01 of z. Since that corresponds to Case (a) of Algorithm 17.7, we read the next 32 bits of z. They are w_1. We add them to the dictionary at index 0000 and we add them to the uncompressed output.*

  (ii) *The next two bits of z are 11, which corresponds to Case (b). Therefore, we read the next four bits 0000 of z, which give us the dictionary index of w_2. We read the word at index 0000 in the dictionary, and write that to the uncompressed output; i.e. w_2, which is a copy of w_1, is written to the uncompressed output.*

  (iii) *The next two bits of z are 00. Therefore, we are in Case (d). The dictionary remains the same. The only addition to the compressed output is the zero word.*

(iv) *The next two bits of z are 01. Therefore, we are in Case (a). Therefore, we read the next 32 bits of z. That gives us the string w_4. We add w_4 to the dictionary at index 0001. We write w_4 to the uncompressed output.*

(v) *The next two bits of z are 10. We are in Case (c). We leave the dictionary alone. We read four more bits 0000 from z. The word in that dictionary entry corresponds to w_1. But, as we are in Case c, we are only interested in the upper 22 bits of that word. Thus, $u_5 = u_1$, which we get by reading the upper 22 bits from the dictionary at index 0000. We write these 22 bits to the uncompressed output. Finally, we read the next 10 bits from the compressed input. They give us l_5, which we write to the uncompressed output.*

After those steps are complete, the uncompressed output contains the string $w_1 w_2 w_3 w_4 w_5$, as required.

Notice that there was no need to save the dictionary from WKdm compression, as it was rebuilt during WKdm decompression.

17.6   Main Memory – to Compress or Not to Compress

In Sections 11.5, 17.4 and 17.5, we talked about compression algorithms. The WKdm algorithm and Ziv-Lempel gives us ways to compress some of the information that is being stored in main memory. But, some extremely important questions about memory management remain. The following questions are all related.

Question 17.9   *If you want to add something to main memory, should it be put in the compressed cache or the uncompressed cache?*

Question 17.10   *If you want to remove something from main memory in order to make room for something else, should you remove item(s) from the compressed cache or should you remove item(s) from the uncompressed cache?*

Question 17.11   *What are the optimal relative sizes of the compressed cache and the regular uncompressed cache in main memory?*

R. S. de Castro et al., [dCdLS03], provides very nice answers to these questions. We should note at this point that Figure 17.3 is misleading, as it gives one the impression that the compressed pages are all in one contiguous region of main memory. This need not be the case. The figure is merely designed to show that part of main memory is a compressed cache, and part if it contains normal, uncompressed information. It should also be noted that the algorithms for this problem work best if they dynamically ("on the fly") determine the relative sizes of the compressed and uncompressed caches, rather than to decide the relative sizes ahead of time.

We now sketch the algorithm used by de Castro et al. in [dCdLS03]. Some preliminary definitions are needed.

Definition 17.12

(a) In a compressed cache, a *cell* is a contiguous region in memory that can be allocated to store one or more compressed pages. All cells have the same size, which must be a constant multiple (often 1, 2, or 4) of the size of an uncompressed page.

(b) The *final free space* of a cell is the contiguous region at the end of a cell that does not currently hold any information. (See Figure 17.6.)

(c) The *free space* of a cell consists of the region(s) of the cell that do not currently hold any information.

(d) The collection of all cells at any instant in time is the *compressed cache*. The remainder of main memory is the *uncompressed cache*.

(e) To *compact* a cell, we shift its contents to the beginning of the cell so that the final free space and the free space of the cell are the same. (i.e. we "defragment" the cell.)

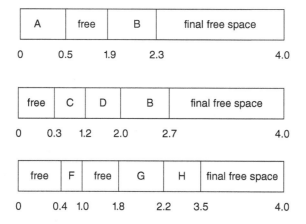

Figure 17.6: Cells 1 (top), 2 (middle), and 3 (bottom) in the compressed cache.

Algorithm 17.13 *Suppose that we wish to add a compressed page to the compressed cache.*

(i) If there is at least one cell that has enough final free space to store that compressed page, then of all of the cells with enough final free space, choose one with the smallest final free space, and store it there starting at the beginning of the final free space.

(ii) If there is no cell with enough final free space to store the compressed page, then we next check to see if there is a cell with enough (total) free space to hold the compressed page. If there is such a cell, pick one, compact it, and store the compressed page at the start of the final free space in the cell.

Additional rules:

(iii) The amount of memory allocated for the compressed cache can only be increased if a page cannot be added via the above rules (i) or (ii), and some page in the compressed cache would have to be removed from it in order to add an additional compressed page.

(iv) If all of the compressed pages of a cell have been released, the region occupied by that cell becomes part of the uncompressed cache. (It might or might not be allocated to some other cell in the future.)

There are some additional rules. First, we introduce two more definitions.

Definition 17.14 A page currently in the compressed cache is a *profit page* if it is in main memory BECAUSE compressed caching is used. It is an *expense page* if it would have been in main memory if compressed caching was NOT used.

Ideally, we will have a lot of profit pages and very few expense pages. So, there are additional rules to Algorithm 17.13 to reflect this.

Algorithm 17.15

(v) If two consecutive pages are read from the expense list, put a temporary freeze on the growth of the compressed cache.

(vi) If a third consecutive page is read from the expense list, try to shrink the compressed cache by first relocating enough compressed pages from one cell to other cells so that it can be freed. If that is not possible, then free the oldest compressed page from

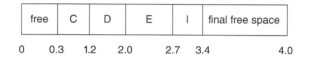

Figure 17.7: Cell 2 after adding a compressed page I of size 0.7.

the compressed cache. After this, remove the freeze on the growth of the compressed cache.

Example 17.16 *Suppose that Cells 1, 2, 3 shown in Figure 17.6 form the compressed cache in main memory at some instant in time, T. The compressed pages $A, B, \ldots, H$ are in the compressed cache at time T. (Note that some pages were added and deleted prior to time T.) Suppose that at time T, we wish to add in compressed page I of size 0.7. It would fit in the final free space of the first two cells, but not in the third cell. Therefore, it must go in either Cell 1 or 2. As Cell 2 has the smaller amount of final free space of those two cells, it goes in Cell 2 at the start of the final free space. After the insertion, Cell 2 is shown in Figure 17.7.*

17.7 Problems

17.1 Construct the LZ tree for the sequence

$$y\,x\,x\,y\,y\,x\,y\,y\,x\,x\,x\,y\,y\,x\,y\,x\,y\,y\,x$$

[See Solution 17.1.]

In Problems 17.2 and 17.3, we use the notation that $a^i = \overbrace{aa \cdots a}^{i}$, if $i > 0$, and a^0 is the string of length 0, where a is a letter of the alphabet.

17.2 Consider Algorithm 17.4, for WKdm compression. Consider the string $s = w_1 w_2 w_3 w_4 w_5 w_6 w_7$ where $w_1 = 0^{16}10^{14}1$, $w_2 = 0^{16}10^{13}11$, w_3 is the zero word, $w_4 = 0^{14}110^{13}110$, $w_5 = 0^{16}10^{14}1$, $w_6 = 0^{14}110^{12}1000$, and w_7 is the zero word. Assume that the dictionary holds 16 32-bit words.

(a) Compress the string $w_1 w_2 w_3 w_4 w_5 w_6 w_7$.

(b) How many bits is the original string s?

(c) How many bits is the compressed version of s?

[See Solution 17.2.]

17.3 (a) Decompress the compressed string $z = 010^{15}1^20^{15}1^20^510^51^20^{25}10^51^50^51^20^31$ using the WKdm decompression algorithm given in Algorithm 17.7 to give the original uncompressed string, which consisted of the concatenation of one or more 32-bit words.

(b) How many bits were there in the compressed input? How many bits were there in the uncompressed output?

[See Solution 17.3.]

17.4 Would it help to save the dictionary at the end of Algorithm 17.4 and then use that dictionary later when decompressing via Algorithm 17.7? [See Solution 17.4.]

17.5 Suppose that we have a compressed cache that consists of three cells, $1, 2, 3$ as shown in Figure 17.8. (In the third cell of the figure, "ffs" refers to the final free space.) We wish to add in a compressed page K of size 0.6 into the compressed cache. Redraw the cell that changes to show it after K is added to the compressed cache. [See Solution 17.5.]

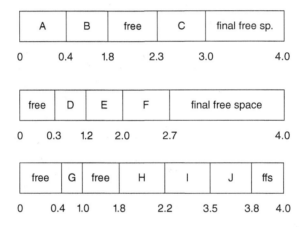

Figure 17.8: Cells 1 (top), 2 (middle), and 3 (bottom) for Problem 17.5.

17.8   Solutions

17.1 Here is the LZ tree:

y	x	$x\,y$	$y\,x$	$y\,y$	$x\,x$	$x\,y\,y$	$x\,y\,x$	$y\,y\,x$
1	2	3	4	5	6	7	8	9
$0y$	$0x$	$2y$	$1x$	$1y$	$2x$	$3y$	$3x$	$5x$

17.2 (a) We follow Algorithm 17.4. The word w_1 is the first word, so this is Case (a) (new word) of the algorithm. Insert w_1 into the dictionary at index 0000. Write the tag 01 to the compressed output. Also write the entire word w_1 to the compressed output.

Next, we consider w_2, which is a partial match to w_1 in the dictionary. We are in case (c), so the dictionary is not modified, the tag 10 is written to the compressed output, the index 0000 of w_1 in the dictionary is written to the compressed output, and the low order 10 bits 0^811 of w_2 are written to the compressed output.

Next is w_3, which is the zero word as in case (d). So we leave the dictionary alone and write the 00 tag to the compressed output.

The upper 22 bits of w_4 are different from that of the only dictionary entry, w_1, so w_4 is a new word, case (a). Therefore, w_4 is inserted into the dictionary at index 0001, the tag 01 is written to the compressed output, and the entire word w_4 is written to the compressed output.

The word w_5 is an exact match to w_1, and we are in case (b). The dictionary is left alone, the tag 11 is written to the compressed output as is the 4-bit index 0000 of w_1 in the dictionary.

The word w_6 agrees with w_4 in the upper 22 bits, but the low-order 10 bits are different. So, we have a partial match as in case (c). We leave the dictionary alone, write the tag 10 to the compressed output, write the 4-bit index 0001 of w_4 in the dictionary to the compressed output, along with the low order 10 bits $l_6 = 0^610^3$.

Next is w_7, which is the zero word as in case (d). So we leave the dictionary alone and write the 00 tag to the compressed output.

Summarizing,

$$01w_1100^40^8110001w_41100001000011l_600$$

$$= 010^{16}10^{14}1100^40^81100010^{14}110^{13}1101100001000010^610^300$$

$$= 010^{16}10^{14}1^20^{13}1^20^310^{14}1^20^{13}1^201^20^410^410^610^5$$

is the compressed output.

(b) The string s contains seven 32-bit words, and $(7)(32) = 224$ bits.

(c) w_1 contributes 34 bits (2 from the tag, and 32 from w_1) to the compressed output. w_2 contributes 16 bits (2 from the tag, 4 from the dictionary index, and 10 from the ten low-order bits). w_3 contributes 2 bits (from the tag). w_4

contributes 34 bits (2 from the tag, 32 from w_4). w_5 contributes 6 bits (2 from the tag, 4 from the dictionary index). w_6 contributes 16 bits (2 from the tag, 4 from the dictionary index, and 10 from the ten low-order bits. w_7 contributes 2 bits (from the tag). Adding these up gives 110 bits.

17.3 (a) We are given the compressed string $z = 010^{15}1^20^{15}1^20^510^51^20^{25}10^51^50^51^20^31$. To uncompress it, we use Algorithm 17.7. We will represent the uncompressed output by $w_1w_2\ldots$. (At the start, we do not know how many 32-bit words w_i there will be in the output.) We begin with an empty dictionary.

The first two bits of z are 01, which is the tag for the first word. That corresponds to case (a) of Algorithm 17.7. Therefore, the next 32 bits represent the first uncompressed word, i.e. $w_1 = 0^{15}110^{15}$. We add w_1 to the dictionary and we write w_1 to the uncompressed output.

We read the next 2 bits from z. They are 11, which corresponds to case (b) (exact match). We read the next four bits from z, which gives us the dictionary index for the match. Looking up the entry at index 0000, we find w_1 is there, so w_2 is identical to w_1 and we write that string to the uncompressed output.

We read the next 2 bits from z, which are 01. This corresponds to case (a), the new word case. So, the next 32 bits from z give us w_3. We add $w_3 = 0^5110^{25}$ to the dictionary at index 0001 and write w_3 to the uncompressed output.

We read the next 2 bits from z, which are 10, corresponding to case (c), the partial match case. Therefore, we read the next four bits from z, 0000, which is the dictionary index for w_1. We use the upper 22 bits $0^{15}1^20^5$ from w_1 (retrieved from the dictionary) for part of w_4. For the low-order 10 bits of w_4, we get those from the next 10 bits 1^50^5 of z. This gives $w_4 = 0^{15}1^20^51^50^5$.

We read the next 2 bits of z, which are 11 corresponding to the exact match case, case (b). We read the next four bits 0001 from the compressed output, and find w_3 in the dictionary at that location. Therefore, w_5 is identical to w_3, and we write that string to the compressed output.

So, the total uncompressed output is

$$w_1w_2w_3w_4w_5 = 0^{15}110^{30}110^{20}110^{40}1^20^51^50^{10}110^{25}.$$

(b) The compressed input has $|z| = 96$ bits. The uncompressed output $w_1w_2w_3$ w_4w_5 has five words of 32 bits each, or $(5)(32) = 160$ bits.

17.4 No. In fact, you **cannot** reuse the dictionary. You **must** start with an empty dictionary when you use the compression algorithm. You **must also** start with an empty dictionary when you use the decompression algorithm. So, do not save a dictionary from compression algorithm. The decompression algorithm will rebuild the dictionary in the same way as the compression algorithm did. If you start with a previous dictionary with entries in it, the words will not end up in the correct location in the dictionary for exact matches and partial matches.

17.5 The first two cells have enough final free space to hold K but the third cell does not, so we must choose either the first or second cell. Of the first and second cells, the first one has less final free space, so that cell is chosen. Figure 17.9 shows the first cell after K has been added.

Figure 17.9: Cell 1 for Solution 17.5.

Part III

Mainly Error-Correction

Chapter 18

Error-Correction, Hadamard, and Bruen–Ott

18.1 General Ideas of Error Correction

Error-correcting and error-detecting codes have their origins in the pioneering work of Hamming and Golay around 1950. The general theory is closely connected to topics in combinatorics and statistics such as block designs, which are also discussed here. On the other hand, we are able to introduce linear codes by the "back door" in order to get an improvement on the (combinatorial) Gilbert–Varshamov bound.

Nowadays, the theory is applied in all situations involving communication channels. The channel might involve a telephone conversation, an encrypted text message, an Internet transaction, and a deep space satellite transmission.

The basic idea is to introduce redundancy – "good redundancy" – with a message in order to improve reliability, and has been discussed in Chapter 12. We review some basic ideas and give several examples here. We also develop some classical bounds on the size of codes.

On the practical side, one of the main problems in coding theory is ton construct codes getting close to the Shannon capacity bound of Chapter 12.

On the theoretical side, the "main" coding theory problem is discussed in Section 18.9.

Cryptography, Information Theory, and Error-Correction: A Handbook for the 21st Century, Second Edition.
Aiden A. Bruen, Mario A. Forcinito, and James M. McQuillan.
© 2021 John Wiley & Sons, Inc. Published 2021 by John Wiley & Sons, Inc.

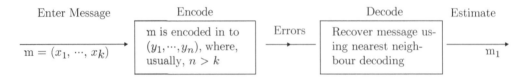

Figure 18.1: Error correction.

The general idea is illustrated in Figure 18.1. As pointed out in Chapter 12, an important special case occurs when

$$(y_1, \cdots, y_n) = (x_1, \ldots, x_k, y_{k+1}, \ldots, y_n) \qquad (18.1)$$

where the message is simply lengthened by adjoining various parity checks $y_{k+1}, \ldots, y_n$ which are linear combinations of the message digits $x_1, \ldots, x_k$. This is the case when we use "systematic linear codes" which are covered in Chapter 20. But there do exist other important examples, some of which are discussed here.

Also, Figure 18.1 mainly illustrates the situation for **error correction**. With **error-detection**, the receiver can tell if there has been a transmission error (or errors) but may not be able to correct the errors. Usually, however the receiver can ask for a re-send. This is the case for example **with TCP and CRC protocols** on the Internet.

18.2   Error Detection, Error Correction

Let us give some examples. (See Hill [Hil86]).

The International Standard Book Number (ISBN)   This is a 10-digit codeword assigned by the publisher. For instance, an ISBN might look like this: ISBN 0-471-12832-8. The first digit refers to the language (0 stands for English) the next three to the publisher, the next five refer to a sequence supplied by the publisher, and the last digit is a check digit. In reality, the position of the hyphens is unimportant (there is some variation in conventions on this matter).

The **check digit** x_{10} is chosen so that the **weighted check sum** of the 10 digits gives a remainder of 0 upon division by 11. In symbols, we have

$$Rem[1x_1 + 2x_2 + \cdots + 9x_9 + 10x_{10}, 11] = 0 \qquad (18.2)$$

In other words, $x_1 + 2x_2 + 3x_2 + \cdots + 9x_9 + 10x_{10} \equiv 0 \pmod{11}$. Since 10 equals -1 modulo 11, we get $x_{10} = x_1 + 2x_2 + 3x_3 + \cdots + 9x_9 = x_{10} \pmod{11}$ giving us the complete ISBN number.

We claim that the ISBN code detects any single error. For if x_j gets changed to $x_j + a$ we must have, from Eq. (18.2) that $Rem[ja, 11] = 0$. Thus 11 divides ja which is impossible since 11 is a prime and j, a are integers lying between 1 and 10 (see Chapter 19).

Generally speaking, with modern technology, multiple errors are rare: one is fairly certain that at most one error has occurred. Still it is important to explore the general theory.

18.3   A Formula for Correction and Detection

We recall from Chapter 12 that the Hamming distance between two code words in a code C of length n over any alphabet is defined to be the number of positions in which they differ. The **minimum distance** d of C is defined to be the minimum distance between any two codewords in C. We have the following two results.

Theorem 18.1 (Error detection result)   *A code C can detect up to $d - 1$ errors.*

To see this, let the codeword $\mathbf{u}$ be transmitted. Assume the received vector $\mathbf{u}_1$ differs from $\mathbf{u}$ is at most $d - 1$ positions. Since the minimum distance between any two words of C is at least d, it follows that $\mathbf{u}_1$ is *not* a codeword so the receiver can detect that an error or errors have occurred, upon receipt of $\mathbf{u}_1$.

For a positive integer e, we say that the code is **e-error correcting** or **corrects e errors** if given any string or vector $\mathbf{v}$ of the given length n there is at most one codeword $\mathbf{c}$ such that $d(\mathbf{v}, \mathbf{c}) \le e$, where d denotes the Hamming distance (between $\mathbf{v}$ and $\mathbf{c}$).

We have also the following result.

Theorem 18.2 (Error-correction result)   *A code C with minimum distance d is e-error correcting if and only if $d \ge 2e + 1$.*

Proof. Suppose that $d \ge 2e + 1$. If a vector $\mathbf{w}$ lies at a distance e or less from two different codewords $\mathbf{c}_1, \mathbf{c}_2$ then

$$d(\mathbf{c}_1, \mathbf{c}_2) \le d(\mathbf{c}_1, \mathbf{w}) + d(\mathbf{w}, \mathbf{c}_2) \le e + e = 2e \qquad (18.3)$$

which contradicts the assumption that the minimum distance of the code is $d \ge 2e + 1$.

On the other hand, suppose $d \le 2e$ and let $\mathbf{c}_1, \mathbf{c}_2$ be codewords at distance d. Put $t = \frac{d}{2}$ if d is even and $t = \frac{d-1}{2}$ if d is odd. Then, $t \le e$ and $d - t \le e$. We can get from $\mathbf{c}_1$ to $\mathbf{c}_2$ by successively changing coordinates one at a time. Let $\mathbf{v}$ be the vector "in the middle." So $\mathbf{v}$ is the vector obtained from $\mathbf{c}_1$ after the first t changes. Then, $d(\mathbf{c}_1, \mathbf{v}) = t$

with $t \le e$ and $d(\mathbf{c}_2, \mathbf{v}) = d - t \le e$. Then there are 2 codewords $\mathbf{c}_1$, $\mathbf{c}_2$ at distance at most e from $\mathbf{v}$. Therefore, C is *not* e-error correcting. ∎

Explanation   *If a code is e-error correcting, it follows that, if at most e transmission errors occur, correct decoding is assured.*

18.4   Hadamard Matrices

Let A be a square matrix of size $n \times n$ in which every entry of A is either 1 or -1. Assume that the dot product of any two distinct rows of A is zero. Then, A is called a **Hadamard matrix**.

Example 18.3 $A = \begin{pmatrix} 1 & 1 \\ 1 & -1 \end{pmatrix}$ *is a 2×2 Hadamard matrix.*

These matrices are at the heart of many mathematical and scientific questions pertaining to cryptography, error correction, statistics, algebra, and geometry.

Let us start with some geometry.

Theorem 18.4 (Hadamard's theorem)   *Let $A = (a_{ij})$ be an $n \times n$ real matrix with $-1 \le a_{ij} \le 1$. Then, denoting the determinant of A by $\det(A)$, we get $|\det(A)| \le n^{\frac{n}{2}}$ where $|\det(A)|$ is the absolute value of $\det(A)$. Equality occurs precisely when A is a Hadamard matrix of size $n \times n$.*

Outline of Proof. We have that $|\det(A)|$ is the volume of the box in Euclidean n-space whose sides are the rows of A. Since $-1 \le a_{ij} \le 1$, the length of the i-th row is at most

$$(a_{i1}^2 + \cdots + a_{in}^2)^{\frac{1}{2}} \le \sqrt{n} \tag{18.4}$$

Then the volume of the box is at most the product of the row lengths with equality exactly when any 2 rows are orthogonal. Then, $|\det(A)| \le (\sqrt{n})^n = n^{\frac{n}{2}}$. Equality occurs if and only if $a_{ij} = \pm 1$ (so the length of each row is $\sqrt{n}$) and any two rows are orthogonal.

For other geometrical characterizations of Hadamard matrices, we refer to [AB76].

What about the existence of Hadamard matrices?

Theorem 18.5 (Existence criterion)   *If A is an $n \times n$ Hadamard matrix, then either $n = 1$ or $n = 2$ or 4 divides n.*

Outline of Proof. Since the dot product of any 2 distinct rows is zero it follows that the number of positions where they agree equals the number of positions where they disagree. Thus, n is even.

If we change the sign of any column, we still have a Hadamard matrix, since the dot product of any 2 rows will still be zero. So we can assume that the first row has all 1s.

Let $n \geq 3$. Let a, b, c, d be the number of columns in which the second and third rows have entries $(+1, +1)$, $(+1, -1)$, $(-1, +1)$, and $(-1, -1)$, respectively. Taking dot products of the 3 rows in pairs, namely $\mathbf{R}_1 \cdot \mathbf{R}_2$, $\mathbf{R}_1 \cdot \mathbf{R}_3$, $\mathbf{R}_2 \cdot \mathbf{R}_3$:

$$
\begin{aligned}
a + b &= c + d = \tfrac{n}{2}, \\
a + c &= b + d = \tfrac{n}{2}, \\
a + d &= c + c = \tfrac{n}{2}
\end{aligned}
\tag{18.5}
$$

Solving we get $a = b = c = d = \tfrac{n}{4}$. So 4 divides n.

A converse would say that if 4 divides n there exists an $n \times n$ Hadamard matrix. This is a famous unsolved problem!

We now turn to constructions. If $A = (a_{ij})$ and B are Hadamard matrices, not necessarily of the same size, then their **tensor product** in block form, namely,

$$
A \otimes B = \begin{pmatrix}
a_{11}B & a_{12}B & \cdots & a_{1n}B \\
a_{21}B & a_{22}B & \cdots & a_{2n}B \\
\cdots & \cdots & \cdots & \cdots
\end{pmatrix}
\tag{18.6}
$$

is a Hadamard matrix.

Example 18.6 *Let* $A = H_2 = \begin{pmatrix} 1 & 1 \\ 1 & -1 \end{pmatrix}$, *and* $B = \begin{pmatrix} 1 & -1 \\ 1 & 1 \end{pmatrix}$. *Then*

$$
A \otimes B = \begin{pmatrix} B & B \\ B & -B \end{pmatrix} = \begin{pmatrix}
1 & -1 & 1 & -1 \\
1 & 1 & 1 & 1 \\
1 & -1 & -1 & 1 \\
1 & 1 & -1 & -1
\end{pmatrix}
\tag{18.7}
$$

Thus, we have from this construction that there exists a Hadamard matrix of size $n \times n$ if $n = 2^m$.

But we would like more possibilities. Although Hadamard matrices are firmly grounded in Euclidean geometry (from Hadamard's theorem above), the next construction involves the more exotic world of finite fields, as follows.

Let F be any finite field of odd order. Thus $|F| = q = p^m$ with p any odd prime. For x in F, the **quadratic character** or **Legendre symbol**, denoted by χ, is defined as follows.

$\chi(x) = 0$ if $x = 0$,

$\chi(x) = 1$ if x is a nonzero square,

$\chi(x) = -1$ if x is a non-square.

Example 18.7 *Let $F = GF(5)$ be the field of order 5. The elements of F are 0, 1, 2, 3, 4. The nonzero squares in F are $1^2 = 1$, $2^2 = 4$, $3^2 = 4$, $4^2 = 1$. Thus, we have $\chi(0) = 0$, $\chi(1) = \chi(4) = 1$ and $\chi(2) = \chi(3) = -1$, since 2 and 3 are non-squares.*

The **Jacobstahl matrix** $R = (r_{ij})$ is a square matrix of size $q \times q$ which is defined by $R = (r_{ij}) = \chi(j - i)$.

Example 18.8 *Let $F = GF(7)$. The elements of F are 0, 1, 2, 3, 4, 5, 6. Index the rows and columns by these elements. Then*

$$R = \begin{pmatrix} 0 & 1 & 1 & -1 & 1 & -1 & -1 \\ -1 & 0 & 1 & 1 & -1 & 1 & -1 \\ -1 & -1 & 0 & 1 & 1 & -1 & 1 \\ 1 & -1 & -1 & 0 & 1 & 1 & -1 \\ -1 & 1 & -1 & -1 & 0 & 1 & 1 \\ 1 & -1 & 1 & -1 & -1 & 0 & 1 \\ 1 & 1 & -1 & 1 & -1 & -1 & 0 \end{pmatrix} \tag{18.8}$$

Here we use the fact that the nonzero squares are 1, 2, 4, and the non squares are 3, 5, 6.

Construction of Paley-type Hadamard matrices Let q be a prime power with $Rem[q, 4] = 3$, i.e. with $q \bmod 4 = 3$. Let R denote the Jacobstahl matrix of size $q \times q$ and let I be the $q \times q$ identity matrix. Let H be the $(q + 1) \times (q + 1)$ matrix that is obtained by bordering the matrix $R - I$ with a column of ones. Then H is a Hadamard matrix which is said to be of **Paley type**.

Example 18.9 *Let $q = 7$. Then*

$$H = \begin{pmatrix} & 1 & \cdots & 1 \\ 1 & & & \\ 1 & & & \\ \vdots & & (R - I) & \\ 1 & & & \end{pmatrix} \tag{18.9}$$

where R is the Jacobstahl matrix obtained previously.

By replacing -1 by 0 in R we get a $(0,1)$ matrix A which is the *incidence matrix* for a special kind of design called a **Hadamard block design**. This design is "symmetric" since the number of points and blocks is q, as explained below.

18.5   Mariner, Hadamard, and Reed–Muller

Imagine a space probe speeding toward a distant planet and transmitting its pictures to far away Earth at the speed of light. An example to work with is Mariner 69. There, each picture was divided into horizontal scans with each scan line being divided into pixels represented by one of 63 possible gray levels with white corresponding to 0, black to 63 and in-between values of gray being indicated by values between 1 and 62.

Each shade of gray sends a message as a binary string of length 6 with black corresponding to (111111) and white to (000000). However, because of the vast distances, errors will corrupt the transmission so error-correction must be performed.

For this purpose, we seek a code C consisting of 64 code-words of reasonably small length such that the Hamming distance between any two words is big.

This was achieved for transmission by the Mariner spacecraft in 1969. The construction of C was as follows. We take any Hadamard matrix H of size 32. Next, define B to be the $2n \times n = 64 \times 32$ matrix as follows

$$B = \begin{pmatrix} H \\ -H \end{pmatrix} \qquad (18.10)$$

Define C to be the matrix obtained from R by replacing -1 by 0. We then have the following, using the fact that H is Hadamard.

If $\mathbf{u}$, $\mathbf{v}$ *are codewords in* C, *then* $d(\mathbf{u}, \mathbf{v}) \geq 16$.

We can now encode each of the gray-code messages. Each message is encoded into the corresponding row of C. For example, shade of gray number 15 (our messages are 0, 1, ..., 63) gets encoded as Row 15 of C. Then, from the error correction result above the following holds. If no more than 7 bit errors are made, the message is decoded correctly. This represents a significant reliability increase over the unencoded transmission. We refer the reader for discussion of the *coding gain*, to Chapter 13.

In general, we have the following result.

Theorem 18.10 (Hadamard code result) *Every Hadamard matrix H of order n gives rise to a binary code of length n with $2n$ codewords and minimum distance $d = \frac{n}{2}$.*

18.6   Reed–Muller Codes

These codes were discovered around 1954. First we need the following result.

Theorem 18.11 (Combining codes)   Let C_1, C_2 be two binary codes of length n with M_1, M_2 codewords and minimum distance d_1, d_2, respectively. Then we can define a third code C_3 of length $2n$, denoted by $C_3 = C_1 \otimes C_2$, with $M_1 M_2$ codewords altogether and minimum distance $d_3 = \min(2d_1, d_2)$.

Proof. (See Welsh [Wel88].) Define

$$C_3 = \{(\mathbf{c}_1, \mathbf{c}_1 + \mathbf{c}_2) \mid \mathbf{c}_1 \text{ in } C_1, \ \mathbf{c}_2 \text{ in } C_2\} \tag{18.11}$$

We can now recursively define the binary m-**th order Reed-Muller code** $C(m, n)$ with $0 \leq m \leq n$ as follows.

$C(m, n)$ has length 2^n.

$C(0, n)$ is $\{(0, \ldots, 0), (1, \ldots, 1)\}$.

$C(n, n)$ is the set of all vectors of length 2^n and

$C(m + 1, n + 1) = C(m + 1, n) \otimes C(m, n)$.

Then, recursively, we have the following codes.

$n = 1$ $C(0, 1) = \{(00), (11)\}$, $C(1, 1) = \{(00), (10), (01), (11)\}$.

$n = 2$ $C(0, 2) = \{(0000), (1111)\}$, $C(1, 2) = C(1, 1) \otimes C(0, 1)$ with codewords (0000), (0011), (1010), (1001), (0101), (0110), (1111), (1100).

We then get that $C(m, n)$ is a code of length 2^n, minimum distance 2^{n-m} and having 2^x codewords altogether, where

$$x = 1 + \binom{n}{1} + \binom{n}{2} + \cdots + \binom{n}{m} \tag{18.12}$$

∎

The connection with Hadamard codes is as follows.

Reed–Muller and Hadamard   The Reed–Muller code $C(1, n)$ is the binary code obtained by forming the m-fold tensor product of $H = \begin{pmatrix} 1 & 1 \\ 1 & -1 \end{pmatrix}$ with itself, having replaced -1 by 0.

18.7 Block Designs

A **block design** $(X, \mathcal{B})$ consists of a finite set X of v points together with a family $\mathcal{B}$ of b subsets called blocks satisfying the following conditions.

(a) Each block contains exactly k points, $k < v$,

(b) Any 2 points are contained in λ blocks, where λ is some constant.

Block designs historically arose in connection with the design of experiments in statistics, and they have been much studied because of their connection with combinatorics and coding theory. Several research journals such as "Designs, Codes and Cryptography" are devoted to these topics. We also mention the books by Assmus and Key entitled "Designs and their Codes.", [AK92], and by Lander, "Symmetric Designs: an Algebraic Approach." [Lan83].

A fundamental result in the theory is as follows.

Theorem 18.12 (Fisher's inequality) *The number of blocks is at least the number of points. In symbols, $b \geq v$.*

Block designs (i.e. "designs") with $b = v$ are called **symmetric designs** and are relatively rare.

Example 18.13 *Let R be the Jacobstahl matrix of Section 18.4. Change each -1 to 0 so we have a $(0,1)$-matrix A of size $q \times q$ with $q \equiv 3(4)$.*

Label the columns of A as $\{0, 1, 2, \ldots, q-1\} = X$. Each row of A yields a subset of X corresponding to those column positions of that row that contain one. Then the set X together with the family of subsets corresponding to the rows of A yields a symmetric design with $b = v = q$ and with $k = \frac{q-1}{2}$, and $\lambda = \frac{1}{4}(q-3)$.

This design is called a **Paley–Hadamard design**. A is called an **incidence matrix** for this design.

In axiom (b) of block designs, if we change 2 to $t \geq 2$ we have a t-**design**. As well as the symmetric designs these t-designs are very rare and have been the subject of much research. The main examples come from finite geometry. If $\lambda = 1$ then we have a **Steiner system** which comes up in connection with the Golay code (Chapter 20). The **inversive plane** over any finite field gives a 3-design which is also a Steiner system. The most-studied symmetric designs are given by the points and hyperplanes of a projective space.

Block designs play a major role in sphere packing (see Thompson and Watkins [TW83]) and coding theory. As examples, we mention the Golay codes which are intimately related to the projective plane of order 4, the Mathieu t-designs, the Leech lattice and the "Monster" in group theory. The Hamming codes are obtained very easily from the design of points and lines in projective space.

Of all the symmetric designs, those with $\lambda = 1$ are the most-studied because of their mathematical allure and the many open problems surrounding them. They are called **projective planes**. Thus, a (finite) projective plane Π is a system of points and lines, with each line having $k = n + 1$ points. The integer n is called the **order of Π**. The total number of points and lines is $n^2 + n + 1$. Any two points lie in a unique line; dually, any two lines will meet in a unique point. These planes will come up also in subsequent chapters.

Remark   Fisher's inequality has been generalized to finite linear spaces in a well-known paper of Erdös and de Bruijn. A very short elegant proof has also been supplied by J.H. Conway. The analogous result for affine planes has been shown independently by P. de Witte and A.A. Bruen. For further references, see [Bru73].

18.8   The Rank of Incidence Matrices

As discussed in MacWilliams and Sloane Chapter 13 [MST73] the Reed–Muller codes are "the simplest examples of the class of geometrical codes, which also includes Euclidean geometry and projective geometry geometrical codes …"

Such geometrical codes require knowledge of the appropriate incidence matrix including its rank. Such ranks are thoroughly studied for the classical case in Assmus and Key [AK92], and Lander [Lan83]. Here we look at the general case for planes.

Let Π denote a finite projective plane. Arbitrarily label the points as $P_1, P_2, \ldots, P_{n^2+n+1}$; label also the lines as $L_1, L_2, \ldots, L_{n^2+n+1}$. Form an incidence matrix $A = (a_{ij})$ which will be a $(0,1)$ matrix of size $(n^2 + n + 1) \times (n^2 + n + 1)$ as follows.

$a_{ij} = 1$ if L_i contains P_j;

$a_{ij} = 0$ if L_i does not contain P_j, $1 \le i, j \le n^2 + n + 1$.

These incidence matrices have been very useful in error-correction, as follows. We can form a **linear code** C by taking all linear combinations of the rows of A – over some given field F – as codewords. There are then several basic questions that can be asked such as

(a) What is the minimum distance of C?

(b) What is the dimension of C?

If the field F is $GF(p)$, for p a prime, the dimension of C is also called the p-rank of C.

There has been a lot of progress with (a). Question (b) was first posed by E.S. Lander in [Lan83]. The main result in the theory is in [BO90] as follows.

Theorem 18.14 (Bruen–Ott theorem) *Let Π be a projective plane of order n and let p be a prime divisor of n. Then, the p-rank of C is at least $n\sqrt{n}+1$.*

If p^2 does not divide n, then it can be shown that the p-rank of C is equal to $\frac{1}{2}(n^2 + n + 2)$.

18.9   The Main Coding Theory Problem, Bounds

Let C be a code with **code parameters** (n, M, d). Thus, n is the length of each codeword, $M = |C|$ denotes the number of codewords and d is the minimum distance. Desirable features of C might include a large value of M, so we can transmit several messages, a large value of d, for reliability, and a small value of n, for fast transmission. These goals are often in conflict with each other. The most common version of the main problem is then the following.

The main coding theory problem

Find the largest code of a given length and given minimum distance (i.e. maximize M) for a given alphabet size q. The maximum value of M is sometimes denoted by $A_q(n, d)$.

In general, this problem is unsolved. This is an understatement. For example, in Hill [Hil86] the author discusses the difficulty of finding $A_2(5, 3)$: it is equal to 4. The existence question for MDS codes discussed below poses an even bigger challenge.

Here is another version of the main problem.

Optimize one of the parameters n, M, d for given values of the other two.

Here we want to obtain some bounds for the construction of codes. Let C be a code of length n. Then each codeword is an n-tuple over some alphabet A of size q, say. For example, C might be linear and A might be F, a finite field of order q. We define the **ball** $B_t(\mathbf{c})$ of radius t about $\mathbf{c}$ to be the set of all strings or vectors $\mathbf{x}$ of length n over A such that $d(\mathbf{x}, \mathbf{c}) \leq t$, where d denotes Hamming distance.

Theorem 18.15 (The Ball theorem)

$$|B_t(\mathbf{c})| = \sum_{i=0}^{t} \binom{n}{i} (q-1)^i \tag{18.13}$$

Proof. Suppose we want a string $\mathbf{x}$ with $d(\mathbf{x}, \mathbf{c}) = i$. First, we choose the i positions in which $\mathbf{x}$ and $\mathbf{c}$ differ. This can be done in $\binom{n}{i}$ ways. In each of these i positions, choose a symbol from A not equal to the symbol that $\mathbf{c}$ has in that position. This can be done in $q - 1$ ways, since $|A| = q$. ∎

Using this we can find *lower bounds* on the size of certain codes.

Theorem 18.16 (The Gilbert–Varshamov bound)   *Given n, q, d, there is a code over an alphabet of size q and minimum distance at least d having at least*

$$q^n \left(\sum_{i=0}^{d-1} \binom{n}{i} (q-1)^i \right)^{-1} \tag{18.14}$$

codewords.

Proof. Start off with any string $\mathbf{c}_1$ of length n over an alphabet A with $|A| = q$. Delete all strings of length n at distance less than d from $\mathbf{c}_1$. Now include in our code any undeleted string $\mathbf{c}_2$ and repeat the process, i.e. delete all strings in the ball $B_{d-1}(\mathbf{c}_2)$. Even assuming no overlap in the balls $B_{d-1}(\mathbf{c}_1)$ and $B_{d-1}(\mathbf{c}_2)$, we are still left with

$$q^n - 2 \sum_{i=0}^{d-1} \binom{n}{i} (q-1)^i \tag{18.15}$$

eligible strings of length n outside the two balls. Proceeding inductively, we end up with M codewords of length n over A at mutual distance d such that no codeword that is distance at least d from all the M codewords already chosen. In other words, the spheres of radius $d - 1$ surrounding the M codewords contain all the vectors. Thus

$$M \geq \frac{q^n}{\sum_{i=0}^{d-1} \binom{n}{i} (q-1)^i} \tag{18.16}$$

∎

Very often it is possible to improve the Gilbert–Varshamov bound by using linear codes. These are discussed in detail in Chapter 20. Here, to simplify, we will work in binary although the proof works for any field. We say that a binary code C is **linear** if whenever $\mathbf{x}, \mathbf{y}$ are in C, then $\mathbf{x} + \mathbf{y}$ is also in C. For such codes it is easy to see that

$$d(\mathbf{x}, \mathbf{y}) = d(\mathbf{x} + \mathbf{y}, 0) = wt(\mathbf{x} + \mathbf{y})$$

where $d(-, -)$ denotes the Hamming distance and "wt" denotes the **weight** of a vector, i.e. the number of nonzero components of that vector.

Theorem 18.17 *There exists a binary linear code satisfying the bound of Theorem 18.16.*

Proof. We proceed inductively constructing linear codes $\{C_0, C_1, C_2, \ldots\}$ having $2^0, 2^1, 2^2, \ldots$ codewords, as follows.

Start off with $C_0 = \{\mathbf{0}\}$. Pick any vector $\mathbf{x}_1 \neq \mathbf{0}$ with $d(\mathbf{x}_1, \mathbf{0}) \geq d$, if possible. Now we have $C_1 = \{\mathbf{0}, \mathbf{x}_1\}$.

Suppose now that

$$|C_1| \left(\sum_{i=0}^{d-1} \binom{n}{i} \right) < 2^n$$

where $|C_1|$ is the size of C_1, which is 2. Then there exists a vector $\mathbf{x}_2$ with $d(\mathbf{x}_2, \mathbf{x}_1) \geq d$ and $d(\mathbf{x}_2, \mathbf{0}) \geq d$.

Now construct the smallest linear code C_2 containing C_1 and $\mathbf{x}_2$. This code C_2, being linear, must contain also all sums of the form $\mathbf{x} + \mathbf{c}$, $\mathbf{c}$ in C_1. Thus

$$C_2 = \{\mathbf{0}, \mathbf{x}_1, \mathbf{x}_2, \mathbf{x}_1 + \mathbf{x}_2\}$$

Now C_2 is a linear code with $|C_2| = 4$. We claim that the distance between any 2 distinct codewords in C_2 is at least d. We need only check the distances between $\mathbf{x}_1 + \mathbf{x}_2$ and the others. For vectors $\mathbf{u}, \mathbf{v}, \mathbf{w}$ of a given length N we have $d(\mathbf{u}, \mathbf{v}) = d(\mathbf{u} + \mathbf{w}, \mathbf{v} + \mathbf{w})$. But

$$d(\mathbf{x}_1 + \mathbf{x}_2, \mathbf{x}_1) = d(\mathbf{x}_1 + \mathbf{x}_2 + \mathbf{x}_1, \mathbf{x}_1 + \mathbf{x}_1) = d(\mathbf{x}_2, \mathbf{0}) \geq d$$

Also

$$d(\mathbf{x}_1 + \mathbf{x}_2, \mathbf{x}_2) = d(\mathbf{x}_1 + \mathbf{x}_2 + \mathbf{x}_2, \mathbf{x}_2 + \mathbf{x}_2) = d(\mathbf{x}_1, \mathbf{0}) \geq d$$

Furthermore,

$$d(\mathbf{x}_1 + \mathbf{x}_2, \mathbf{0}) = d(\mathbf{x}_1 + \mathbf{x}_2 + \mathbf{x}_2, \mathbf{x}_2) = d(\mathbf{x}_1, \mathbf{x}_2) \geq d$$

Now, suppose that

$$|C_1| \sum_{i=0}^{d-1} \binom{n}{i} = 4 \sum_{i=0}^{d-1} \binom{n}{i} < q^n$$

Then, as in Theorem 18.16, there exists a vector $\mathbf{x}_3$ with $d(\mathbf{x}_3, \mathbf{c}) \geq d$ for any $\mathbf{c}$ in C_2. Now we construct the smallest linear code C_2 containing $\mathbf{x}_3$ and C which will have $2^3 = 8$ codewords. Moreover, $d(\mathbf{u}, \mathbf{v}) \geq d$ for any $\mathbf{u} \neq \mathbf{v}$ in C_3.

Eventually, we end up with a binary linear code C_t, where $|C_t| = 2^t$ such that $d(\mathbf{u}, \mathbf{v}) \geq d$ for $\mathbf{u} \neq \mathbf{v}$ in C_t and such that $|C_t| \left(\sum_{i=0}^{d-1} \binom{n}{i} \right) \geq q^n$. Then, C_t is the required linear code, proving the theorem. ∎

Example   Let $n = 15, d = 3$. Then $\binom{15}{0} + \binom{15}{1} + \binom{15}{2} = 121$. Now Theorem 18.17 guarantees a code C (with the same distance property) with C linear and $|C| \geq 512$. So we get a big improvement on the bound of Theorem 18.16.

We now turn our attention to *upper bounds*.

Theorem 18.18 (The Hamming bound)   *Suppose that $d \geq 2e + 1$. A q-ary code over A, $|A| = q$, of length n and minimum distance d has at most*

$$\frac{q^n}{\sum_{i=0}^{e} \binom{n}{i} (q-1)^i} \tag{18.17}$$

codewords.

Proof.   Since $d \geq 2e + 1$, the balls of radius e about the codewords in C must be disjoint as we saw in Section 18.3. Since the total number of strings of length n over A is q^n, we must have

$$|C| \sum_{i=0}^{e} \binom{n}{i} (q-1)^i \leq q^n \tag{18.18}$$

giving the result. ∎

If equality occurs in the above we have a **perfect code**. This means that every vector lies in one of the balls of radius e about a codeword in C.

For $e = 1$, the Hamming codes are perfect. In fact they are the only examples which are linear with $e = 1$.

After much work by van Lint, Tietäväinen, Zinov'ev, and Leont'ev, we have the following result.

Theorem 18.19 *Let q be a prime power and let $e > 1$. Then the only perfect e-error-correcting codes of length n are the binary repetition codes (with $q = 2$, $n = 2e + 1$) and the binary and ternary Golay codes (with $q = 2$, $e = 3$, $n = 23$ and $q = 3$, $e = 2$, $n = 1$, respectively).*

For an interesting discussion of perfect codes in the general case we refer to the paper of O. Heden, "On perfect codes over non prime power alphabets," [Hed10]

Remark The following also holds. Let C be any perfect binary code, linear or not, of length n which is e-error correcting. Then the support of the codewords of smallest weight $2e + 1$ in C are the blocks of a t-design with $t = e + 1$, $v = n$, $k = 2e + 1$, $\lambda = 1$. Here, the support of a codeword is the set of positions where the codeword is nonzero. In this way, we get t-designs associated with the binary Golay codes and Hamming codes.

We want now to describe a fundamental upper bound in connection with the main coding theory problem.

Theorem 18.20 (The MDS bound = The Singleton bound) *Let C be a code of length n over an alphabet of size q with minimum distance d. Then $|C| \leq q^{n-d+1}$.*

Proof. We examine any set of $n - d + 1$ coordinate positions, for example, the first $n - d + 1$ positions. Two distinct words of C cannot agree in all these $n - d + 1$ positions, for otherwise they could differ in at most the remaining $d - 1$ positions, contradicting the fact that the minimum distance of C is d. Thus the number of codewords is at most the number of $(n - d + 1)$-tuples over an alphabet of size q. This number is at most $\underbrace{(q)(q)\cdots(q)}_{n-d+1}$, i.e. $|C| \leq q^{n-d+1}$. ∎

Theorem 18.21 *In 18.20 assume that $|C| = q^{n-d+1}$. Then given any set of $n - d + 1$ coordinate positions and any set of $n - d + 1$ symbols from the alphabet, there is a unique codeword in C having the given symbols in the given positions.*

Proof. This follows from the argument in the proof of Theorem 18.20. ∎

Theorem 18.22 *Let C be a code of length n over an alphabet of size q satisfying the following condition:*

Given any set of $n - d + 1$ coordinate positions and any set of $n - d + 1$ symbols from the alphabet, there is a unique codeword having the given symbols in the given position.

Then

(a) $|C| = q^{n-d+1}$.

(b) C *has minimum distance* d.

Proof. Map each codeword $\mathbf{x} = \{x_1, x_2, \ldots, x_n\}$ in C to, say, its projection on the first $n - d + 1$ positions. So $\mathbf{x}$ gets mapped to $f(x) = (x_1, x_2, \ldots, x_{n-d+1})$. The given condition implies that f is one-to-one and onto the set of $(n - d + 1)$-tuples over an alphabet of size q. Thus $|C| = q^{n-d+1}$. This proves (a).

The given condition implies that no two distinct codewords can agree in as many as $n - d + 1$ positions. So the minimum distance of C is $d^* \geq d$. If $d^* > d$, then by Theorem 18.20 we have $|C| \leq q^{n-d^*+1} < q^{n-d+1}$ which contradicts Part (a). ∎

18.10 Update on the Reed–Muller Codes: The Proof of an Old Conjecture

As pointed out in [MST73], Reed–Muller codes (RM codes) are one of the oldest and best understood families of codes. Also, they are relatively easy to decode using majority-logic circuits. RM codes are the simplest examples of the class of geometrical codes which also includes Euclidean geometry and projective geometry codes, all of which can be decoded by majority logic. RM codes were discovered around 1954 by I.S. Reed and D.E. Muller and also came to prominence with the Mariner space probe in the transmission of pictures from space.

Many properties of RM codes are best stated in the language of finite geometries. The affine geometry $AG(m, 2)$ of dimension m over $GF(2)$ contain 2^m points whose coordinates are all possible binary vectors $(v_1, \ldots, v_m)$ of length m. (In the binary case, if we omit the zero vector, the points of the projective geometry $PG(m - 1, 2)$ remain.)

Then codewords of the RM code $R(r, m)$ can be identified with subsets of $AG(m, 2)$. The codewords of minimum weight of $R(r, m)$ are well-known. They correspond exactly to the subspaces of dimension $m - r$ in $AG(m, 2)$.

In his Ph.D. thesis (D. Erickson, "Counting zeros of polynomials over finite fields," [Eri73]), the author tackled the problem of finding low-weight codewords, i.e. the next-to-minimum weight of the generalized Reed–Muller codes (GRM codes).

The problem is solved in a four-page paper in 2010 (see Bruen, "Blocking sets and low-weight codewords in the generalized Reed–Muller codes," [Bru10]).

We need some definitions. $K = GF(q)$ is the field being used. K^m is the vector space of dimension m over K. $P = P(x_1, x_2, \ldots, x_m)$ is a polynomial in m variables over K. Each polynomial P yields a mapping from K^m to K, but it may be that different polynomials P_1, P_2 yield the same mapping. This, however, cannot happen if all polynomials P are reduced such that, for each i, $1 \leq i \leq m$, there is no term x^i in P with $i \geq q$. A polynomial P can be reduced by reducing modulo $(x_1^q - x_1)(x_2^q - x_2) \cdots (x_m^q - x)$.

A polynomial P and its reduction P_1 yield the same mapping from K^m to K. Two reduced polynomials yield different mappings. Thus, the number of reduced polynomials in m variables over $GF(q)$ is equal to the number of mappings from K^m to K which is q^{q^m}.

$PG(m, q)$ denotes the set of reduced polynomials in m variables over $GF(q)$. Those polynomials in $PG(m, q)$ with degree less than or equal to R are denoted by $P_R(m, q)$.

If the elements of K^m are ordered as $\boldsymbol{\alpha_1}, \boldsymbol{\alpha_2}, \ldots, \boldsymbol{\alpha_{q^m}}$, the **value table** with respect to this ordering is defined to be the q^m-tuple $P(\boldsymbol{\alpha_1}), P(\boldsymbol{\alpha_2}), \ldots, P(\boldsymbol{\alpha_{q^m}})$. The set of value tables of polynomials in $P_R(m, q)$ is called the *Rth-order generalized Reed–Muller code of length q^m* denoted by $GRM_R(m, q)$. Note that $GRM_R(q)$ is a block code of length q^m.

In Theorem 3.1 of his thesis [Eri73], the author shows that if one knows the next-to-minimum weight of $P_R(m, q)$ for $m = 2$ one knows it for all m.

Blocking sets, $m = 2$, the main result As in the thesis [Eri73], let $R = s(q-1) + t$, $0 \leq t < q - 1$. Then, $d_R^m = (q - t)q^{m-s-1}$ is the minimum weight of $P_R(m, q)$. $d_t^2 + c_t$ denotes the next-to-minimum weight of $P_t(2, q)$.

In the thesis [Eri73], we have the following

Definition 18.23 Let Π be a finite affine plane and let S be a subset of the points of Π. Then S is called a *blocking set of order n in Π* if each line of Π contains at least n points of S and at least n points of Π that are not in S. (**Caution:** this is not the standard definition.)

If P is a polynomial in $P_t(2, q)$, we denote the *support of P*, i.e. the set of points (α_1, α_2) in K^2 at which P is nonzero, by $S(P)$. The following is Lemma 4.2 in the thesis [Eri73].

Lemma 18.24 *If $P \in P_t(2, q)$, $0 \leq t < q - 1$ such that P has no linear factors and $|P| \leq d_t^2 + (t - 1)$, then $S(P)$ is a blocking set of order $q - t$ in K^2.*

Recall that $d_t^2 + c_t$ denotes the next-to-minimum weight of $P_t(2, q)$. In [Eri73], the author makes the following conjecture (see Conjecture 4.14).

Conjecture 18.25 *Let Π be the affine plane $AG(2, q)$. If S is a blocking set of order n in Π, then S contains at least $nq + (q - n)$ points. In symbols, $|S| \geq nq + q - n$.*

Erickson points out that the validity of the conjecture would imply that $c_t = t - 1$ for $q \geq 4$. We will now see how the conjecture follows from work of the author (see [Bru92,Bru06]). If S is a blocking set of order n in $AG(2, q)$ as defined above by Erickson, [Eri73], then, in particular, it follows that each line must contain at least n points of S. A set W of points in $AG(v, q)$ satisfying the property that each hyperplane of $AG(v, q)$ intersects W in at least n points is called an *n-intersection set* in $AG(v, q)$. The following result is shown in [Bru92] and [Bru06].

Theorem 18.26 *Let W be an n-intersection set in the affine space $AG(v, q)$. Then W contains at least $(n + v - 1)(q - 1) + 1$ points.*

In particular when $v = 2$, and hyperplanes become lines, we have $|W| \geq nq + q - n$. Thus any blocking set in $AG(2, q)$ of order n contains at least $nq + q - n$ points, proving Conjecture 18.25.

The main result (Theorem 5.1 in the thesis [Eri73]) yields a complete account of the next-to-minimum weight of all GRM codes in all dimensions.

Theorem 18.27 *The next-to-minimum weight of $P_r(m, q)$ is $d_r^m + cq^{m-q+2}$ where $d_R^m = (q - t)q^{m-s-1}$ is the minimum weight, $r = s(q - 1) + t$, $0 \leq t < q - 1$ and c is as defined in [Bru10, Theorem 3.1] but with $c = t - 1$ for $q \geq 4$.*

For the lengthy statement of Theorem 3.1 of [Bru10], we refer to that 4 page paper.

Historical background   In his thesis in 1974, Erickson thanks the late Professor Marshall Hall for alerting him to a paper of Bruen (see [Bru71a]). In the thesis, he expresses great pessimism on establishing the conjecture even for the case $n = 1$.

Around this time, Dr. Leonard Baumert kindly forwarded Bruen a copy of the thesis. He briefly read over it and put it on a shelf where it lay for the next 36 years.

Then in 2010, Bruen looked again and noticed that a special case of one of his results in a 1992 paper proved the conjecture.

Such are the ways of mathematical research!

18.11   Problems

18.1   Let Π be a projective plane of order 2. Let A be any incidence matrix for Π. Regard A as a binary vector space. What is the dimension of A? (See Solution 18.1.)

18.2   Show that there exists a binary code C of length 7 containing at least 5 words such that the minimum distance between any 2 distinct words in C is at least 3. (See Solution 18.2.)

18.3 Show that the bound in Problem 18.2 can be improved to give $|C| \geq 8$. (See Solution 18.3.)

18.4 Does there exist a binary code C of length 7 with $|C| = 16$ such that any 2 distinct codewords in C are separated by a Hamming distance of 3 or more? (See Solution 18.4.)

18.5 Does there exist a binary code C of length 7 with $|C| \geq 17$ such that the distance between any 2 distinct codewords in C is at least 3? (See Solution 18.5.)

18.12 Solutions

18.1 The rank is 4. In general for a projective plane of order n with incidence matrix M, let the prime p divide n but assume that p^2 does not divide n. Then over the field $GF(p)$, the rank of M is $\frac{1}{2}(n^2 + n + 2)$. When p is 2 and n is 2, we get 4. See Bruen and Ott [BO90, p. 39].

   (We can use Theorem 18.14 to get that the rank $\geq 2\sqrt{2} + 1 = 3.8$. Since the rank is an integer the rank is at least 4.)

18.2 We have $\binom{7}{0} + \binom{7}{1} + \binom{7}{2} = 29$. Then by using the argument in Theorem 18.16 we have a code C with at least $\frac{2^7}{29} = 4.4$ codewords, so $|C| \geq 5$ since $|C|$ is an integer.

18.3 Use the argument in Theorem 18.17 to get a linear code C with $|C| \geq 2^3 = 8$.

18.4 Yes. We can use the code in Problem 18.1. This is also a Hamming code as discussed in Chapter 20.

18.5 No, since the Hamming upper bound is violated: we have $d \geq 2(1) + 1$. So pick $e = 1$. If such a code C exists, then $(17)[\binom{7}{0} + \binom{7}{1}] \leq 2^7$, i.e. $144 \leq 128$, which is impossible. Note that $16[\binom{7}{0} + \binom{7}{1}] = 2^7$ and indeed there does not exist a code C of length 7 with $|C| = 16$. As in Problem 18.4, C also has the property that the distance between any two distinct codewords is at least 3.

Chapter 19

Finite Fields, Modular Arithmetic, Linear Algebra, and Number Theory

Goals, Discussion

We present a rigorous treatment of modular arithmetic. This leads into linear algebra, which is important for its applicability to coding, especially the class of linear codes.

We also prove several results that have been deferred from earlier chapters. In particular, we prove the correctness of the Rivest, Shamir, Adleman (RSA) algorithm, and demonstrate that our more efficient choice of d is a valid one. The Euclidean algorithm is discussed, and we point out how it can be used to find multiplicative inverses modulo N.

The chapter exhibits a construction procedure for finite fields. We also discuss polynomials in terms of this construction procedure, and then mention a few results regarding polynomials that are of use in other contexts. This chapter also has a discussion on complexity issues and a factoring algorithm is described. For additional information on these topics, we refer to Chapter 29.

Cryptography, Information Theory, and Error-Correction: A Handbook for the 21st Century, Second Edition.
Aiden A. Bruen, Mario A. Forcinito, and James M. McQuillan.
© 2021 John Wiley & Sons, Inc. Published 2021 by John Wiley & Sons, Inc.

19.1   Modular Arithmetic

We use the **integers** Z and the **nonnegative integers** or **natural numbers** N consisting of $\{0, 1, 2, \ldots\}$. A positive integer divisible only by itself and 1 is called a **prime**. (1 is not considered prime.) So 19 is a prime number, but $10 = 2 \times 5$ is not a prime.

A useful fact is the following. If two integers a, b are relatively prime, that is, $\gcd(a, b) = 1$, and they both divide another integer c, then their product ab divides c as well. In particular, if a and b are both prime with $a \neq b$, and a divides c, and b divides c, then ab divides c. For example, this holds true with $a = 5$, $b = 3$, and $c = 30$. In the above, $\gcd(a, b)$ denotes the greatest common divisor of a and b. For example $\gcd(15, 6) = 3$, $\gcd(15, 225) = 15$, and $\gcd(-3, 6) = 3$.

Recall that in Chapter 3, we used the symbol $Rem[u, v]$ to denote the unique remainder that lies between 0 and $v - 1$ when we divide u by v. Thus, $Rem[57, 10] = 7$.

Fix v and think of u as varying, so that we are always dividing by v. Then we can denote $Rem[u, v]$ by $Rem[u]$ or $Remu$. In Chapter 3, we used the following principle, which greatly simplified our calculations.

$$Rem[xy] = Rem[Remx \times Remy] \tag{19.1}$$

This is easily proven as follows. Let $Rem[x] = \alpha$, so $x = \lambda_1 v + \alpha$ with $0 \leq \alpha \leq v - 1$, and let $Rem[y] = \beta$, so $y = \lambda_2 v + \beta$ with $0 \leq \beta \leq v - 1$. Then

$$xy = (\lambda_1 v + \alpha)(\lambda_2 v + \beta)$$
$$= \lambda_1 \lambda_2 v^2 + v(\lambda_1 \beta + \lambda_2 \alpha) + \alpha\beta$$
$$= v(\lambda_1 \lambda_2 v + \lambda_1 \beta + \lambda_2 \alpha) + \alpha\beta$$

Thus, when we divide xy by v, the remainder equals the remainder of $\alpha\beta$ divided by v, establishing formula (19.1).

Before going any further, we need to introduce a few ideas. First, we have the notion of a **group**. A group is a set equipped with an operation, such as addition or multiplication. The operation is **associative**, meaning that the order of adding (or multiplying) is not significant. The operation has a **neutral element** or **unity** which, when added to (or multiplied by) any element of the group, say a, results in the same element a. Also, each element a has an inverse which, when added to (or multiplied by) the given element, results in the unity element. Groups can be written multiplicatively, or additively, and these properties are listed below.

Multiplicative group	Additive group
$(a \cdot b) \cdot c = a \cdot (b \cdot c)$	$(a + b) + c = a + (b + c)$
Unity is 1 so that $a \cdot 1 = a$	Unity is 0 so that $a + 0 = a$
Given a, there exists a^{-1}	Given a, there exists $-a$
so that $a \cdot a^{-1} = 1$	so that $a + (-a) = 0$

where a, b, and c are group elements. Concrete examples of groups abound. The integers, the rationals, and the real numbers with the usual addition each form an additive group. The rationals and reals, **without zero**, each form a multiplicative group with the usual multiplication.

We will be dealing with mainly **commutative** or **abelian** groups, wherein the order of operation does not matter. That is, written multiplicatively, $a \cdot b = b \cdot a$, or written additively, $a + b = b + a$. Unless otherwise stated, assume we are working with abelian groups.

If the group has finitely many elements, then the number of elements of a group is called the **order** of the group. In the case of the real numbers, the order is the cardinality of the infinite set, but as we shall see, many groups have finite order.

Returning to our main narrative, the set of remainders obtained when we divide all numbers by v, consisting of the set $Z_v = \{0, 1, 2, \ldots, v - 1\}$ forms a mathematical structure known as a **ring**. This means that we have addition, with neutral element 0, and multiplication, with neutral element 1, connected by two distributive laws, namely $x(y + z) = xy + xz$ and $(x + y)z = xz + yz$. In fact, the set under addition is an additive group. The set under multiplication cannot be a group because of the zero element. However, a subset of Z_v will form a group under multiplication. To add or multiply two elements in Z_v, we add or multiply them in the usual way and obtain the remainder upon division by v.

The resulting structure is called the **ring of integers modulo** v, denoted by Z_v. As an example, let $v = 6$. Then $Z_v = Z_6 = \{0, 1, 2, 3, 4, 5\}$. So $3 + 5 = 2$, $(2)(5) = 4$ in this ring.

Each element of Z_v can be viewed as an equivalence class over the integers. If $Rem[u, v] = w$, so that $u = \alpha v + w$, $0 \le w < v - 1$, we also use the notation, called

modular notation that

$$u \ (\mathrm{mod} \ v) = w \qquad\qquad (19.2)$$

which implies

$$u \equiv w \ (\mathrm{mod} \ v) \qquad\qquad (19.3)$$

Equation (19.2) says that w is the remainder when u is divided by v, and Eq. (19.3) holds if and only if v divides $u - w$.

(We use notation similar to the above for polynomials. So we say that $U(x) \equiv W(x) \ (\mathrm{mod} \ V(x))$ if $U(x) - W(x)$ is divisible by $V(x)$. In (19.3), if v is prime, then Z_v is a field. Similarly, if $V(x)$ is irreducible (no factors), then the ring of polynomials mod $V(x)$ is a field. We use this when constructing finite fields.)

With this notation, Eq. (19.1) can be written as follows:

$$xy \ (\mathrm{mod} \ v) = ((x \ (\mathrm{mod} \ v))(y \ (\mathrm{mod} \ v))) \ (\mathrm{mod} \ v) \qquad\qquad (19.4)$$

In the ring Z_v, given any element x in Z_v, we can find another element y in $\{0, 1, \ldots, v-2, v-1\}$ so that $(x + y) \ (\mathrm{mod} \ v) = 0$. This element y is unique (with $y = v - x$), and is called the **additive inverse** of x modulo v, and we can denote it by $-x$. Thus, we have $(x + (-x)) \ (\mathrm{mod} \ v) = 0$. For example, with $v = 6$ and $x = 2$, we get $-x = 4$ so that $(2 + 4) \ (\mathrm{mod} \ 6) = 0$.

The difficulty in the ring Z_v lies with multiplication and multiplicative inverses. Given x in Z_v, we want to find its **multiplicative inverse** y in Z_v. Thus, we want to find y in Z_v with $xy \ (\mathrm{mod} \ v) = 1$. It turns out that y can be found if and only if x is **relatively prime** to v, i.e. the **greatest common divisor** of x and v is 1. In symbols, $\gcd(x, v) = 1$, or more simply, $(x, v) = 1$. This means that the only positive integer dividing both x and v is 1.

This important fact concerning inverses will be shown later. It is also true that if x_1 and x_2 are both relatively prime to v, then so is their product $x_1 x_2$. The elements x of Z_v which have $\gcd(x, v) = 1$ are called the **multiplicative units** or **units** of Z_v. From above, the multiplicative units are "closed under multiplication," i.e. the product of two multiplicative units is also a multiplicative unit. In other words, the multiplicative units form a group (under multiplication). The number of elements in this group is denoted by $\varphi(v)$; φ is called the **Euler phi-function**, so the group of multiplicative units has order $\varphi(v)$.

Let us give some examples. Take $v = 10$. Then $Z_v = Z_{10} = \{0, 1, \ldots, 8, 9\}$. The multiplicative units are 1, 3, 7, and 9. In Z_{10}, the multiplicative inverses of 1, 3, 7, 9 are 1, 7, 3, 9 respectively. This can be seen from the facts that $(3 \times 7) \ (\mathrm{mod} \ 10) = 1$, and $(9 \times 9) \ (\mathrm{mod} \ 10) = 1$. Next, let $v = 7$, so $Z_v = Z_7 = \{0, 1, \ldots, 6\}$. Then, **all nonzero**

elements are multiplicative units since each of them is relatively prime to 7. This holds since 7 is a prime so, $\varphi(7) = 7 - 1$. This can be generalized as follows:

$$\varphi(p) = p - 1 \tag{19.5}$$

when p is prime. **Thus, the group of units in Z_p has order $p - 1$.**

In general, it is easy to calculate $\varphi(v)$ using Eq. (19.5), generalized to prime powers, and using the nontrivial fact that φ is **multiplicative**. We express these two observations as follows:

$$\varphi(p^t) = p^t - p^{t-1} = p^{t-1}(p - 1) \tag{19.6}$$

where p is prime and t is an integer. Also,

$$\varphi(ab) = \varphi(a)\varphi(b) \tag{19.7}$$

when a and b are relatively prime. The fact that $\varphi(v)$ can be calculated easily from Eqs. (19.6) and (19.7) follows from the **Fundamental Theorem of Arithmetic**, to the effect that any positive integer can be factored uniquely as the product of prime powers.[1]

For example, suppose $v = 36$. We have $\varphi(36) = \varphi(4)\varphi(9) = \varphi(2^2)\varphi(3^2) = (2^2 - 2^1)(3^2 - 3^1) = 12$. So, in Z_{36} there are 12 multiplicative units. They are 1, 5, 7, 11, 13, 17, 19, 23, 25, 29, 31, 35.

19.2   A Little Linear Algebra

The **rank** of a matrix is an important concept; it is the maximum number of linearly independent rows of a matrix. For example, the matrix

$$I = \begin{pmatrix} 1 & 0 & 0 \\ 0 & 1 & 0 \\ 0 & 0 & 1 \end{pmatrix}$$

has rank 3, since the rows are linearly independent. However, the matrix

$$A = \begin{pmatrix} 1 & 2 & 2 \\ 1 & 1 & 0 \\ 2 & 3 & 2 \end{pmatrix}$$

---

[1] $2^2 \times 3 \times 5$ and $2 \times 5 \times 3 \times 2$ are considered the same factorizations of 60. Uniqueness means up to an ordering of the factors.

has rank 2 since $(1, 2, 2) + (1, 1, 0) = (2, 3, 2)$ but $(1, 2, 2)$ and $(1, 1, 0)$ are linearly independent. We write $\text{rank}(A) = 2$. The rank of a matrix can be found through the process of row reduction.

A useful fact about the rank of a matrix A is that the rank is equal to the rank of its transpose. In symbols, $\text{rank}(A) = \text{rank}(A^{\text{t}})$. Since the rows of A^{t} are the columns of A, we could have said that the rank of a matrix is the maximum number of linearly independent columns; **the maximum number of linearly independent columns equals the maximum number of linearly independent rows.** It follows that the rank of a matrix must be less than or equal to the number of rows, and less than or equal to the number of columns. That is, if A is an $n \times m$ matrix, then $\text{rank}(A) \leq n$ and $\text{rank}(A) \leq m$.

Now, the important fact for this section is simply this: A has full rank exactly when it is invertible. That is, when A is an $n \times n$ matrix, $\text{rank}(A) = n$ if and only if there is another matrix A^{-1} such that $AA^{-1} = I$, where I is the identity matrix, which plays the role of 1 for matrix multiplication. This fact is important for solving systems of linear equations, which can be represented in the form $A\mathbf{x} = \mathbf{b}$, where $\mathbf{x}$ is a column matrix of variables, and $\mathbf{b}$ is the column matrix of constant terms; we can solve for $\mathbf{x}$ uniquely when A is invertible. In fact, $\mathbf{x} = A^{-1}\mathbf{b}$, and so rank is an important concept in terms of its relation to invertibility.

Rank is also important when we deal with the generator matrices of linear codes. In this case, the rank of the generator matrix is exactly the dimension of the linear code.

The Vandermonde technique

Let V be a Vandermonde matrix, i.e. a matrix of the following form,

$$V = \begin{pmatrix} 1 & 1 & \cdots & 1 \\ \alpha_1 & \alpha_2 & \cdots & \alpha_n \\ \alpha_1^2 & \alpha_2^2 & \cdots & \alpha_n^2 \\ \vdots & \vdots & \ddots & \vdots \\ \alpha_1^{n-1} & \alpha_2^{n-1} & \cdots & \alpha_n^{n-1} \end{pmatrix}$$

where the α_i are in some field F. Fields were introduced in Section 5.2 and are discussed in detail in Section 19.7, but for now it is enough to say that a field is a special kind of a ring in which all nonzero elements have a multiplicative inverse. Then, it can be shown that the determinant of V has a special form. In fact,

$$\det(V) = \prod_{1 \leq i < j \leq n} (\alpha_j - \alpha_i) \tag{19.8}$$

What this means is that if we take the product of terms $(\alpha_j - \alpha_i)$ where $i < j$, then we will have the determinant. In particular, $\det(V) = 0$ if and only if at least one of the terms $(\alpha_j - \alpha_i)$ is zero. Now, since $\det(V) \neq 0$ if and only if V is invertible, we know by Eq. (19.8) that V is invertible if and only if no two elements α_i, α_j are equal, for $i \neq j$.

This is of particular use in coding theory where Vandermonde matrices are used, since it tells us that the matrix V^{-1} exists exactly when the various α_i are distinct.

Subspaces

We also need the notion of a subspace of a vector space. A subspace is a set of vectors which is closed under addition and closed under scalar multiplication. For example if we suppose that V is a vector space, and S is a subset of V, then S is a subspace provided that

1. $\mathbf{u} + \mathbf{v}$ is in S whenever $\mathbf{u}$ and $\mathbf{v}$ are in S.

2. $a\mathbf{u}$ is in S whenever $\mathbf{u}$ is in S and a is a scalar.

When we are working in binary, the only nonzero scalar is 1, and multiplication by 1 has no effect. However, the second condition with $\alpha = 0$ guarantees that the zero vector is in the subspace.

For example, within the vector space consisting of all binary vectors of length 3, the set

$$S = \{(000), (101), (110)\}$$

is not a subspace since the vector $(101) + (110) = (011)$ is not in the set S. However, if we adjoined this vector, then we would have a set which is a subspace.

19.3 Applications to RSA

We use the notation from Chapter 3 where $N = pq$ and $p \neq q$ are primes. Then, from equations (19.5) and (19.7), we have $\varphi(N) = (p-1)(q-1)$. Since e was chosen with $\gcd(e, \varphi(N)) = 1$ (see Section 3.3), it follows that e is a multiplicative unit in $Z_{\varphi(N)}$. Also, d is chosen so that $(M^e)^d \pmod{N} = M$.

A fundamental fact, holding for any multiplicative group G is this: if we multiply any element g in G by itself t times, where t denotes the order of G (i.e. the number of elements in G), we get the unity element 1. In symbols, $g^t = 1$.

We now apply this principle to obtain two famous results in number theory.

Euler's theorem

$$x^{\varphi(N)} \ (\text{mod } N) = 1 \qquad (19.9)$$

whenever $\gcd(x, N) = 1$. As a special case, when N is prime in (19.9) we get the following.

Fermat's little theorem

$$x^{p-1} \ (\text{mod } p) = 1 \qquad (19.10)$$

whenever the integer x is not divisible by p.

Justification of Equations (19.9), (19.10)

Strictly speaking we have only justified (19.9) in the case when x is one of the multiplicative units in Z_N, with $1 \leq x < N$. Suppose x is any integer relatively prime to N. Dividing x by N we get $x = Nu + y$, with $0 < y < N$. Note that if $y = 0$, then x would be divisible by N so that $\gcd(x, N) = N$, contradicting $\gcd(x, N) = 1$. If a number $d > 1$ were to divide y and N then since $x = Nu + y$, d would divide x, so d would divide N and x, contradicting that $\gcd(x, N) = 1$.

We conclude that $\gcd(y, N) = 1$. Now $x^{\varphi(N)} = (Nu + y)^{\varphi(N)}$. When we multiply $Nu + y$ by itself $\varphi(N)$ times, all terms are divisible by N save for $y^{\varphi(N)}$. Then $x^{\varphi(N)}$ equals $y^{\varphi(N)}$ (mod N). Now we can think of y as an element of Z_N, since $0 \leq y < N$; moreover, $\gcd(y, N) = 1$. So (19.9) follows, and this in turn implies (19.10).

Question 1

What is the remainder when 2^{86} is divided by 55? This is tantamount to finding x such that $2^{86} \ (\text{mod } 55) = x$.

We have $55 = 5 \times 11$, so $\varphi(55) = \varphi(5)\varphi(11) = (5-1)(11-1) = 40$. Further, $86 = 2 \times 40 + 6$, and $\gcd(2, 55) = 1$. Then $2^{86} = (2^{40})^2(2^6)$, so

$$2^{86} \equiv (2^{40})(2^{40})(2^6) \ (\text{mod } 55)$$

$$\equiv (1)(1)(2^6) \ (\text{mod } 55)$$

$$\equiv 64 \ (\text{mod } 55)$$

$$\equiv 9 \ (\text{mod } 55)$$

We now prove a result that was mentioned in Chapter 3. We know that $M^e = C + t_0 N$ for some integer t_0, and we claimed that this admits a converse; if $(C + tN)^{\frac{1}{e}}$ is an integer for any integral value of t, with t not necessarily equal to t_0, then $(C + tN)^{\frac{1}{e}} \pmod{N} = M$. This is important from the point of view of an attacker, as guessing t would let the attacker find M.

So, suppose that $x = (C + tN)^{\frac{1}{e}}$ is an integer. We want to show that $x \pmod{N} = M$. Now,

$$x^e = C + tN, \tag{19.11}$$

and also, since the RSA algorithm works, we know that

$$(x^e)^d \equiv x \pmod{N} \tag{19.12}$$

Thus, by Eq. (19.12) $x^{ed} = x + \lambda N$ for some integer λ. So, by Eq. (19.11) we get that $x + \lambda N = x^{ed} = (C + tN)^d$. Now, when we multiply $(C + tN)$ by itself d times, we find that all terms are divisible by N except for C^d. It follows that there is a μ so that $x + \lambda N = C^d + \mu N$, and from this, we get that $x + (\lambda - \mu)N = C^d$, which says that $x \equiv C^d \equiv M \pmod{N}$.

19.4 Primitive Roots for Primes and Diffie–Hellman

For the Diffie–Hellman key exchange, we need to find a **generator** for the multiplicative group of units in Z_p where p is a prime (such a generator is also called a **primitive root**). What we mean by a generator is a number g so that the set of all powers of $g \pmod{p}$ is the nonzero elements of Z_p. That is, $\{1, 2, 3, \ldots, p-1\} = \{g^t \mid t = 1, 2, 3, \ldots, p-1\}$. In this situation, the quantity $\varphi(p-1)$ plays an important role. We have the following result.

The number of primitive roots g with

$$1 \leq g \leq p - 1 \tag{19.13}$$

is $\varphi(p-1)$. Thus, there is always at least one generator.

Solving congruence equations

Suppose N_1, N_2 are positive integers with $\gcd(N_1, N_2) = 1$. Given $0 \leq a_1 < N_1$ and $0 \leq a_2 < N_2$, we can formulate the following result.

Chinese remainder theorem

Let α_1, α_2 be given with $0 \le a_1 < N_1$ and $0 \le a_2 < N_2$. Then, there is one and only one x with $0 \le x < N_1 N_2$ such that both $x \pmod{N_1} = a_1$ and $x \pmod{N_2} = a_2$. In fact,

$$x \equiv a_1 N_2 m_1 + a_2 N_1 m_2 \pmod{N_1 N_2}$$

where $N_2 m_1 \pmod{N_1} = 1$ and $N_1 m_2 \pmod{N_2} = 1$.

This can be generalized from two relatively prime integers N_1, N_2 to any number of relatively prime integers, as follows.

Let $x \pmod{N_i} = a_i$ for $i = 1, 2, \ldots, k$ be a set of congruence equations, where the N_i are pairwise relatively prime. Then x has a unique solution modulo $N = N_1 \times N_2 \times \cdots \times N_k$, in fact,

$$x \equiv a_1 M_1 m_1 + a_2 M_2 m_2 + \cdots + a_k M_k m_k \pmod{N}$$

where $M_i = \frac{N}{N_i} = \frac{N_1 N_2 \cdots N_k}{N_i}$ and $M_i m_i \pmod{N_i} = 1$.

Question 2

Solve Question 1 using Eq. (19.5) and the Chinese Remainder Theorem.

First, we want to find $2^{86} \pmod 5$. Now $\varphi(5) = 4$ and $86 = 21 \times 4 + 2$. So

$$2^{86} \equiv (2^4)^{41} (2^2) \pmod 5$$
$$\equiv (1^{41})(2^2) \pmod 5$$
$$\equiv 4 \pmod 5$$

Next, we find $2^{86} \pmod{11}$. We know that $86 = 8 \times 10 + 6$, and thus

$$2^{86} \equiv (2^{10})^8 (2^6) \pmod{11}$$
$$\equiv (1^8)(2^6) \pmod{11}$$
$$\equiv 64 \pmod{11}$$
$$\equiv 9 \pmod{11}$$

So we seek the unique x with $0 \le x < 55$ so that $x \pmod 5 = 4$ and $x \pmod{11} = 9$. This forces $x = 9$.

Primes and primality testing

The famous **prime number theorem** asserts that the number of prime numbers less than the positive integer n is approximately $\frac{n}{\ln n}$. Since this quantity grows at a reasonable rate as n gets large, we can say that there is no shortage of primes! From the prime number theorem, the probability that a number n, represented as a binary string of length m, is prime is a bit bigger than $\frac{\log_2 e}{m}$ as n gets large. It has been shown that we can test quickly (in polynomial time) to see if a given integer is a prime. See [AKS04].

Calculating inverses and the Euclidean algorithm

Given two positive integers a, b with $a > b$, and we want to do the following.

- Calculate the greatest common divisor d, of a and b, $\gcd(a, b) = d$.

- Express d in the form $d = ax + by$ where x, y are integers, not necessarily positive.

To see how this works, we first divide a by b. This gives the equation

$$a = bq + R, \ \ 0 \le R < b \tag{19.14}$$

Note now that any number x dividing a and b must divide R. Thus, x divides both b and R. On the other hand, any number dividing b and R must divide a. What this all means is the following: $\gcd(a, b) = \gcd(b, R)$.

Now the numbers b, R are smaller than a, b, respectively, so we proceed until we reach "the bottom." Let us take an example. Find $\gcd(657, 75)$.

$$657 = 75 \times 8 + 57$$

$$75 = 57 \times 1 + 18$$

$$57 = 18 \times 3 + 3$$

$$18 = 3 \times 6 + 0$$

We know then that $\gcd(657, 75) = \gcd(75, 57) = \gcd(57, 18) = \gcd(18, 3) = 3$.

Working backward from the bottom we get the following result. There are integers x, y so that

$$d = ax + by \tag{19.15}$$

In the above example, we have $3 = 657x + 75y$ giving $x = 4$, $y = -35$, and this can be verified directly, while a simpler method for finding x, y will be shown later. Note that, in Eq. (19.15), if $\gcd(a, b) = 1$, then we have $ax + by = 1$, and so $xa = b(-y) + 1$. So $ax \pmod{b} = 1$, and x is the inverse of a in the group of multiplicative units in Z_b. On the other hand, if $d > 1$, then we cannot find an x, y so that $1 = ax + by$, and so a cannot have a multiplicative inverse in Z_b. In summary, as mentioned earlier, the invertible elements under multiplication in Z_b are exactly those elements in Z_b that are relatively prime to b.

It is important to note, too, that a Euclidean algorithm exists even for polynomials, since we have a notion of the divisibility of polynomials. In fact, irreducible polynomials, which will be discussed later, play the role of prime numbers for polynomials, and many analogies can be made between integers and polynomials.

19.5   The Extended Euclidean Algorithm

We can use the Euclidean algorithm to express the greatest common divisor d of two numbers a, b as a **linear combination** of a and b, as in $d = ax + by$. However, using the method described above can be tiresome as we are forced to work backward after having found "the bottom."

Instead, we present a slightly modified version which keeps track of the numbers x, y as the algorithm runs. It proceeds as follows.

	x_i	y_i	$657x_i + 75y_i$	
r_1	1	0	657	
r_2	0	1	75	
r_3	1	-8	57	$r_3 = r_1 - 8r_2$
r_4	-1	9	18	$r_4 = r_2 - r_3$
r_5	4	-35	3	$r_5 = r_3 - 3r_4$
r_6	-25	219	0	$r_6 = r_4 - 6r_5$

The initialization of the algorithm is presented in rows r_1 and r_2. At each step, we take a sum of the previous two rows, say r_i and r_{i-1} to find the next row, say r_{i+1} and this sum uses the quotient when the last entry of r_{i-1} is divided by the last entry of r_i. The algorithm stops when the last entry of a row is zero. Compare the above extended process with the previous worked example to see the parallels. It follows that $\gcd(657, 75) = 3$, and $657x + 75y = 3$, where $x = 4$ and $y = -35$.

This algorithm can, of course, be generalized to find the greatest common divisor of any two numbers.

The theory of integers and the integers (mod n) is very similar to the theory of polynomials in one variable over a field. For example, the gcd of two integers u and v is analogous to the gcd of two polynomials $u(x), v(x)$, which is the polynomial of highest degree dividing both $u(x)$ and $v(x)$. This gcd is expressible as a combination (with polynomial coefficients) of $u(x)$ and $v(x)$. $Rem[u, v]$ gets replaced by $Rem[u(x), v(x)]$ which will have a degree lying between 0 and $t - 1$ where t is the degree of $v(x)$. Similarly, the ring Z_n is analogous to the ring of polynomials (mod f) where f is any polynomial of degree n. In coding, $f(x) = x^n - 1$ is often used.

19.6 Proof that the RSA Algorithm Works

We have two distinct primes, p, q and $N = pq$. Also, e is relatively prime to $\varphi(N) = (p-1)(q-1)$. Next, let t be any integer which is divisible by both $p-1$ and $q-1$. So, in particular, t may be $(p-1)(q-1)$, or t may be the least common multiple of $p-1$ and $q-1$. Finally, we have d so that ed (mod t) $= 1$, and so $ed = 1 + \lambda t$, for some integer λ.

We want to show that for any integer message M,

$$C^d \equiv (M^e)^d \equiv M \pmod{N} \tag{19.16}$$

Assume first that the message M has $\gcd(M, p) = 1$. Then, $M^{ed} = M^{1+\lambda t} = M(M^{p-1})^u$ where u is an integer satisfying $u(p-1) = \lambda t$. It is followed by Fermat's little theorem that $M^{ed} \equiv M \pmod{p}$. Now, when $\gcd(M, p) \neq 1$, we have that p divides M, as p is prime, and then $M^{ed} \equiv M \pmod{p}$ still holds.

Similarly, we can show that M^{ed} (mod q) $= M$. Thus, we have shown that $M^{ed} - M$ is divisible by both p and q, and so it must be divisible by pq, since p, q are prime and therefore relatively prime. That is, Eq. (19.16) is satisfied.

19.7 Constructing Finite Fields

A **field**, F, is a ring with the added stipulation that every nonzero element of the set have a multiplicative inverse. Another way of putting this is that a field is a set F with two operations, addition and multiplication, such that F under addition is an additive group, and F without zero under multiplication is a multiplicative group, and addition and multiplication are linked by the usual distributive laws, $x(y + z) = xy + xz$ and $(x + y)z = xz + yz$. Also, the groups are commutative. Examples of such are the rational numbers, the real numbers, and the complex numbers. A **finite field**, F, is a field which has only a finite number of elements. The number of elements in F is called the **order** of F. Z_2 is a field, and so is Z_p for any prime p, since the number of multiplicative units in Z_p is $\varphi(p) = p - 1$, which is exactly the number of nonzero elements of Z_p. That is in Z_p every nonzero element has a multiplicative inverse.

It is a remarkable fact that a field of order q exists if and only if q is a power of a prime, say $q = p^k$ where p is prime, and k is a positive integer. In fact, the field of order p^k is unique (in that all fields of order p^k are essentially the same, or **isomorphic**), and is denoted $GF(p^k)$, where GF stands for "Galois Field" in honor of Galois, the founder of the subject. Further, the smallest number of ones that adds to zero in $GF(q)$ is called the **characteristic** of the field, and this number is guaranteed to be a prime number p. In fact, going back to Diffie–Hellman, just like in Z_p there is a generator for the field $GF(q)$. That is, there is an element α of $GF(q)$ such that the nonzero elements of the field are the successive powers of α, i.e. $GF(q) = \{0, \alpha^1, \alpha^2, \dots, \alpha^{q-1}\}$.

When $GF(q)$ has characterstic p, $GF(q)$ will contain $GF(p)$ as a subfield, and ultimately, $GF(q)$ can be built up from $GF(p)$ using the polynomial construction procedure we are about to illustrate. Unfortunately, Z_{p^k} is not a field when $k \geq 2$, for example, consider Z_4. It is a simple exercise to check that 2 has no multiplicative inverse in Z_4, and so Z_4 is not a field. However, finite fields turn up again and again in coding theory, so we need to be able to construct fields of order p^k.

An example is in order. Let us construct $GF(4)$ using Z_2 and the polynomial $f(x) = x^2 + x + 1$. Note that f has **degree** 2, since it has an x^2 term, and it does not have a term like x^3 or another higher exponent. Then our field elements are all polynomials over Z_2 of degree strictly less than 2, using a "variable" α. Thus, $GF(4) = \{0, 1, \alpha, 1 + \alpha\}$. Here, 2 comes from the fact that the degree of f is 2. Also, the polynomial f has a special property; it is **irreducible** over Z_2, meaning that it cannot be factored. This is discussed in more detail later.

Addition is straightforward polynomial addition. For example, in Z_2, $(\alpha) + (1) = (\alpha + 1)$ and, $(\alpha) + (1 + \alpha) = (1)$. Multiplication, however, has a twist. It seems that we can multiply $\alpha \times \alpha$ to get α^2, which is not a field element. However, we work around this difficulty by saying that $f(\alpha) = 0$, i.e. that $\alpha^2 + \alpha + 1 = 0$, or $\alpha^2 = -\alpha - 1 = \alpha + 1$. We can now completely describe the addition and multiplication in $GF(4)$ in the following Cayley tables, setting $\omega = \alpha$ and $\omega^2 = \alpha + 1$.

+	0	1	ω	ω^2
0	0	1	ω	ω^2
1	1	0	ω^2	ω
ω	ω	ω^2	0	1
ω^2	ω^2	ω	1	0

×	0	1	ω	ω^2
0	0	0	0	0
1	0	1	ω	ω^2
ω	0	ω	ω^2	1
ω^2	0	ω^2	1	ω

Polynomials

For the sake of completeness, we need a few notions. A **polynomial over** Z_v is a polynomial $f(x) = a_0 + a_1 x + a_2 x^2 + \cdots + a_k x^k$ wherein each a_i is an element of Z_v. That is, a_i is in $\{0, 1, 2, \ldots, p-1\}$. Polynomial addition and multiplication proceed as usual, except that the coefficients are added modulo v. That is,

$$(a_0 + a_1 x + a_2 x^2 + \cdots) + (b_0 + b_1 x + b_2 x^2 + \cdots) =$$
$$(a_0 + b_0 \ (\text{mod } v)) + (a_1 + b_1 \ (\text{mod } v))x + (a_2 + b_2 \ (\text{mod } v))x^2 + \cdots \qquad (19.17)$$

where each of the above polynomials is finite. Also, the **degree** of f is the highest value of i for which a_i is nonzero. So, if $a_k \neq 0$ in $f(x)$, then the degree of f is k.

A polynomial is **irreducible** provided that it cannot be factored into lower degree terms. For example, $x^2 + x + 1$ is irreducible both as a polynomial over the real numbers, and as a polynomial over Z_2. However, as a polynomial in Z_2, $(x+1)^2 = x^2 + 1$ is not irreducible. Polynomials which can be factored, that is, polynomials which are not irreducible are **reducible**.

We also need to be able to tell when a polynomial is irreducible. For now, we are satisfied to say that a polynomial $f(x)$ of degree 2 or 3 is irreducible over Z_p provided that for all a in Z_p, $f(a) \neq 0$. That is to say, f has no roots in Z_p. Also, another method to test the irreducibility of a polynomial is to attempt to divide it by all polynomials of lesser degree, and if any divide evenly, then the polynomial is not irreducible.

A useful, if tedious, procedure for finding all irreducible polynomials of degree k is to take all polynomials of degree less than k, and find the products of these which multiply to have degree k. This produces a list of all polynomials of degree k which are *not* irreducible, so any unlisted polynomials of degree k must be irreducible.

Example 19.1 *To find all irreducible polynomials over Z_2 of degree 2, we begin by listing the polynomials of lesser degree. They are x and $x + 1$. Note that we do not list 0 or 1, since these will not provide any useful results. Now, $(x)(x) = x^2$, $(x)(x + 1) = x^2 + x$, and $(x + 1)(x + 1) = x^2 + 1$, and the only unlisted polynomial of degree 2 is $x^2 + x + 1$, so it must be irreducible.*

We also point out that over any field F, there always exists an irreducible polynomial of degree k, for $k \geq 2$.

The general construction procedure

We can now describe how to construct finite fields $GF(p^k)$ of order p^k in general.

- We choose a prime p and an irreducible polynomial $f(x)$ over Z_p of degree k.

- The field elements are all polynomials of degree $< k$ over Z_p.

- Addition of the field elements is as described in Eq. (19.17). That is, we use normal polynomial addition and reduce the coefficients by taking them to be the remainder upon division by p.

- Multiplication is like addition in that the coefficients are reduced modulo p, but with the extra stipulation that α^k has a reduced version since $f(\alpha) = 0$. That is, if $f(x) = b_0 + b_1 x + \cdots + b_k x^k$ with $b_k \neq 0$, then

$$\alpha^k = b_k^{-1}(-b_0 - b_1\alpha - \cdots - b_{k-1}\alpha^{k-1}) \qquad (19.18)$$

An example: constructing $GF(8)$

We use the irreducible polynomial $f(x) = 1 + x + x^3$. Our field elements are then polynomials of the form $a_0 + a_1\alpha + a_2\alpha^2$, where $a_i = 0$ or 1.

Polynomial in α	Power of ω
0	—
1	$\omega^0 = 1$
α	ω^1
α^2	ω^2
$1 + \alpha$	ω^3
$\alpha + \alpha^2$	ω^4
$1 + \alpha + \alpha^2$	ω^5
$1 + \alpha^2$	ω^6

For this field, the element α is a multiplicative generator ω, i.e. put $\omega = \alpha$. We have used this presentation rather than the table format since it is less cumbersome. Addition proceeds as usual, and is easily done using the left column, with the added stipulation that the coefficients are reduced modulo 2, so that $(1 + \alpha) + \alpha = 1 + 2\alpha = 1$. Multiplication requires that $f(\alpha) = 0$, i.e. that $\alpha^3 = \alpha + 1$. We can easily do multiplication using the right column and the usual exponent laws, namely that $\omega^a \omega^b = \omega^{a+b}$. We also need to know that $\omega^7 = 1$, and we can see this from the fact that $\alpha^3 = \alpha + 1$, as follows,

$$\omega^7 = \alpha^7$$
$$= \alpha^{1+3+3}$$
$$= \alpha(\alpha + 1)(\alpha + 1)$$
$$= \alpha(\alpha^2 + 1)$$
$$= \alpha^3 + \alpha$$
$$= (\alpha + 1) + \alpha$$
$$= 1.$$

A useful polynomial for coding

We mention here a fact that will be later useful when we discuss coding, especially linear codes. The polynomial $x^{q-1} - 1$ over a field of order q is of particular importance. In fact,

$$x^{q-1} - 1 = \prod_{i=1}^{q-1}(x - \alpha_i)$$
$$= (x - \alpha_1)(x - \alpha_2) \cdots (x - \alpha_{q-1})$$

where $\alpha_1, \alpha_2, \ldots, \alpha_{q-1}$ are the distinct nonzero field elements. This means that a polynomial of the form $(x - b_1)(x - b_2) \cdots (x - b_k)$, divides $x^{q-1} - 1$, where $k < q$ and the b_i's are distinct.

For example, over Z_5, we have that

$$x^4 - 1 = (x - 1)(x - 2)(x - 3)(x - 4).$$

Another example: constructing $GF(16)$

We use the polynomial $f(x) = 1 + x + x^4$, which is irreducible. Our field elements are $\{a_0 + a_1\alpha + a_2\alpha^2 + a_3\alpha^3 \mid a_i = 0 \text{ or } 1\}$. Then, using $f(\alpha) = 0$, which means that $\alpha^4 = \alpha + 1$, we can describe the field as follows:

Polynomial in α	Power of ω
0	—
1	$\omega^0 = 1$
α	ω^1
α^2	ω^2
α^3	ω^3
$1 + \alpha$	ω^4
$\alpha + \alpha^2$	ω^5
$\alpha^2 + \alpha^3$	ω^6
$1 + \alpha + \alpha^3$	ω^7
$1 + \alpha^2$	ω^8
$\alpha + \alpha^3$	ω^9
$1 + \alpha + \alpha^2$	ω^{10}
$\alpha + \alpha^2 + \alpha^3$	ω^{11}
$1 + \alpha + \alpha^2 + \alpha^3$	ω^{12}
$1 + \alpha^2 + \alpha^3$	ω^{13}
$1 + \alpha^3$	ω^{14}

As before, we can use the left column to quickly compute addition, and the right column to quickly compute multiplication, with $\omega^{15} = 1$.

19.8   Pollard's $p - 1$ Factoring Algorithm

Suppose that we want to factor some positive integer n which is not a prime. For example, we might be trying to crack RSA, in which case n is the product of two large primes.

Now, there exists some prime p dividing n. The number $p - 1$ is uniquely expressible as a product of prime powers. We have $p - 1 = p_1^{a_1} p_2^{a_2} \cdots p_s^{a_s}$, where $p_1, p_2, \ldots, p_s$ are the distinct primes dividing $p - 1$. Thus, no two of $p_1^{a_1}, p_2^{a_2}, \ldots, p_s^{a_s}$ are equal. We can assume, by relabelling if necessary, that $p_1^{a_1} < p_2^{a_2} < \cdots < p_s^{a_s}$. Now assume that $p_s^{a_s}$ is less than or equal to some small number B. Then, $p_i^{a_i}$ is less than or equal to B for $1 \leq 1 \leq s$. The algorithm proceeds as follows:

1. Pick some integer t that is a multiple of all integers less than or equal to B. For instance, take $t = factorial(B) = B!$ Or choose t to be the least common multiple of $\{1, 2, 3, \ldots, B\}$.

2. Choose the integer x randomly, with $2 < x < n - 2$.

3. Calculate $y = x^t \pmod{n}$ by repeated squaring as in Chapter 3.

4. Let d be the greatest common divisor of $x^t - 1$ and n. In symbols, $d = gcd(x^t - 1, n) = gcd(y - 1, n)$.

5. We have that d divides n. In fact, we can guarantee that $d > 1$. This means that $x^t - 1$ is a multiple of n, d is a proper factor of n.

To see this, proceed as follows. Any two of the numbers $p_1^{a_1}, p_2^{a_2}, \ldots, p_s^{a_s}$ are relatively prime and each of them is less than B. By choice of t, it follows that their product, namely $p - 1$, divides t. Thus, t is some multiple of $p - 1$, say $t = \lambda(p - 1)$.

Therefore, $x^t = x^{(p-1)\lambda}$. By Fermat's little theorem $x^{p-1} = 1 \pmod{p}$ so $x^{(p-1)\lambda} = (x^{(p-1)})^\lambda = 1 \pmod{p}$.

Thus, $x^t = 1 \pmod{p}$. Therefore, p divides $x^t - 1$, and we already know that p divides n. Now because $d = gcd(x^t - 1, n)$, it follows that p divides d. This means that we have factored n.

The above algorithm is due to Pollard [Pol74]. The method is a predecessor of Lenstra's [Len87] method with elliptic curves.

An example

Let $n = 2117$, $B = 7$. Then choose t to be the least common multiple of the integers $2, 3, 4, 5, 6, 7$, so $t = 420$. Choose $x = 2$ (randomly). Then, $x^{420} \pmod{2117} = 1451$. Thus, $y = 1451$. So $d = gcd(y - 1, n) = gcd(1450, 2117) = 29$. It follows that n is a multiple of 29 and $n = 29 \cdot 73$.

19.9 Latin Squares

A matrix A is an $m \times n$ matrix if it has m rows and n columns. A **latin square** A is an $n \times n$ matrix whose entries come from a set S, $|S| = n$, such that each element of S appears exactly once in each row and each column of A. In this case, n is the *order* of the latin square. (Often S is chosen to be $\{1, 2, \ldots, n\}$.)

Two latin squares $A = [a_{ij}]$ and $B = [b_{ij}]$ with entries from a set S are **orthogonal** if the set of ordered pairs of corresponding elements of the form $\{a_{ij}, b_{ij}\}$ (with $i, j \in \{1, \ldots, n\}$) contains each possible ordered pair from $S \times S$ exactly once. In other words, when we place A on top of B the n^2 ordered paris are all distinct.

Example 19.2 *Let*

$$A = \begin{pmatrix} 1 & 2 & 3 \\ 2 & 3 & 1 \\ 3 & 1 & 2 \end{pmatrix}, \qquad B = \begin{pmatrix} 1 & 2 & 3 \\ 3 & 1 & 2 \\ 2 & 3 & 1 \end{pmatrix}.$$

Superposition yields 9 distinct ordered pairs, i.e.

$$\begin{pmatrix} 11 & 22 & 33 \\ 23 & 31 & 12 \\ 32 & 13 & 21 \end{pmatrix}.$$

So A, B are a pair of orthogonal latin squares of order 3.

Counterexample 19.3 *Let*

$$A = \begin{pmatrix} 1 & 2 & 3 \\ 2 & 3 & 1 \\ 3 & 1 & 2 \end{pmatrix}, \qquad B = \begin{pmatrix} 1 & 2 & 3 \\ 3 & 2 & 1 \\ 2 & 3 & 1 \end{pmatrix}$$

When superimposed we get

$$\begin{pmatrix} 11 & 22 & 33 \\ 23 & 32 & 11 \\ 32 & 13 & 21 \end{pmatrix}$$

Note that (11) is repeated twice and (31) is missing. So, A, B are not orthogonal.

A set of latin squares is a set of *mutually orthogonal latin squares (MOLS)*, if every pair of them are orthogonal.

A well-known theorem is the following:

Theorem 19.4 *There are at most $n - 1$ latin squares of order n that are mutually orthogonal.*

If n is a prime or a prime power, there exists such a system yielding a plane of order n. No other examples have been found.

A latin square is the vehicle for perfect secrecy as pointed out in Chapter 15. Systems of MOLS are very important for MDS codes and are equivalent to structures known as Bruck nets. They are discussed in Chapter 23. The subject has a long and interesting history; see also Chapter 23.

Euler conjectured that if $n \equiv 2 \pmod{4}$, then there does not exist a pair of orthogonal latin squares of order n. This conjecture is true for $n = 6$. However, in 1960, Bose,

Shrikhande, and Parker showed that Euler's conjecture is **false** if $n \geq 10$. (See [BSP60] and [BS59].)

Sudoku puzzles are popular and are available in newspapers, magazines, and online wherever crossword puzzles can be found. A **Sudoku latin square** is a 9×9 latin square using the numbers from a set S that contains exactly nine distinct elements (often chosen to be $S = \{1, 2, \ldots, 9\}$) with the extra requirements that the following nine 3×3 submatrices each contains all of the elements of S: the upper left 3×3 submatrix, the lower left 3×3 submatrix, the 3×3 submatrix in between them; the 3×3 submatrices immediately to the right of each of those; and the 3×3 submatrices immediately to the right of each of those. Usually S is chosen to be $\{1, 2, \ldots, 9\}$.

A **Sudoku puzzle** is a 9×9 matrix with some entries from S and some entries blank that can be completed in a unique way to a Sudoku latin square.

Sudoku latin squares and Sudoku puzzles can be generalized by replacing "3" with n and "9" with n^2. An n^2-**Sudoku latin square** is a $n^2 \times n^2$ latin square using the numbers from a set S that contains exactly n^2 distinct elements (often chosen to be $S = \{1, \ldots, n^2\}$) with the extra requirements that the following nine $n \times n$ submatrices each contains all of the elements of S: the upper left $n \times n$ submatrix, the $n \times n$ submatrix immediately below it, $\ldots$, the lower left $n \times n$ submatrix; each of the $n \times n$ submatrices immediately to the right of those; each of the $n \times n$ submatrices immediately to the right of those; etc. An n^2-**Sudoku puzzle** is an $n^2 \times n^2$ matrix with some entries from S and some entries blank that can be completed in a unique way to an n^2-Sudoku latin square.

The general problem of solving Sudoku puzzles on $n^2 \times n^2$ grids of $n \times n$ blocks is known to be NP-complete, or more precisely, the problem of determining whether a partially filled $n^2 \times n^2$ array with some entries in S, $|S| = n^2$, (and the remaining entries blank) can be completed to an n^2-Sudoku latin square is an NP-complete problem. See Section 19.10.

19.10 Computational Complexity, Turing Machines, Quantum Computing

In previous chapters (such as Chapters 3, 4, and 6), we discussed public key algorithms such as RSA and pointed out that their security depends on the unproved assumptions that, given a cipher text, it is not possible to calculate the underlying message in a reasonable amount of time. This kind of security is called *computational security*. We want to briefly expand on such ideas in the context of **computational complexity**, which is a much-studied topic in theoretical Computer Science. It also ties in with Information Theory.

Roughly, the complexity of a mathematical problem, algorithm or calculation is a measure of the computational resources needed to solve it. These resources might involve time, space in memory or other considerations. Here we focus on time.

Example 19.5   *Let us take multiplication. Suppose that $x = x_1 x_2 \cdots x_n$ is an n digit decimal number. Assume the same for $y = y_1 y_2 \cdots y_n$. To multiply x by y, we can use the school method of "long multiplication." So, we multiply x by y_1, shift that to the left, multiply x by y_2, shift both of those to the left, and so on. Then, we sum these up to get x times y.*

*Each multiplication by $y_1, y_2, \ldots$ takes about n **bit operations**. The summing up of the n products accounts for approximately n^2 bit operations. Thus, this long multiplication algorithm uses $t(n)$ bit operations, where $t(n)$ is $O(n^2)$ as explained below. Note that the actual time taken for the multiplication will depend on the processor being used, so $t(n)$ is just an estimate. This is why we use the big O notation, which is machine independent.*

Big O notation

We say that $F(n)$ is $O(G(n))$ for functions F, G provided that there exists some positive constant c so that $F(n) < cG(n)$ for all n greater than some integer n_0.

In general, we need not find (or know) the numbers c, n_0. All we need to know is that, eventually, some positive multiple of G is larger than F. We think of F as being dominated by G and sometimes write $F << G$. An easy example is provided by the log function: here $\log n$ is $O(n)$. To see this, just take $c = 1$ and $n_0 = 1$ in the definition.

In the multiplication example above, it is possible to devise a better algorithm that uses only $O((n \log n)(\log \log n))$ bit operations.

Input

The complexity of a problem or class of problems depends on the size, n, of the input data. How can this size be defined or measured? Here we fall back on Information Theory and define the **input size** to be the minimum number of Shannon bits of information needed to present the input data.

As an example, consider the following class of problems called PRIME: given an integer N, decide whether N is prime. We can represent N as a sequence of N ones. However, it is shorter to represent N as a binary string which will have just $m = 1 + \lceil \log N \rceil$ binary digits corresponding to m Shannon bits (see Chapter 9). It was shown in [AKS04] that the PRIME problem is in the class P of polynomial algorithms as explained below. To discuss this, we need to talk about Turing machines.

Turing machines

A Turing machine is a theoretical computer which provides the model for all possible computers. This unprovable assumption is known as Church's thesis, and it is generally accepted as being correct. A Turing Machine has an infinite "tape" which is divided into squares. All but a finite number of these squares are blank. So the machine has infinite memory but only a finite part is used at any stage. There is a "head" positioned over the tape, and it can read what is on any square on the tape – or write a symbol in any square. The Turing machine has a finite number of internal states. Each location on the tape can have a symbol from some finite alphabet A (or a blank) written in it.

In one cycle, the machine can write or read a symbol on the tape, move one position left or right or stay, and change the internal state. The **output** of the machine, for a given input, is the characters remaining on the tape when the machine has reached its final state. The time taken from the input to the final state is the number of steps (or cycles).

Remarkably, any computation possible on a present-day computer can be performed by a Turing machine. Also, any processor that can be designed can perform only the equivalent of a bounded number of Turing machine steps.

A function f mapping a string X over the finite alphabet A to another string $f(x)$ over A is **computable** by the Turing machine M if for any input x the machine M stops (or halts) with $f(x)$ as its output. The **time complexity** of f with respect to M is a function $t_M(n)$, which is the maximum time taken to compute $f(x)$ over all strings x of length n, $n > 0$.

A function or algorithm f is computable in **polynomial time** or is a **polynomial algorithm** if there exists some Turing machine M that computes f and some polynomial $G(x)$ such that $t_M(n) \leq G(n)$ for all n.

Using the previous terminology, we can then say that the algorithm f has complexity $O(G)$. Note also that $t_M(n)$ corresponds to the "worst-case" scenario.

Example 19.6 *Suppose that we are given n objects to be sorted in an order. What we want is a procedure of algorithm which accepts as input the unsorted list and outputs a sorted list. It can be shown that there exists an algorithm f which can carry out this procedure with complexity $O(n \log n)$. (Also, this bound is "best possible" for this problem). Since $\log n \leq n$, we can also say that f is $O(n^2)$, and therefore that f is a polynomial time algorithm.*

Example 19.7 *We consider the PRIME problem. We want an algorithm which accepts as input a positive integer N and outputs "Yes" if N is prime and "No" otherwise. When* *the output must be "Yes" or "No," the problem is called a **decision problem**. It has been shown [AKS04] that there exists a polynomial algorithm for the problem PRIME.*

Example 19.8   *We consider the problem of constructing a Huffman code given n source words using the Huffman algorithm in Chapter 11. The algorithm can be shown to have complexity $O(n^2)$.*

A class of decision problems is said to belong to the class NP (for **nondeterministic polynomial**) if for any problem for which the answer is "Yes," there is a "certificate," i.e. an extra piece of information that can be used to verify the correctness of the answer in polynomial time.

For example, consider the question "is the positive integer N non-prime." If the answer is "Yes" a certificate could be a pair of positive integers u, v with $1 < u, v < N$ such that $N = uv$.

It can be shown that, as class, $P \subset NP$. Whether or not $P = NP$ is a major unsolved problem in theoretical computer science. It should also be pointed out that there do exist decision problems which are not even in NP.

From a practical point of view, a fundamental unsolved problem is whether or not a given function is computable in polynomial time. In other words, we want to know whether there exists an algorithm implementing f in polynomial time. If so, the function is called "feasible" or tractable" or "computable in a reasonable amount of time," etc. because these algorithms can be effectively implemented on a modern computer.

As an example, we mention that the factoring problem or the RSA problem discussed in Chapters 2 and 3. It is assumed, but has not been proved, that the factoring problem cannot be solved in polynomial time.

Ideally, to guarantee good security for a public key algorithm, we want the encryption function e to be a "one-way function." This means that the public key e is computable in polynomial time whereas the inverse of e, i.e. the private key d corresponding to the decryption index is not computable in polynomial time.

However, to date, nobody has been able to prove the existence of such a one-way function.

If we do not restrict ourselves to Turing machines but allow quantum computers, then factoring can be done in polynomial time. This would spell the end of RSA.

We should mention also that various "probabilistic algorithms" have been used with some success such as the **index calculus** method for the Diffie–Hellman problem in Chapter 3. We refer to McCurley [McC90].

Finally, it is worth noting, as pointed out in Mollin [Mol00], that for an input n of size 10^6, an algorithm with complexity n takes under a second, where the unit of time for a machine cycle is $\frac{1}{10^6}$ of a second, but an algorithm of complexity n^2 will take days while an algorithm of complexity n^3 will take thousands of years. **Exponential algorithms** with complexity of order $2^{f(n)}$, with f a polynomial, are "off the scale" here.

19.11 Problems

19.1 Use trial division to find the prime factorization of 4023390. (See Solution 19.1.)

19.2 Calculate $\varphi(4023390)$. (See Solution 19.2.)

19.3 Calculate the remainder when 2^{605} is divided by 783. (See Solution 19.3.)

19.4 Use the Euclidean algorithm to find the greatest common divisor, d, of 2925 and 3055, and find x, y so that $d = 2925x + 3055y$. (See Solution 19.4.)

19.5 Repeat the above question for 1547 and 1265. (See Solution 19.5.)

19.6 Show that if $d = \gcd(a, b)$, and $d = ax + by$, then there are integers x_0, y_0 with $x_0 \neq x$ and $y_0 \neq y$ so that $d = ax_0 + by_0$. (See Solution 19.6.)

19.7 Use the Chinese Remainder Theorem to find $x < 7 \times 11 \times 13$ so that $x \equiv 4 \pmod 7$, $x \equiv 3 \pmod{11}$, and $x \equiv 8 \pmod{13}$. (See Solution 19.7.)

19.8 Is the requirement that the moduli be pairwise relatively prime in the Chinese Remainder Theorem necessary? What happens if we remove that restriction? (See Solution 19.8.)

19.9 Find all irreducible second degree polynomials over Z_3. (See Solution 19.9.)

19.10 Construct $GF(9)$, writing out the Cayley tables. (See Solution 19.10.)

19.11 Show that if a, b are elements of a field F, then $ab = 0$ implies that $a = 0$ or $b = 0$. (See Solution 19.11.)

19.12 What happens if we try to construct $GF(9)$ using the reducible polynomial $(x + 1)(x + 2) = x^2 + 2$. Why is the resulting structure not a field? What is a better term for the resulting structure? (See Solution 19.12.)

19.13 We work over Z_7 for this question.

- Does $(x - 3)(x - 6) = x^2 + 5x + 4$ divide $x^6 - 1$?
- Does $(x - 2)^2 = x^2 - 4x + 4$ divide $x^6 - 1$?

What is a quick way to come to these conclusions? (See Solution 19.13.)

19.14 Verify that over Z_5, the equation $x^4 - 1 = (x-1)(x-2)(x-3)(x-4)$ is true. That is, expand the right hand side, and show that it is the left hand side. (See Solution 19.14.)

19.12   Solutions

19.1 $4023390 = 2 \times 3 \times 5 \times 7^3 \times 17 \times 23$.

19.2   We refer to equations (19.6) and (19.7).

$$\varphi(4023390) = \varphi(2)\varphi(3)\varphi(5)\varphi(7^3)\varphi(17)\varphi(23)$$

$$= (2-1)(3-1)(5-1)(7^3 - 7^2)(17-1)(23-1)$$

$$= (1)(2)(4)(7^3 - 7^2)(16)(22)$$

$$= 827904$$

19.3   We find $2^{605} \pmod{783}$. Now, $783 = 3^3 \times 29$, so $\varphi(783) = \varphi(3^3 \times 29) = \varphi(3^3)\varphi(29) = 3^2(3-1)(28) = 504$, so $2^{605} \equiv 2^{101} \pmod{783}$. We now use the repeated squaring technique of Chapter 3 to find that the answer is 50.

19.4 $d = 65$, $x = 23$, $y = -22$.

19.5 $d = 1$, $x = -157$, $y = 192$.

19.6   We can use $x_0 = x + \frac{b}{d}t$ and $y_0 = y - \frac{a}{d}t$ for any integer t, so that $ax_0 + by_0 = a(x + \frac{b}{d}t) + b(y - \frac{a}{d}t) = ax + by = d$.

19.7   We find $N = 7 \times 11 \times 13$, and then $M_1 = 143$, $M_2 = 91$ and $M_3 = 77$. Using the Euclidean algorithm, we calculate that $m_1 = 5$, $m_2 = 4$ and $m_3 = 12$. This leads to finding that $x = 333$.

19.8   The pairwise relatively prime condition implies that the set of congruences is actually solvable. Consider $x \equiv 1 \pmod 2$, and $x \equiv 2 \pmod 4$. Then no such x exists, as $x \equiv 2 \pmod 4$ implies that x is even, whereas $x \equiv 1 \pmod 2$ forces that x is odd.

   However, it is possible to have a solvable set of congruence equations wherein the moduli are not pairwise relatively prime. To deal with this situation, one can reduce the congruence equations into a set of pairwise relatively prime moduli, and then apply the Chinese Remainder Theorem.

19.9   The six irreducible polynomials are $x^2 + 1$, $x^2 + x + 2$, $x^2 + 2x + 2$, $2x^2 + 2$, $2x^2 + 2x + 1$, and $2x^2 + x + 1$.

To find these polynomials, one could list the first degree polynomials and find all products of exactly two of them. The resulting list will be all polynomials which are not irreducible, so any unlisted polynomials are irreducible.

Also, one could list all second degree polynomials and test if each polynomial has a root. If a polynomial has no root, then it is irreducible (but this test only works for polynomials of degree 2 or 3).

19.10 We use the polynomial $f(x) = x^2 + 1$ to find the field, so $\alpha^2 + 1 = 0$, that is, $\alpha^2 = 2$. This is sufficient to let us completely describe the addition and multiplication of the field.

19.11 Assume that $b \neq 0$. Then b has an inverse, say b^{-1}. Multiplying $ab = 0$ by b^{-1}, we get $(ab)b^{-1} = 0b^{-1} = 0$, so $a = 0$. It follows that either $a = 0$ or $b = 0$.

19.12 Using $f(x) = x^2 + 2$, we set $f(\alpha) = 0$, i.e. $\alpha^2 + 1 = 0$. So, we find that the field elements $\alpha + 1$ and $\alpha + 2$ multiply to $(\alpha + 1)(\alpha + 2) = \alpha + 2 = 0$. That is, the condition proven to hold for all fields in the previous problem is violated. This kind of structure is more properly called a ring.

19.13 Using long division, we find:

- $(x^2 + 5x + 4)g(x) = x^6 - 1$, where $g(x) = x^4 + 2x^3 + 6x + 5$, so that it does divide evenly.
- $(x - 4x + 4)h(x) + (3x + 1) = x^6 - 1$ where $h(x) = x^4 + 4x^3 + 6x^2 + 5x + 2$, so that it does not divide evenly.

We can conclude these quickly, since we know that

$$x^6 - 1 = (x - 1)(x - 2)(x - 3)(x - 4)(x - 5)(x - 6) \tag{19.19}$$

and so it follows that $(x - 3)(x - 6) = x^2 + 5x + 4$ must divide evenly. Further, we know that the factorization of $x^6 - 1$ over $GF(7)$ is unique, so that if $(x - 2)^2$ were to divide $x^6 - 1$, it would also have to divide the right hand side of (19.19). However, this is impossible, and thus we can conclude that $(x - 2)^2$ does not divide $x^6 - 1$ evenly, without having to do the long division.

19.14 We take $[(x - 1)(x - 2)][(x - 3)(x - 4)]$ and expand inside the square braces to find $[(x - 1)(x - 2)][(x - 3)(x - 4)] = [x^2 - 3x + 2][x^2 - 7x + 12]$. Adjusting the coefficients modulo 5, we get $[x^2 - 3x + 2][x^2 - 7x + 12] = [x^2 + 2x + 2][x^2 + 3x + 2]$. Expanding again, we have that this is equal to $(x^4 + 3x^3 + 2x^2) + (2x^3 + 6x^2 + 4x) + (2x^2 + 6x + 4)$. Collecting like terms and reducing modulo 5, we get $x^4 + 4 = x^4 - 1$.

Chapter 20

Introduction to Linear Codes

Goals, Discussion   We introduce the basics of linear codes and give several examples including the "perfect" Hamming and Golay codes. The McEliece cryptographic protocol is described as an application of the theory of linear codes.

New, Noteworthy   We include a discussion of the "football pools" problem. Basic ideas from Shannon's fundamental theorem are revisited using Hamming codes over a binary symmetric channel. We discuss some of the fascinating history of the perfect ternary Golay code of length 11, which was in fact discovered independently and published in the Finnish soccer magazine *Veikkaaja* a year and a half before Golay published the same code.

20.1   Repetition Codes and Parity Checks

We want to revisit some of the general ideas of Chapter 18 and to amplify on them. Mathematical error correction is concerned with the errors which occur when information is transmitted from one place to another. As an example, the binary message 010101 may be received as 011101 because of a problem in the transmission process. These problems are referred to as "noise" and may be due to electromagnetic radiation, thermal radiation (heat), cross talk, deterioration of storage devices such as

Cryptography, Information Theory, and Error-Correction: A Handbook for the 21st Century, Second Edition.
Aiden A. Bruen, Mario A. Forcinito, and James M. McQuillan.
© 2021 John Wiley & Sons, Inc. Published 2021 by John Wiley & Sons, Inc.

hard disks, or even operator (human) error. The detection of errors is important because it sometimes allows for correction by transmitting the information a second time. The correction of the received message to the correct message is even more desirable, but usually harder to accomplish. Both of these objectives can be realized by transmitting the information in a redundant form. For example the binary message 010111 could be repeated three times by transmitting 010111010111010111. Then if only one error was made in the 18 digits transmitted, it would be easy to pick the correct message, since the correct message would occur twice and the wrong message would occur only once.

Repeating the message a large number of times would almost certainly guarantee the received message to be corrected to the sent message, but this process is inefficient and may be too time consuming. For example the digital encoding of music on a compact disc is decoded by a digital-to-analog converter, but early CD players did not read the data on the disc fast enough to be able to read multiple copies of each note encoded on the disc. Nor would the disc have been able to contain 75 minutes of music if everything were recorded multiple times on the disc. Coding theory is concerned with finding the most efficient methods of transmitting information so that some error detection and usually some error correction is possible. Part of the secret of efficient coding is to carefully choose which sequences of numbers are used in representing the transmitted information.

We now give some examples of linear codes.

Example 20.1 *The repetition code consists of repeating each transmitted digit n times. The map from elements in a field F to n-tuples over F given by $f_n : x \rightarrow (x, x, \ldots, x)$ expresses the encoding. The encoding is a linear map from $F^{(1)}$ to $F^{(n)}$, where $F^{(n)}$ is the standard n dimensional vector space over F. If n is odd these will give rise to perfect codes.*

As indicated above, this is not a very efficient approach to coding.

Example 20.2 *A commonly used coding technique is to add an overall parity check. This is used in places where errors are not likely to occur and the detection of an error is all that is required. This code does not supply enough information to determine what the original message might be if there is an error in transmission. The map from vectors of length $n-1$ to vectors of length n over F given by $\psi_n : (x_1, x_2, \ldots, x_{n-1}) \rightarrow (x_1, x_2, \ldots, x_{n-1}, -x_1 - \cdots - x_{n-1})$ defines this code. It can also be expressed in matrix form by*

$$(x_1, x_2, \ldots, x_{n-1}) \rightarrow (x_1, x_2, \ldots, x_{n-1}) \begin{pmatrix} 1 & & & -1 \\ & 1 & & -1 \\ & & \ddots & \vdots \\ & & & 1 & -1 \end{pmatrix}.$$

Note that, if we are working in binary, 2222the effect of this is to adjoin a 1 at the end if the message $(x_1, x_2, \ldots, x_{n-1})$ has an odd number of 1s and to adjoin a 0 otherwise.

Example 20.3 *Suppose that we want to encode messages which consist of four binary digits. The code map f maps a vector $\mathbf{u}$ to $\mathbf{u}G$ where $\mathbf{u}G$ is considered to be a vector of length seven over the binary field. We transmit the seven binary digits which correspond to the seven components of $\mathbf{u}G$. This gives us a linear code C. The matrix G is*

$$\begin{pmatrix} 1 & 0 & 0 & 0 & 0 & 1 & 1 \\ 0 & 1 & 0 & 0 & 1 & 0 & 1 \\ 0 & 0 & 1 & 0 & 1 & 1 & 0 \\ 0 & 0 & 0 & 1 & 1 & 1 & 1 \end{pmatrix}$$

Using this matrix, we find all of the codewords C:

$$(0,0,0,0)G = (0,0,0,0,0,0,0), \quad (0,0,0,1)G = (0,0,0,1,1,1,1)$$
$$(0,0,1,0)G = (0,0,1,0,1,1,0) \quad (0,0,1,1)G = (0,0,1,1,0,0,1)$$
$$(0,1,0,)G = (0,1,0,0,1,0,1) \quad (0,1,0,1)G = (0,1,0,1,0,1,0)$$
$$(0,1,1,0)G = (0,1,1,0,0,1,1) \quad (0,1,1,1)G = (0,1,1,1,1,0,0)$$
$$(1,0,0,0)G = (1,0,0,0,0,1,1) \quad (1,0,0,1)G = (1,0,0,1,1,0,0)$$
$$(1,0,1,0)G = (1,0,1,0,1,0,1) \quad (1,0,1,1)G = (1,0,1,1,0,1,0)$$
$$(1,1,0,0)G = (1,1,0,0,1,1,0) \quad (1,1,0,1)G = (1,1,0,1,0,0,1)$$
$$(1,1,1,0)G = (1,1,1,0,0,0,0) \quad (1,1,1,1)G = (1,1,1,1,1,1,1)$$

20.2 Details of Linear Codes

Let $\mathbf{u} = (u_1, u_2, \ldots, u_k)$ be any element of the k-dimensional vector space over the finite field $GF(q)$ of order q. Thus, $\mathbf{u}$ is a vector of length k over some finite field F of order q, $q = p^m$. For example if $q = 2$ then we are talking about binary strings of length k. So, $\mathbf{u}$ is a **message** of length k.

Let G be a matrix with k rows and n columns over F, of rank k. This implies that $k \leq n$. This is because the column rank must also be k so there must be at least k columns. The fact that G has rank k means that the k rows of G are linearly independent. These rows are a set of linearly independent (row) vectors in F_q^k. First, we break up our messages into blocks of length k. Then, a block $\mathbf{u}$ gets encoded to the codeword $\mathbf{u}G$. This is our **encoding algorithm**.

Thus, $\mathbf{u}$ has length k and $\mathbf{u}G$ has length n.

The set $C = \{\mathbf{u}G \mid \mathbf{u} \text{ in } F_q^k\}$ is called a **linear code of dimension** k **over** F, because C is a linear subspace of F_q^n. F_q^n means the set of vectors of length n, with entries taken from $GF(q)$. To see this, let $\mathbf{v}_1, \mathbf{v}_2$ be in C. So, $\mathbf{u}_1 G = \mathbf{v}_1$ and $\mathbf{u}_2 G = \mathbf{v}_2$. Then, $\alpha \mathbf{v}_1 + \beta \mathbf{v}_2$ is in C since

$$(\alpha \mathbf{u}_1 + \beta \mathbf{u}_2)G = \alpha(\mathbf{u}_1 G) + \beta(\mathbf{u}_2 G)$$

$$= \alpha \mathbf{v}_1 + \beta \mathbf{v}_2$$

The matrix G is called a **generator matrix** for C. We say that C is **a linear** (n, k) **code**, since each row in C has length n and C has dimension k.

Properties of the encoding

(a) the mapping $\mathbf{u} \to \mathbf{u}G$ is one to one. Thus, given $\mathbf{u}G \,(= \mathbf{v})$ there is a unique $\mathbf{u}$ such that $\mathbf{u}G = \mathbf{v}$. We find $\mathbf{u}$ by solving the appropriate system of linear equations.

(b) usually $d(\mathbf{u}G, \mathbf{v}G) \geq d(\mathbf{u}, \mathbf{v})$ where d denotes the Hamming distance.

Example 20.4 *Let G be as in Example 20.3. Let $\mathbf{u} = (0010)$, $\mathbf{v} = (0100)$. Then $d(\mathbf{u}, \mathbf{v}) = 2$. But $\mathbf{u}G = (0010110)$, $\mathbf{v}G = (0100101)$. Then $d(\mathbf{u}G, \mathbf{v}G) = 4$.*

How linear encoding works

The data stream (= message stream) is blocked off into segments of length k. Then, each segment $\mathbf{u}$ of length k is encoded to $\mathbf{u}G$. The code word $\mathbf{u}G$ is then transmitted. The receiver has a list of the code words in C and decodes the received vector to the nearest codeword in C. From this codeword, the receiver calculates the message since the encoding function $\mathbf{u} \to \mathbf{u}G$ is one-to-one. For the moment we ignore the possibility that there may not be a unique "nearest codeword" in C.

The fact that C is linear has several advantages. For example if $\mathbf{v}_1, \mathbf{v}_2$ are in C, then $d(\mathbf{v}_1, \mathbf{v}_2) = d(\mathbf{v}_1 - \mathbf{v}_2, \mathbf{0})$ where $\mathbf{0}$ is the all-zero codeword. Then, $d(\mathbf{v}_1 - \mathbf{v}_2, \mathbf{0})$ is the number of nonzero elements in $\mathbf{v}_1 - \mathbf{v}_2$. This is called the **weight** of $\mathbf{v}_1 - \mathbf{v}_2$. Now $\mathbf{v}_1 - \mathbf{v}_2$ is in C. We have shown the following.

The minimum distance between any 2 codewords in a linear code C equals the minimum weight d of any nonzero codeword in C.

This is useful, because instead of testing all pairs of words in C we need only measure the weight of words in C.

Example 20.5 *The minimum distance between any 2 distinct codewords in the code in Example 20.3, i.e. the minimum distance of the code C, is 3. This follows from the fact that the minimum weight of any codeword in C is 3.*

The above encoding method is called minimum distance coding which is optimal for the kinds of codes with which we deal.

We describe another approach to linear codes C, as follows. Two vectors of length n are said to be **orthogonal** if their dot product is zero.

Example 20.6 *The binary vectors* (1100) *and* (1111) *are orthogonal since* $(1)(1) + (1)(1) + (0)(1) + (0)(1) = 1 + 1 = 0$ *(in binary).*

Example 20.7 (1100) *is orthogonal to itself (in binary). Thus, if C is the linear code consisting of* $\{(1100), (0000)\}$ *we have $C \subset C^{\perp}$.*

This is in sharp contrast to the Euclidean situation over the reals. However, the dimension formula still works: it can be shown by solving a system of linear equations.

Dimension formula

Let C be a linear (n, k) code. Then $C^{\perp}$, the set of all vectors that are orthogonal to each vector in C, is a linear $(n, n - k)$ code.

To check if a vector $\mathbf{x}$ is in $C^{\perp}$, we need only check that $\mathbf{x}$ is orthogonal to each row of a generator matrix G. The code $C^{\perp}$ is called the **dual code** or the **orthogonal code** of C.

We now examine $(C^{\perp})^{\perp}$ the set of all vectors orthogonal to all vectors in $C^{\perp}$. By definition, C is contained in $(C^{\perp})^{\perp}$. Also, dimension $(C^{\perp})^{\perp} = n - (n - k) = k = \dim C$.

Double dual formula $(C^{\perp})^{\perp} = C$.

Two linear codes over the finite field $GF(q)$ are said to be **equivalent** if one can be obtained from the other by a combination of operations of the following types.

(A) Permutations of the positions of the code.

(B) Multiplication of the symbols appearing in a fixed position by a nonzero scalar.

Note that (A) corresponds to a permutation or re-arrangement of the columns of the matrix of the code when the code C is thought of as a matrix whose rows are the codewords in C.

Thus, two $k \times n$ matrices generate equivalent linear (n, k) codes over $GF(q)$ if one matrix can be obtained from the other by a sequence of operations of the following types:

E1 Permutation of the rows.

E2 Multiplying a row by a nonzero scalar.

E3 Adding a multiple of one row to another.

E4 Permutation of the columns.

E5 Multiplying a column by a nonzero scalar.

Operations E1, E2, and E3 replace one basis of the code by another one of the same code. Operations E4 and E5 convert a generator matrix to one for an equivalent code.

For general codes, we are allowed to use any permutation of the symbols instead of the permutation in (B) in the definition of equivalent codes.

Note that if two linear codes are equivalent, the distances between codewords are unchanged by the operations E1 to E5.

Thus, C can equally well be described as the set of all vectors orthogonal to $(C^\perp)$.

A linear (n, k) code C is said to be in **systematic form** if a generator matrix for C is of the form $G = [I_k \mid A]$ where I is the $k \times k$ identity matrix and A is some matrix of size $k \times (n - k)$. In such a case the first k entries of $\mathbf{u}G$ are just the k entries of the message $\mathbf{u}$ and are called the **information** or **message** digits. The remaining $n - k$ digits are called **parity bits** or **parity digits**.

The following result is shown in [Hil86, p. 63], and Welsh [Wel88, p. 55]. Let G be a generator matrix of an (n, k) code. Then, by performing operations of type E1 to E5, G can be transformed to systematic or standard form $(I_k \mid A)$.

We can now establish the following result.

Algebraic representation of $C^\perp$

Let $G = (I_k \mid A)$ be a generator matrix for a linear (n, k) code C. Then, $H = (-A^t \mid I_{n-k})$ is a generator matrix for $C^\perp$, where A^t is the transpose matrix of A. The code C can be described as the set of all vectors $\mathbf{v}$ whose dot product with each row of H is zero. In other words, $C = \{\mathbf{v} \mid \mathbf{v}H^t = 0\}$.

To see that H is a generator matrix for $C^\perp$, we need to only check that the corresponding dot products are zero. H is called a **parity check matrix** for C (or G).

Remark

Do not confuse a parity check matrix with an "overall parity check."

Example 20.8 *Let G be the matrix in Example 20.3 and C the corresponding binary $(7, 4)$ code. Then C is in systematic form. A parity check matrix H is given by the matrix*

$$H = \begin{pmatrix} 0 & 1 & 1 & 1 & 1 & 0 & 0 \\ 1 & 0 & 1 & 1 & 0 & 1 & 0 \\ 1 & 1 & 0 & 1 & 0 & 0 & 1 \end{pmatrix}$$

Example 20.9 *The repetition code of length n in Example 20.1 is dual to the parity check code in Example 20.2 over any field.*

To see this, we can check that the relevant dot products are zero and that the dimensions add up.

For example let $n = 3$. Then the overall parity check mapping takes (x_1, x_2) to $(x_1, x_2, -x_1 - x_2)$. The repetition code maps x_1 to (x_1, x_1, x_1) and x_2 to (x_2, x_2, x_2). Each of (x_1, x_1, x_1), (x_2, x_2, x_2) and any linear combination of them has dot product zero with $(x_1, x_2, -x_1 - x_2)$.

The operation of **row reduction** of a matrix is familiar from linear algebra. Let G be any generator matrix for an (n, k) linear code C. Then by row reduction we can reduce G to systematic form. The resulting code C_1 may not be the same as C (since we may permute columns in the process) but is **equivalent to** C in that distances are preserved.

20.3 Parity Checks, the Syndrome, and Weights

Let C be an (n, k) linear code over F. We can show the following result.

Theorem 20.10 *C has a codeword of weight t if and only if some t columns of H are linearly dependent, where H is a parity check matrix for C.*

For, suppose $\mathbf{c}$ in C has weight t. Now $\mathbf{c}H^t = 0$; so we get a dependence relation among t rows of H^t, i.e. among the corresponding t columns of H. The converse also holds.

Take an easy example. Suppose the sum of the first 2 columns of H is zero. Then the dot product of $(110 \ldots 0)$ with each row of H is zero. So $(1100 \ldots 0)$ is in C – and has weight 2.

Next, let $\mathbf{w}$ be any vector of length n. The **syndrome** of $\mathbf{w}$ is defined to be $\mathbf{w}H^t$, which is a row vector over F. Using our previous discussions, we have part of the following result.

Theorem 20.11

(a) *The vector $\mathbf{w}$ is in C if and only if the syndrome of $\mathbf{w}$ is the zero vector.*

(b) *The syndromes of $\mathbf{w}$ and $\mathbf{w} + \mathbf{c}$ are equal for any codeword $\mathbf{c}$ in C.*

(c) *If $\mathbf{w}_1, \mathbf{w}_2$ have the same syndrome, then $\mathbf{w}_1 = \mathbf{w}_2 + \mathbf{c}$ for some codeword $\mathbf{c}$ in C. Thus, the set of all vectors having a given syndrome forms a coset.*

To see (c) observe that if $\mathbf{w}_1 H^t = \mathbf{w}_2 H^t$ then $(\mathbf{w}_1 - \mathbf{w}_2)H^t = \mathbf{0}$, so $\mathbf{w}_1 - \mathbf{w}_2$ is in C giving $\mathbf{w}_1 = \mathbf{w}_2 + \mathbf{c}$. Then, the set of all vectors $\mathbf{w}_1$ having the same syndrome as $\mathbf{w}_2$ is the coset $\mathbf{w}_2 + C$.

We can use the syndrome idea for decoding. Let C be any linear (n, k) code over F where F is any finite field. Then the set of all vectors of the form $\mathbf{c} + \mathbf{x}$, $\mathbf{c}$ in C, which is denoted by $C + \mathbf{x}$ is called a **coset of C**.

Example 20.12   *Let $\mathbf{x}$ be any codeword $\mathbf{c}$. Then $C + \mathbf{x} = C + \mathbf{c} = C$. The reason is that C, being a subspace, is closed under addition.*

Example 20.13   *For any $\mathbf{x}$, the coset $C + \mathbf{x}$ equals the coset $C + \mathbf{x}_1$ where $\mathbf{x}_1$ is any vector in the coset $C + \mathbf{x}$.*

To see this, we have $C + \mathbf{x}_1 = C + (\mathbf{c} + \mathbf{x}) = (C + \mathbf{c}) + \mathbf{x} = C + \mathbf{x}$.

From Theorem 20.11 above we see that two vectors have the same syndrome if and only if they lie in the same coset of C. A **coset leader** for a coset $C + \mathbf{x}$ is a vector $c_0 + \mathbf{e}$ of minimal weight in $C + \mathbf{x}$. Of course, there may be several coset leaders in $C + \mathbf{x}$.

The syndrome decoding procedure works on the assumption that a *small number of errors is more likely than a large number of errors*. Suppose that $\mathbf{y}$ is received. We calculate $\mathbf{y}H^t = S(\mathbf{y})$, the syndrome of $\mathbf{y}$. If $S(\mathbf{y}) = \mathbf{0}$ then, since $\mathbf{y}$ is in C, we assume that no errors occurred and that $\mathbf{y}$ was transmitted. We note in passing that for **any** c in C, $S(\mathbf{c}) = \mathbf{0}$.

Now suppose $S(\mathbf{y}) = \mathbf{z} \neq \mathbf{0}$. The set of all vectors of length n having syndrome $\mathbf{z}$ consists of a coset $C + \mathbf{x}$, and this coset contains $\mathbf{y}$. Thus, $\mathbf{y}$ is one of the vectors $\{\mathbf{c}_1 + \mathbf{x}, \mathbf{c}_2 + \mathbf{x}, \ldots, \mathbf{c}_t + \mathbf{x}\}$ where $t = q^k$ is the total number of codewords in C. We can think of $\mathbf{y}$ as having been obtained by transmitting some $\mathbf{c}_i$ which gets distorted by the error pattern $\mathbf{x}$ in transmission, so $\mathbf{y} = \mathbf{c}_i + \mathbf{x}$.

Now let $\mathbf{e}$ be the coset leader in the coset $C + \mathbf{x}$. So $C + \mathbf{x} = C + \mathbf{e}$ as in Example 20.13. and $wt(\mathbf{e}) \leq wt(\mathbf{x})$, with wt denoting weight, by definition of the coset leader.

Then, $C + \mathbf{x} = C + \mathbf{e} = \{\mathbf{c}_1 + \mathbf{e}, \mathbf{c}_2 + \mathbf{e}, \ldots, \mathbf{c}_t + \mathbf{e}\}$. So $\mathbf{y}$ is also equal to $\mathbf{c}_j + \mathbf{e}$ and $\mathbf{y}$ could have been obtained by transmitting $\mathbf{c}_t$ which gets distorted to $\mathbf{c}_j + \mathbf{e}$ with error pattern $\mathbf{e}$. If $wt(\mathbf{e}) < wt(\mathbf{x})$ this is more likely than having $\mathbf{c}_i$ transmitted as above, with error pattern $\mathbf{x}$.

Now to our punch line. We assume $\mathbf{y} = \mathbf{c}_j + \mathbf{e}$ so we decode $\mathbf{y}$ as $\mathbf{c}_j = \mathbf{y} - \mathbf{e}$. This explains the following decoding algorithm.

Syndrome decoding algorithm

(a) For a received vector $\mathbf{y}$ calculate $\mathbf{y}H^t$, the syndrome $S(\mathbf{y})$ of $\mathbf{y}$.

(b) Find a coset leader $\mathbf{w}$ in that coset having the property that each coset vector has $S(\mathbf{y})$ as its syndrome.

(c) Decode $\mathbf{y}$ as $\mathbf{y} - \mathbf{w}$. If there are several coset leaders make an arbitrary choice.

Example 20.14 *Working in binary, let the $(4,2)$ linear code C have systematic generator matrix* $G = \begin{pmatrix} 1 & 0 & 0 & 1 \\ 0 & 1 & 1 & 1 \end{pmatrix}$. *Then the codewords in C are*

$\{(0000), (1001), (0111), (1110)\}$. *Now* $H = \begin{pmatrix} 0 & 1 & 1 & 0 \\ 1 & 1 & 0 & 1 \end{pmatrix}$. *Suppose the codeword*

$\mathbf{y} = (1101)$ *is received. Now* $S(\mathbf{y}) = \mathbf{y}H^t = (1101) \begin{pmatrix} 0 & 1 \\ 1 & 1 \\ 1 & 0 \\ 0 & 1 \end{pmatrix} = (11)$.

The coset $C + (0100) = \{(0100), (1101), (0011), (1010)\}$ has the property that the syndrome of each of its members is $(1,1)$. The unique coset leader is $\mathbf{w} = (0100)$. So we decode $\mathbf{y}$ are $\mathbf{y} - \mathbf{w} = \mathbf{y} + \mathbf{w} = (1101) + 0100) = (1001)$.

For the record, we write down the cosets of C here with the coset leaders and the syndromes.

Coset	Coset leader	Syndrome
(0000) (1001) (0111) (1110)	(0000)	(00)
(1000) (0001) (1111) (0110)	(1000) [or(0001)]	(01)
(0100) (1101) (0011) (1010)	(0100)	(11)
(0010) (1011) (0101) (1100)	(0010)	(10)

20.4   Hamming Codes, an Inequality

Initially, we work in binary. Pick any positive integer $m \geq 3$. Form the matrix H_m of size $m \times s$, $s = 2^m - 1$ whose columns are all possible *nonzero* binary m-tuples. Using this matrix H_m as a parity check matrix form the $(2^m - 1 - m) \times (2^m - 1)$ binary linear code C_m. This code C_m is called the **Hamming code** of length $2^m - 1$. Of course the words in C_n will depend on our ordering of the columns of H_m.

Theorem 20.15 C_m *has length* $2^m - 1$, *dimension* $2^m - 1 - m$ *and minimum weight* $w = 3$. *Moreover* C_m *is a perfect code.*

Proof. Since the columns in H contain the standard basis vectors

$$\begin{pmatrix} 1 \\ 0 \\ \vdots \\ 0 \end{pmatrix}, \begin{pmatrix} 0 \\ 1 \\ \vdots \\ 0 \end{pmatrix}, \ldots, \begin{pmatrix} 0 \\ 0 \\ \vdots \\ 1 \end{pmatrix}$$

of length m, the rank of H is m. Since the columns of H are distinct it follows from Theorem 20.10 of Section 20.3 that $w = 3$. C_m is perfect since by calculation the Hamming balls of radius 1 about the codewords in C_m are pairwise disjoint and fill up the space, i.e. the sphere-packing criterion is satisfied as described in Chapter 12.

Decoding is easy for the Hamming codes. Suppose that we index the columns of H in accordance with the binary representations of $1, 2, 3, \ldots, 2^m - 1$. So for $m = 3$ we get

$$H = \begin{pmatrix} 0 & 0 & 0 & 1 & 1 & 1 & 1 \\ 0 & 1 & 1 & 0 & 0 & 1 & 1 \\ 1 & 0 & 1 & 0 & 1 & 0 & 1 \end{pmatrix}.$$

Now suppose $\mathbf{u}$ is transmitted and $\mathbf{v} = \mathbf{u} + \mathbf{e}$ is received, where the error vector $\mathbf{e}$ is either the zero vector or else has exactly one 1 in it. Now the syndrome is $\mathbf{v}H^t = (\mathbf{u} + \mathbf{e})H^t = \mathbf{e}H^t$. We are getting the dot product of $\mathbf{e}$ with the rows of H. Suppose H is as above and $\mathbf{e} = (0001000)$. Then (the transpose) of $\mathbf{v}H^t$ will be $\begin{pmatrix} 1 \\ 0 \\ 0 \end{pmatrix}$, corresponding to the fourth column of H. We then know that the error is in the fourth slot. So we correct the received word $\mathbf{v}$ by adding 1 in the fourth slot, since this operation will change 1 to 0 or 0 to 1. ∎

Example 20.16 *Let $m = 3$ and let H be as above. Let the received word by $\mathbf{v} = (1010011)$. The transpose of the syndrome is $\mathbf{v}H^t = \begin{pmatrix} 0 \\ 1 \\ 1 \end{pmatrix}$. So there is an error in position number three. Thus, $\mathbf{v}$ gets decoded to $\mathbf{v} + (0010000) = (1000011)$.*

We now obtain an inequality involving the minimum distance and dimension of a linear code. For convenience, we restrict our attention to the binary case.

Theorem 20.17 *If a binary linear code C of length n and dimension k has minimum distance $d \geq 2t + 1$ then $2^{n-k} \geq \binom{n}{0} + \binom{n}{1} + \binom{n}{2} + \cdots + \binom{n}{t}$.*

Proof. Let $\mathbf{u}, \mathbf{v}$ be distinct vectors, each of which has weight at most t. If the syndrome of $\mathbf{u}$ were equal to the syndrome of $\mathbf{v}$ then the syndrome of $\mathbf{u} + \mathbf{v}$ is $\mathbf{0}$, implying that $\mathbf{u} + \mathbf{v} = \mathbf{c}$ in C. Then $\mathbf{c}$ would be a nonzero codeword in C whose weight is at most $t + t = 2t < d$. This is impossible. Thus, since there are exactly $\binom{n}{i}$ binary vectors of length i, $0 \leq i \leq t$, the number of distinct syndromes is at least $\binom{n}{0} + \binom{n}{1} + \binom{n}{2} + \cdots + \binom{n}{t}$. ∎

20.5 Perfect Codes, Errors, and the BSC

Suppose C is an (n, k) linear code over a field $F = GF(q)$ of order q. Then the number M of codewords in C is q^k. The **rate of** C is defined to be $\frac{\log_q M}{n} = \frac{k \log q}{n}$. Note that when $q = 2$ this accords with our previous definition in Part II of this book.

Now suppose also that C is perfect and can correct up to t errors. *Then, if at most t errors occur, all transmissions of codewords will be decoded correctly* since **every** vector lies within the (Hamming) ball of some codeword in C of radius t. However, if more than t errors occur in a transmission, then **there is certain to be a decoding error**. For, if $\mathbf{c}$ is transmitted and $\mathbf{w}$ is received with $d(\mathbf{c}, \mathbf{w}) > t$ then $\mathbf{w}$ will be decoded to the unique codeword $\mathbf{c}_1$ with $d(\mathbf{c}_1, \mathbf{w}) \leq t$. So $\mathbf{c}_1 \neq \mathbf{c}$ and we have a decoding error.

For example let us look at the case when $C = C_m$ is a Hamming code (which is perfect), with $t = 1$. The rate of C_m is $\frac{2^m - 1 - m}{2^m - 1}$ so **the rate tends to 1 as m gets**

large. Suppose we transmit over the binary symmetric channel (BSC) with parameter p. From the above, there is a decoding error if there is more than a one-bit transmission error.

The code length is $n = 2^m - 1$. We have $\Pr(0 \text{ or exactly } 1 \text{ errors}) = q^n + \binom{n}{1} q^{n-1} p^1$, $q = 1 - p$. Thus the probability of a decoding error is $1 - \left[q^n + \binom{n}{1} q^{n-1} p^1 \right]$. This tends to 1 as n gets large as pointed out in Jones and Jones [JJ00].

This gives a nice vindication of Shannon's channel capacity theorem. Here, the rate tends to 1 when n is large. In particular for large n, the rate is greater than the capacity function $1 - H(p)$. Shannon's result only guarantees accuracy of decoding when the rate is less than the capacity. Here, as we have seen, the error probability tends to 1!

20.6   Generalizations of Binary Hamming Codes

Instead of working in binary, we can work over $GF(q)$. Each column of H is defined to be a nonzero vector of length m, and no two columns are allowed to be scalar multiples of each other. We then get a matrix H of size $m \times \left(\frac{q^m - 1}{q - 1} \right)$ of rank k. H is a parity check matrix for a Hamming code $C_m(q)$ which is a perfect one-error correcting code over $GF(q)$. The columns of H are the points of a projective space of (projective) dimension $m - 1$. For $m = 3$, $q = 2$, we get the famous seven point Fano projective plane (Figure 20.1).

The following matrix covers the case when $q = 3$, $m = 3$.

$$H = \begin{pmatrix} 1 & 1 & 0 & 1 & 2 & 0 & 2 & 2 & 1 & 2 & 1 & 0 & 0 \\ 1 & 0 & 1 & 1 & 1 & 2 & 0 & 1 & 2 & 2 & 0 & 1 & 0 \\ 0 & 1 & 1 & 1 & 0 & 1 & 1 & 1 & 1 & 1 & 0 & 0 & 1 \end{pmatrix}.$$

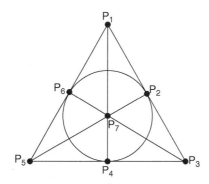

Figure 20.1: Fano's geometry with seven lines and seven vertices.

20.7 The Football Pools Problem, Extended Hamming Codes

We present here a surprising application of Hamming codes to the topic of Football pools, a topic which does not appear to be directly related to the errors that occur in the transmission of messages. Suppose that a **football pool** consists of m soccer matches, each of which can end in either a draw(0), a loss(1), or a win(2) for the home team. Any outcome for all m games can be considered a vector over $GF(3)$ of length m. The number of possible outcomes of all m games is 3^m. A first or second prize is awarded to any person who guesses at least $m-1$ games correctly. We want to solve the following problem. *What is the fewest number of guesses required to be certain of winning at least a second prize?*

Winning at least a second prize corresponds to choosing a ternary m-tuple that differs from the winning m-tuple in at most one slot. We choose as our set of guesses all of the codewords in the ternary Hamming code of length $m = 3^n + 3^{n-1} + \cdots + 3 + 1$. From the nature of the Hamming code, one can show that this set of guesses is optimal for guaranteeing at least a second prize. Since a Hamming code is a perfect code in which every vector lies in exactly one Hamming ball of radius 1 centered at a codeword, we know that the codewords are sufficiently close to every vector. Let C_m be the Hamming code which comes from the n- dimensional projective geometry over $GF(3)$. Then the number of rows in a parity-check matrix is $n+1$ and the number of columns is the number of points in the geometry, which is $m = 3^n + \cdots + 3 + 1$. Hence the number of rows in a generator matrix for C_m is $m - n - 1$. Thus, the number of codewords is 3^{m-n-1}. Each value of n determines a possible value of m. For example, if $n = 1$, then $m = 4$. If $n = 2$, then $m = 13$. In this case, the number of guesses required to win at least a second prize in a pool of 13 games is $3^{m-n-1} = 3^{10}$.

If the value of m does not equal the number of points in some projective geometry over $GF(3)$, then a different approach is required.

Extended Hamming codes

Let H be a parity-check matrix for a Hamming code. We create a new matrix H^* by first adding a row of ones at the top of H. Then, we add a column of zeros to the left side of H. Next, we change the number in the upper left hand corner of this new matrix to -1. This new matrix H^* is a parity-check matrix for a linear code C, called an **extended Hamming code**. The words in C are the words in the Hamming code with a new first digit which is the sum of all the other digits in the code. Extended Hamming codes are not perfect codes, but they do correct any one error in transmission and are capable of detecting any two errors.

Example 20.18 *The following matrix is a parity-check matrix for the extended Hamming code arising from the Fano geometry.*

$$H^* = \begin{pmatrix} 1 & 1 & 1 & 1 & 1 & 1 & 1 & 1 \\ 0 & 0 & 1 & 1 & 1 & 1 & 0 & 0 \\ 0 & 1 & 0 & 1 & 1 & 0 & 1 & 0 \\ 0 & 1 & 1 & 0 & 1 & 0 & 0 & 1 \end{pmatrix}.$$

20.8   Golay Codes

In this section, we will discuss all perfect codes which can correct more than one error. The easy examples are the repetition codes over $GF(2)$. The repetition code of length $2k+1$ corrects any k errors. It is perfect over $GF(2)$ since any $(2k+1)$-tuple will have either $k+1$ zeros or $k+1$ ones and hence, will be corrected to one of the two possible code words: $(000 \ldots 0)$ and $(111 \ldots 1)$.

Golay searched for perfect linear codes C of length n. In addition to finding the repetition codes and some of the Hamming codes, he also found some nontrivial examples. He looked for solutions to the sphere packing condition which must be satisfied by a perfect code. There are altogether q^n vectors. Also $|C|$, the number of vectors in C is q^j. As in Chapter 18, we have

$$\sum_{i=0}^{t} \binom{n}{i} (q-1)^i = q^{n-j} \tag{20.1}$$

One solution is $q=3$, $n=11$, $j=6$, and $t=2$. Golay created the following parity-check matrix for the corresponding ternary code G_{11}.

$$H = \begin{pmatrix} 1 & 1 & 1 & 2 & 2 & 0 & 1 & 0 & 0 & 0 & 0 \\ 1 & 1 & 2 & 1 & 0 & 2 & 0 & 1 & 0 & 0 & 0 \\ 1 & 2 & 1 & 0 & 1 & 2 & 0 & 0 & 1 & 0 & 0 \\ 1 & 2 & 0 & 1 & 2 & 1 & 0 & 0 & 0 & 1 & 0 \\ 1 & 0 & 2 & 2 & 1 & 1 & 0 & 0 & 0 & 0 & 1 \end{pmatrix}.$$

The five rows of H are linearly independent over $GF(3)$, the field of order 3. Here we refer to Jones and Jones [JJ00]. They comment as follows. "With considerable patience one can show that there are no sets of four or fewer linearly independent columns whereas there is a set of five linearly dependent columns (for instance, $\mathbf{c}_2 - \mathbf{c}_7 - \mathbf{c}_8 + \mathbf{c}_9 + \mathbf{c}_{10} = \mathbf{0}$)."

Thus, $H^\perp = G_{11}$ has minimum distance 5 and can correct up to 2 errors so $t = 2$. Then, since $\Sigma_{i=0}^{2} \binom{n}{i} (q-1)^i = 243 - 3^5$, we conclude that G_{11} is perfect.

There are many other ways of representing this Golay code including quadratic residue codes.

Another solution, $q = 2$, $n = 23$, $j = 12$, and $t = 3$ leads to the binary Golay code G_{23} with a parity-check matrix $H = [A^t \mid I]$ where

$$A^t = \begin{pmatrix} 1 & 0 & 0 & 1 & 1 & 1 & 0 & 0 & 0 & 1 & 1 & 1 \\ 1 & 0 & 1 & 0 & 1 & 1 & 0 & 1 & 1 & 0 & 0 & 1 \\ 1 & 0 & 1 & 1 & 0 & 1 & 1 & 0 & 1 & 0 & 1 & 0 \\ 1 & 0 & 1 & 1 & 1 & 0 & 1 & 1 & 0 & 1 & 0 & 0 \\ 1 & 1 & 0 & 0 & 1 & 1 & 1 & 0 & 1 & 1 & 0 & 0 \\ 1 & 1 & 0 & 1 & 0 & 1 & 1 & 1 & 0 & 0 & 0 & 1 \\ 1 & 1 & 0 & 1 & 1 & 0 & 0 & 1 & 1 & 0 & 1 & 0 \\ 1 & 1 & 1 & 0 & 0 & 1 & 0 & 1 & 0 & 1 & 1 & 0 \\ 1 & 1 & 1 & 0 & 1 & 0 & 1 & 0 & 0 & 0 & 1 & 1 \\ 1 & 1 & 1 & 1 & 0 & 0 & 0 & 0 & 1 & 1 & 0 & 1 \\ 0 & 1 & 1 & 1 & 1 & 1 & 1 & 1 & 1 & 1 & 1 & 1 \end{pmatrix}$$

In addition to being extremely useful codes, Golay codes are related to other mathematical structures such as simple groups, lattices, block designs, and Steiner systems. These connections give insight into how Golay chose a correct parity-check matrices for these codes. The reader is referred to Anderson [And89] for details of the block design on 24 points with block size 8, denoted by $S(5, 8, 24)$.

20.9 McEliece Cryptosystem

In order to correct the errors in a linear code, it is necessary to know something about how the code is constructed, such as the parity-check matrix. It is possible to create codes that are so complicated that correcting a message with many errors is infeasible without this knowledge. This fact can be used to enhance the security of a cryptosystem. The McEliece cryptosystem is based on the sender purposely putting errors into the message, but not so many that the message cannot be decoded if the receiver has knowledge of the code. Eavesdroppers, without this knowledge, have little hope of correcting the message and therefore cannot determine what the message is.

The codes which are often used for this purpose are Goppa codes, defined over $GF(2)$. The word length is $n = 2^m$ and the distance between codewords is $2t + 1$ for some integer t. A generator matrix G for the code is of size $k \times n$ where $k = n - mt$. For example if $m = 9$ and $t = 30$, the generator matrix is 242×512, the word length is 512 and the code can correct as many as 30 errors.

The encryption works as follows. A message M of length k is multiplied on the right by the product $G^+ = SGP$ where S is an invertible $k \times k$ matrix, G is a $k \times n$ generator matrix for the code, and P is a $n \times n$ permutation matrix. (A permutation matrix over $GF(2)$ is characterized by the fact that every row and every column of P contains exactly one 1.) **The receiver keeps these matrices secret**. Only G^+, the product of the three matrices, is made public. The sender then adds an error E of weight at most t to the product $M \cdot G^+$. (Making the weight of the error E close to t will make the message harder to correct.) So the transmitted message is $M_1 = MG^+ + E$.

The receiver multiplies M_1 by P^{-1} to get $M_1' = M_1 P^{-1} = MSG + EP^{-1}$. Since P is a permutation matrix, it has the effect of permuting the components of any vector. Hence, EP^{-1} has at most t ones, just as E does. The vector M_1' is decoded, using knowledge of the code, by the receiver producing MSG which is a codeword. Assuming that the matrix G is in systematic form, i.e. has the form $G = [I|A]$, MS gives the first k components of MSG. Multiplying MS on the right by S^{-1} produces the intended message M.

One problem with this encryption (which offers only computational security) is that the public key G^+ must be a very large matrix.

20.10   Historical Remarks

Soccer pools

Suppose we have a soccer pool with 12 matches with the outcomes being a home win, home loss, or draw for each game. Let us assume that even a novice is guaranteed to know one "sure thing." We are now down to a pool with 11 matches. So now our problem is to buy as few tickets as possible in such a way that we differ by at most two from the real outcome. In other words, we want to be sure that we are off by at most two results out of the eleven matches.

This is reminiscent of the football pools problem using Hamming codes, except that now we allow ourselves to be wrong on two matches instead of just one match.

The most economical way of purchasing the tickets is by buying exactly those tickets – regarded as ternary 11-tuples that are in the Golay code G_{11}. Indeed, Juhani Virtakillio published the code G_{11} in issues 27, 28, and 33 of the Finnish soccer magazine *Veikkaja*, one and a half years before Golay published G_{11}. The history of this is described in H. Hämäläinen and S. Rankinen [HR91], and in the following (unpublished) paper by I. Honkala, *On the early history of the ternary Golay code*, which is an appendix to the paper above in the *Journal of Combinatorial Theory*.

Quoting from Bary quoting from Honkola, Virtakallio puts it laconically in this way.

The following system with 729 columns [= codewords] was born in my brain during a period of depression in football-pool prizes. Because the prizes were too small at that time to compensate the investments that would have been required if the system had been used week after week, the system remained unpublished and was forgotten among other systems. When during the last winter the football-prizes reached a peak, there was talk with the editors about publishing the system but they could not fit the 729 columns into the magazine. Only now, when I discovered a method to obtain the required saving of space, does this system get a chance to enrich the possibilities of players, and perhaps the players themselves.

If the match chosen to be sure has been forecast correctly, the system guarantees at least 10 correct results. In the model we only present how to forecast the 11 other matches, the sure match has not been written down.

In his famous and remarkable half-page paper in 1949 [Gol49], Golay describes not just the two Golay codes, but also the (perfect) binary Hamming codes and the perfect binary repetition codes of odd length.

20.11 Problems

20.1 Find all the codewords in the linear code C, over the field of order 3, if a generator matrix for C is $G = [I|A]$ where $A = \begin{pmatrix} 1 & 2 \\ 2 & 1 \end{pmatrix}$. Also, find all the codewords in the dual code $C^{\perp}$. (See Solution 20.1.)

20.2 If $G = \begin{pmatrix} 2 & 4 & 2 & 3 \\ 1 & 2 & 0 & 1 \end{pmatrix}$ is a generator matrix for the linear code C over the field $GF(5)$, find a generator matrix G' in the form $G' = [I|A]$ for an equivalent code C'. (See Solution 20.2.)

20.3 Suppose that the minimum weight of any nonzero codeword in the linear code C is 8. How many errors can the code correct? (See Solution 20.3.)

20.4 What is the rank of a generator matrix G if G encodes 3 digit messages in binary? (See Solution 20.4.)

20.5 The following vectors were received from a transmission using a linear code over the field $GF(5)$ or order 5: (224332), (412311), and (324410). The code corrects 1 error.

(a) Which of the 3 vectors can be corrected to the nearest codeword if the generator matrix was $G = [I|A]$ and $A = \begin{pmatrix} 1 & 1 & 4 \\ 0 & 2 & 4 \\ 2 & 3 & 4 \end{pmatrix}$?

(b) In each case where the vector can be corrected, find the nearest codeword.

(See Solution 20.5.)

20.6   What is the information rate for the binary Hamming code of length 15? (See Solution 20.6.)

20.7   What finite field is used to create the Hamming code of length 156? (See Solution 20.7.)

20.8   Find the columns of a parity-check matrix for a binary Hamming code of length 15. (See Solution 20.8.)

20.9   How many bets need to be placed in a football pool of four games in order to be sure of winning at least second prize? (See Solution 20.9.)

20.10   If C is a k dimensional code over $GF(q)$, then how many words are in C? (See Solution 20.10.)

20.11   If B is the following matrix, then how many words $\mathbf{u}B$ are there? That is how many codewords does B generate? We are working over $GF(3)$.

$$B = \begin{pmatrix} 1 & 2 & 1 & 1 \\ 2 & 2 & 1 & 2 \\ 0 & 1 & 2 & 0 \end{pmatrix}$$

(See Solution 20.11.)

20.12   How many codewords would we have expected using B in the previous question? Why is B an ineligible choice for a generator matrix of a linear code? (See Solution 20.12.)

20.13   Find a code C equivalent to

$$D = \begin{pmatrix} 2 & 1 & 2 & 1 \\ 1 & 2 & 2 & 1 \end{pmatrix}$$

that is in the form $[I|A]$ over the field $GF(3)$. Then find $C^{\perp}$, the code dual to C. (See Solution 20.13.)

20.14 The matrix G below is a generator matrix for a Hamming code of length 7. The vector $\mathbf{y} = (1110101)$ is received. Given that the only possible transmission errors are binary vectors of weight 1, what was the transmitted message?

$$G = \begin{pmatrix} 1 & 0 & 0 & 0 & 0 & 1 & 1 \\ 0 & 1 & 0 & 0 & 1 & 0 & 1 \\ 0 & 0 & 1 & 0 & 1 & 1 & 0 \\ 0 & 0 & 0 & 1 & 1 & 1 & 1 \end{pmatrix}$$

(See Solution 20.14.)

20.15 Repeat Question 20.14 with $\mathbf{y} = (1001100)$. (See Solution 20.15.)

20.16 Use $\mathbf{y} = (0111011)$ to do Question 20.14 again. (See Solution 20.16.)

20.17 Consider a binary code C with generator matrix G given by

$$G = \begin{pmatrix} 1 & 0 & 0 & 1 & 1 & 0 \\ 0 & 1 & 0 & 1 & 0 & 1 \\ 0 & 0 & 1 & 0 & 1 & 1 \end{pmatrix}$$

Find the generator matrix for $C^{\perp}$. (See Solution 20.17.)

20.18 For the generator matrix G above, find all of the codewords belonging to C. (See Solution 20.18.)

20.19 What is the information rate for the code given in Problem 20.18? (See Solution 20.19.)

20.20 Using the parity-check matrix H of a given binary code with generator matrix G, determine whether a transmission error can be detected given that the received message was $(1, 0, 1, 0, 1, 0)$, where

$$H = \begin{pmatrix} 1 & 1 & 1 & 1 & 0 & 0 \\ 1 & 1 & 0 & 0 & 1 & 0 \\ 1 & 0 & 1 & 0 & 0 & 1 \end{pmatrix}.$$

(See Solution 20.20.)

20.21 Find the Hamming distance between the two vectors $\mathbf{u}, \mathbf{v}$ given by $\mathbf{u} = (1, 1, 0, 0, 1, 0, 1, 0)$, $\mathbf{v} = (0, 1, 0, 1, 0, 1, 0, 1)$ (See Solution 20.21.)

20.22 If the probability of a bit error is p, what is the probability that a received message obtained from the binary repetition code of length 5 is received correctly? (See Solution 20.22.)

20.23 What is the fewest number of guesses required to be certain of winning at least second prize in a pool of 40 games? (See Solution 20.23.)

20.24 Find an upper bound on the fewest number of guesses required to be certain of winning at least a second prize in a pool of three games. (See Solution 20.24.)

20.25 Find an upper bound on the fewest number of guesses required to be certain of winning at least a second prize in a pool of m games. (See Solution 20.25.)

20.12 Solutions

20.1 The codewords are $(0,0)G = (0,0,0,0)$, $(1,0)G = (1,0,1,2)$, $(2,0)G = (2,0,2,1)$, $(0,1)G = (0,1,2,1)$, $(0,2)G = (0,2,1,2)$, $(1,1)G = (1,1,0,0)$, $(2,2)G = (2,2,0,0)$, $(1,2)G = (1,2,2,1)$, and $(2,1)G = (2,1,1,2)$. The code words in $G^\perp$ are those vectors which are orthogonal to every row in the matrix G. They are $(0,0,0,0)$, $(0,0,1,1)$, $(0,0,2,2)$, $(1,2,0,1)$, $(2,1,0,2)$, $(1,2,1,2)$, $(2,1,2,1)$, $(1,2,2,0)$, and $(2,1,1,0)$.

By choosing two nonzero, linearly independent vectors, say $(0,0,1,1)$ and $(2,1,1,0)$ in the dual space and getting all possible combinations of them over the field of order 3, including the zero vector, we generate the nine vectors in the dual code.

20.2 We apply row operations to G. First, we interchange the two rows of G. Then, we subtract 2 times the new top row from the bottom row. This produces the matrix $G_2 = \begin{pmatrix} 1 & 2 & 0 & 1 \\ 0 & 0 & 2 & 1 \end{pmatrix}$. Interchanging the second and third columns gives $G' = \begin{pmatrix} 1 & 0 & 2 & 1 \\ 0 & 2 & 0 & 1 \end{pmatrix}$. Dividing the second row by two yields the matrix $\begin{pmatrix} 1 & 0 & 2 & 1 \\ 0 & 1 & 0 & 3 \end{pmatrix}$ since $\frac{1}{2} = 3$ in the field of order 5.

20.3 We set $2t + 1 = 8$. The solution is $t = 3.5$, but t must be an integer. So the correct answer is $t = 3$; the code can correct up to t errors.

20.4 $Rank(G) = 3$.

20.5 We construct a parity-check matrix $H = \begin{pmatrix} 4 & 0 & 3 & 1 & 0 & 0 \\ 4 & 3 & 2 & 0 & 1 & 0 \\ 1 & 1 & 1 & 0 & 0 & 1 \end{pmatrix}$. Multiplying each of these vectors by H^t, we obtain $(224332)H^t = (300)$, $(412311)H^t = (043)$, and $(324410)H^t = (324)$. Since (300) is 3 times the fourth column of H, we need to subtract 3 from the fourth component of (224332) to obtain the codeword (224032). Since (043) is three times the second column of H, we need to subtract 3 from the second component of (412311) to obtain the codeword (432311). Since (324) is not a multiple of any column of H, we know that more than one error has been made. In this case, it is not possible to determine a unique nearest codeword to (324410).

20.6 We know that $2^r - 1 = 15$, where r is the rank of H. Thus, $r = 4$, and it follows that G has $15 - 4$ rows, giving an information rate of $\frac{11}{15}$.

20.7 We need to find values of q and n such that $q^n + q^{n-1} + \cdots + q + 1 = 156$. Since $156 - 1 = 155$, the value of q must divide 155. We try $q = 5$ and notice that $1 + 5 + 25 + 125 = 156$. So the field is $GF(5)$.

20.8 We simply take all possible nonzero columns. One such example is

$$\begin{pmatrix} 1 & 1 & 1 & 1 & 0 & 1 & 1 & 1 & 0 & 0 & 0 & 1 & 0 & 0 & 0 \\ 1 & 1 & 1 & 0 & 1 & 1 & 0 & 0 & 1 & 1 & 0 & 0 & 1 & 0 & 0 \\ 1 & 1 & 0 & 1 & 1 & 0 & 0 & 1 & 1 & 0 & 1 & 0 & 0 & 1 & 0 \\ 1 & 0 & 1 & 1 & 1 & 0 & 1 & 0 & 0 & 1 & 1 & 0 & 0 & 0 & 1 \end{pmatrix}.$$

20.9 If $m = 4$ then $n = 1$. Hence, the required number of bets is $3^{m-n-1} = 3^{4-2} = 9$.

20.10 A typical vector in k dimensions is of the form $(x_1, x_2, \ldots, x_k)$, where x_i is an element of $GF(q)$. So we have altogether q^k possibilities.

20.11 As we let $\mathbf{u}$ range over all 3^3 possibilities, we get nine codewords. They are (0000), (0120), (0210), (2212), (2002), (2122), (1121), (1211), (1001).

20.12 This is because B has rank 2 because the rows are linearly independent. For example the first and second rows of B sum to the third row. This makes B a poor choice because it means that several messages will get encoded to the same codeword, and thus we will not be able to decode uniquely. For example the word (0000) could have been made by the message (000) or by (112).

To fix this problem, we could simply remove the third row of B to get the matrix

$$B' = \begin{pmatrix} 1 & 2 & 1 & 1 \\ 2 & 2 & 1 & 2 \end{pmatrix}$$

which could be used to generate a linear code.

20.13 We take the matrix D and switch the rows to get

$$\begin{pmatrix} 1 & 2 & 2 & 1 \\ 2 & 1 & 2 & 1 \end{pmatrix}.$$

Then adding the rows and storing the result into the second row, we have

$$\begin{pmatrix} 1 & 2 & 2 & 1 \\ 0 & 0 & 1 & 2 \end{pmatrix}.$$

Switching the second and third columns, we get

$$\begin{pmatrix} 1 & 2 & 2 & 1 \\ 0 & 1 & 0 & 2 \end{pmatrix}.$$

Finally, subtracting twice the second row from the first row, we get

$$[I|A] = \begin{pmatrix} 1 & 0 & 2 & 0 \\ 0 & 1 & 0 & 2 \end{pmatrix}$$

A matrix for $C^\perp$ is

$$[-A^t|I] = \begin{pmatrix} 1 & 0 & 1 & 0 \\ 0 & 1 & 0 & 1 \end{pmatrix}$$

20.14 A parity check matrix is

$$H = \begin{pmatrix} 0 & 1 & 1 & 1 & 1 & 0 & 0 \\ 1 & 0 & 1 & 1 & 0 & 1 & 0 \\ 1 & 1 & 0 & 1 & 0 & 0 & 1 \end{pmatrix}$$

and when we take the product $\mathbf{y}H^t$ we get (101). Since (101) is the second column of H, we conclude that there was an error in the second position. To correct this error, we add 1 to the second position, meaning that (1010101) was sent.

20.15 We have $\mathbf{y}H^t = (000)$, from which we conclude that there was no error in transmitting $\mathbf{y}$.

20.16 We find that $\mathbf{y}H^t = (111)$, and as (111) is the fourth column of H, we know that there was an error in the fourth position. Correcting this error, we reason that (0110011) was sent.

20.17 In $GF(2)$, $A = -A$. Therefore, the generator matrix for $C^\perp$ is given by

$$H = [-A^t | I] = [A^t | I] = \begin{pmatrix} 1 & 1 & 0 & 1 & 0 & 0 \\ 1 & 0 & 1 & 0 & 1 & 0 \\ 0 & 1 & 1 & 0 & 0 & 1 \end{pmatrix}$$

20.18 To find the codewords for C, we just need to carry out the multiplication $\mathbf{v}G$, where $\mathbf{v}$ is a codeword in C. Doing so yields the following $2^3 = 8$ vectors:

$(0,0,0,0,0,0)$ $(0,1,0,1,0,1)$ $(1,0,0,1,1,0)$ $(1,1,0,0,1,1)$
$(0,0,1,0,1,1)$ $(0,1,1,1,1,0)$ $(1,0,1,1,0,1)$ $(1,1,1,0,0,0)$

20.19 The information rate is $\frac{3}{6} = \frac{1}{2}$.

20.20 To determine if an error was sent, we need to compute $(1,0,1,0,1,0)H^t$ where H is the parity-check matrix. Since we end up with the vector $(0,0,0)$, we can conclude that no transmission error can be detected. An alternative (albeit much longer) solution can be obtained by determining the generator matrix G and identifying all of the codewords in C. By doing so, we notice that the codeword $(1,0,1,0,1,0)$ is contained in our code list.

20.21 6.

20.22 The binary repetition code of length 5 is given by $(0,0,0,0,0), (1,1,1,1,1)$. Suppose we send the message $(0,0,0,0,0)$. If our received message contains no less than three zeros, we can assume that the transmitted message was $(0,0,0,0,0)$. The probability of at least three zeros is:

$$(1-p)^5 + 5(1-p)^4 p + 10(1-p)^3 p^2$$

To see this note that $1 - p$ is the probability of a correct transmission. Then we calculate, successively, the probability that five zeros are transmitted correctly, the probability that exactly four and exactly three zeros are correctly transmitted. The we add the probabilities to get the answer.

20.23 $40 = 3^3 + 3^2 + 3 + 1$. So m is 40, $n = 4$, and as in Section 20.7 the answer is $3^{40-4} = 3^{36}$.

20.24 Think of the three possible outcomes of the matches as column vectors $\mathbf{x}, \mathbf{y}, \mathbf{z}$, where $\mathbf{x} = \begin{pmatrix} x_1 \\ x_2 \\ x_3 \end{pmatrix}$, $\mathbf{y} = \begin{pmatrix} y_1 \\ y_2 \\ y_3 \end{pmatrix}$, $\mathbf{z} = \begin{pmatrix} z_1 \\ z_2 \\ z_3 \end{pmatrix}$. If we make the following nine guesses, namely x_1y_1z, x_1y_2z, x_1y_3z, x_2y_1z, x_2y_2z, x_2y_3z, x_3y_1z, x_3y_2z, x_3y_3z, where z is a random choice of z_1 or z_2 or z_3 in each case then we are certain of winning at least a second prize. So nine is an upper bound here.

20.25 3^{m-1} is an upper bound. This number is much bigger than 3^{m-1-n} where m is of the form $n^2 + n + 1$.

Chapter 21

Cyclic Linear Codes, Shift Registers, and CRC

Goals, Discussion   We present some basic material concerning linear cyclic codes from a very elementary point of view while covering all the main ideas. We then develop some more advanced results on linear cyclic codes.

New, Noteworthy   We clarify the fact that a cyclic linear code may have several generators of various degrees. Standard treatments sometimes imply that the "canonical" generator and its scalar multiples are the only ones.

We show how linear feedback shift registers dovetail beautifully with linear cyclic codes using our approach to generators. Using this connection, we describe a simple but powerful algorithm for finding all shift registers and finding the period given the tap polynomial.

The algebraic theory of shift registers is related to a cyclic redundancy check (CRC) protocol which is frequently used on the Internet and elsewhere. We summarize some results in the area.

Cryptography, Information Theory, and Error-Correction: A Handbook for the 21st Century, Second Edition.
Aiden A. Bruen, Mario A. Forcinito, and James M. McQuillan.
© 2021 John Wiley & Sons, Inc. Published 2021 by John Wiley & Sons, Inc.

454 *CHAPTER 21. CYCLIC LINEAR CODES, SHIFT REGISTERS, AND CRC*

21.1 Cyclic Linear Codes

As motivation, we mention some practical advantages of these codes. They are compactly described and easy to store. Encoding and decoding becomes quite simple. Some of the main codes used in industry, namely the Reed–Solomon codes, are special kinds of cyclic linear codes.

A code C is said to be **cyclic** if the following holds. Whenever $\mathbf{c}$ is in C with $\mathbf{c} = (w_0, w_1, \ldots, w_{n-1})$, then also the n-tuple $\mathbf{c}_1 = (w_{n-1}, w_0, w_1, \ldots, w_{n-2})$ is also in C. The codeword $\mathbf{c}_1$ denoted by $\sigma(\mathbf{c})$ is called the **cyclic shift** of $\mathbf{c}$. Not all cyclic codes are **linear**.

In the following two examples, C is binary.

Example 21.1 *Let $C = \{(1,1,1,1)\}$. Then C is cyclic but not linear.*

Example 21.2 *Let $C = \{(0,0,0,0), (1,1,1,1)\}$. Then C is cyclic and linear.*

Here is a **construction for a linear cyclic code C.** First, pick any finite field F and any positive integer n for the length of C. Next, pick **any** vector $\mathbf{w} = (w_0, w_1, \ldots, w_{n-1})$.

Step 1 Form all vectors S obtained by repeatedly shifting $\mathbf{w}$, i.e. all vectors of the form $\mathbf{w}, \sigma\mathbf{w}, \sigma^2(\mathbf{w}), \ldots$. Here $\mathbf{w} = \sigma^0(\mathbf{w})$ where σ^0 is the null shift.

Step 2 The set $\langle S \rangle$ of all possible linear combinations of vectors in S is then a cyclic linear code C containing $\mathbf{w}$. Note that when all coefficients of the linear combination are zero we get the zero vector.

Theorem 21.3 *C is linear and cyclic. It is the smallest linear cyclic code containing $\mathbf{w}$.*

Proof. Certainly any cyclic code containing $\mathbf{w}$ must contain all vectors in S. Now if C is linear and C contains S then C must contain $\langle S \rangle$.

It remains to show that C is cyclic. Let $\mathbf{c}$ be any vector in C. We want to show that $\sigma(\mathbf{c})$ is in C. First, suppose that $\mathbf{c}$ is in S. Then $\mathbf{c} = \sigma^i(\mathbf{w})$. Then $\sigma(\mathbf{c}) = \sigma\sigma^i(\mathbf{w}) = \sigma^{i+1}(\mathbf{w})$ so $\sigma(\mathbf{c})$ is in S.

Next, let $\mathbf{c}$ be a linear combination of two or more vectors in S. It suffices to consider the case when $\mathbf{c}$ is a linear combination of two such vectors.

So let $\mathbf{c} = \alpha\mathbf{u} + \beta\mathbf{v}$ with α, β in F and u, v in S. We want to show that $\sigma(\mathbf{c})$ is in C. Now $\mathbf{u} = \sigma^i(\mathbf{w})$. Then $\sigma(\mathbf{u}) = \sigma^{i+1}(\mathbf{w})$ so $\sigma(\mathbf{u})$ is in S. Similarly, $\sigma(\mathbf{v})$ is in S. We have $\sigma(\mathbf{c}) = \sigma(\alpha\mathbf{u} + \beta\mathbf{v}) = \alpha\sigma(\mathbf{u}) + \beta\sigma(\mathbf{v})$ since σ is a linear mapping. Since $\sigma(\mathbf{u}), \sigma(\mathbf{v})$ are in S we have that $\sigma(\mathbf{c})$ is a linear combination of 2 vectors in S. Thus, $\sigma(\mathbf{c})$ is in C. ∎

The code C in Theorem 21.3 is said to be **generated by w** and we denote it by $\langle \mathbf{w} \rangle$.

Example 21.4 *Let $n = 3$, $F = \{0,1\}$, $\mathbf{w} = (1,0,1)$. Then*

$$\langle \mathbf{w} \rangle = \{(1,0,1),(1,1,0),(0,1,1),(0,0,0)\}$$

It is a two-dimensional vector space with $2^2 = 4$ codewords.

Example 21.5 *Take $n = 4$, $F = \{0,1\}$, and $\mathbf{w} = (1,0,1,0)$. Then*

$$\langle \mathbf{w} \rangle = \{(1,0,1,0),(0,1,0,1),(1,1,1,1),(0,0,0,0)\}$$

Here $\langle \mathbf{w} \rangle$ is a two-dimensional space sitting inside a four-dimensional space.

The next step is to *"go algebraic."* Thus, with each codeword $\mathbf{c}$ in a cyclic linear code of length n we associate a polynomial $c(x)$ of degree $n-1$ or less. Namely, if

$$\mathbf{c} = (c_0, c_1, c_2, \ldots, c_{n-1})$$

then

$$c(x) = c_0 + c_1 x + c_2 x^2 + \cdots + c_{n-1} x^{n-1}.$$

The main reason for this is the following principle.

Fundamental Principle 21.6 *Cyclically shifting a codeword in a cyclic linear code C of length n is equivalent to multiplying the corresponding polynomial by x and, if necessary, dividing this polynomial by $x^n - 1$ (i.e. reducing mod $x^n - 1$): the remainder yields the polynomial corresponding to the shifted codeword. Similarly, t shifts of the codeword $\mathbf{c}$ corresponds to multiplying the polynomial $c(x)$ by x^t and if necessary (i.e. if $x^t c(x)$ has terms of degree n or more) reducing mod $x^n - 1$: the remainder yields the polynomial corresponding to the resulting codeword.*

*The polynomials corresponding to the vectors in the code C form a set R_n of polynomials reduced modulo $(x^n - 1)$ (i.e. modulo $x^n + 1$ if we are working in the binary field). The sum and difference of any 2 polynomials in R_n is also in R_n. Because C is cyclic, it will follow that for any polynomial $f(x)$ of any degree and any $c(x)$ in R_n the product $f(x)c(x)$ is in R_n in that $f(x)c(x)$ modulo $(x^n - 1)$ is equal to $c_1(x)$ for some $c_1(x)$ in R_n. If $C = \langle \mathbf{w} \rangle$ then since R_n has the algebraic properties above it is called the **ideal** generated by $w(x)$ and is denoted by $\langle w(x) \rangle$. So $R_n = \langle w(x) \rangle$.*

Notation

Caution. Some authors use the symbol R_n to denote the set of all polynomials modulo $x^n - 1$. Our symbols indicates a subset of such polynomials namely those that correspond to vectors in the code in question.

Remark 21.7 *Suppose that in Theorem 21.3 $w(x)$ is relatively prime to $x^n - 1$. Then there exists polynomials $A(x)$ and $B(x)$ such that*

$$A(x)w(x) + B(x)(x^n - 1) = 1$$

Thus

$$A(x)w(x) \equiv 1 \bmod (x^n - 1)$$

Since R_n contains all multiples of $w(x)$, we see that 1 is in R_n. Thus, all multiples of 1 by any polynomial reduced mod $(x^n - 1)$ are in R_n. Thus, R_n contains ALL polynomials– including constants–of degree $\leq n - 1$.

Note that the polynomial $w(x)$ is not the polynomial of smallest degree in R_n in this case, but it does generate R_n. The polynomial 1 is also a generator as is any polynomial in R_n which is relatively prime to $x^n - 1$.

Concerning the Fundamental Principle 21.6, we present two examples.

Example 21.8 *Let $c(x) = c_0 + c_1 x + \cdots + c_{n-1}x^{n-1}$, $c_{n-1} \neq 0$. Then $xc(x) = c_0 x + c_1 x^2 + \cdots + c_{n-2}x^{n-1} + c_{n-1}x^n$. We have $c_{n-1}x^n = c_{n-1}(x^n - 1) + c_{n-1}$. Since we are reducing mod $x^n - 1$, we get $c_{n-1}x^n = c_{n-1}$. Or we can replace x^n by 1 right away, so $c_{n-1}x^n = c_{n-1}$. Thus, $xc(x) = c_{n-1} + c_0 x + c_1 x^2 + \cdots + c_{n-2}x^{n-1}$. This corresponds to the codeword $\sigma(\mathbf{c})$, i.e. the cyclic shift of $\mathbf{c}$, where $\mathbf{c}$ is the codeword corresponding to $c(x)$.*

Example 21.9 *In Example 21.5, let $\mathbf{c} = (0101)$. The corresponding polynomial is $x + x^3$. Here $n = 4$. When we multiply by x we get the polynomial $x^2 + x^4$. We divide this by $x^4 + 1$. The long division method is presented as follows.*

$$
\begin{array}{r}
1 \\
x^4 + 1 \overline{)\, x^4 + x^2} \\
\underline{x^4 \quad + \quad 1} \\
x^2 - 1
\end{array}
$$

So the remainder is $x^2 - 1 = x^2 + 1$ since we are working in binary. This gives the codeword (1010). *(Or, we can argue that $x^4 = 1$ so $x^2 + x^4 = x^2 + 1$ in R_n.) We have $\sigma(0101) = (1010)$ as promised by the principle above. Now since $x\mathbf{c}(x)$ corresponds to $\sigma(\mathbf{c})$ we have that $x^2\mathbf{c}(x)$ corresponds to $\sigma^2(\mathbf{c})$ and so on.*

21.2 Generators for Cyclic Codes

Suppose that C is known to be a cyclic linear code. Thus for each codeword $\mathbf{c}$ in C, $\sigma\mathbf{c}$ is also in C.

Question

Must there exist a codeword $\mathbf{w}$ in C such that $C = \langle\mathbf{w}\rangle$, i.e. C is generated by $\mathbf{w}$ as in Theorem 21.3?

From Remark 21.7, we see that $\mathbf{w}$ need not be unique. Let us take another informative example.

Example 21.10 *In Theorem 21.3, let $\mathbf{w} = (0110)$. We are working in the binary field with $n = 4$. Let $C = \langle\mathbf{w}\rangle$. Then C contains cyclic shifts of $\mathbf{w}$ and linear combinations of vectors. The code C has dimension 3 and has 8 vectors, namely $\{(0110, (0011), (1001), (1100)\}$ together with $\{(0000), (0101), (1010), (1111)\}$. R_n has the polynomials $x + x^2$, $x^2 + x^3$, $1 + x^3$, $1 + x$ and their combinations. These are all divisible by $w(x) = x + x^2$. However, the polynomial $1 + x$ is in R_n and divides the others. (For example, $1 - x^3 = (1 - x)(1 + x + x^2)$ so in binary $1 + x^3 = (1 + x)(1 + x + x^2)$.) Actually it is enough to show that $1 + x$ divides $w(x) = x(1 + x)$ in order to conclude that $1 + x$ is also a generator. Note that $1 + x$ divides $x^n + 1 = x^4 + 1$, since $x^2 + 1 = (x + 1)^2$ in binary, so that $x^4 + 1 = (x + 1)^4$ in binary. However, we note that $w(x) = x + x^2$ does not divide $x^4 + 1$. To see this, the roots of $x^2 + x$, i.e. the values of x that make it zero are 0 and 1. If $w(x)$ were to divide $x^4 + 1$ then 0 and 1 must be roots of $x^4 + 1$. But 0 is not a root of $x^4 + 1$, even though 1 is, since $1^4 + 1 = 1 + 1 = 2 = 0 \pmod 2$. We refer to Theorem 21.12.*

Back to our question. The answer is that C always contains a generator $\langle\mathbf{w}\rangle$. As we have seen, $\mathbf{w}$ is not unique. However, there is a special generator called the *canonical polynomial generator* of R_n and any nonzero scalar multiple of it is also a generator.

Then, to recap, let C be a cyclic code of length n. Each codeword $\mathbf{c} = (c_0, c_1, c_2, \ldots, c_{n-1})$ in C yields a polynomial $c(x) = c_0 + c_1 x + c_2 x^2 + \cdots c_{n-1} x^{n-1}$ whose degree is at most $n - 1$. Let R_n be the set of all such polynomials. In R_n choose any polynomial $g(x)$ of smallest degree. Let $g(x) = g_0 + g_1 x + g_2 x^2 + \cdots + g_{n-k} x^{n-k}$, $g_{n-k} \neq 0$.

With the above notation we have the following result.

Theorem 21.11 *The polynomial $g(x)$ has the following properties:*

1. *$g(x)$ divides $\mathbf{c}(x)$, for every $\mathbf{c}$ in C.*

2. *$g(x)$ divides $x^n - 1$.*

3. *The codewords corresponding to $g(x), xg(x), x^2 g(x), \ldots, x^{k-1} g(x)$ form a basis for C and C has dimension k. The rows of the matrix G form a basic for C. Here*

$$G = \begin{pmatrix} g_0 & g_1 & \cdots & \cdots & g_{n-k} & 0 & 0 & \cdots & 0 \\ 0 & g_0 & g_1 & \cdots & & g_{n-k} & 0 & \cdots & 0 \\ & & \ddots & & \ddots & & & \ddots & \\ 0 & 0 & 0 & \cdots & g_0 & g_1 & g_2 & \cdots & g_{n-k} \end{pmatrix} \qquad (21.1)$$

4. *Conversely, if $g(x)$ is a polynomial of degree $n - k$ such that $g(x)$ divides $x^n - 1$ then $g(x)$ generates a linear cyclic code C of length n, dimension k. Moreover, $g(x)$ is a polynomial of lowest degree in R_n.*

Proof. Suppose $g(x)$ does not divide $c(x)$, where $c(x)$ corresponds to a codeword $\mathbf{c}$ in C. Then $c(x) = v(x)g(x) + R(x)$. Now $v(x)g(x)$ is in C, as is $c(x)$. Thus $R(x)$, their difference, is in R_n and has smaller degree than g, a contradiction.

To prove 2, if we divide $x^n - 1$ by $g(x)$ we get $x^n - 1 = g(x)q(x) + R(x)$. Suppose $R(x) \neq 0$. Since $x^n - 1$ is zero mod $(x^n - 1)$, we get that $R(x)$ is a multiple of $g(x)$ mod $(x^n - 1)$ and so is in C. But the degree of $R(x)$ is less than that of $g(x)$, a contradiction. Thus, $g(x)$ divides $x^n - 1$.

The $n - (n - k) = k$ rows of G are linearly independent because each column containing $g_0 \neq 0$ has all zeros below g_0. These k rows represent the codewords $g(x), xg(x), \ldots, x^{k-1} g(x)$ corresponding to the null shift and $k - 1$ other shifts. The rows of G consist of $n - k$ cyclic shifts of the first row corresponding to $g(x)$. From part 1, C (i.e. the ideal R_n corresponding to C) is generated by $g(x)$. Thus, each codeword $\mathbf{c}$ is a linear combination of at most n cyclic shifts of the first row. As before, if $c(x)$ corresponds to $\mathbf{c}$ in C it is divisible by $g(x)$ so that $c(x) = g(x)v(x)$. This is an equality of polynomials not requiring any reduction modulo $x^n - 1$. The degree of $c(x)$ is at most $n - 1$ and that of g is $n - k$. So $v(x)$ has degree at most $k - 1$. Then

$$c(x) = v(x)(g(x)) = (v_0 + v_1 x + v_2 x^2 + \cdots + v_{k-1} x^{k-1})g(x)$$

$$= v_0 g(x) + v_1 x g(x) + v_2 x^2 g(x) + \cdots + v_{k-1} x^{k-1} g(x).$$

Thus, $\mathbf{c}$ is a linear combination of at most k cyclic shifts – including the null shift – of the first row of G. Thus, the rows of G span C and so form a basis.

To prove part 4, we first show the following result. ∎

Theorem 21.12 *Let C be a cyclic linear code of length n generated by a vector $\mathbf{w}$. Then the greatest common divisor (=gcd) of $w(x)$ and $x^n - 1$ is a polynomial of least degree in R_n and generates C.*

Proof. From Chapter 19 we have polynomials $A(x), B(x)$ such that $A(x)w(x) + B(x)(x^n - 1) = v(x)$. Thus, in R_n, $A(x)w(x) = v(x)$ and $v(x)$ is in the code C generated by $w(x)$.

On the other hand $w(x)$ is divisible by $v(x)$, since $v(x)$ by hypothesis is a divisor of $w(x)$. Thus, $w(x)$ is in the code generated by $v(x)$. Therefore, $v(x)$ generates C. Let us suppose that $v(x)$ has degree $n - k$.

Let $g(x)$ be a polynomial of least degree in R_n, the ideal corresponding to C. Then $v(x)$ must be a multiple of $g(x)$. For if not then $v(x) = q(x)g(x) + R(x)$, for polynomials $q(x), R(x)$. But then if $R(x) \neq 0$ then $R(x)$ has degree less than $g(x)$ which is in C, a contradiction. So we have $v(x) = f(x)g(x)$. Then $g(x)$ has degree $n - k_1$, say. Since $g(x)$ divides $v(x)$, the degree of $g(x)$ is less than or equal to the degree of $v(x)$. Thus, $n - k_1 \leq n - k$. Then $k_1 \geq k$. The code C has dimension k_1 as $g(x)$ generates a code of dimension k_1. But by hypothesis $g(x)$ generates C which has dimension k. We conclude that $g(x)$, a polynomial of least degree in R_n, has the same degree as the polynomial $v(x)$. So $v(x)$ is a polynomial of least degree in R_n and generates C. ∎

Proof of Part 4 of Theorem 21.11 We are given that $g(x)$ divides $x^n - 1$. Thus, the gcd of $x^n - 1$ and $g(x)$ is $g(x)$. Then, from Theorem 21.12, the polynomial $g(x)$ is one of least degree in R_n.

Comment 21.13 *Let $g(x)$ be as in Theorem 21.11. Although $g(x)$ divides $x^n - 1$ this does not imply that the highest nonzero coefficient g_{n-k} of $g(x)$ is 1, i.e. that $g(x)$ is* *monic. For example, $x^3 - 1 = (x - 1)(x^2 + x + 1)$. Thus $x^2 + x + 1$ divides $x^3 - 1$. But so does $\alpha x^2 + \alpha x + \alpha$ for any $\alpha \neq 0$ since*

$$x^3 - 1 = \frac{1}{\alpha}(x - 1)(\alpha x^2 + \alpha x + \alpha)$$

$$= \left(\frac{1}{\alpha}x - \frac{1}{\alpha}\right)(\alpha x^2 + \alpha x + \alpha).$$

*If $g(x)$ is not monic, then dividing $g(x)$ by g_{n-k} we get a monic polynomial $g_1(x)$ of least degree in R_n which also divides $x^n - 1$ using the argument above. This unique generator of smallest degree can be called the **canonical linear generator** of R_n and is referred to as THE generator in several treatments of this topic.*

21.3   The Dual Code

Let C be a linear cyclic code of length n, dimension k with generator polynomial $g(x) = g_0 + g_1 x + g_2 x^2 + \cdots + g_{n-k} x^{n-k}$ of degree $n - k$ as above. The dual code of C will be linear, of dimension $n - k$, and cyclic. To develop this, we know that $g(x)$ divides $x^n - 1$ so that $g(x)h(x) = x^n - 1$ with $deg(h(x)) = n - (n - k) = k$.

The polynomial $h(x)$ is known as the **check polynomial of C**. We have $g(x)h(x) = x^n - 1 \equiv 0 \mod (x^n - 1)$. For any $c(x)$ in C, we have $c(x) = A(x)g(x)$. Then

$$c(x)h(x) = A(x)g(x)h(x) \equiv 0 \mod (x^n - 1)$$

Conversely, let $c(x)$ satisfy $c(x)h(x) \equiv 0 \mod (x^n - 1)$. By the division algorithm, when dividing by $g(x)$, we get $c(x) = A(x)g(x) + r(x)$ (where $\deg r(x) < \deg g = n - k$). Then $c(x)h(x) \equiv 0 \mod (x^n - 1)$ implies that $r(x)h(x) \equiv 0 \mod (x^n - 1)$. But, the degree of $r(x)h(x)$ is less than $n - k + k = n$. Thus, as polynomials, $r(x)h(x) = 0$. Therefore, $r(x) = 0$ so that $c(x) = A(x)g(x)$ and $c(x)$ is in C.

All the above might suggest that $h(x)$ is the generator polynomial of the dual code $C^\perp$. (Adding to this is the fact that $h(x)$, of degree k, divides $x^n - 1$ and that $h(x)$ therefore generates a code of dimension $n - k$ which is the dimension of $C^\perp$.)

But this is not quite true. The product of $g(x)$ and $h(x)$ being 0 mod $(x^n - 1)$ is not the same as the corresponding vectors being orthogonal. First, we need some notation.

The **reverse polynomial** of

$$h(x) = h_0 + h_1 x + \cdots + h_k x^k, \qquad h_0 \neq 0, h_k \neq 0$$

is

$$h_1(x) = x^k h\left(\frac{1}{x}\right) = h_k + h_{k-1} x + h_{k-2} x^2 + \cdots + h_1 x^{k-1} + h_0 x^k$$

The roots of $h_1(x)$ are the reciprocals of the roots of $h(x)$.

Example 21.14 *We work over $GF(5)$ with $n = 4$ and $g(x) = (x-1)(x-2) = x^2 - 3x + 2$. Then $h(x) = (x-3)(x-4) = x^2 + 3x + 2$ since $x^n - 1 = x^4 - 1 = (x-1)(x-2)(x-3)(x-4)$. Then the reverse polynomial $h_1(x)$ is given by $1 + 3x + 2x^2$. The roots of $h_1(x)$ are the inverses or reciprocals of the roots of $h(x)$: in this case the roots of $h_1(x)$ are $\{\frac{1}{3}, \frac{1}{4}\} = \{2, 4\}$.*

Theorem 21.15 *Let C be a cyclic $[n, k]$ code of length n, dimension k with check polynomial $h(x) = h_0 + h_1 x + \cdots + h_k x^k$. Then*

(i) a parity check matrix for C is

$$H = \begin{pmatrix} h_k & h_{k-1} & & \cdots & & h_0 & 0 & 0 & 0 & \cdots & 0 \\ 0 & h_k & h_{k-1} & & \cdots & & h_0 & 0 & 0 & \cdots & 0 \\ & & & & & \ddots & & & & & \\ 0 & 0 & 0 & \cdots & 0 & h_k & h_{k-1} & & \cdots & & h_0 \end{pmatrix}$$

(ii) $C^\perp$ is generated by the polynomial $h_1(x)$.

Proof. We have seen that $c(x) = c_0 + c_1 x + \cdots + c_{n-1} x^{n-1}$ is a codeword if and only if $c(x)h(x) \equiv 0 \bmod (x^n - 1)$. For this to hold (see "Explanation" below) we have in particular that the coefficients of $x^k, x^{k+1}, \ldots, x^{n-1}$ must all be zero, i.e.

$$c_0 h_k + c_1 h_{k-1} + \cdots + c_k h_0 \qquad\qquad = 0$$
$$c_1 h_k + c_2 h_{k-1} + \cdots + c_{k+1} h_0 \quad = 0$$
$$\ddots$$
$$c_{n-k-1} h_k + \cdots + c_{n-1} h_0 = 0.$$

Thus, each row of C is orthogonal to the cyclic shifts of the vector $(h_k, h_{k=1}, \ldots, h_0, 0, 0, 0)$. So the rows of H above are codewords of $C^\perp$. Since $g(x)h(x) = x^n - 1$, we have that $h_k \neq 0$. Thus, the rows of H are linearly independent and there are $n - k$ of them which is the dimension of $C^\perp$. Thus, as with G in Section 20.2, H is a generator matrix of $C^\perp$. If we can show that $h_1(x)$ divides $x^n - 1$, then we have that h_1 is a polynomial generator of $C^\perp$ of smallest degree.

Now $h_1(x) = x^k h(x^{-1})$. Since $h(x^{-1})c(x^{-1}) = (x^{-1})^n - 1$ we have $x^k h(x^{-1})x^{n-k}$ $c(x^{-1}) = x^n(x^{-n} - 1) = 1 - x^n$ so that $h_1(x)$ is a factor of $x^n - 1$. ∎

Explanation

By hypothesis we have that, as polynomials, $c(x)h(x) = A(x)(x^n - 1)$ where $A(x) = a_0 + a_1 x + \cdots + a_t x^t$. The highest term on the right has degree $t + n$. On the left, the degree of highest term is at most $(n-1) + k$. Thus, $t \leq k - 1$. Apart from terms of degree at least n, the remaining terms in the product have degree at most $k - 1$.

21.4   Linear Feedback Shift Registers and Codes

Here we work in the binary field. There are various connections between such shift registers and codes. One such connection covered in Peterson and Weldon [PW72] involves the recurrence relation

$$\sum_{j=0}^{k} h_j a_{i+j} = 0 \tag{21.2}$$

Recall that $h_0 \neq 0$, $h_k = 1$ and that the elements $h_0, h_1, \ldots, h_k = 1$ are fixed elements of the binary field. The connection is established through the following theorem.

Theorem 21.16 *Let* $h(X) = \sum_{j=0}^{k} h_j X^j$ *with* $h_0 = h_k = 1$. *Let* n *be the smallest positive integer such that* $X^n + 1$ *is divisible by* $h(X)$. *Then*

(a) *All solutions of (21.2) are periodic with period dividing* n.

(b) *Set* $g(X) = \frac{X^n + 1}{h(X)}$. *Then each solution in (21.2) corresponds to a codeword in the code* C *generated by the reverse polynomial of* $g(X)$. *All solutions lie in the row space of* G *a generator matrix for* C.

In order to prove Theorem 21.16, we first present some background and then proceed to Lemma 21.17.

Let H denote the cyclic linear code generated by $h(X)$. Since $h(X)$ divides $X^n + 1$ we have from Theorem 21.12 that $\mathbf{h} = (h_0, h_1, \ldots, h_{k-1}, 0, 0, 0)$ is a generator for H. Since $h(X)$ has degree k the dimension of H is $n - k$. Thus, the dimension of $C = H^\perp$ is k.

We have $g(X)h(X) = X^n - 1$. Thus, the degree of $g(X)$ is $n - k$ which is also the degree of $g_1(X)$ the reverse polynomial of $g(X)$. Note that $g_1(X)$ generates C which follows from the earlier work in the chapter. Recall that $h_k = 1$ and that, for binary, $h_0 = 1$.

Lemma 21.17 *Let* $\mathbf{c} = (a_0, a_1, \ldots, a_{n-1})$ *be any nonzero vector in* $C = H^\perp$. *Then, the periodic sequence* $a_0 a_1 a_2 \ldots a_{n-1} a_0 a_1 a_2 \ldots$ *is a solution of the recurrence (21.2).*

Proof. Since $\mathbf{c}$ is in $H^\perp$ the dot product of $\mathbf{c}$ with $\mathbf{h}$ and its n cyclic shift is zero. Thus, we get a series of equations

$$h_0 a_0 + h_1 a_1 + \cdots + h_{k-1} a_{k-1} + h_k a_k = 0 \tag{21.3}$$

$$h_0 a_1 + h_1 a_2 + \cdots + h_{k-1} a_k + h_k a_{k+1} = 0 \tag{21.4}$$

$$\vdots$$

$$h_0 a_{n-k-2} + h_1 a_{n-k-1} + \cdots + h_{k-1} a_{n-2} + h_k a_{n-1} = 0. \tag{21.5}$$

Thus, $\mathbf{c}$ itself (as a sequence) conforms with (21.2). The next shift, i.e. the $(n-k)$-th shift of $\mathbf{h}$ (the identity shift is the first) yields

$$h_0 a_{n-k-1} + h_1 a_{n-k} + \cdots + h_k a_{n-1} + h_k a_0 = 0$$

If we then define $a_n = a_0$ we have a sequence $a_0 \ldots a_{n-1} a_n$, an extension of $a_0 a_1 \ldots a_{n-1}$ conforming with (21.2). Performing k more shifts of $\mathbf{h}$, we obtain an extension of $\mathbf{c}$ conforming with (21.2) such that $a_{n+t} = a_t$, $0 \le t \le k$. Now from Eq. (21.4), if we put $a_{n+k+1} = a_{k+1}$ we extend the sequence. Continuing down to Eq. (21.5), we extend the sequence which still conforms with (21.2). For Eq. (21.5) it follows that if we put $a_{n+(n-1)} = a_{n-1}$ the sequence $a_0 a_1 \ldots a_{n-1} a_0 a_1 \ldots a_{n-1}$ conforms with (21.2). Continuing this process, putting $a_{n+t} = a_n$, for all $t \ge 1$ we arrive at a periodic sequence with first block $(a_0, \ldots, a_{n-1})$ which satisfies the recurrence. ∎

Proof of Theorem 21.16 We have that $C = H^\perp$ has dimension 2^k. The polynomial $g_1(X)$ – the reverse polynomial of $g(X)$, of degree $n-k$ – generates the ideal corresponding to $g_1(X)$. A generator matrix G consists of the vector corresponding to $g_1(X)$ and its k cyclic shifts. The row space of G then provides 2^k solutions of the recurrence.

On the other hand, the equations in (21.2) are linear, any linear combination of solutions is a solution and the solutions form a vector space. Knowing $a_0, a_1, \ldots, a_{k-1}$ we can find a_k and, recursively, the entire solution. The k solutions for which one of $a_0, a_1, a_2, \ldots, a_{k-1}$ is 1 and the rest are zero form a basis for the k-dimensional solution space of the recurrence. Thus, all told there are 2^k solutions. Each of them therefore corresponds to a periodic solution of period n obtained from C as above. This proves the theorem.

Example 21.18 *Let*

$$h(X) = X^4 + X^3 + X + 1 = (X+1)^2(X^2 + X + 1)$$

The polynomial $X + 1$ divides $X^3 + 1$ as does $X^2 + X + 1$. However the smallest value of n for which $X^n + 1$ is divisible by $h(X)$ is $n = 6$. The solutions to Eq. (21.2) will have period dividing 6 but there must be at least one solution of period 6. We have

$$g(X) = \frac{X^6 + 1}{h(X)} = X^2 + X + 1$$

G is the code whose row space equals the solutions to Eq. (21.2). G consists of the vectors corresponding to $g(x)$ and its cyclic shifts. Thus

$$G = \begin{pmatrix} 1 & 1 & 1 & 0 & 0 & 0 \\ 0 & 1 & 1 & 1 & 0 & 0 \\ 0 & 0 & 1 & 1 & 1 & 0 \\ 0 & 0 & 0 & 1 & 1 & 1 \end{pmatrix}$$

The sum of the first two rows, i.e. (100100) has period 3 and the sum of the first three rows, i.e. (101010) has period 2. The corresponding LFSR has four registers with recurrence generated by $x_4 = x_3 + x_1 + x_0$ since the tap polynomial is $X^4 + X^3 + X + 1$.

The general case follows along on the same lines. The procedure is as follows:

(a) Form the tap polynomial

$$h(X) = \sum_{j=0}^{k} h_j X^j, \qquad h_0 \neq 0, \ h_k = 1$$

(b) Find n, the smallest integer such that $X^n + 1$ is divisible by $h(X)$.

(c) The solutions to Eq. (21.2) regardless of input will have period dividing n. At least one of them will have period n.

(d) Let $g(X) = \frac{X^n + 1}{h(X)}$, let $C = \langle g_1(X) \rangle$, the code of length n corresponding to the polynomial $g(X)$ and its cyclic shifts, where $g_1(X)$ is the reverse polynomial of $g(X)$.

(e) Then, all solutions lie in the row space of the $k \times n$ matrix corresponding to C.

Note: For an LFSR with k registers there are only $2^k - 1$ possible nonzero state vectors so the most that n can be is k.

Here is another connection between cyclic linear codes and shift registers.

Theorem   21.19 *Let the column vectors $\mathbf{x}, A\mathbf{x}, A^2\mathbf{x}, \ldots, A^t\mathbf{x} = \mathbf{x}$ denote the output of state vectors of a LFSR with k registers and nonzero input $\mathbf{x}$. Let $H = \{\mathbf{x}, A\mathbf{x}, A^2\mathbf{x}, \ldots, A^{t-1}\mathbf{x}\}$ denote the resulting $k \times t$ matrix. If H is chosen as the parity check matrix of a binary linear code C, then the code C is cyclic.*

Proof. Let $\mathbf{w}$ be a nonzero codeword with $H\mathbf{w}^t = \mathbf{0}$ where $\mathbf{w} = (w_1, w_2, \ldots, w_t)$. Then

$$w_1\mathbf{x} + w_2 A\mathbf{x} + \cdots + w_t A^{t-1}\mathbf{x} = \mathbf{0}$$

Multiplying by A, given that $A^t\mathbf{x} = \mathbf{x}$, we get that $H(w_t, w_1, \ldots, w_{t-1}) = \mathbf{0}$. Thus $(w_t, w_1, \ldots, w_{t-1})$ is also a codeword, as required. ∎

21.5 Finding the Period of a LFSR

This was also discussed in Chapter 16. If the tap polynomial does not factor over the binary field, then the period divides $x^n + 1$ for some n. If we start with $h(x) = x^8 + x^6 + x^5 + x^3 + 1$, the smallest n such that $h(x)$ divides $x^n + 1$ is when $n = 255$. Thus, the period is 255 which is the maximum length possible for a shift register with 8 registers. To see this the total number of nonzero vectors of length 8, i.e. of state vectors is $2^8 - 1 = 255$. In Table 21.1 we give factorizations of $x^n + 1$ over the binary field.

n	Factorization
1	$1 + x$
2	$(1 + x)^2$
3	$(1 + x)(1 + x + x^2)$
4	$(1 + x)^4$
5	$(1 + x)(1 + x + x^2 + x^3 + x^4)$
6	$(1 + x)^2(1 + x + x^2)^2$
7	$(1 + x)(1 + x + x^3)(1 + x^2 + x^3)$
8	$(1 + x)^8$
9	$(1 + x)(1 + x + x^2)(1 + x^3 + x^6)$
10	$(1 + x)^2(1 + x + x^2 + x^3 + x^r)^2$
11	$(1 + x)^2(1 + x + \cdots + x^{10})$
12	$(1 + 4)^4(1 + x + x^2)^4$
13	$(1 + x)(1 + x + \cdots + x^{12})$
14	$(1 + x)^2(1 + x + x^3)^2(1 + x^2 + x^3)^2$
15	$(1 + x)(1 + x + x^2)(1 + x + x^2 + x^3 + x^4)(1 + x + x^4)(1 + x^3 + x^4)$
16	$(1 + x)^{16}$

Table 21.1: Factorization of $x^n + 1$ over $GF(2)$

21.6   Cyclic Redundancy Check (CRC)

In the Internet, the CRC (**cyclic redundancy check**) and the Internet checksum have different functions. The CRC is used to detect link-level transmission errors while the Internet checksum, used by most Internet protocols, is designed to detect higher level transmission errors. For interesting details on this, we refer to [SP00].

CRCs use polynomial arithmetic. As mentioned in Chapter 19, the polynomials over any field form a ring analogous to the ring of integers modulo n. We will use the binary field.

Associated with each binary string, say 11101, there is a binary polynomial: in this case, the polynomial is $1x^0 + 1x^1 + 1x^2 + 0x^3 + 1x^4$, which yields the polynomial $1 + x + x^2 + x^4$. Also, given a polynomial in binary, we obtain a corresponding binary string. As we have seen in this chapter, it is sometimes convenient to reverse the polynomial associated with a string, and vice versa.

How do polynomials relate to error detection? Let us start with an example, corresponding to the binary parity check. Suppose we transmit a binary message M which has *even parity*, i.e. the string has an even number of ones in it, $M(x)$ is divisible by $x + 1$.

Example 21.20   *Let $M = (10111101)$. Then*

$$M(x) = 1 + x^2 + x^3 + x^4 + x^5 + x^7$$
$$= (1 + x^2) + (x^3 + x^4) + (x^5 + x^7)$$
$$= (1 + x)(1 + x) + x^3(1 + x) + x^5(1 + x)(1 + x).$$

*In summary, $M(x)$ **is divisible by** $1 + x$ **since** M **has even parity.***

Now suppose that M is transmitted and R is received. In polynomial terms,

$$R(x) = M(x) + E(x)$$

where $E(x)$ corresponds to the error term.

Example 21.21   *In the above suppose that there is a bit error in the received string in, say, the third position. Then the received string is $R = (10011101)$, giving the polynomial $R(x) = 1 + x^3 + x^4 + x^5 + x^7$. Now $R(x)$ is not divisible by $x + 1$. One way to see this is to argue that if $x + 1$ divides a polynomial, that polynomial must have an even number of terms. But $R(x)$ has 5 (nonzero) terms. We conclude that there has been an error and ask for a retransmission. Alternatively, we have*

$$M(x) - R(x) = -E(x)$$

Or, since we are working in binary,

$$M(x) + R(x) = E(x)$$

Now, $x + 1$ divides $M(x)$. If $x + 1$ also divides $E(x)$, then $x + 1$ divides $R(x)$. Thus the error would go undetected if $x + 1$ divides $E(x)$. In our case, $E = (00100000)$, $E(x) = x^2$ and $E(x)$ is not divisible by $x + 1$, so the transmission error is detected.

The above is the basic idea. One example is CRC is CRC-32. It uses the following polynomial.

$$f(x) = 1 + x + x^2 + x^4 + x^5 + x^7 + x^8 + x^{10} + x^{11} + x^{12} + x^{16} + x^{22} + x^{23} + x^{26} + x^{32}$$

Using the above notation, suppose $M(x)$ is divisible by $f(x)$. The binary string for f (it is usually reversed) is a string of length 33 – do not forget the constant term. *So, if there are 32 or fewer errors–but at least one error–in the first 32 bits, then this will be detected.* To see this, $E(x) \neq 0$ has degree less than 32. Thus, $f(x)$ cannot divide $E(x)$ so a transmission error will be detected.

What about detecting a pair of errors? Suppose that $E(x) = x^a + x^b$ with $a < b$. Then $E(x) = x^a(x^{b-a} + 1) = x^a(x^n + 1)$. Then $f(x)$ can only divide $E(x)$ if $f(x)$ divides $x^n + 1$. But this is precisely the reason why we chose the particular polynomial $f(x)$! For $f(x)$ to divide $x^n + 1$, n must be very big. In fact, $f(x)$ is **primitive**! Thus, n is at least $2^{32} - 1$. (We have met primitive polynomials before when discussing shift registers.)

We conclude that the CRC of degree 32 detects all two-bit errors in the first $2^{32} - 1$ positions.

For further mathematical discussions on CRC, we refer to Paul Garrett [Gar04].

21.7 Problems

21.1 In each case decide if the given code is (i) cyclic and (ii) linear.

1. the binary code $\{(0000), (1111), (1010), (0101)\}$.

2. the ternary code $\{(0000), (1111), (2222), (1100), (2200), (0011), (0022), (1122), (2211)\}$, where ternary means over $Z_3 = \{0, 1, 2\}$.

(See Solution 21.1.)

21.2   Which of the following codes are (i) cyclic? and (ii) linear?

1. the ternary code $\{(000), (121), (212), (111), (222), (202), (010), (101), (020)\}$.

2. the binary code $\{(101), (110), (011)\}$.

(See Solution 21.2.)

21.3   Repeat Problem 21.2 for the following codes.

1. the ternary code $\{(000), (211), (121), (112)\}$.

2. the code of length n over $GF(q)$ such that each nonzero codeword has weight r.

(See Solution 21.3.)

21.4   We have a notion of **equivalent codes**, which is discussed in Chapter 20. It turns out that when we permute the columns of a code C to get another code D, then we have an equivalent pair of codes. For example, if we take C and switch the fourth column with the second column in all codewords, then we have a new, equivalent code. For those codes in the previous three questions that are linear but not cyclic, find an equivalent code that is linear and cyclic by switching the order of the columns. For those codes that are not linear, find a code that is linear by adjoining codewords to the existing nonlinear code. (See Solution 21.4.)

21.5   Find all of the codewords v of length 6 over Z_3 such that $x^2v(x) = v(x)$, when we reduce modulo $(x^6 - 1)$. (See Solution 21.5.)

21.6   Form the code S from the vector $\mathbf{w} = (021)$ over Z_3 as detailed in the text. (See Solution 21.6.)

21.7   Repeat Problem 21.6 with $\mathbf{w} = (11000)$, working over the binary field. Is the generator polynomial of the resulting code equal to $\mathbf{w}(x)$? (See Solution 21.7.)

21.8   How could we alter the linear cyclic code construction procedure to create a linear cyclic code containing the codewords $\mathbf{w}_1$, $\mathbf{w}_2$ of equal length, instead of just the codeword $\mathbf{w}$? (See Solution 21.8.)

21.9   Working over Z_5, express the codewords in $A = \{(1243), (1414)\}$ as linear combinations of the codewords in $B = \{(1130), (0113)\}$, and vice versa. (See Solution 21.9.)

21.10   Starting with the polynomial $g(x) = 3 + 4x + x^2$, which generates a linear cyclic code over Z_5 of length 4, use the two methods described in the text to find generator matrices for the code dual to $g(x)$. How can we see that these two codes are the same in this case? (See Solution 21.10.)

21.11 Working in binary, suppose that we have a shift register Γ generated by the recurrence $x_2 = x_1 + x_0$.

  (a) Find the corresponding tap polynomial, $h(x)$.

  (b) Find the smallest n such that $h(x)$ divides $x^n - 1$.

  (c) Find the maximum period of Γ over various inputs.

  (d) Give an input which generates an output having maximum period.

  (e) Given an arbitrary input for Γ, what can you say about the period of the output of the resulting LFSR?

  (See Solution 21.11.)

21.12 Repeat Problem 21.11, using instead the recurrence $x_3 = x_2 + x_0$. (See Solution 21.12.)

21.13 Working over Z_3, repeat Problem 21.11 with the recurrence $x_3 = 2x_0$. (See Solution 21.13.)

21.8 Solutions

21.1 (a) Linear and cyclic.

  (b) Linear and not cyclic; $\sigma(1100) = (0110)$ is not in the code.

21.2 (a) Linear but not cyclic; $\sigma(121) = (112)$ is not a codeword.

  (b) Cyclic but not linear; (000) is not a codeword.

21.3 (a) Cyclic and not linear; $(211) + (121) = (002)$ is not a codeword.

  (b) This code is always cyclic; if we shift a codeword of weight r, we still have a codeword of weight r. However, the code is not guaranteed to be linear. Consider the code of weight 0 with length 3 over Z_3, where $(111) + (221) = (001)$, but (001) has weight 2 and is therefore not a codeword.

21.4   (a) No change.

   (b) We switch the second and third columns to arrive at the code

$$\{(0000), (1111), (2222), (1010), (2020), (0101), (0202), (1212), (2121)\} \quad (21.6)$$

   (c) No such cyclic code exists. To see this, one can take all possible permutations of the columns without finding such a code.

   (d) We can make the code linear by adding (000) to the code.

   (e) We adjoin the codewords (002), (020), and (200). Note that after this is complete, the code is still cyclic.

   (f) To make this code linear, we follow the method as described in the text and take the set of all linear combinations of these codewords. In fact, this process is exactly what we did for the previous two codes.

21.5   The condition implies that if we cyclically shift the six components of a codeword two places to the right, we get the same word. That is $\sigma^2(v) = v$, so if $v = (v_0, v_1, v_2, v_3, v_4, v_5)$, we have $v = (v_0, v_1, v_2, v_3, v_4, v_5) = (v_4, v_5, v_0, v_1, v_2, v_3) = \sigma^2(v)$. Thus, $v_0 = v_2 = v_4$ and $v_1 = v_3 = v_5$. Therefore, v must be of the form $(ababab)$, where a, b are any elements of $Z_3 = GF(3)$. The nine possibilities are: (000000), (111111), (222222), (010101), (101010), (121212), (212121), (020202), and (202020).

21.6 $S = \{(021), (102), (201)\}$, so that

$$S = \left\{ \begin{array}{ccc} (000) & (012) & (021) \\ (102) & (111) & (120) \\ (201) & (210) & (222) \end{array} \right\}.$$

21.7 $S = \{(11000), (01100), (00110), (00011), (10001)\}$ and taking all linear combinations, we get

$$S = \left\{ \begin{array}{cccc} (00000) & (00011) & (00101) & (00110) \\ (01001) & (01010) & (01100) & (01111) \\ (10001) & (10010) & (10100) & (10111) \\ (11000) & (11011) & (11101) & (11110) \end{array} \right\} \quad (21.7)$$

with generator $g = (00011)$, which in this case is not **w**.

21.8   When constructing S, we would simply take it to be the set of all cyclic shifts of both $\mathbf{w}_1$ and $\mathbf{w}_2$. Constructing S from S in the same manner, we would find that S is a linear cyclic code containing both $\mathbf{w}_1$ and $\mathbf{w}_2$. To prove that it all works, we use the fact that the shift operator σ is a linear mapping.

21.9   We get that

$$(1, 1, 3, 0) = 4(1, 2, 4, 3) + 2(1, 4, 1, 4)$$
$$(0, 1, 1, 3) = 2(1, 2, 4, 3) + 3(1, 4, 1, 4)$$

and

$$(1, 2, 4, 3) = 1(1, 1, 3, 0) + 1(0, 1, 1, 3)$$
$$(1, 4, 1, 4) = 1(1, 1, 3, 0) + 3(0, 1, 1, 3).$$

21.10 Using method 1, we get

$$C_1^{\perp} = \begin{pmatrix} 2^0 & 2^1 & 2^2 & 2^3 \\ 4^0 & 4^1 & 4^2 & 4^3 \end{pmatrix} = \begin{pmatrix} 1 & 2 & 4 & 3 \\ 1 & 4 & 1 & 4 \end{pmatrix} \tag{21.8}$$

and using method 2, we get that

$$C_2^{\perp} = \begin{pmatrix} 1 & 1 & 3 & 0 \\ 0 & 1 & 1 & 3 \end{pmatrix} \tag{21.9}$$

These can be seen to be equivalent by the work of Problem 21.10; since each row in $C_1^{\perp}$ can be expressed as a linear combination of the rows in $C_2^{\perp}$, and vice versa, it follows that the set of all linear combinations of the rows of $C_1^{\perp}$ is equivalent to the set of all linear combinations of the rows of $C_2^{\perp}$. That is the codes are the same.

21.11 (a) The tap polynomial is $h(x) = x^2 + x + 1$.

(b) $n = 3$.

(c) The maximum period is three.

(d) Any nonzero input generates output with maximum period. The output sequence could be $\{110110110 \ldots\}$.

(e) If the input is nonzero, then the output has period three, as noted above. If the input is zero, then the output is $\{00000 \ldots\}$, which has period 1. In either case, the period divides 3.

21.12 (a) The tap polynomial is $h(x) = x^3 + x^2 + 1$.

    (b) $n = 7$.

    (c) The maximum period is seven.

    (d) Any nonzero input generates output with maximum period. The output sequence could be $\{10011101001110 \ldots\}$.

    (e) If the input is nonzero, then the output has period seven, as noted above. If the input is zero, then the output is $\{00000 \ldots\}$, which has period 1. In either case, the period divides 7.

21.13 (a) The tap polynomial is $h(x) = x^3 + 1$.

    (b) $n = 6$.

    (c) The maximum period is six.

    (d) An input that achieves maximum period is $(x_0 x_1 x_2) = (120)$. The output is then $\{120210120210 \ldots\}$.

    (e) Regardless of what the input is, the output period will divide 6.

Chapter 22

Reed-Solomon and MDS Codes, and the Main Linear Coding Theory Problem (LCTP)

Goals, Discussion We present the main features of Reed–Solomon (RS) codes – both encoding and decoding – which are central for many industrial applications. These codes generalize to MDS codes and arcs. We discuss the main results due to one of the authors and others on the 50-year old problem of finding the largest arc and therefore the longest MDS code, of a given dimension over a given field. This question can also be phrased as a version of "The main coding theory problem" discussed in Chapter 18. From the Singleton bound, $d \leq n - k + 1$. We want d to be large and therefore the longer the code, the bigger the minimum distance, so the question is of considerable interest in coding theory. Part of our result is that at least when q is large, the longest MDS code is equivalent to an extended Reed–Solomon code and $n \leq q + 1$ (q odd) and $n \leq q + 2$ (q even).

For more details on MDS codes, we refer to Chapter 29.

Cryptography, Information Theory, and Error-Correction: A Handbook for the 21st Century, Second Edition.
Aiden A. Bruen, Mario A. Forcinito, and James M. McQuillan.
© 2021 John Wiley & Sons, Inc. Published 2021 by John Wiley & Sons, Inc.

New, Noteworthy We do not discuss general BCH codes which are usually covered as an introduction to the RS codes. Instead we get down to business quickly. We prefer to present RS codes in the context of general MDS codes.

In [McE78], the author states the following: "It is fairly clear that the deepest and most impressive theoretical result in coding theory (block or convolutional) is the algebraic decoding of BCH-RS codes."

We want to comment on this. Certainly, this work is deep and impressive. In a fascinating paper by Alexander Barg [Bar93], the author points out that in fact the basic decoding problem was solved in 1795 by Gaspard-Clair-François-Marie baron Riche de Prony. Later, it was also solved for special cases by the legendary Srinivasa Ramanujan in a two-page paper in 1912. Barg also refers to related work of several others, including work of Peterson and Gorenstein-Zierler.

However, it is our opinion that the geometrical work on MDS codes and arcs developed by the late Beniamino Segre must be put on an equally high pedestal. Segre was the pioneer in exploiting the famous Hasse–Weil theorem in algebraic geometry to the study of arcs and MDS codes. Segre's work in the case of q odd, developed also by J.A. Thas let to the main known result on arcs. We give a very brief discussion of arcs in Section 22.8.

22.1 Cyclic Linear Codes and Vandermonde

Let us work over some finite field $F = \mathrm{GF}(q)$: then, necessarily, $q = p^m$, where p is a prime and m is a positive integer. We put $n = q - 1$.

Let $\alpha_1, \ldots, \alpha_{n-k}$ be any set of $n - k$ distinct elements of F. Put

$$g(x) = (x - \alpha_1) \cdots (x - \alpha_{n-k})$$

Since

$$\prod_{\alpha \neq 0 \ \text{in} \ F} (x - \alpha) = x^{q-1} - 1 \quad \text{(see Chapter 19)}$$

it follows that $g(x)$, of degree $n - k$, divides $x^n - 1 = x^{q-1} - 1$ As in Chapter 21 we can construct the linear cyclic code C of length $q - 1$ with generator polynomial $g(x)$. Then, as in Chapter 21, the codewords formed from the polynomials

$$\{g(x), xg(x), \ldots, x^{k-1}g(x)\}$$

form a basis for C which has dimension k. Thus, C is a linear code of length n and dimension k, i.e. C is an (n, k) **linear code**.

Let $g(x) = g_0 + g_1 x + \cdots + g_{n-k} x^{n-k}$. Then, the corresponding code word for g of length n is $(g_0, g_1, \ldots, g_{n-k}, 0, \ldots, 0)$. Since $g(\alpha_i) = 0$, we have that

$$g_0 + g_1 \alpha_i + \cdots + g_{n-k} \alpha_i^{n-k} = 0, \quad 1 \leq i \leq n - k$$

It follows that the dot product of the codeword $(g_0, g_1, \ldots, g_{n-k}, 0, \ldots, 0)$ and each of its cyclic shifts with the vector

$$(1, \alpha_i, \alpha_i^2, \ldots, \alpha_i^{n-k}, \alpha_i^{n-k+1}, \ldots, \alpha_i^{n-1})$$

is zero, $1 \leq i \leq n - k$.

We have shown the following result.

Theorem 22.1 *Each row of the matrix*

$$H = \begin{pmatrix} 1 & \alpha_1 & \alpha_1^2 & \cdots & \alpha_1^{n-1} \\ 1 & \alpha_2 & \alpha_2^2 & \cdots & \alpha_2^{n-1} \\ \vdots & \vdots & \vdots & \ddots & \vdots \\ 1 & \alpha_{n-k} & \alpha_{n-k}^2 & \cdots & \alpha_{n-k}^{n-1} \end{pmatrix}$$

lies in the dual space of the code C generated by $g(x) = (x - \alpha_1) \cdots (x - \alpha_{n-k})$.

Now the matrix H is of size $(n - k) \times n$. The transpose, H^t, is then of size $n \times (n - k)$ and is of the following form:

$$H^t = \begin{pmatrix} 1 & 1 & \cdots & 1 \\ \alpha_1 & \alpha_2 & \cdots & \alpha_{n-k} \\ \alpha_1^2 & \alpha_2^2 & \cdots & \alpha_{n-k}^2 \\ \vdots & \vdots & \ddots & \vdots \\ \alpha_1^{n-1} & \alpha_2^{n-1} & \cdots & \alpha_{n-k}^{n-1} \end{pmatrix}$$

The first $n - k$ rows of H^t give a Vandermonde matrix of the type:

$$V = \begin{pmatrix} 1 & 1 & \cdots & 1 \\ \alpha_1 & \alpha_2 & \cdots & \alpha_{n-k} \\ \alpha_1^2 & \alpha_2^2 & \cdots & \alpha_{n-k}^2 \\ \vdots & \vdots & \ddots & \vdots \\ \alpha_1^{n-k-1} & \alpha_2^{n-k-1} & \cdots & \alpha_{n-k}^{n-k-1} \end{pmatrix}$$

Now, as mentioned in Chapter 19 we have a Vandermonde determinant. Thus,

$$\det V = \prod (\alpha_i - \alpha_j)$$

where the product is over all pairs (i, j) with $1 \le i < j \le n - k$. Since $\alpha_i \ne \alpha_j$ if $i \ne j$, we see that the determinant of V is nonzero. So the first $n - k$ rows of H^t are linearly independent. In fact, by manipulating determinants, we see that any set of $n - k$ rows of H^t is a linearly independent set. Thus, the first $n - k$ columns (and in fact any $n - k$ columns) of H are linearly independent. Since H is of size $(n - k) \times n$, we have that, a priori, $\text{rank}(H) \le n - k$. Putting these together shows that $\text{rank}(H) = n - k$.

We have now shown the following result.

Theorem 22.2

(a) *A parity check matrix of C, corresponding to the dual code $C^\perp$, is given by the matrix H of Theorem 22.1.*

(b) *Any set of $n - k$ columns of H is linearly independent.*

Proof. The dimension of C is k. Thus, the dimension of $C^\perp$ is $n - k$. Each row of H is in $C^\perp$. H is of size $(n - k) \times n$ and the rank of H is $n - k$. This proves Part (a). Part (b) has already been shown. ∎

22.2   The Singleton Bound for Linear Codes

This calculates the maximum possible distance that an (n, k) linear code can have.

Theorem 22.3 *Let C be any linear (n, k)-code with generator matrix G of size $k \times n$ and parity check matrix H with length n, minimum distance d over some finite field F. Then $d \le n - k + 1$. Moreover, $d = n - k + 1$, if and only if no set of $n - k$ or fewer columns of the parity-check matrix H is linearly dependent.*

Proof. There exists a codeword $\mathbf{c}$ of weight m in the code C if and only if $\mathbf{c}H^t = \mathbf{0}$ where H^t is the transpose of H. This is equivalent to saying that some m columns of H are linearly dependent. (For example $\mathbf{c} = (1, 1, -1, 0, \ldots, 0)$ is in C if and only if the sum of the first two columns in H is equal to the third column.)

Now, since C has dimension k, the rank of H is $n - k$. Thus, the maximum number of linearly independent columns of H is $n - k$. So some set of $n - k + 1$ columns of H are linearly dependent and C then has a word of weight $n - k + 1$.

The Hamming distance between this word and the all-zero word $\mathbf{0}$ in C is $n - k + 1$. Note that the distance between any two words $\mathbf{u}, \mathbf{v}$ in the linear code C is equal to the distance between $\mathbf{0}$ and $\mathbf{v} - \mathbf{u}$, i.e. $d(\mathbf{u}, \mathbf{v}) = d(\mathbf{0}, \mathbf{v} - \mathbf{u})$, which is the Hamming weight of $\mathbf{u} - \mathbf{v}$. ∎

If C is a linear (n, k) code with $d = n - k + 1$, then C is called a **Maximum Distance Separable Code** (=**MDS code**). Later on in a subsequent Chapter 23, we will discuss **nonlinear MDS codes**.

Remark

If C is MDS then no nonzero codeword $\mathbf{c}$ in C can have as many as k zeros in it. For if it did then the Hamming distance between $\mathbf{c}$ and $\mathbf{0}$ is at most $n - k$ which is less than $n - k + 1$.

Theorem 22.4 *If C is MDS then so is $C^{\perp}$, the dual code of C.*

Proof. Let C have length n and dimension k. From the above, no set of $n - k$ (or fewer) columns of H is linearly dependent. H is of size $(n - k) \times n$. Now suppose a codeword in $C^{\perp}$ is zero on as many as $n - k$ coordinates. Then, the corresponding square submatrix of H of size $(n - k) \times (n - k)$ has rank at most $n - k - 1$. It follows that the corresponding $n - k$ columns of H would be linearly dependent which is impossible since C is MDS. Thus, no codeword in $C^{\perp}$ is zero or as many as $n - k$ coordinates. Therefore, the minimum distance d of $C^{\perp}$ is at least $n - (n - k - 1) = k + 1$. From the Singleton bound $d \leq k + 1 = n - (n - k) + 1$ so that $C^{\perp}$ is an MDS code. ∎

In Section 22.1 we considered the cyclic code C with generator $g(x) = (x - \alpha_1)(x - \alpha_2) \cdots (x - \alpha_{n-k})$. From Theorem 22.2 part (b) any set of $n - k$ (or fewer) columns of H is linearly independent. Thus, from Theorem 22.3, C is an MDS code. We have now the following.

Theorem 22.5 *The linear code C generated by $g(x) = (x - \alpha_1) \cdots (x - \alpha_{n-k})$ is an MDS code where $n = q - 1$ and $\alpha_1, \ldots, \alpha_{n-k}$ are distinct elements in $F = \mathrm{GF}(q)$. C need not be a Reed–Solomon code.*

Alternative proof of the first part of Theorem 22.3 In Chapter 18, we showed that for any code of length n, linear or not, having minimum distance d over an alphabet of size q, and having exactly M codewords, then $M \leq q^{n-d+1}$. In the case of Theorem 22.3, $M = q^k$, so $k \leq n - d + 1$, giving $d \leq n - k + 1$. □

We want to develop several other properties of linear MDS codes. Some of these results can actually be shown using the work in Chapter 18.

Theorem 22.6 *Let G be a generator matrix for a linear (n, k) code C with $k \leq n$. Then*

(1) If C is MDS, then any set of k columns of G is linearly independent.

(2) If any set of k columns of G is linearly independent, then C is MDS.

(3) If C is MDS, then the linear code generated by deleting any set of t columns is MDS, $t \leq n - k$.

(4) C is MDS if and only if every $k \times k$ submatrix of G is non-singular.

Proof. G generates C. Thus, no set of k columns of C is linearly dependent and Part (1) follows.

For Part (2), note that the condition implies that $C^{\perp}$ is MDS from Theorem 22.3. But then, from Theorem 22.4, $(C^{\perp})^{\perp} = C$ is MDS.

Part (3) is proved as follows. Any subset of a linearly independent set is linearly independent. From Part (1), the columns of C are linearly independent. The result now follows from Part (2).

Part (4) follows by noting that since G has rank k, the given condition is equivalent to the statement that any set of k columns of G is linearly independent. ∎

Insight

Since G has rank k it follows that some set of k columns of G is linearly independent since the row rank of a matrix equals its column rank. But for an MDS code with generator matrix G of size $k \times n$, $k \leq n$, we have from Part (1) the remarkable fact that **each** of the $\binom{n}{k}$ k-sets of columns of G forms a linearly independent set of columns and a basis for the column space of G.

Another way of putting it is as follows. The k rows of G are linearly independent by hypothesis. But if G represents an MDS code we have something stronger. Namely, we have that the k **truncated rows** of G cut out by any of the $\binom{n}{k}$ sets of k columns of G are also linearly independent.

22.3 Reed–Solomon Codes

These codes are widely used in industry. The applications are everywhere, ranging from computer-based disk drives to CD players, satellite communications, and space probes. According to [MS78], they first appeared as *codes* in the paper by Reed and Solomon in 1960. However, they had already been explicitly constructed by K.A. Bush [Bus52] in 1952 using the language of statistics and orthogonal arrays. Geometrically (see [BTB88]), they have been known for a very long time as **normal rational curves**.

Let F be any finite field with $|F| = q = p^m$. Let α be a generator of the multiplicative group of F. Put $n = q - 1$. Define a **Reed–Solomon** (RS) code over F to be the linear cyclic code C generated by $g(x) = (x - \alpha^b)(x - \alpha^{b+1}) \cdots (x - \alpha^{b+n-k-1})$. For example if $b = 1$, then

$$g(x) = (x - \alpha)(x - \alpha^2) \cdots (x - \alpha^{n-k})$$

and C is the linear cyclic code generated by C, with $0 \le k < n$, $n = q - 1$.

The integer b can have any value. For instance, if $b = 0$ we get $x - 1$ as the first term.

Theorem 22.7 *C is a cyclic linear code of length n and dimension k. Moreover, C is an MDS code of minimum distance $d = n - k + 1 = \deg(g) + 1$, where $\deg(g)$ is the degree of C. A parity check matrix for C is given by the matrix H in Theorem 22.1 of Section 22.1, where $\alpha_i = \alpha^i$, $1 \le i \le n - k$.*

Proof. The fact that C has dimension k follows from Chapter 21. The rest follows using also Theorem 22.5. ∎

22.4 Reed-Solomon Codes and the Fourier Transform Approach

As in Section 22.3, let C be the linear (n, k) generated by $g(x)$ with

$$g(x) = (x - \alpha)(x - \alpha^2) \cdots (x - \alpha^{n-k})$$

In what follows, we describe these codes in a completely different way using, implicitly, the Mattson–Solomon polynomial (which we cannot discuss here). This method is also called the **Discrete Fourier Transform approach**.

Let $f(x) = f_0 + f_1 x + \cdots + f_{k-1} x^{k-1}$ be any polynomial of degree at most $k-1$. We have the following result (see van Lint [vL98] and MacWillians, Sloane [MS78]).

Theorem 22.8 $C = \{(c_0, c_1, \ldots, c_{n-1})\}$ with $c_i = f(\alpha^i)$, $0 \leq i \leq n-1$, and with f being a polynomial of degree at most $k-1$.

Remark

Note that we have moved from a representation involving the original $n-k$ field elements to *a representation involving* **all nonzero elements** *of the field F.*

A generator matrix for C and for the dual code $C^{\perp}$ can be calculated from the generator matrix $g(x)$ using the method in Chapter 21. Alternatively, we can proceed as follows.

We examine the set of all polynomials over $F = \mathrm{GF}(q)$ of degree at most $k-1$. From Theorem 22.8 we get the following result, where β_i denotes α^i, $0 \leq i \leq q-2$.

Theorem 22.9 *A generator matrix for C is given by the matrix G below. Given k information bits $f = (f_0, f_1, \ldots, f_{k-1})$ the encoding of f is just the codeword*

$$(f(\beta_0), f(\beta_1), \ldots, f(\beta_{q-2}))$$

where $f(x) = f_0 + f_1 x + \cdots + f_{k-1} x^{k-1}$.

$$G = \begin{pmatrix} 1 & 1 & \cdots & 1 \\ \beta_0 & \beta_1 & \cdots & \beta_{q-2} \\ \beta_0^2 & \beta_1^2 & \cdots & \beta_{q-2}^2 \\ \vdots & \vdots & \ddots & \vdots \\ \beta_0^{k-1} & \beta_1^{k-1} & \cdots & \beta_{q-2}^{k-1} \end{pmatrix}$$

Remarks

The elements $\beta_0, \beta_1, \ldots, \beta_{q-2}$ give a complete listing of all the nonzero elements of F. The matrix G is a generator for a linear cyclic code of length $n = q-1$ and dimension k. G has size $k \times (q-1)$. The code C is MDS with minimum distance $d = n-k+1$. Also, $C^{\perp}$ is MDS. Thus, any set of k columns of G are linearly independent, $0 \leq k < q-1$.

Generalizations of the Reed–Solomon codes are discussed in van Lint [vL98] and MacWilliams et al. [MST73]. We also refer to a nice discussion by Madhu Sudan in "The Princeton Companion to Mathematics," edited by Gowers et al. [GBGL09], in Part VII,

"The Influence of Mathematics" part 6. There is also a nice discussion of "Mathematics and Cryptography" by Clifford Cocks whose name is associated with the Diffie–Hellman algorithm.

Importance of Reed–Solomon codes

1. If we need a code of length less than q they can be used. Since they are MDS the minimum distance is as big as possible.

2. They can be combined and concatenated with other codes to build strong error correcting codes.

3. The encoding of f is very easy from Theorem 22.9.

4. They are very useful for correcting bursts of errors either individually or when interleaved with other codes.

5. They have a highly developed decoding theory, discussed later.

6. If $q = 2^r$, we can represent them as binary codes since each element of $F = \mathrm{GF}(2^r)$ can be represented as a binary string of length r.

22.5   Correcting Burst Errors, Interleaving

Very often, errors are not random but occur in clusters or bursts. This is sometimes due to physical constraints. For example for compact disc players, laser tracking makes it desirable that in the binary representation of each codeword, there must be at least 2 and at most 10 zeros between any two ones.

A **burst of length** b is a vector whose only nonzero elements are among b successive coordinate positions, the first and last of which are nonzero.

Binary codes obtained from Reed–Solomon codes (RS codes) are particularly useful for burst error correction because of their big minimum distance d. Such a code (over the field $\mathrm{GF}(q)$ with $q = 2^r$) can correct up to $\lfloor \frac{d-1}{2} \rfloor$ errors, where $\lfloor x \rfloor$ denotes the integer part of x: for example $\lfloor \frac{5}{2} \rfloor = 2$.

Theorem 22.10 (*See [MS78]*)   *A binary burst of length b can affect at most m adjacent symbols from $\mathrm{GF}(2^r)$, where $m \leq b \leq (m-1)r + 1$.*

To see this, think of the situation where the left-most one of the b bits is the right-most element of a symbol from $\mathrm{GF}(2^r)$.

Thus, if d (or e) is much bigger than m, long bursts can be corrected.

Interleaving is a technique that is used for improving the burst error correcting capability of a code.

Let us take an example. Suppose we have a code C of length n, and we take three codewords in C, namely, the three codewords:

$$\begin{aligned}
\mathbf{x} &= X_1, \ldots, X_n, \\
\mathbf{y} &= Y_1, \ldots, Y_n, \\
\mathbf{z} &= Z_1, \ldots, Z_n
\end{aligned}$$

We could send the three codewords $\mathbf{x}, \mathbf{y}, \mathbf{z}$ one after the other. Another option is to transmit column by column. Then our transmitted code-word $\mathbf{w}$ would look like this:

$$\mathbf{w} = X_1 Y_1 Z_1 \ldots X_n Y_n Z_n$$

Now suppose that each codeword in C can correct a burst of length 1. Then each codeword $\mathbf{w}$ corrects all bursts of length 3. We have **interleaved the code C to depth 3**. In general, we have the following result (see [HLL$^+$92]).

Theorem 22.11 *Let C be a b burst error-correcting code. If C is interleaved to depth w then all bursts of length at most bw will be corrected provided that each interleaved codeword will be subjected to at most one burst of errors.*

The proof depends on the fact that any burst of errors of length at most bw in an interleaved codeword will cause a burst error pattern of length at most b in a codeword $\mathbf{c}$ of C.

22.6 Decoding Reed-Solomon Codes, Ramanujan, and Berlekamp–Massey

Let C be a Reed–Solomon code as described in Section 22.3 with $b = 0$ and generator

$$g(x) = (x - 1)(x - \alpha) \cdots (x - \alpha^{n-k-1})$$

To simplify the treatment (and to tie in with shift registers), we assume that F is a field of characteristic 2, so $-1 = 1$.

Recall that the parity check matrix is

$$H = \begin{pmatrix} 1 & 1 & \cdots & 1 \\ 1 & \beta_1 & \cdots & \beta_1^{n-1} \\ \vdots & \vdots & \vdots & \vdots \\ 1 & \beta_{n-k-1} & \cdots & \beta_{n-k-1}^{n-1} \end{pmatrix}$$

where $\beta_i = \alpha^i$ and α is a generator of the field $F = \mathrm{GF}(2^r)$.

Suppose that the codeword $\mathbf{c}$ with corresponding polynomial $\mathbf{c}(x)$ is transmitted and that the string $\mathbf{w}$ corresponding to the polynomial $\mathbf{w}(x)$ is received. Then we may calculate the $2t$ **syndromes**

$$s_i = \mathbf{w}(\alpha^i) \quad \text{for } 1 \leq i \leq n - k, \ n = q - 1$$

Write

$$\mathbf{w}(x) = \mathbf{c}(x) + \mathbf{E}(x)$$

where $\mathbf{E}(x)$ is the **error polynomial**.

The code C has dimension k and minimum distance $d = n - k + 1$.

Let $t = \frac{d-1}{2} = \lfloor \frac{n-k}{2} \rfloor$. Then the code C can correct up to t errors. Here $\lfloor x \rfloor$ denotes the integer part of x. So, when decoding we assume that at most t transmission errors occur.

Since $\mathbf{c}$ is in the code C, the polynomial $\mathbf{c}(x)$ is a multiple of $g(x)$. Since $g(\alpha^i) = 0$, we have then that $\mathbf{c}(\alpha^i) = 0$. Thus

$$\mathbf{w}(\alpha^i) = \mathbf{c}(\alpha^i) + \mathbf{E}(\alpha^i) = \mathbf{E}(\alpha^i)$$

for $1 \leq i \leq n - k$. Now $\mathbf{E}(x)$ is some polynomial of degree at most t. Suppose that there are exactly e errors, $e \leq t$. Let

$$\mathbf{E}(x) = b_1 x^{i_1} + b_2 x^{i_2} + \cdots + b_e x^{i_e}$$

Then, for any j with $0 \leq j \leq n - k - 1$, we have

$$
\begin{aligned}
s_j &= \mathbf{E}(\alpha^j) \\
&= b_1 (\alpha^j)^{i_1} + b_2 (\alpha^j)^{i_2} + \cdots + b_e (\alpha^j)^{i_e} \\
&= b_1 (\alpha^{i_1})^j + b_2 (\alpha^{i_2})^j + \cdots + b_e (\alpha^{i_e})^j \\
&= b_1 \alpha_1^j + b_2 \alpha_2^j + \cdots + b_e \alpha_e^j
\end{aligned}
$$

where $a_1 = \alpha^{i_1}$, $a_2 = \alpha^{i_2}$, ..., $a_e = \alpha^{i_e}$ are the so-called "**error locations**" and $b_1, b_2, \ldots, b_t$ are the **error magnitudes**.

If $e < t$, it is convenient to define $a_i = 0$ for $e + 1 \leq i \leq t$ even though the corresponding error locations do not exist.

So the **decoding problem** comes down to solving the nonlinear system of $2t$ equations given by

$$\sum_{i=1}^{t} b_i a_i^j = s_j \tag{22.1}$$

for the $2e$ unknowns $a_1, a_2, \ldots, a_e$ and $b_1, b_2, \ldots, b_e$.

However, an astonishing fact, pointed out by Hill [Hil86] is that the system was solved over 100 years ago! The solution was provided in a little known two-page paper in 1912 by the legendary Indian mathematician Srinivasa Ramanujan [Ram12]. Ramanujan's elegant method used partial fractions and power series. (In fact, as mentioned above and pointed out by Barg, the solution goes back to de Prony in 1795.)

A more modern method involves the **error-locator polynomial**

$$\sigma_A(x) = (x - a_1) \cdots (x - a_e) \tag{22.2}$$

Note that the roots of σ_A are $a_1, \ldots, a_e$. Recall that we are in characteristic 2. Expanding this polynomial we get

$$\sigma_A(x) = \sigma_0 + \sigma_1 x + \cdots + \sigma_{e-1} x^{e-1} + x^e \tag{22.3}$$

where the σ_i are the so called elementary symmetric functions, so that we also have $\sigma_A(a_i) = 0$, $1 \leq i \leq e$. If we multiply both sides of (22.3) by $b_i a_i^j$, substitute $x = a_i$ and sum both sides from $i = 1$ to $i = t$, we get the equation

$$s_{j+e} = s_j \sigma_0 + s_{j+1} \sigma_1 + \cdots + s_{j+e-1} \sigma_{e-1} \tag{22.4}$$

as in [HLL$^+$92]. This equation certainly has the look of something we have seen in this book more than once: we are talking *shift-registers*!

This is where the **Berlekamp–Massey algorithm** discussed in Chapter 16 comes in to play, leading to an iterative solution of the decoding problem. For details and many examples, we refer to [PW72] and to [HLL$^+$92].

22.7   An Algorithm for Decoding and an Example

We have from the above that

$$s_{j+e} = s_j \sigma_0 + s_{j+1} \sigma_1 + \cdots + s_{j+e-1} \sigma_{e-1}$$

We know the values $s_1, s_2, \ldots, s_e$ and so we get a linear system of the following form:

$$
\begin{pmatrix}
s_0 & s_1 & \cdots & s_{e-1} \\
s_1 & s_2 & \cdots & s_e \\
\vdots & \vdots & \ddots & \vdots \\
s_{e-1} & s_e & \cdots & s_{2e-2}
\end{pmatrix}
\begin{pmatrix}
\sigma_0 \\
\sigma_1 \\
\vdots \\
\sigma_{e-1}
\end{pmatrix}
=
\begin{pmatrix}
s_e \\
s_{e+1} \\
\vdots \\
s_{2e-1}
\end{pmatrix}
\tag{22.5}
$$

Denote the coefficient matrix in the above by P. On the assumption that $a_1, \ldots, a_e$ are distinct and $a_1, \ldots, a_e$, $b_1, \ldots, b_e$ are all nonzero, we can solve Eq. (22.5) for $\sigma_0, \sigma_1, \ldots, \sigma_{e-1}$ thereby obtaining the error locator polynomial $\sigma_A(x)$. Since the roots of $\sigma_A(x)$ are $a_1, a_2, \ldots, a_e$, we can then find these. Finally, we can find $b_1, b_2, \ldots, b_e$ from the linear system in Eq. (22.1) above. These can be represented in matrix form as follows.

$$
\begin{pmatrix}
a_1^0 & a_2^0 & \cdots & a_e^0 \\
a_1^1 & a_2^1 & \cdots & a_e^1 \\
\vdots & \vdots & \ddots & \vdots \\
a_1^{e-1} & a_2^{e-1} & \cdots & a_e^{e-1}
\end{pmatrix}
\begin{pmatrix}
b_1 \\
b_2 \\
\vdots \\
b_e
\end{pmatrix}
=
\begin{pmatrix}
s_0 \\
s_1 \\
\vdots \\
s_{e-1}
\end{pmatrix}
\tag{22.6}
$$

Now we have found the locations of the errors (corresponding to the a_i) and the "magnitude" of the errors corresponding to the b_i, $1 \le i \le e$, completing the decoding.

To summarize, we have our Reed–Solomon decoding algorithm.

Reed–Solomon Decoding Algorithm

1. Calculate the $2t$ syndromes $s_1, s_2, \ldots, s_{2t}$, $s_i = E(\alpha^i)$, where E is the error polynomial.

2. The rank of the matrix P in Eq. (22.5) yields the number e.

3. Having found e, solve the system (22.5) for $\sigma_0, \sigma_1, \ldots, \sigma_{e-1}$.

4. Find the roots of the error locator polynomial. These give the *error locations* $a_1, a_2, \ldots, a_e$.

5. Solve the linear system in (22.6) for $b_1, b_2, \ldots, b_e$. We now have found the errors and their locations.

A Worked Example

Let C be the linear code generated by $g(x)$, where

$$g(x) = (x + \alpha^0)(x + \alpha)(x + \alpha^2)(x + \alpha^3) = (x + 1)(x + \alpha)(x + \alpha^2)(x + \alpha^3)$$

Here, α is a generator for a field F of order $2^3 = 8$ obtained from the irreducible polynomial $u(x) = x^3 + x + 1$ (see Chapter 19). Thus, $n = q - 1 = 7$. The degree of the polynomial $g(x)$ (which is 4) is $n - k = 7 - k$. So $7 - k = 4$, giving $k = 3$. Thus the code C has dimension 3. Since C is MDS, the minimum distance is $n - k + 1 = 7 - 3 + 1 = 5$. It follows that C can correct as many as t errors where $t = \frac{5-1}{2} = 2$.

Now let us suppose that the received vector is the vector $\mathbf{w} = (1, \alpha, 0, \alpha, \alpha^6, 1, 0)$. On the assumption that at most two errors have been made, we want to find the transmitted codeword from our algorithm.

First, we calculate the syndromes. The syndrome polynomial $\mathbf{w}(x)$ is $1 + \alpha x + \alpha x^3 + \alpha^6 x^4 + x^5$. We calculate now $\mathbf{w}(1) = \mathbf{w}(\alpha^0), \mathbf{w}(\alpha), \mathbf{w}(\alpha^2), \mathbf{w}(\alpha^3)$. We have $\mathbf{w}(1) = 1 + \alpha + \alpha + \alpha^6 + 1$. Since the field F has characteristic 2, we have $1 + 1 = 0$, $\alpha + \alpha = 0$. Thus

$$\mathbf{w}(1) = \mathbf{w}(\alpha^0) = s_0 = \alpha^6$$

Then $s_0 = \alpha^6$.

Now $\mathbf{w}(\alpha)$ can be written as the dot product of $\mathbf{w}$ with the vector $(1, \alpha, \alpha^2, \alpha^3, \alpha^4, \alpha^5, \alpha^6)$. So we have

$$(1, \alpha, 0, \alpha, \alpha^6, 1, 0) \cdot (1, \alpha, \alpha^2, \alpha^3, \alpha^4, \alpha^5, \alpha^6) = 1 + \alpha^2 + \alpha^4 + \alpha^3 + \alpha^5$$

(Since $\alpha^7 = 1$.) Now using the addition tables (or remembering that $\alpha^3 = \alpha + 1$ so $\alpha^4 = \alpha^2 + \alpha$), we get $\mathbf{w}(\alpha) = \alpha^5$. Therefore, $s_1 = \alpha^5$.

To get s_2, we dot product $\mathbf{w}$ with $(1, \alpha^2, (\alpha^2)^2, \ldots, (\alpha^2)^6)$. Then $s_2 = 1$. Similarly, $s_3 = 0$.

Our system (22.5) now gives the following

$$\begin{pmatrix} \alpha^6 & \alpha^5 \\ \alpha^5 & 1 \end{pmatrix} \begin{pmatrix} \sigma_0 \\ \sigma_1 \end{pmatrix} = \begin{pmatrix} s_2 \\ s_3 \end{pmatrix} = \begin{pmatrix} 1 \\ 0 \end{pmatrix}$$

So we have the system

$$\begin{aligned} \alpha^6 \sigma_0 + \alpha^5 \sigma_1 &= 1, \\ \alpha^5 \sigma_0 + \sigma_1 &= 0 \end{aligned}$$

The rank of the system is 2 so $e = 2$. Solving gives $\sigma_0 = \alpha^3$ and $\sigma_1 = \alpha^5 \sigma_0 = \alpha^8 = \alpha$.

The error locator polynomial is given by the quadratic $\alpha^3 + \alpha x + x^2$. The roots are $x = 1$ and $x = \alpha^3$. Thus, $a_1 = 1$ and $a_2 = \alpha^3$. To solve for b_1, b_2, we have from Eq. (22.6) that

$$\begin{pmatrix} a_1^0 & a_2^0 \\ a_1^1 & a_2^1 \end{pmatrix} \begin{pmatrix} b_1 \\ b_2 \end{pmatrix} = \begin{pmatrix} \alpha^6 \\ \alpha^5 \end{pmatrix}$$

i.e.

$$\begin{pmatrix} 1 & 1 \\ 1 & \alpha^3 \end{pmatrix} \begin{pmatrix} b_1 \\ b_2 \end{pmatrix} = \begin{pmatrix} \alpha^6 \\ \alpha^5 \end{pmatrix}$$

Solving gives $b_2 = 1$ and $b_1 = \alpha^2$. Summing up then, on the assumption of at most two errors, we get that the two errors occurred in the α^0 and α^3 positions with magnitudes α^2 and 1. The received vector was $\mathbf{w} = (1, \alpha, 0, \alpha, \alpha^6, 1, 0)$. The (likely) error pattern is $(\alpha^2, 0, 0, 1, 0, 0, 0)$. Thus, the (likely) transmitted codeword is the sum of these, namely,

$$(1 + \alpha^2, \alpha, 0, \alpha + 1, \alpha^6, 1, 0) = (\alpha^6, \alpha, 0, \alpha^3, \alpha^6, 1, 0)$$

This is indeed a codeword $\mathbf{c}$ in C (see Problem 22.1).

22.8 Long MDS Codes and a Partial Solution of a 60 Year-Old Problem

In Section 22.3, we discussed a Reed–Solomon code C with generator matrix

$$G = \begin{pmatrix} 1 & 1 & \cdots & 1 \\ \beta_0 & \beta_1 & \cdots & \beta_{q-2} \\ \beta_0^2 & \beta_1^2 & \cdots & \beta_{q-2}^2 \\ \vdots & \vdots & \ddots & \vdots \\ \beta_0^{k-1} & \beta_1^{k-1} & \cdots & \beta_{q-2}^{k-1} \end{pmatrix}$$

where the nonzero elements of a given finite field $F = \mathrm{GF}(q)$ are denoted by $\beta_0, \beta_1, \ldots, \beta_{q-2}$. The matrix G is of size $k \times n = k \times (q-1)$ with $k \leq n-1$. The code C is MDS so that (see Section 22.2) any $k \times k$ submatrix of G is non-singular. Thus, any set of k columns are linearly independent. The rows of G are linearly independent: however, from the previous remark, the **truncated rows** of G, i.e. the rows corresponding to any k positions, are also linearly independent. Let us record some properties of MDS codes, some of which were discussed also in Chapter 18.

We have that no two codewords in C can agree on as many as $k = n - d + 1$ positions.
For suppose two distinct codewords in C agreed in k positions. Then, their difference
which is a nonzero vector in C has at most $n - k$ nonzero entries. But, since C is MDS,
any nonzero vector in C has at least $d = n - k + 1$ nonzero entries.

Take any k-tuple of nonzero entries from F, say $\gamma_1, \ldots, \gamma_k$. Pick any set of coordinate
(column) positions, say the first k positions. No two codewords in C have $\gamma_1, \ldots, \gamma_k$ in
their first k coordinate positions. So, from this, the total number of codewords in C is
at most $(q)\cdots(q) = q^k$. But $|C| = q^k$ since C has dimension k. It follows that there is a
unique codeword which has $\gamma_1, \ldots, \gamma_k$ in its first k coordinate positions. The same holds
true no matter which k positions we choose.

An interesting property of MDS codes which follows from the above is this. Even if
we lose the data in any $d - 1$ positions of a codeword, we can still recover the entire word
since we are left with $n - (d - 1) = k$ data pieces.

(A related idea involves the use of MDS error correction in the RAID [Redundant
Array of Independent Disks] system which is a collection of drives collectively acting as
a storage system which can tolerate the failure of an individual drive without losing data
and which can act independently of each other.)

It is possible to extend G by two more columns, namely

$$\begin{pmatrix} 1 \\ 0 \\ \vdots \\ 0 \\ 0 \end{pmatrix} \text{ and } \begin{pmatrix} 0 \\ 0 \\ \vdots \\ 0 \\ 1 \end{pmatrix}$$

while still preserving the MDS property, and get a doubly extended RS code D. (When
$k = 3$ and $F = \mathrm{GF}(q) = \mathrm{GF}(2^m)$ we can get a further extension. In this case, we can take
the matrix

$$G = \begin{pmatrix} 1 & \cdots & 1 & 1 & 0 & 0 \\ \alpha_1 & \cdots & \alpha_{q-1} & 0 & 0 & 1 \\ \alpha_1^2 & \cdots & \alpha_{q-1}^2 & 0 & 1 & 0 \end{pmatrix}$$

so the length of the MDS code C is now $q - 1 + 3 = q + 2$. Similarly, for C here the code
$C^\perp$ also has length $q + 2$.)

We may now pose the following question.

Question

For given k, q what is the length $m(k, q)$ of the longest linear MDS code of dimension k over $\mathrm{GF}(q)$?

Conjecture

$$m(k, q) = \begin{cases} q + 1 & \text{for } 2 \le k \le q, \\ k + 1 & \text{for } q < k \end{cases}$$

apart from the cases, $m(3, q) = m(q - 1, q) = q + 2$ if $q = 2^r$, as detailed above.

Let us return to the double-extended RS code D of length $q + 1$ with generator matrix G, obtained from G by adjoining two extra columns. A typical column of G looks like

$\begin{pmatrix} 1 \\ t \\ \vdots \\ t^{k-1} \end{pmatrix}$ with t in $\mathrm{GF}(q)$. (Allowing t to be infinite gives $\begin{pmatrix} 0 \\ 0 \\ \vdots \\ 1 \end{pmatrix}$.) We can regard this

column either as a vector in a k-dimensional vector space over $\mathrm{GF}(q)$ **or** as a point in a projective space $\sum = \mathrm{PG}(k - 1, q)$ of dimension $k - 1$ over $\mathrm{GF}(q)$.

Let us take $k - 1 = 2$. Then, our point looks like $\begin{pmatrix} 1 \\ t \\ t^2 \end{pmatrix}$ which we can identify with

the Euclidean point $\begin{pmatrix} t \\ t^2 \end{pmatrix}$ – all of which lie on the curve $y = x^2$, which is a conic.

For $t = 0$, we get the Euclidean point $\begin{pmatrix} 0 \\ 0 \end{pmatrix}$, the origin.

For $t = \infty$, we get a single "infinite point" $\begin{pmatrix} 0 \\ 0 \\ 1 \end{pmatrix}$ or point at infinity which we met in

Chapter 6.

Let us take $k - 1 = 3$. Then, our point set is a "twisted cubic" in $\mathrm{PG}(3, q)$. In general, we get a **normal rational curve** in $\mathrm{PG}(k - 1, q)$.

Any MDS code of dimension k will yield an **arc** S in $\sum = \mathrm{PG}(k - 1, q)$, i.e. a set of points S such that no k points lie in a hyperplane $\mathrm{PG}(k - 2, q)$ where $|S| \ge k \ge 3$, and conversely.

We can now extend the MDS conjecture to arcs. Here is a version.

Conjecture

Any arc in $\mathrm{PG}(k-1,q)$, $2 \leq k \leq q$, has at most $q+1$ points unless $k=3$ or $k=q-1$ and $q=2^r$ in which case the arc has at most $q+2$ points.

In Wicker [Wic95], the author refers to the problem related to this conjecture as "one of the more interesting problems in projective geometry over Galois fields."

In fact this famous problem had indeed been open for about 50 years. The arc conjecture was asymptotically proven in the late 1960s for q odd following pioneering work by the late B. Segre. A similar result for an even q was finally obtained in 1988 by the senior author of this book along with two co-authors (see [BTB88]). Here are two typical results from that paper.

Theorem 22.12 *Let K be an arc of $\sum = \mathrm{PG}(k-1,q)$, $q=2^s$, $k \geq 5$ and $|K| \geq q+k-1-\sqrt[3]{q}$. Then K lies in a unique normal rational curve.*

Theorem 22.13 *In $\mathrm{PG}(k-1,q)$, $q=2^s$, let K be an arc. Then*

(a) $|K| \leq q+1$ if $k=4$.

(b) $|K| \leq q+1$ if $k \geq 5$ and $q \geq (k-3)^3$.

(c) For $k \geq 6$, if $|K| > q+1$ then $|K| < q+k-1-\sqrt[3]{q}$.

In the projective plane, it is known that, for an arc K, $|K| \leq q+1$ (q odd) and $|K| \leq q+2$ (q even).

Results similar to Theorem 22.13 for q odd have also been shown. The method of the proof for Theorem 22.13 involves the celebrated Hasse–Weil estimates for algebraic curves along with the geometry of quadrics and some combinatorics. For further background, we refer to [BTB88].

22.9   Problems

22.1   Why is the vector $\mathbf{c} = (\alpha^6, \alpha, 0, \alpha^3, \alpha^6, 1, 0)$ in C? (See Solution 22.1.)

22.2   Using the code C with generator polynomial $g(x)$ over the field of order 8 as in the text, suppose the received vector is the vector $(\alpha^6, \alpha^6, \alpha^4, \alpha^3, \alpha^4, \alpha^2, 1)$. What is the (most likely) transmitted codeword? (See Solution 22.2.)

22.3   Construct an MDS code of minimum distance 4. (See Solution 22.3.)

22.4 Show that the dual of the Reed–Solomon code C with generator matrix given by

$$g(x) = (x - \alpha)(x - \alpha^2) \cdots (x - \alpha^t)$$

is also a Reed–Solomon code. (See Solution 22.4.)

22.5 Let $F = \mathrm{GF}(5)$ and let $g(x) = (x - 1)(x - 2)$ denote the generator matrix for the cyclic code of length $q - 1 = 5 - 1 = 4$. Sketch two different methods for constructing the code $C^{\perp}$ of length 4 and dimension 2. (See Solution 22.5.)

22.10 Solutions

22.1 The first two rows of a generator matrix G for C are

$$\begin{pmatrix} \alpha^6 & \alpha^5 & \alpha^5 & \alpha^2 & 1 & 0 & 0 \\ 0 & \alpha^6 & \alpha^5 & \alpha^5 & \alpha^2 & 1 & 0 \end{pmatrix}$$

The sum of these is $\mathbf{c}$.

22.2 We assume that, most likely, at most two errors occur. The first three rows of a generator matrix for C are

$$\begin{pmatrix} \alpha^6 & \alpha^5 & \alpha^5 & \alpha^2 & 1 & 0 & 0 \\ 0 & \alpha^6 & \alpha^5 & \alpha^5 & \alpha^2 & 1 & 0 \\ 0 & 0 & \alpha^6 & \alpha^5 & \alpha^5 & \alpha^2 & 1 \end{pmatrix}$$

Recall that $\alpha^3 = \alpha + 1$ so $\alpha^4 = \alpha^2 + \alpha$, $\alpha^5 = \alpha^3 + \alpha^2 = 1 + \alpha + \alpha^2$ and $\alpha^6 = \alpha(\alpha^5) = \alpha(1 + \alpha + \alpha^2) = \alpha + \alpha^2 + \alpha^3 = \alpha + \alpha^2 + \alpha + 1 = \alpha^2 + 1$. Therefore, $\alpha^5 + \alpha^6 = 1 + \alpha + \alpha^2 + \alpha^2 + 1 = \alpha$. The codeword $\mathbf{c}$ given by the sum of Rows 1 and 3 is

$$= (\alpha^6, \alpha^5, \alpha^5 + \alpha^6, \alpha^2 + \alpha^5, 1 + \alpha^5, \alpha^2, 1)$$

$$= (\alpha^6, \alpha^5, \alpha, \alpha^3, \alpha^4, \alpha^2, 1)$$

The received word is $(\alpha^6, \alpha^5, \alpha, \alpha^3, \alpha^4, \alpha^2, 1)$. The Hamming distance between $\mathbf{c}$ and the received word is 1 as they differ in positions $2, 5$ reading entries $1, 2, 3, 4, 5, 6, 7$ from the left.

The conclusion is that the (most likely) transmitted codeword is $(\alpha^6, \alpha^5, \alpha, \alpha^3, \alpha^4, \alpha^2, 1)$.

22.3 There are many options. Since the minimum distance is 4, the length of each codeword is at least 4. So if we work over a field $F = \mathrm{GF}(q)$ of order q, the length, namely $q - 1$, must be at least 4. Thus, $q - 1 \geq 4$ so $q \geq 5$. We work with GF(5) and pick a generator $\alpha = 2$ of the multiplicative group.

Now choose the generator polynomial to construct a code C with

$$g(x) = (x - 2^0)(x - 2^1)(x - 2^2) = (x - 1)(x - 2)(x - 4)$$

22.4 From Chapter 21, the code $C^\perp$ has a generator polynomial $h_1(x)$ whose roots are the inverses of the elements $\alpha^{t+1}, \alpha^{t+2}, \dots, \alpha^{q-1} = 1$. The roots of h_1 are then $(\frac{1}{\alpha})^{t+1}, (\frac{1}{\alpha})^{t+2}, \dots$. Thus, $C^\perp$ is a Reed–Solomon code since $\frac{1}{\alpha}$ is also a generator: we take $b = t + 1$ in the definition, with $\frac{1}{\alpha}$ being the generator.

22.5 **Method 1.** From Chapter 19,

$$h(x) = \frac{x^{q-1} - 1}{g(x)} = \frac{x^4 - 1}{(x - 1)(x - 2)} = \frac{(x - 1)(x - 2)(x - 3)(x - 4)}{(x - 1)(x - 2)}$$
$$= (x - 3)(x - 4) = x^2 - 7x + 12 = x^2 + 3x + 2$$

since, in GF(5), $-7 = 3$ and $12 = 2$.

Then, $h_1(x)$ has roots $\{\frac{1}{3}, \frac{1}{4}\} = \{2, -1\}$. The generator polynomial for $C^\perp$ is $(x - 2)(x + 1) = x^2 - x - 2$. A generator matrix for $C^\perp$ is

$$\begin{pmatrix} -2 & -1 & 1 & 0 \\ 0 & -2 & -1 & 1 \end{pmatrix}$$

Method 2. Here $n = 4$, $q = 5$, $k - 2$.

$$G = \begin{pmatrix} 2 & -3 & 1 & 0 \\ 0 & 2 & -3 & 1 \end{pmatrix}$$

From Theorem 22.1, a generator matrix for $C^\perp$ is

$$\begin{pmatrix} 1 & 1^2 & 1^3 & 1^4 \\ 2 & 2^2 & 2^3 & 2^4 \end{pmatrix} = \begin{pmatrix} 1 & 1 & 1 & 1 \\ 2 & 4 & 3 & 1 \end{pmatrix}$$

Chapter 23

MDS Codes, Secret Sharing, and Invariant Theory

Goals, Discussion   We want to give a quick summary of some nonlinear MDS codes and their applications to secret sharing schemes and combinatorics. The MacWilliams identities are presented and used in connection with ideas from invariant theory applied to linear codes related to projective planes. In particular, the "computer algebra theorem of the twentieth century" – namely the nonexistence of a projective plane of order 10 – is discussed. We also mention Euler's famous "36 officers" problem.

For more information on MDS codes, latin squares, and related topics, we refer to Chapter 29.

New, Noteworthy   Much of this material has only appeared in research papers, so, from a textbook point of view, it is new.

23.1   Some Facts Concerning MDS Codes

In Chapter 22, we discussed **linear** MDS codes using Reed–Solomon codes as examples. Basically, what we need for a linear MDS code C over a finite field $F = GF(q)$ is a $k \times n$ generator matrix G of rank k over F, with $n \geq k$, such that **every set of** k columns of

Cryptography, Information Theory, and Error-Correction: A Handbook for the 21st Century, Second Edition. Aiden A. Bruen, Mario A. Forcinito, and James M. McQuillan.
© 2021 John Wiley & Sons, Inc. Published 2021 by John Wiley & Sons, Inc.

G is linearly independent. (We know from linear algebra that **some set** of k columns is linearly independent since the row rank equals the column rank.)

The code C will have the property that, given any k entries $\beta_1, \beta_2, \ldots, \beta_k$ from F in columns $y_1, y_2, \ldots, y_k$ say, there is a unique codeword $\mathbf{c}$ in C such that $\mathbf{c}$ has entry β_1 in column y_1, entry β_2 in column $y_2, \ldots,$ and entry β_k in column y_k. We have that two codewords in C cannot agree in as many as k positions, i.e. $d(\mathbf{c}_1, \mathbf{c}_2) \geq n - (k-1) = n + 1 - k$ for any two codewords $\mathbf{c}_1, \mathbf{c}_2$ in C, where d denotes the Hamming distance. Since G has rank k, the code C can be regarded as a k-dimensional vector space with basis the rows of G so C has exactly q^k codewords.

In general, an (n, k, q) MDS code, linear or not, is defined as follows. *It is a set C of q^k codewords of length n over an alphabet A of size q with $k \leq n$, where q is some positive integer, satisfying the following property P.*

Property P No two codewords in C agree in as many as k positions.

Explanation of Property P

Choose any set $y_1, y_2, \ldots, y_k$ of k column positions. For example, we might choose the first k column positions of C. Now map each codeword $\mathbf{c}$ to its entries in these column positions. So we have a projection mapping $f : C \to A^k$, the set of k-tuples over A. From property P, this projection mapping f is one-to-one. Since $|C| = q^k = |A^k|$, we have that f is an onto mapping. It follows that the following conclusion holds.

Property Q Given any k elements $\beta_1, \beta_2, \ldots, \beta_k$ from the alphabet A and any set of k column positions $y_1, y_2, \ldots, y_k$ there is a unique codeword $\mathbf{c}$ having entry β_i in column position y_i, for $1 \leq i \leq k$.

We also discussed this condition in Chapter 18.

23.2 The Case $k = 2$, Bruck Nets

Suppose $k = 2$. Then C is a set of q^2 codewords of length n, where $2 \leq n$, over some alphabet A of size q satisfying the following property P (or the analogous condition Q).

Property P No two codewords in C agree in as many as 2 positions.

Example 23.1 *Suppose A is the binary alphabet of size 2, so $q = 2$. Let $n = 3$. So $|C| = 4$, and each word in C is a binary triple. Such a code is given as follows.*

$$C = \{(000), (011), (101), (110)\}$$

It is convenient to discuss C from a geometrical standpoint. We define a structure N of points and lines as follows.

1. *Points of N.* All q^2 points of C.

2. *Lines of N.* All codewords in C that have a given symbol in a given position.

It follows that there are qn lines of N altogether. Each line has q points.

To see that there are qn lines altogether, let us suppose that we are looking at all codewords $\mathbf{c}$ having a symbol, α_1 say, in the first position. Fix any other position, say the second position and pick any α in A. There is exactly one codeword $\mathbf{c}$ having α_1 in the first position and α in the second position. There are q choices for α. So, altogether, there are exactly q codewords $\mathbf{c}$ having α_1 in the first position. So each line will have q points. We are using properties P, Q here.

Letting α_1 vary we get q distinct lines corresponding to the different symbols that a codeword can have in the second position. These lines form a **parallel class** of q lines. This means that

1. No two of these lines meet, and

2. Each point of N lies on exactly one line of this parallel class.

Examining the codewords having a given symbol from A in the ith position, $1 \leq i \leq n$, we get altogether a set of qn lines. Each line consists of all the codewords that have a given symbol in a given position. The lines are therefore arranged into n parallel classes of lines satisfying the following axioms.

1. Two lines from the same parallel class are parallel, i.e. they have no points in common.

2. Two lines from distinct parallel classes meet in a unique point.

Each line has q points. Each point is on n lines.

To see Axiom 2, we can use Property Q Section 23.1. Now we make the following definition.

A **Bruck net** N of order q and degree n is a set of q^2 points and qn lines, $n \geq 3$, satisfying the following axioms.

1. Any 2 points lie on at most one line.

2. Given any line l and any point P off l there is a unique line on P failing to meet l. This line is said to be **parallel** to l.

From the above it can be seen that any MDS code with $k = 2$ yields a Bruck net of order q and degree n.

For the converse, let N be such a Bruck net. There will then be n parallel classes of lines, as defined earlier. Label the n parallel classes as $1, 2, \ldots, n$ in some fashion, and label the q lines $1, 2, \ldots, q$ within each parallel class. Then, with each point P associate a codeword $(x_1, x_2, \ldots, x_n)$ where x_i is the number of the line in the ith parallel class that goes through P.

In this way, we get a MDS code with q^2 codewords of length n with $k = 2$. *We have thus shown that MDS codes with $k = 2$ are equivalent to Bruck nets.*

Example 23.2 *In Example 23.1, we have $q^2 = 2^2 = 4$ points and $qn = (2)(3) = 6$ lines. Let us draw a Bruck net of order 2 and degree 3 (Figure 23.1).*

We have 4 points and 6 lines and 3 parallel classes of lines, namely horizontal, vertical, and diagonal. (Note that the line 14 is parallel to the line 23.)

Then, labeling the lines within each parallel class as 0 or 1 we get, for each point, a codeword as follows.

$$3 \to (000)$$
$$4 \to (011)$$
$$1 \to (101)$$
$$2 \to (110)$$

This is just the code described in Example 23.1 above!

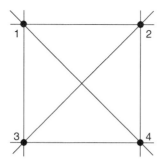

Figure 23.1: Bruck net of order 2 and degree 3.

23.3   Upper Bounds on MDS Codes, Bruck–Ryser

For $k = 2$, one can show that $n \leq q + 1$. If $n = q + 1$ the corresponding Bruck net N is in fact an **affine plane** of order q. This means that **any 2 points of N are joined by a unique line.**

An example is obtained by using a field $F = GF(q)$ as alphabet A when q is a prime power with $q = p^n$. The affine plane $\Pi_A = AG(2, q) = AG(2, F)$ over F is easily described. The points of Π_A are all possible ordered pairs (a, b) with a, b in F. The lines are sets of points (x, y) satisfying linear equations of the form $y = mx + b$ or $x = c$ where m, b, c are fixed elements of F. (This is exactly the construction of the Euclidean plane when $F = R$, the field of real numbers, as following Descartes.) These particular affine planes satisfy the **Desargues axiom**, but there also exist non-Desarguesian planes of order q. (The Desargues axiom states that if two triangles are in perspective from a point in a projective plane then the intersections of corresponding lines are collinear.) The MDS code obtained from $AG(2, F)$ is equivalent to a linear code but the code obtained from a non-Desarguesian plane will **not** be equivalent to a linear code.

Given any affine plane of order q we can adjoin $q + 1$ "points of infinity" to end up with a projective plane of order q. These were discussed in Chapter 22. Conversely, given a projective plane of order q, we obtain an affine plane of order q by deleting a line. So the two concepts are, in a sense, equivalent. The affine plane of order q has q^2 points and $q^2 + q$ lines. The projective plane of order q has $q^2 + q + 1$ points and lines.

It is not known for which values of q affine (or projective) planes exist. If q is a prime power they certainly exist, as we have seen, by using a field of order q. This existence question has been studied intensively but there has been no general result since the **Bruck–Ryser Theorem** [BR49] in 1949 – generalized to the **Bruck–Ryser–Chowla Theorem** for symmetric designs – which rules out all of those values of q with $q \bmod 4 = 1$ or $q \bmod 4 = 2$, whenever q is not the sum of 2 integer squares. This theorem rules out infinitely many values of q, e.g. $q = 6, 14, \ldots$ but leaves open the possibility of a plane of order q for infinitely many values of q such as $q = 10, 18, \ldots$ (since $10 = 3^2 + 1^2$ and $18 = 3^2 + 3^2$) which are not prime powers. We shall have more to say about the case $q = 10$ shortly. *There is no known plane whose order is not a prime power.*

Even when there is no plane of order q, the question remains as to how big n can be in a Bruck net for a given q. A famous case occurs when $q = 6$, dating back to Euler and the "36 officers problem" in 1782. The 36 officer problem is as follows. "Officers can have 6 distinct ranks. The problem is to choose 36 officers from 6 regiments, no two officers from the same regiment having the same rank, such that when they are on parade in a 6 by 6 square, no column or row shall contain 2 officers of the same regiment or of the same rank." It was shown by G. Tarry in 1901 that for $q = 6$, n is less than or equal to 3. Tarry's result is equivalent to showing that the 36 officer's problem has no solution. Tarry's method of proof was exhaustive trial and error. A shorter proof was constructed by D.R. Stinson [Sti84]. Hill [Hil86] discusses this in the context of "the main coding theory problem." (The usual version of this problem is to find the largest code of a given length and given minimum distance.) A famous theorem of Bruck, which also relates to work on **derivation** by T.G. Ostrom, is that if n is close to $q + 1$ then the corresponding Bruck net can be embedded in a unique plane. Bruen [Bru71b] showed that the existence of large unembeddable nets close to the Bruck bound using a centuries-old geometrical result known as **Galluci's Theorem** or the **Theorem of Dandelin.** Further references are given in Beutelspacher-Rosenbaum [BR98] and Alderson [Ald02]. In summary, in order to mimic general q ary MDS codes with $k = 2$, we are forced to deal with Bruck nets or equivalently, of systems of mutual orthogonal latin squares, i.e. MOLS (see Hill [Hil86, Theorem 10.20]). For the above, a Bruck net with n parallel classes is equivalent to $n - 2$ mutually orthogonal latin squares of size $q \times q$. See also "Maximum distance separable codes and arcs in projective spaces" by Alderson et al. [ABS07].

For $k \geq 3$ very little is known. It is known that $n \leq q + k - 1$. If $k \geq 4$, $q > 2$ and there exists a MDS code with $n = q + k - 1$ then 36 divides q so that q cannot be a prime power. This result is proved in [BS83] and [BS88], where related results are given. For $k = 3$ and $n = q + 2$, the only known examples are closely related to Desarguesian planes. We refer the reader to [BS88]. A specific example due to Alderson [Ald02] is described in Figure 23.2, with $n = 6$, $k = 3$, and $q = 4$.

$(1,1,1,1,1,1)$	$(1,1,2,2,2,2)$	$(1,1,3,3,3,3)$	$(1,1,4,4,4,4)$
$(1,2,4,3,2,1)$	$(1,2,3,4,1,2)$	$(1,2,2,1,4,3)$	$(1,2,1,2,3,4)$
$(1,3,2,4,3,1)$	$(1,3,1,3,4,2)$	$(1,3,4,2,1,3)$	$(1,3,3,1,2,4)$
$(1,4,3,2,4,1)$	$(1,4,4,1,3,2)$	$(1,4,1,4,2,3)$	$(1,4,2,3,1,4)$
$(2,1,4,2,3,1)$	$(2,1,3,1,4,2)$	$(2,1,2,4,1,3)$	$(2,1,1,3,2,4)$
$(2,2,1,4,4,1)$	$(2,2,2,3,3,2)$	$(2,2,3,2,2,3)$	$(2,2,4,1,1,4)$
$(2,3,3,3,1,1)$	$(2,3,4,4,2,2)$	$(2,3,1,1,3,3)$	$(2,3,2,2,4,4)$
$(2,4,2,1,2,1)$	$(2,4,1,2,1,2)$	$(2,4,4,3,4,3)$	$(2,4,3,4,3,4)$
$(3,1,2,3,4,1)$	$(3,1,1,4,3,2)$	$(3,1,4,1,2,3)$	$(3,1,3,2,1,4)$
$(3,2,3,1,3,1)$	$(3,2,4,2,4,2)$	$(3,2,1,3,1,3)$	$(3,2,2,4,2,4)$
$(3,3,1,2,2,1)$	$(3,3,2,1,1,2)$	$(3,3,3,4,4,3)$	$(3,3,4,3,3,4)$
$(3,4,4,4,1,1)$	$(3,4,3,3,2,2)$	$(3,4,2,2,3,3)$	$(3,4,1,1,4,4)$
$(4,1,3,4,2,1)$	$(4,1,4,3,1,2)$	$(4,1,1,2,4,3)$	$(4,1,2,1,3,4)$
$(4,2,2,2,1,1)$	$(4,2,1,1,2,2)$	$(4,2,4,4,3,3)$	$(4,2,3,3,4,4)$
$(4,3,4,1,4,1)$	$(4,3,3,2,3,2)$	$(4,3,2,3,2,3)$	$(4,3,1,4,1,4)$
$(4,4,1,3,3,1)$	$(4,4,2,4,4,2)$	$(4,4,3,1,1,3)$	$(4,4,4,2,2,4)$

Figure 23.2: An MDS code with $k = 3$, $n = 6$, $q = 4$ with $4^3 = 64$ codewords.

23.4   MDS Codes and Secret Sharing Schemes

Suppose a combination lock with 100 dial positions has combination 13-32-93. The classical way of sharing this secret combination would be to first dissect the secret into three shares, each share consisting of a position and a two-digit number. Each share is then distributed to different users, 13 to Alice, 32 to Bob, and 93 to Charles, where each user is told the position of his or her number within the secret combination.

There are two difficulties with this secret sharing protocol. Firstly, knowledge of any given share reduces the security of the secret. In the above example, before being given her share, Alice can determine the secret with a probability of $1/100^3$. After she is given her share, the probability is increased to $1/100^2$. If Alice were privy to Bob's share, the probability would be further increased to $1/100$.

Secondly, all shares are required to determine the secret. Indeed, if Alice were to lose her share then the remaining share holders would be left with only experimentation to determine the secret.

These two shortcomings led to the formulation of (S, T) **threshold schemes** for secret sharing due to Shamir, Blakely, and others (see Trappe and Washington [TW01] and also Beutelspacher and Rosenbaum [BR98]) in which a secret is dissected into an *ordered list of S shares*. As above, a share consists of its value and position within the list. We have two requirements or postulates.

(P1) Knowledge of T shares reveals the secret

(P2) Knowledge of $T - 1$ or fewer shares reveals no information regarding the secret.

Now, to construct such a scheme, assume that the given secret is a member of some finite alphabet A. Consider an (n, k) MDS code C over A, linear or not. So the code has length n and any k entries from A in k given positions determine a unique codeword.

We may construct an $(S = n - 1, T = k)$ threshold scheme as follows. The code C is made known to all. The secret is the final coordinate a_n, where $a = (a_1, a_2, \ldots, a_n)$ is a given codeword. The share list is $\{a_1, a_2, \ldots, a_{n-1}\}$. Since any k coordinate positions in C form an information set, property (P1) is satisfied for $T = k$. Moreover, given t shares where $t < k$, no information regarding the secret is divulged. For example, suppose the first t coordinates are known. There are $|A|^{k-t}$ words in C having $a_1, a_2, \ldots, a_t$ as the first t coordinates.

Let B be this set of codewords. If α and β are elements in A, then, among the words of B, just as many, namely $|A|^{k-t-1}$, have final coordinate α as have β. So property (P2) is satisfied.

This scheme will work for any MDS code, linear or not. It is more general than previous schemes such as the Shamir scheme, which is closely related to linear MDS codes.

23.5   MacWilliams Identities, Invariant Theory

The celebrated MacWilliams identities relate the weight distribution of a linear code C to that of the dual code $C^\perp$. Let C have length n and denote by A_i the number of codewords in C that have weight equal to i. Then the **weight enumerator** of C is defined as follows.

$$W_C(X, Y) = \sum_{i=0}^{n} A_i X^i Y^{n-i}$$

Let B_i denote the number of vectors of weight i in the dual code $C^\perp$.

In the binary case we have the following result, which shows that the weight enumerator polynomial of the dual code $C^\perp$ is entirely determined by W_C and is in fact a linear transformation of $W_C(X, Y)$. We have the **MacWilliams identities**

$$W_{C^\perp}(X, Y) = \frac{1}{|C|} W_C(X + Y, X - Y) \tag{23.1}$$

where $|C|$ denotes the number of codewords in C.

Now suppose that $C = C^\perp$. Then $n = 2k$. Define

$$f(X, Y) = 2^{n-k} \sum_{i=0}^{n} A_i X^i Y^{n-i} \tag{23.2}$$

Multiplying across by $|C| = 2^k$ in Eq. (23.1), we obtain

$$f(X,Y) = f(2^{-\frac{1}{2}}(Y-X), 2^{-\frac{1}{2}}(Y+X)) \tag{23.3}$$

In other words, we have

$$f(X,Y) = f(\frac{1}{\sqrt{2}}(Y-X), \frac{1}{\sqrt{2}}(Y+X)) \tag{23.4}$$

23.6 Codes, Planes, and Blocking Sets

Let Π be a finite projective plane of order n. In this section, we assume that $n \bmod 4 = 2$, that is, the remainder when n is divided by 4 equals 2. Thus, 2 divides n but 4 does not divide n. An example (the only known example) is when $n = 2$ (see Chapter 20).

Let A be any incidence matrix for Π. Thus, the $n^2 + n + 1$ points of Π give a (0,1) matrix A of size $(n^2 + n + 1) \times (n^2 + n + 1)$. If we denote the points and lines of Π by $P_1, P_2, \dots, P_{q^2+q+1}$ and $L_1, L_2, \dots, L_{q^2+q+1}$, then $A = (a_{ij})$ where

$$a_{ij} = \begin{cases} 1 & \text{if } L_i \text{contains} P_j \\ 0 & \text{otherwise.} \end{cases}$$

Now the rows of A generate a linear code D, working over the binary field. Using a parity check for D we arrive at the code C. One of the show-pieces of the theory, which uses the Smith canonical form for matrices in the proof, was mentioned in Chapter 18. Applied to our special case we have the following result.

Theorem 23.3 *The dimension of C is $\frac{1}{2}(n^2 + n + 2)$.*

Example

Let Π denote the projective plane of order 2 (the Fano plane) as diagrammed in Figure 20.1. It has seven points, namely $P_1, P_2, \dots, P_7$ and seven lines $l_1, l_2, \dots, l_7$ labeled as follows

$$l_1 = \{P_1, P_6, P_5\}, \ l_2 = \{P_1, P_7, P_4\}, \ l_3 = \{P_1, P_2, P_3\},$$
$$l_4 = \{P_5, P_4, P_3\}, \ l_5 = \{P_5, P_7, P_2\}, \ l_6 = \{P_3, P_7, P_6\},$$
$$l_7 = \{P_6, P_4, P_2\}$$

Thus, the incidence matrix A is as follows.

$$A = \begin{pmatrix} 1 & 0 & 0 & 0 & 1 & 1 & 0 \\ 1 & 0 & 0 & 1 & 0 & 0 & 1 \\ 1 & 1 & 1 & 0 & 0 & 0 & 0 \\ 0 & 0 & 1 & 1 & 1 & 0 & 0 \\ 0 & 1 & 0 & 0 & 1 & 0 & 1 \\ 0 & 0 & 1 & 0 & 0 & 1 & 1 \\ 0 & 1 & 0 & 1 & 0 & 1 & 0 \end{pmatrix}$$

A suitable set of 4 rows of A serves as a generator matrix for the code D. To obtain a generator matrix for C, simply adjoin a column of 1's to a generator matrix for A. A generator matrix for a code equivalent to C is given in Chapter 20.

The minimum weight of D is 3, corresponding to the lines. In the general case, the minimum weight of a codeword in D is $n + 1$.

The minimum weight of C is $n + 1$ corresponding to the "extended lines" and the hyperovals which are sets of $n + 2$ points with no 3 collinear. For $n = 2$, these are just quadrangles of which there are exactly 168.

Note that $n^2 + n + 2$ is the length of the code C. Each row of a generator matrix of C corresponds to a line of Π. This line has $n + 1$ points, which is odd, since n is even. Thus, when the parity check is applied, the corresponding line will have a one at the "infinite coordinate," i.e. in column number $n^2 + n + 2$.

Any two distinct lines meet in a unique finite point. But they also each have 1 in column number $n^2 + n + 2$. So two distinct lines intersect in two coordinate points when regarded as codewords in C. Now the lines generate C. If follows that C is contained in $C^\perp$. Therefore, $\dim(C) \le \dim(C^\perp)$, where dim denotes the dimension. But $\dim(C^\perp) = n^2 + n + 2 - \dim(C) = \frac{1}{2}(n^2 + n + 2) = \dim(C)$. We now have the following result.

Theorem 23.4 C *is self-dual, i.e.* $C = C^\perp$.

From Eq. (23.4) of the Section 23.5 $f(X, Y)$ is invariant under the matrix

$$\begin{pmatrix} a & b \\ c & d \end{pmatrix} = \frac{1}{\sqrt{2}} \begin{pmatrix} -1 & 1 \\ 1 & 1 \end{pmatrix} = M_1 \tag{23.5}$$

Here we say that f is invariant under the matrix $M = \begin{pmatrix} a & b \\ c & d \end{pmatrix}$ if $f(X, Y) = f(aX + bY, cX + dY)$.

Each row $\mathbf{u}, \mathbf{v}$ in the generator matrix for C has weight $(n + 1) + 1 = n + 2$. So each row has weight divisible by 4. Now, for binary, $\text{wt}(\mathbf{u} + \mathbf{v}) = \text{wt}(\mathbf{u}) + \text{wt}(\mathbf{v}) - 2\text{wt}(\mathbf{u} \cap \mathbf{v})$, where $\mathrm{wt}(\mathbf{u} \cap \mathbf{v})$ means the number of ones that $\mathbf{u}, \mathbf{v}$ have in common. Since $C \subset C^{\perp}$, $\mathrm{wt}(\mathbf{u} \cap \mathbf{v})$ is even. In summary, each word in C has weight divisible by 4. Thus, f is invariant under the matrix

$$\begin{pmatrix} \omega & 0 \\ 0 & 1 \end{pmatrix} = M_2 \tag{23.6}$$

where $\omega^2 = -1$. Then (see Broué and Enguehard [BE72], Assmus and Mattson [AM74])

$$(M_1 M_2)^3 = \frac{1+\omega}{\sqrt{2}} \begin{pmatrix} 1 & 0 \\ 0 & 1 \end{pmatrix}$$

which is a **primitive 8th root of unity** and acts to multiply X and Y by this primitive 8th root. We have shown the following result.

Theorem 23.5 *The length $n^2 + n + 2$ is divisible by 8.*

This is a nice example of the use of codes in combinatorial questions. As an immediate consequence, we have the following result.

Theorem 23.6 *There are no projective planes of order n with $n \bmod 8 = 6$.*

Proof. We have that $n^2 + n + 2$ would have to be divisible by 8 from Theorem 23.5. This contradicts the fact that $n \bmod 8 = 6$ since in that case $n^2 + n + 2$ leaves a remainder of 4 (not 0) upon division by 8. ∎

Let us return to the linear code D for which C is the parity check code. We know that each word in C has weight divisible by 4. Thus, each codeword in D has a weight w such that $w \bmod 4 = 0$ or 1.

The codewords of smallest weight in D are the lines, which have weight $n + 1$. The next question is this.

Question

What is the smallest weight of a codeword $\mathbf{c}$ in D having odd weight bigger than $n + 1$?

Given such a codeword $\mathbf{c}$ we associate a set S of points of Π corresponding to those columns of $\mathbf{c}$ with 1 in them. Assume that $|S| < 2n + 3$. Such a set S then has the following properties.

1. Each line of Π contains at least one point of S.

2. Each line of Π contains at least one point not in S.

(Bruen studied such sets for his doctoral dissertation at Toronto. His friend and class-mate J. C. Fisher urged that they be called "amiable sets." Bruen went with the name **blocking sets**. This name was vindicated by existing papers in the literature due to Di Paola [dP69] where the terminology "blocking conditions" was used, stemming from the connections to game theory).

The following result is shown in [Bru70] and [Bru71a].

Theorem 23.7 *If S is a blocking set then $|S| \geq n + \sqrt{n} + 1$. If equality occurs, then S is a projective subplane of order $\sqrt{n}$, i.e. a Baer subplane.*

It should be mentioned that, working independently in Hungary, Jan Pelikán [Pel70] had a result which came close to Theorem 23.7. The case of multiple blocking sets was not handled for another 20 years [Bru92].

The case of equality in Theorem 23.7 is of particular interest when $n = 10$. For a quick history, we refer the reader to Cameron and van Lint [CvL80].

The issue was whether or not there was a plane of order 10. This was the first case that was left open by the Bruck–Ryser theorem.

Using invariant theory, it was known that the entire weight distribution was known if the values A_{12}, A_{15}, A_{16} were found, where A_{12}, A_{15}, A_{16} denote the number of codewords in D of weight $12, 15, 16$, respectively. A computer search showed that A_{12} was zero. Bruen had shown in [Bru71a] that A_{15} was zero unless Π had a subplane of order 2. The possible configurations were also classified there by hand. A computer search by Denniston [Den69] and independently by MacWilliams et al. [MST73] showed that A_{15} was zero.

We now come to A_{16}. The configurations corresponding to words of weight 15 and weight 16 are closely connected. Using Bruen's classification, Larry Carter, in his dissertation at Berkeley, showed that A_{16} was zero.

Finally, Lam et al. [LTS89] showed that there were no codewords of weight 19 by a lengthy computer analysis leading to the conclusion that *there is no projective plane of order 10*. The result garnered much publicity and was discussed in the New York Times. A shorter proof of Theorem 23.7 appears, jointly with B.L. Rothschild and coworker [BR85].

23.7 Long Binary Linear Codes of Minimum Weight at Least 4

Let $\mathbf{u}, \mathbf{v}$ be vectors in a linear code C over any field. Then $d(\mathbf{u}, \mathbf{v})$, the Hamming distance between $\mathbf{u}$ and $\mathbf{v}$ equals $d(\mathbf{u} - \mathbf{v}, \mathbf{0})$ which is the weight of $\mathbf{u} - \mathbf{v}$. Thus, the minimum distance between two distinct vectors equals the minimum weight of a nonzero codeword in C. In other words, for a linear code we have that "minimum distance equals minimum weight."

The determination of codes in the title above would appear to be a specialized task. But, in fact, a great deal of discrete mathematics is involved. We now want to outline some of this by discussing codes obtained from caps, i.e. cap codes.

In $PG(n, F)$ the projective space of (projective) dimension n over any field F, a **cap** is any set of points with no 3 collinear. We concentrate here on the case when F is $GF(2)$, the binary field.

There is a correspondence between caps in $PG(n, 2)$ and binary linear codes C of length N, dimension k and minimum weight at least 4. Let $C^\perp$ be the dual code.

A basis for C yields a $k \times N$ generator matrix and $C^\perp$ has a generator matrix M of size $(N - k) \times N$. Note that none of the columns can be the all zero vector.

(a) For suppose the ith column is zero. Then the vector $(000 \cdots 010 \cdots 000)$ with 1 in the ith position has dot product zero with each row of M and thus is a vector in C. But its weight is just $1 < 4$.

(b) Suppose that 2 columns of M, say columns 1 and 2 are equal or scalar multiples of each other, so that column 2 is equal to λ times column 1. Then as above the vector $(\lambda 100 \cdots 0)$ is in C but has weight 2.

(c) Similarly assume that, say, (column 1) $+ \alpha$(column 2) $+ \beta$(column 3) is the all zero column with α and β nonzero. Then, the vector $(1, \alpha, \beta, 0, 0, \ldots, 0)$ is in C but has weight 3.

Each column is a nonzero vector of length $n - k$ so can be viewed as a point in $PG(n, F)$ where $n = N - k - 1$.

From (b) two of the points from different columns cannot be the same. Thus the columns yield a set of N points in $PG(n, F)$.

From (c) no 3 of the N points are collinear se we have found a cap with N points.

Conversely, suppose we start with a large cap of size N which spans a projective space $PG(n)$ with $n = N - k - 1$. The points of the cap yield N columns of length $N - k$ in a matrix M of rank $N - k$ and M generates a linear code D. The dual code $D^\perp$ has rank k and length N and, as above, has minimum weight 4 because the cap is a set of N distinct points in projective space with no 3 collinear.

In Bruen and Wehlau [BW99], it is pointed out that a cap is maximual if and only if the corresponding code is non-lengthening, i.e. has covering radius 2. This topic leads to many questions in $PG(n, 2)$.

It was W. Tutte who investigated the connection between graphs and sets of points in $PG(n, 2)$. A 2-block in $PG(n, 2)$ is a set S of points such that every $(n-2)$-dimensional subspace intersects S. A tangential 2-block is a 2-block S with additional properties generalizing the notion of a tangent at S. The only known 2-blocks occur when $n = 2$, 3, or 5. A result that there exist no other examples would, as a very special case, imply the famous four-color theorem for graphs.

23.8 An Inverse Problem and a Basic Question in Linear Algebra

The question of the maximum length n of linear MDS codes of dimension k over a finite field of size q is related to the following:Given a $k \times n$ matrix M over $GF(q)$ of rank k, where $k < n, q$, such that **all** of the $\binom{n}{k}$ sets of columns of M are linearly independent, how large can n be?

In particular, it is conjectured that, for q odd, $n \le q + 1$, and that, for q even, $n \le q + 2$.

An "inverse" question is the following:Given a $k \times n$ matrix M of rank k over a field F (for example, F might be the real numbers), what is the **minimum** number of column sets of size k that form a basis?

This problem has been solved in Bruen and Bruen, "The basics of bases," The Mathematical Intelligencer, [BB10], when a line has enough points. It is shown in Theorem 3 that the number of bases is at least $\binom{t-n+2}{2}$ for $n \ge 3$ and $\binom{t}{2}$ for $n = 2$. Here n is the dimension of the vector space and t [k in the above] is the number of columns, where no column is a scalar multiple of another column. The result is for general fields, not just finite fields.

Chapter 24

Key Reconciliation, Linear Codes, and New Algorithms

The authors are very grateful to Professor David Wehlau of the Royal Military College (RMC) in Kingston, Ontario and the Communications Security Establishment (CSE) for his help with this work. Work related to this chapter has appeared in a joint paper co-authored with Dr. Wehlau (Bruen, Forcinito, Wehlau, "Error Correcting Codes, Block Designs, Perfect Secrecy and Finite Fields," *Acta Applicandae Mathematica*, **93** (2006) 253–278 [BWF06]).

Goals, Discussion In traditional symmetric key cryptography, the communicating parties **A**, **B** must both be in possession of a common secret key in order to communicate in secret. Here we give a very broad generalization of this. Namely, we assume that **A**, **B** are each in possession of keys **U**, **V** of a suitable common length N such that the mutual information $I(X : Y)$ of the corresponding random variables X, Y is nonzero. Under suitable assumptions, we show that a common secret key can be constructed by "public discussion." This algorithm has been used commercially.

Cryptography, Information Theory, and Error-Correction: A Handbook for the 21st Century, Second Edition.
Aiden A. Bruen, Mario A. Forcinito, and James M. McQuillan.
© 2021 John Wiley & Sons, Inc. Published 2021 by John Wiley & Sons, Inc.

New, Noteworthy We show how to construct new hash functions derived from linear codes in connection with the algorithms. Our methods can be modified to apply to error-correction but for reasons of space, we focus only on the cryptographic applications. This chapter brings together several ideas from Chapters 12 and 13. The new checking hash function discussed in Section 24.5 has been used as "information reconciliation" in quantum cryptography and in other key-exchange protocols.

24.1　Symmetric and Public Key Cryptography

The ancient difficulty for establishing a common cryptographic secret key between two communicating parties Alice and Bob is nicely summarized by the catch-22 dictum of Lomonaco [Lom99], to wit: "in order to communicate in secret one must communicate in secret." In other words, to establish a common secret key, Alice and Bob must already have a "shared secret."

In this chapter, we show how to establish such a common secret key by public discussion where Alice and Bob are initially in possession of keys A and B, respectively, of a common length N, which are not necessarily equal but are such that the mutual information $I(A, B)$ is nonzero. This is tantamount to assuming that the corresponding statistical variables a_i, b_i are correlated. Under additional assumptions, the common secret key generated will enjoy the property of "perfect secrecy" in the sense of Shannon. Such initial keys A, B arise in quantum cryptography using the laws of quantum physics. Other methods, using classical physics (such as measurements of a bit stream from a common satellite), have also been proposed for generating the correlated keys A and B.

Finally, we note that if Alice and Bob are in possession of a "shared secret" such as an error-correcting code then a common secret key can also be generated using a variation of the well-known McEliece cryptosystem. However, we point out that this key will no longer enjoy perfect secrecy but only computational security. Some such systems are in commercial use.

In Chapters 4, 12, and 15, we have seen that under capacity restrictions a code can be transmitted and received with an error probability close to zero. The search then goes on to find such codes with capacity close to the Shannon bound. Here we can think of the single vector A transmitting to B. We know the Shannon bound from entropy considerations. The problem then is to find ways of "extracting" the mutual information between A and B.

24.2 General Background

In his foundational paper [Sha48], Shannon pointed out that for cryptographic systems, two different kinds of security methodologies can be considered as follows.

1. *Computational security.* Here, although the system can be broken given sufficient time and computational resources, it is assumed that this cannot be done in a sufficiently short time frame as to pose a real threat.

2. *Perfect Shannon security (perfect secrecy).* Here the system can mathematically never be broken even assuming that an adversary has unlimited time and computational resources.

An example of (1) is the well-known RSA public key algorithm. The main algorithm in connection with (2) is the so-called *Vernam cipher* or *one-time pad* which was used extensively during the cold war in the 1950s and 1960s and still remains in use for military purposes. A secret message encoded with a one-time pad will remain secret forever. As Schneier [Sch96] puts it "Even after the aliens from Andromeda land with their massive spaceships and undreamed-of computing power, they will not be able to read the Soviet spy messages encrypted with one-time pads (unless they can go back in time and get the one-time pads)."

The difficulty with (1) is that no system has yet been devised that is provably computationally secure. In particular, the security, even computational security, of the RSA system rests on mathematical assumptions about the difficulty of factoring integers which remain unproven.

The problem with (2), as exemplified by the one-time pad, is the difficulty of providing the two communicating parties Alice and Bob with a secret key to enable encryption. During the cold war, and throughout history the two parties were provided with the common secret key using trusted couriers.[1]

One of the goals of this chapter is to provide some new results relating to the problem of key establishment. We aim to show how a secret key exchange can be designed by **public discussion**. Public discussion here means that Alice and Bob can exchange information in the open (e.g. over the Internet, so that anyone can listen in), and yet end up with a common secret key concerning which an eavesdropper will have only a vanishingly small amount of information as measured in Shannon bits.

---

[1] As Professor Lomonaco so eloquently put it we are confronted by a catch-22. *Catch-22 of modern cryptography*: In order to communicate in secret we must first communicate in secret.

Such a procedure has, of course, been sought for a considerable amount of time. We must point out that there are two aspects to our procedure, namely

(i) Physical

(ii) Mathematical.

For (i), *we take it as given that Alice and Bob are each in possession of a binary string of length N*. The physical process that generates these two strings is assumed to have the property that the two strings are not completely random with respect to each other, i.e. their bit correlation (which is their total number of bit agreements divided by N) is bounded away from $1/2$.

Such physical systems arise in various applications. We mention the well-known quantum encryption procedure developed by Bennett, Brassard, and others (see for example [BBR88]). Other physical examples have also been patented and are currently in industrial use. We will not dwell on the details here other than to exploit them mathematically.

Assuming the existence of the two sufficiently long strings A and B, in the respective possession of Alice and Bob, *we show how to construct a common secret key by public discussion using information theory and other mathematical techniques*. In the case where an eavesdropper, Eve, has no initial information about the strings A and B, we prove that Eve will have no information about the common secret key distilled from A and B. (The situation where Eve has some initial information about either A or B [or both] is more complicated.) We also point out that our algorithm for constructing a common secret key has an **intruder detection system** built into it.

Wireless devices cannot support long keys required by popular public key cryptosystems such as RSA. It is hoped that the methods in this chapter may lead to a key-exchange procedure where the keys are reasonably short and therefore more suitable.

Unfortunately, in previously published discussions of these techniques, the question of the length of the final secret key Alice and Bob obtain has not been specified. Of course, this is crucial in practical applications. In practical situations, Alice and Bob know ahead of time the desired length n of their secret key. They need to know what length N their initial keys should be. Indeed, if N is chosen too small, they may end up with the empty string as their final key. Conversely, if N is too large they will waste time and computing resources generating a final key whose length significantly exceeds n. We provide here a method for estimating N from n. Our analysis may also be used by Alice and Bob to predict how much time and effort will be required to generate their common secret key.

The basic method requires the choice of a block length for each round. We show here that for information theoretic and experimental reasons, choosing ℓ to be an integer power of 2 gives especially good results.

In order to verify that the secret key possessed by Alice is indeed exactly equal to the secret key possessed by Bob, we design a new kind of hash function customized for this purpose based on the theory of error-correcting codes.

24.3 The Secret Key and the Reconciliation Algorithm

We consider two communicating parties (cryptographic stations), Alice and Bob who are each in possession of a binary string $A = (a_1, a_2, \ldots, a_N)$, $B = (b_1, b_2, \ldots, b_N)$, respectively. We define the bit correlation between A and B, denoted by bitcorr(A, B) as follows

$$\text{bitcorr}(A, B) = \frac{\#\{i \mid a_i = b_i, 1 \le i \le N\}}{N}$$

Thus, we have bitcorr$(A, B) = 1 - d(A, B)/N$ where $d(A, B)$ denotes the usual Hamming distance between A and B, i.e. the number of indices i for which $a_i \neq b_i$. We assume that the events $\{\Pr(a_i) = b_i\}$ are independent, $1 \le i \le N$.

Let us explain our philosophy. We assume that the probabilities $\Pr(a_i = b_i)$ with a_i in A and b_i in B are independent. For the key agreement protocol denoted by KAP, we assume for the moment that X and Y are two strings of equal length with $1/2 <$ bitcorr$(X, Y) < 1$. Then, if U and V are substrings of X, Y and if f is a suitable (hash) function such that $f(U) = f(V)$, it is likely that bitcorr$(U, V) >$ bitcorr(X, Y). Assume further that we partition X and Y into corresponding substrings $U_1, U_2, \ldots, U_t$ and $V_1, V_2, \ldots, V_t$ and that we modify, by reducing or even deleting, those substrings U_i, V_i for which $f(U_i) \neq f(V_i)$.

Then, for the remnant strings X_1 and Y_1 it is reasonable to expect that bitcorr$(X_1, Y_1) >$ bitcorr(X, Y). By pursuing this iteratively, after a suitable number of iterations, say s, the two initial strings "converge" to two equal substrings $X_s = Y_s$.

This is the essence of the method. Of course, the procedure is complicated by the fact that care must be taken to account for any information that might be revealed to the eavesdropper, Eve, during the entire process.

Special cases of the above procedure were suggested as an algorithm for quantum encryption in the paper [BBB+90]. A general, but abstract, approach is outlined by Maurer [Mau93]. This general philosophy dates back to the basic methodology used in error-correcting codes going back to Hamming and Shannon in the 1940s.

Let us begin. In the first phase of the KAP, called the *convergence phase*, the following procedure is applied repeatedly.

1. A random permutation σ (better still a *shuffle* of a certain type, as described in Section 24.8) is applied equally to each of the two keys A and B.

2. A block size $\ell \geq 2$ is chosen.

3. The two keys are divided into blocks of length ℓ. If the length of the keys is not evenly divisible by ℓ, the excess bits are discarded.

4. For each block, Alice and Bob publicly compare the total parity of that block.

5. If the parities agree then the two blocks are tentatively accepted as agreeing. In this case, the remnant string from that block consists of the entire block, save the last bit. Alice and Bob each delete this last bit from their block to offset the information revealed to Eve when announcing their two parities.

   If the parities do not agree, Alice and Bob perform a binary search in order to locate an error.

6. Having started with two keys A and B and applied the previous five steps, Alice and Bob are now in possession of two remnant keys A_1 and B_1. They now apply steps 1–5 using A_1 and B_1 in the roles of A and B. They continue to iterate steps 1–5 until the estimated correlation of the remnant keys satisfies a certain halting condition described in Section 24.4.

Each time steps 1–5 of the convergence phase is performed we say that one *round* of the convergence phase has been performed.

To elaborate on how Alice and Bob carry out the binary search in step 5 when the parities disagree, we first define functions $P_1, P_2, P_3, \ldots$ inductively as follows. The function $P_i(S_A, S_B)$ for $i \geq 1$ is defined on ordered pairs of strings, S_A and S_B of common length i. The function value of P_i is an ordered pair of strings of a common length.

For $i = 1$, we define $P_i(S_A, S_B) = (\emptyset, \emptyset)$ where $\emptyset$ is the null string of length 0. For $i = 2$ write $S_A = (\alpha_1, \alpha_2)$ and $S_B = (\beta_1, \beta_2)$. If $\alpha_1 \neq \beta_1$ we put $P_2(S_A, S_B) = ((\alpha_2), (\beta_2))$. Otherwise, we put $P_2(S_A, S_B) = (\emptyset, \emptyset)$.

For $i \geq 3$ define procedure P_i as follows. Put $t := \lceil i/2 \rceil$ and write $S_A = (\alpha_1, \ldots, \alpha_t, \alpha_{t+1}, \ldots, \alpha_i)$ and $S_B = (\beta_1, \ldots, \beta_t, \beta_{t+1}, \ldots, \beta_i)$. Thus, S_A is the concatenation of M_A and N_A where $M_A := (\alpha_1, \ldots, \alpha_t)$ and $N_A := (\alpha_{t+1}, \ldots, \alpha_i)$. Define M_B and N_B similarly from S_B. Also put $M'_A := (\alpha_1, \ldots, \alpha_{t-1})$ and $M'_B := (\beta_1, \ldots, \beta_{t-1})$.

If the parities of M_A and M_B agree, then $P_i(S_A, S_B) := (R_A, R_B)$. Here R_A is the concatenation of the string M'_A with that string which is the first component of the ordered pair $P_{i-t}(N_A, N_B)$. Similarly, R_B is the concatenation of the string M'_B with the second component of the ordered pair $P_{i-t}(N_A, N_B)$.

On the other hand, suppose the parities of M_A and M_B disagree. Then, $P_i(S_A, S_B) :=$ (Q_A, Q_B). Here Q_A is the concatenation of the first component of $P_{t-1}(M'_A, M'_B)$ with the string N_A. Similarly, Q_B is the concatenation of the second component of $P_t(M'_A, M'_B)$ with the string N_B.

Having thus defined $P_i(S_A, S_B)$, we now easily obtain recursively Alice's and Bob's remnant strings for each block as follows. Denote the strings in their blocks of length ℓ by S_A and S_B, respectively. Also let S'_A be the string obtained from S_A by deleting the last bit and define S'_B similarly. Alice and Bob publicly announce the parities of S_A and S_B. If the parities of S_A and S_B agree then the remnant strings are S'_A and S'_B as specified in step 5. Should the parities disagree, then the remnant strings are obtained recursively as $P_\ell(S'_A, S'_B)$ with the relevant parities being announced at each stage by Alice and Bob. Having computed a remnant string for each block, both Alice and Bob concatenate all of their remnants from each block to obtain their whole remnant string.

To illustrate, let us describe the procedure for blocks of size 2 and blocks of size 3.

Blocks of size 2

Let $N = 6$ and $\ell = 2$. Then, $A = (a_1, \ldots, a_6)$ and $B = (b_1, \ldots, b_6)$. We first consider the blocks $S_A = (a_1, a_2)$ and $S_B = (b_1, b_2)$. Alice announces the parity $(a_1 + a_2) \pmod 2$ and Bob announces $(b_1 + b_2) \pmod 2$. If the two announced parities are equal, the remnant string from this block for Alice is (a_1) and the remnant string from this block for Bob is the string (b_1). If the announced values are different, the remnant string for both Alice and Bob is the null string. Alice then proceeds to her next block comprised of the string (a_3, a_4) and Bob proceeds to his next block (b_3, b_4). They then proceed to their third and final blocks (a_5, a_6) and (b_5, b_6), respectively. To end this round, they concatenate their three remnant strings obtaining an overall remnant string.

To give a concrete example suppose $A = (1, 1, 0, 0, 0, 1)$ and $B = (1, 1, 0, 1, 1, 0)$. For the first block, the remnant string for both Alice and for Bob is (1). For the second block, the remnant string for both Alice and Bob is the null string. For the third block, the remnant string for Alice is (0) and for Bob it is (1). Thus, the overall remnant string for Alice is $A_1 = (1, 0)$ and for Bob it is $B_1 = (1, 1)$.

Blocks of size 3

Again let $N = 6$. Write $A = (a_1, \ldots, a_6)$ and $B = (b_1, \ldots, b_6)$. Alice's first block is the string $S_A = (a_1, a_2, a_3)$ and Bob's first block is $S_B = (b_1, b_2, b_3)$. Alice announces $(a_1 + a_2 + a_3) \pmod 2$ and Bob announces $(b_1 + b_2 + b_3) \pmod 2$. If these announced parities agree, then Alice keeps the remnant string (a_1, a_2) and Bob keeps the remnant string (b_1, b_2).

Assume on the contrary that the announced parities differ. Then Alice announces (a_1) and Bob announces (b_1). If these two bits agree, then the remnant strings for this block of length 3 for Alice and for Bob is the null string. If the two bits disagree, then the remnant string for Alice is (a_2) and for Bob it is (b_2). Alice and Bob then proceed to calculate their remnant strings from the second and final block. Concatenating their remnant strings from each of their two blocks give them their overall remnant string.

As an example let $A = (1, 1, 0, 0, 0, 1)$ and $B = (1, 1, 0, 1, 1, 0)$ as above. Then the remnant string for both Alice and for Bob from their first block is $(1, 1)$. The remnant string from the second block of length 3 for Alice is (0) and for Bob it is (1). Thus, the overall remnant string for Alice is $A_1 = (1, 1, 0)$ and for Bob it is $B_1 = (1, 1, 1)$.

Remark 24.1 *In the above two concrete examples, the initial bit correlation,* bitcorr$(A, B) = 3/6$. *When $\ell = 2$, the bit correlation of the remnant strings is still 1/2, whereas for $\ell = 3$, the bit correlation has risen to 2/3. We will show that, in the general case, the bit correlation increases to 1 with arbitrarily high probability. We then employ a suitable hash function to ensure that the two remnant strings are actually equal.*

Remark 24.2 *Note that the "binary search procedure" differs from the usual binary search in that we never "get lucky" early on. If their first comparison, on blocks of length $k + 1$, indicates that the block's disagree, Alice and Bob have to each discard one bit and then perform their binary search using P_k. This binary search consists of either $\lceil \log_2(k + 1) \rceil$ or $\lfloor \log_2(k + 1) \rfloor$ comparisons and for each of these comparisons, Alice and Bob must both discard a corresponding bit from their original block.*

Remark 24.3 *As indicated above, the motivation for deleting a bit in a sub-string in various steps of the algorithm is to offset information revealed when the parities are publicly announced.*

24.4 Equality of Remnant Keys: The Halting Criterion

Let us recap the situation. Alice and Bob initially have generated, by physical means or otherwise, two strings or keys A, B of common length N such that the corresponding random variables are not independent. In fact, without loss of generality, it can be assumed that $1/2 < x = $ bitcorr$(A, B) \le 1$. The case where $x < 1/2$ can be reduced to the above case; this will be clarified at the end of this section.

Alice and Bob carry out one round of the convergence phase, using block size ℓ_1, obtaining remnant keys A_1 and B_1. It will transpire (see Section 24.6) that, on average, $\text{bitcorr}(A_1, B_1) > x = \text{bitcorr}(A, B)$. The expected correlation of A_1 and B_1 is given by $x_1 := \phi_{\ell_1}(x)$.

Performing the algorithm, after a suitable number of rounds, say i rounds, Alice and Bob end up with two keys A_i, B_i of common length $n := N_i$ and whose expected correlation, $y := x_i = \phi_{\ell_i}(x_{i-1}) = \phi_{\ell_i}(\phi_{\ell_{i-1}}(\cdots(\phi_{\ell_1}(x))\cdots))$, satisfies the following condition:

$$\textbf{Halting Criterion} \qquad n(1 - y) \leq \theta$$

Here $\theta < 1$ is a suitable pre-determined positive constant.

Write $p = 1 - y$. Then the expected number of disagreements between the keys A_i and B_i is np. The number of disagreements is a *Bernoulli process* which in turn is approximated by a normal distribution with mean np and variance $np(1 - p)$. For a given positive number t one can estimate the probability that $np > t$. In particular, this holds for $t = 1$. By a suitable choice of θ we can make this probability arbitrarily small. Thus the probability that A_i and B_i differ in even a single bit can be made arbitrarily small.

To further ensure that A_i and B_i are indeed identical we employ a hash function f based on an error-correcting code of a suitable minimum distance, say 4.

If $f(A_i) = f(B_i)$ we can then be assured that $A_i = B_i$. In the unlikely case that $f(A_i) \neq f(B_i)$ Alice and Bob repeat the convergence algorithm until the hash function agrees on the two remnant keys.

Let us clarify our earlier statement that we can assume $\text{bitcorr}(A, B) > 1/2$ provided that $\text{bitcorr}(A, B) \neq 1/2$.

Theorem 24.4 *If* $\text{bitcorr}(A, B) \neq 1/2$ *we may assume that* $\text{bitcorr}(A, B) > 1/2$.

Proof. If Alice and Bob know in advance that $x = \text{bitcorr}(A, B) < 1/2$ then $\text{bitcorr}(A, \overline{B}) = 1 - x > 1/2$ where $\overline{B}$ is the boolean complement of B obtained by interchanging 0's and 1's in B. Bob can then replace B by $\overline{B}$.

Assume that nothing about $\text{bitcorr}(A, B)$ is known in advance save that $\text{bitcorr}(A, B) \neq 1/2$. If Alice and Bob begin with block size ℓ then they can estimate $x = \text{bitcorr}(A, B)$ from the length of the remnant strings A_1 and B_1 (see Theorem 24.13). Since $L_\ell(x)$ is not a one-to-one function, its value indicates a few possible values for x. Applying another round of the convergence procedure (with another block length ℓ') gives a new remnant length $L_{\ell'}(L_\ell(x))$. This gives further information about the original value x. After a few rounds Alice and Bob may estimate x and the current correlation x'. Then if the value of x' is less than $1/2$ Bob simply replaces B by $\overline{B}$. ∎

Remark 24.5 *Choosing the block length ℓ to be an integer power of 2 can have advantages. Experiments show (see Table 24.4) that for many values of x the optimal value of ℓ is a power of 2. Furthermore, for ℓ a power of 2, $\phi_\ell(x) = \phi_\ell(1-x)$.*

Remark 24.6 *In practice, Alice and Bob will have decided in advance on the desired length of the final common secret key (as well as on the value of the constant θ). On the basis of these two values together the value of the correlation y can be calculated. For example, we have worked with $n = 160$ and $\theta = 0.25$ where $y > \frac{639}{640}$. Knowing the values of n, θ, and $\text{bitcorr}(A, B)$, the required length N of the initial keys can be estimated with high precision. We give some details of this in Section 24.6.*

24.5   Linear Codes: The Checking Hash Function

Traditionally, in error correction, linear codes are used as follows. A message m is embedded in a codeword $\tilde{m}$ belonging to some linear code C where $\tilde{m}$ is obtained from m by adjoining to m certain "parity" bits. The vector $\tilde{m}$ is transmitted to a receiver. Classical approaches, on the assumption of few errors, attempt to decode $\tilde{m}$ and thus to recover m.

Here we provide a new approach, as follows. Recall that in cryptographic and other applications a hash function f is constructed to help decide with high probability whether two binary vectors u and v are equal. Consider the special situation where it is known (with high probability) that the Hamming distance between u and v is less than some small integer t. In other words, it is known that the number of bits where u and v differ is very likely less than t.

Consider next an $r \times n$ matrix H which is the parity check matrix of a code, C, of minimum distance at least t. This implies that the subspace, C, of vectors orthogonal to each row of H contains only one vector of Hamming weight less than t, namely the zero vector.

For each row w of H, define a function f_w, by taking for any binary vector z of length n, the value $f_w(z)$ to be the dot product of the row w with z. Then, given vectors u and v as above such that $f_w(u) = f_w(v)$ for all r rows w of H, it follows that $u + v$ is an element of the code, C, which has minimum distance t. Therefore, either $u = v$ or else the Hamming distance between u and v is at least t.

Let us summarize the above remarks.

Theorem 24.7 *Let u, v be binary vectors of length n whose Hamming distance is less than t. Let f be the syndrome, i.e. let f be the hash function given by*

$$f(z) := (f_{w_1}(z), f_{w_2}(z), \ldots, f_{w_r}(z))$$

where $w_1, w_2, \ldots, w_r$ are the r rows of the $r \times n$ parity check matrix H of a code of minimum distance at least t. Here $f_{w_i}(z)$ is the dot product of the row w with the binary vector z of length n. Then, if $f(u) = f(v)$, it follows that $u = v$.

Motivated by this, we define the hash function $f(z) := (f_{w_1}(z), f_{w_2}(z), \ldots, f_{w_r}(z))$ where $w_1, w_2, \ldots, w_r$ are the r rows of the check matrix H.

This technique of constructing hash functions applies in particular to the cryptographic situation in the Section 24.5 where, in the notation there, $u = A_i$ and $v = B_i$.

Using the notation of the Section 24.5, we have now the following result.

Theorem 24.8 *Fix any number ϵ, no matter how small, with $0 < \epsilon < 1$. Let A_i and B_i be Alice and Bob's remnant keys. Assume $f(A_i) = f(B_i)$ where f is the hash function of Theorem 24.7. Then with probability at least $1 - \epsilon$, $A_i = B_i$ and Alice and Bob are in possession of a common secret key.*

Remark 24.9 *In the Section 24.4, compliance with the stopping condition ensured that $A_i = B_i$ with high probability. If, subsequently, it is also verified that $f(A_i) = f(B_i)$, then the probability of equality is even higher.*

Example 24.10 *Suppose that n is some integer with $64 < n \leq 128$ and that A and B are binary vectors of length n. We will construct an 8×128 parity check matrix H. First, we construct a 7×128 matrix $\overline{H}$ where the 128 columns of $\overline{H}$ are all distinct. Take the first eight columns of $\overline{H}$ to be*
$$\begin{pmatrix} 0 & 1 & 0 & 0 & 0 & 0 & 0 & 0 \\ 0 & 0 & 1 & 0 & 0 & 0 & 0 & 0 \\ 0 & 0 & 0 & 1 & 0 & 0 & 0 & 0 \\ 0 & 0 & 0 & 0 & 1 & 0 & 0 & 0 \\ 0 & 0 & 0 & 0 & 0 & 1 & 0 & 0 \\ 0 & 0 & 0 & 0 & 0 & 0 & 1 & 0 \\ 0 & 0 & 0 & 0 & 0 & 0 & 0 & 1 \end{pmatrix}$$
. The remaining 120 distinct columns of $\overline{H}$ may be arranged in any order, say in lexicographic order. Now H is obtained from $\overline{H}$ by adding a row of length 128 consisting entirely of 1's to the top of $\overline{H}$.

Then, as can be seen from projective geometry, H is the parity check matrix for a code of minimum distance 4. We form eight functions $f_1, f_2, \ldots, f_8$ by defining $f_i(z)$ to be the dot product of the i-th row of H with z where z is a binary vector of length 128. Now if $n < 128$, we extend A and B to new binary strings A' and B' of length 128 by adding 0's to the right end of A and B. Note that the Hamming distance between A' and B' is the same as the Hamming distance between A and B. If $f_i(A') = f_i(B')$ then either $A' = B'$ or else the Hamming distance from A' to B' is at least 4. Thus, clearly either $A = B$ or else the Hamming distance from A to B is at least 4.

Security

Finally, consider the extra condition that it is desired to conceal information about the values of A and B from some eavesdropper, Eve, who has learned say the eight values $f_1(A'), f_2(A'), \ldots, f_8(A')$. In this case the first eight bits may be deleted from A (and B) leaving shortened strings $\overline{A}$ and $\overline{B}$ of length $n - 8$. Although eight bits have been lost from A and B, this is compensated for by the fact that Eve's knowledge of the eight values $f_j(A)$ provides her with no information about A (or B).

24.6   Convergence and Length of Keys

As above Alice and Bob are in possession of two keys A and B of common length N with $x = \mathrm{bitcorr}(A, B)$ where $1/2 < x \leq 1$. Let $\phi_\ell(x)$ denote the expected correlation of the two keys after applying one round of the convergence procedure of Section 24.3 where ℓ denotes the block length. Our goal now is to calculate $\phi_\ell(x)$ and also the expected length of various remnant keys.

We begin by considering the case $\ell = 2$.

Theorem 24.11
$$\phi_2(x) = \frac{x^2}{2x^2 - 2x + 1}$$

Thus, $\phi_2(x)$ is a strictly increasing function on the interval (1/2,1). In particular, for every $x \in (1/2, 1)$ and for all $\epsilon > 0$, there exists $i \in N$ such that the i-th iteration $\phi_2^i(x)$ is greater than $1 - \epsilon$.

Proof. We divide A and B into sub-blocks of length 2 discarding the last bit of A and B if N is odd. Consider a typical pair of sub-blocks (α_1, α_2) and (β_1, β_2) belonging to Alice and Bob respectively. If the parities $\alpha_1 + \alpha_2 \pmod{2}$ and $\beta_1 + \beta_2 \pmod{2}$ disagree both sub-blocks are deleted and there are no surviving (remnant) bits from these sub-blocks.

If the two parities agree then the surviving (remnant) bits are α_1 and β_1. The two parities only agree if either $\alpha_1 = \beta_1$ and $\alpha_2 = \beta_2$ or else if $\alpha_1 \neq \beta_1$ and $\alpha_2 \neq \beta_2$. Thus the conditional probability that $\alpha_1 = \beta_1$ given that the parities are equal is $\frac{x^2}{x^2+(1-x)^2}$. Averaging over the disjoint blocks of length 2, we conclude that the expected value for the bit correlation of the two remnant strings A_1 and B_1 is $\phi_2(x) = \frac{x^2}{x^2+(1-x)^2} = \frac{x^2}{2x^2-2x+1}$. Thus $\phi_2(x) > x$ if and only if $x > 2x^2 - 2x + 1$ if and only if $x \in (1/2, 1)$. The final assertion of the theorem then follow by a calculus argument. ∎

We proceed to the case $\ell = 3$.

Theorem 24.12
$$\phi_3(x) = \frac{3x^3 - 3x^2 + 2x}{6x^3 - 8x^2 + 3x + 1}$$

Thus, $\phi_3(x)$ is a strictly increasing function on the interval (1/2,1). In particular, for every $x \in (1/2, 1)$ and for all $\epsilon > 0$, there exists $i \in N$ such that the i-th iteration $\phi_3^i(x)$ is greater than $1 - \epsilon$.

Proof. As before we divide A and B into sub-blocks of length 3 discarding leftover bits if any. Again we consider a typical pair of sub-blocks $\alpha := (\alpha_1, \alpha_2, \alpha_3)$ and $\beta := (\beta_1, \beta_2, \beta_3)$.

An analysis of the KAP algorithm reveals the following.

1. There are remnant keys of length 2, namely (α_1, α_2) for Alice and (β_1, β_2) for Bob if $\alpha_1 + \alpha_2 + \alpha_3 \pmod 2$ equals $\beta_1 + \beta_2 + \beta_3 \pmod 2$.

2. There are remnant keys of length 1, namely (α_2) and (β_2) if $\alpha_1 + \alpha_2 + \alpha_3 \pmod 2$ differs from $\beta_1 + \beta_2 + \beta_3 \pmod 2$ and also $\alpha_1 \pmod 2$ differs from $\beta_1 \pmod 2$.

3. In the remaining case the remnant keys are null.

Note that the parity of α is equal to the parity of β if and only if the bitwise sum (exclusive OR), $\alpha + \beta$, has an even number of 1's.

We construct a Table 24.1 as follows. The eight entries in the first column enumerate the eight possibilities for $\alpha + \beta$. The second column expresses the probability of occurrence of the triple in its row. The third column is the length of the two corresponding remnant strings from the sub-blocks. The fourth column is the number of bit agreements between these two remnant strings. See Table 24.1.

Case 1 corresponds to rows 1, 5, 6, and 7. Case 2 corresponds to rows 4 and 8. The remaining rows correspond to Case 3.

	$\alpha + \beta$	Probability	Remnant length	Remnant agreements
1	(0,0,0)	x^3	2	2
2	(0,0,1)	$x^2(1-x)$	0	0
3	(0,1,0)	$x^2(1-x)$	0	0
4	(1,0,0)	$x^2(1-x)$	1	1
5	(0,1,1)	$x(1-x)^2$	2	1
6	(1,0,1)	$x(1-x)^2$	2	1
7	(1,1,0)	$x(1-x)^2$	2	0
8	(1,1,1)	$(1-x)^3$	1	0

Table 24.1: Bit agreements between two remnant strings

From the entries in Table 24.1 we can easily calculate $\phi_3(x)$ by dividing the average number of remnant bit agreements by the average length of the remnants.

Thus the numerator is $2x^3 + x^2(1-x) + 2 \times (x(1-x)^2)$ and the denominator is $2x^3 + x^2(1-x) + 3 \times (2x(1-x)^2) + (1-x)^3$ giving the desired formula for $\phi_3(x)$. Thus $\phi_3(x) > x$ if and only if $\frac{3x^3 - 3x^2 + 2x}{6x^3 - 8x^2 + 3x + 1} > x$ if and only if $3x^2 - 3x + 2 > 6x^3 - 8x^2 + 3x + 1$ if and only if $6x^3 - 11x^2 + 6x - 1 < 0$. Since $6x^3 - 11x^2 + 6x - 1 = 6(x - 1/3)(x - 1/2)(x - 1)$ we see that $\phi_3(x) > x$ for all $x \in (1/2, 1)$. The final assertion of the theorem again follows easily using calculus. ∎

Let $L_\ell(x)$ be the fraction of the initial key that is expected to remain after one round of the convergence algorithm. We also consider $M_\ell(x) = \phi_\ell(x) \cdot L_\ell(x)$ which when multiplied by N gives the predicted number of bit agreements in the remnant keys after one round of the convergence algorithm. A remarkable fact is that, after one round of the KAP algorithm, Alice and Bob can estimate the initial correlation by comparing the length of their remnant keys with that predicted by the function L_ℓ. After this round they can also monitor any distortion of signals from an intruder ("intruder detection") by means of knowledge of $L_\ell(x)$.

Suppose we begin with a pair of keys A and B of length n and correlation x. Applying one round of the convergence algorithm we obtain the pair A_1 and B_1. Then $L_\ell(x) \cdot n$ is the expected length of the keys A_1 and B_1 and $M_\ell(x) \cdot n = \phi_\ell(x) \cdot L_\ell(x) \cdot n$ is the expected number of bits which agree in the two new keys A_1 and B_1.

We summarize the resulting formulae for $M_\ell(x)$ and $L_\ell(x)$ for $\ell \leq 24$.

Theorem 24.13 *Let A and B denote binary strings of length N and let $0 \leq x \leq 1$. Then for $2 \leq \ell \leq 24$ the values for the quantities $M_\ell(x)$ and $L_\ell(x)$ are as in Tables 24.2 and 24.3. The quantity $\phi_\ell(x)$ is then calculated from the formula $\phi_\ell(x) = M_\ell(x)/L_\ell(x)$.*

In order to be certain that the convergence phase terminates one needs to prove that if $x > 1/2$ then $\phi_\ell(x) > x$ for each block size ℓ used. If each of the block sizes used is at most 24 then by Theorem 24.13 we know that $\phi_\ell(x) > x$. *Furthermore, using the explicit formulae for $L_\ell(x)$ we can accurately predict the length of the final common secret key from the initial length N and the correlation x of the initial keys.* Explicitly, the expected length of the keys A_i and B_i, produced by the convergence phase, is given by the expression $L_{\ell_i}(x_{i-1})N_{i-1} = L_{\ell_i}(L_{\ell_{i-1}}(\cdots(L_{\ell_1}(x))\cdots))N$. Taking into account an estimate for the number of bits required to be discarded while verifying equality with the hash function allows Alice and Bob to estimate the length, n, of their final secret key. Similarly, they may begin with n and use this desired length to determine the length, N, of the initial key required to produce a common final key of length n.

We emphasize again that **the initial bit correlation**, even if unknown, **can be estimated with high precision** based on the length of the remnant key after one round of the algorithm.

24.7 Main Results

A *word of caution* is in order. In Parts 1 and 2 of the procedure in Section 24.3, it is important that, for block size $\ell > 2$, the shuffle ensures that two elements a_i, a_j (opposite b_i, b_j) end up in different blocks of the (new) shuffle. This is done so that the independence of the probabilities of the set $\Pr(a_k = b_k)$ is preserved.

Let us summarize. Alice and Bob start off equipped only with two strings A and B of a common length N with nonzero mutual information $I(A, B) \neq 0$, i.e. with $\mathrm{bitcorr}(A, B) \neq 1/2$. These keys may be thought of as having been produced by some physical means as is the case for quantum encryption using the laws of quantum physics. (Other physical means using classical physics have recently been advanced.) We have shown that Alice and Bob can then proceed by *public discussion* to obtain a final common secret key. We summarize as follows.

Theorem 24.14 *Assume that two cryptographic stations Alice and Bob are in possession of keys A and B of a common length N where the probabilities $\Pr(a_i = b_i)$ are independent for a_i in A and b_i in B and such that $x = \mathrm{bitcorr}(A, B) \neq 1/2$. If N is sufficiently long then Alice and Bob can generate, by public discussion, a common secret key of length n using the convergence algorithm. If x is known, the expected value of N required to*

ℓ	$M_{\ell(x)}$
2	$(x^2)/2$
3	$(3x^3 - 3x^2 + 2x)/3$
4	$(10x^4 - 18x^3 + 11x^2)/4$
5	$(18x^5 - 38x^4 + 30x^3 - 10x^2 + 4x)/5$
6	$(40x^6 - 100x^5 + 94x^4 - 38x^3 + 5x^2 + 4x)/6$
7	$(88x^7 - 272x^6 + 348x^5 - 236x^4 + 90x^3 - 18x^2 + 6x)/7$
8	$(192x^8 - 704x^7 + 1120x^6 - 1016x^5 + 580x^4 - 214x^3 + 49x^2)/8$
9	$(400x^9 - 1648x^8 + 2984x^7 - 3112x^6 + 2050x^5 - 872x^4 + 231x^3 - 33x^2 + 8x)/9$
10	$(832x^{1}0 - 3808x^9 + 7744x^8 - 9168x^7 + 6916x^6 - 3388x^5 + 1036x^4 - 172x^3 + 9x^2 + 8x)/10$
11	$(1728x^{11} - 8704x^{10} + 19\ 632x^9 - 26\ 048x^8 + 22\ 420x^7 - 12\ 996x^6 + 5096x^5 - 1328x^4 + 225x^3 - 25x^2 + 10x)/11$
12	$(3584x^{12} - 19\ 712x^{11} + 48\ 896x^{10} - 72\ 000x^9 + 69\ 696x^8 - 46\ 448x^7 + 21\ 784x^6 - 7288x^5 + 1764x^4 - 306x^3 + 33x^2 + 8x)/12$
13	$(7424x^{13} - 44\ 800x^{12} + 123\ 456x^{11} - 205\ 248x^{10} + 229\ 072x^9 - 180\ 704x^8 + 103\ 320x^7 - 43\ 176x^6 + 13\ 098x^5 - 2812x^4 + 407x^3 - 37x^2 + 12x)/13$
14	$(15\ 360x^{14} - 100\ 864x^{13} + 305\ 408x^{12} - 564\ 608x^{11} + 711\ 104x^{10} - 644\ 384x^9 + 432\ 048x^8 - 216\ 528x^7 + 80\ 568x^6 - 21\ 624x^5 + 3916x^4 - 408x^3 + 13x^2 + 12x)/14$
15	$(31\ 744x^{15} - 225\ 280x^{14} + 742\ 912x^{13} - 1\ 509\ 888x^{12} + 2\ 114\ 688x^{11} - 2\ 161\ 408x^{10} + 1\ 664\ 576x^9 - 982\ 400x^8 + 446\ 904x^7 - 156\ 048x^6 + 41\ 184x^5 - 7956x^4 + 1053x^3 - 81x^2 + 14x)/15$
16	$(65\ 536x^{16} - 499\ 712x^{15} + 1\ 781\ 760x^{14} - 3\ 944\ 448x^{13} + 6\ 070\ 272x^{12} - 6\ 888\ 448x^{11} + 5\ 964\ 288x^{10} - 4\ 020\ 096x^9 + 2\ 132\ 160x^8 - 893\ 152x^7 + 294\ 800x^6 - 75\ 992x^5 + 15\ 028x^4 - 2206x^3 + 225x^2)/16$
17	$(133\ 120x^{17} - 1\ 079\ 296x^{16} + 4\ 107\ 264x^{15} - 9\ 743\ 360x^{14} + 16\ 136\ 192x^{13} - 19\ 795\ 712x^{12} + 18\ 622\ 336x^{11} - 13\ 713\ 792x^{10} + 7\ 996\ 656x^9 - 3\ 708\ 272x^8 + 1\ 364\ 616x^7 - 394\ 768x^6 + 88\ 062x^5 - 14\ 614x^4 + 1680x^3 - 112x^2 + 16x)/17$

Table 24.2: Expressions for $M_\ell(x)$ for $2 \leq \ell \leq 24$

ℓ	$M_{\ell(x)}$
18	$(270\ 336x^{18} - 2\ 322\ 432x^{17} + 9\ 396\ 224x^{16} - 23\ 783\ 424x^{15} + 42\ 190\ 848x^{14} - 55\ 675\ 904x^{13} + 56\ 599\ 552x^{12} - 45\ 273\ 856x^{11}$ $+ 28\ 840\ 864x^{10} - 14\ 704\ 928x^9 + 5\ 990\ 864x^8 - 1\ 931\ 984x^7 + 483\ 236x^6 - 90\ 176x^5 + 11\ 630x^4 - 866x^3 + 17x^2 + 16x)/18$
19	$(548\ 864x^{19} - 4\ 980\ 736x^{18} + 21\ 350\ 400x^{17} - 57\ 444\ 352x^{16} + 108\ 703\ 744x^{15} - 153\ 607\ 680x^{14} + 167\ 923\ 200x^{13}$ $- 145\ 129\ 216x^{12} + 100\ 441\ 824x^{11} - 56\ 014\ 624x^{10} + 25\ 187\ 360x^9 - 9\ 086\ 784x^8 + 2\ 600\ 832x^7 - 579\ 464x^6 + 97\ 620x^5$ $- 11\ 948x^4 + 1020x^3 - 60x^2 + 18x)/19$
20	$(1\ 114\ 112x^{20} - 10\ 649\ 600x^{19} + 48\ 218\ 112x^{18} - 137\ 437\ 184x^17 + 276\ 410\ 368x^{16} - 416\ 587\ 776x^{15} + 487\ 615\ 488x^{14}$ $- 453\ 193\ 728x^{13} + 338\ 967\ 296x^{12} - 205\ 485\ 184x^{11} + 101\ 154\ 944x^{10} - 40\ 326\ 016x^9 + 12\ 925\ 328x^8 - 3\ 293\ 216x^7 + 657\ 544x^6$ $- 101\ 464x^5 + 11\ 968x^4 - 1046x^3 + 57x^2 + 16x)/20$
21	$(2\ 260\ 992x^{21} - 22\ 708\ 224x^{20} + 108\ 281\ 856x^{19} - 325\ 902\ 336x^{18} + 694\ 210\ 560x^{17} - 1\ 112\ 119\ 296x^{16} + 1\ 389\ 661\ 696x^{15}$ $- 1\ 386\ 181\ 632x^{14} + 1\ 120\ 237\ 696x^{13} - 740\ 054\ 912x^{12} + 401\ 422\ 560x^{11} - 178\ 885\ 184x^{10} + 65\ 294\ 632x^9 - 19\ 391\ 816x^8$ $+ 4\ 635\ 488x^7 - 877\ 440x^6 + 128\ 282x^5 - 13\ 930x^4 + 1064x^3 - 56x^2 + 20x)/21$
22	$(4\ 587\ 520x^{22} - 48\ 300\ 032x^{21} + 241\ 958\ 912x^{20} - 766\ 902\ 272x^{19} + 1\ 725\ 038\ 592x^{18} - 2\ 927\ 468\ 544x^{17} + 3\ 889\ 661\ 952x^{16}$ $- 4\ 144\ 225\ 280x^{15} + 3\ 597\ 054\ 464x^{14} - 2\ 569\ 691\ 392x^{13} + 1\ 520\ 272\ 128x^{12} - 746\ 976\ 192x^{11} + 304\ 787\ 392x^{10} - 102\ 955\ 728x^9$ $+ 28\ 598\ 440x^8 - 6\ 454\ 040x^7 + 1\ 158\ 856x^6 - 159\ 596x^5 + 15\ 770x^4 - 970x^3 + 21x^2 + 20x)/22$
23	$(9\ 306\ 112x^{23} - 102\ 498\ 304x^{22} + 538\ 214\ 400x^{21} - 1\ 792\ 081\ 920x^{20} + 4\ 245\ 225\ 472x^{19} - 7\ 608\ 737\ 792x^{18} + 10\ 712\ 315\ 904x^{17}$ $- 12\ 140\ 961\ 792x^{16} + 11\ 261\ 769\ 728x^{15} - 8\ 645\ 957\ 120x^{14} + 5\ 534\ 317\ 440x^{13} - 2\ 966\ 481\ 920x^{12} + 1\ 333\ 880\ 288x^{11}$ $- 502\ 825\ 312x^{10} + 158\ 404\ 672x^9 - 41\ 446\ 528x^8 + 8\ 916\ 772x^7 - 1\ 553\ 252x^6 + 214\ 016x^5 - 22\ 464x^4 + 1680x^3 - 80x^2$ $+ 22x)/23$
24	$(18\ 874\ 368x^{24} - 217\ 055\ 232x^{23} + 1\ 192\ 230\ 912x^{22} - 4\ 161\ 011\ 712x^{21} + 10\ 355\ 343\ 360x^{20} - 19\ 548\ 471\ 296x^{19}$ $+ 29\ 073\ 178\ 624x^{18} - 34\ 925\ 461\ 504x^{17} + 34\ 474\ 221\ 568x^{16} - 28\ 296\ 159\ 232x^{15} + 19\ 472\ 275\ 456x^{14} - 11\ 295\ 878\ 144x^{13}$ $+ 5\ 541\ 159\ 936x^{12} - 2\ 301\ 116\ 160x^{11} + 808\ 267\ 648x^{10} - 239\ 427\ 968x^9 + 59\ 503\ 808x^8 - 12\ 311\ 968x^7 + 2\ 098\ 512x^6$ $- 290\ 376x^5 + 31\ 948x^4 - 2702x^3 + 161x^2 + 16x)/24$

Table 24.2: *Continued*

ℓ	$L_{\ell(x)}$
2	$(2x^2 - 2x + 1)/2$
3	$(6x^3 - 8x^2 + 3x + 1)/3$
4	$(16x^4 - 32x^3 + 24x^2 - 8x + 3)/4$
5	$(36x^5 - 88x^4 + 86x^3 - 42x^2 + 10x + 2)/5$
6	$(80x^6 - 232x^5 + 276x^4 - 172x^3 + 60x^2 - 12x + 5)/6$
7	$(176x^7 - 608x^6 + 896x^5 - 728x^4 + 350x^3 - 98x^2 + 14x + 4)/7$
8	$(384x^8 - 1536x^7 + 2688x^6 - 2688x^5 + 1680x^4 - 672x^3 + 168x^2 - 24x + 7)/8$
9	$(800x^9 - 3584x^8 + 7136x^7 - 8288x^6 + 6188x^5 - 3080x^4 + 1022x^3 - 218x^2 + 27x + 5)/9$
10	$(1664x^10 - 8256x^9 + 18\,432x^8 - 24\,384x^7 + 21\,160x^6 - 12\,576x^5 + 5180x^4 - 1460x^3 + 270x^2 - 30x + 9)/10$
11	$(3456x^{11} - 18\,816x^{10} + 46\,496x^9 - 68\,832x^8 + 67\,832x^7 - 46\,736x^6 + 22\,988x^5 - 8084x^4 + 1998x^3 - 332x^2 + 33x + 7)/11$
12	$(7168x^{12} - 42\,496x^{11} + 11\,5200x^{10} - 188\,800x^9 + 208\,384x^8 - 163\,296x^7 + 93\,296x^6 - 39\,248x^5 + 12\,096x^4 - 2664x^3 + 396x^2 - 36x + 11)/12$
13	$(14\,848x^{13} - 95\,744x^{12} + 284\,544x^{11} - 515\,968x^{10} + 636\,832x^9 - 564\,928x^8 + 370\,576x^7 - 182\,032x^6 + 66\,984x^5 - 18\,252x^4 + 3586x^3 - 482x^2 + 39x + 9)/13$
14	$(30\,720x^{14} - 214\,016x^{13} + 691\,712x^{12} - 1\,374\,464x^{11} + 1\,875\,328x^{10} - 1\,857\,856x^9 + 1\,377\,376x^8 - 775\,648x^7 + 332\,976x^6 - 108\,248x^5 + 26\,180x^4 - 4564x^3 + 546x^2 - 42x + 13)/14$
15	$(63\,488x^{15} - 475\,136x^{14} + 1\,658\,880x^{13} - 3\,584\,000x^{12} + 5\,358\,080x^{11} - 5\,870\,592x^{10} + 4\,868\,864x^9 - 3\,111\,680x^8 + 1\,544\,400x^7 - 5\,948\,80x^6 + 176\,176x^5 - 39\,312x^4 + 6370x^3 - 700x^2 + 45x + 11)/15$
16	$(131\,072x^{16} - 1\,048\,576x^{15} + 3\,932\,160x^{14} - 9\,175\,040x^{13} + 14\,909\,440x^{12} - 17\,891\,328x^{11} + 16\,400\,384x^{10} - 11\,714\,560x^9 + 6\,589\,440x^8 - 2\,928\,640x^7 + 1\,025\,024x^6 - 279\,552x^5 + 58\,240x^4 - 8960x^3 + 960x^2 - 64x + 15)/16$
17	$(266\,240x^{17} - 2\,260\,992x^{16} + 9\,035\,776x^{15} - 22\,568\,960x^{14} + 39\,459\,840x^{13} - 51\,251\,200x^{12} + 51\,204\,608x^{11} - 40\,195\,584x^{10} + 25\,099\,360x^9 - 12\,538\,240x^8 + 5\,010\,720x^7 - 1\,592\,864x^6 + 397\,852x^5 - 76\,440x^4 + 10\,910x^3 - 1090x^2 + 68x + 12)/17$

Table 24.3: Expressions for $L_\ell(x)$ for $2 \le \ell \le 24$

ℓ	$L_{\ell(x)}$
18	$(540\,672x^{18} - 4\,857\,856x^{17} + 20\,611\,072x^{16} - 54\,870\,016x^{15} + 102\,707\,200x^{14} -$ $143\,546\,368x^{13} + 155\,244\,544x^{12}$ $-\,132\,840\,448x^{11} + 91\,172\,160x^{10} - 50\,564\,480x^9 + 22\,714\,560x^8 -$ $8\,245\,056x^7 + 2\,400\,216x^6 - 552\,720x^5$ $+\,98\,460x^4 - 13\,092x^3 + 1224x^2 - 72x + 17)/18$
19	$(1\,097\,728x^{19} - 10\,403\,840x^{18} + 46\,706\,688x^{17} - 132\,022\,272x^{16} +$ $263\,415\,808x^{15} - 394\,171\,392x^{14}$ $+\,458\,734\,592x^{13} - 424\,885\,760x^{12} + 317\,820\,608x^{11} - 193\,683\,456x^{10} +$ $96\,557\,472x^9 - 39\,378\,496x^8$ $+\,13\,083\,616x^7 - 3\,510\,760x^6 + 74\,9812x^5 - 124\,588x^4 + 15\,538x^3 - 1370x^2 +$ $76x + 14)/19$
20	$(2\,228\,224x^{20} - 22\,216\,704x^{19} + 105\,218\,048x^{18} - 314\,720\,256x^{17} +$ $666\,787\,840x^{16} - 1\,063\,632\,896x^{15} + 1\,325\,410\,304x^{14}$ $-\,1\,321\,125\,888x^{13} + 1\,069\,758\,976x^{12} - 710\,588\,160x^{11} + 389\,309\,184x^{10} -$ $176\,227\,712x^9 + 65\,798\,304x^8 - 20\,155\,808x^7$ $+\,5\,017\,280x^6 - 999\,616x^5 + 155\,720x^4 - 18\,280x^3 + 1520x^2 - 80x + 19)/20$
21	$(4\,521\,984x^{21} - 47316\,992x^{20} + 235\,732\,992x^{19} - 743\,686\,144x^{18} +$ $1\,666\,752\,512x^{17} - 2\,821\,943\,296x^{16} + 3\,746\,638\,848x^{15}$ $-\,3\,996\,544\,000x^{14} + 3\,480\,948\,480x^{13} - 2\,502\,096\,896x^{12} + 1\,493\,944\,896x^{11} -$ $743\,277\,248x^{10} + 308\,170\,096x^9 - 106\,161\,952x^8$ $+\,30\,195\,096x^7 - 7\,016\,936x^6 + 1\,311\,108x^5 - 192\,264x^4 + 21\,318x^3 -$ $1682x^2 + 84x + 16)/21$
22	$(9\,175\,040x^{22} - 100\,532\,224x^{21} + 525\,598\,720x^{20} - 1\,744\,240\,640x^{19} +$ $4\,123\,131\,904x^{18} - 7\,384\,875\,008x^{17}$ $+\,10\,407\,481\,344x^{16} - 11\,829\,676\,032x^{15} + 11\,027\,932\,160x^{14} -$ $8\,527\,770\,112x^{13} + 5\,510\,624\,768x^{12} - 2\,988\,261\,504x^{11}$ $+\,1\,361\,817\,600x^{10} - 520\,937\,824x^9 + 166\,608\,112x^8 - 44\,231\,440x^7 +$ $9\,638\,728x^6 - 1\,695\,584x^5 + 234\,916x^4$ $-\,24\,684x^3 + 1848x^2 - 88x + 21)/22$

Table 24.3: *Continued*

ℓ	$L_{\ell(x)}$
23	$(18\ 612\ 224x^{23} - 213\ 123\ 072x^{22} + 1\ 166\ 737\ 408x^{21} - 4\ 063\ 166\ 464x^{20} +$
	$10\ 103\ 521\ 280x^{19} - 19\ 087\ 310\ 848x^{18}$
	$+\ 28\ 458\ 741\ 760x^{17} - 34\ 339\ 606\ 528x^{16} + 34\ 116\ 040\ 704x^{15} -$
	$28\ 240\ 956\ 416x^{14} + 1\ 963\ 6367\ 104x^{13}$
	$-\ 11\ 526\ 520\ 064x^{12} + 5\ 726\ 300\ 736x^{11} - 2\ 407\ 951\ 232x^{10} + 855\ 159\ 584x^{9} -$
	$255\ 255\ 264x^{8} + 63\ 533\ 352x^{7}$
	$-\ 13\ 031\ 904x^{6} + 2\ 165\ 468x^{5} - 284\ 268x^{4} + 28\ 378x^{3} - 2026x^{2} + 92x + 18)/23$
24	$(37\ 748\ 736x^{24} - 450\ 887\ 680x^{23} + 2\ 579\ 496\ 960x^{22} - 9\ 406\ 251\ 008x^{21} +$
	$24\ 545\ 329\ 152x^{20} - 48\ 780\ 017\ 664x^{19}$
	$+\ 76\ 717\ 031\ 424x^{18} - 97\ 942\ 405\ 120x^{17} + 103\ 305\ 461\ 760x^{16} -$
	$91\ 143\ 421\ 952x^{15} + 67\ 845\ 869\ 568x^{14}$
	$-\ 42\ 855\ 499\ 776x^{13} + 23\ 047\ 305\ 216x^{12} - 10\ 565\ 132\ 800x^{11} +$
	$4\ 124\ 555\ 520x^{10} - 1\ 367\ 061\ 248x^{9}$
	$+\ 382\ 566\ 912x^{8} - 89\ 630\ 784x^{7} + 17\ 366\ 304x^{6} - 2\ 734\ 240x^{5} + 341\ 040x^{4} -$
	$32\ 432x^{3} + 2208x^{2} - 96x + 23)/24$

Table 24.3: *Continued*

produce a secret key of desired length n can also be calculated as a function of N. If x is not known in advance it can be estimated from the length of the remnant keys produced by a few rounds of the convergence algorithm. Despite the public discussion, an eavesdropper who has no initial information concerning A and B will have no information whatsoever, measured in Shannon bits, about the final common secret key.

Remark 24.15 (Perfect secrecy)   *If an eavesdropper, Eve, is in fact in possession of initial information concerning A or B the procedure can be modified so that Eve's average information about the final secret key can be made arbitrarily small.*

Remark 24.16 (Optimal key length)   *In any given industrial application, users will make a choice between, on the one hand, a slow convergence (many rounds of the algorithm) with a long final key and, on the other hand, rapid convergence with a shorter final secret key. Much depends on the initial value of x as indicated in Theorem 24.13. This choice manifests itself in the choice of the value of the block length ℓ used in each successive round of the algorithm.*

Correlation range	Best ℓ
$0.5 < x \leq 0.812\ 602\ 86$	2
$0.812\ 602\ 86 < x \leq 0.905\ 491\ 62$	4
$0.905\ 491\ 62 < x \leq 0.908\ 795\ 24$	5
$0.908\ 795\ 24 < x \leq 0.909\ 674\ 05$	6
$0.909\ 674\ 05 < x \leq 0.912\ 556\ 08$	7
$0.912\ 556\ 08 < x \leq 0.951\ 358\ 77$	8
$0.951\ 358\ 77 < x \leq 0.952\ 644\ 88$	9
$0.952\ 644\ 88 < x \leq 0.953\ 455\ 73$	10
$0.953\ 455\ 73 < x \leq 0.954\ 638\ 45$	11
$0.954\ 638\ 45 < x \leq 0.955\ 128\ 70$	12
$0.955\ 128\ 70 < x \leq 0.956\ 239\ 24$	13
$0.956\ 239\ 24 < x \leq 0.956\ 878\ 48$	14
$0.956\ 878\ 48 < x \leq 0.957\ 950\ 73$	15
$0.957\ 950\ 73 < x \leq 0.975\ 235\ 00$	16
$0.975\ 235\ 00 < x \leq 0.975\ 614\ 11$	17
$0.975\ 614\ 11 < x \leq 0.975\ 885\ 34$	18
$0.975\ 885\ 34 < x \leq 0.976\ 247\ 47$	19
$0.976\ 247\ 47 < x \leq 0.976\ 452\ 35$	20
$0.976\ 452\ 35 < x \leq 0.976\ 800\ 92$	21
$0.976\ 800\ 92 < x \leq 0.977\ 043\ 05$	22
$0.977\ 043\ 05 < x \leq 0.977\ 375\ 59$	23
$0.977\ 375\ 59 < x \leq 0.977\ 528\ 90$	24
$< x \leq$	

Table 24.4: Optimal values for ℓ

Remark 24.17 (Theory and practice) *In actual experiments, there is strong agreement between theory and practice. We include some experimental data in Tables 24.4 and 24.5. In Table 24.5, the column labelled x gives the initial correlation of two $N = 400$ bit strings. The column n_f denotes the expected bit length of the remnant keys and x_f denotes the expected value of the correlation between the two remnant keys after the indicated number of rounds of the algorithm using optimal choices for the block length. The final column shows the expected number of errors in the remnant strings.*

x	Rounds	n_f	x_f	Expected errors
0.60	5	10.02	0.9800	0.20
0.61	5	11.29	0.9912	0.10
0.62	4	14.25	0.9847	0.21
0.63	4	16.74	0.9845	0.25
0.64	4	19.64	0.9822	0.34
0.65	4	22.22	0.9844	0.34
0.66	4	23.82	0.9908	0.21
0.67	3	29.09	0.9803	0.57
0.68	4	31.35	0.9866	0.42
0.69	4	37.37	0.9802	0.74
0.70	4	40.57	0.9854	0.59
0.71	4	43.10	0.9913	0.37
0.72	3	52.16	0.9808	1.00
0.73	3	56.78	0.9818	1.03
0.74	3	61.78	0.9827	1.07
0.75	3	64.46	0.9876	0.80
0.76	3	72.95	0.9824	1.28
0.77	3	79.97	0.9815	1.47
0.78	3	83.04	0.9867	1.10
0.79	3	86.35	0.9907	0.79
0.80	2	102.88	0.9781	2.24
0.81	2	105.93	0.9825	1.84
0.82	3	111.56	0.9872	1.42
0.83	3	125.83	0.9826	2.19
0.84	3	137.52	0.9825	2.41
0.85	3	142.61	0.9882	1.68
0.86	3	149.37	0.9917	1.24
0.87	2	175.48	0.9815	3.24
0.88	2	187.59	0.9820	3.37
0.89	2	200.77	0.9826	3.49
0.90	2	206.28	0.9876	2.56

Table 24.5: Reconciling two 400 bit keys

Remark 24.18 (Man-in-the-middle attack, intruder disruption) *One classical method of attack on a cryptosystem is the so-called "man in the middle attack" where an active intruder impersonates Alice to Bob and Bob to Alice. The usual suggested remedy for this as in quantum encryption is a separate authentication channel. For the present algorithm an intruder might attempt to disrupt communications by changing the announced parities en route between Alice and Bob. After the first round, Alice and Bob can estimate the initial correlation from the remnant key. Based on this, Alice and Bob can calculate the correlation at the end of the second round using the function L_ℓ. On the other hand, Alice and Bob can also estimate the correlation at the end of the second round on the basis of the length of the remnant key. If these estimates differ significantly one can conclude that the parity signals have been altered by an intruder. Similarly, Alice and Bob can carry out this procedure on any round after the first one. Thus the algorithm has some built-in intruder detection.*

It may be that Eve constructs a separate key K_1 between Eve and A and another key K_2 between Eve and B.

As is done in the BB84 protocol, we assume that A and B communicate at the end over an authenticated public channel. Then A and B can use the checking hash function or exchange a number of bits to check if this has happened, i.e. that Eve has keys K_1, K_2 with $K_1 \neq K_2$.

Remark 24.19 *In [BBB⁺90] the authors correctly suggest that the original correlation* $\text{bitcorr}(A, B)$ *can be estimated at the end from the "errors corrected during reconciliation." However, as pointed out above* $\text{bitcorr}(A, B)$ *can be estimated after the first round of the convergence algorithm.*

In [BBB⁺90] the authors give an example of two strings, A and B generated using a quantum channel. These keys were of length 640 and had $x = \text{bitcorr}(A, B) = 0.956\,25$. There, two rounds of the convergence algorithm were performed using $\ell_1 = 10$ and $\ell_2 = 20$ and yielding strings (A_1, B_1) and (A_2, B_2) with lengths $N_1 = 509$ and $N_2 = 457$ and correlations $x_1 = \text{bitcorr}(A_1, B_1) = 501/509 \approx 0.984\,28$ and $x_2 = \text{bitcorr}(A_2, B_2) = 455/457 \approx 0.995\,62$.

The expected values are $N_1 = 640$, $L_{10}(x) = 510.76$, $x_1 = \phi_{10}(0.956\,25) \approx 0.984\,73$, $N_2 = 509 L_{20}(x_1) \approx 457.12$ or $N_2 = 640 L_{20}(\phi_{10}(x)) \approx 459.25$ and $x_2 = \phi_{20}(\phi_{10}(x)) \approx 0.996\,10$. These numbers predict $(1 - 0.996\,10)(459.25) \approx 1.79$ errors.

Instead, for example using $\ell_1 = 14$, $\ell_2 = 32$, and $\ell_3 = 64$ gives the expected values of $N_1 = 640$, $L_{14}(x) \approx 530.56$, $x_1 = \phi_{14}(x) \approx 0.980\,25$, $N_2 \approx 484.00$, $x_2 \approx 0.991\,11$, $N_3 \approx 460.45$ and $x_3 \approx 0.996\,37$.

24.8   Some Details on the Random Permutation

In order to ensure convergence it is important that in step 1 of the convergence phase Alice and Bob first agree on a random permutation of their two strings to better randomize the location of errors. In practice, we have found it preferable to perform a specific kind of permutation which has some of the properties of a shuffle.

During the first round it is useful to apply a random permutation in order to randomize the location of the bits where the two keys disagree. However, in subsequent rounds, what is desired is that two or more errors lying in the same block should not be permuted into the same (new) block. Rather than relying on a random permutation to do this, we have found it more useful, experimentally, to use a specific permutation designed to prevent this. For example an effective procedure is given by applying the permutation that changes the order from $(1, 2, 3, \ldots, n)$ into the order $(1, \ell + 1, 2\ell + 1, \ldots, n - \ell + 1, 2, \ell + 2, 2\ell + 2, \ldots, n - \ell + 2, \ldots, \ell - 1, 2\ell - 1, 3\ell - 1, \ldots, n - \ell - 1, \ell, 2\ell, 3\ell, \ldots, n)$. For example if $\ell = 4$ and $n = 20$, this shuffling produces the order $(1,5,9,13,17,2,6,10,14,18,3,7,11,15,19,4,8,12,16,20)$.

The advantage of this permutation is that it minimizes the occurrences of pairs of bits occurring in the same block (of length ℓ) twice in a row. Furthermore, since it is pre-determined, Alice and Bob do not have to spend time choosing and communicating a random permutation.

Experiments suggest that using such permutations performs better than choosing random permutations and is faster to perform. The permutation above ensures that two pairs (a_i, b_i) and (a_j, b_j) which lie in the same block will not be together in a block in the next round. Thus, independence of the set $\{\Pr(a_k = b_k)\}$ will be preserved as mentioned earlier.

24.9   The Case Where Eve Has Nonzero Initial Information

In practice, it may happen that an eavesdropper, Eve, has some (but not all) initial information about the keys A and/or B. Regardless of this, Alice and Bob can perform the convergence algorithm as described in Section 24.3 in order to achieve a common secret key. If Eve begins with no information the algorithm is such that she cannot acquire any information from Alice's and Bob's public discussions. However, if Eve's initial information about A or about B is nonzero, this initial information, in concert with the public discussion, may generate further information for Eve. The amount of information about the final secret key that Eve possesses can however be estimated.

In [BBB+90], this estimate is made based on physical considerations. In the mathematical setting, additional techniques from information theory can be used to obtain bounds on the amount of Eve's possible information.

The procedure for generating the common secret key, X, by public discussion must now take account of Eve's information.

Let us say that Alice and Bob are in possession of a common key of length n and that the amount of Eve's information about X is at most k bits. Let the integer $s > 0$ denote a security parameter that Alice and Bob may adjust as desired. A result of Bennett et al. [BBR88] is that, by using a suitable hash function, Alice and Bob can construct from X a new common key, Y, of length $n - k - s$ such that Eve's average knowledge about Y is less than $2^{-s}/\ln(2)$ bits. In effect then, Alice and Bob are now in possession of a common secret key of length $n - k - s$.

24.10 Hash Functions Using Block Designs

In connection with the hash function mentioned above, it is pointed out in [BBB+90] that a suitable hash function is given by $n - (k - s) = n - t$ independent random subset parities where $t = k - s$.

Related hash functions are also of interest, as follows. Let $v = (v_1, v_2, \ldots, v_n)$ be a binary vector of length n. We construct a set of $n - t$ functions $f_1, f_2, \ldots, f_{n-t}$ where $t > 0$ as follows. Choose first a family $F = F_1, F_2, \ldots, F_{n-t}$ of $n - t$ subsets of $\Omega := \{1, 2, 3, \ldots, n\}$. We identify each set F_i with its characteristic function. Thus, each F_i is a binary vector of length n. We require that these corresponding $n - t$ binary vectors are linearly independent over the field with two elements.

Define $f_j(v)$ as the dot product of v with the binary vector corresponding to F_j. Finally put $f(v) = (f_1(v), f_2(v), \ldots, f_{n-t}(v))$. This gives the desired hash function.

In a preferred embodiment, when f is utilized as a hash function to maximize the difficulty of eavesdropping, we want f to be constructed in such a way that it has regularity properties. That is, it is desirable that the subsets in the family F be "well spread out." Ideally, the family F would also have the property that any two elements of Ω lie in a constant number of subsets in F. Further, it is desirable that each subset in F have the same cardinality and also, under suitable conditions, that every two different subsets in F intersect in a constant number of elements. Indeed these are precisely the criteria that motivated the design of experiments in statistics leading to the combinatorial study of designs (see [BJL86]).

In cryptography, a condition known as the *Avalanche criterion* (AC) is used in the analysis of S-boxes or substitution boxes (see for example [Mol00,Nic99]). S-boxes take a string as input and produce an encoded string as output. The Avalanche criterion requires that if any one bit of the input to an S-box is changed, about half of the bits that are output by the S-box should change their values.

Here we wish to adapt this criterion to hash functions. Given a set of hash functions with values in $\{0,1\}$, if one bit of the input string is changed then the Avalanche criterion requires that about half of the hash functions should change their output values.

Here we now show how to use design theory to construct a large set of hash functions which satisfy all of these criteria, as follows. A particular kind of block design arises from Sylvester matrices, the so-called Hadamard designs. Let H denote a $4m \times 4m$ Hadamard matrix. This means that every entry in H is a 1 or -1 and that $HH^t = 4mI_{4m}$. We assume that such a matrix exists. (There is a long standing open conjecture that at least one $4m \times 4m$ Hadamard matrix exists for every m. This conjecture has been verified for all $m \leq 117$. Furthermore, for infinitely many larger values of m, it is known that $4m \times 4m$ Hadamard matrices do exist.)

We suppose that H has been normalized so that its first row and first column consist entirely of 1's. We construct a new $4m - 1 \times 4m - 1$ matrix $\overline{H}$ all of whose entries are either 0 or 1 as follows. First, we delete the first row and first column (consisting of all 1's) from H and then we convert all the -1's in the remaining matrix to 0's. The resulting matrix is $\overline{H}$. This matrix is the incidence matrix of a block design with $v = 4m$, $k = 2m - 1$, and $\lambda = m - 1$. This design is called a Hadamard 2-design.

For each row, w, of $\overline{H}$, we define a hash function h_w which maps a $(4m - 1)$-vector to its dot product with the row w. These $4m - 1$ different hash functions satisfy the Avalanche criterion as well as the other desirable conditions listed above.

If m is odd then these $4m - 1$ linear hash functions are linearly independent. This fails if m is even. (However, in that case a large subset of the $4m - 1$ hash functions is linearly independent.)

Suppose that $n \not\equiv 3 \pmod 4$. Then, there do not exist any Hadamard designs of size n. In this case, we may choose the least integer $n' > n$ with $n' \equiv 3 \pmod 4$ and then we extend our input strings to length n' by padding on the right with zeros.

24.11   Concluding Remarks

We have not given any detailed discussion of a fundamental problem for all cryptosystems, whether they be based on symmetric encryption or on the public key methodology. This problem is that of transmission errors in hardware and physical communication channels. Such errors seem impossible to eliminate. (Many estimates for transmission errors have been given in various applications.) Also, some form of checking hash functions are essential in key generation algorithms between two parties Alice and Bob in order to ensure that each party has the same key.

This probabilistic element pervades all of cryptography and indeed all communication methods. In many cryptographic protocols, the problem is handled by explicitly including a suitable error correction methodology with the encryption.

We also should point out that in a great many applications, including for example digitized speech such as in the GSM wireless protocols, the encryption is often a so-called stream cipher. In such a case, a discrepancy of a few bits between the two final secret keys used by Alice and Bob will have a negligible effect.

Chapter 25

New Identities for the Shannon Function with Applications

Goals, Discussion   This work beautifully illustrates the connections between the three subjects in the title of this book. Information theory tells us the bound. The identities suggest possibilities for constructing algorithms that come close to producing a common secret key which attains, or gets close to, the information theory bound.

Coding theory is then used to ensure that the two communicating parties have a common secret key by using the hash function described in Chapter 24 relating to a code C. In fact, error correction can ensure that the common secret key can be obtained without using another round of the algorithm and shortening the common key if the difference between the keys of A and B is small and less than the minimum distance of the dual code of C.

New, Noteworthy   In Renyi's *A Diary on Information Theory*, [Ren87], he points out that the entropy formula, i.e.

$$H(X) = p_1 \log \frac{1}{p_1} + p_2 \log \frac{1}{p_2} + \cdots + p_N \log \frac{1}{p_N}$$

Cryptography, Information Theory, and Error-Correction: A Handbook for the 21st Century, Second Edition.
Aiden A. Bruen, Mario A. Forcinito, and James M. McQuillan.
© 2021 John Wiley & Sons, Inc. Published 2021 by John Wiley & Sons, Inc.

was arrived at, independently, by Claude Shannon and Norbert Wiener in 1948. This famous formula was the revolutionary precursor of the information age. Renyi goes on to say that

> this formula had already appeared in the work of Boltzmann which is why it is also called the Boltzmann–Shannon Formula. Boltzmann arrived at this formula in connection with a completely different problem. Almost half a century before Shannon he gave essentially the same formula to describe entropy in his investigations of statistical mechanics. He showed that if, in a gas containing a large number of molecules the probabilities of the possible states of the individual molecules are $p_1, p_2, \ldots, p_N$ then the entropy of the system is $H = c(p_1 \log \frac{1}{p_1} + p_2 \log \frac{1}{p_2} + \cdots + p_N \log \frac{1}{p_N})$ where c is a constant. (In statistical mechanics the natural logarithm is used and not base 2 ...). The entropy of a physical system is the measure of its disorder ...

Since 1948, there have been many advances in the mathematical theory of entropy. A well-known paper of Dembo et al. [DCT91] is devoted to inequalities in information theory. Here, we concentrate on equalities. We show for the first time how a Shannon function $H(p, q)$ can be expanded in infinitely many ways in an infinite series of functions each of which is a linear combination of Shannon functions of the type $H(f_1, f_2, \ldots, f_n)$ where the f_i are rational functions of (p, q), for any $n \geq 2$. Apart from its intrinsic interest, this also gives insight into the algorithm in this chapter for constructing a common secret key between two communicating parties A and B and suggests possible ways in which it might be improved. We refer also to the end of this chapter, for more details.

This chapter is closely connected to research by the authors (see [BWF06] and https://arxiv.org) and to Chapter 24.

25.1   Extensions of a Binary Symmetric Channel

In Chapter 12, we discussed the binary symmetric channel C. We want to talk about the nth extension of C. It will be helpful later on if we *change the notation* now. So we write the channel matrices $P = \begin{pmatrix} p & q \\ q & p \end{pmatrix}$. Here, p is the probability of *success*, i.e. p denotes the probability that 0 is transmitted to 0 and also the probability that 1 gets transmitted to 1. (Formerly, p denoted the probability of a transmission error. This change in notation makes it consistent with the notation in Chapter 14.) The second extension $P^{(2)}$ of P

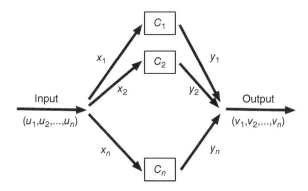

Figure 25.1: n copies of C acting independently and in parallel.

has input and output probabilities $\{00, 01, 10, 11\}$ and channel matrix

$$P^{(2)} = \begin{pmatrix} p^2 & pq & qp & q^2 \\ pq & p^2 & q^2 & qp \\ qp & q^2 & p^2 & pq \\ q^2 & qp & pq & p^2 \end{pmatrix} = \begin{pmatrix} pP & qP \\ qP & pP \end{pmatrix}$$

An alternative way to think of an nth extension of a channel C is to regard it as n copies of C acting independently and in parallel. See Figure 25.1.

Let us assume also that, for C, the input probability of 0 and the input probability of 1 are both equal to $\frac{1}{2}$.

Theorem 25.1 *Let* $\mathbf{X} = (X_1, \ldots, X_n)$ *and* $\mathbf{Y} = (Y_1, \ldots, Y_n)$ *denote an input–output pair for* $C^{(n)}$. *Then*

(a) $H(\mathbf{X}) = H(X_1, \ldots, X_n) = n$

(b) $H(\mathbf{Y}) = H(Y_1, \ldots, Y_n) = n$

(c) $H(\mathbf{X}|\mathbf{Y})$ *is equal to* $nH(p,q)$

(d) The capacity of C *is* $n(1 - H(p,q))$.

(a) Since, by definition, the X_i are independent, $H(\mathbf{X}) = H(X_1) + H(X_2) + \cdots + H(X_n)$ (see Chapter 10). We have

$$H(X_i) = -[\Pr(X_i = 0) \log \Pr(X_i = 0) + \Pr(X_i = 1) \log \Pr(X_i = 1)]$$

$$= -[\frac{1}{2} \log \left(\frac{1}{2}\right) + \frac{1}{2} \log \left(\frac{1}{2}\right)]$$

$$= -\log \left(\frac{1}{2}\right)$$

$$= -[\log 1 - \log 2] = \log 2 = 1$$

Thus, $H(\mathbf{X}) = n$.

(b) The value of Y_i only depends on X_i. The X_i are independent. Thus, $Y_1, Y_2, \ldots, Y_n$ are independent. For any Y_i we have

$$\Pr(Y_i = 0) = \Pr(X_i = 0)(p) + \Pr(X_i = 1)(q) = \frac{1}{2}(p + q) = \frac{1}{2}$$

Also $\Pr(Y_i = 1) = \frac{1}{2}$. Then, as for X_i, $H(Y_i) = 1$. Thus, $H(\mathbf{Y}) = H(Y_1, Y_2, \ldots, Y_n) = n$.

(c) We have $H(\mathbf{X}) - H(\mathbf{X}|\mathbf{Y}) = H(\mathbf{Y}) - H(\mathbf{Y}|\mathbf{X})$ (see Theorem 10.17). Since $H(\mathbf{X}) = H(\mathbf{Y}) = n$ we have $H(\mathbf{X}|\mathbf{Y}) = H(\mathbf{Y}|\mathbf{X})$. Now

$$H(\mathbf{Y}|\mathbf{X}) = \sum_{\mathbf{x}} \Pr(\mathbf{x}) H(\mathbf{Y} \mid \mathbf{X} = \mathbf{x})$$

where $\mathbf{x}$ denotes a given value of the random vector $\mathbf{X}$. Since the channel is memoryless,

$$H(\mathbf{Y} \mid \mathbf{X} = \mathbf{x}) = \sum_i H(Y_i \mid \mathbf{X} = \mathbf{x}) = \sum_i H(Y_i \mid X_i = x_i)$$

(*Note*: for this last step, see Problem 25.1. Then

$$H(\mathbf{Y} \mid \mathbf{X}) = \sum_{\mathbf{x}} \Pr(\mathbf{x}) \sum_i H(Y_i \mid X_i = x_i)$$

$$= \sum_i \sum_u H(Y_i \mid X_i = u) \Pr(X_i = u)$$

Thus

$$H(\mathbf{Y} \mid \mathbf{X}) = \sum_{i=1}^{n} H(Y_i \mid X_i) = nH(p, q)$$

(d) The capacity of C is the maximum value over all inputs of $H(X) - H(X \mid Y)$. Since X is random, the input probability of a 1 or 0 is 0.5. This input distribution maximizes $H(X) - H(X \mid Y)$ for C, the maximum value being $1 - H(p, q)$. Then, the capacity of $C^{(n)}$ is $n(1 - H(p, q))$. $\square$

25.2   A Basic Entropy Equality

First we need some additional discussion on entropy.

Extending Theorem 10.17

The theorem shows that $H(X) + H(Y|X) = H(Y) + H(X|Y)$. A corresponding argument may be used to establish similar identities involving more than two random variables. For example

$$H(X,Y,Z) = H(X) + H(Y|X) + H(Z \mid X,Y)$$
$$= H(X,Y) + H(Z \mid X,Y)$$

Also

$$H(X,Y,Z) = H(X) + H(Y,Z \mid X)$$

From Random Variables to Random Vectors

For any random variable X taking only a finite number of values with probabilities $p_1, p_2, \dots, p_n$ such that

$$\sum p_i = 1 \quad \text{and} \quad p_i > 0 \quad (1 \le i \le n)$$

we define the entropy of X using the Shannon formula by

$$H(X) = -\sum_{k=1}^{n} p_k \log p_k = \sum_{k=1}^{n} p_k \log \frac{1}{p_k}$$

Analogously, if $\mathbf{X}$ is a *random vector* which takes only a finite number of values $\mathbf{u}_1, \mathbf{u}_2, \dots, \mathbf{u}_m$, we define its entropy by the formula

$$H(\mathbf{X}) = -\sum_{k=1}^{m} \Pr(\mathbf{u}_k) \log \Pr(\mathbf{u}_k)$$

For example, when $\mathbf{X}$ is a two-dimensional random vector, say $\mathbf{X} = (U,V)$ with $p_{ij} = \Pr(U = a_i, V = b_j)$, then we can write

$$H(\mathbf{X}) = H(U,V) = -\sum_{i,j} p_{ij} \log p_{ij}$$

More generally, if $X_1, X_2, \ldots, X_m$ is a collection of random variables each taking only a finite set of values, then we can regard $\mathbf{X} = (X_1, X_2, \ldots, X_m)$ as a random vector taking a finite set of values and define the **joint entropy** of $X_1, \ldots, X_m$ by

$$H(X_1, X_2, \ldots, X_m) = H(\mathbf{X}) = -\sum \Pr(X_1 = x_1, X_2 = x_2, \ldots, X_m = x_m)$$
$$\log \Pr(X_1 = x_1, X_2 = x_2, \ldots, X_m = x_m).$$

Standard results for random variables then carry over to random vectors.

The Grouping Axiom for Entropy   This axiom or identity can shorten calculations. It reads as follows ([Wel88, p. 2], [Ash90, p. 8], Section 9.6).

Let $p = p_1 + p_2 + \cdots + p_m$ and $q = q_1 + q_2 + \cdots + q_n$ where each p_i and q_j is nonnegative. Assume that p, q are positive with $p + q = 1$. Then

$$H(p_1, p_2, \ldots, p_m, q_1, q_2, \ldots, q_n) = H(p, q) + pH\left(\frac{p_1}{p}, \frac{p_2}{p}, \ldots, \frac{p_m}{p}\right)$$
$$+ qH\left(\frac{q_1}{q}, \frac{q_2}{q}, \ldots, \frac{q_n}{q}\right)$$

For example, suppose $m = 1$ so $p_1 = p$. Then we get

$$H(p_1, q_1, q_2, \ldots, q_n) = H(p, q) + qH\left(\frac{q_1}{q}, \ldots, \frac{q_n}{q}\right)$$

This is because $p_1 H\left(\frac{p_1}{p_1}, 0, \ldots, 0\right) = p_1 H(1, 0, \ldots, 0) = 0$.

Theorem 25.2 *Let* $\mathbf{X}, \mathbf{Y}, \mathbf{Z}$ *be random vectors such that* $H(\mathbf{Z} \mid \mathbf{X}, \mathbf{Y}) = 0$. *Then*

(a) $H(\mathbf{X}|\mathbf{Y}) = H(\mathbf{X}, \mathbf{Z} \mid \mathbf{Y})$.

(b) $H(\mathbf{X}|\mathbf{Y}) = H(\mathbf{X} \mid \mathbf{Y}, \mathbf{Z}) + H(\mathbf{Y} \mid \mathbf{Z})$.

Proof.

$$H(\mathbf{X} \mid \mathbf{Y}) = H(\mathbf{X}, \mathbf{Y}) - H(\mathbf{Y})$$
$$= H(\mathbf{X}, \mathbf{Y}, \mathbf{Z}) - H(\mathbf{Z} \mid \mathbf{X}, \mathbf{Y}) - H(\mathbf{Y})$$
$$= H(\mathbf{X}, \mathbf{Y}, \mathbf{Z}) - H(\mathbf{Y}) \quad [\text{since } H(\mathbf{Z} \mid \mathbf{X}, \mathbf{Y}) = 0]$$
$$= H(\mathbf{Y}) + H(\mathbf{X}, \mathbf{Z} \mid \mathbf{Y}) - H(\mathbf{Y})$$
$$= H(\mathbf{X}, \mathbf{Z} \mid \mathbf{Y}), \quad \text{proving (a)}$$

For (b): Using (a) we have

$$H(\mathbf{X} \mid \mathbf{Y}) = H(\mathbf{X}, \mathbf{Z}, \mathbf{Y}) - H(\mathbf{Y})$$
$$= H(\mathbf{X}, \mathbf{Z}, \mathbf{Y}) - H(\mathbf{Y}, \mathbf{Z}) + H(\mathbf{Y}, \mathbf{Z}) - H(\mathbf{Y})$$
$$= H(\mathbf{X} \mid \mathbf{Y}, \mathbf{Z}) + H(\mathbf{Z} \mid \mathbf{Y})$$

■

25.3   The New Identities

We will use the above identity in Theorem 25.2, part (b), namely,

$$H(\mathbf{X} \mid \mathbf{Y}) = H(\mathbf{X} \mid \mathbf{Y}, \mathbf{Z}) + H(\mathbf{Z} \mid \mathbf{Y}) \tag{25.1}$$

which holds under the assumption that $H(\mathbf{Z} \mid \mathbf{X}, \mathbf{Y}) = 0$. We start with arrays $A = \begin{pmatrix} a_1 \\ a_2 \\ \vdots \\ a_n \end{pmatrix}$, $B = \begin{pmatrix} b_1 \\ b_2 \\ \vdots \\ b_n \end{pmatrix}$, where n is even. We assume that A, B are random binary strings subject to the condition that, for each i, we have $\Pr(a_i = b_i) = p$. We also assume that the set of outcomes $(a_i = b_i)$ is an independent set. We divide A, B into blocks of size 2. To start, put $\mathbf{X} = \begin{pmatrix} x_1 \\ x_2 \end{pmatrix}$, $\mathbf{Y} = \begin{pmatrix} y_1 \\ y_2 \end{pmatrix}$, $\mathbf{Z} = x_1 + x_2$.

Lemma 25.3

$$H(\mathbf{Z} \mid \mathbf{X}, \mathbf{Y}) = 0$$

Proof. We want to calculate $\sum_{\mathbf{x},\mathbf{y}} H(Z \mid \mathbf{x}, \mathbf{y}) \Pr(X = \mathbf{x}, Y = \mathbf{y})$. Given $\mathbf{x}, \mathbf{y}$, say $\mathbf{x} = \begin{pmatrix} \alpha_1 \\ \alpha_2 \end{pmatrix}$, $\mathbf{y} = \begin{pmatrix} \beta_1 \\ \beta_2 \end{pmatrix}$ the value of $\mathbf{Z}$ is $\alpha_1 + \alpha_2$ which is 1 or 0. There is no uncertainty in the value of $\mathbf{Z}$ given $\mathbf{x}, \mathbf{y}$, i.e. each term in the above sum for H is $H(1,0)$ or $H(0,1)$ which is 0. Therefore, $H(Z \mid \mathbf{X}, \mathbf{Y}) = 0$.

From this we can use identity (25.1) from Theorem 25.2 for this block of size 2. We can think of this block as the second extension of a binary symmetric channel from $\mathbf{X}$ to $\mathbf{Y}$ (or from $\mathbf{Y}$ to $\mathbf{X}$). We have

$$H(\mathbf{X} \mid \mathbf{Y}) = H(\mathbf{X} \mid \mathbf{Y}, \mathbf{Z}) + H(\mathbf{Z} \mid \mathbf{Y})$$

From Theorem 25.1 the left side, i.e. $H(\mathbf{X} \mid \mathbf{Y})$ is equal to $2H(p,q)$. Next we calculate the right side beginning with $H(\mathbf{Z} \mid \mathbf{Y})$, i.e. $H\left(\mathbf{Z} \mid \begin{pmatrix} y_1 \\ y_2 \end{pmatrix}\right)$. We have

$$H(\mathbf{Z} \mid \mathbf{Y}) = H\left(\mathbf{Z} \mid (y_1 + y_2 = x_1 + x_2)\right) \Pr(y_1 + y_2 = x_1 + x_2)$$
$$+ H\left(\mathbf{Z} \mid (y_1 + y_2 \neq x_1 + x_2)\right) \Pr(y_1 + y_2 \neq x_1 + x_2)$$

We know that $\Pr(x_1 + x_2 = y_1 + y_2) = p^2 + q^2$ and $\Pr(x_1 + x_2 \neq y_1 + y_2) = 1 - (p^2 + q^2) = 2pq$ since $p + q = 1$. Thus, $H(\mathbf{Z} \mid \mathbf{Y}) = (p^2 + q^2) \log\left(\frac{1}{p^2+q^2}\right) + 2pq \log\left(\frac{1}{2pq}\right)$ i.e. $H(\mathbf{Z} \mid \mathbf{Y}) = H(p^2 + q^2, 2pq)$.

Next we calculate

$$H\left(\begin{pmatrix} x_1 \\ x_2 \end{pmatrix} \mid \begin{pmatrix} y_1 \\ y_2 \end{pmatrix}, (x_1 + x_2)\right) = H(\mathbf{X} \mid \mathbf{Y}, \mathbf{Z})$$

Again we have two possibilities, i.e. $y_1 + y_2 = x_1 + x_2$ and $y_1 + y_2 \neq x_1 + x_2$. The corresponding probabilities are $p^2 + q^2$ and $2pq$ respectively. We obtain

$$H(\mathbf{X} \mid \mathbf{Y}, \mathbf{Z}) = (p^2 + q^2) H\left(\frac{p^2}{p^2 + q^2}, \frac{q^2}{p^2 + q^2}\right) + 2pq H\left(\frac{pq}{2pq}, \frac{pq}{2pq}\right)$$

This comes about from the facts that

(a) If $y_1 + y_2 = x_1 + x_2$ then we either have $y_1 = x_1$ and $y_2 = x_2$ or $y_1 = 1 - x_1$, $y_2 = 1 - x_2$.

(b) If $y_1 + y_2 \neq x_1 + x_2$ then either $y_1 = x_1$ and $y_2 \neq x_2$ or $y_1 \neq x_1$ and $y_2 = x_2$.

Using the fact that $H(\frac{1}{2}, \frac{1}{2}) = 1$ and identity (25.1) we get:

Theorem 25.4 Part A

$$2H(p,q) = (p^2 + q^2) H\left(\frac{p^2}{p^2 + q^2}, \frac{q^2}{p^2 + q^2}\right) + 2pq\, H(p^2 + q^2, 2pq) \qquad (25.2)$$ ∎

Blocks of Size 3

Here, $\mathbf{X} = \begin{pmatrix} x_1 \\ x_2 \\ x_3 \end{pmatrix}$, $\mathbf{Y} = \begin{pmatrix} y_1 \\ y_2 \\ y_3 \end{pmatrix}$, $\mathbf{Z} = x_1 + x_2 + x_3$. As in Lemma 25.3 we have $H(\mathbf{Z} \mid \mathbf{X}, \mathbf{Y}) = 0$ so we can use identity (25.1) again, i.e.

$$H(\mathbf{X} \mid \mathbf{Y}) = H(\mathbf{X} \mid \mathbf{Y}, \mathbf{Z}) + H(\mathbf{Z} \mid \mathbf{Y})$$

Our assumptions guaranteed that we have a channel from $\mathbf{X}$ to $\mathbf{Y}$ (or from $\mathbf{Y}$ to $\mathbf{X}$) which is in effect the third extension $C^{(3)}$ of a binary symmetric channel C.

From Theorem 25.1, we have $H(\mathbf{X}|\mathbf{Y}) = 3H(p,q)$. Just as for blocks of size 2, we have $H(\mathbf{Z}|\mathbf{Y}) = H(p^3 + 3pq^2, q^3 + 3qp^2)$. This is because the probabilities that $Z = y_1 + y_2 + y_3$ or $Z \neq y_1 + y_2 + y_3$ are, respectively, $p^3 + 3pq^2$ or $q^3 + 3qp^2$.

If $Z = y_1 + y_2 + y_3$, then either $x_1 = y_1$, $x_2 = y_2$, $x_3 = y_3$ or else, for some i, $1 \leq i \leq 3$ (three possibilities) $x_i = y_i$ and for the other two indices j,k, $x_j \neq y_j$ and $x_k \neq y_k$.

A similar analysis can be carried out for the case where $Z \neq y_1 + y_2 + y_3$. We then get $H(\mathbf{X} \mid \mathbf{Y}, \mathbf{Z}) = f(p,q) + f(q,p)$ where

$$f(p,q) = (p^3 + 3pq^2) \left\{ H \left(\frac{p^3}{p^3 + 3pq^2}, \frac{pq^2}{p^3 + 3pq^2}, \frac{pq^2}{p^3 + 3pq^2}, \frac{pq^2}{p^3 + 3pq^2} \right) \right\}$$

We now use the grouping axiom for $m = 1$. The p in the grouping axiom then refers to $\frac{p^3}{p^3 + 3pq^2}$ and the q there is now replaced by $\frac{3pq^2}{p^3 + 3pq^2}$. Then

$$f(p,q) = (p^3 + 3pq^2) \left\{ H \left(\frac{p^3}{p^3 + 3pq^2}, \frac{3pq^2}{p^3 + 3pq^2} \right) + \frac{3pq^2}{p^3 + 3pq^2} H \left(\frac{1}{3}, \frac{1}{3}, \frac{1}{3} \right) \right\}$$

$$= (p^3 + 3pq^2) H \left(\frac{p^3}{p^3 + 3pq^2}, \frac{3pq^2}{p^3 + 3pq^2} \right) + 3pq^2 \log 3$$

$f(q,p)$ is obtained by interchanging p with q. We note that, since $p + q = 1$, $3pq^2 \log 3 + 3qp^2 \log 3 = 3pq \log 3$.

Putting this all together, using blocks of size 3 we get

Theorem 25.4 Part B

$$3H(p,q) = H(p^3 + 3pq^2, q^3 + 3qp^2) + (p^3 + 3pq^2) H \left(\frac{p^3}{p^3 + 3pq^2}, \frac{3pq^2}{p^3 + 3pq^2} \right)$$

$$+ (q^3 + 3qp^2) H \left(\frac{q^3}{q^3 + 3qp^2}, \frac{3qp^2}{q^3 + 3qp^2} \right) + 3pq \log 3 \qquad (25.3)$$

Using the same method, we can find a formula analogous to formulas (25.2) and (25.3) for obtaining $nH(p,q)$ as a linear combination of terms of the form $H(u,v)$ where u,v involve terms in $p^n, p^{n-2}q^2, \ldots, q^n, q^{n-2}p^2, \ldots$ plus extra terms such as $3pq \log 3$ as in Theorem 25.4.

For blocks of size 2, formula (25.2) can be put in a more compact form in terms of capacities, as follows,

Theorem 25.4 Part C

$$2\left(1 - H(p,q)\right) = [1 - H(p^2 + q^2, 2pq)] + \left[(p^2 + q^2) \left(1 - H \left(\frac{p^2}{p^2 + q^2}, \frac{q^2}{p^2 + q^2} \right) \right) \right] \qquad (25.4)$$

25.4   Applications to Cryptography and a Shannon-Type Limit

The above method of using blocks of various sizes is reminiscent of the algorithm for the key exchange in Chapter 24. Indeed the identities above were informed by the details in the algorithm.

Let us take an example. Suppose we have two binary arrays $(a_1, \ldots, a_n)$ and $(b_1, \ldots, b_n)$ of length n with n even, $n = 2t$, say. The events $a_i = b_i$ are assumed independent, with probability p, $1 \leq i \leq n$. We subdivide the arrays into corresponding blocks of size 2 as in Chapter 24. For blocks $\begin{pmatrix} a_1 \\ a_2 \end{pmatrix}$ and $\begin{pmatrix} b_1 \\ b_2 \end{pmatrix}$, we discard those blocks if the parities disagree. If the parities agree, which happens with probability $p^2 + q^2$, we keep a_1 and b_1, discarding a_2 and b_2. Thus, on average, we keep $(p^2 + q^2)\frac{n}{2}$ partial blocks of size 1 and discard $\left[1 - (p^2 + q^2)\right]\frac{n}{2}$ blocks of size 2.

Let us suppose $n = 100$ and $p = 0.7$. The information that Y has about X, i.e. that B has about A is $100[1 - H(0.7, 0.3)] \approx 100(1 - 0.8813) \approx 11.87$ Shannon bits.

We are seeking to find a sub-array of A, B such that corresponding bits are equal. Our method is to publicly exchange parities. The (average) length of this secret key will be at most 11.

Back to the algorithm. We keep on average, $(50)(p^2 + q^2)$ blocks of size 2, i.e. $(50)(0.58) = 29$ blocks of size 2. A and B remove the bottom element of each block. To repeat, the initial information that Y has about X (i.e. that B has about A) is $I(X : Y) = 100[1 - H(0.7, 0.3)] \approx 100(1 - 0.8813) \approx 11.87$ Shannon bits. We are then left with 29 pairs of elements (a_1, b_1). The probability that $a_1 = b_1$ given that $a_1 + a_2 = b_1 + b_2$ is $\frac{p^2}{p^2 + q^2}$, i.e. $\frac{(0.7)^2}{(0.7)^2 + (0.3)^2} = \frac{0.49}{0.58} \approx 0.845$. Next, $1 - H(0.845, 0.155) \approx (1 - 0.6221) \approx 0.3779$. To summarize, we started with 100 pairs (a_i, b_i) with $\Pr(a_i = b_i) = 0.7$. The information revealed to B by A is $(100)(1 - H(0.7, 0.3)) = 11.87$ *Shannon bits of information.*

We are left with 29 pairs (a_j, b_j) with $\Pr(a_j = b_j) = 0.845$. The amount of information revealed to the remnant of B by the remnant of A is $29(0.3779) \approx 10.96$ *Shannon bits of information.* So we have "wasted" about $11.87 - 10.96 \approx 0.91$ bits, i.e. the wastage is about 8%. Mathematically, we have $100\left(1 - H(0.7, 0.3)\right) = 29\left(1 - H(0.845, 0.155)\right) + $ Wastage. In general, we have

$$n[1 - H(p, q)] = \frac{n}{2}(p^2 + q^2)\left[1 - H\left(\frac{p^2}{p^2 + q^2}, \frac{q^2}{p^2 + q^2}\right)\right] + W$$

where W denotes the wastage. Dividing by $\frac{n}{2}$ we get

$$2[1 - H(p, q)] = (p^2 + q^2)\left[1 - H\left(\frac{p^2}{p^2 + q^2}, \frac{q^2}{p^2 + q^2}\right)\right] + \frac{2W}{n}$$

Comparing with Theorem 25.4 Part C, we see that $W = \frac{n}{2} \left[1 - H(p^2 + q^2, 2pq) \right]$. In this case, $W = 50 \left[1 - H(0.58, 0.42) \right] \approx 50(1 - 0.9815) = (50)(0.0185) = 0.925$ bits.

To sum up then the new identities tell us exactly how much information was not utilized or wasted. *Moreover, the algorithm yields valuable insights into Theorem 25.4 Part C.*

One of the original motivations for work in linear coding was that the Shannon fundamental theorem in Chapter 12 showed how capacity was the bound for accurate communication. The problem was to construct linear codes or other codes such as turbo codes that came close to the bound.

Here we have an analogous problem. In the example just considered, the average length of a cryptographic common secret key obtained as a common subset of A, B is bounded by $n(1 - H(p))$. The problem is to find algorithms which produce such a common secret key coming close to this Shannon bound of $n(1 - H(p))$.

25.5 Problems

25.1 Give an example to show why $H(\mathbf{Y} \mid \mathbf{X} = \mathbf{x}) = \sum_i H(Y_i \mid X_i = x_i)$ in the proof of Theorem 25.1. (See Solution 25.1.)

25.2 Draw a Venn Diagram to illustrate formula (25.1) in Section 25.3 in the case where $Z = x_1 + x_2$. (See Solution 25.2.)

25.3 Write down a formula for $H(p, q)$ using blocks of size 4. (See Solution 25.3.)

25.4 Is $H\left(\frac{2}{5}, \frac{3}{5}\right)$ the same as $H\left(\frac{2}{5}, \frac{1}{5}, \frac{1}{5}, \frac{1}{5}\right)$? (See Solution 25.4.)

25.6 Solutions

25.1 Let us suppose that $n = 2$ and that $\mathbf{x}_i = (1, 0)$. To calculate the conditional entropy $H(\mathbf{Y} \mid \mathbf{X} = \mathbf{x}_i)$ we proceed as follows.

We have four terms to calculate, corresponding to the four possible values for $\mathbf{Y}$, i.e. $(y_1, y_2) = (0, 0), (0, 1), (1, 0), (1, 1)$ given that $(x_1, x_2) = (1, 0)$. We get $\Pr\left((0, 0) \mid (1, 0)\right) = \Pr(y_1 = 0 \mid x_1 = 1) \Pr(y_2 = 0 \mid x_2 = 0)$, i.e. qp. The resulting contribution to the conditional entropy is $qp \log \frac{1}{qp}$. For the term $((0, 1) \mid (1, 0))$, we get $q^2 \log \frac{1}{q^2}$. For the term $((1, 0) \mid (1, 0))$, we get $p^2 \log \frac{1}{p^2}$. For the term

$((1,1) \mid (1,0))$, we get $pq \log \frac{1}{pq}$. Our sum is

$$qp \log \frac{1}{qp} + q^2 \log \frac{1}{q^2} + p^2 \log \frac{1}{p^2} + pq \log \frac{1}{pq}$$

$$= qp \left(\log \frac{1}{p} + \log \frac{1}{q} \right) + q^2 \left(\log \frac{1}{q} + \log \frac{1}{q} \right)$$

$$+ p^2 \left(\log \frac{1}{p} + \log \frac{1}{p} \right) + pq \left(\log \frac{1}{p} + \log \frac{1}{q} \right)$$

$$= \log \frac{1}{p} \left[qp + 2p^2 + pq \right] + \log \frac{1}{q} \left[qp + 2q^2 + pq \right]$$

$$= \log \frac{1}{p} [2p(p+q)] + \log \frac{1}{q} [2q(p+q)]$$

(In the above, we use the fact that $\log \left(\frac{1}{uv} \right) = \log \frac{1}{u} + \log \frac{1}{v}$.)

Since $p + q = 1$ we get

$$2p \log \frac{1}{p} + 2q \log \frac{1}{q} = 2 \left[p \log \frac{1}{p} + q \log \frac{1}{q} \right]$$

$$= 2H(p,q)$$

$$= H(Y_1 \mid X_1 = 1) + H(Y_2 \mid X_2 = 0)$$

The case for general n can be shown by induction.

25.2   Since $Z = x_1 + x_2$, the information that Z contains is a subset of the information contained in $\mathbf{X}$. So we get the following diagram.

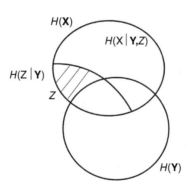

25.3   We use the formula that

$$H(\mathbf{X} \mid \mathbf{Y}) = H(\mathbf{X} \mid \mathbf{Y}, Z) + H(Z \mid \mathbf{Y}) \tag{25.5}$$

We note that $1^4 = 1 = (p+q)^4 = p^4 + 4p^3q + 6p^2q^2 + 4pq^3 + q^4$. Then,

$$H(Z \mid \mathbf{Y}) = H(p^4 + 6p^2q^2 + q^4, 4p^3q + 4pq^3) \qquad (25.6)$$

To calculate $H(\mathbf{X} \mid \mathbf{Y}, Z)$ with $Y = \begin{pmatrix} y_1 \\ y_2 \\ y_3 \\ y_4 \end{pmatrix}$, $Z = x_1 + x_2 + x_3 + x_4$ we consider cases (a) $Z = y_1 + y_2 + y_3 + y_4$, (b) $Z \neq y_1 + y_2 + y_3 + y_4$.

We have $\Pr(Z = y_1 + y_2 + y_3 + y_4) = p^4 + q^4 + 6p^2q^2$; $\Pr(Z \neq y_1 + y_2 + y_3 + y_4) = 4p^3 + 4pq^3$. Set $\lambda = p^4 + q^4 + 6p^2q^2$, $\mu = 4p^3q + 4pq^3$. The term of $6p^2q^2$ in λ corresponds to $x_1 = y_1$, $x_2 = y_2$; $x_1 = y_1$, $x_3 = y_3$; $x_1 = y_1$, $x_4 = y_4$; $x_2 = y_2$, $x_3 = y_3$; $x_2 = y_2$, $x_4 = y_4$; $x_3 = y_3$, $x_4 = y_4$. Then,

$$H(\mathbf{X} \mid \mathbf{Y}, Z) = \lambda H \left(\frac{p^4}{\lambda}, \frac{q^4}{\lambda}, \frac{pq^2}{\lambda}, \frac{pq^2}{\lambda}, \frac{pq^2}{\lambda}, \frac{pq^2}{\lambda} \right)$$
$$+ \mu H \left(\frac{p^3q}{\mu}, \frac{p^3q}{\mu}, \frac{p^3q}{\mu}, \frac{p^3q}{\mu}; \frac{pq^3}{\mu}, \frac{pq^3}{\mu}, \frac{pq^3}{\mu}, \frac{pq^3}{\mu} \right) \qquad (25.7)$$

Thus, $4H(p) = H(\mathbf{Z} \mid \mathbf{Y}) + H(\mathbf{X} \mid \mathbf{Y}, Z)$ as calculated in (25.6) and (25.7). We also refer to Problem 25.4.

25.4

$$H \left(\frac{2}{5}, \frac{3}{5} \right) = \frac{2}{5} \log \frac{5}{2} + \frac{3}{5} \log \frac{5}{3}$$

$$H \left(\frac{2}{5}, \frac{1}{5}, \frac{1}{5}, \frac{1}{5} \right) = \frac{2}{5} \log \frac{5}{2} + \frac{1}{5} \log 5 + \frac{1}{5} \log 5 + \frac{1}{5} \log 5$$

$$= \frac{2}{5} \log \frac{5}{2} + \frac{3}{5} \log 5$$

Since $\log \frac{5}{3} \neq \log 5$, the two expressions are different.

Addendum

The first two laws of thermodynamics are easily stated, i.e. energy is conserved: entropy always increases. (Informally! You can't win: you can't even break even.)

It was Boltzmann who took the atomic point of view and essentially showed how to prove the second law using a purely probabilistic argument. The formula $S = k \log W$ is on his tombstone where k is Boltzmann's constant and W is the entropy. It was Boltzmann who introduced the H notation for entropy.

A good discussion can be found in "Entropy Demystified: The Second Law Reduced to Plain Common Sense" by Arieh Ben-Naim, [BN07].

Chapter 26

Blockchain and Bitcoin

Goals, Discussion   A blockchain uses hash pointers to construct an append-only secure ledger. In the bitcoin application of the blockchain, each page of the ledger corresponds to a block and the entries in the page are transactions.

New, Noteworthy   Based on the work in Chapter 24, we detail a new hash function X which uses properties of error-correcting codes. Unlike the usual situation with hashes, we are able to calculate the exact probability that $X(A) = X(B)$ for two unequal strings A, B of the same length. This will show whether it is unlikely that, for $A \neq B$, we have $X(A) = X(B)$. That property is a prerequisite for a secure hash function. In Section 26.8, we offer a new elementary mathematical proof of how double spending can be thwarted. The proof is quite different than the informal proof by Nakamoto, [Nak08].

According to *Inside Higher Education* (2018), [Pia18],

> Blockchain is the underlying technological innovation behind Bitcoin – the rise of digital currency. The technology itself solves one of the great problems of society: how to create a system where many people keep verified, trusted information. Today, for example, the record of who owns a plot of land is kept at the town hall. Imagine if every town hall was linked so that every town hall had a copy of a land title?

Cryptography, Information Theory, and Error-Correction: A Handbook for the 21st Century, Second Edition.
Aiden A. Bruen, Mario A. Forcinito, and James M. McQuillan.
© 2021 John Wiley & Sons, Inc. Published 2021 by John Wiley & Sons, Inc.

This issue of *Inside Higher Education* also points out that

> Already, the single most in-demand skill for freelancers is blockchain. LinkedIn postings for blockchain jobs are up 6,000 percent year over year, and starting developer salaries are over $100,000 . . .

It is then pointed out that universities "may put student portfolios or other work on the blockchain to enable discovery by employers or other partners," that "Blockchain is likely the death knell for the embossed transcript" and that it "can help to solve one of higher education's most vexing challenges: making the case for a system where many people keep verified, trusted information."

Obviously, legal disputes over patents can benefit from Blockchain since a timestamp facility will help in assessing priority of discoveries. Legal and medical records are well-suited to storage on a blockchain.

In April 2020, during the COVID-19 pandemic, IBM used blockchains to help the healthcare industry. In [Wei20], Weiss writes that IBM is using blockchains to connect "pop-up medical mask and equipment makers with hospitals." They quote Mark Treshock, the IBM blockchain solutions leader for IBM healthcare and life sciences as saying, "It's the immutability component. If I am a supplier and I create a profile and include my information for onboarding as a new supplier, there's a qualification process I have to go through . . . It is done to determine if they are legitimate, ethical, that they comply with required laws and, in this case, with needed FDA certifications" [Wei20].

Another industry that can benefit heavily from blockchains is the video game industry. Many video games allow players to earn some type of "token" that they can use for purchases within the games. In the article "Atari CEO touts future of blockchain in gaming," [Gre20], Jonathan Greig notes that Atari is working with Arkane Network which specializes in blockchain applications. Greig says, "Game makers are innovating with blockchain to address the risks involved with online purchasing and to create new use cases." Greig quotes Frédéric Chesnais, Chairman and CEO of *Atari* as saying,

> Atari created the video game industry, and we see blockchain from two different angles. The first one is the vision from the gamer. So as a gamer you want to be able to buy games and use games on the blockchain. There is going to be a big business in grinding and selling avatars. It's already big, but it is going to be much, much bigger. We are trying to help our users by using the blockchain and playing on the blockchain or playing or buying on the blockchain as an individual. That's why we're creating the Atari Token.

On 20 April 2020, *The Wall Street Journal* announced that, "China's central bank has introduced a homegrown digital currency across four cities as part of a pilot program, marking a milestone on the path toward the first electronic payment system by a major central bank ...," [Che20].

The financial technology industry has been a big driver of blockchain development due in part to the success of bitcoin. This has contributed also to a boom in blockchain-related patents in the financial sector. By August 2018, the Bank of America had no fewer than 50 blockchain-related patents! According to Mearian at *Computerworld*, [Mea18], blockchain developer is first in the top five emerging careers. The future for blockchain looks bright!

26.1 Ledgers, Blockchains

The idea of a ledger is the starting point for studying blockchains. It is a place to record all transactions, using timestamping, in a given system.

The ledger is such that a participant can add new transactions but cannot remove, modify, or change the order of existing transactions. In other words, it is "**append-only**." It should be open and trusted by the participants. We are now getting close to the idea of a blockchain.

Recall that in programming, a **pointer**, denoted by P say, is a variable whose value is the address of another variable, for example the address of the variable Q. We can think of a pointer as a "locator" as it tells us where to locate another value.

A **hash pointer** is a pointer to where some information is stored, together with a cryptographic hash of the information. A regular pointer gives a way to retrieve the information. A hash pointer also gives a way to verify that the information is consistent with the hash so that it has not been changed.

Formally (see Narayanan et al. [NBF$^+$16, Section 1.2]) a **blockchain** is the data structure obtained from a linked list that uses hash pointers.

In a regular linked list you have a series of blocks, each block has data and a pointer to the previous block in the list. For a block chain, the previous block pointer is replaced by a hash pointer. Bitcoin converts a blockchain structure for recording payments into a currency. (Actually, in a programming or data structures class, when linked lists are first introduced, it is usually phrased as a node has a pointer to the "next" node in the linked list. But, with blockchain there is instead a link to the "previous node." In the case of doubly linked lists, a node has a link to the next node and a link to the previous node.)

We can think of a blockchain as a virtual chain of blocks forming a digital ledger where each block of data contains several interrelated transactions. These transactions occur on a decentralized peer-to-peer network. This peer-to-peer network consists of a network of computers each called a node. Each block contains a cryptographic hash of the previous block. As mentioned, the ledger is append-only so that a participant can add to it but cannot change previous transactions.

26.2   Hash Functions, Cryptographic Hashes

As discussed in Chapter 4, hashes are a basic part of data storage and cryptography. A hash is a form of (lossy) compression and can be thought of as a digest or summary of the data being hashed. As a general idea of a message digest, we can think of a zipped file or the DNA or fingerprints of a person. We have seen many examples of mathematical hash functions in this book. As a "bad" example, suppose we have a group of N people with a data set for each such as the name, social security number, date of birth, and so on. We could, for identification purposes, use the hash function which maps each person to his or her date of birth. However, as we have seen in Section 7.11, if $N \geq 24$ it is likely that some two people will have the same birthday. A good hash function, on the other hand, ensures that the probability of two different objects hashing to the same value, i.e. the *collision probability* is small.

Several hash functions are discussed in Sections 4.4 and 24.10. A **cryptographic hash function** takes as input a message of arbitrary length and outputs a message digest of fixed length. To see examples of such hashes, just Google "Hash generator" and input a message.

For work with blockchains, we require that our hash functions work on inputs of arbitrary length. If we have a hash function X that works on inputs of fixed length, we can use the Merkle–Damgard transform. The **Merkle–Damgard transform** (see [NBF$^+$16]) converts X to a hash function H that accepts arbitrary-length inputs. SHA-256 uses this method.

The method is as follows. Suppose X, the "**compression function**" accepts inputs of length m with outputs of length n, $n < m$. The input to H is divided into **blocks** of length $m - n$. Pass each such block *together with the output of the previous block* into the compression function X. This can be done since the length of the input is $(m - n) + n = m$ which is the length of the input to X. For the first block for which there is no previous block output to use, we use instead an Initialization Vector (IV) which is reused for every call of the hash function. The input of H is padded so that its length is a multiple of $m - n$.

As an example, SHA-256 uses a compression function that accepts strings of length 768 as input and produces 256-bit outputs. Thus, $m = 768$, $n = 256$, $m - n = 512$. The input for SHA-256 is of arbitrary length x but is padded so that x is a multiple of 512.

Let us take another look at a "new hash function on the block" which is discussed but from a different point of view in Section 24.5. It has the advantage that we can calculate the probability that two strings hash to the same value.

We start with a binary linear (n, k) code C. A basis for C is given by any k vectors in C (of length n, $k < n$) which are linearly independent. Denote these k vectors by

$\{\mathbf{u}_1, \mathbf{u}_2, \ldots, \mathbf{u}_k\}$. Suppose $\mathbf{w}$ is any string of length n. Then define the hash H of $\mathbf{w}$, i.e. $H(\mathbf{w})$ to be the binary string $\{\mathbf{w} \cdot \mathbf{u}_1, \mathbf{w} \cdot \mathbf{u}_2 \ldots, \mathbf{w} \cdot \mathbf{u}_k\}$ of length k. Now suppose that $\mathbf{x}$ is another string of length n such that $H(\mathbf{x}) = H(\mathbf{w})$. Then

$$(\mathbf{x} + \mathbf{w}) \cdot \mathbf{u}_1 = (\mathbf{x} + \mathbf{w}) \cdot \mathbf{u}_2 = \cdots = (\mathbf{x} + \mathbf{w}) \cdot \mathbf{u}_k = 0$$

It follows that $\mathbf{x} + \mathbf{w}$ is in the dual code $C^{\perp}$.

Conversely if $\mathbf{x} + \mathbf{w}$ is in $C^{\perp}$, $H(\mathbf{x}) = H(\mathbf{w})$.

(For *strong security*, we want the probability to be very small that $H(\mathbf{x}) = H(\mathbf{w})$, i.e. we want H to be a **collision-resistant** hash function.)

So, if $\mathbf{x}$ is a random binary string, what is the probability that $\mathbf{x} + \mathbf{w}$ is in $C^{\perp}$? The number of binary strings $\mathbf{x}$ of length n is 2^n. Now $\mathbf{x} + \mathbf{w}$ is in $C^{\perp}$ if and only if $\mathbf{x} + \mathbf{w} = \mathbf{y}$, $\mathbf{y}$ some vector in $C^{\perp}$, i.e. $\mathbf{x}$ is in $C^{\perp} + \mathbf{y}$. C has dimension k, length n, so $C^{\perp}$ has dimension $n - k$, length n. The number of vectors in $C^{\perp}$ is 2^{n-k} which is the number of vectors in $C^{\perp} + \mathbf{y}$. The conclusion is that the probability that $\mathbf{x}$ and $\mathbf{u}$ have the same hash is $\frac{2^{n-k}}{2^n} = \frac{1}{2^k}$ which gets arbitrarily small as k gets large.

Note that by the Merkle–Damgard transform method, the hash function H accepts inputs of *arbitrary length*. We mention also that the hash function works over *arbitrary finite fields* such as fields of order 2^t and not just the binary field.

26.3   Digital Signatures

We have seen several examples of public key cryptosystems such as RSA, El Gamal, and the one by McEliece that uses error-correcting codes. In such a system, we have the set M of possible messages. There are encryption and description functions E_k and D_k which depend on a key k. For example, in RSA, a key is a triple e, d, n with $ed \equiv 1 \pmod{\phi(n)}$, where $n = pq$ and $\phi(n) = (p-1)(q-1)$. Once k is fixed, the encryption functions $E_k = E$ and $D_k = D$ map M to M and are inverses of each other. This enables us to construct digital signatures and verify them with the public key as in Sections 4.1 and 4.7. In Bitcoin, the El Gamal digital signature, which is based on elliptic curves, is used.

26.4   Bitcoin and Cryptocurrencies

Building on earlier work on blockchains, the foundational paper entitled "Bitcoin: A Peer-to-Peer Electronic Cash System" was published by Satoshi Nakamoto in 2008, [Nak08]. In the paper, he proposes a decentralized electronic payment system that is based on cryptographic proof instead of trust. Bitcoin relies on a peer-to-peer, trusted, decentralized network which is also distributed, so that anyone can get a copy of the network.

Bitcoin aspires to

1. Peer-to-peer payments over an online network.

2. The replacing of third parties replacing trust with verification.

3. Transactions which are irreversible.

4. A peer-to-peer distributed timestamp server which generates mathematical proof of the chronological order of transactions.

A bitcoin refers to a unit of digital currency to the online bank but without the centralized authority of a regular bank. Later on we will see how, instead of linking documents and transactions individually, *we collect them into blocks and link blocks together in a chain.* Within a block, the documents are linked together, not linearly, but in a tree structure.

Before proceeding it is good to have a few pictures in mind.

Each block has two hashes A_i, B_i, as shown in Figure 26.1. A_i is a hash of itself in its own block and B_i is a hash of A_{i-1}, the predecessor block. In general, each block *contains a hash of the block that it is being built on top of*, i.e. *a hash of the previous block.*

The second picture, Figure 26.2, is one of backward hash pointers as in Narayanan et al., [NBF$^+$16, p. 33].

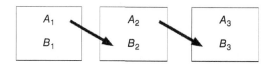

Figure 26.1: Blocks linked into a chain.

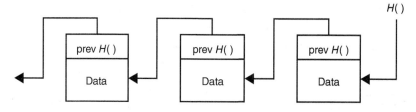

Figure 26.2: Backward hash pointers. See [NBF$^+$16, p. 33]. Source: Narayanan et al. (2016). © 2016, Princeton University Press.

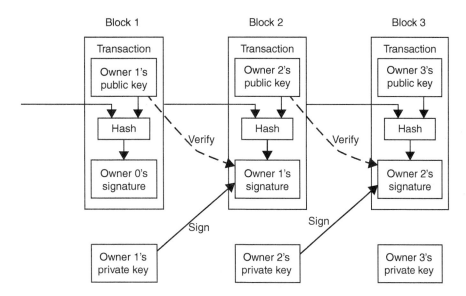

Figure 26.3: The foundation of Bitcoin.

Our initial discussion focuses on the paper of Nakamoto, [Nak08], the bitcoin pioneer, which starts with the diagram in Figure 26.3.

Think of Bob as the owner of Block 2, i.e. Owner 2. He broadcasts the message or transaction that, say, he is giving Charlie, who is Owner 3, a bitcoin. Here, broadcasting means signing a hash of the proposed transaction and sending it out publicly over the network. Bob actually signs a hash of Block 2, which includes the proposed transaction, and transmits it over the entire network. The question now arises, does Bob own the bitcoin that he is giving to Charlie?

All participants on the network including Charlie have access to all of Bob's prior transactions, including the previous transaction, i.e. the one that shows that Bob received from Alice the bitcoin that Bob is now giving to Charlie. Also, Charlie can check that the hash of this previous transaction is identical to the hash signed by Bob. From this hash, Bob has also signed that he is giving the coin to Charlie.

To be rigorous, we can travel all the way back through the blocks validating the successive transactions until we come to the "end block." This may be the "Genesis block" where bitcoins were first started in 2009. Otherwise "the end" is a block containing a special "coinbase transaction." With the exception of the Genesis block, every block of transactions in the blockchain starts with a special coinbase transaction. This is the transaction that rewards the miner who validated this block of transactions (more on this and mining later). The coinbase transaction has a null hash pointer to indicate it does not redeem a previous output since it is minting new bitcoins and not spending existing coins. The reward for the miner in 2016 was around 25 bitcoins.

26.5   The Append-Only Network, Identities, Timestamp, Definition of a Bitcoin

We want to ensure that the framework allows data to form a block which is then appended to the blockchain, but *prevents previous data from being altered without being detected.* Let us suppose that Eve, an intruder, alters data in a previous block, say block n. The existing hash in block $n + 1$, which is a hash of the entire block n, will not match up. This is because the hash is collision-resistant, i.e. the altered content, when hashed, will not be equal to the hash of the unaltered (previous) content already in block $n + 1$. So Eve has to change the contents of that new block, block $n + 1$. But then, the hash of that block will not match the hash of the unaltered block that is already in block $n + 2$. Eve can keep on doing this, but the strategy will fail at the block at the very end so long as the hash pointer is stored where Eve does not have access to it.

The earlier discussion tells us how a given bitcoin gets transferred along the blockchain. This explains why Nakamoto states in [Nak08, Section 2] that, *"We define an electronic coin as a chain of digital signatures."*

We call them Alice, Bob, and Charlie, but each participant in a network is anonymous. Their address is just a hash of their public key. A participant may have several public keys in order to increase their mining power discussed later or for other reasons.

Bitcoin also has a timestamping service to which clients send documents to timestamp. Initially, when the server received a document, it signed the document with the current time and a pointer to the previous document and issued a certificate with this information. The timestamps show that at least a piece of data was in existence at a given time. When transactions are linked together in a block, the timestamp shows the relative time ordering of transactions in a tamper-resistant way.

26.6   The Bitcoin Blockchain and Merkle Roots

As mentioned in Section 26.4, related transactions are collected into a block. We can think of a block as being a page of the ledger that is the blockchain. The blockchain combines two different hash-based data structures. The first is a hash chain of blocks. Each block has a block header, a hash pointer to data, and a hash pointer to the previous block. The second data structure is a binary tree of the transactions in the block itself. So the second data structure is internal to the given block.

We start with a block B in the blockchain. Within B we have a number of "sub-blocks" of data in B such as transactions. These sub-blocks are the leaves of the tree. The sub-blocks are ordered in some fashion such as chronological ordering. They are grouped into pairs. For each pair, we construct a data structure that has two pointers, one to each of these two blocks. Such data structures make the next level up the tree. Then, for each pair, we create a new data structure containing the hash of each. This is continued until we reach a single block, the Merkle root of the tree. (If the number of sub-blocks is odd, we can insert a copy of the last sub-block with itself.)

Now, starting with the root, we can travel down to any data block at the bottom and check it, analogous to the situation for the blockchain.

The tree is also useful in other ways. For any sub-block in our set, we can prove membership by simply showing the path from the root to it.

To prove non-membership of a sub-block Z, we find paths from the root to an item that would be just before Z and one that would be just after Z. If these two items are consecutive in the tree, then we conclude that Z is not included in the tree.

Note that we can check membership in about $\log n$ steps, where n is the number of nodes in the Merkle tree.

26.7   Mining, Proof-of-Work, Consensus

In a normal bank, cheating, such as double spending, is taken care of by the central authority in the bank. In Bitcoin, where there are no identities, save for public keys, the situation is different. Basic questions include the following:

1. Who maintains the ledger?

2. Who decides which transactions are valid?

3. How are bitcoins created?

In bitcoin, consensus is reached on a block-by-block basis. By way of answering the questions above, we list the steps outlined by Nakamoto for running the Bitcoin peer-to-peer network, which are as follows (Bitcoin Whitepaper [Nak08]):

1. New transactions are broadcast to all nodes/computers in the network.

2. Each node collects new transactions into a block.

3. Each node works on finding a difficult *proof-of-work* for its block.

4. When a node finds a proof-of-work, it broadcasts the block to all nodes.

5. Nodes accept the block only if all transactions in it are valid and the bitcoins involved are not already spent.

6. Nodes express their acceptance of the block by working on creating the next block in the chain, using the accepted block as the previous block.

Note that there may be some valid outstanding transaction that was "left out," i.e. did not get included in the approved block. This is not a problem as it can be put into the next block or subsequent blocks. It can get into the next block.

Next we have to talk about *proof-of-work*. It starts with a "hash puzzle," requiring a node to find a particular number, the "nonce." The process is called **mining**. It is carried out by nodes called **miners** who have specially equipped computers. The **block header** of each block consists of a number of items, including the Merkle root (i.e. all of the transactions in the block hashed together), the time, and the hash of the previous block. By a hash of a block we mean the hash of the block header. A miner appends a 32-bit number, call it x, to the miner's block header, and hashes the resulting input in the hopes that the "hash puzzle" is solved, i.e. that the hash value will be below a pre-assigned target. The miners vary x. In approximately 10 minutes some miner solves the puzzle by finding an x such that the hash value is less than or equal to the target. The lower the target number, the more zeros will be needed in the front of the number and the more difficult the "hash puzzle."

Each miner has the same target. It is adjusted every 2016 blocks, i.e. approximately every 2 weeks so that a new bitcoin is mined every 10 minutes on average. The successful miner is the one who is first at solving the puzzle. The miner receives a bitcoin reward and a transaction fee. The reward is cut in half every four years, limiting the total supply of bitcoins to 21 million. The winning miner broadcasts the block to all nodes and the winning value of x, which can then be checked by all other nodes. Then, subject to step 5 above, the other nodes and miners accept the block and work on the next block.

Cryptojacking

As an aside, while considering mining, we mention a solution by *BlackBerry* and *Intel* for the problem of cryptojacking. **Cryptojacking** is malware that infects a computer for the purpose of using the computer's resources for the mining of cryptocurrencies. See "BlackBerry partners with Intel to detect cryptojacking malware" by Vigliarolo, [Vig20]. Vigliarolo notes that "Coin mining malware can slow down infected machines, increase electricity costs, and damage hardware, so while it may not be out to steal data it can still be just as damaging." The advantage of using the solution from *BlackBerry* and

Intel is that it is hardware-based security that has "virtually no processor impact" on Windows 10 Systems that use their solution.

26.8 Thwarting Double Spending

Occasionally, a fork will appear in a blockchain. This can happen, for example, if two miners discover a winning nonce and validate a block almost simultaneously. Some nodes will update their blockchain one way and others update their blockchain in the opposite way. The rule is that, if a fork occurs, the nodes keep an eye on both forks, with the understanding that miners work on the longest fork. If fork B becomes longer, then the miners working on fork A switch to working on fork B. Still-pending transactions in A will still be pending for the miners working on fork B and all valid transactions will eventually be validated. No matter what the outcome, the process ensures that the blockchain has an agreed-upon ordering of the blocks.

For double spending, it may be that Alice tries to double spend by awarding the same bitcoin in her possession to both Bob and Charlie. She can try to validate a new block that includes both transactions. Even with a small percentage of the computing power, she might succeed in solving the proof-of-work hash puzzle. But then (see step 5 in Section 26.7) the double spending will be seen immediately by the other nodes.

But what if Alice=Bob, i.e. what if Alice tries to spend a coin with Charlie which she is also spending with herself. (It is easy for Alice to assume two or more identities in the network.)

Alice's strategy (Alice is the attacker and Charlie is the receiver) is to wait until Charlie accepts the bitcoin. Charlie's strategy is that, when Alice sends him the bitcoin, he should not try to verify the transaction alone. Instead, he should broadcast the possible transaction to the entire network and ask for help to determine whether the transaction is legitimate. This happens only after the transaction has been confirmed z times, with $z \geq 6$, by blocks in the longest existing chain of blocks, i.e., after at least 6 blocks have been added to the block chain after the block in which the transaction is included. Then Charlie accepts the infocoin. (Nakamoto in [Nak08, Section 11] suggests also that Charlie should generate a new key pair and only give the public key to Alice shortly before signing. The idea is that "This prevents the sender from preparing a chain of blocks ahead of time by working on it continuously ..." until the sender (i.e. Alice) gets ahead and then executes the transaction.)

Once Charlie accepts the bitcoin, Alice will try to fork the chain before the transaction with Charlie, adding a block which includes a transaction in which she pays herself. Now the fun starts. Miners are working on the longer fork and Alice is already at least z blocks behind the longer fork, let us call it fork C.

Nakamoto mathematically models this as follows. He assumes that Alice has a probability q of constructing the next block and that the corresponding probability for an honest node is p where $p + q = 1$. This set-up is related to the famous "gambler's ruin" problem going back to Pascal. In that problem, the hypothesis is that the gambler has a probability q of winning in a given round and the casino has a probability $p = 1 - q$. The outcomes of the rounds are independent.

For each round, the gambler gets \$1 for a win and the casino gets \$1 if he loses. The question to be decided is whether the gambler becomes rich by getting ahead at any stage by \$$N$, where N is an arbitrarily large positive integer, or whether he gets ruined from the fact that his initial gambling money is lost before he gets ahead by N.

The answer is that if $q \leq 0.5$ then the gambler will inevitably get ruined first. If $q > 0.5$ there is a positive probability that the gambler will never get ruined but, instead, will become arbitrarily rich.

We model the bitcoin situation at hand by thinking of Alice as the gambler. Each new block gets created by Alice with probability q. We assume that $q < p$. Nakamoto models the situation by a continuous probability distribution, i.e. a Poisson distribution. His conclusion then is that the probability of Alice catching up to the honest nodes in N trials goes to zero as N gets large. For an excellent discussion of the Poisson distribution we refer to the MIT notes of Dr. Rota's course by John Guidi, [Rot98].

Here we sketch a much more elementary approach fitting in with Chapter 10 where we mention Chebyshev's inequality. In N trials, the average number of wins by the honest nodes is Np, and for Alice we have Nq wins. Thus, after N independent trials, on average Alice is behind by $\mu = Np - Nq = N(p - q)$ in addition to the z that she was behind originally. The variance V is Npq. The Chebyshev inequality says that $\Pr[|X - \mu| \geq a] \leq \frac{\text{variance}X}{a^2}$. In this case, we have that the probability that Eve catches up, which is the left side with $a = z + N(p - q)$, is at most $\frac{Npq}{z+N(p-q)^2}$ which goes to zero in the limit as N, z get large.

Note that the argument above can be replaced by more powerful statistical bounds to show that Alice's probability of catching up in N trials goes to zero much faster as N gets large.

The above gives an outline of blockchains and Bitcoin. For reasons of space we have not discussed the programming language that goes along with Bitcoin, the situation when several bitcoins or portions of a bitcoin are exchanged with an outside merchant and several other topics. For further details, we refer the reader to *Bitcoin and Cryptocurrency Technologies* by Narayanan et al., [NBF+16], and to other discussions of Bitcoin.

Chapter 27

IoT, The Internet of Things

Goals, Discussion The *Internet of Things, IoT*, encompasses any object or device that is connected to the Internet. The Internet of Things is experiencing an explosion of growth, with a "smart" prefix being added to almost anything and everything. Consumer devices can be equipped with small radios that enables wireless communication with the Internet. Then all you need is some imagination to decide what information to collect from, or to transmit to that object.

What advantages will there be in that object being "smart"? Sensors can be added for the collection of data. Types of sensors include ambient environment phenomena such as light intensity, temperature, humidity, pressure, etc. GPS to identify device location, accelerometer/gyroscope to measure speed/angular velocity to name a few. As a result, there are smart phones, smart wearables (such as smart watches), smart light bulbs, smart speakers, smart homes, self-driving cars, precision agriculture connected farm tractors, and smart cities.

Along with this explosion of new IoT devices comes *privacy and security concerns!* Privacy concerns include: Who has access to the information your smart device is collecting? Are your conversations being recorded and transmitted elsewhere? Security concerns include confidentiality, integrity, and availability. Many IoT applications are mission critical in nature; therefore, data security is of utmost importance to such applications.

Cryptography, Information Theory, and Error-Correction: A Handbook for the 21st Century, Second Edition.
Aiden A. Bruen, Mario A. Forcinito, and James M. McQuillan.
© 2021 John Wiley & Sons, Inc. Published 2021 by John Wiley & Sons, Inc.

Since IoT devices tend to be constrained in computational speed and power, mechanisms designed for traditional Internet devices may not be applicable/appropriate.

New, Noteworthy   We discuss privacy and security concerns of the Internet of Things, the scope and vastness of different Internet of Things devices, and give tips for the disposal of such devices.

27.1   Introduction

How many "smart" devices have you purchased recently? Do you have a smart watch, or smart speakers, or smart light bulbs? Does your smart alarm clock wake you up earlier than normal if your commute time might be longer because of heavy traffic?

We have gone from using basic computers to transmit information over the Internet to using smart phones, wearables such as smart watches, smart light bulbs, speakers, TVs and larger appliances, smart homes, smart cars, and smart cities. Consumer devices like Amazon's Alexa [Ama19] and HomeKit [App19] are widely adopted technologies.

The *Internet of Things, IoT*, refers to the collection of devices, in particular those that can act over the physical world, that are connected to the Internet. The IoT is experiencing an explosion of growth, with an estimated "installed base" of 30 billion devices by 2020 growing to 75 billion by the year 2025 [Dep19].

The exponential growth on the variety and quantity of "smart" (and connected) devices in the last few years is due to the convergence of several technologies that were developed in the second half of the twentieth century, analog/digital converters, programmable logic controller (PLC), embedded operating systems (EOS), database technology, and networking protocols.

Researchers at Microsoft, Carnegie Mellon University, Inria, and MIT have developed a prototype privacy and security product label for IoT devices, [PPFH20]. A product label would provide information about an IoT device that one could read before purchasing a product in an analogous way to what nutrition labels do for food. The title of [Tka20], "IoT labels will help consumers figure out which devices are spying on them" describes a possible benefit of having product labels on IoT devices.

27.2   Analog to Digital (A/D) Converters

Given that in the physical world the relevant parameters and variables are continuous (or analog) and computers work only with digital information, a key functionality to allow computers to get information about the physical world, and to affect it, is the ability to convert, back and forth, between an analog signal and a digital one. It is worth to remark here the pioneering work by Nyquist [Nyq28], although it was Shannon [Sha49a] who formalized the mathematical proof.

Analog to digital (A/D) converters sample the amplitude of the analog signal at discrete intervals, converting them into digital values. The sampled signal is typically a variable voltage resulting from the conversion of a physical variable by the sensor. The resolution of an A/D converter (the number of discrete values it can produce over a range of analog values) is expressed by the number of bits, i.e. a 4-bit converter will produce 16 different binary values over the allowed input range of the signal. To give an idea of the order of magnitude, the standard resolution for CDs and MP3s is 16 bits.

Sampling is the process of reading the amplitude values of the analog signal at discrete (and constant) time intervals and it governs the maximum frequency of the signal that can be digitalized. We refer to Chapter 13 of this book for the full mathematical details of the Whittaker–Shannon sampling theorem. Sampling rates are specified in samples/s.

With the advent of the transistor and the advances in miniaturization of electronic components, analog to digital (and digital to analog) converters became faster, efficient, and more ubiquitous.

27.3 Programmable Logic Controller

A PLC is a type of computer which has been ruggedly constructed and adapted for the control of processes. Of widespread use in commercial and industrial applications such as assembly lines, chemical processing plants, pipelines, utilities, or robotic tools, these devices are specially adapted for any activity that requires high reliability control, ease of programming, and process fault diagnostics.

The PLC's input circuitry converts the signals provided by the various switches and sensors into logic signals that can be processed by the CPU that evaluates the status of inputs, outputs, and other variables according to a predetermine algorithm. The CPU sends the signals through the PLC output circuits that are in turn connected to actuators, the inputs of other PLCs, or logging facilities.

PLCs and microcontrollers are both used in IoT applications. PLCs are typically used in Industrial Control Systems (ICSs), as they are required to be less programmer heavy and reliable and because they are subjected to rigorous industrial environments. PLCs are of robust design against extreme temperatures, humidity, vibration, and electrical disturbances. Newer applications for consumer devices are all based on microcontrollers (e.g. Arduino).

27.4   Embedded Operating Systems

An embedded operating system, or embedded system is a type of operating system that is coded into a piece of hardware or a device. This system is specifically configured for the hardware, and typically runs a constant routine for configuration and operation of the device. EOS are usually used for hardware that have very little computing power, little RAM/ROM, and a slow CPU, so they tend to be very specific in their applications and scope. Because of the limitations of the hardware that uses them, EOS are designed to be lightweight and compact, setup to perform one (or just a few) tasks in a very efficient way.

EOS are also known as real-time operating systems (RTOS). They are usually written using assembly or machine language and thus very difficult to be ported from one hardware architecture (or chipset) to another.

27.5   Evolution, From SCADA to the Internet of Things

A/D converters, PLCs, and EOS are the building blocks of Supervisory Control and Data Acquisition (SCADA) systems. Nowadays, these systems constitute the control architecture of almost all critical industrial infrastructures and processes. The flow of gas and oil through pipes, the processing and distribution of water, the management of the electricity grid, the operation of chemical plants, and the signaling network for railways are all managed and supervised through networked data communications and graphical user interfaces that use computers for high-level processing of information, as well as PLCs to interface with the process plant or machinery. Only a few years ago the terms "process control" and "SCADA" were unknown outside a niche area in industry. Today, securing SCADA systems is a key issue for infrastructure protection.

Very slowly at first, but with increasing speed, SCADA-type systems started to find their way into the homes and office spaces being deployed to control lighting fixtures, sound systems, door openers, heating, ventilation, and air conditioning (HVAC), and home security systems. Concurrently with these developments, the Internet infrastructure was developing very rapidly.

The next, natural step on the evolution of automation concepts was to allow the control systems to communicate over public links through a common protocol such as the Internet Protocol (IP). This additional connectivity greatly enhances the functionality of the system by enabling the ability to have the functions that were normally reserved to the "control room" to be virtually anywhere in the world. Not only that, now the raw computing and data storage power of the whole network can be leveraged to help with the control and reporting tasks, in particular, by using powerful and widely available database query technologies. The availability of accurate geo-location information (typically through access to GPS signals) enhances the functionality of the devices and the aggregation databases.

The combination of all these technologies constitute what is known as the Internet of Things (IoT) with open endless possibilities in terms of automation. In theory, a two-way communication channel between any two connected devices can be established, in real time, at a very low cost, anywhere in the world over wired or wireless networks.

The IP provides the routing of messages between devices that need to be individually addressed. The IPv6 standard provides an addressing space of $2^{128} = 3.4 \times 10^{38}$ unique IP addresses. A special mention is due here to routers, the devices that compartmentalize (or segment) networks in such a way that only the right message gets to the right device, thus making possible the IoT. The development of fast and affordable routers made possible the wide adoption of Internet connected devices. Proper configuration of routers and their firmware is key to network security.

Being open to the Internet gives devices new dimensions in terms of capabilities; however, with the Internet being a generally hostile environment, the protection of assets against malicious attacks is a titanic task. Strong encryption and robust authentication schemes are of paramount importance.

NIST Special Publication 800-82 [SPL$^+$15] outlines concrete steps for restricting unauthorized access to ICSs giving clear instructions to industrial organizations to secure SCADA systems, and PLCs thus protecting individual components from exploitation, while maintaining functionality in the presence of adversarial attacks.

27.6 Everything is Fun and Games until Somebody Releases a Stuxnet

Stuxnet, which was discovered in 2011, was not the first computer virus capable of causing actual physical loses by damaging equipment, but it was one of the paradigms for highly sophisticated virtual weapons. Designed to penetrate a computer network, to seek and destroy the enemy's assets, it is the best-known example of an industrial grade cyber-weapon.

There has been public disclosure elsewhere [FMC11] on the technical details related to Stuxnet; to summarize here, we will only mention that the malware had the capabilities to infect a computer network and lie dormant looking for opportunities to self-replicate and spread to computers connected to specific pieces of industrial equipment. Once the right equipment was found, the malware was capable of reprogramming the PLCs with the objective of sabotaging the facility by forcing the machinery to operate outside of its design range while, at the same time, reporting false parametric information to mislead the operators. Under these conditions, mechanical parts, and the targeted machinery failed catastrophically without an apparent cause and without warning signs. The infection was very difficult to detect thanks to its ability to use several techniques designed to hide and update the malware avoiding detection.

Stuxnet was also the first example of a cyber-weapon whose existence and functioning was discovered and initially publicly disclosed by private security companies. Although it has been certainly developed by one or more state agents, the countries suspected of its creation have denied any involvement with it.

The uncovering of Stuxnet brought to the fore the realization that the Internet has become a battlefield. Several countries have already established special units to defend against cyber-attacks as well as to conduct offensive operations with the intent to inflict damage on enemy's military and civil infrastructure.[1]

In September 2018, three entrepreneurial gamers in their early 20s were each sentenced to serve a five-year period of probation, 2500 hours of community service, ordered to pay restitution in the amount of US\$ 127 000, and have voluntarily abandoned significant amounts of cryptocurrency seized during the course of the investigation.[2] This was a reduced sentence after entering a plea bargain with the FBI whereby they helped the Feds to understand the technology and to dismantle hacking networks. Their crime? Over a few months period between 2016 and 2017, they successfully infected over 100 000 computing devices, such as home Internet routers and IoT devices with malicious software that caused the devices to join the powerful botnet known as Mirai botnet, that was later used to stage Distributed Denial-of-Service (DDoS) attacks. Mirai was one of the most active botnets in 2018 and, although not as sophisticated as Stuxnet, Mirai networks scan the Internet for devices that have factory default security credential using different vectors to infect the targets. Once a new device is infected, the virus deletes all its files and hides in the memory, contacts the Command and Control center (CnC) and tries to spread itself to other devices using the Telnet port. Whenever required, the CnC will issue commands that the bots will follow to mount DDoS attacks or for any purpose that the owners of the botnet so choose. The creators of this virus published the code on hacker's forums, and many others have started botnets that use the same code base and adaptations of it, many botnets are still active. To defend against this type of

---

[1] This is in addition of the traditional role that the intelligence agencies had spying on military and industrial secrets or creating misinformation campaigns.

[2] https://www.justice.gov/usao-ak/pr/hackers-cooperation-fbi-leads-substantial-assistance-other-complex-cybercrime.

attack IT professionals and users in general must follow good practices to protect network accessible devices from exploitation by using strong credentials and keeping the devices updated with the latest security patches. Mirai is known to have exploited weak security and zero-day vulnerabilities. Analyzing network traffic for hints about the location of the CnC also is a good strategy because if the CnC is neutralized, the whole network falls down.

In October 2016, the Mirai network was used to attack a DNS server that brought down many top tier websites such as Amazon, Reddit, Netflix, Twitter, Soundcloud, Spotify, Etsy, and Github.

27.7 Securing the IoT, a Mammoth Task

From the point of view of the average user, the IoT takes the form of a multitude of small computational devices embedded in appliances and "smart-things" that collect information from sensors, perform (at least) small calculations or tasks, and exchange information with other devices across the Internet. Such devices can provide information to computers or people to help us make good decisions, save us time, or improve our lives in other ways. Goals might include saving energy, reducing waste, and saving time. At the same time, these devices can leak sensitive information or open a control channel into vital systems at user's homes or vehicles.

27.8 Privacy and Security

Along with the explosion of new IoT devices comes privacy and security concerns. They include the following.

Privacy concerns

Who has access to the information your smart device is collecting? Are your conversations being recorded and transmitted elsewhere? Other concerns are physical security, data integrity due to man-in-the-middle attacks, eavesdropping, lack of authentication, and proper access control.

Security concerns

Could someone else remotely access your smart device and affect what it does? Could they cause it to send a message that impersonates you? Could they remotely turn off your car or apply your car's breaks remotely? Could they shut off your furnace, or turn on your lights in your smart house remotely?

So far, the experience indicates that the short answer to all these questions is a resounding YES. The IoT is going through the initial phases of its widespread deployment where achieving fast connectivity and proper exchange of information is the primary goal, while security and privacy considerations, although perceived as important, are secondary. Encryption is at least a partial answer to many privacy and security concerns. Strong Authentication schemes are necessary also. A big problem, however, is that many of the IoT devices are small and/or portable with constrained resources. Many have extremely limited battery life. Any extra computational overhead might drain the batteries and make the devices useless. Therefore, energy efficient encryption and key exchange algorithms would be ideal for many of the IoT devices.

The National Institute of Standards and Technology (NIST) is working on this issue. As of late 2019, NIST is in the process of selecting authenticated encryption and hashing schemes for constrained environments for use in the IoT, sensor networks and cyber physical systems. They describe the project at [NIS19d], provide a status report from the first round of the selection process at [TMcc+19], and provide a list of the Round 2 Candidates at [NIS19e]. Of the 56 Round 1 candidates, 32 were selected to be evaluated in Round 2. They say,

> The National Institute of Standards and Technology (NIST) has initiated the Lightweight Cryptography (LWC) standardization process to solicit, evaluate, and standardize lightweight cryptographic algorithms that are suitable to be used in constrained environments (e.g., radio frequency identification, sensor networks) where the performance of current NIST cryptographic standards is not acceptable. The initial focus is on symmetric cryptography, and one or more authenticated encryption and hashing schemes are expected to be selected through a public, competition-like process.

As in many other applications, the degree of security of the IoT will be determined in part by the trade-off between how much "inconvenience" the users are willing to accept versus the consequences of suffering an intrusion. Many of the horror stories about data breaches published in the specialized magazines have at the root of it some actor that took a shortcut or was sloppy handling the security procedure.[3]

The open nature of the new products development process lends itself to a proliferation of badly designed, from the security point of view, systems. Typically, the product

---

[3] Notoriously, many intrusions have occurred because hard-coded or easy to guess passwords used by programmers during the development process made it to the final versions of the firmware.

development process starts with a useful device, whose design has been optimized from the mechanical and electrical point of view, to which Internet connectivity is added. This means that a protocol for data exchange has to be included in the design by people specialized in the physical aspects of the application that may lack the knowledge or the resources to understand the fine points of data security. A telling anecdote by one of the authors goes to show this point: "few years ago on an Oil Show I was talking to a vendor of field equipment designed to control flow from oil wells remotely through a radio-link. When asked about the potential for third parties to snoop on the data, the vendors replied categorically, 'Oh no, that is impossible! We use a proprietary way to encode the data that nobody would guess'." The pressure to get to market first put even big companies with access to the right resources on a position in which major design decisions are taken based on faulty assumptions about the capabilities and determination of hackers.

Examples of Protocols Commonly Used for Industrial Control Systems (ICS)
In the earlier stages of its development, a variety of SCADA/ICS communication protocols proliferate as a consequence of the incentive different vendors had to try to exclude equipment from other vendors in their applications. Thus, many protocols started as "proprietary." All the dominant companies such as Siemens, Honeywell, Toshiba, Allen-Bradley, Mitsubishi, GE, Schneider Electric, and Rockwell Automation had one or more protocols attached to their names.

Several protocols evolved from these to include interoperability as the networks grew larger and the end users demand the functionality. We are going to mention here a few protocols that have become of widespread use in industrial applications.

The **Modbus Protocol** was the first protocol to be widely accepted standard. Modbus is built around messages that have the same structure regardless the physical interface over which they are transmitted. The structure of a modbus message over RS-232 is the same as for a message sent over TCP/IP, characteristic that gave this protocol a remarkable long lifetime (it was introduced in 1979). Modbus messages are always started by a master in the network and directed to a slave node. Every other node in the network just ignores the packet if the address header does not include it. Modbus protocol is very flexible yet easy to implement. Micro-controllers PLCs and intelligent devices have interfaces for Modbus, and there are extensions modules of Modbus for wireless communications.

Distributed Network Protocol (DNP3) is also a widely used, open communications protocol based on an object model, which reduces the bit mapping of data traditionally needed by other protocols. It is used in SCADA and remote monitoring systems and was introduced in 1993 as a readily available solution for critical infrastructure monitoring and remote control. Because of its open nature, any vendor can develop equipment that is compatible with any other vendor's equipment using DNP3. This protocol is based on an implementation of IEC 60870-5 standard introduced by Westronic Inc. (now GE-Harris Canada), while the standard was still under development. DNP3 was adopted as IEEE Standard 1815-2010, and secure authentication features were added to the protocol which make it applicable for smart grid application where several networks share the same TCP/IP infrastructure.

The **CANbus** protocol was developed by Robert Bosch and has been widely adopted by the automotive and aerospace industries as a building block for vehicular diagnostic and control systems. CANbus or Controller Area Network serial bus was designed to connect individual systems and sensors over a single or dual wire to replace multi-wire looms of cables with the consequential savings in cost and weight brought by the elimination of miles of cable. CANbus is a low-level protocol and has no built-in security or authentication scheme, making it vulnerable to man-in-the-middle attacks.

Given that there is a large number of hardware vendors, many of whom have developed their own communication and networking protocols, it is useful to standardize the functionality of the necessary parts of a network into a reference model. Because of its wide acceptance within the realm of industrial applications, we will briefly present here the seven layers Open System Interconnection reference model, OSI Model for short. It is a conceptual abstraction of the necessary elements to construct and understand networks, and it was published in 1984 by the International Organization for Standardization (ISO). This model is similar to the five-layer TCP/IP logical model created by the DoD, presented elsewhere in this book.

7. **Application layer** or top layer is the layer that the end user sees or interacts with. Allows applications to request network services.

6. **Presentation layer** translate and formats data so that systems that use different data formats can exchange information and handles syntax processing and encryption/decryption needed by the Application layer.

5. **Session layer** establishes sessions between network applications, that is, it manages the sequence and flow of events that initiate and remove network connections and must provide support to multiple types of dynamically created connections.

4. **Transport layer** provides for reliable delivery of packets guaranteeing error correction and error-free connection between hosts.

3. **Network layer** is where the routing protocols act to find the shortest and time-efficient way to route packets between the sender and the receiver to perform routing protocols, switching, error detection, and addressing techniques. The main function of this layer is to analyze routing data inside each frame and determine if the data has reached its final destination or not. When data reaches the final destination, it formats the data into packets delivered to the Transport layer.

2. **Data link layer** is where bits are combined into frames. The important functions of error detection (not correction) and managing physical addressing schemes (such as MAC addresses) is performed at this level.

1. **Physical layer** is where the actual bits are exchanged between devices, highly dependent on the underlying hardware making the communicating devices and the network. Hub repeaters and ethernet cables are the basic devices that constitute this layer.

A correspondence between the OSI models and the TCP/IP layer model can be established by lumping together the application, the presentation, and the session layers onto what is known as the application layer for the TCP/IP protocol. Transport and network layers map to the homonomous layers in TCP/IP, whereas the data link and the physical layers map onto the data link layer of TCP/IP.

Communication Protocols for IoT As in the case of industrial systems, there are almost as many communications protocols as applications of IoT technologies. Each protocol seems to have been developed as the best fit for a particular purpose. An exhaustive inventory of all the protocols, their characteristics, advantages, and drawbacks will take an entire volume. For a current and more complete catalogue of protocols, the interested reader is encouraged to consult the myriad of freely available references that an Internet search of the term "IoT protocols" will provide. A short description of the most widely used ones is given below as examples of their characteristics.

Protocols can be classified, depending on the range or distance between nodes as Low Power Wide Area Networks (LPWAN) or Short Range Networks. Two examples of LPWANs protocols are SigFox and Cellular.

SigFox is designed for communication of small amounts of data, 10-1000 bits/s, over ranges of up to 50 km. It uses low-power wireless and Ultra Narrow Band technology and is used to provide communication to a diverse range of low-energy sensors and machine-to-machine applications.

Cellular technology is better suited for applications where high data transmission rates over long distances are needed as it can take advantage of the infrastructure already in place for GSM, 3G, 4G (and 5G) cellular communication. This also affords a high degree of connectivity to the Internet, which makes it ideal for the IoT. The main drawback is that the cellular modems have a relatively high power consumption. On the other hand, cellular communication protocol can be used for applications that involve mobile devices.

Short Range Networks

6loWPAN is a standard protocol created by the Internet Engineering Task Force (IETF) with the finality of enabling IPv6 packets to be carried on top of low-power wireless networks (specifically IEEE 802.15.4). It utilizes IPv6, meaning that it can address 2^{128} unique devices communicating over low power. The hierarchical nature of the addressing gives it the flexibility to use different address lengths. It is of low cost, low bandwidth, and low power consumption and supports mesh and star topologies.

ZigBee alliance created an alternative to 6loWPAN also based on the IEEE 802.15.4 physical layer. The ZigBee protocol is suited for low consumption (30 mA peak current), short range (up to 100 m), and high speed (250 kbps) high-level communication. It uses AES for security, similarly to 6loWPAN.

Z-Wave is a low-power (2.5 mA peak current), low-range (up to 30 m indoors, 100 m outdoors) radio frequency communication protocol. It is primarily used for home automation applications featuring data throughput rates of up to 40 kbps. It builds on top of a Wireless Personal Area Network (WPAN) and uses AES-128 encryption for security. Z-Wave support mesh network topology.

BLE Bluetooth Low Energy designed by the Bluetooth Special Interest Group (Bluetooth SIG) and marketed as Bluetooth Smart, is a protocol optimized for short-range, low-bandwidth, and low-latency IoT applications. The advantages of BLE classic Bluetooth. BLE has low power consumption (0.5 W) and base its security on a streamed version of AES-128. It operates in the same band that Bluetooth operates although with a different set of channels. IoT applications of this protocol are related to health care and fitness, automotive, and wearables.

RFID consists of a reader device and small radio frequency transponders (called RF tags) that store static information. There are tags that work with high frequency and are battery powered (active tags) and tags that use the power radiated by the reader to transmit information at lower frequencies (passive tags). The information in the tag has to be programmed and is of a static nature. Tags have a characteristic distance at which the information can be read. They are typically used for inventory control and smart shopping.

Near Field Communication (NFC) is a set of protocols designed to enable data transmission among devices brought in close proximity or contact. It is in many aspects similar to RFID but the data in the "tag" is rewritable and allows two-way communications. Mobile phones use this protocol extensively for many applications such as contact-less payments and access. The range of communication is very short, from a few centimeters to a meter, and it uses RSA/AES encryption for security.

Chapter 28

In the Cloud

Goals, Discussion

Mathematicians often have their heads "in the clouds," contemplating their next big conjecture or theorem. In this chapter, we are interested in *cloud storage* and *cloud computing*. Here, data is stored "in the cloud." Cloud computing is increasingly being used because:

1. Your data is always available – anytime, anywhere, and from any device.

2. Applications that are important and useful are provided.

According to Gartner, "The worldwide public cloud services market is forecast to grow 17% in 2020 to total $266.4 billion, up from $227.8 billion in 2019...," [Gar19]. In 2020 during the COVID-19 pandemic, Macy Bayern at TechRepublic wrote an article entitled, "91% of IT leaders are shifting cloud strategy to accommodate the new normal," [Bay20], Bayern noted that "More than half (56%) of [IT leaders] said they expect to increase their cloud spending."

In Section 28.2, we provide some background information on distributed computing. (Distributed computing is also very important for blockchains, Chapter 26.) In Section 28.3, we discuss *Copyset Replication*, which is of extreme importance for cloud

Cryptography, Information Theory, and Error-Correction: A Handbook for the 21st Century, Second Edition.
Aiden A. Bruen, Mario A. Forcinito, and James M. McQuillan.
© 2021 John Wiley & Sons, Inc. Published 2021 by John Wiley & Sons, Inc.

storage providers. Copyset Replication helps them to ensure that we can always access our data (24 hours a day, 7 days a week), i.e. Copyset Replication helps ensure the *availability* of our data. In Section 28.4, we consider *homomorphic encryption*, which, if developed further, would allow for an increased use of cloud computing while maintaining privacy for users' data. Section 28.5 gives an overview of the important area of cybersecurity.

New, Noteworthy

When computers and networks are used, faults occur. A file being stored or transmitted might become corrupted. A computer or a network device might fail. However, no one wants to lose any data that they have. We want it to be accessible all the time. There was a major breakthrough in cloud computing in 2013 regarding the availability of data stored in the cloud based on the replication of data.

Having three replicas of each chunk of data results in most people's data being accessible almost all of the time. However, if a cloud provider has a large-scale correlated failure, such as a cluster power outage, the probability that **someone's data would be lost** might have been as much as **99.99%** in 2013. Cidon et al., [CRS$^+$13], showed that it is possible to dramatically reduce this probability. They gave a new algorithm that cloud providers can use whey they decide **which** nodes might be used to store the three replicas of a particular chunk.

It turns out that a purely random strategy is not always the best approach! Cidon et al. [CRS$^+$13] show that "... Copyset Replication provides a near optimal solution to [the] problem." They "... also show that this problem has been partly explored in a different context in the field of combinatorial design theory." This gives another application of combinatorial designs. Please see Chapters 18, 20, 23, and 24, including Section 18.7, for more on combinatorial designs.

We provide details of Copyset Replication in Section 28.3. First, we provide some background material in Sections 28.1 and 28.2.

Section 28.4 gives a discussion of homomorphic encryption, which is the subject of much current research because of the privacy benefits it could yield for cloud computing applications.

We conclude this chapter with a discussion about cybersecurity in Section 28.5. Cybersecurity is of fundamental importance to governments and companies. Many universities now have entire degrees in cybersecurity.

28.1 Introduction

Cloud computing is now a multibillion dollar business. Its popularity has exploded because

1. The data you have in the cloud is always available – anytime, anywhere, and from any device.

2. Important and useful applications are provided.

Cloud storage and computing companies provide large amounts of storage and impressive applications that are always (or almost always) accessible.

If you store some files in the cloud, you can access them from home, school, work, or anywhere in the world, as long as you have access to the Internet. You may be able to access them from multiple devices, such as your smartphone, tablet, laptop, or desktop computer via dedicated apps or perhaps a web browser on those devices. Allowing users to access their files and applications seamlessly from the point where they last left off, possibly while using a different device, makes cloud computing very attractive.

The files you store in the cloud could include photos from your photo library, essays, assignments, or other files for school, and documents or spreadsheets for work. Devices as simple as a tablet or a smartphone might be sufficient to access the data and some of the services. Some (cloud) applications are accessible without having to first download much or perhaps any additional code or data to your device.

Cloud providers have the advantage that they can afford to have many expensive machines with powerful software. Alternatively, they can have many "regular" machines that collectively provide powerful software that an individual could not hope to run on their own personal machines. They can do many computations in parallel so as to perform certain tasks extremely quickly. They can remember what you have done in the past so ask to predict what you might do in the future, and get you to your goal(s) faster.

You might recall when IBM's Watson computer won on Jeopardy back in 2013. Watson had 10 racks of 10 Power 750 servers (see [Bes13], for example). IBM made heavy use of Watson's ability to do many tasks in parallel.

Cloud storage is an important part of cloud computing. Microsoft OneDrive, Google Drive, Apple iCloud Drive, and Dropbox are just some of the cloud storage providers. The industry standard for cloud storage providers is to store three replicas of each chunk of data. This is for protection against faults. Consider some data that you have stored in the cloud, such as a favorite photo from your photo library or an important essay or document for school or work. Suppose that you try to access that file (that is stored in the cloud). What happens if that file becomes corrupted? Or, what happens if a node storing your data has a failure? You could imagine someone being at least a little, if not extremely upset if that important photo, document, etc. was not available!

With three replicas of each chunk of data, if there is a problem with one replica (or the node containing that replica), then the cloud provider immediately goes to one of the other two replicas and gives you access to it. The cloud provider's goal is do this in a *transparent* way that *masks the failure*, i.e. they want to give you access to one of the other replicas almost immediately and without you ever knowing that there was a problem! This happens regularly.

In Section 28.3, we provide details of Copyset Replication, a new algorithm due to Cidon et al. [CRS+13] that cloud providers can use whey they decide **which** nodes might be used to store the multiple replicas of a particular chunk.

28.2   Distributed Systems

In a distributed system, there can be a wide variety of different types of computational devices, networks, operating systems, programming languages, and applications. The various components communicate and coordinate their actions by passing messages. The main purpose of distributed systems is the sharing of resources. The Internet is an example of a distributed system.

In the early days of distributed systems, a main goal might have been something simple like allowing a dozen computers to share a printer. Early distributed systems were very homogeneous, with companies trying to use identical computers, operating systems, and applications so that it was easier for maintenance, communication, and cooperation.

Today, distributed systems are extremely heterogeneous, with a wide variety of computers and other devices, operating systems, programming languages, and applications. People have desktops, laptops, tablets, smart phones, smart watches, and IoT devices. Information is available from different countries via the Internet. Cloud computing has changed the way we store and access photos, and other applications.

Three important characteristics that distributed systems have are the concurrency of components, the lack of a global clock, and the possible independent failures of components of a system. For details on these, please see a wonderful book by Coulouris et al. *Distributed Systems: Concepts and Design*, fifth edition, [CDKB11], which we highly recommend! We very briefly discuss failures here.

When computers and networks are used, faults occur. When a message is sent, it might never arrive at its destination, in which case an *omission failure* has occurred, or, much worse, the message might become corrupted in transit so that the message that arrives is different from the message that was sent. The latter situation is an example of an *arbitrary failure*.

Failures that have been detected can often be *masked*, i.e. they can be hidden or made less severe. This can often be done without the users knowing that the failure occurred. For example if a corrupt message arrives, it can be dropped (a less severe type of error). If a message does not arrive, the message can be resent. If a file becomes corrupt, a replica of the file can be used in its place. (Checksums are often used to detect arbitrary failures in which data has become corrupted.)

Cloud computing providers try to mask failures. As mentioned in Section 28.1, with three replicas of each chunk of data, if there is a problem with one replica (or the node containing that replica), then the cloud provider immediately goes to one of the other two replicas and gives you access to it. The cloud provider's goal is do this in a *transparent* way that *masks the failure*, i.e. they want to give you access to one of the other replicas without you ever knowing that there was a problem. If at all possible, problems should be corrected without the clients knowing that there was a problem in the first place.

It is hard to go a day without hearing about security issues with distributed systems. There are security concerns, privacy concerns, and availability concerns. We rely on cloud storage and cloud computing providers to ensure that our data and applications are always available.

28.3 Cloud Storage – Availability and Copyset Replication

In this section, we consider the availability of data in the cloud. Cidon's work from his PhD thesis on "Data Durability in Cloud Storage Systems," [Cid14], 2014, and Cidon et al.'s USENIX ATC '13 paper, [CRS+13], will be key in the section. As noted in Section 28.1, there has been a dramatic rise in cloud storage and cloud computing in recent years. Individuals and businesses might have various types of files [stored] "in the cloud," including word processing documents, spreadsheets, digital photos, email messages, etc. Students in elementary school through high school, College, or university might use Microsoft OneDrive or Google Drive, for example so as to work on their homework and assignments from school and from home, via their smart phones, Chromebooks, iPads, desktops, or other such devices.

Some terminology and definitions relating to cloud computing and storage are in order. A company might have a *cluster* of *nodes* that they can use for storing data. We use N to denote the number of nodes in a cluster. The value of N might be as high as 5000 or 10 000 nodes. Some of the nodes are put in the same *rack*. It is more efficient for two nodes in the same rack to communicate with each other than it is for two nodes in different racks to exchange messages.

Systems partition their data into *chunks*. Since a node can fail, it is important to store multiple replicas of each chunk in different nodes, so that if one node fails or becomes unavailable, or if an entire rack fails, then there is no loss of availability. Companies sometimes insist that some or perhaps all of the different replicas of a chunk are stored in nodes that are in different racks. As noted in Section 28.2, the cloud provider will try to mask (hide) failures whenever possible. If one node, X say, becomes unavailable, the cloud provider will go to other the nodes that contain replicas of the chunks in X. This is usually done without the user even realizing that a failure occurred – a successful masking of the failure.

The *replication factor*, R, is the number of replicas that are made of each chunk. The *primary replica* is the first copy of a chunk that is stored in some node. The other copies of the same chunk that are stored are *secondary replicas*.

Question 28.1 *Suppose that a cloud storage provider has N nodes. What value should be used for the replication factor R?*

The industry standard is to have three replicas of each chunk of data, i.e. $R = 3$. That way, if one node, X say, goes down, there are still $R - 1 = 2$ replicas of each of X's chunks somewhere among the remaining $N - 1$ nodes. Of course, it is possible for multiple nodes to go down at roughly the same time. The hope is that at least one replica of each chunk is available at all times. Having $R = 3$ replicas of each chunk (instead of a smaller value) increases the chances of this. But, there is **no guarantee** that a particular chunk of data will always be available. If R was bigger than 3, then more nodes would be required to store the extra copies of each chunk of data, which would significantly increase the cost of providing the storage service. Therefore, most companies opt for $R = 3$ for the replication factor.

Question 28.2 *Suppose that a cloud storage provider has a large-scale correlated failure such as a power outage in the cluster. What impact might this have?*

Cidon et al. [CRS+13] focuses on the fact that a replication factor of 3 does not mean that data will not be lost. Indeed, in 2013, if many major cloud providers had a large-scale correlated failure such as a power outage for a cluster, the probability that **someone's**

data would be lost might have been as much as **99.99%**. Cidon et al. [CRS$^+$13] showed that it is possible to dramatically reduce this probability. They implemented Copyset Replication on a RAMCloud storage system and showed that it reduces the probability of data loss from 99.99% to 0.15%. Note that this is the probability of losing **some** data. They also showed that, for Facebook's Hadoop Distributed File System (HDFS) storage in 2013, Copyset Replication reduces the probability of data loss from 22.8% to 0.78%. (Facebook was ahead of most cloud providers in this regard in 2013.) The key to this lies in the answer to Question 28.3:

Question 28.3 *Suppose that a cloud storage provider has N nodes, and it uses a replication factor of R. Which nodes should it pick for storing the R replicas of a chunk of data?*

The simplest answer is provided by Algorithm 28.4, which is based on randomness.

Algorithm 28.4 (Simple random replication) *When storing R replicas of a chunk, randomly pick a node for the primary replica, randomly pick a different node (usually on a different rack) for the next replica, and continue like this until all R replicas have been assigned to different nodes.*

Unfortunately, this algorithm can result in a 99.99% probability that **someone's** data will be lost in a large-scale correlated failure such as a power outage in a cluster, as discussed above. In [CRS$^+$13], they quote Kannan Muthukkaruppan, the Tech Lead of Facebook's HBase engineering team:

> Even losing a single block of data incurs a high fixed cost, due to the overhead of locating and recovering the unavailable data. Therefore, given a fixed amount of unavailable data each year, it is much better to have fewer incidents of data loss with more data each than more incidents with less data. We would like to optimize for minimizing the probability of incurring any data loss.

This suggests that we should look for an alternative to Algorithm 28.4. Before proceeding to the alternative algorithms, we introduce several important concepts.

Definition 28.5 A *set* is a group of R distinct nodes. A *copyset* is a set that stores ALL of the replicas of SOME chunk.

The main significance of a copyset is, if all of the nodes of some copyset are down, then some chunk of data is not available, which is what Muthukkaruppan (Facebook) said they would like to avoid. We illustrate this with an example.

Example 28.6 *Suppose that a cluster has $N = 5000$ nodes $X_1, \ldots, X_{5000}$, and the replication factor is $R = 3$. If chunk A is stored in nodes X_{23}, X_{834}, and X_{4232}, then $\{X_{23}, X_{834}, X_{4232}\}$ is a copyset. If chunk B is stored in nodes X_{256}, X_{3535}, and X_{3982}, then $\{X_{256}, X_{3535}, X_{3982}\}$ is another copyset.*

Suppose that at some time T the nodes $X_{23}, X_{834}, X_{3535}, X_{4232}$, and X_{3982} are all down but X_{256} is not down. Then chunk A is not available because all the nodes in the copyset $\{X_{23}, X_{834}, X_{4232}\}$ are all down, However, chunk B is currently available because there is a node in the copyset $\{X_{256}, X_{3535}, X_{3982}\}$ that is not down, namely X_{256}.

That gives us a clear goal:

Goal 28.7 *There should always be at least one node available from each copyset. (Never have all of the nodes of a copyset down at the same time.)*

How likely is it for Goal 28.7 to be violated? We return to Algorithm 28.4. If a cluster has $N = 5000$ nodes, for example and there is a large-scale correlated failure such as a power outage, then approximately 0.5% to 1% of them will not come back up. Assuming the more conservative 0.5%, approximately 25 nodes of the 5000 will not come back up. Is there a copyset among those 25 nodes? With Algorithm 28.4, the more chunks there are, the more likely it is that there is a copyset among the 25 nodes. If there are a lot of chunks, then it is almost certain that some data is unavailable! This gives us a very unhappy answer to Question 28.2.

This is somewhat akin to winning a lottery. With some lotteries, there are sometimes one or perhaps a few winners; sometimes there are no winners. But, lotteries tend to not have a lot of winners. In particular, the odds that a particular individual will win the lottery tends to be very low.

For our problem, and the analogy of losing someone's data compared to winning a lottery, we do not want to "win." (We do not want one of OUR chunks to be lost.) With simple random replication, if there is a large-scale correlated failure, then the odds of a particular individual losing data tends to be very low. But, the odds of **someone** losing data tends to be extremely high. If all the nodes of a few copysets go down, then some user(s) will probably lose some data. Most users would not lose their data, but one or perhaps a few will lose some data.

We are almost ready to improve on the simple random replication algorithm. We need another term. To motivate it, consider the following quote from Luiz André Barroso, a Google Fellow in [CRS+13]:

> Having a framework that allows a storage system provider to manage the profile of frequency vs. size of data losses is very useful, as different systems prefer different policies. ...

Definition 28.8 The *scatter width*, S, is the number of nodes that store replicas of each node's data.

The scatter width is a measure of how "scattered" or "spread out" a node's data is.

Example 28.9 (See [CRS+13])
Let $N = 9$ and $R = 3$. Consider the N nodes $X_1, \ldots, X_9$. If the copysets are

$$C_1 = \{X_1, X_2, X_3\}, \quad C_2 = \{X_4, X_5, X_6\}, \quad C_3 = \{X_7, X_8, X_9\},$$
$$C_4 = \{X_1, X_4, X_7\}, \quad C_5 = \{X_2, X_5, X_8\}, \quad C_6 = \{X_3, X_6, X_9\},$$

then $S = 4$. To see this, note that some of the chunks in node X_1 are replicated in X_2 and X_3 (see copyset C_1) while the others are replicated in X_4 and X_7 (see copyset C_4). So, for the chunks in X_1, there are four nodes that store its replicas. Similarly, for X_2, the other nodes that store replicas of its chunks are $X_1, X_3, X_5, X_8\}$ (see C_1 and C_5). For X_3, the other nodes that store replicas of its chunks are X_1, X_2, X_6, X_9 (see C_1 and C_6). For X_4, the other nodes that store replicas of its chunks are X_5, X_6, X_1, X_7 (see C_2 and C_4). One can check that there are four such nodes for each of $X_5, \ldots, X_9$ as well.

What is the importance of the scatter width? It is related to the quote above by Luiz André Barroso. Some companies want to avoid having too low a scatter width. If the scatter width is low then that can put a burden on some of the nodes. For example if a node X goes down, then that will put a burden on the few nodes that contain replicas of that node's data, both to make a replacement for X, and to access other replicas of X's chunks in the meantime. If the scatter width is higher, then this will be less of a problem.

A key to Facebook's success of having a lower probability of data loss as compared to others in 2013 is that their HDFS team had modified the default HDFS implementation to add restrictions to the placement of replicas of chunks. This brings us to the second answer to Question 28.3: use a more general algorithm based on randomness.

Algorithm 28.10 (General random replication) *Pick some ordering of the N nodes, $X_1, X_2, \ldots, X_N$. (You might opt to require that no $S + 1$ consecutive nodes in the ordering $X_1, \ldots, X_N$ belong to the same rack so that replicas of a chunk are not stored in the same rack.) We take the indices modulo N, so index $N + 1 = 1$, $N + 2 = 2$, etc. When storing R replicas of a chunk, randomly pick a node for the primary replica. The remaining $R - 1$ secondary replicas are randomly picked from the next S nodes (following the given ordering), while requiring that the R nodes chosen must be distinct, i.e. if the primary replica is X_i, for some $i \in \{1, \ldots, N\}$, then the (different) secondary replicas are chosen at random from $X_{i+1}, \ldots, X_{i+S}$, (where we use the indices modulo N).*

Note that if S equals $N - 1$, then Algorithms 28.4 and 28.10 yield the same results.

Cidon et al. improved on this significantly with Algorithm 28.13. The key is to realize the problem with the random replication approach – namely that if there are a lot of chunks, then there will be a lot of copysets. For example if there are no restrictions on having multiple replicas in the same rack, then for Algorithm 28.4, the

$$\text{probability of data loss} = \frac{\text{number of copysets}}{\text{maximum number of sets}}$$

Instead, one should try to minimize the number of copysets, subject to the scatter width conditions set forth by the company. One way to accomplish this is to determine the possible copysets ahead of time, and then randomly pick one of them each time you wish to add a new chunk to the cloud. Toward this, we need another definition.

Definition 28.11   A *TOL* is a totally ordered list of all of the N nodes in the cluster with no repetitions.

(Note: in [CRS$^+$13], Cidon et al. use the term *permutation* to mean a TOL of all of the N nodes in the cluster with no repetitions.)

Given a TOL w, we can make copysets from it by taking the first R nodes of w to be one copyset, the next R nodes of w to be another copyset, etc. This gives us $\lfloor N/R \rfloor$ copysets. Note that we only used those copysets, then the scatterwidth would be exactly $R - 1$.

Example 28.12   *Let $N = 9$ and $R = 3$. Consider the N nodes $X_1, \ldots, X_9$. If $\{X_1, X_2, \ldots, X_9\}$ is one TOL and $\{X_1, X_4, X_7, X_2, X_5, X_8, X_3, X_6, X_9\}$ is another TOL, then the resulting copysets would be $C_1 = \{X_1, X_2, X_3\}$, $C_2 = \{X_4, X_5, X_6\}$, $C_3 = \{X_7, X_8, X_9\}$, $C_4 = \{X_1, X_4, X_7\}$, $C_5 = \{X_2, X_5, X_8\}$, $C_6 = \{X_3, X_6, X_9\}$. As there are no duplicate copysets, the scatter width is $S = P(R - 1) = 2(2) = 4$, which agrees with Example 28.9.*

If P TOLs are generated at random, then we will have approximately $\frac{PN}{R}$ copysets. (There might be some duplicate copysets.) Note also that $S \approx P(R-1)$ because each additional TOL increases the scatter width by approximately $R - 1$. (See Example 28.12 above.) Therefore, we should generate $\frac{S}{R-1}$ TOLs to get the desired scatter width. Therefore, the P TOLs give us approximately

$$\left(\frac{S}{R-1} \right) \left(\frac{N}{R} \right)$$

copysets. We summarize with Algorithm 28.13:

Algorithm 28.13 **(Copyset replication)** *There are two phases:*

1. *Permutation phase generates $\lceil \frac{S}{R-1} \rceil$ TOLs. Each TOL can be generated at random, or additional constraints can be applied (so as to limit two replicas of a chunk from being in nodes in the same rack, for example). Each TOL gives rise to some copysets, as described above.*

2. *Replication phase: Given a chunk, assign its replicas to the nodes of a copyset chosen at random from the copysets generated in the TOL phase.*

Example 28.14 *Suppose that there are $N = 9$ nodes $X_1, \ldots, X_9$ in a cluster, and that a replication factor of $R = 3$ is used. Suppose that a scatter width of 4 is desired. Following Algorithm 28.13, we generate two TOLs at random:*

$$X_5, X_2, X_6, X_9, X_7, X_3, X_8, X_1, X_4 \text{ and}$$
$$X_8, X_3, X_9, X_5, X_1, X_6, X_2, X_7, X_4$$

This gives us copysets

$$\{X_5, X_2, X_6\}, \{X_9, X_7, X_3\}, \{X_8, X_1, X_4\},$$
$$\{X_8, X_3, X_9\}, \{X_5, X_1, X_6\}, \{X_2, X_7, X_4\}$$

Suppose we wish to add chunk A to our cluster of nine nodes. We choose one of those copysets at random and store the three replicas of A in those nodes. If copyset $\{X_8, X_1, X_4\}$ is chosen, then the replicas of A are stored in X_8, X_1, and X_4.

We conclude this section with some further remarks about Copyset Replication.

Remark 28.15

1. *Cidon et al. prevented replicas of a chunk from being assigned to multiple nodes within a rack by generating a replacement TOL for any TOL in which this would have happened.*

2. *Is there a downside to using Copyset Replication? There are some trade-offs. We have already mentioned that some companies want to specify the scatter width. We also note that, while having fewer copysets reduces the probability that some data will be lost, if some data is lost, then the amount of data lost will be higher. Many companies prefer this, though.*

3. *Cidon notes on his website [Cid] that Copyset Replication was adopted in Facebook's LogDevice and Warm Storage, in Apache Ozone, in TIBCO ActiveSpaces, and in HyperDex.*

28.4   Homomorphic Encryption

Homomorphic encryption is a fast-growing area in large part because of cloud computing. We provide some background, references to some of the latest research, and links to current state-of-the-art software. We begin with a definition.

Definition 28.16   *Homomorphic encryption* is a type of encryption in which computations can be done on the encrypted data while the data is in encrypted form (i.e. without first decrypting it).

The idea for homomorphic encryption dates back to 1978, shortly after the birth of RSA. In 1978, Rivest, Adleman, and Dertouzous introduced homomorphic encryption using the name "privacy homomorphisms," [RAD78]. They offered the example of a loan company that wished to store their data in a data bank in an encrypted form, since there would be a lot of sensitive information.

At first glance, this sounds tricky, and it is! Which encryption algorithms will allow this? How does one do calculations on encrypted data so that, after the data is decrypted, the correct results are obtained?

Progress on this problem had been slow, with initial algorithms allowing for one operation on encrypted data, such as one addition. Progress began to accelerate around the year 2000. Significant progress was made on this problem in 2009 by Gentry, [Gen09a, Gen09b]. Recently, Chakarov and Papazov, [CP19], have evaluated the complexity of some homomorphic algorithms.

Google has a patent based on some of Gentry's work, [Goo15]. They also have a 2019 whitepaper describing how they protect the cloud data that they store. They use homomorphic encryption to protect data when it is being used by servers to run computations. See [Goo19].

Microsoft has developed the *Microsoft Simple Encrypted Arithmetic Library* or *SEAL* [Mic16], "a library with the goal of making homomorphic encryption available in an easy-to-use form both to experts and to non-experts." They note that *Microsoft SEAL* "... powered by open-source homomorphic encryption technology – provides a set of encryption libraries that allow computations to be performed directly on encrypted data. This enables software engineers to build end-to-end encrypted data storage and computation services where the customer never needs to share their key with the service." [Mis].

Applications

Suppose that there is a cloud provider that you would like to use, but you do not want to trust them to have access to your sensitive data. You might choose to store your data in the cloud in encrypted form. What if, in addition, you would like to do some calculations on that data while it is stored in the cloud. You could first decrypt it, perform the calculations, and then re-encrypt it. But then we have the original problem that you do not wish there to be an unencrypted copy in the cloud. Here, homomorphic encryption might be able to help!

We now make this even more concrete.

Example 28.17 *(DNA testing)*

Consider an individual who would like to do a DNA test to see if they have a medical condition, for example or perhaps to compare their DNA to someone else's DNA. This individual is concerned about their privacy, and does not want their DNA information stored in an unencrypted form. Could it suffice for a doctor to merely submit their encrypted DNA for testing? What tests could be performed on that encrypted DNA, and could homomorphic encryption help with these tests?

The Hamming distance between two vectors was defined in Section 12.6. It is an extremely useful quantity to calculate. (Indeed, Hamming distance calculations were used in Chapters 12, 18, 20, 22, 23, and 24.) In 2013, Yasuda et al., [YSK+13], proposed a new packing method for the computation of multiple Hamming distance values on encrypted values, thus enabling them to compare two patterns, such as two strands of DNA. There work was based on the 2011 work of Lauter et al., [LNV11]. In 2015, Miran Kim and Kristin Lauter described how to calculate the Hamming distance and approximate Edit distance between two encrypted DNA sequences, [KL15]. In 2015, Lu et al. proposed using homomorphic encryption for genome-wide association studies (GWASs) that look for variations in DNA that are associated with particular diseases. See [LYS15].

As mentioned above, Microsoft has released a public tool, *Microsoft SEAL*, for doing homomorphic encryption. It is available for Windows as well as Linux and MacOS. Dowlin et al. have written a manual for homomorphic encryption specifically for the important area of bioinformatics, [DGBL+15]. Their goal is to help practitioners in bioinformatics to use the *SEAL* library.

28.5 Cybersecurity

Cybersecurity is the protection in a connected world from threats to governments', companies', and individual's data, devices, infrastructure, and services. It deals with

(i) the privacy of information, whether stored, online, or in transit;

(ii) the security of our connected resources, including data, code, hardware, and other resources; and

(iii) the ability of our connected devices to operate without obstruction from unauthorized individuals.

Cybersecurity has become an area of enormous concern to governments and companies world-wide. The United States Department of Homeland Security has multiple agencies dedicated to cybersecurity. The *Cybersecurity & Infrastructure Security Agency*, or *CISA* has provided an overview of cybersecurity at [CIS19]. In [Cry18], they note that,

> Cyberspace is particularly difficult to secure due to a number of factors: the ability of malicious actors to operate from anywhere in the world, the linkages between cyberspace and physical systems, and the difficulty of reducing vulnerabilities and consequences in complex cyber networks.

The *Computer Security Resource Center*, [Cen19], at the *National Institute of Standards and Technology (NIST)* has recommendations for cryptographic algorithms, [Cry18]. They "... research, develop, engineer, and produce guidelines, recommendations and best practices for cryptographic algorithms, methods, and protocols." For example they note that, as of April 2018, the approval for DES, the Data Encryption Standard, has been withdrawn, [Cen19]. For more on DES, see Section 1.6.

Canada has a *Canadian Centre for Cyber Security*, [Can19]. It "... is the single unified source of expert advice, guidance, services and support on cyber security for government, critical infrastructure owners and operations, the private sector and the Canadian public."

The United Kingdom has a *UK National Cyber Security Centre, NCSC*, [NCS19]. The NCSC "... support[s] the most critical organisations in the UK, the wider public sector, industry, SMEs as well as the general public."

The demand for cybersecurity professionals is growing at a dramatic rate. Alison DeNisco Rayome reported in 2018 that "Cybersecurity engineers will be the highest-paying and most recruited tech job for 2019 ...," [Ray18]. She also noted that, "... 50–90% of all companies depending on industry experienced a cyberattack in 2018 ..." and " ... [there will be an] estimated 3.5 million unfilled positions in the industry by 2021." Cybersecurity is a very large area, with foundations that include security and privacy. Accordingly, there is a critical need to train students to fill these necessary cybersecurity positions.

Universities and colleges now offer entire degrees in cybersecurity. This focus on cybersecurity has resulted in curricular guidelines being established for this new area. The two main Computer Science organizations – the *Association for Computing Machinery, ACM*, and the *Institute of Electrical and Electronics Engineers–Computer Society, IEEE-CS* – have announced their first curricular guidelines for a four-year post-secondary degree in Cybersecurity, [BBB+17].

The ACM and IEEE have identified **six crosscutting concepts** that should be included in a cybersecurity degree so as to "... help students explore connections among the knowledge areas, and are fundamental to an individual's ability to understand the knowledge area regardless of the disciplinary lens." These are ([BBB+17, p. 22]),

(i) confidentiality

(ii) integrity

(iii) availability

(iv) risk

(v) adversarial thinking

(vi) systems thinking

They have also identified important Knowledge Units that should be included in a cybersecurity program.

Toward a similar goal, the *National Security Agency, NSA*, has established *Centers of Academic Excellence (CAE)*. Included in these are CAEs in *Cyber Defense Education, CAE-CDE*, [NSA20b]. They list important *Knowledge Units* that can be used toward achieving such a *CAE-CDE* designation at [NSA20a].

This book could be used for one or more important courses that are part of a cybersecurity major.

28.6 Problems

28.1 Suppose that there is a cluster with $N = 9$ nodes $X_1, \ldots, X_9$ and the replication factor is $R = 3$. Consider the copysets

$$C_1 = \{X_1, X_2, X_3\}, \quad C_2 = \{X_1, X_4, X_5\}, \quad C_3 = \{X_1, X_6, X_7\},$$
$$C_4 = \{X_5, X_6, X_8\}, \quad C_5 = \{X_2, X_6, X_9\}, \quad C_6 = \{X_2, X_4, X_8\},$$
$$C_7 = \{X_4, X_7, X_9\}, \quad C_8 = \{X_3, X_7, X_8\}, \quad C_9 = \{X_3, X_5, X_9\}.$$

(a) If nodes X_1, X_6, X_7, X_9 all become unavailable, would some data be inaccessible?

(b) If nodes X_2, X_3, X_6, X_8 all become unavailable, would some data be inaccessible?

(c) What is the scatter width?

(See Solution 28.1.)

28.7   Solutions

28.1   (a) Yes. All of the nodes in the copyset C_3 are unavailable.

(b) No. At least one node in each copyset is still available.

(c) $S = 6$. To see this, note that some of the chunks in node X_1 are replicated in X_2 and X_3 (see copyset C_1) while the others are replicated in X_4 and X_5 (see copyset C_2) and others are replicated in X_6 and X_7. So, for the chunks in X_1, there are six nodes that store its replicas. Similarly, for X_2, the other nodes that store replicas of its chunks are $X_1, X_3, X_6, X_9, X_4, X_8$ (see C_1, C_5, and C_6). For X_3, the other nodes that store replicas of its chunks are $X_1, X_2, X_7, X_8, X_5, X_9$ (see C_1, C_8, and C_9). One can check that there are six such nodes for each of $X_4, \ldots, X_9$ as well.

Chapter 29

Review Problems and Solutions

29.1 Problems

Latin Squares

29.1 Describe an easy way of constructing an $n \times n$ latin square for any n. (See Solution 29.1.)

29.2 Let

$$A = \begin{pmatrix} 1 & 2 & 3 & 4 & 5 \\ 5 & 1 & 2 & 3 & 4 \\ 4 & 5 & 1 & 2 & 3 \\ 3 & 4 & 5 & 1 & 2 \\ 2 & 3 & 4 & 5 & 1 \end{pmatrix}$$

Find a latin square orthogonal to A. (See Solution 29.2.)

Cryptography, Information Theory, and Error-Correction: A Handbook for the 21st Century, Second Edition.
Aiden A. Bruen, Mario A. Forcinito, and James M. McQuillan.
© 2021 John Wiley & Sons, Inc. Published 2021 by John Wiley & Sons, Inc.

29.3   Analogous to A in Problem 29.2, can you find a latin square orthogonal to the latin
       square

$$A = \begin{pmatrix} 1 & 2 & 3 & 4 \\ 4 & 1 & 2 & 3 \\ 3 & 4 & 1 & 2 \\ 2 & 3 & 4 & 1 \end{pmatrix}?$$

(Hint: Do not spend too much time on it!) (See Solution 29.3.)

29.4   Does there exist even a pair of mutually orthogonal latin squares of order 4?
       (See Solution 29.4.)

29.5   Let $n = p^\alpha$ where p is a prime and α is a positive integer. Then for $n \geq 3$ there
       exists a complete set of $n - 1$ mutually orthogonal latin squares of order n. To
       see this, denote the elements of the field by $a_0 = 0, a_1 = 1, a_2, \ldots, a_{n-1}$. Define
       the $n - 1$ matrices of order n to get $n - 1$ MOLS, as follows:

$$A_l = [a_{ij}^{(l)}], \quad i, j = 0, 1, \ldots, n - 1, \quad l = 1, 2, \ldots, n - 1$$

where $a_{ij}^{(l)} = a_l a_i + a_j$. *Carry out this procedure when* $n = 3$. (See Solution 29.5.)

29.6   Carry out the procedure in Problem 29.5 for $n = 4$. (See Solution 29.6.)

Linear Algebra and Codes

29.7   Let A be a 3×4 matrix, say

$$A = \begin{pmatrix} a_{11} & a_{12} & a_{13} & a_{14} \\ a_{21} & a_{22} & a_{23} & a_{24} \\ a_{31} & a_{32} & a_{33} & a_{34} \end{pmatrix}$$

What does $\mathbf{x}A$ "look like" if $\mathbf{x}$ is a row vector, say $\mathbf{x} = (x_1 \ x_2 \ \ldots \ x_n)$.
(See Solution 29.7.)

29.8   Let A be a 3×4 matrix as above and let $\mathbf{y}$ be a column vector, say $\mathbf{y} = \begin{pmatrix} y_1 \\ y_2 \\ \vdots \\ y_n \end{pmatrix}$.

What does $A\mathbf{y}$ look like? (See Solution 29.8.)

29.9   Can you describe a fundamental theorem in linear algebra involving the rank of a
       matrix? (See Solution 29.9.)

29.10 Let $G = (g_{ij})$, $1 \le i \le k$, $1 \le j \le n$ be a generator matrix for a linear (n, k) code C with $k \le n$ and of rank k. Let H be a generator matrix for the dual code $C^{\perp}$. Then

(a) each row of H has the property that its dot product with each row of G is zero.

(b) Any vector $\mathbf{v}$ satisfying the property in (a) is a linear combination of the rows of H.

What is the size of H? (See Solution 29.10.)

29.11 If G is a generator matrix for a linear (n, k) code with G of size $k \times n$ and rank k, what does it mean to say that a different generator matrix G_1 is **equivalent** to G? (See Solution 29.11.)

29.12 Is there a restriction on (29.1.11) (see Solution 29.11) for linear codes? (See Solution 29.12.)

29.13 How can we simplify the generator matrix G of a linear $[n, k]$ code by obtaining an equivalent code? (See Solution 29.13.)

29.14 If $A = \begin{pmatrix} a & b \\ c & d \end{pmatrix}$ then find A^{-1} assuming it exists. (See Solution 29.14.)

29.15 How is det A calculated for 3×3 matrices and higher? (See Solution 29.15.)

29.16 The following question arises in the theory of shift registers: If A is invertible can it happen that $A^n \mathbf{x} = \mathbf{0}$ where $\mathbf{x}$ is a nonzero column vector and n is a positive integer? (See Solution 29.16.)

29.17 Let C be a linear (n, k) code and let H be a generator matrix for the dual code $C^{\perp}$, so H has size $(n - k) \times n$. We are given that some codeword in C has exactly t nonzero coordinates. What information does this convey about the columns of H? (See Solution 29.17.)

29.18 Is the converse of Problem 29.17 true? I.e. does information about linear dependence of columns in H yield information about codewords in C? (See Solution 29.18.)

29.19 Let C be as in Problem 29.17, and let G be a generator matrix of C of size $k \times n$. Show that the minimum distance between codewords in C is at most $n - k + 1$. (See Solution 29.19.)

29.20 C is MDS if and only if $d = n - k + 1$, where d is the minimum distance. If C is MDS, what does this say about the columns of H? (See Solution 29.20.)

29.21 If C is MDS must every set of k columns of its generator matrix be linearly independent? (See Solution 29.21.)

29.22 Is the converse of Problem 29.21 true, i.e. if every set of k columns of G is linearly independent must C be MDS? (See Solution 29.22.)

29.23 If C is MDS must $C^{\perp}$ be MDS? (See Solution 29.23.)

Logs, Entropy

29.24 Intuitively why does entropy involve logarithms? (See Solution 29.24.)

29.25 Let X, Z be random variables such that $H(X \mid Z) = 0$. Show that X is a function of Z, say $X = f(Z)$. (See Solution 29.25.)

29.26 Conversely if X is a function of Z must $H(X \mid Z) = 0$? (See Solution 29.26.)

29.27 A single unbiased die is tossed once. If the face of the die is 1,2,3, or 4 then a fair coin is tossed once. If the face of the die is 5 or 6 then the fair coin is tossed twice. Find the information conveyed about the face of the die by the number of heads obtained. (See Solution 29.27.)

29.28 Given a table of logs to base 10, how does one convert it to a table of logs to the base 2 if base 2 logs are needed? (See Solution 29.28.)

29.29 We have $H(p, q) = p \log \frac{1}{p} + q \log \frac{1}{q}$. For the function $p \log \frac{1}{p}$, $0 < p \leq 1$ find its maximum value and the value of p at which the maximum is attained. (See Solution 29.29.)

29.30 In Chapter 25 we discuss entropy involving three random variables and vectors. How do we define $H(X \mid Y, Z)$? (See Solution 29.30.)

29.31 Can you think of another approach to calculating $H(X \mid Y, Z)$? (See Solution 29.31.)

Finite Fields

29.32 If F is a finite field of order n, i.e. if F has elements, what can you say about n? (See Solution 29.32.)

29.33 If $n = p^t$

    (a) Does there exist a finite field of order n?

    (b) Are all fields of order n "the same"?

(See Solution 29.33.)

29.34 How are finite fields F constructed? (See Solution 29.34.)

29.35 In the example in Solution 29.34, what is the inverse of $2 + \alpha$? (See Solution 29.35.)

29.36 Let $F = \mathrm{GF}(q)$, $q = p^t$. Show that all nonzero elements a in F satisfy $a^{q-1} = 1$. (See Solution 29.36.)

29.37 If q is a prime, for any positive integer u not divisible by p, we have $u^{p-1} \equiv 1 \pmod{p}$. Why is this so? (See Solution 29.37.)

29.38 In $\mathrm{GF}(q)$, let $\{\alpha_1, \alpha_2, \dots, \alpha_{q-1}\}$ be the nonzero elements. Show that $x^{q-1} - 1 = (x - \alpha_1)(x - \alpha_x) \cdots (x - \alpha_{q-1})$. (See Solution 29.38.)

29.39 Does the multiplicative group of $\mathrm{GF}(q)$ always have a **multiplicative generator**, i.e. a nonzero element a such that

    1. $a^{q-1} = 1$ and

    2. no smaller power of a is 1?

(See Solution 29.39.)

29.40 Find a generator for $\mathrm{GF}(9)$ above. (See Solution 29.40.)

Modular Arithmetic

29.41 Is Z_n a field? (See Solution 29.41.)

29.42 Does some subset of Z_n form a multiplicative group? (See Solution 29.42.)

29.43 What is the main property of the Euler phi-function ϕ? (See Solution 29.43.)

29.44 Fermat's little theorem says that $a^{p-1} \equiv 1 \bmod p$ for any nonzero a in Z_p. Is there a general theorem that works $(\bmod\ n)$ and specializes to this? (See Solution 29.44.)

29.45 How are n and $\phi(n)$ connected when we take powers? (See Solution 29.45.)

29.2   Solutions

Latin Squares

29.1   Let the first row be (1 2 3 $\cdots$ n) (or any permutation of it). Then apply right cyclic shifts to get the remaining rows. For example, if $n = 3$ and we start with (1 2 3) we get the latin square

$$\begin{pmatrix} 1 & 2 & 3 \\ 3 & 1 & 2 \\ 2 & 3 & 1 \end{pmatrix}$$

29.2   The method is to set the top row as in A, i.e. (1 2 3 4 5). Then cyclically shift it twice to the right to get the new second row. Then cyclically shift each of the new second, third, fourth rows twice to get B. So

$$B = \begin{pmatrix} 1 & 2 & 3 & 4 & 5 \\ 4 & 5 & 1 & 2 & 3 \\ 2 & 3 & 4 & 5 & 1 \\ 5 & 1 & 2 & 3 & 4 \\ 3 & 4 & 5 & 1 & 2 \end{pmatrix}$$

29.3   The method for Problem 29.2 will not work. It is known that a cyclic latin square of order n with n even does not have an orthogonal mate.

29.4   In Chapter 23 it is pointed out that if n is a power of a prime (such as $4 = 2^2$) there exists $n - 1$ mutually orthogonal latin squares of order n.

29.5   The field elements are $a_0 = 0$, $a_1 = 1$, $a_2 = 2 \equiv -1 \pmod 3$.

$$A_1 = \begin{pmatrix} a_{00}^1 & a_{01}^1 & a_{02}^1 \\ a_{10}^1 & a_{11}^1 & a_{12}^1 \\ a_{20}^1 & a_{21}^1 & a_{22}^1 \end{pmatrix}, \quad A_2 = \begin{pmatrix} a_{00}^2 & a_{01}^2 & a_{02}^2 \\ a_{10}^2 & a_{11}^2 & a_{12}^2 \\ a_{20}^2 & a_{21}^2 & a_{22}^2 \end{pmatrix}$$

$a_{00}^1 = a_1 a_0 + a_0 = a_0 = 0$ $a_{01}^1 = a_1 a_0 + 1 = 1$, $a_{02}^1 = 2$.
$a_{10}^1 = a_1 a_1 + a_0 = 1$, $a_{11}^1 = a_1 a_1 + 1 = 2$, $a_{12}^1 = a_1 a_1 + 2 = 0$.
$a_{20}^1 = a_1 a_2 + a_0 = 2$, $a_{21}^1 = a_1 a_2 + a_1 = 0$, $a_{22}^1 = a_1 a_2 + a_2 = 1$

So

$$A_1 = \begin{pmatrix} 0 & 1 & 2 \\ 1 & 2 & 0 \\ 2 & 0 & 1 \end{pmatrix}. \quad \text{Similarly } A_2 = \begin{pmatrix} 0 & 1 & 2 \\ 2 & 0 & 1 \\ 1 & 2 & 0 \end{pmatrix}$$

If we change {012} to {123} we get the same pair of orthogonal latin squares as in the text.

29.6 For a field of order 4, start with an irreducible (=non-factoring) polynomial of degree 2. The polynomial $x^2 + 1$ factors as $(x + 1)(x + 1)$. Also the polynomial $x^2 + x$ will not work as $x^2 + x = x(x + 1)$. So the only choice is $x^2 + x + 1$ which is irreducible. Thus our field elements are $\{a + b\omega\}$ where a, b are in binary and $\omega^2 + \omega + 1 = 0$.

We have four field elements. Addition is easy since $(a + b\omega) + (c + d\omega) = a + c + (b + d)\omega$. How do we get the product, say $(1 + \omega)(1 + \omega)$? $(1 + \omega)(1 + \omega) = 1 + \omega + \omega + \omega^2 = 1 + \omega^2 = 1 + \omega + 1 = \omega$. Note that $\omega^3 = \omega(\omega^2) = \omega(1 + \omega) = \omega + \omega^2 = \omega + \omega + 1 = 1$. In summary, $\omega^3 = 1$.

Carrying out the procedure above we get three matrices, i.e. three latin squares, any two of which are orthogonal. Each of the three matrices has for its first row $(0\ 1\ 2\ 3)$ if we label the elements as $0 + 0\omega = 0$, $1 + 0\omega$ as 1, ω as 2, and $1 + \omega$ as 3. None of the three latin squares will be cyclic! (See Problem 29.3.)

The three mutually orthogonal latin squares of order 4 are

$$\begin{pmatrix} 0 & 1 & 2 & 3 \\ 1 & 0 & 3 & 2 \\ 2 & 3 & 0 & 1 \\ 3 & 2 & 1 & 0 \end{pmatrix}, \quad \begin{pmatrix} 0 & 1 & 2 & 3 \\ 2 & 3 & 0 & 1 \\ 3 & 2 & 1 & 0 \\ 1 & 0 & 3 & 2 \end{pmatrix}, \quad \begin{pmatrix} 0 & 1 & 2 & 3 \\ 3 & 2 & 1 & 0 \\ 1 & 0 & 3 & 2 \\ 2 & 3 & 0 & 1 \end{pmatrix}$$

Linear Algebra and Codes

29.7 We are multiplying on the left by a matrix of size $1 \times n$. So we want the matrix product $(1 \times n)(3 \times 4)$. The matrix product is not defined unless $n = 3$. In that case the product is a vector of size 1×4, i.e. a row vector with four components. In this case, if $\mathbf{x} = (x_1\ x_2\ x_3)$ then

$$\mathbf{x}A = x_1(\text{first row of } A) + x_2(\text{second row of } A) + x_3(\text{third row of } A)$$

i.e. $\mathbf{x}A$ is a linear combination of the rows of A.

29.8 We are looking at $(3 \times 4)(n \times 1)$. For this matrix product to exist n must be 4 and the product is a 3×1 matrix, i.e. a column vector with three components. The vector is

$$y_1(\text{Column 1}) + y_2(\text{Column 2}) + y_3(\text{Column 3})) + y_4(\text{Column 4})$$

29.9 The row rank of the matrix M is the maximum number of linearly independent rows in M. The column rank is the maximum number of linearly independent columns. The big theorem is that row rank = column rank = rank of M.

29.10 In order for the dot product to be defined H must have n columns. Let $\mathbf{h} = (h_1 \; h_2 \; \ldots \; h_n)$ be a row of H. Then

$$h_1 g_{11} + h_2 g_{12} + \cdots + h_n g_{1n} = 0$$

$$h_1 g_{21} + h_2 g_{22} + \cdots + h_n g_{2n} = 0$$

$$\vdots$$

$$h_1 g_{k1} + h_2 g_{k2} + \cdots + h_n g_{kn} = 0$$

The conditions on $\mathbf{h}$ are linearly independent since G has rank k so the rows of G are linearly independent. So we impose k linearly independent conditions on $\mathbf{h}$. Thus the dimension of the solution space is $n - k$. So H is of size $(n - k) \times n$.

29.11 Two codes over a given alphabet are equivalent if one can be obtained from the other by a combination of operations of the following types:

1. Permutation of the positions of the code, i.e. permuting the columns.

2. Permutation of the symbols appearing in a fixed position.

Distances of the code are preserved by the above operations and the codes have the same parameters n and d (the length of the codewords and the minimum distance) and the same number of codewords.

29.12 Yes, this permutation is restricted to one caused by multiplying the symbols in a given column by a nonzero scalar. For linear codes, row operations are also allowed.

29.13 By using row operations and equivalence operations we can transform G to standard form $(I_k \mid A)$, where I_k is the $k \times k$ identity matrix and A is a $k \times (n - k)$ matrix.

29.14 Define $A^{-1} = \frac{1}{ad - bc} \begin{pmatrix} d & -b \\ -c & a \end{pmatrix}$ assuming $ad - bc \neq 0$. If $ad - bc = 0$ then A does not have an inverse. The number $ad - bc$ is called the determinant of A. The determinant of A is denoted by det A.

29.15 Let $A = \begin{pmatrix} a_{11} & a_{12} & a_{13} \\ a_{21} & a_{22} & a_{23} \\ a_{31} & a_{32} & a_{33} \end{pmatrix}$. We can expand by any row or column. Expanding by the first row we get

$$\det A = a_{11} \det \begin{pmatrix} a_{22} & a_{23} \\ a_{32} & a_{33} \end{pmatrix} - a_{12} \det \begin{pmatrix} a_{21} & a_{23} \\ a_{31} & a_{33} \end{pmatrix} + a_{13} \det \begin{pmatrix} a_{21} & a_{22} \\ a_{31} & a_{32} \end{pmatrix}$$

We proceed by induction for 4×4 and $n \times n$ matrices. A^{-1} exists if and only if det $A \neq 0$. If A^{-1} exists, we say that A is invertible or non-singular. Otherwise we say that A is not invertible or singular.

29.16 No. To see this, let n be the smallest positive integer such that $A^n \mathbf{x} = \mathbf{0}$. Then $AA^{n-1}\mathbf{x} = \mathbf{0}$. Multiplying on the left by A^{-1} we get $A^{-1}(AA^{n-1}\mathbf{x}) = A^{-1}\mathbf{0} = \mathbf{0}$. Thus $(A^{-1}A)A^{n-1}\mathbf{x} = \mathbf{0}$ so $IA^{n-1}\mathbf{x} = \mathbf{0}$ where I is the identity matrix. Then $A^{n-1}\mathbf{x} = \mathbf{0}$. We have a contradiction since $n-1$ is positive and less than n unless $n = 1$ so that $A\mathbf{x} = \mathbf{0}$. Multiplying by A^{-1} we get

$$A^{-1}(A\mathbf{x}) = (A^{-1}A)\mathbf{x} = \mathbf{x} = A^{-1}\mathbf{0} = \mathbf{0}$$

forcing $\mathbf{x} = \mathbf{0}$, a contradiction. Thus $A^n \mathbf{x}$ cannot be zero if $\mathbf{x} \neq \mathbf{0}$ and $n \geq 1$.

29.17 A corresponding set of t columns of H is linearly independent. To see this, let us assume that, for ease of notation, the first t entries of the given codeword $\mathbf{c}$ in C are nonzero and the rest are zero, i.e. $\mathbf{c} = (c_1, c_2, \ldots, c_t, 0, 0, \ldots, 0)$. Since $\mathbf{c}$ is in C, the dot product of $\mathbf{c}$ with each row of H is nonzero. Then $c_1 h_{i1} + c_2 h_{i2} + \cdots + c_t h_{it} = 0$, $1 \leq i \leq n - k$. Thus, the first t columns of H are linearly dependent.

29.18 Yes. To see this, assume that some set of t columns of H, say the first t columns of H, satisfy the relationship given by $\alpha_1 C_1 + \alpha_2 C_2 + \cdots + \alpha_t C_t = 0$, with $\alpha_i \neq 0$, $1 \leq i \leq t$. Then the vector $\mathbf{c} = (\alpha_1, \alpha_2, \ldots, \alpha_t, 0, 0, \ldots, 0)$ is such that the dot product of $\mathbf{c}$ with each row of H is zero. Thus, the dot product of $\mathbf{c}$ with every vector in $C^\perp$ is zero. Therefore $\mathbf{c}$ is in $(C^\perp)^\perp = C$.

29.19 Using equivalence and row operations, G can be transformed to the standard form $(I_k \mid A)$ where I_k is the $k \times k$ identity matrix. Each row of I_k has just 1 nonzero entry in the first k positions. So the total number of nonzero entries in this row is at most $n - k + 1$. Then the distance from that vector to the all zero word is at most $n - k + 1$. Since $d(\mathbf{u}, \mathbf{v}) = d(\mathbf{u} - \mathbf{v}, \mathbf{0})$ for linear codes, we have $d \leq n - k + 1$.

29.20 The MDS requirement is equivalent to saying that any nonzero codeword in C contains at most $k - 1$ zeros, i.e. at least $n - k + 1$ nonzero elements. From Problems 29.17 and 29.18, we get that C is MDS if and only if every set of $n - k$ columns is linearly independent.

29.21 Yes. Otherwise the corresponding $k \times k$ submatrix of G is such that the rows are dependent since row rank = column rank. Then some nontrivial linear combination of the rows is the zero vector. The corresponding codeword $\mathbf{c}$ in C has k

zeros in the positions corresponding to the given set of dependent columns. Then **c** has at most $n - k$ nonzero elements, contradicting the MDS property of C.

29.22 Yes. C is MDS if and only if no nonzero codeword **c** in C has as many as k zeros. If C is not MDS, some nonzero codeword **c** in C has at least k zeros. Suppose it has zeros in positions $1, 2, \ldots, k$. The $k \times k$ submatrix of G formed from the first k columns and the k (truncated) rows of C has the property that a nontrivial linear combination of the (truncated) rows of G is zero. Since row rank = column rank a linear combination of k of the columns of G is the zero column. Thus, if every set of k columns of C is linearly independent C is MDS. The converse is shown in Problem 29.21.

29.23 Yes. From Problems 29.21 and 29.22, C is MDS if and only if every set of k columns of G is linearly independent. Since $C^{\perp}$ has rank $n - k$ we have from the solution to Problem 29.20 that $C^{\perp}$ is MDS if and only if any set of $n - (n - k)$ columns of the generator matrix of $(C^{\perp})^{\perp}$ is linearly independent. Thus $C^{\perp}$ is MDS if and only if any set of k columns of G is linearly independent if and only if C is MDS.

Logs, Entropy

29.24 Let us look at the result that, if the pair X, Y are independent random variables then $H(XY) = H(X) + H(Y)$. If X has probabilities $p_1, \ldots, p_m$ and Y has probabilities $q_1, \ldots, q_n$ then the variable (X, Y) has probabilities involving products $\{p_i q_j\}$. So in a very rough sense, the entropy function converts products to sums. This is what the logarithm function does: it converts products to sums since $\log(ab) = \log a + \log b$.

29.25 $H(X \mid Z)$ is a sum of terms of the form $H(X, Z) \Pr(Z = z)$. Each of these terms is nonnegative. So if $H(X \mid Z) = 0$ then $H(X, z) = 0$ for all values z. Thus, once Z is known then X is known, there is no uncertainty as the only terms in calculating $H(X, z)$ involve probabilities 1 and 0. Thus X is a function of Z.

29.26 Yes, as we have that $H(1, 0) = H(0, 1) = 0$ where H is the Shannon function, and these are the only entropy terms that arise in the calculation.

29.27 Let X denote the random variable relating to the face of the die and let Y denote the random variable corresponding to the number of heads obtained. The question asked for the information conveyed about X by $Y = I(X : Y) = H(X) - H(X \mid Y) = I(Y : X) = H(Y) - H(Y \mid X)$. We calculate $H(Y) - H(Y \mid X)$.

The number of heads obtained is 0, 1, or 2 with probabilities $\left(\frac{5}{12}, \frac{1}{2}, \frac{1}{12}\right)$. So $H(Y) = H\left(\frac{5}{12}, \frac{1}{2}, \frac{1}{12}\right)$. To calculate $H(Y \mid X)$ we have

$$H(Y \mid \text{face is } 1, 2, 3, \text{or } 4)\frac{2}{3} + H(Y \mid \text{face is } 5 \text{ or } 6)\frac{1}{3}$$

Thus, $H(Y \mid X) = \frac{2}{3}H\left(\frac{1}{2}, \frac{1}{2}\right) + \frac{1}{3}H\left(\frac{1}{4}, \frac{1}{2}, \frac{1}{4}\right)$. So

$$H(Y) - H(Y \mid X)$$

$$= H\left(\frac{5}{12}, \frac{1}{2}, \frac{1}{12}\right) - \frac{2}{3}H\left(\frac{1}{2}, \frac{1}{2}\right) - \frac{1}{3}H\left(\frac{1}{4}, \frac{1}{2}, \frac{1}{4}\right)$$

$$= -\frac{5}{12}\log\frac{5}{12} - \frac{1}{2}\log\frac{1}{2} - \frac{1}{12}\log\frac{1}{12} - \frac{2}{3} - \frac{1}{3}\left[-\frac{1}{4}\log\frac{1}{4} - \frac{1}{2}\log\frac{1}{2} - \frac{1}{4}\log\frac{1}{4}\right]$$

Using the fact that $\log\frac{1}{x} = -\log x$ we get

$$-\frac{5}{12}\log\frac{5}{12} - \frac{1}{2}(-1) - \frac{1}{12}\log\frac{1}{12} - \frac{2}{3} - \frac{1}{3}\left[\frac{1}{2} + \frac{1}{2} + \frac{1}{2}\right]$$

$$= -\frac{5}{12}\log\frac{5}{12} - \frac{1}{12}\log\frac{1}{12} - \frac{2}{3} = 0.158 \text{ bits}$$

29.28   Use the equation $\log_2 a = \frac{\log_{10} a}{\log_{10} 2}$. To see this put $\log_2 a = x$. Thus $2^x = a$. Taking logs to the base 10 on both sides we have $\log_{10}(2^x) = \log_{10} a$. Thus $x\log_{10} 2 = \log_{10} a$. Therefore $x = \frac{\log_{10} a}{\log_{10} 2}$, i.e. $\log_2 a = \frac{\log_{10} a}{\log_{10} 2}$.

29.29   Changing from p to x we want the maximum value of $x\log\frac{1}{x}$, $0 < x \leq 1$ We have

$$f(x) = x\log_2\left(\frac{1}{x}\right) = -x\log_2 x = -x\frac{\ln x}{\ln 2}$$

$$f'(x) = -\frac{\ln x}{\ln 2} - x\left(\frac{1}{x}\right)\frac{1}{\ln 2} = \frac{1}{\ln 2}(-\ln x) - \frac{1}{\ln 2}$$

$$f'(x) = 0 \Rightarrow \ln x = -1, \quad x = e^{-1} = \frac{1}{e}$$

The maximum value occurs when $x = \frac{1}{e}$ and $f(x) = \frac{1}{e}\log_2 e$.

29.30   We can treat the pair $[Y, Z]$ as a single random variable W. Then $H(X \mid Y, Z) = H(X \mid W)$.

29.31 $H(X \mid Y, Z) = \sum_z H(X \mid Y, Z = z)\Pr(Z = z)$.

Finite Fields

29.32 The order must be a prime power, i.e. $n = p^t$ where p is a prime and t is an arbitrary positive integer.

29.33 (a) Yes.

(b) Yes. This means that if F_1, F_2 are fields of order n, there exists a 1–1 and onto mapping f from the elements of F_1 to the elements of F_2 such that f preserves addition and multiplication, i.e. If $f(u_1) = v_1$ and $f(u_2) = v_2$ then

(a) $f(u_1 + u_2) = f(u_1) + f(u_2) = v_1 + v_2$,

(b) $f(u_1 u_2) = f(u_1) f(u_2) = v_1 v_2$.

29.34 If F has order $p' = p$, a prime, this is easy. The field is just Z_p the field of integers (mod p). If $p = 5$, say, the elements are $0, 1, 2, 3, 4$ and addition works mod 5. So for example $(3)(4) = 2$ in F since $\text{Rem}[12, 5] = 2$, i.e. $12 \equiv 2 \pmod 5$ since $12 - 2 = 10$ is divisible by 5. The multiplicative inverse of 3 is 2 since $(3)(2) \equiv 1 \pmod 5$. The additive inverse of 4 is 1 since $4 + 1 \equiv 0 \pmod 5$. Alternatively, $-4 \equiv 1 \pmod 5$ since $-4 - 1$ is divisible by 5.

The case when F has order p^t, $t > 1$ is more difficult. The ring Z_{p^n} with $n > 1$ is not a field. For example, Z_4 is not a field since, for example, 2 has no multiplicative inverse. To construct F we construct a polynomial $v(x)$ of degree n which does not factor over Z_p.

Examples. We use the polynomial $g(x) = x^2 + 1$ which does not factor in Z_3. The field of order 9 consists of all elements $a + b\alpha$ with a, b in Z_3 and with α satisfying $\alpha^2 + 1 = 0$. The field of order 4 was constructed in Solution 29.6. The field of order 8 is constructed in connection with AES (Chapter 5).

29.35 Let it be $(x + \alpha y)$. Then $(x + \alpha y)(2 + \alpha) = 1$. Comparing coefficients we get

(a) $2x + \alpha^2 y = 2x - y = 1$.

(b) For the terms involving α, $x + 2y = 0$.

From (b), $x = -2y = y$, so $x = y$ since $-2 \equiv 1 \pmod 3$. From (a), $x = 1$, $y = 1$. So $(2 + \alpha)^{-1} = (1 + \alpha)$. To check, since $\alpha^2 = -1 \equiv 2 \pmod 3$, $(2 + \alpha)(1 + \alpha) = 2 + \alpha^2 + \alpha(3) = 2 - 1 = 1$.

29.36 **Proof.** List the nonzero elements of F as $\{x_1 = 1, x_2, \ldots, x_{q-1}\}$. Let a be any element in this list. Then the set $\{ax_1, ax_2, \ldots, ax_{q-1}\}$ equals the set $\{x_1, x_2, \ldots, x_{q-1}\}$.

[Example. Let $F = \mathrm{GF}(5)$, $a = 2$. Then $\{x_1, x_2, x_3, x_4\} = \{1, 2, 3, 4\}$, and $\{2x_1, 2x_2, 2x_3, 2x_4\} = \{2, 4, 1, 3\} = \{1, 2, 3, 4\}$.]

Thus the products of all elements in both sets are equal and nonzero. So $(x_1)(x_2) \cdots (x_{q-1}) = (ax_1)(ax_2) \cdots (ax_{q-1})$. Therefore $x_1 x_2 \cdots x_{q-1} = a^{q-1}(x_1 x_2 \cdots x_{q-1})$. Dividing through by the product of the nonzero element $x_1 x_2 \cdots x_{q-1}$ we get that $a^{q-1} = 1$ for any $a \neq 0$ in F_q.

The fact that $a^{q-1} = 1$ in $\mathrm{GF}(q)$ is known as "Fermat's little theorem" when $q = p$, a prime and the beautiful proof is due to Fermat. ["Fermat's last theorem" about solving equations of the type $x^n + y^n = z^n$ is discussed in Chapter 6.] ∎

29.37 Let us take an example to illustrate the general proof.

Claim. 39^6 leaves a remainder of 1 when divided by 7. Note that 39 is not divisible by 7 and 7 is a prime number.

Proof: $39 = (5)(7) + 4$. Then $(4 + 35)^6 \equiv 4^6 \pmod 7 \equiv 1$. We are skipping a few steps here. One solution is to say that $(4 + 35)^6 = 4^6 + 4^5(35) + 4^4(35)^2 + \cdots + (35)^6$. Thus, mod 35, $(4 + 35)^6 \equiv 4^6 \equiv 1$ as the remaining terms in the binomial expansion above are divisible by 35. Or we can say that if $u \equiv u_1 \pmod n$ and $v \equiv v_1 \pmod n$ then $uv \equiv u_1 v_1 \pmod n$. So let $u = 39$, $u_1 = 4$, $v = 35$, $v_1 = 4$, $n = 7$ to get $(39)^2 \equiv 4^2 \pmod 7$. Continuing we get $(39)^6 = 4^6 \pmod 7 = 1$, using $\alpha^{q-1} = 1$ in $\mathrm{GF}(q)$. Here we have $q = p$ and $\mathrm{GF}(p) = Z_p$.

29.38 From Problem 29.37, α_i is a root of $x^{q-1} - 1$ since $\alpha^{q-1} - 1 = 0$. We claim that $x - \alpha_1$ divides $x^{q-1} - 1$. If not, then dividing we get $x^{q-1} - 1 = (x - \alpha_1)u(x) + R(x)$. Here $R(x)$ being of smaller degree than $x - \alpha_1$ is a constant w. So $x^{q-1} - 1 = (x - \alpha_1)u(x) + w$. Substituting α_1 for x we get $\alpha_1^{q-1} - 1 = (\alpha_1 - \alpha_1)u(\alpha_1) + w$ so $0 = 0 + w$. Thus $w = 0$ and $(x - \alpha_1)$ divides $x^{q-1} - 1$ as does $x - \alpha_i$ for $1 \leq i \leq q - 1$. So $x^{q-1} - 1 = (x - \alpha_1)(x - \alpha_2) \cdots (x - \alpha_{q-1})f(x)$. But both $x^{q-1} - 1$ and $(x - \alpha_1) \cdots (x - \alpha_{q-1})$ have the same degree and the coefficient of x^{q-1} is 1 for both. So $f(x) = 0$, and $x^{q-1} - 1 = (x - \alpha_1)(x - \alpha_2) \cdots (x - \alpha_{q-1})$.

29.39 Yes. Thus if α is a multiplicative generator, each nonzero element in the field is a power of α.

29.40 $z = 1 + \alpha$ is a generator, since $(1 + \alpha)^8 = 1$ and no smaller power of $1 + \alpha$ is 1. Since $\alpha^2 = -1$ we have $z = 1 + \alpha$, $z^2 = 1 + \alpha^2 + 2\alpha = 2\alpha$, $z^4 = 4\alpha^2 = \alpha^2 = -1$, $z^8 = (-1)^2 = 1$.

Modular Arithmetic

29.41 No because unless n is a prime, the nonzero elements do not form a group under multiplication. For example in Z_4, 2 does not have a multiplicative inverse even though like all elements in Z_n it has an additive inverse.

29.42 Yes, those elements less than n and relatively prime to n. There are $\phi(n)$ of these.

29.43 If a, b are relatively prime then $\phi(ab) = \phi(a)\phi(b)$.

29.44 Yes. Euler's theorem says that if a is relatively prime to n then $a^{\phi(n)} \equiv 1 \pmod{n}$. For $n = p$, $\phi(n) = p - 1$ with p a prime.

29.45 If $u \equiv v \pmod{\phi(n)}$ then $a^u \equiv a^v \pmod{n}$.

Example. Let n be a prime. Then in Z_p if $a \neq 0$ and $u \equiv v \pmod{p-1}$ then $a^u \equiv a^v \bmod p$. To see this we have $u - v = \lambda(p-1)$, so $u = v + \lambda(p-1)$. Then

$$a^u \equiv a^{v+\lambda(p-1)} \equiv a^v(a^{(p-1)})^\lambda \equiv a^v \pmod{p}$$

Appendix A

A.1 ASCII

ASCII (American Standard Code for Information Interchange), is a standard code set for representing characters. It consists of 128 characters including letters, numbers, punctuation, and symbols. Each character has been assigned a unique binary string.

Char	Binary	Char	Binary	Char	Binary	Char	Binary
(nul)	00000000	(sp)	00100000	@	01000001	'	01100001
(soh)	00000001	!	00100001	A	01000010	a	01100010
(stx)	00000010	"	00100010	B	01000011	b	01100011
(etx)	00000011	#	00100011	C	01000100	c	01100100
(eot)	00000100	$	00100100	D	01000101	d	01100101
(enq)	00000101	%	00100101	E	01000110	e	01100110
(ack)	00000110	&	00100111	F	01000111	f	01100111
(bel)	00000111	'	00101000	G	01001000	g	01101000
(bs)	00001000	(	00101001	H	01001001	h	01101001
(ht)	00001001	)	00101010	I	01001010	i	01101010
(nl)	00001010	*	00101011	J	01001011	j	01101011
(vt)	00001011	+	00101100	K	01001100	k	01101100
(np)	00001100	,	00101101	L	01001101	l	01101101
(cr)	00001101	-	00101110	M	01001110	m	01101110
(so)	00001110	.	00101111	N	01001111	n	01101111
(si)	00001111	/	00110000	O	01010000	o	01110000
(dle)	00010000	0	00110001	P	01010001	p	01110001
(dc1)	00010001	1	00110010	Q	01010010	q	01110010
(dc2)	00010010	2	00110011	R	01010011	r	01110011
(dc3)	00010011	3	00110100	S	01010100	s	01110100
(dc4)	00010100	4	00110101	T	01010101	t	01110101
(nak)	00010101	5	00110110	U	01010110	u	01110110
(syn)	00010110	6	00110111	V	01010111	v	01110111
(etb)	00010111	7	00111000	W	01011000	w	01111000
(can)	00011000	8	00111001	X	01011001	x	01111001
(em)	00011001	9	00111010	Y	01011010	y	01111010
(sub)	00011010	:	00111011	Z	01011011	z	01111011
(esc)	00011011	;	00111100	[	01011100	{	01111100
(fs)	00011100	<	00111101	\	01011101	|	01111101
(gs)	00011101	=	00111110	]	01011110	}	01111110
(rs)	00011110	>	00111111	^	01011111	~	01111111
(us)	00011111	?	01000000	_	01100000	(del)	10000000

Table A.1: ASCII table

Appendix B

B.1 Shannon's Entropy Table

Here we give different values for Shannon's famous entropy function: $H(p, 1-p) = p \log \frac{1}{p} + (1-p) \log \frac{1}{1-p}$

p	$1-p$	$H(p, 1-p)$	p	$1-p$	$H(p, 1-p)$
0.000	1.000	0.0000	0.250	0.750	0.8113
0.010	0.990	0.0808	0.260	0.740	0.8267
0.020	0.980	0.1414	0.270	0.730	0.8415
0.030	0.970	0.1944	0.280	0.720	0.8555
0.040	0.960	0.2423	0.290	0.710	0.8687
0.050	0.950	0.2864	0.300	0.700	0.8813
0.060	0.940	0.3274	0.310	0.690	0.8932
0.070	0.930	0.3659	0.320	0.680	0.9044
0.080	0.920	0.4022	0.330	0.670	0.9149
0.090	0.910	0.4365	0.340	0.660	0.9248
0.100	0.900	0.4690	0.350	0.650	0.9341
0.110	0.890	0.4999	0.360	0.640	0.9427
0.120	0.880	0.5294	0.370	0.630	0.9507

Table B.1: Shannon's entropy table.

p	$1-p$	$H(p, 1-p)$	p	$1-p$	$H(p, 1-p)$
0.130	0.870	0.5574	0.380	0.620	0.9580
0.140	0.860	0.5842	0.390	0.610	0.9648
0.150	0.850	0.6098	0.400	0.600	0.9710
0.160	0.840	0.6343	0.410	0.590	0.9765
0.170	0.830	0.6577	0.420	0.580	0.9815
0.180	0.820	0.6801	0.430	0.570	0.9858
0.190	0.810	0.7015	0.440	0.560	0.9896
0.200	0.800	0.7219	0.450	0.550	0.9928
0.210	0.790	0.7415	0.460	0.540	0.9954
0.220	0.780	0.7602	0.470	0.530	0.9974
0.230	0.770	0.7780	0.480	0.520	0.9988
0.240	0.760	0.7950	0.490	0.510	0.9997
0.250	0.750	0.8113	0.500	0.500	1.0000

Table B.1: *(Continued)*

Glossary

Most of these terms appear in numerous chapters in the book. We include a sample section or chapter number for each term in the Glossary. Please consult the Table of Contents and the Index for additional relevant sections and chapters for each term.

A

AES Advanced Encryption Standard. The standard block cipher algorithm designated by the NIST for symmetric key cryptography. It is also known as Rijndael code. See Chapter 5 and Section 5.2.

ASCII American Standard Code for Information Interchange. The code generally used by most computer systems to translate characters into binary numbers. See Appendix A.

B

Block Coding Any encoding function that encodes a block of words instead of one word at a time. See Section 11.1.

BSC Binary Symmetric Channel. A communication channel transporting the binary symbols $(0, 1)$ for which the probabilities p of receiving a 1 when 0 is transmitted is equal to the probability of receiving 0 when 1 is transmitted the same error. See Section 12.2.

C

CAE Centers of Academic Excellence. The *National Security Agency* established Centers of Academic Excellence. https://www.iad.gov/nietp/CAERequirements.cfm

CAE-CDE   Center of Academic Excellence in Cyber Defence Education. https://www
.iad.gov/NIETP/documents/Requirements/CAE-CD_2020_Knowledge_Units.pdf

Certificate   An electronic file, typically containing a public key, that is digitally signed
by a Certificate Authority. Certificates are used as a means of authentication over the
Internet. See Section 3.9.

Certificate Authority   The trusted party that signs and distribute certificates. See
Section 3.9.

Cryptanalysis   The art and science of deciphering encrypted messages. See Section 4.1.

CRC   Cyclic Redundancy Check. A widely used error detection code. See Section 21.6.

D

DES   Data Encryption Standard. The standard block cipher algorithm adopted by
NIST for symmetric key cryptography in the late 70's. It has been superseded by AES.
See Section 1.6.

Digital Signature   A protocol by which the recipient of a message can verify that the
sender of the message is in possession of the private key corresponding to a given public
key and that the message itself has not been tampered with. Digital signatures should
be used in conjunction with certificates to avoid the possibility of impersonation. See
Chapter 4 and Section 4.7.

DNA   Desoxyribonucleic Acid. The molecule were the genetic information of all live
organisms is encoded. DNA is split and copied within the nuclei of each cell during
multiplication. See Section 28.4.

DSS   Digital Signature System. A protocol used to electronically sign documents. See
Chapter 4.

E

ECC   Elliptic Curve Cryptography. A public key cryptographic system based on the
mathematical properties of elliptic curves. See Chapter 6.

ENIGMA   The generic name given to a family of mechanical-rotor based ciphering devices utilized by the German forces during World War II. See Section 2.7.

Entropy   A measure of the amount of uncertainty. Entropy is directly related to the number of *a priori* possible outcomes of a given event. For example, the entropy of a random binary string of length n is $\log(2^n) = n$. See Section 1.5, 8.3, and 9.2.

F

FIPS   Federal Information Processing Standards. The collective name for a series of standards related to information processing issued by NIST. See Section 7.20.

G

GPG   GNU Privacy Guard. Open source, freeware version of PGP. See Section 3.10.

GSM   Global System for Mobile telecommunications. The international standard for satellite phones. See Section 4.2.

H

Hacker   Originally, the terms were used for creative programmers who program in an unorthodox way but it is now used to described those who use their technical skills to gain illegal access into computer networks to steal or vandalize information. A good hacker must have cryptanalytic skills. See Chapter 8.

Hamming Distance   The number of characters in which two strings (words) differ, measured with the metric of the corresponding alphabet. See Section 12.6.

Hash Function   A function that output a shorter version or digest of an input message. For cryptographic applications the hash function must be one-way (the input cannot be easily derived from the output) and has collisions-free (low probability that two different inputs will give the same output). See Section 4.4.

K

Kerberos   A trusted server-based protocol that provides authentication and key exchange for symmetric encryption systems. It is the logical equivalent of PKI. Windows 2000 operative systems authentication is based on Kerberos. See Section 4.13.

Key Reconciliation   A protocol by which two communicating entities obtain the same secret string after exchanging information over a public network. See Chapter 24.

L

LAN   Local Area Network. See Section 8.9.

LFSR   Linear Feedback Shift Register. A pseudo-random sequence generator based on a recurrence relation. See Chapter 16.

M

Markov Chain (or Source)   A chain (source) of symbols source such that the next symbol of the chain depends only on the current value, not on any previous symbol. See Section 14.3.

McEliece Cryptosystem   A public key cryptosystem based on linear error correcting codes. See Section 20.9.

Memoryless Source (or Channel)   A source of symbols for which the probabilities of output a given symbol does not depend on any of the previously output symbols. See Section 11.1.

N

NCSC   UK National Cyber Security Centre. It supports organizations in the United Kingdom, industries, and the public. URL: www.ncsc.gov.uk See Section 28.5.

NIST   National Institute of Standards and Technologies. The United States' federal agency that develops and promotes measurement, standards, and technology. URL: www .nist.gov. See Section 28.5.

NSA   National Security Agency. The United States' intelligence agency responsible for the security and cryptanalysis of electronic communications. It grew from a small US Navy task group in the World War II to be the largest employer of cryptographers in the world nowadays. URL: www.nsa.gov See Section 28.5.

O

One-time pad   A perfectly secure symmetric key encryption system that uses a random, secret key of the same length of the message to transmit. See Section 4.3.

P

PGP   Pretty Good Privacy. Data and message encryption computer software developed by Phil Zimmermann on the basis of standard algorithms and public key encryption. See Section 3.10.

PKI   Public Key Infrastructure. A Public Key directory database, often associated with key-pair generation functions, that provides authentication over medium to large networks. See Section 7.4.

Private Key   The element of an asymmetric-key system key-pair that is kept secret by each user. This part of the key-pair is used for decryption. See Section 3.1.

Public Key   The element of an asymmetric-key system key-pair that is shared with other users. This part of the key-pair is used by senders to encrypt a message. See Section 3.1.

Q

Quantum cryptography   A form of cryptography that employs quantum properties of photons to exchange a random key over a public channel with perfect secrecy. See Chapter 4.

R

RSA   A public-key cryptosystem patented by Rivest, Shamir, and Adleman in 1976. It is based on the computational difficulty of factoring large composite numbers. It the most widely implemented of the public key algorithms, included in applications such as PGP and SSL. See Chapter 3.

S

Shannon bit   The amount of information gained (or entropy removed) upon learning the answer to a question whose two possible answers were equally likely, a priori. See Section 1.5.

SNR   Signal to Noise Ratio. See Section 13.2.

SSL   Secure Socket Layer. A protocol that was used mainly for authentication of Internet transactions. It has been replaced by TLS, the Transport Layer Security protocol. See Section 3.9.

T

TCP/IP   Transmission Control Protocol/Internet Protocol. Protocols used for the transmission of information within networks of computers. TCP/IP have became the *de facto* standard for all networks connected to the Internet. See Section 27.8.

TLS   Transport Layer Security. A protocol that is used mainly for authentication of Internet transactions. It replaces SSL, the Secure Socket Layer protocol. See Section 3.9.

Triple-DES   Symmetric key encryption system based on the successive application of three DES ciphers having different keys.

Trojan Horse   A malicious program that causes damage or compromises the security, but does not replicates itself. See Section 7.20.

V

Virus   A program or code that replicates by attaching itself, or infecting, another program, boot sector, partition sector, or document. Viruses are mostly malicious software that can cause large amounts of damage to sensitive data. See Section 27.6.

VoIP   Voice Over IP. Any of the protocols used to digitize and pack a voice channel signal to be sent over a TCP/IP link. See Section 8.10

W

WAN Wide Area Network. See Section 8.9.

WEP Wired Equivalent Privacy. IEEE protocol used for data encryption of wireless LANs. See Section 8.9.

Worm A, usually malicious, program that makes copies of itself, inside the same computer or by copying itself through email. Worms may do damage and compromise the security of the computer and its network. See Section 7.20.

X

X.509 Certificate A widely used standard for digital certificates.

References

[ABD+19]   Adrian, D., Bhargavan, K., Durumeric, Z. et al. (2019). Imperfect forward
            secrecy: how Diffie-Hellman fails in practice. *Communications of the ACM*
            62. https://dl.acm.org/doi/pdf/10.1145/3292035.

[AKS04]   Agrawal, M., Kayal, N., and Saxena, N. (2004). PRIMES is in P. *Annals of
            Mathematics* 160: 791–793. https://doi.org/10.4007/annals.2004.160.781.

[AASA+19]   Alagic, G., Alperin-Sheriff, J., Apon, D. et al. (2019). NISTIR 8240 Sta-
            tus Report on the First Round of the NIST Post-Quantum Cryptography
            Standardization Process. National Institute of Standards and Technology,
            NIST. https://doi.org/10.6028/NIST.IR.8240.

[Ald02]   Alderson, T.L. (2002). On MDS codes and Bruen-Silverman codes. PhD
            thesis. University of Western Ontario. Mathematical Reviews: http://www
            .ams.org/mathscinet-getitem?mr=2703431 (accessed 17 September 2020).

[ABS07]   Alderson, T.L., Bruen, A.A., and Silverman, R. (2007). Maximum distance
            separable codes and arcs in projective spaces. *Journal of Combinatorial
            Theory, Series A* 114. https://doi.org/10.1016/j.jcta.2006.11.005.

[Ale02]   Aleksander, I. (2002). Understanding information, bit by bit. Shannon's
            equations. In: *It Must be Beautiful: Great Equations of Modern Science*
            (ed. G. Farmelo). Granta Publications. https://granta.com/products/it-
            must-be-beautiful/.

[AB76]   Ali, M.M. and Bruen, A.A. (1976). BIB designs and the hadamard problem. *Proceedings of Statistics Days*. Ball State University, pp. 68–74. https://mathscinet.ams.org/mathscinet-getitem?mr=0431318 (accessed 17 September 2020).

[Ama19]   AmazonAlexa (2019). https://developer.amazon.com/en-US/alexa. (accessed November 2019).

[USA19]   Analytics.usa.gov (2019). https://analytics.usa.gov (accessed December 2019).

[And89]   Anderson, I. (1989). *A First Course in Combinatorial Mathematics*. Oxford. https://mathscinet.ams.org/mathscinet-getitem?mr=1029023.

[Appb]   macOS Mojave 10.14 User Guide. https://support.apple.com/guide/mac-help/save-energy-mh35848/mac (accessed 17 September 2020).

[App18]   Apple Inc. (2018). Use FileVault to encrypt the startup disk on your Mac. https://support.apple.com/en-us/HT204837.

[App19]   Apple Inc. (2019). https://www.apple.com/ios/home/ (accessed November 2019).

[Ash90]   Ash, R.B. (1990). *Information Theory*. Dover Publications. https://store.doverpublications.com/0486665216.html.

[AK92]   Assmus, E.F. and Key, J.D. (1992). *Designs and Their Codes*. Cambridge University Press. https://doi.org/10.1017/CBO9781316529836.

[AM74]   Assmus, E.F. Jr. and Mattson, H.F. Jr. (1974). Coding and combinatorics. *SIAM Review* 16: 349–388. https://doi.org/10.1137/1016056.

[Bar93]   Barg, A. (1993). At the dawn of the theory of codes. *The Mathematical Intelligencer* 15. https://doi.org/10.1007/BF03025254.

[Bar16]   Barker, E. (2016). NIST special publication 800-57 Part 1 revision 4. Recommendation for key management. Part 1: general. http://dx.doi.org/10.6028/NIST.SP.800-57pt1r4.

[BD15]   Barker, E. and Dang, Q. (2015). NIST special publication 800-57 Part 3 revision 1: key management. Part 3: application-specific key management guidance. http://dx.doi.org/10.6028/NIST.SP.800-57pt3r1.

[Bau02]   Bauer, F.L. (2002). *Decrypted Secrets, Methods and Maxims of Cryptology*, 3e. Berlin: Springer-Verlag. https://www.springer.com/gp/book/9783540245025.

[Bay20]   Bayern, M. (2020). 91% of it leaders are shifting cloud strategy to accommodate the new normal. *TechRepublic*, June 2020. https://www.techrepublic.com/article/91-of-it-leaders-are-shifting-cloud-strategy-to-accommodate-the-new-normal/.

[Bel64]   Bell, J.S. (1964). On the einstein podolsky rosen paradox. *Physics Physique Fizika* 1. http://dx.doi.org/10.1103/PhysicsPhysiqueFizika.1.195.

[BN07]   Ben-Naim, A. (2007). *Entropy Demystified:The Second Law Reduced to Plain Common Sense*. World Scientific. https://doi.org/10.1142/6261.

[BBB+90]   Bennett, C.H., Bessette, F., Brassard, G. et al. (1990). Experimental quantum cryptography. *EUROPCRYPT 90*, Arhus, Denmark, pp. 253–265. https://dx.doi.org/10.1007/3-540-46877-3_23.

[BB84]   Bennett, C.H. and Brassard, G. (1984). Quantum cryptography: public key distribution and coin tossing. *International Conference on Computers, Systems & Signal Processing.* http://researcher.watson.ibm.com/researcher/files/us-bennetc/BB84highest.pdf (accessed 18 September 2020).

[BBR88]   Bennet, C.H., Brassard, G., and Robert, J.-M. (1988). Privacy amplification by public discussion. *SIAM Journal of Computing* 17 (2): 210–229. https://doi.org/10.1137/0217014.

[BBD09]   Bernstein, D.J., Buchmann, J., and Dahmen, E. (eds.) (2009). *Post-Quantum Cryptography*. Springer-Verlag. https://doi.org/10.1007/978-3-540-88702-7_1.

[Bes13]   Best, J. (2013). IBM Watson: the inside story of how the Jeopardy-winning supercomputer was born, and what it wants to do next. *TechRepublic*. https://www.techrepublic.com/article/ibm-watson-the-inside-story-of-how-the-jeopardy-winning-supercomputer-was-born-and-what-it-wants-to-do-next/ (accessed 18 September 2020).

[BR98]   Beutelspacher, A. and Rosenbaum, U. (1998). *Projective Geometry: From Foundations to Applications*. Cambridge University Press. Mathematical Reviews: https://mathscinet.ams.org/mathscinet-getitem?mr=1629468?.

[BJL86]   Beth, T., Jungnickel, D., and Lenz, H. (1986). *Design Theory*. Cambridge Univerisy Press. URL for second edition Volume 1: https://doi.org/10.1017/CBO9780511549533, URL for second edition Volume 2: https://doi.org/10.1017/CBO9781139507660.

[Beu94]   Beutelspacher, A. (1994). *Cryptology*. New York: The Mathematical Association of America. https://www.maa.org/press/books/cryptology (accessed 18 September 2020).

[BS90]   Biham, E. and Shamir, A. (1990). Differential cryptanalysis of DES-like cryptosystems. *Advances in Cryptology-CRYPTO'90*, pp. 2–21. https://doi.org/10.1007/3-540-38424-3_1.

[Bon99]   Boneh, D. (1999). Twenty years of attacks on the RSA cryptosystem. *Notices of the AMS* 51. https://www.ams.org/notices/199902/boneh.pdf.

[Bon19]   Boneh, D. (2019). Attacking cryptographic key exchange with precomputation. *Communications of the ACM* 62. https://dl.acm.org/doi/pdf/10.1145/3292033.

[BDF98]   Boneh, D., Durfee, G., and Frankel, Y. (1998). An attack on RSA given a small fraction of the private key bits. Advances in Cryptology – ASIACRYPT'98. (ed. Ohta, K. and Pei, D.). *International Conference on the Theory and Applications of Cryptology and Information Security*. https://link.springer.com/chapter/10.1007%2F3-540-49649-1_3

[BB75]   Borwein, D. and Bruen, A.A. (1975). A problem of Erdös. *The Canadian Mathematical Bulletin* 17: 220.

[BS59]   Bose, R.C. and Shrikhande, S.S. (1959). On the consturction of sets of mutually orthogonal latin squares and the falsity of a conjecture of euler. *Proceedings of the National Academy of Sciences of the United States of America* 45. https://doi.org/10.1073/pnas.45.5.734.

[BSP60]   Bose, R.C., Shrikhande, S.S., and Parker, E.T. (1960). Further results on the construction of mutually orthogonal latin squares and the falsity of Euler's conjecture. *The Canadian Journal of Mathematics* 12. https://doi.org/10.4153/CJM-1960-016-5.

[BE72]   Broué, M. and Enguehard, M. (1972). Polynômes des poids de certains codes et fonctions thêta de certains réseaux. *Annales Scientifiques de l'École Normale Supérieure* 5 (1): 157–181. https://doi.org/10.24033/asens.1223.

[Bru70]   Bruen, A.A. (1970). Baer subplanes and blocking sets. *Bulletin of the American Mathematical Society* 76: 342–344. https://www.ams.org/journals/bull/1970-76-02/S0002-9904-1970-12470-3/S0002-9904-1970-12470-3.pdf.

[Bru71a]   Bruen, A.A. (1971). Blocking sets in finite projective planes. *SIAM Journal on Applied Mathematics* 21: 380–392. https://doi.org/10.1137/0121041.

[Bru71b]   Bruen, A.A. (1971). Partial spreads and replaceable nets. *The Canadian Journal of Mathematics* 20: 381–391. https://doi.org/10.4153/CJM-1971-039-x.

[Bru73]   Bruen, A.A. (1973). The number of lines determined by n^2 points. *The Journal of Combinatorial Theory, Series A* 15: 225–241. https://doi.org/10.1016/S0097-3165(73)80009-3.

[Bru84]   Bruen, A.A. (1984). Arcs and multiple blocking sets. *Symposia Mathematica* 28: 15–29. Mathematical Reviews: https://mathscinet.ams.org/mathscinet-getitem?mr=873770.

[Bru92]   Bruen, A.A. (1992). Polynomial multiplicities over finite fields and intersection sets. *The Journal of Combinatorial Theory, Series A* 60: 19–33. https://doi.org/10.1016/0097-3165(92)90035-S.

[Bru06]   Bruen, A.A. (2006). Applications of finite fields to combinatorics and finite geometries. *Acta Applicandae Mathematicae* 93. https://doi.org/10.1007/s10440-006-9051-4.

[Bru10]   Bruen, A.A. (2010). Blocking sets and low-weight codewords in the generalized reed-muller codes. In: *Error-Correcting Codes, Finite Geometries and Cryptography: Contemporary Mathematics*, vol. 523 (ed. A.A. Bruen and D.L. Wehlau): 161–164. The Americal Mathematical Society. http://dx.doi.org/10.1090/conm/523.

[BR49]   Bruck, R.H. and Ryser, H.J. (1949). The non-existence of certain finite projective planes. *The Canadian Journal of Mathematics* 1: 88–93. https://doi.org/10.4153/CJM-1949-009-2.

[BB10]   Bruen, A.A. and Bruen, T.C. (2010). The basics of bases. *The Mathematical Intelligencer* 32. https://doi.org/10.1007/s00283-010-9149-4.

[BH88]   Bruen, A.A. and Hirschfeld, J.W.P. (1988). Intersections in projective space II; pencils of quadrics. *The European Journal of Combinatorics* 9: 255–270. https://doi.org/10.1016/S0195-6698(88)80017-9.

[BHW11]   Bruen, A.A., Hirschfeld, J.W.P., and Wehlau, D.L. (2011). Cubic curves, finite geometry and cryptography. *Acta Applicandae Mathematicae* 115. http://dx.doi.org/10.1007/s10440-011-9620-z.

[BO90]   Bruen, A.A. and Ott, U. (1990). On the p-rank of incidence matrices and a question of E.S. Lander. In: (ed. E.S. Kramer and S.S. Magliveras). *Finite Geometries and Combinatorial Designs*, 39–45. AMS. https://www.ams .org/books/conm/111/.

[BR85]   Bruen, A.A. and Rothschild, B.L. (1985). Lower bounds on blocking sets. *Pacific Journal of Mathematics* 118 (2). https://projecteuclid.org/euclid .pjm/1102706440.

[BS83]   Bruen, A.A. and Silverman, R. (1983). On the non-existence of certain MDS codes and projective planes. *Mathematische Zeitschrift* 183: 171–175. https://doi.org/10.1007/BF01214819.

[BS88]   Bruen, A.A. and Silverman, R. (1988). On extendable planes, M.D.S. codes and hyperovals in PG(2,q), q = 2^t. *Geometriae Dedicata* 28: 31–43. https://doi.org/10.1007/BF00147798.

[BTB88]   Bruen, A.A., Thas, J.A., and Blokhuis, A. (1988). On M.D.S. codes, arcs in PG(n,q) with q even and a solution of three fundamental problems of B. Segre. *Inventiones Mathematicae* 92: 441–459. https://doi.org/10.1007/BF01393742.

[BW99]   Bruen, A.A. and Wehlau, D. (1999). Long binary linear codes and large caps in projective space. *Designs, Codes and Cryptography* 17: 37–60. https://doi.org/10.1023/A:1008346303015.

[BWF06]   Bruen, A.A., Wehlau, D.L., and Forcinito, M. (2006). Error correcting codes, block designs, perfect secrecy and finite fields. *Acta Applicandae Mathematica* 93. https://doi.org/10.1007/s10440-006-9043-4.

[Buc04]   Buchmann, J. (2004). *Introduction to Cryptography*. Springer-Verlag. https://www.springer.com/us/book/9780387207568.

[BBB+17]   Burley, D.L., Bishop, M., Buck, S. et al. (2017). Cybersecurity curricula 2017: curriculum guidelines for post-secondary degree programs in cybersecurity. A report in the computing curricula series joint task force on cybersecurity education. https://www.acm.org/binaries/content/ assets/education/curricula-recommendations/csec2017.pdf (accessed 18 September 2020).

[Bus52]   Bush, K.A. (1952). Orthogonal arrays of index unity. *The Annals of Mathematical Statistics* 23: 426–434. https://www.jstor.org/stable/2236685.

[Bus19]   Bushwick, S. (2019). *New Encryption System Protects Data from Quantum Computers*. Scientific American. https://www.scientificamerican.com/article/new-encryption-system-protects-data-from-quantum-computers/.

[CvL80]   Cameron, P.J. and van Lint, J.H. (1980). *Graphs, Codes and Designs*, vol. 43. Cambridge. https://doi.org/10.1017/CBO9780511662140.

[Can19]   Canadian Centre for Cyber Security (2019). https://cyber.gc.ca/en/. (accessed October 2019).

[CBC14]   CBC (2014). Retailers use smartphones to track your habits in the store. https://www.cbc.ca/news/business/retailers-use-smartphones-to-track-your-habits-in-the-store-1.2653566 (accessed 18 September 2020).

[CK74]   Cerf, V.G. and Kahn, R.E. (1974). A protocol for packet network intercommunication. *IEEE Transactions on Communications* 22. https://doi.org/10.1109/TCOM.1974.1092259.

[CP19]   Chakarov, D. and Papazov, Y. (2019). Evaluation of the complexity of fully homomorphic encryption schemes in implementations of programs. *Proceedings of the 20th International Conference on Computer Systems and Technologies.* https://doi.org/10.1145/3345252.3345292.

[Che20]   Cheng, J. (2020). China rolls out pilot test of digital currency. Milestone for world's biggest central banks in path toward launching electronic payment system. *The Wall Street Journal.* https://www.wsj.com/articles/china-rolls-out-pilot-test-of-digital-currency-11587385339.

[Cho19]   Choudhury, S.R. (2019). Automated hacking, deepfakes are going to be major cybersecurity threats in 2020. https://www.cnbc.com/2019/12/18/automated-hacking-deepfakes-top-cybersecurity-threats-in-2020.html (accessed 18 September 2020).

[Cic65]   Cicchese, M. (1965). Sulle cubiche di un piano di Galois. *Rendiconti di Matematica e delle sue Applicazioni* 24: 291–330. Mathematical Reviews: https://mathscinet.ams.org/mathscinet-getitem?mr=205144.

[Cic71]   Cicchese, M. (1971). Sulle cubiche di un piano lineare $S_{2,\,q}$, con $q \equiv 1 (\mathrm{mod}\ 3)$. *Rendiconti di Matematica* 4: 349–383. Mathematical Reviews: https://mathscinet.ams.org/mathscinet-getitem?mr=0309944.

[Cid]   Cidon, A. http://www.asafcidon.com (retrieved 23 August 2019).

[Cid14]   Cidon, A. (2014). Data durability in cloud storage systems. PhD thesis. Stanford University. http://www.asafcidon.com/uploads/5/9/7/0/59701649/thesis.pdf (accessed 18 September 2020).

[CRS+13]   Cidon, A., Rumble, S.M., Stutsman, R. et al. (2013). Copysets: reducing the frequency of data loss in cloud storage. *2013 Proceedings of the USENIX Annual Technical Conference (USENIX ATC '13)*, pp. 37–48. https://www.usenix.org/system/files/conference/atc13/atc13-cidon.pdf (accessed 18 September 2020).

[Cle80]   Clemens, C.H. (1980). *A Scrapbook of Complex Curve Theory*, 2e. Plenum Press. https://bookstore.ams.org/gsm-55/.

[Coo87]   Cooper, N.G. (1987). *Reflections on the Life and Legacy of Stanislaw Ulam*. Los Alamos Science Special Issue. Los Alamos National Laboratory.

[CDKB11]   Coulouris, G., Dollimore, J., Kindberg, T., and Blair, G. (2011). *Distributed Systems: Concepts and Design*, 5e. Addison Wesley. http://www.cdk5.net/wp/.

[Cov02]   Golomb, S.W. Berlekamp, E., Cover, T.M., Gallager, R.G., Massey, .L., and Viterbi, A. (2002). Cover and Claude Elwood Shannon (1916-2001). *Notices of the AMS* 49 (1): 8–16. https://www.ams.org/notices/200201/200201FullIssue.pdf.

[CIS19]   Cybersecurity & Infrastructure Security Agency (2019). Cybersecurity overview. https://www.dhs.gov/cisa/cybersecurity-overview. (accessed October 2019).

[Age20]   Cybersecurity & Infrastructure Security Agency (2020). Alert (TA18-086A): brute force attacks conducted by cyber actors. https://www.us-cert.gov/ncas/alerts/TA18-086A. Initial Version March 27, 2018, Updated May 6, 2020.

[DR99]   Daemen, J. and Rijmen, V. (1999). AES proposal: Rijndael. https://csrc.nist.gov/CSRC/media/Projects/Cryptographic-Standards-and-Guidelines/documents/aes-development/Rijndael-ammended.pdf (accessed 18 September 2020).

[DdOFH+19]   Dahlberg, A., de Oliveira Filho, J., Hanson, R. et al. (2019). A link layer protocol for quantum networks. *Proceedings of the ACM Special Interest*

Group on Data Communication - SIGCOMM '19. http://dx.doi.org/10.1145/3341302.3342070.

[Dar05]   Darling, D. (2005). *Teleportation: The Impossible Leap*. Wiley. https://www.daviddarling.info/books3.html.

[Dav19]   Davis, J. (2019). Biometric screening at airports is spreading fast, but some fear the face-scanning systems. https://www.nbcnews.com/mach/science/biometric-screening-airports-spreading-fast-some-fear-face-scanning-systems-ncna982756 (accessed 18 September 2020).

[dB88]   den Boer, B. (1988). Cryptanalysis of F.E.A.L. *EUROCRYPT 1988*. https://doi.org/10.1007/3-540-45961-8_27.

[dCdLS03]   de Castro, R.S., do Lago, A.P., and Da Silva, D. (2003). Adaptive compressed caching: design and implementation. *Proceedings of the 15th Symposium on Computer Architecture and High Performance Computing*. http://linuxcompressed.sourceforge.net/linux24-cc/files/docs/paper.pdf (accessed 18 September 2020).

[DCT91]   Dembo, A., Cover, T.M., and Thomas, J.A. (1991). Information theoretic inequalities. *IEEE Transactions on Information Theory* 37. https://doi.org/10.1109/18.104312.

[Den69]   Denniston, R.H.F. (1969). Non-existence of a certain projective plane. *Journal of the Australian Mathematical Society* 10: 214–218. https://doi.org/10.1017/S1446788700007096.

[Dil13]   Dilger, D.E. (2013). Compressed memory in OS X 10.9 Mavericks aims to free RAM, extend battery life. *Appleinsider*. https://appleinsider.com/articles/13/06/12/compressed-memory-in-os-x-109-mavericks-aims-to-free-ram-extend-battery-life (accessed 23 September 2020).

[dP69]   Di Paola, J.W. (1969). On minimum blocking coalitions in small projective plane games. *SIAM Journal on Applied Mathematics* 17: 378–392. https://www.jstor.org/stable/2099569.

[DGBL+15]   Dowlin, N., Gilad-Bachrach, R., Laine, K. et al. (2015). Manual for using homomorphic encryption for bioinformatics. https://www.microsoft.com/en-us/research/publication/manual-for-using-homomorphic-encryption-for-bioinformatics/ (accessed 18 September 2020).

[EPR35]   Einstein, A., Podolsky, B., and Rosen, N. (1935). Can quantum-mechanical description of physical reality be considered complete? *Physical Review* 47. https://doi.org/10.1103/PhysRev.47.777.

[Bri97]   *Encyclopedia Britannica* (1997), 15e. Chicago. https://www.britannica.com/topic/cryptology/Developments-during-World-Wars-I-and-II.

[Eri73]   Erickson, D.E. (1973). Counting zeros of polynomials over finite fields. PhD dissertation. California Institute of Technology.

[FMC11]   Falliere, N., Murchu, L.O., and Chien, E. (2011). W32.stuxnet dossier version 1.4. https://www.symantec.com/content/en/us/enterprise/media/security_response/whitepapers/w32_stuxnet_dossier.pdf (accessed 18 September 2020).

[FCC19]   Federal Communications Commission (2019). Wireless connections and bluetooth security tips. https://www.fcc.gov/consumers/guides/how-protect-yourself-online (accessed 18 September 2020).

[FTC19]   Federal Trade Commission Consumer Information (2019). How to Recognize and Avoid Phishing Scams. https://www.consumer.ftc.gov/articles/how-recognize-and-avoid-phishing-scams (accessed 18 September 2020).

[Fel50]   Feller, W. (1950). *Introduction to Probability Theory*. Wiley.

[FS03]   Ferguson, N. and Schneier, B. (2003). *Practical Cryptography*. Wiley. https://www.wiley.com/en-us/Practical+Cryptography-p-9780471223573 (accessed 18 September 2020).

[Fey00]   Feynman, R.P. (2000). *Feynman Lectures on Computation*. CRC Press. https://www.crcpress.com/Feynman-Lectures-On-Computation/Feynman/p/book/9780738202969 (accessed 18 September 2020).

[gif]   Flickinger, M. (2005). What's in a GIF. http://giflib.sourceforge.net/whatsinagif/lzw_image_data.html (retrieved August 2019).

[FDC11]   Francillon, A., Danev, B., and Capkun, S. (2011). Relay attacks on passive keyless entry and start systems in modern cars. *The Network and Distributed System Security Symposium (NDSS)*. https://www.ndss-symposium.org/wp-content/uploads/2017/09/franc.pdf (accessed 18 September 2020).

[Fun13]   Fung, B. (2013). How stores use your phone's WiFi to track your shopping habits. https://www.washingtonpost.com/news/the-switch/wp/2013/10/19/how-stores-use-your-phones-wifi-to-track-your-shopping-habits/ (accessed 18 September 2020).

[Gar04]   Garrett, P. (2004). *The Mathematics of Coding Theory*. Prentice Hall. https://www.pearson.com/us/higher-education/product/Garrett-Mathematics-of-Coding-Theory-The/9780131019676.html (accessed 18 September 2020).

[Gar19]   Gartner® (2019). Gartner Forecasts Worldwide Public Cloud Revenue to Grow 17% in 2020. https://www.gartner.com/en/newsroom/press-releases/2019-11-13-gartner-forecasts-worldwide-public-cloud-revenue-to-grow-17-percent-in-2020 (accessed 18 September 2020).

[Gen09a]   Gentry, C. (2009). A fully homomorphic encryption scheme. PhD thesis. Stanford University. https://crypto.stanford.edu/craig/craig-thesis.pdf (accessed 18 September 2020).

[Gen09b]   Gentry, C. (2009). Fully homomorphic encryption using ideal lattices. *Proceedings of the 41st Annual ACM Symposium on Theory of Computing, STOC '09*. https://doi.org/10.1145/1536414.1536440.

[Goo15]   Inventor: Gentry, C.B. (2015). Fully homomorphic encryption. https://patents.google.com/patent/US9083526B2/en (accessed 18 September 2020).

[Gil95]   Gillogly, J. (1995). Ciphertext-only cryptanalysis of ENIGMA. *Cryptologia* 19 (4). https://doi.org/10.1080/0161-119591884060.

[gzib]   GNU Gzip (2018). GNU Gzip: General file (de)compression, Manual for GNU Gzip version 1.10. http://www.gnu.org/software/gzip/manual/gzip.html (accessed 18 September 2020).

[Gol49]   Golay, M.J.E. (1949). Notes on digital coding. *Proceedings of the I.R.E.*, Volume 37. https://ieeexplore.ieee.org/stamp/stamp.jsp?tp=&arnumber=1698057 (accessed 18 September 2020).

[GP91]   Goldie, C.M. and Pinch, R.G.E. (1991). *Communication Theory*. Cambridge. https://doi.org/10.1017/CBO9781139172448.

[Gol82]   Golomb, S. (1982). *Shift Register Sequences*, 2e. Aegean Park Press. https://dl.acm.org/doi/book/10.5555/578271.

[GBC⁺02]   Golomb, S., Berlekamp, E., Cover, T.M. et al. (2002). *Claude Elwood Shannon (1916–2001)*. Notices of the American Mathematical Society. https://www.ams.org/notices/200201/fea-shannon.pdf (accessed 18 September 2020).

[Goo]   Google. compcache. https://code.google.com/archive/p/compcache/ (retrieved August 2019).

[Goo19]   Google (2019). *Encryption in Transit in Google Cloud*. https://cloud.google.com/security/encryption-in-transit/ (retrieved September 2019).

[Goo20]   Goodin, D. (2020). Flaw in billions of Wi-Fi devices left communications open to eavesdropping. *Ars Technica*. https://arstechnica.com/information-technology/2020/02/flaw-in-billions-of-wi-fi-devices-left-communications-open-to-eavesdroppng/ (accessed 18 September 2020).

[GBGL09]   Gowers, T., Barrow-Green, J., and Leader, I. (eds.) (2009). *The Princeton Companion to Mathematics*. Princeton University Press. https://press.princeton.edu/books/hardcover/9780691118802/the-princeton-companion-to-mathematics.

[Gra00]   Graff, J.C. (2000). *Cryptography and E-commerce: Cryptography Basics for Non-Technical Managers Working with E-business Products and Services (Wiley Tech Brief S.)*. Wiley. https://dl.acm.org/citation.cfm?id=517390.

[Gra19]   Graham, J. (2019). Sorry, readers. Your bluetooth device is a security risk. *USA Today*. https://www.usatoday.com/story/tech/talkingtech/2019/08/22/alexa-airdrop-ring-any-device-with-bluetooth-big-security-risk/2074164001/ (accessed 18 September 2020).

[Gre20]   Greig, J. (2020). Atari CEO touts future of blockchain in gaming. *TechRepublic*, June 2020. https://www.techrepublic.com/article/atari-ceo-touts-future-of-blockchain-in-gaming/ (accessed 18 September 2020).

[Gri13]   Grime, J. (2013). Flaw in the Enigma Code - Numberphile. Films by Brady Haran. https://www.youtube.com/watch?v=V4V2bpZlqx8, https://www.numberphile.com (accessed 18 September 2020).

[Guy82]   Guy, R. (1982). Sets of integers whose subsets have distinct sums. *North-Holland Mathematics Studies* 60: 141–154. Part of volume: Theory and practice of combinatorics: a collection of articles honoring Anton

Kotzig on the occasion of his sixtieth birthday. https://doi.org/10.1016/S0304-0208(08)73500-X.

[Guy88]   Guy, R. (1988). The strong law of small numbers. *American Math Monthly* 95: 697–792. https://www.maa.org/sites/default/files/pdf/upload_library/22/Ford/Guy697-712.pdf (accessed 18 Septmeber 2020).

[gzia]   gzip. http://www.gzip.org (accessed 18 September 2020).

[Ham89]   Hamming, R.W. (1989). *Digital Filters*, 3e. Dover Publications. https://store.doverpublications.com/048665088x.html.

[Hay01]   Haykin, S. (2009). *Communication Systems*, 5e. Wiley, 2001. https://www.wiley.com/en-us/Communication+Systems%2C+5th+Edition-p-9780471697909.

[Hea18]   Heath, N. (2018). 'Moore's Law is dead': three predictions about the computers of tomorrow. https://www.techrepublic.com/article/moores-law-is-dead-three-predictions-about-the-computers-of-tomorrow/ (accessed 18 September 2020).

[Hed10]   Heden, O. (2010). On perfect codes over non prime power alphabets. In: *Error-Correcting Codes, Finite Geometries and Cryptography: Contemporary Mathematics*, vol. 523 (ed. A.A. Bruen and D.L. Wehlau). The Americal Mathematical Society. http://dx.doi.org/10.1090/conm/523.

[HSH+08]   Halderman, J.A., Schoen, S.D., Heninger, N. et al. (2008). Lest we remember: cold boot attacks on encryption keys. *17th USENIX Security Symposium (USENIX Security 08)*, San Jose, CA: USENIX Association. https://www.usenix.org/conference/17th-usenix-security-symposium/lest-we-remember-cold-boot-attacks-encryption-keys (accessed 18 September 2020).

[HR91]   Hämäläinen, H. and Rankinen, S. (1991). Upper bounds for football pool problems and mixed covering codes. *Journal of Combinatorial Theory, Series A* 56. https://doi.org/10.1016/0097-3165(91)90024-B.

[HP17]   Hennessy, J.L. and Patterson, D.A. (2017). *Computer Architecture: A Quantitative Approach*, 6e (ed. M. Kaufmann). https://www.elsevier.com/books/computer-architecture/hennessy/978-0-12-811905-1.

[Hil86]   Hill, R. (1986). *A First Course in Coding Theory*. Oxford. https://
                global.oup.com/academic/product/a-first-course-in-coding-theory-
                9780198538035?cc=us&lang=en&.

[HLL⁺92]   Hoffman, D.G., Leonard, D.A., Lindner, C.C. et al. (1992). *Coding Theory,
                The Essentials*. Marcel Dekker. Mathematical Reviews: https://mathscinet
                .ams.org/mathscinet-getitem?mr=1150977.

[Hon85]   Honsberger, R. (1985). *Mathematical Gems III*. New York: The Mathemat-
                ical Association of America. https://www.maa.org/press/maa-reviews/
                mathematical-gems-iii.

[Hor90]   Horgan, J. and Claude, E. (1990). Shannon, unicyclist, juggler and father of
                information theory. *Scientific American*. https://www.scientificamerican
                .com/article/claude-e-shannon/.

[Hor16]   Horwitz, S. (2016). More than 30 states offer online voting, but experts
                warn it isn't secure. https://www.washingtonpost.com/news/post-nation/
                wp/2016/05/17/more-than-30-states-offer-online-voting-but-experts-
                warn-it-isnt-secure/ (accessed 18 September 2020).

[Int19]   Intel. Moore's law and Intel innovation. https://www.intel.com/content/
                www/us/en/history/museum-gordon-moore-law.html (accessed November
                2019).

[Int15]   Intel newsroom (2015). Intel and Micron produce breakthrough memory
                technology. https://newsroom.intel.com/news-releases/intel-and-micron-
                produce-breakthrough-memory-technology/ (accessed 18 September
                2020).

[Int18]   Intel newsroom (2018). Intel Optane Technology. https://newsroom
                .intel.com/press-kits/introducing-intel-optane-technology-bringing-3d-
                xpoint-memory-to-storage-and-memory-products/#gs.lzsqqx (accessed
                18 September 2020).

[KBG19]   Irving Kaplansky and June Barrow-Green (2019). évariste Galois. French
                Mathematician. https://www.britannica.com/biography/Evariste-Galois.
                (accessed December 2019).

[JJ00]   Jones, G.A. and Jones, J.M. (2000). *Information and Coding Theory*.
                Springer-Verlag. https://www.springer.com/gp/book/9781852336226.

[Kah67]   Kahn, D. (1967). *The Codebreakers*. New York: Macmillan.

[Kera]   KernelNewbies. KernelNewbies: Linux_3.14. https://kernelnewbies.org/ Linux_3.14 (accessed 18 September 2020).

[Kerb]   KernelNewbies. KernelNewbies: Linux_3.15. https://kernelnewbies.org/ Linux_3.15 (accessed 18 September 2020).

[KL15]   Kim, M. and Lauter, K. (2015). Private genome analysis through homomorphic encryption. *BMC Medical Informatics and Decision Making 2015*, Volume 15. https://dx.doi.org/10.1186%2F1472-6947-15-S5-S3.

[Kin08]   King, K.N. (2008). *C Programming: A Modern Approach*, 2e. W. W. Norton & Company. http://knking.com/books/c2/index.html.

[Koc96]   Kocher, P.C. (1996). Timing attacks on implementations of Diffie-Hellman, RSA, DSS, and other systems. *Proceedings of CRYPTO'96*. https://doi.org/10.1007/3-540-68697-5_9.

[LTS89]   Lam, C., Thiel, L., and Swiercz, S. (1989). The nonexistence of finite projective planes of order 10. *The Canadian Journal of Mathematics* 41: 1117–1123. https://doi.org/10.4153/CJM-1989-049-4.

[Lan83]   Lander, E.S. (1983). *Symmetric Designs: An Algebraic Approach*. Cambridge. https://doi.org/10.1017/CBO9780511662164.

[LNV11]   Lauter, K., Naehrig, M., and Vaikuntanathan, V. (2011). Can homomorphic enctyption be practical? *Proceedings of the 3rd ACM workshop on Cloud computing security workshop*. https://doi.org/10.1145/ 2046660.2046682.

[Lea96]   Leary, T.P. (1996). *Cryptology in the 16th and 17th Centuries*. Cryptologia.

[Len87]   Lenstra, H.W. Jr. (1987). Factoring integers with elliptic curves. *Annals of Mathematics* 126: 649–673. https://doi.org/10.2307/1971363.

[Lic]   Library of Congress. Sustainability of digital formats: planning for the library of congress collections. https://www.loc.gov/preservation/digital/ formats/fdd/fdd000135.shtml (last significant update on 14 February 2012.

[Lom98]   Lomonaco, S. (1998). *Quick Glance at Quantum Cryptography*, American Mathematical Society Lecture Series.

[Lom99]   Lomonaco, S.J. (1999). A quick glance at quatum cryptography. *Cryptologia* 23 (1): 1–41.

[Lov79]   Lovasz, L. (1979). On the shannon capacity of a graph. *IEEE Transactions on Information Theory* 25. https://doi.org/10.1109/TIT.1979.1055985.

[Luc15]   Luckerson, V. (2015). Netflix accounts for more than a third of all Internet traffic. *Time.com.* https://time.com/3901378/netflix-internet-traffic/ (accessed 18 September 2020).

[Lue06]   Luenberger, D.G. (2006). *Information Science.* Princeton, NJ. https://press.princeton.edu/books/hardcover/9780691124186/information-science.

[LYS15]   Lu, W.-J., Yamada, Y., and Sakuma, J. (2015). Privacy-preserving genome-wide association studies on cloud environment using fully homomorphic encryption. *BMC Medical Informatics and Decision Making 2015*, Volume 15. http://www.biomedcentral.com/1472-6947/15/S5/S1 (accessed 18 September 2020).

[MS78]   MacWilliams, F.J. and Sloane, N.J.A. (1978). *The Theory of Error-Correcting Codes.* North Holland. https://www.elsevier.com/books/the-theory-of-error-correcting-codes/macwilliams/978-0-444-85193-2.

[MST73]   MacWilliams, F.J., Sloane, N.J.A., and Thompson, J.G. (1973). On the existence of a projective plane of order 10. *Journal of Combinatorial Theory, Series A* 14: 66–79. https://doi.org/10.1016/0097-3165(73)90064-2.

[Mas69]   Massey, J.L. (1969). Shift-register synthesis and BCH decoding. *IEEE Transactions on Information Theory* 15: 122–127. https://doi.org/10.1109/TIT.1969.1054260.

[Mas02]   Massey, J.L. (2002). Shannon and the development of cryptography. *AMS Notices* 49 (1). https://www.ams.org/journals/notices/200201/200201FullIssue.pdf.

[Mau93]   Maurer, U.M. (1993). Secret key agreement by public discussion from common information. *IEEE Transactions on Information Theory* 39: 733–742. https://doi.org/10.1109/18.256484.

[McC90]   McCurley, K.S. (1990). The discrete logarithm problem. *Proceedings of Symposia in Applied Mathematics.* Cryptology and computational number theory, Volume 42. American Mathematical Society Short Course. https://www.ams.org/books/psapm/042/psapm042-endmatter.pdf (accessed 18 September 2020).

[McE78]   McEliece, R.J. (1978). *The Theory of Information and Coding*. Addison-Wesley.

[MC19]   McKay, K.A. and Cooper, D.A. (2019). *Guidelines for the selection, configuration, and use of Transport Layer Security (TLS) implementations*. National Institute of Standards and Technology, NIST. https://doi.org/10.6028/NIST.SP.800-52r2.

[Mea18]   Mearian, L. (2018). LinkedIn: 'Blockchain developer' is the no. 1 emerging job. *Computerworld*. https://www.computerworld.com/article/3327135/linkedin-blockchain-developer-is-the-no-1-emerging-job.html.

[Mic16]   Microsoft (2016). Homomorphic encryption. https://www.microsoft.com/en-us/research/project/homomorphic-encryption/ (accessed 18 September 2020).

[Mis]   Microsoft. https://www.microsoft.com/en-us/research/project/microsoft-seal/ (retrieved September 2019).

[Cen18]   Microsoft Ignite (2018). Windows Dev Center. File compression and decompression. https://docs.microsoft.com/en-us/windows/win32/fileio/file-compression-and-decompression (accessed 18 September 2020).

[Mil19]   Mills, S. (2019). Toyota, Lexus owners warned about thefts that use 'relay attacks'. https://www.cbc.ca/news/canada/ottawa/toyota-lexus-relay-attack-1.5380947 (accessed 18 September 2020).

[MSW02]   Mitnick, K.D., Simon, W.L., and Wozniak, S. (2002). *The Art of Deception: Controlling the Human Element of Security*. Indianapolis: Wiley Publishing. https://www.wiley.com/en-us/The+Art+of+Deception%3A+Controlling+the+Human+Element+of+Security-p-9780764542800.

[Mol00]   Mollin, R.A. (2000). *Introduction to Cryptography*, 2e. Chapman & Hall/CRC Press. https://www.crcpress.com/An-Introduction-to-Cryptography/Mollin/p/book/9781584886181.

[Mol02]   Mollin, R.A. (2002). *RSA and Public-key Cryptography*. Chapman & Hall/CRC Press. https://www.crcpress.com/RSA-and-Public-Key-Cryptography/Mollin/p/book/9781584883388.

[Mor18]   Morris, C. (2018). *Netflix Consumes 15% of the World's Internet Band-width*. Fortune.com. https://fortune.com/2018/10/02/netflix-consumes-15-percent-of-global-internet-bandwidth/.

[Nak08]   Nakamoto, S. (2008). Bitcoin: a peer-to-peer electronic cash system. https://bitcoin.org/bitcoin.pdf (accessed 18 September 2020).

[NBF⁺16]   Narayanan, A., Bonneau, J., Felten, E. et al. (2016). *Bitcoin and Cryptocurrency Technologies*. official version published by Princeton University Press. with a preface by Jeremy Clark. Draft — 9 February 2016. https://d28rh4a8wq0iu5.cloudfront.net/bitcointech/readings/princeton_bitcoin_book.pdf.

[NSA20a]   National Security Agency CAE-CD 2020 Knowledge Units (2020). https://www.iad.gov/NIETP/documents/Requirements/CAE-CD_2020_Knowledge_Units.pdf.

[NSA20b]   National Security Agency CAE requirements and resources (2020). https://www.iad.gov/nietp/CAERequirements.cfm.

[New19a]   Newman, D. (2019). *Amazon's Alexa: Why it Will Become Even More of a Fixture in Our Lives*. FUTURUM. https://futurumresearch.com/amazons-alexa-why-it-will-become-even-more-of-a-fixture-in-our-lives/.

[New19b]   Newman, D. (2019). *Facial Recognition Software: Where Are We Now?* FUTURUM. https://futurumresearch.com/facial-recognition-software-2/.

[NC10]   Nielsen, M.A. and Chung, I.L. (2010). *Quantum Computation and Quantum Information*. Cambridge University Press. https://doi.org/10.1017/CBO9780511976667.

[Nic99]   Nichols, R.K. (ed.) (1999). *ICSA Guide to Cryptography*. McGraw Hill. https://dl.acm.org/doi/book/10.5555/552688.

[Cry18]   NIST (2018). Cryptographic Technology. https://csrc.nist.gov/Groups/Computer-Security-Division/Cryptographic-Technology (accessed 18 September 2020).

[NIS19a]   NIST (2019). Back to basics: multi-factor authentication (MFA). https://www.nist.gov/itl/applied-cybersecurity/tig/back-basics-multi-factor-authentication (accessed 24 September 2020).

[Cen19]   NIST (2019). Computer Security Resource Center. Block Cipher Tech-
            niques. National Institute of Standards and Technology (NIST). https://
            csrc.nist.gov/Projects/block-cipher-techniques (accessed 18 September
            2020).

[NIS19b]   NIST (2019). Cryptographic standards and guidelines. https://csrc
            .nist.gov/Projects/Cryptographic-Standards-and-Guidelines/Archived-
            Crypto-Projects/AES-Development (updated 17 July 2019).

[NIS19c]   NIST (2019). Elliptic curve cryptography ECC. https://csrc.nist.gov/
            Projects/elliptic-curve-cryptography (accessed 24 September 2020).

[NIS19d]   NIST (2019). Lightweight cryptography. https://csrc.nist.gov/projects/
            lightweight-cryptography. (updated 21 October 2019).

[NIS19e]   NIST (2019). Lightweight cryptography. Round 2 Candidates. https://
            csrc.nist.gov/Projects/lightweight-cryptography/round-2-candidates.
            (updated 21 October 2019).

[NIS19f]   NIST (2019). Post-quantum cryptography. https://csrc.nist.gov/projects/
            post-quantum-cryptography (updated 23 September 2019).

[NIS20]   NIST (2020). Transport Layer Security (TLS). https://csrc.nist.gov/
            glossary/term/Transport-Layer-Security (accessed January 2020).

[Nyq28]   Nyquist, H. (1928). Certain topics in telegraph transmission theory. *Trans-
            actions of the American Institute of Electrical Engineers* 47 (2): 617–644.
            https://doi.org/10.1109/T-AIEE.1928.5055024.

[Oli19]   Oliver, D. (2019). Facial recognition scanners are already at some us
            airports. Here's what to know. *USA Today*, August 2019. https://www
            .usatoday.com/story/travel/airline-news/2019/08/16/biometric-airport-
            screening-facial-recognition-everything-you-need-know/1998749001/
            (accessed 26 September 2020).

[Orm19]   Orman, H. (2019). Online voting: we can do it! (we have to). *Communi-
            cations of the ACM* 62. https://cacm.acm.org/magazines/2019/9/238963-
            online-voting.

[PT16]   Paulsen, C. and Toth, P. (2016). Small business information security:
            the fundamentals. NISTIR 7621 Revision 1. https://doi.org/10.6028/
            NIST.IR.7621r1.

[Pel70]   Pelikán, J. (1970). Properties of balanced incomplete block designs. *Combinatorial Theory and its Applications* Vol. III, North-Holland, Amsterdam. 869–889, MR0309754.

[PW72]   Peterson, W. and Weldon, E.J. (1972). *Error-Correction Codes*, 2e. M.I.T. Press. https://mitpress.mit.edu/books/error-correcting-codes-second-edition.

[Pew19a]   Pew Research Center (2019). Internet/Broadband Fact Sheet. https://www.pewresearch.org/internet/fact-sheet/internet-broadband/ (accessed December 2019).

[Pew19b]   Pew Research Center (2019). Mobile Fact Sheet. https://www.pewresearch.org/internet/fact-sheet/mobile/ (accessed December 2019).

[Pia18]   Pianko, D. (2018). *What Every College Leader Should Know About Blockchain*. Inside Higher Ed. https://www.insidehighered.com/digital-learning/views/2018/09/05/what-every-college-leader-should-know-about-blockchain-opinion.

[Pie79]   Pierce, J.R. (1979). *An Introduction to Information Theory*. Dover. https://store.doverpublications.com/0486240614.html.

[PM02]   Piper, M. and Murphy, S. (2002). *Cryptography: A Very Short Intorduction*. Oxford University Press. https://global.oup.com/academic/product/cryptography-a-very-short-introduction-9780192803153?cc=us&lang=en&.

[Poe93]   Poe, E.A. (1993). *Tales of Mystery and Imagination*. Wadsworth.

[Pol74]   Pollard, J.M. (1974). Theorems on factorization and primality testing. *Mathematical Proceedings of the Cambridge Philosophical Society* 76. https://doi.org/10.1017/S0305004100049252.

[PPFH20]   Protzenko, J., Parno, B., Fromherz, A., and Hawblitzel, C. (2020). Evercrypt: a fast, verified, cross-platform cryptographic provider. *2020 IEEE Symposium on Security and Privacy*. https://doi.ieeecomputersociety.org/10.1109/SP40000.2020.00043.

[Ram12]   Ramanujan, S. (1912). Note on a set of simultaneous questions. *The Journal of Indian Mathematical Society* 4: 94–96.

[Ray18]   Rayome, A.D.N. (2018). Top 5 highest-paying tech jobs of 2019. https://www.techrepublic.com/article/top-5-highest-paying-tech-jobs-of-2019/ (accessed 26 September 2020).

[DHS19]   REAL ID (2019). https://www.dhs.gov/real-id (accessed December 2019).

[Ren87]   Renyi, A. (1987). *A Diary on Information Theory*. Wiley. https://mathscinet.ams.org/mathscinet-getitem?mr=904052.

[Res18]   Rescorla, E. (2018). The transport layer security (TLS) protocol version 1.3. https://doi.org/10.17487/RFC8446.

[RAD78]   Rivest, R.L., Adleman, L., and Dertouzos, M.L. (1978). On data banks and privacy homomorphisms. In: *Foundations of Secure Computation* (ed. R.A. De Millo, D.P. Dobkin, A.K. Jones, and R.J. Lipton), 165–179. Academic Press. http://people.csail.mit.edu/rivest/RivestAdlemanDertouzos-OnDataBanksAndPrivacyHomomorphisms.pdf.

[RR03]   Robbins, K.A. and Robbins, S. (2003). *UNIX Systems Porgramming: Communication, Concurrency, and Threads*. Prentice Hall. URL for the second edition (2016). https://www.pearson.com/us/higher-education/program/Robbins-UNIX-Systems-Programming-Communication-Concurrency-and-Threads-Communication-Concurrency-and-Threads-2nd-Edition/PGM332591.html (accessed 26 September 2020).

[RNGC19]   Rose, S., Nightingale, J.S., Garfinkel, S., and Chandramouli, R. (2019). Trustworthy email. NIST Special Publication 800-177 Revision 1. https://doi.org/10.6028/NIST.SP.800-177r1.

[Rot98]   Rota, G.-C. (1998). Lecture Notes by John N. Guidi - Spring 1998. MIT Course 18.313. Professor Gian-Carlo Rota. Volume 1 of 2. (Lectures 1-21). http://www.ellerman.org/wp-content/uploads/2016/06/Guidi-Notes-Rota-Probability-Vol-1-2.pdf (accessed March 2020).

[R8..7]   Rück, H. (1987). A note on elliptic curves over finite fields. *Mathematics of Computation* 49: 301–304. https://www.ams.org/journals/mcom/1987-49-179/S0025-5718-1987-0890272-3/S0025-5718-1987-0890272-3.pdf.

[Rue86]   Rueppel, R. (1986). *Analysis and Design of Stream Ciphers*. New York: Springer-Verlag. https://link.springer.com/book/10.1007/978-3-642-82865-2.

[RF11]   Ruggiero, P. and Foote, J. (2011). Cyber Threats to Mobile Phones. https://www.us-cert.gov/sites/default/files/publications/cyber_threats-to_mobile_phones.pdf (accessed 26 September 2020).

[Rys63]   Ryser, H.J. (1963). *Combinatorial Mathematics*. Mathematical Association of America. https://doi.org/10.5948/UPO9781614440147.

[Sch96]   Schneier, B. (1996). *Applied Cryptography: Protocols, Algorithms, and Source Code in C*. Wiley. 20th Anniversary Edition website https://www.wiley.com/en-us/Applied+Cryptography%3A+Protocols%2C+Algorithms+and+Source+Code+in+C%2C+20th+Anniversary+Edition-p-9781119096726.

[Sch03]   Schneier, B. (2003). *Beyond Fear*. Copernicus Books. https://www.springer.com/us/book/9780387026206.

[Sch08]   Schneier, B. (2008). Quantum cryptography: as awesome as it is pointless. *Wired Magazine* (October 2008). https://www.wired.com/2008/10/quantum-cryptography-as-awesome-as-it-is-pointless/ (accessed 26 September 2020).

[Sea13]   Seacord, R.C. (2013). *Secure Coding in C and C++*, 2e. Addison-Wesley Professional.   https://www.pearson.com/us/higher-education/program/Seacord-Secure-Coding-in-C-and-C-2nd-Edition/PGM142190.html.

[SR85]   Semple, J.G. and Roth, L. (1985). *Introduction to Algebraic Geometry*. Oxford: Clarendon Press.

[Sha19]   Shaban, H. (2019). *Twitter Reveals its Daily Active User Numbers for the First Time*. The Washington Post. https://www.washingtonpost.com/technology/2019/02/07/twitter-reveals-its-daily-active-user-numbers-first-time/ (accessed 26 September 2020).

[Sha77]   Shafarevich, I.R. (1977). *Basic Algebraic Geometry*. Springer-Verlag. https://www.springer.com/us/book/9783540082644.

[SH19]   Shale-Hester, T. (2019). Ford launches new keyless fob to combat relay attacks. https://www.msn.com/en-nz/motoring/news/ford-launches-new-keyless-fob-to-combat-relay-attacks/ar-BBVOUas (accessed 26 September 2020).

[Sha38]   Shannon, C.E. (1938). A symbolic analysis of relay and switching circuits. *Electrical Engineering* 57: 713–723. https://doi.org/10.1109/EE.1938.6431064.

[Sha40]   Shannon, C.E. (1940). *A Symbolic Analysis of Relay and Switching Circuits*. Massachusetts Institute of Technology. https://dspace.mit.edu/handle/1721.1/11173.

[Sha48]   Shannon, C.E. (1948). A mathematical theory of communication. *Bell Systems Tech Journal* 27: 379–423, 623–656. https://doi.org/10.1002/j.1538-7305.1948.tb01338.x.

[Sha49a]   Shannon, C.E. (1949). Communication in the presence of noise. *Proceedings of the Institute of Radio Engineers* 37 (1): 10–21.

[Sha49b]   Shannon, C.E. (1949). Communication theory of secrecy systems. *Bell Systems Tech Journal* 28: 656–715. https://doi.org/10.1002/j.1538-7305.1949.tb00928.x.

[SW49]   Shannon, C.E. and Weaver, W. (1949). *The Mathematical Theory of Communication*. University of Illinois Press. https://www.press.uillinois.edu/books/catalog/67qhn3ym9780252725463.html.

[Sho97]   Shor, P.W. (1997). Polynomial-time algorithms for prime factorization and discrete logarithms on a quantum computer. *SIAM Journal on Computing* 26. https://doi.org/10.1137/S0097539795293172.

[Shu18]   Shultz, G. (2018). How to monitor memory compression in Windows 10. *TechRepublic*. https://www.techrepublic.com/article/how-to-monitor-memory-compression-in-windows-10/.

[SGG18]   Silberschatz, A., Galvin, P.B., and Gagne, G. (2018). *Operating Systems Concepts*, 10e. Wiley. https://os-book.com/OS10/index.html.

[Bri19]   Simmons, G.J. (2019). *Encyclopædia Britannica*. https://www.britannica.com/topic/cryptology (accessed October 2019).

[Sim16]   Simonite, T. (2016). Moore's law is dead. Now what? https://www.technologyreview.com/s/601441/moores-law-is-dead-now-what/ (accessed 26 September 2020).

[Smi02]   Smith, R.E. (2002). *Authentication: From Passwords to Public Keys*. Addison Wesley. https://www.pearson.com/us/higher-education/program/Smith-Authentication-From-Passwords-to-Public-Keys/PGM81511.html.

[Dep19]   Statista Research Department (2019). Internet of things (IOT) connected devices installed base worldwide from 2015 to 2025 (in billions). https://www.statista.com/statistics/471264/iot-number-of-connected-devices-worldwide/ (accessed 10 December 2019).

[Sti84]   Stinson, D.R. (1984). A short proof of the nonexistence of a pair of orthog-
            onal latin squares of order six. *Journal of Combinatorial Theory, Series A*
            36: 373–376. https://doi.org/10.1016/0097-3165(84)90044-X.

[SP00]   Stone, J. and Partridge, C. (2000). When the CRC and TCP checksum
            disagree. In *SIGCOMM '00: Proceedings of the conference on Applications,
            Technologies, Architectures, and Protocols for Computer Communication.*
            https://doi.org/10.1145/347059.347561.

[SPL⁺15]   Stouffer, K., Pillitteri, V., Lightman, S. et al. (2015). Guide to indus-
            trial control systems (ICS) security. NIST Special Publication 800-82, rev2.
            http://dx.doi.org/10.6028/NIST.SP.800-82r2.

[Syv94]   Syverson, P. (1994). A taxonomy of replay attacks. *Proceed-
            ings of the Computer Security Foundations Workshop (CSFW94).*
            https://doi.org/10.1109/CSFW.1994.315935.

[Eco18]   The Economist (2018). How airports use biometric technology. https://
            www.economist.com/the-economist-explains/2018/11/12/how-airports-
            use-biometric-technology (accessed 18 September 2020).

[TW83]   Thompson, T.M. and Watkins, W. (1983). *From Error-Correcting Codes
            through Sphere Packings to Simple Groups*, Carus Mathematical Mono-
            graphs 21. Mathematical Association of America. https://www.maa.org/
            press/maa-reviews/from-error-correcting-codes-through-sphere-packings-
            to-simple-groups.

[Tib19]   Tibken, S. (2019). CES 2019: Moore's law is dead, says Nvidia's CEO.
            https://www.cnet.com/news/moores-law-is-dead-nvidias-ceo-jensen-
            huang-says-at-ces-2019/ (accessed 26 September 2020).

[Tka20]   Tkacik, D. (2020). IoT labels will help consumers figure out which devices
            are spying on them. https://cylab.cmu.edu/news/2020/05/27-iot-labels-
            consumers.html (accessed 26 September 2020).

[TW01]   Trappe, W. and Washington, L. (2001). *Introduction to Cryptography with
            Coding Theory*, 2e. Prentice Hall. https://www.pearson.com/us/higher-
            education/product/Trappe-Introduction-to-Cryptography-with-Coding-
            Theory-2nd-Edition/9780131862395.html.

[Tsu18]   Tsukayama, H. (2018). *Tshould Your Car Keys Be Wearing a Tin-
            foil Hat?* The Washington Post. https://www.washingtonpost.com/
            technology/2018/07/12/should-your-car-keys-be-wearing-tinfoil-hat/.

[Tur76]   Turan, P. (1976). *Selected Papers of A. Renyi*. Akademiai Kiado.

[TMcc⁺19]   Turan, M.S., McKay, K.A., Çalik, c.C. et al. (2019). Status report on the first round of the NIST lightweight cryptography standardization process. https://doi.org/10.6028/NIST.IR.8268.

[USC19]   United States Census 2020 (2019). https://2020census.gov/en/ways-to-respond.html (accessed December 2019).

[NCS19]   UK National Cyber Security Centre (2019). NCSC. https://www.ncsc.gov.uk (accessed in October 2019).

[vL98]   van Lint, J.H. (1998). *Introduction to Coding Theory*, 3e. Springer-Verlag. https://www.springer.com/us/book/9783540641339.

[Vig20]   Vigliarolo, B. (2020). Blackberry partners with Intel to detect cryptojacking malware. *TechRepublic*, June 2020. https://www.techrepublic.com/article/blackberry-partners-with-intel-to-detect-cryptojacking-malware/ (accessed 26 September 2020).

[VR15]   Vila, J. and Rodríguez, R.J. (2015). Practical experiences on NFC relay attacks with Android: virtual pickpocketing revisited. *International Workshop on Radio Frequency Identification: Security and Privacy Issues*. https://doi.org/10.1007/978-3-319-24837-0_6.

[Wal01]   Waldrop, M.M. (2001). Claude Shannon: reluctant father of the digital age. *Technology Review*, p. 64, July/August 2001. https://www.technologyreview.com/s/401112/claude-shannon-reluctant-father-of-the-digital-age/ (accessed 26 September 2020).

[Wat69]   Waterhouse, W.C. (1969). Abelian varieties over finite fields. *Annales scientifiques de l'École normale supérieure* 4 (2): 521–560. https://mathscinet.ams.org/mathscinet-getitem?mr=0265369.

[Wei20]   Weiss, T.R. (2020). Covid-19: Ibm using blockchain to connect pop-up medical mask and equipment makers with hospitals. *TechRepublic*, April 2020. https://www.techrepublic.com/article/covid-19-ibm-using-blockchain-to-connect-pop-up-medical-mask-and-equipment-makers-with-hospitals/ (accessed 26 September 2020).

[Wel85]   Welch, T.A. (1985). A technique for high-performance data compression. *Computer* 17: 8–19. https://doi.org/10.1109/MC.1984.1659158.

[Wel88]   Welsh, D. (1988). *Codes and Cryptography*. Oxford University Press. https://mathscinet.ams.org/mathscinet-getitem?mr=959137.

[Whi15]   Whittaker, E.T. (1915). On the functions which are represented by the expansion of the interpolation theory. *Proceedings of the Royal Society of Edinburgh* 35. https://doi.org/10.1017/S0370164600017806.

[WW46]   Whittaker, E.T. and Watson, G.N. (1946). *A Course of Modern Analysis*, 4e. Cambridge University Press. https://doi.org/10.1017/CBO9780511608759.

[Wic95]   Wicker, S.B. (1995). *Error Control Systems for Digital Communication and Storage*. Prentice Hall. https://www.pearson.com/us/higher-education/program/Wicker-Error-Control-Systems-for-Digital-Communication-and-Storage/PGM203436.html.

[Wie90]   Wiener, M.J. (1990). Cryptanalysis of short RSA secret exponents. *IEEE Transactions on Information Theory* 36 (3): 188–190. https://doi.org/10.1109/18.54902.

[Wie83]   Wiesner, S. (1983). Conjugate coding. *ACM SIGACT* 15 (1). https://doi.org/10.1145/1008908.1008920.

[Wil91]   Wilson, P.R. (1991). Operating system support for small objects. *International Workshop on Object Orientation in Operating Systems*. https://doi.org/10.1109/IWOOOS.1991.183026.

[Wil99]   Wilson, P.R. (1999). Some issues and strageties in heap management and memory hierarchies. *OPPSLA/ECOOP '90 Workshop on Garbage Collection in Object-Oriented Systems*. https://doi.org/10.1145/122167.122173.

[WKS99]   Wilson, P.R., Kaplan, S.F., and Smaragdakis, Y. (1999). The case for compressed caching in virtual memory systems. *Proceedings of the USENIX Annual Technical Conference*. https://www.usenix.org/legacy/event/usenix99/full_papers/wilson/wilson.pdf (accessed 26 September 2020).

[Win19]   Microsoft (2019). https://docs.microsoft.com/en-us/windows/whats-new/whats-new-windows-10-version-1507-and-1511?redirectedfrom=MSDN#bitlocker (accessed 26 September 2020).

[Wol61]   Wolfowitz, J. (1961). *Coding Theorems of Information Theory*. Englewoods Cliffs, NJ: Prentice-Hall. https://mathscinet.ams.org/mathscinet-getitem?mr=0143674.

[YSK+13]   Yasuda, M., Shimoyama, T., Kogure, J. et al. (2013). Secure pattern matching using somewhat homomorphic encryption. *Proceedings of the 2013 AMC Workshop on Cloud Computing Security Workshop*, pp. 65–76. https://doi.org/10.1145/2517488.2517497.

[Yur17]   Yurieff, K. (2017). Facebook hits 2 billion monthly users. *CNN*. https://money.cnn.com/2017/06/27/technology/facebook-2-billion-users/index.html (accessed 26 September 2020).

[Yuv79]   Yuval, G. (1979). How to swindle Rabin. *Cryptologia* 3: p. 187–190.

[ZL77]   Ziv, J. and Lempel, A. (1977). A universal algorithm for sequential data compression. *IEEE Transactions on Information Theory* 23: 337–343. https://doi.org/10.1109/TIT.1977.1055714.

[ZL78]   Ziv, J. and Lempel, A. (1978). Compression of individual sequences via variable-rate coding. *IEEE Transactions on Information Theory* 24: 530–536. https://doi.org/10.1109/TIT.1978.1055934.

Index

Cryptography, Information Theory, and Error-Correction: A Handbook for the 21st Century, Second Edition.
Aiden A. Bruen, Mario A. Forcinito, and James M. McQuillan.
© 2021 John Wiley & Sons, Inc. Published 2021 by John Wiley & Sons, Inc.

GROSS AND TUCKER
Topological Graph Theory

HALL
Combinatorial Theory, Second Edition

HOOKER
Logic-Based Methods for Optimization: Combining Optimization and Constraint Satisfaction

IMRICH AND KLAVⱥZAR
Product Graphs: Structure and Recognition

JANSON, LUCZAK, AND RUCINSKI
Random Graphs

JENSEN AND TOFT
Graph Coloring Problems

KAPLAN
Maxima and Minima with Applications: Practical Optimization and Duality

LAWLER, LENSTRA, RINNOOY KAN, AND SHMOYS, Editors
The Traveling Salesman Problem: A Guided Tour of Combinatorial Optimization

LAYWINE AND MULLEN
Discrete Mathematics Using Latin Squares

LEVITIN
Perturbation Theory in Mathematical Programming Applications

MAHMOUD
Evolution of Random Search Trees

MAHMOUD
Sorting: A Distribution Theory

MARTELLI
Introduction to Discrete Dynamical Systems and Chaos

MARTELLO AND TOTH
Knapsack Problems: Algorithms and Computer Implementations

McALOON AND TRETKOFF
Optimization and Computational Logic

MERRIS
Combinatorics, Second Edition

MERRIS
Graph Theory

MINC
Nonnegative Matrices

MINOUX
Mathematical Programming: Theory and Algorithms (Translated by S. Vajda-)

MIRCHANDANI AND FRANCIS, Editors
Discrete Location Theory

NEMHAUSER AND WOLSEY
Integer and Combinatorial Optimization

NEMIROVSKY AND YUDIN
Problem Complexity and Method Efficiency in Optimization (Translated by E. R. Dawson)

PACH AND AGARWAL
Combinatorial Geometry